STUDIES IN LINGUISTICS
IN HONOR OF
RAVEN I. McDAVID, JR.

RAVEN I. McDAVID, JR.

STUDIES IN LINGUISTICS
IN HONOR OF
RAVEN I. McDAVID, JR.

General Editor: Lawrence M. Davis

THE UNIVERSITY OF ALABAMA PRESS
University, Alabama 35486

410
St9
99756
Jan.1977

CONTENTS

STRUCTURE OF LANGUAGE

HISTORY OF LANGUAGE

† Deceased

RAVEN IOOR McDAVID, JR.

Like a great many linguists of his generation, Raven McDavid came into the field almost accidentally. After very thorough training in the intricacies of Milton scholarship under Allan Gilbert at Duke University, where he took his Ph.D. in 1935, he began his teaching career at The Citadel, the Charleston, South Carolina, school which trains many officers for the Armed Services.

While at The Citadel, he gathered data for an *American Speech* article on the in-group language of the students, indicating that the students had more than a superficial acquaintance with the shady ladies of that graceful Southern city, and this caused him to be persona non grata with that military establishment. During the summer of 1937, he attended his first linguistic institute at the University of Michigan, where Bernard Bloch who was teaching a course in dialect geography used him as an informant because of his Greenville, South Carolina, dialect.

It would not be quite correct to say that these two events had convinced him he had found his profession, because it was an exciting time in the development of a new discipline. The great descriptive linguists, Edward Sapir and Leonard Bloomfield, were demonstrating that every language must be studied in its own framework; scholars of historical linguistics—like Franklin Edgerton, Edgar H. Sturtevant, and Adelaide Hahn—were in regular attendance and extending our knowledge of language reconstruction; C. C. Fries was working on a comparative grammar of the American English of social classes; and Hans Kurath and Bernard Bloch were editing the *Linguistic Atlas of New England*. Linguistics was no longer philology nor an auxiliary tool for anthropological field work. In those days the Linguistic Society of America was still a small family. In fact, the meetings were smaller than many family reunions. But what a family it was! Here were people who seemed to know almost everything about language, who had mastered several languages, many of them exotic. It is small wonder that young scholars were eager to become members of that illustrious company, and equally exciting was the enthusiasm of these young scholars newly trained in the handling of language data and language design.

Of the group perhaps no one had more influence upon McDavid than the retired mechanical engineer, John Kepke, a man who published little and made only one formal talk to the Society. Respected for his knowledge by all the well-known scholars, Kepke had (as had so many of that day) a profound interest in young scholars, and he and McDavid became firm friends.

Teaching posts were hard to find. McDavid taught at Southeastern Louisiana College, where the student body was mostly of Acadian French background, and McDavid saw that their peculiar English problems could be illuminated by application of linguistics procedures. A brief stay on the English staff at Michigan State University (then, college) showed him that even native users of American English could also benefit by study of their problems from a linguistic point of view.

Shortly after the American entry into World War II, McDavid was selected to work with the linguists assembled at 165 Broadway in New York City, a military-civilian unit under the direction of J Milton Cowan and Henry Lee Smith, Jr., in order to prepare materials of use to the war effort: phrase books, grammars, and dictionaries in many languages, some little known in this country. McDavid was assigned to two projects, the development of materials for the study of Burmese and materials for Italians to learn English. The group included many of today's prominent linguists; and Kepke, who had left the communications project at Arlington Hall to assume the direction of the military dictionary project, extended his gemütlich hospitality to them.

In 1945, shortly after the war, McDavid began full-time field work for the *Linguistic Atlas of the South Atlantic States*, intensifying his close association with Kurath, who was in general charge of Atlas work on the Eastern Seaboard. He resumed his interviews in South Carolina and Georgia and completed the work begun by Guy S. Lowman, who had been killed in an automobile accident. McDavid quickly became an interviewer of extraordinary skills. His manner put his informants at ease; his intimate knowledge of the various layers of Southern culture and prodigious memory were combined with an "accurate ear." He later completed the field work for the Middle Atlantic States (in upstate New York) and finished that of the North Central States (in Illinois, Ohio, Michigan, Kentucky, and part of Ontario). His several hundred field records are marked by phonetic detail and an unusually large number of conversational items. They nearly always represent the relaxed speech of his informants as they would talk to an old friend. They also represent thousands of hours of intense concentration, countless bad meals in country restaurants, and hundreds of uncomfortable nights in second-rate hotels (or worse).

While in New York State he became associated with the linguists at Cornell University. After a visiting lectureship at the University of Illinois, he joined them in preparing the "General Form," a model textbook for the teaching of English overseas; in 1949–50 he was a visiting lecturer at the University of Illinois. He held his first regular academic post in English linguistics at Western Reserve University in Cleveland, Ohio, where he directed his first doctoral students (1952–57). In 1957 he became visiting associate professor in the English department of the University of Chicago and associate professor in the following year, and was promoted to a professorship in 1964.

In 1950 he married Virginia Glenn, then a dialectology student of Harold B. Allen's at the University of Minnesota. She now is Professor of English at Chicago State University where she continues her research in American English. They have a daughter and three sons, none showing any burning interest in becoming linguists, though all have an aptitude for foreign languages. It would be fascinating if I could report that the offspring of a Minneapolis speaker and a South Carolinian would show phonemic splits and mergers of a novel kind, but they speak the Standard Inland Northern of their peers.

In addition to his teaching, research, and article-review writing, McDavid has condensed the three-volume H. L. Mencken *The American Language* into one large volume (1963), revising it and bringing it up-to-date. He was a most suitable choice for the task. In the volume it is difficult at times to know which parts McDavid has added because the styles match so well. I feel sure there was little, if any, conscious effort to achieve this, because of McDavid's natural exuberance in writing. He seldom has to search for the right phrase and is prolific in epithet, as those know who are acquainted with his articles or public speeches.

With Hans Kurath he published *Pronunciation of English in the Atlantic States* (1961)—a radically different book, written by scholars for scholars. Here there was little occasion for more than the straightforward account. It is a sober book based on the data of the Linguistic Atlas field records, carefully organized into dialect regions and sub-areas.

For more than a decade he has been engaged with problems facing the classroom teacher of English, by taking part in U.S. Office of Education projects, lecturing and writing articles of practical application. At every opportunity he expresses common sense approaches to English linguistics and to teaching situations.

As a scholar during most of the controversy over what linguistic church— surely "school" can only be applied to the less fierce loyalties of Siwash football fans of the 1920's—one attends, McDavid has tried to keep to a course which depends upon exhaustive analysis of data. It would be strange if an experienced field worker did otherwise. He is aware of the limitations of such data, but he also knows the traps that a person can fall into by using himself as informant. The Trager-Smith model of English phonology has seemed to him inadequate to account for the great variety of American English, let alone that of the British Isles, without a recourse to phonemic-phonetic gymnastics. Similarly he has been unable to accept transformational models readily since so much may depend upon a narrow view of *what* people say in the language.

Perhaps no one today has a more encyclopedic knowledge of American English than McDavid or has written more extensively. He has trained many students and colleagues in dialectology. Only his tremendous energy has enabled him to achieve this and at the same time give his aid so freely to the furtherance of the practical application of linguistics.

Recognition has come to McDavid. He has received honorary doctorates from Furman University, his undergraduate alma mater, and from Duke University, where he earned his Ph.D. In 1969 he received the David H. Russell Award for Distinguished Research in the Teaching of English from the National Council of Teachers of English. In 1965 he was Fulbright Professor at Johannes Gutenburg University, Germany. In 1970 he was sponsored by the USIS office in Bonn on a lecture tour of German universities culminating in an address to the Gesellschaft für Amerikastudien, in Berlin. In 1964 he became editor of the Linguistic Atlas of the Middle Atlantic and South Atlantic States, succeeding Kurath.

This volume has been prepared to honor an eminent scholar and a good friend. Happy Birthday, Raven Ioor McDavid, Jr.!

Illinois Institute of   A. L. DAVIS
   Technology

SELECTED PUBLICATIONS OF
RAVEN I. McDAVID, JR.
(total bibliography amounts to more than 300 items)

1946: Dialect Geography and Social Science Problems. *Social Forces* 25: 168–72.

1948: Post vocalic /–r/ in South Carolina: A Social Analysis. *American Speech* 23: 194–203.

1949: Derivatives of Middle English *o*: in the South Atlantic Area. *Quarterly Journal of Speech* 35: 496–506.

1950: The Linguistic Atlas Project. Washington, *Americus*, Council of Learned Societies.

1951: (with Virginia G. McDavid) *A Compilation of Worksheets of the Linguistic Atlas of the United States and Canada and Associated Projects.* Ann Arbor; *Linguistic Atlas of the U.S. and Canada* (second ed., with A. L. Davis and Virginia G. McDavid, University of Chicago Press, 1970).

1951: The Folk Vocabulary of New York State. *New York Folklore Quarterly* 8: 173–92.

1951: (with Marjorie M. Kimmerle and Virginia G. McDavid) Problems of Linguistic Geography in the Rocky Mountain Area. *Western Humanities* R, 5: 249–64.

1951: (with Virginia G. McDavid) The Relationship of the Speech of American Negroes to the Speech of Whites. *American Speech* 26: 3–17.

1952: Some Social Differences in Pronunciation. *Language Learning* 4: 102–116.

1952: (with Virginia G. McDavid) *h* Before Semivowels in the Eastern United States. *Language* 28: 41–62.

1954: Linguistic Geography in Canada: an Introduction. *Journal of the Canadian Linguistic Association*, Preliminary No., 3–8.

1955: The Position of the Charleston Dialect. *Publication of the American Dialect Society* 23: 35–53.

1957: Social Differences in Pronunciation: A Problem in Methodology. *General Linguistics* 2: 15–21.

1958: The Dialects of American English. Chapter 9 of W. Nelson Francis' *The Structure of American English* (New York, Ronald Press Company) 480–543.

1958: Linguistic Geography and the Study of Folklore. *New York Folklore Quarterly* 14: 242–262.

1960: A Study in Ethnolinguistics. *Southern Speech Journal* 25: 247–254.

1960: (with Virginia G. McDavid) Grammatical Differences in the North-Central States. *American Speech* 35: 5–15.

1961: (with Hans Kurath) *The Pronunciation of English in the Atlantic States.* Ann Arbor, University of Michigan Press.

1963: (ed., with the assistance of David W. Maurer) H. L. Mencken, *The American Language,* one-volume abridged edition with new material, New York, Alfred A. Knopf, Inc.

1964: The Dialectology of an Urban Society, *Communications et Rapports du Premier Congres International de Dialectologie Generale.* Premier Partie (Louvain, Belgium) 68–80.

1964: Mencken Revisted. *Harvard Educational Review* 34: 211–225.

1964: (with Virginia McDavid) Plurals of Nouns of Measure in the United States. *Studies in Honor of C. C. Fries* (Ann Arbor, Michigan University Press) 271–311.

1964: American Social Dialects. *College English* 26: 254–260.

1965: Social Dialects: Cause or Symptoms of Social Maladjustment. *Social Dialects and Language Learning* ed. Roger W. Shuy (Champaign, Ill., National Council of Teachers of English) 3–9.

1965: The Cultural Matrix of American English. *Elementary English* 42: 13–21, 41.

1966: Sense and Nonsense about American Dialects, *Publications of the Modern Language Association* 81, No. 2, 7–17.

1966: Dialect Study and English Education. *New Trends in English Education,* ed. David Stryker (Champaign, Ill; National Council of Teachers of English) 45–52.

1966: Dialect Differences and Social Differences in an Urban Society. *Sociolinguistics,* ed. William Bright, 72–83.

1966: The Impact of Mencken on American Linguistics. *Menckeniana* 17.1. 1–7.

1966: (with William M. Austin) *Communication Barriers to the Culturally Deprived.* Cooperative Research Project 2107 (U.S. Office of Education) Chicago.

1967: Historical, Regional and Social Variation. *Journal of English Linguistics* 1: 24–40.

1967: A Checklist of Significant Features for Discriminating Social Dialects.

Dimensions of Dialect, ed. Eldonna Evertts (Champaign, Ill., National Council of Teachers of English) 7–11.

1968: Needed Research in Southern Dialects. *Perspectives on the South Agenda for Research.* ed. Thompson.

1969: (with Virginia McDavid) The Late Unpleasantness: Folk Names for the Civil War. *Southern Speech Journal.*

1970: Changing Patterns of Southern Dialects. *Studies for C. M.,* Wisconsin.

1970: The Sociology of Language. *In Yearbook of the National Society for the Study of Education.,* ed. A. H. Marckwardt.

1970: (with Lawrence M. Davis) The Dialects of Negro Americans. *Studies in Honor of George Trager.*

1970: *Essays in General Dialectology.* ed. Lee A. Pederson, Roger W. Shuy, and Gerald Udell (University of Alabama Press).

1970: The Urbanization of American English: *Proceedings of the Gesellschaft für Amerikastudien* (originally a talk given before the Gesellschaft at its May meeting in Berlin).

DIRECTORY OF CONTRIBUTORS

Harold B. Allen
University of Minnesota

†**William M. Austin**
Illinois Institute of Technology

Walter S. Avis
Royal Military College of Canada

William Card
Chicago State University

Marvin Carmony
Indiana State University

Frederic G. Cassidy
University of Wisconsin

Sara Chapman
Ohio University

Thomas J. Creswell
Chicago State University

Alva L. Davis
Illinois Institute of Technology

Lawrence M. Davis
Illinois Institute of Technology

Bozena Dostert
California Institute of Technology

†**Léon Dostert**
Occidental College

Audrey R. Duckert
University of Massachusetts

†**Karl W. Dykema**
Youngstown State University

Paul L. Garvin
State University of New York at
Buffalo

Clyde T. Hankey
Youngstown State University

Atcheson L. Hench
University of Virginia

Archibald A. Hill
University of Texas at Austin

Melvin Hoffman
State University College at Buffalo

Hans Kurath
University of Michigan

William Labov
University of Pennsylvania

Rosemary M. Laughlin
Mundelein College

Donald W. Lee
University of Houston

†**Kemp Malone**
Johns Hopkins University

David W. Maurer
University of Louisville

John McKenna
Ohio University

Lee Pederson
Emory University

Johnnie D. Ragsdale, Jr.
Ohio University

Thomas Pyles
Northwestern University

Carroll E. Reed
University of Massachusetts

David W. Reed
Northwestern University

Roger W. Shuy
Georgetown University

Henry Lee Smith, Jr.
State University of New York at Buffalo

George L. Trager
Northern Illinois University

Edith Crowell Trager-Johnson
University of California, Santa Barbara; and San José State University

Gerald Udell
Ohio University

Francis Lee Utley
The Ohio State University

Josef Vachek
Czechoslovak Academy of Sciences (Prague)

†Deceased

William R. Van Riper
Louisiana State University

Wolfgang Viereck
Johannes Gutenberg University (Mainz)

Juanita V. Williamson
LeMoyne-Owen College

H. Rex Wilson
University of Western Ontario

Gordon R. Wood
Southern Illinois University

Francis Xavier
Ohio University

DIALECTOLOGY

CURDS AND CHECKLISTS IN THE UPPER MIDWEST

HAROLD B. ALLEN
University of Minnesota

During the preparation of the contents of what will be the first volume, that on the vocabulary, of the Linguistic Atlas of the Upper Midwest, the basic fieldwork findings have frequently been confirmed by the supplementary evidence of the mailed checklists. With certain items queried, however, problems arise because of special influences affecting the typical westward movement of regional variants from the Atlantic Coast into the Middle West. One such item is that which includes the terms for the curds of very sour milk, drained and used as food.

The Linguistic Atlas of the Upper Midwest, for which the fieldwork was carried on from 1947 to 1953, is now being edited for publication in four volumes. The fieldwork practice closely followed that of the Linguistic Atlas of New England; and the New England short worksheets, with some modifications to adapt them to non-coastal investigation, were used for the interviewing. But for 137 lexical items, additional information was obtained when the Upper Midwest Atlas became the first American regional survey to utilize also the mailed checklist approach devised by Georg Wenker for the German dialect atlas three-quarters of a century earlier. Except for some slight revision the particular checklist employed was almost entirely that originally prepared by A. L. Davis for use in his 1949 University of Michigan doctoral study, *A Word Atlas of the Great Lakes Region*. The checklist made available, for this particular "curds" item, the responses of 1,036 Upper Midwest residents to supplement the field recorded replies of the 208 personally interviewed informants. These checklist responses are distributed as follows: Minnesota 263, Iowa 250, North Dakota 131, South Dakota 171, and Nebraska 221.

To serve as field informants, the now familiar three types of lifelong residents were sought: I, old and uneducated; II, middle-aged with high school education; III, younger, with college education. Because of the less carefully controlled selection of mail respondents, a similar classification for them turned out to be impracticable. The respondents represent all but two counties in the five states and reflect the full range covered by the three types of field informants, but with heavy concentration among persons about 60 years old and with less than full high school education. Except for the self-selecting circumstance that they were persons willing to take time to mark and return the checklist, these respondents constitute more nearly a random sample than does the selected small group of field informants. It is probably unnecessary to add that the data from one group are not simply added to those from the other. They are editorially treated as two distinct bodies of information useful for comparison. But despite the admittedly lower validity of the information provided by the unselected mail respondents, it has proved to be useful not only in confirming the field findings but also in supplementing what otherwise would be the only information at hand about the dialect features of the area.

Even by the time of the field investigations for the Linguistic Atlas of New England (1931–33), the various regional terms for strained milk curds were meeting strong competition from what Hans Kurath, in *A Word Geography of the Eastern United States*, called a trade name, *cottage cheese*. It is clearly an Americanism, with its first cited occurrence in *A Dictionary of Americanisms* as early as 1848. The tendency for trade names to replace regional designations would have made possible in 1933 a prediction that the western dialect studies would show *cottage cheese* in an even stronger position. The Upper Midwest investigation, made twenty years afterward, does indeed reveal the accuracy of such a prediction. In these five states the uniformity induced by commercialization has so accelerated the acceptance of *cottage cheese* that nearly nine out of ten of the 208 field informants consider it their normal everyday term. That this influence is still active is attested further by the fact that thirteen of the 187 informants using *cottage cheese* volunteered during their interviews that their adoption of the term had been recent. The actual percentages for the states are as follows: Minnesota 89%, Iowa 88%, North Dakota 80%, South Dakota 85%, and Nebraska 97%, for a general average of 89% for the whole region. Differences among the states are so insignificant that no regional pattern emerges for this particular term.

Since the proportion of instances of *cottage cheese* is higher than that on the East Coast, one may suspect whether the selected sample of only 208 informants adequately represents the entire Upper Midwest. At this point, then, the mailed returns of the 1,036 respondents become important. These returns, collected between 1949 and 1953, indicate a proportional frequency for *cottage cheese* as follows: Minnesota 91%, Iowa 80%, North Dakota 91%, South Dakota 90%, and Nebraska 92%, with the over-all average of 88%. The extremely close correspondence between the two sets of data strongly supports the conclusion that at least for widely spread items the field investigation did constitute an adequate sampling. The addition of extra informants would soon have reached the point of diminishing returns.

The pervasive dominance of *cottage cheese* both in Upper Midwest markets and in Upper Midwest homes is accompanied by the conspicuously increasing obsolescence of the two principal competing terms, *Dutch cheese* and *smearcase*, the appearance of several other originally eastern variants only as feebly surviving relics, and the complete absence of the common Hudson Valley expression, *pot cheese*, that might have been expected to persist among at least a few speakers with New York state background.

Along with *cottage cheese*, New England and New York state *Dutch cheese* was carried west on the population wave into the North Central states and the Upper Midwest. But even in part of the Northern speech area, it suffered a setback when in northern Minnesota and part of North Dakota the much more numerous late nineteenth century immigrants, largely Scandinavian, found the dynamic form to be that heard in stores and dairies, *cottage cheese*. By 1951 *Dutch cheese* was clearly on its way out. Thirty-two of the seventy-six informants familiar with the expression acknowledged that for them it was old-fashioned; they no longer said it. A few others, like the writer of this article, retain it at home only, since its use in markets and restaurants makes for a communication gap. By states the proportion of Upper Midwest informants still familiar with *Dutch cheese* is: Minnesota 15%, Iowa 20%, North Dakota 36%, South Dakota 33%, and Nebraska 16%, with an over-all average of 22%. Nearly all the Iowa instances are in the northern half of the state, 26%, not in the southern half, which is characteristically Midland with its 8%. Again the checklist returns substantiate the field reports with the following proportional distribution: Minnesota 19%, Iowa 28%, North Dakota 23%, South Dakota 28%, and Nebraska 18%, with the general average of 23%. The Iowa division is attested particularly by the contrast between the northern section, with 19%, and the southern section, with only 10%.

Smearcase presents a quite different situation. Not found in New England, it is an expression originating in the Pennsylvania German area [from German *Schmierkäse*], whence, according to Kurath, it spread into Delaware, Maryland, and West Virginia. From this population base it apparently then moved with the westward migration into the Midland speech areas of southern Iowa and Nebraska. Of the eighteen informants reporting the word, all but three have one or both parents with birthplaces in the Midland migration path—Pennsylvania, Ohio, Indiana, and Illinois. Of the three exceptions one has Swedish parents, one has German parents, and one has New York state parents. At least the second and third of these presumably acquired the word from Midland-speaking neighbors. The relative proportions for actual users of *smearcase* are: Minnesota 0, Iowa 12%, North Dakota 0, South Dakota 4%, and Nebraska 5%, with the general average (here almost meaningless) of 4%. It should also be observed that the drift appears in the volunteered remarks of seven of the eighteen informants that they once used *smearcase* but had switched to *cottage cheese*.

Now the checklist returns do not at first appearance corroborate these findings. The mailed data indicate a wider, though relatively inconsequential, spread into all the states: Minnesota 4%, Iowa 12%, North Dakota 5%, South Dakota 5%, and Nebraska 9%, for an average of 7%. Since they indicate the occurrence of *smearcase*, a Midland feature, in Minnesota and North Dakota, where distinctively Midland terms do not ordinarily occur among older residents, a question is immediately raised by the discrepancy between these two sets of data. It is a question resolvable, however, by a close examination of the biographical data for the checklist respondents. Six of the ten *smearcase* respondents in Minnesota have two German-born parents and a seventh has one German-born parent. All seven are familiar with German. Each of the two remaining respondents has a parent born in Pennsylvania and putatively considered a carrier of the Midland term. Only one of the ten cannot thus be accounted for, a respondent with Canadian and Scottish parentage. In view of the fact that the fieldworkers typically sought representatives of the early westward population movement and hence would not have chosen an informant of German parentage unless one of native-born parentage could not be found, it is not likely that *smearcase* would appear in the Minnesota records unless the term had escaped from German speakers into general community usage as it had earlier done in Pennsylvania. The evidence supports the inference that in the Upper Midwest it has not done this and that, on the contrary, its incidence in Minnesota is due simply to its use by first generation Americans of German descent who bring it into English directly from German rather than from the speech of possible Midland-speaking neighbors.

In North Dakota the situation is similar. There five respondents encircled *smearcase* as their normal expression. But three of these belong to the Russian German settlement group and a fourth has German-born parents. All four speak German. The fifth has Pennsylvania and West Virginia background but also speaks German. Clearly in North Dakota, too, the incidence of *smearcase* is due to its use by respondents who have carried it into English from German rather than from the Midland population wave. In Nebraska on the other hand, the incidence of *smearcase* is attributable not only to the fact that ten of the twenty respondents speak German but also to the fact that the ten others all possess a Midland family background.

When only a few instances of a variant occur, however, inferences can not safely be much more than guesses. An example is provided by *clabber cheese*, a South Midland and southern Atlantic coast term that the field records report with four occurrences along the Des Moines river in southern Iowa, one near the Missouri river in southwestern Iowa, and one in southeastern Nebraska also near the Missouri river. These are not unexpected, for the settlement history reveals an influx of South Midland families in these areas. But the checklists, in addition to their confirmation of *clabber cheese* in these localities, also have two examples from South Dakota, one from a respondent with Swedish and Danish parents and the other from a respondent with Norwegian background. Since *clabber* is of Gaelic, not Scandinavian, origin, presumably the variant *clabber cheese* was adopted by at least some persons outside the South Midland population group before the domination by *cottage cheese*. This particular problem with *clabber cheese*, like a fairly large number of similar problems appearing in the Upper Midwest files, cannot of course be solved without a much more intensive local survey than can be provided in a general regional investigation.

Other relic variants appear in the Upper Midwest, almost always in the speech of the oldest, Type I, speakers. *Country cheese* occurs once in Nebraska, *cream cheese* one each in southern Minnesota and in central Iowa, *curd* in North Dakota and *curds and whey* in Minnesota (perhaps a reflex of the historic British *curds* still found in Maine and New Hampshire), *primost* in Minnesota (a Norwegian loanword for a cheese made by boiling down the whey), *Scotch cheese* in southern Minnesota (perhaps an unwitting transfer from *Dutch cheese*), and *sour milk cheese* (from eastern New England) twice in southern Minnesota and once in Nebraska. None of these appeared in the checklists. But the checklists did offer one instance of simple *curds* in the usage of an Iowan of Maine and Canadian background and of simple *crud*, perhaps a shortening of South Midland *crud cheese*, in the usage of a Nebraskan with some South Midland background.

But for general coverage the usual confirming support of the checklist data, as with *cottage cheese* and *Dutch cheese*, suggests the validity of the basic fieldwork findings for vocabulary in the Linguistic Atlas of the Upper Midwest. When sufficient examples occur, resort to biographical information of checklist respondents can often resolve such inconsistencies as that between the field data for *smearcase* and the checklist findings for it. When insufficient examples occur, as with *clabber cheese*, an inspired guess can be based upon analogous situations, but such an inspired guess can be no more than that without further investigation.

ASPECTS OF REGIONAL SPEECH IN INDIANA

Marvin Carmony
Indiana State University

Although casual modern observers of Indiana speech tend to lump all Hoosier voices together as characteristically southern Middlewestern, an early observer of the state's people noted both diversity of tongues and a northern turn of speech. At a time when the young state's citizens were concentrated near the Ohio River,[1] Timothy Flint noted that "most of the newly arrived settlers that I addressed, were from Yankee land," and added that the southern element among the settlers feared that Indiana, like Ohio, would indeed become a Yankee state.[2] For a brief period, the apprehension of the southerners appeared to be well founded, judging from Flint's remark elsewhere of Indiana:

> Here, too, we first find the number and manners of northern people predominating among the immigrants. Here we first discover, in many places, a clear ascendency of New England dialect, manners and population.[3]

But the steady flow of southerners into the southeastern section of which Flint was writing apparently soon overwhelmed the northern element. Despite traces of New England speech which have survived in this part of Indiana, today one discovers rather in the southernmost counties a dialect manifestly related to Southern speech. It was from this area, in fact, that Edward Eggleston, writing in 1894, drew examples of "extreme Hoosier" remembered from the speech of Indianans living along the Ohio River thirty years earlier.[4]

In 1900, following continued immigration from the South, the settlement of the northern tier of counties by substantial numbers of Yankees, and the movement of Pennsylvanians into the state across the old National Road, two observers of the Hoosier dialect situation divided rural Indiana into northern and southern areas, offering as one evidence of this division their observation that *right smart*, an expression heard in central and southern Indiana, was rarely met with farther north.[5] A generation later, a confirm-

atory observation was made by historian Logan Esarey, who considered the
Hoosier dialect to be "distinctive" only in the southern part of the state.[6]

The modern investigation of Indiana speech may be said to have begun
with Hans Kurath, who in a 1928 essay on dialect differences in American
English noted that, as was the case in Ohio and Illinois, the southern portion of Indiana received most of its early population from the Valley of
Virginia and the Piedmont, where the Scotch-Irish predominated.[7] Although
the Middle Atlantic states especially made important contributions to the
later Indiana population, the Southern turn of much Indiana speech was
evidenced in the survey of the speech of the Great Lakes Region undertaken in 1938 by Albert Marckwardt. Like Hempl before him, Marckwardt
used the pronunciation of *greasy* as one touchstone, finding the South Midland and Southern /z/ to prevail south of an inverted V stretching across
the state, its apex reaching nearly to the northernmost part of central
Indiana.[8]

Following this preliminary survey of Great Lakes speech, disclosing as it
did the existence of considerable variation and the consequent need for a
systematic study of the speech of the area, A. L. Davis used a checklist for
his study of the regional vocabularies of the Great Lakes Region. Davis
found that Indiana speech was essentially Midland in character, with a small
Northern area along the Michigan border and North and South Midland
sections below.[9]

For the most part, efforts to assay Indiana speech have been based on interviews carried out for the Linguistic Atlas of the North Central States
(hereafter LANCS), which grew out of the earlier survey and was directed
by Marckwardt and his assistant, Raven I. McDavid, Jr. Both men published
important studies of the situation, McDavid in a 1956 paper surveying Atlas
work in the country as a whole[10] and Marckwardt a year later in an article
delineating the major and minor dialect areas of the North Central States.[11]
In his study Marckwardt presented a number of isoglosses representative of
the distribution of Northern, Midland, and Southern words in the North-
Central States, using the Eastern Seaboard study directed by Hans Kurath
as the basis of evaluation and making tentative extensions of Kurath's Eastern
boundary lines.[12] In 1958 McDavid used the LANCS material and his own
observations to extend Kurath's boundary lines as far westward as investigation up to that time permitted.[13] Further observations by Raven and
Virginia McDavid appeared in 1960,[14] and other Atlas-oriented studies were
carried out during the next few years.[15]

As drawn by McDavid, the Northern–North Midland boundary in Indiana is shaped like a thin Y lying on its side and open to the east, with
Allen County (Fort Wayne) inside the Y. Since for practical purposes, the
forty-first parallel can be taken as the boundary line and inasmuch as the
state divides into four major sections on the basis of the parallels crossing it,

one can depict vocabulary differences by frequency of occurrence of items within sections.[16]

The viability of the Northern-North Midland boundary line may be illustrated by LANCS informants' use of words for the bone from the chicken breast. From the North sector to the South, one finds the frequency of occurrence of the Northern *wishbone* as follows:

100
35
43
17

The Southern *pullybone*, on the other hand, has a distribution that sets off the Northern sector even more clearly:

0
50
53
72

One observes in passing that on the basis of this single item one could posit the existence of three dialect areas in the state, the two central sectors constituting a transitional area between the northern and southern sectors.

Another lexical item that supports the Northern-North Midland line as drawn by McDavid involves terms for the yard adjoining the barn. The principal expression among Northern and Midland informants generally is *barnyard*, while Southern informants use terms involving *lot*, as in *barn lot*, *cow lot*, etc. The responses of the Indiana LANCS informants were as follows:

barnyard	*barn* (etc.) *lot*
100	0
45	55
45	55
11	80

Other pertinent items include *snack*, *fishing worm*, *salad* as a term for edible tops of turnips etc., and *weatherboarding*, the frequency of occurrence of these expressions setting the northern sector apart from the remainder of the state:

snack	*fishing worm*	*salad*	*weatherboarding*
14	0	0	0
25	27	25	25
48	38	24	81
78	73	22	61

While this cursory reference to frequency of occurrence percentages, by sections, of a small number of lexical items is strongly confirmatory of the

1958 analysis, one should note that several traditional Midland expressions spill over the North-North Midland line and thus bear mention here. *Skillet* prevails throughout the state, as does *till* in *quarter till*. *Snake feeder* prevails in all sections, with *snake doctor* a strong rival in the north. Finally, Midland and Southern *roasting ears* predominates throughout the state.

The extension of the North Midland-South Midland boundary line to Indiana, as drawn by McDavid, crosses the north central part of the state, following closely the west-flowing portion of the Wabash River. The line thus lies about halfway between the forty-first and the fortieth parallels. Isoglosses that support this placement of the line include the southern limit of Northern *armful,* the northernmost extension of the predominance of *nicker,* and the northernmost extension of the predominance of *pallet.* If one keeps in mind that the line bisects the north central sector, one can ascertain something of the distribution by reference to frequency of occurrence percentages of these words:

armful	*nicker*	*pallet*
29	14	14
10	55	35
0	53	77
0	61	90

It is interesting to note that the frequency of occurrence of all three of the items support the North-North Midland line, .even more clearly than the North Midland-South Midland boundary. In addition, the distribution of *armful* and *pallet,* the latter in particular, offers support for the existence of a dialect boundary around the fortieth parallel, the traditional marker of the North Midland-South Midland boundary. In terms of the seventy or so items examined during early stages of the development of a line manuscript of the Indiana materials, indeed, the 1958 analysis is not very well supported, a fact that bears further treatment in this discussion.

The line bisecting the South Midland area of Indiana appears to follow closely the east branch of the White River, which on the western side of the state marks the boundary line between Gibson County and Knox County, the seat of which is Vincennes, the oldest town in the state. The isogloss marking the southernmost extension of the expression *quarter of* corresponds closely on the western side but dips southward below the White River on the east. The other pertinent LANCS items examined, however, indicate that the line should be drawn farther to the north in the interior of the state, taking in both Brown County and Monroe County and ending midway between Vincennes and Terre Haute. Lexical items that support this placement of the boundary include the isogloss marking the southernmost extension of the predominance of *husk* for the outer cover of an ear of corn, the line marking the northernmost extension of the predominance of *hay loft,* the isogloss for the northern limits of *totter horse* and *rocky horse,* the isogloss marking the northern limits of the predominance of *fish-*

ing worm, and the line marking the southernmost penetration of Northern *comforter.* Because the suggested line corresponds somewhat to the thirty-ninth parallel separating the south central sector from the southern quarter of the state, the percentages of frequency of occurrence of some of these forms are of value:

husk	hay loft	fishing worm
86	29	0
55	20	27
58	38	38
30	84	73

This appraisal of a fragment of the LANCS materials on Indiana speech suggests that the lexical data in general supports the division of the state into three principal dialect areas—apparently corresponding to the eastern seaboard Northern, North Midland, and South Midland areas—and a division of the South Midland into two parts. Although some of the phonological data raises questions about this view of Indiana dialects, not until all of the LANCS materials have been edited can we expect to gain a reasonably good understanding of the state's dialect situation as reflected in the speech of the two older generations of Indianans living in the fifties. In the meantime, a useful check on the validity of the LANCS findings can be made by comparing them with the results of a recent ancillary Indiana study and by looking further into the Indiana LANCS project in the light of that comparison.

During the past several years, the Western Indiana Regional Dialect Study (hereafter WIRDS) has accumulated a growing body of data concerning the nature and background of Indiana speech. In addition to a number of county settlement history and regional speech studies, two principal projects have been carried out. The study drawn upon in this paper used a modification of the Davis-McDavid questionnaire to ascertain the nature of the regional vocabularies of several hundred Indiana State University students.[17] It hardly needs to be pointed out that the WIRDS and LANCS projects differ in several respects. The latter study involved sixty-five informants from twenty-one counties, counting three informants from the Terre Haute study, all of whom presumably were typical Atlas informants interviewed in characteristic Atlas fashion by field workers using the Short Work Sheets as modified by McDavid and Davis. Though undifferentiated in this paper, thirty-three of the informants were classified by field workers as Type I, twenty-seven as Type II, and five as Type III. The WIRDS project, on the other hand, involved an IBM-scored checklist consisting of one hundred lexical items, many of which were known to have a regional distribution in Indiana and others of which were felt to be potential regional expressions. WIRDS evidence was drawn from four hundred forty-nine informants from ninety of Indiana's ninety-two counties.

Appraisal of the WIRDS data, both for its own sake and in conjunction with LANCS evidence, must be made in the light of certain facts about these young informants. Nearly all of them were college freshmen, some ten per cent being second or third year students. Although all of the informants had lived for a period of time in the counties with which they are identified in the study, not all of them were natives of these counties, the exact figures being obscured by the fact that some ten per cent did not respond to the appropriate questions. Nevertheless an overwhelming majority of the students were born in the part of the state from which they entered college. In addition, nearly seventy per cent of their fathers and at least sixty per cent of their mothers were born in Indiana and an additional fifteen per cent elsewhere in the North Central States. Twelve informants born south of the Ohio River represent widely scattered Indiana counties.

According to the responses, about seventy per cent of the fathers had at least a high school education, about ten per cent a four year college education, and five per cent had completed a master's degree or equivalent. Similarly, the mothers of some three-fourths of the informants had completed at least a high school education, but only five per cent possessed a bachelor's degree. At the time they completed the questionnaire, then, these students were by and large high school graduates a few weeks removed, and children of parents with about the same degree of formal education. Ninety percent of the informants, as first generation college students, represented a middle group of young Indianans standing between those whose parents were college educated and those who, like their parents, had high school educations or less and would not, in most cases, go on to college. There appears to be good reason to take their responses to regional words as fairly indicative of the speech of young Indianans generally.

When one turns to the maps based upon the lexical data provided by the WIRDS project, one seldom finds the relatively simple spatial distribution of forms that marks the maps based upon LANCS materials. The nearly eight-fold increase in the number of informants, coupled with the frequent interpenetration of competing forms, makes resorting to frequency of occurrence tables essential more often than not, and desirable even where the distribution does permit somewhat idealized lines to be drawn. Spacial distributions are strikingly evident, however, in the case of previously undetected subsidiary areas.

In the speech of young Indianans, not many of the one hundred lexical features surveyed indicate the continuation of the Northern-North Midland boundary near the forty-first parallel. One supportive expression is "sick *to* the stomach," which prevails only in the northernmost counties except in the northeast, where the word is the usual choice in the second tier of counties as well. The distribution thus matches almost perfectly the early settlement history of these counties. Although the position of the isogloss is somewhat north of the forty-first parallel, except in the northeast, a four-section picture of the distribution of "sick *to* his stomach" is informative:

"sick *to* his stomach"
72
38
31
33

Another lexical item which reflects a degree of viability of the line is *bag* used in preference to any of several other words for the paper container for groceries, including *sack*, *toot*, and *poke*.[18] Thus *bag* has the following distribution by sections:

bag
28
13
12
9

Differentials of ten per cent or so occur with a few other forms, including Northern *angleworm*, *dog irons*, and Midland *belling*, which have the following frequency of occurrence percentages:

angleworm	*dog irons*	*belling*
13	16	20
5	6	10
4	5	5
3	7	10

The strength of the South Midland *dog irons* in the northern quarter of the state is centered in Marshall and Newton Counties, where the frequency of occurrence is one hundred per cent; Starke County, with a frequency of occurrence of eighty per cent; and Porter county, with a percentage of seventy-five. Given the strength of the underlying Southern element in these northern counties, only the Porter County figure seems to be subject to speculation.

Complementing lexical items with a northern distribution are several expressions that have considerable strength in the southern three quarters of the state. Of these items, *sack*, Midland "sick *at* his stomach," and *fishing worm* are the most prominent, their frequency of occurrence in the southern three quarters exceeding that in the northern section by at least twenty per cent:

sack	"sick *at* his stomach"	*fishing worm*
16	18	16
46	53	38
41	55	53
37	49	65

If the WIRDS data makes less than a compelling case for the continued vitality of the Northern-North Midland boundary separating the northern counties of Indiana from those of the southern three quarters, it is equally unsupportive of the current placement of the North Midland-South Midland line. An analysis of the responses does indicate, however, that a substantial bundle of isoglosses exists farther to the south, most of the lines falling between the traditional dialect marking line, the old National Road, and U.S. 36, some forty miles to the north. Lexical items involved include *eaves troughs, eaves spouts, hay mow, bottom land, fish worm, sugar camp*, and *carting*, all of which have decidedly more currency in the northern half of the state than in the southern half; and *shivaree, weather boards /-boarding, gaum, mow the grass, hop toad, cow lot, bottoms, pully bone, cake doughnut, gutters, yahoo, flitters, comfort, pallet, hoe cakes*, and *salt pork*, most of which are considerably more prominent in southern than in northern Indiana.

As one would expect, few isoglosses fall on the fortieth parallel, which divides the state into halves; nevertheless the clustering near the parallel is such that frequency of occurrence percentages are revealing. For example, the southern extension of North Midland *haymow*, North Midland *bottom land*, and Northern and North Midland *fish worm* is indicated as follows:

haymow	bottom land	fish worm
27	40	21
26	36	32
9	24	7
6	13	8

The distribution of *fishing worm*, referred to earlier, complements that of *fish worm* and evidences clearly a northern-southern pattern. Although the terms are not unknown in the southern half of the state, Northern *eaves troughs* and *eaves spouts*, Northern *carting*, and western Pennsylvania *sugar camp* also have an essentially northern distribution, as indicated below:

eaves troughs	eaves spouts	carting	sugar camp
33	7	7	21
38	10	8	30
10	1	2	14
11	4	4	8

The related *eaves* is known through the state and was the response of seventeen per cent of the informants of the north central sector, thus giving that section a total of fifty-five per cent *eaves*-related responses.

Several of the checklist items, most of them South Midland or Southern words, have a relatively high degree of currency in the southern half of Indiana. Among them are *bottoms, pully bone, comfort, pallet*, and *hoe cakes*, which have the following patterns of distribution among WIRDS informants:

bottoms	pully bone	comfort	pallet	hoe cakes
6	4	12	12	2
7	13	24	15	1
20	27	41	32	6
30	41	36	31	9

It is instructive to note that *pully bone* clearly marks the Northern-North Midland boundary among LANCS informants and that the LANCS isogloss of *pallet* supports the 1958 North Midland-South Midland boundary. Thus both expressions are retreating southward and at the same time are sharply recessive, in terms of WIRDS data.

The case of *gutters* in Indiana speech is worthy of mention not only because of the southern distribution among WIRDS informants but also because the LANCS evidence in regard to the form is at odds with the eastern distribution of the word. According to Kurath, the term occurs widely in parts of the North and South, is fairly common in the North Midland, but does not occur in the South Midland.[19] Among Indiana LANCS informants, however, the expression is limited virtually to the central half of the state and is strongest in the south central sector, considered to be a part of the South Midland dialect area. Among young Indianans the term prevails in the southern half of the state and is strong in all four sections, thus supporting Kurath's observation in 1949 that the term was gaining ground. Note that *gutters* remains stronger in south central Indiana than elsewhere in the state:

gutters

LANCS	WIRDS
0	36
15	29
24	62
6	51

With at least thirty of the one hundred items utilized in the WIRDS questionnaire evidencing a southern-half distribution, coupled with a dozen or so forms with a northern pattern of incidence, one finds valid the concept of a major dialect boundary in Indiana based on a rather broad but substantial band of isoglosses across the middle of the state. The strength of this boundary appears to be directly related to the dimming of the Northern-North Midland boundary as Northern words have moved southward and at least some Midland and Southern words have retreated.

As the LANCS evidence suggests and as residents of both central and southern Indiana know, something of a linguistic boundary line exists between the central and the southernmost parts of the state. The seedbed counties are especially rich in regionalisms, a reflection not only of their early settlement and diverse settlement history but also of their conservatism, which is revealed in the retention of expressions that have lost ground in the remainder of the state. Pertinent expressions include such familiar Southern terms as *shuck, lightbread, French harp, barn lot,* and *cow lot.* Of these terms only *shuck* is strong in the state as a whole, and *barn lot* and *French harp* are sharply recessive. The isoglosses of most of these expressions fall near the thirty-ninth parallel and thus are reflected rather well in terms of frequency of occurrence percentages:

shuck	lightbread	French harp	barn lot	cow lot
36	6	6	9	1
26	4	4	12	3
37	8	4	13	7
58	16	13	21	14

The strength of Southern *shuck* in the northern sector is matched by the frequency of occurrence of Northern *husk* in the southernmost sector, where it has an incidence of thirty per cent.

The fate of two traditional Midland expressions lends support to the notion that the southern quarter of the state is to an increasing extent a relic area. For example, Midland *hull* as a term for shelling beans prevails among LANCS informants except in the northernmost sector, where it occurs as a minority form. Among WIRDS informants the term apparently has lost no ground in the north but has lost most of its strength elsewhere, especially in the central half of the state. Midland *weatherboards /-boarding*, the prevailing expressions for "overlapping horizontal boards on outside of house" among LANCS informants in the southern half of the state, are hardly used among WIRDS informants, except those from the southern quarter of the state. The comparative percentages of these forms are revealing:

hull		*weatherboards /-boarding*	
LANCS	WIRDS	LANCS	WIRDS
14	17	0	2
65	12	25	1
62	15	81	8
61	26	61	23

Of interest also is the strength of Northern *salt pork* in the southern quarter of the state, where it was the choice of thirty-nine per cent of the WIRDS informants, compared with eighteen per cent of the informants from the northern quarter of the state.

The retreat of Midland *hull* before *shell* and of *weatherboards /-boarding* before *siding* is representative of changes now taking place in the regional vocabulary of the state. Only the sparest of accounts of such changes can be given here. Something of the extent of obsolescence and replacement may be observed in the consideration of *increasing* forms, expressions with higher state-wide frequency of occurrence percentages among WIRDS informants than among LANCS informants; and *decreasing* forms, those with lower percentages among WIRDS informants than among LANCS informants.[20] Although the fate of some regionalisms seems beyond question, one should keep in mind the differences in the two studies, especially in terms of the small and relatively arbitrary selection of items from LANCS and of the considerably larger sampling of WIRDS informants.

Of sixty-one regional expressions that are common to both studies and that have undergone change, fifty-nine per cent (36) appear to be in retreat; and forty-one percent (25) appear to be increasing. While regional forms related to all three major dialect areas in the country seem to be receding, Northern expressions have nearly held their own, the ratio of losses to gains being about 1.2 to 1. Midland losses exceed gains by a ratio of 3:2, the same as the over-all average; and nearly twice as many Southern forms are receding as gaining. Inasmuch as the replacements for these Midland and Southern terms are generally recognized as national expressions, vocabulary change in Indiana at the present time appears to be characterized principally by the loss of regionalisms in general and by the retreat of Midland and Southern expressions before national terms, fostered either by commercial use or by the changing customs of the central and southern parts of the state.

If the WIRDS data has contributed to the delineation of the principal dialect areas of Indiana and to an understanding of vocabulary change in the state, the usefulness of the project does not end there. Of no less interest are evidences of the existence of several subsidiary dialect areas within the state. An examination of the WIRDS maps enables us to chart, tentatively to be sure, at least six such subareas, either adumbrated or not revealed by the wide-meshed LANCS project. Two are in the northern part of the state, one a Southern enclave between the Kankakee and Iroquois Rivers, including Jasper, Pulaski, Starke, and Marshall Counties; and the other a Southern enclave in Lagrange County, on the Michigan line. Although the middle counties of the state constitute a transition area, some evidence exists that the mid-section of the state, constituting the Pennsylvania wedge, has some characteristics of its own. Within this area, east central Shelby, Rush, and Decatur Counties have several features in common;[21] and on the eastern side of the state, Wayne County, the seat of which is Richmond, settled by North Carolina Quakers, and adjoining Fayette County, are often in consonance. Finally, in the southernmost part of the state a substantial bundle of isoglosses sets apart Clark, Washington, and Lawrence Counties, which lie astraddle the Wilderness Road. Only the first and last of these subareas will be singled out for discussion here.

That there may well be several substantial subsidiary dialect areas in Indiana is hardly surprising. Such a development could have been anticipated, and indeed was anticipated by Albert Marckwardt.[22] What is likewise noteworthy is the connection between WIRDS evidence of these subareas and the disclosure of certain deficiencies in the gathering carried out by LANCS fieldworkers in northern and southern Indiana, reflecting, it would appear, insufficient attention to the state's settlement history.

A study carried out in 1950 of immigration to northern Indiana making use of the 1850 Census figures revealed that the northernmost counties have a decidedly heavier underlying New England element than does the second tier of counties west of Noble County.[23] In the northernmost tier, the counties having the highest ratio of Yankees to Southerners were overlooked by fieldworkers; in the second tier, only one county is represented, although the evidence from the other counties would have been of great interest in view of the fact that all of these counties except one had from over two to more than ten times as many Southerners as New Englanders within their borders as of 1850. Of the third tier of northern Indiana counties, only one is represented in the survey, too small a sampling to give much of a hint of the complexity of the situation and of the strength of the Southern element. For example, distributed roughly according to the Northern, Midland, and Southern dialect areas on the Eastern Seaboard, the eastern population of third-tier Jasper County in 1850 had a Northern element of four per cent, a Midland population of six per cent, and a Southern element of nearly thirteen per cent, the remainder coming from the North Central States. In three other third tier counties, the Southern element comprised the largest part of the eastern population in 1850. When one considers the fact that many young native Indianans of the day were children of Southerners, the influence of the South on the speech of northern Indiana today is easily understood. Even without re-enforcements from later immigrations, which have taken place in some parts of this area, the young people of these counties would be likely to have a knowledge of a good many Southern expressions. Thus Southern *barn lot* occurs in Jasper, Pulaski, Starke, and Marshall Counties, almost uniformly in Pulaski County. *Pallet* likewise occurs here, although not only here in the northern sector. While the Southern cast of the speech of these counties is obvious in these and several other expressions, the area retains some relics of Northern speech, such as *coal hod*. Surely one of the principal tasks ahead in the investigation of Indiana speech is a study of the dialect of the old Kankakee swamp lands and adjoining areas and further study of the speech of the oldest generation of northern Indianans generally. Additional study seems likely to confirm the existence of a Southern enclave on the west and at the same time to compress considerably the Northern dialect area on the western side of the state.

No less interesting than the Southern enclave in the northern part of the state is a heavily demarked subsidiary area in southeastern Indiana involving Clark, Washington, and Lawrence Counties, and to a lesser extent several other counties along a northwesterly line drawn from Clark County on the Ohio River. Although these counties lie in the path of the Wilderness Road migration route into the interior of the state, only Clark County was selected for study by Atlas field workers, and as a result, LANCS records give little inkling of the existence of this subarea. Among the features common to these counties but not always exclusive to them and rarely prevailing in them are such expressions as *gallery, stoop, press, spider, spicket / spigot, turn, drawing, carrying, toting, garden corn, green corn, wart / warty toad frog, baby cab, coal pail, coal hod, carbon oil, lodge* (for *pallet* or other expressions), *corn dodger, hoe cake, raised donut,* and *lunch* (for "snack between meals"). Until interviews with informants of the oldest generation can be carried out in all of these counties, one can only remark on the mixed nature of the regional forms and speculate on the relative importance of the original settlement, recent immigration, the proximity to Louisville,[24] and the conservatism of the area. In view of the presence of a number of seemingly aberrant Northern expressions and pronunciations in the speech of some southeastern Indiana LANCS informants, in fact, it is not especially surprising to find WIRDS evidence in support of Timothy Flint's observations of a century and a half ago concerning the Northern turn of speech in this area. Indeed, the spinning off along the Wilderness Road of settlers from all parts of the eastern seaboard might have created something very like the picture that presents itself today.

Assuming that the existence of a Southern enclave in northwestern Indiana is confirmed by fieldwork, and that in consequence of this fact and of the results of further gathering in the northern sector the LANCS North-North Midland boundary is moved farther northward, all of the state except a narrow band at the top would be designated as the Midland, a very substantial part of the northern third of the state as North Midland, and the southern two-thirds as South Midland. Although the question of Indiana's relationship with the Eastern Seaboard is complicated by recent movements of isoglosses, when one turns to LANCS phonological evidence—in particular to the incidence of certain prime markers—one finds support for the characterization of the northern part of the state as North Midland rather than Northern. Thus the pronunciation of /ay/ as [ʌy], a Northern feature, is recorded but a single time in the northern quarter of the state.[25] Furthermore, the neutralization of the /o/ : /ɔ/ contrast, a North Midland feature, is most prevalent in the northernmost sector, occurring as far north as the top tier of counties. As one moves southward, the neutralization of this contrast continues to be a prominent phonological feature, but the surviving vowel is more often /o/ than /ɔ/, the usual survivor farther north. This shift to /o/ sets off the central part of the state from the northernmost and southernmost areas.

The strength of the neutralization of /o/ : /ɔ/ in the northern three quarters of the state is only part of the evidence to support the observation that something less than the southern two-thirds of Indiana should be considered a part of the South Midland. It is not until one gets down close to the Ohio River counties that one encounters with any consistency, either in the LANCS records or in conversation, the prime phonological marker of the South Midland, the monophthongal or near-monophthongal allophone of /ay/. It is here, too, that one notices a tenser version of /ɪ/ than is characteristic of the counties to the north. Although a preliminary examination of the LANCS records was not very revealing, one would expect to find [ɪ] as an allophone of /ɪ/ where the tense /ɪ/ occurs, in contrast to [ɪ] as an allophone of /ʊ/, as in *should, sure,* etc., as it seems to be in the remainder of the state. Other Southern and South Midland features that do not seem to have much currency in much if any of the area designated as the South Midland include /æ/ in *stairs*; /ju/ in *Tuesday, new,* etc.; and /ʌ/ in *put* and *took.* On the other hand, [aeu] in *down,* etc. is fairly common south of the fortieth parallel; /z/ prevails over much of the state in *greasy* and seems to be losing no ground among the young; and /o/ is common in the pronunciation of *your,* much less so in *poor.*[26]

Given the relative importance of phonological data in the determination of dialect boundary lines and one's observation that the recent movement of Northern and Southern words toward the center of the state has not been paralleled by a like movement of Northern and Southern pronunciations, one is tempted to suggest on the basis of this limited study that a redesignation of the dialect areas of the state might be appropriate. Aside from the question whether or not the area of the state designated as the South Midland reflects as a whole the characteristics of the seedbed South Midland areas, one can be sure that the southern two-thirds of Indiana is far from homogeneous, the southern quarter of the state being set off from central Indiana by numerous expressions and pronunciations.[27] But the determination of the place of Hoosier speech in relation to that of the Eastern Seaboard as well as that of the North Central States must await editing and publication of the Linguistic Atlas of the North Central States, for only on the basis of a full examination of that rich linguistic resource can we expect to make the necessary judgments.

To be sure, there are other urgent matters, other opportunities. In Indiana a careful study of the subsidiary dialect areas as indicated by the WIRDS project should be undertaken, and major studies should be undertaken of the speech of Indianapolis and the Calumet Region, to name only two urban areas the dialects of which need study for both historical and social reasons. In the studies of the speech of Terre Haute and of Fort Wayne, we have a basis for an increasingly sophisticated and insightful study of the urban speech. In the investigation of such speech, we face, as Kurath has pointed out, "one of the most important tasks confronting the student of American English." [28] Inasmuch as the wide-meshed surveys of the Atlas projects provide the data and insights so crucial to an understanding of urban speech, however, it would seem wise, if not imperative, to continue to press toward a clear understanding of the speech of the countryside as the investigation of urban speech goes forward.

Notes

1. Charles O. Paullin and John K. Wright, *Atlas of the Historical Geography of the United States* (Washington and New York, 1932), plate 76.

2. Timothy Flint, *Recollections of the Last Ten Years, passed in Occasional Residences and Journeyings in the Valley of the Mississippi* (Boston, 1826), pp. 56–57.

3. *A Condensed Geography and History of the Western States, or the Mississippi Valley* (Cincinnati, 1828), II, 18.

4. Edward Eggleston, "Folk Speech in America," *Century Illustrated Monthly Magazine*, XLVIII (1894), 867–875.

5. Paul L. Haworth and O.G.S., "Folk-Speech in Indiana," *Indiana Magazine of History*, I (1905), 163–172.

6. Logan Esarey, *History of Indiana from Its Exploration to 1922* (Dayton, 1922), I, 475.

7. Hans Kurath, "The Origin of the Dialectal Differences in Spoken American English," *Modern Philogy*, XXV (May, 1928), 392. Kurath's observation that the Scotch-Irish did not diphthongize their long vowels may possibly be reflected in the relative infrequency of diphthongization of these vowels in Indiana.

8. Albert H. Marckwardt, "Folk Speech in Indiana and Adjacent States," *Indiana Historical Bulletin*, XVII (1940), 120–140. George Hempl, in "Grease and Greasy," *Dialect Notes*, I (1896), 438–444, found that [s] in 1) *to grease* and 2) *greasy* fell into three patterns of distribution in Indiana, as indicated by the following percentages: northern Indiana (77–70), middle Indiana (31–17), and southern Indiana (0–0). Hempl found a significantly lower incidence of [s] in northern Indiana than in the middle North area of the country as a whole. E. Bagby Atwood, in "Grease and Greasy: A Study of Geographical Variation," *Studies in English*, XXIX (1950), p. 256, noted that [z] in *greasy* "takes in almost the whole of Indiana. . . ."

9. A. L. Davis, "A Word Atlas of the Great Lakes Region" (unpublished Ph.D. dissertation, University of Michigan, 1948).

10. Raven I. McDavid, Jr., "Regional Linguistic Atlases in the United States," *Orbis*, V (1956), 349–386.

11. Albert H. Marckwardt, "Principal and Subsidiary Dialect Areas in the North-Central States," *Publication of the American Dialect Society*, XXVII (April, 1957), 3–15.

12. Hans Kurath, *A Word Geography of the Eastern United States* (Ann Arbor, 1949).

13. Raven I. McDavid, Jr., "The Dialects of American English," in W. Nelson Francis, *The Structure of American English* (New York, 1958), Ch. 9.

14. Raven I. McDavid, Jr., and Virginia G. McDavid, "Grammatical Differences in the North Central States," *American Speech*, XXXV (February, 1960), 5–19. Also of value is Virginia McDavid's "Verb Forms in the North-Central States and Upper Midwest" (unpublished Ph.D. dissertation, University of Minnesota, 1956).

15. V. E. Gibbens, "Progress Report on a Word Geography of Indiana," *Midwest Folklore*, XI (Fall, 1961), 151–154. Also of interest are Marvin Carmony, "The Speech of Terre Haute: a Hoosier Dialect Study" (unpublished Ph.D. dissertation, Indiana University, 1965) and Charles Edward Billiard, "Dialect Features Affecting the Social Mobility and Economic Opportunities of the Disadvantaged in Fort Wayne, Indiana" (unpublished Ph.D. dissertation, Purdue University, 1969).

16. The analysis of LANCS data presented here is based on a fragment of a line manuscript of the Indiana LANCS records, developed by the writer while assisting Professor McDavid in editing the forthcoming *Linguistic Atlas of the Middle and South Atlantic States*. Thanks are due to Professor Marckwardt for permission to use the LANCS records and to Professor McDavid and Miss Catherine Ham for their hospitality during an enjoyable sabbatical. The regional provenience of features discussed is based generally on Kurath's *Word Geography* but designations also reflect McDavid's discussion in *Orbis* and in Chapter 9 of *The Structure of American English*. For the tentative boundary lines drawn by McDavid, see p. 580 in the latter.

17. ISU graduate student James Harner administered the questionnaires and made the preliminary analysis of the data gathered for this project.

18. *Toot* and *poke*, which do not appear in the Indiana LANCS records, have percentages of occurrence of 2,0,1,5 and 0,1,4,7, respectively.

19. *Word Geography*, Table VI, p. 49.

20. For a detailed study of lexical change in another Midwestern state, see Gary N. Underwood, "Vocabulary Change in the Upper Midwest," *Publication of the American Dialect Society*, XLIX (April, 1968), 8–28.

21. *Flitters* for *pancakes* is nearly uniform in this area.

22. "Principal and Subsidiary Dialect Areas," p. 15.

23. Elfrieda Lang, "Immigration to Northern Indiana 1800–1850" (unpublished Ph.D. dissertation, Indiana University, 1950). See also John D. Barnhardt and Donald F. Carmony, *Indiana: From Frontier to Industrial Commonwealth* (New York, 1954), I, 176–78.

24. See Robert Ray Howren, Jr., "The Speech of Louisville, Kentucky" (unpublished Ph.D. dissertation, Indiana University, 1958).

25. The LANCS records indicate that the pronunciation of /ay/ as [ʌy] occurs primarily in southeastern Indiana.

26. [ɪ] or [ʊ] is exceedingly common in the pronunciation of *little* and *children*, the vowel often being /ʊ/; but *sister* seems to have [ɪ] throughout the state.

27. Among them are the use of "indefinite" *whenever* in the sense of "definite" *when*; *plus* as a coordinate conjunction (now widespread, however); regardless *to*; and many pronunciations, including Wisconsin as [wɛs kan sɪn], *Saint Louis* as [sænt] _____, *evening* as [í nin] or [íniŋ], the rounding of [ʌ] to [ɔ] in *hull*, *gulf*, etc. *registration* as [rɛ̀j stɚ é šɪn], and many others. These features may or may not be characteristic of other southern middlewestern areas.

28. Hans Kurath, "The Investigation of Urban Speech and Some Other Problems Confronting the Student of American English," *Publication of the American Dialect Society*, XLIX (April, 1968), 1–7.

THE SOURCE OF "JACK MANDORA"

Frederic G. Cassidy
University of Wisconsin

A continuing puzzle to folklorists and creolists has been the phrase *Jack Mandora* used regularly in Jamaica, W.I., as the concluding formula for "Nancy stories." It has hovered on the edge of intelligibility, folk-etymologized and guessed at, without a real solution. Obviously not an original form, whether it conceals an African or European source, or some blend of both, has been part of the puzzle. The Nancy stories, spread by slavery throughout the Caribbean (Jamaica, Bahamas, Surinam, Curaçao, etc.) are themselves in origin partly African, partly European; they take their name from their hero, Anancy the spider, who can change into man's shape and back again as need requires. But many Nancy stories do not include Anancy or his animal brothers: they are European fairy-tales which have been assimilated to the Anancy canon.

The attempt to explain *Jack Mandora* has produced a story in Jamaica according to which there is a girl named Dora, the daughter of Jackman. Put in first place in the Pioneer Press volume of *Anancy Stories and Dialect Verse*[1] it is palpably a recent attempt to fill the vacuum by folk-etymology.

The earliest record of the phrase comes from 1868, *Jacmandorah, Don't want none.*[2] Jekyll (1907) recorded it in two forms, *Jack Mantora, me no choose any*, and (more frequently) *Jack Mantora, me no choose none.*[3] He notes:

> All Annancy stories end with these or similar words. The Jack is a member of the company to whom the story is told, perhaps its principal member; and the narrator addresses him and says: "I do not pick you out, Jack, or any of your companions, to be flogged as Tiger and Annancy were by the monkeys." Among the African tribes stories we know are often told with an object. The Negro is quick to seize a parable, and the point of a cunningly constructed story directed at an individual obnoxious to the reciter would not miss. So when the stories were merely told for diversion, it may have been thought good manners to say: "This story of mine is not aimed at anyone." [4]

In other words, Jekyll took the latter part as perhaps a polite denial that the story had been told to point to a member of the audience.

Beckwith (1924) recorded the stories with far less editing,[5] whereupon the phrase turns out to be far more variable, as follows:

> *Jack man dora*—8 examples, seven of which have no second part;
> *Jack man dory*—12 examples; five of which have no second part;
> *choose none*—4 examples;
> *choose now*—1 example;
> *choose one*—1 example.

Other fuller forms:

> *Jack man dory, Dat's de end of de story* (p. 86)
> *Jack man dory, me story done* (p. 76)
> *Jack man dory, this story done* (p. 160)
> *Jack man dory fe dat.* (p. 105)

It would seem plausible that the sequence of alteration or reduction which proceeds as the phrase turns into a formula and comes to mean merely "that's all" goes from the full rhyme, "Jack man dory, That's the end of the story," to obscuring of the rhyme, "Jack man dory, my/this story's done," to "Jack man dory for that," to the forms with "choose," and finally to "Jack man dory" alone and "Jack man dora," which last change triggers the explanation with Jackman and his daughter. "Choose none" would also appear to be the form from which "choose now" (perhaps a slip of the tongue or an error in recording) and "choose one" are deviations. Jekyll's surmise is not borne out; the phrase might just as well be merely terminal, meaning "I choose to go no further" or (as in the earliest record) "I want to tell no more." And "dory" is certainly better than "dora" unless the presence of rhyme is taken to show modern sophistication. But this is unlikely: traditional formulas frequently do have rhyme—for example the English "Be bow bended, My story is ended," the source of the common Bahamian terminal formula, "E bo ben, Dis story en." [6]

I confess my own earlier failure to solve the problem either in *Jamaica Talk*[7] or in the *Dictionary of Jamaican English*;[8] the best I could do was to suggest the possibility of an African source and to throw out (without conviction) "cf. Sp-Pg *mentira*, a lie." Since *Jamaica Talk* the only reference I have seen to Jack Mandora is in Joey Dillard's article and note[9] in which he recognizes the presence of folk-etymology but takes us no further: "the source form seems to be unknown." [10]

Yet the solution to this puzzle was closer and simpler than any of us realized: had we thought sooner of Mother Goose we would have found it in the verse used to put off an importunate child who wants to be told a story at an awkward time:

> I'll tell you a story
> About Jack a Nory,
> And now my story's begun;
> I'll tell you another
> About Jack and his brother,
> And now my story is done.[11]

So the *Oxford Dictionary of Nursery Rhymes*, No. 260, where other citations are given from c.1760 (Jacky Nory) forward, with mention of several variants: Mother Morey (c.1825), Peg Amo-re (c.1840), Jack a Manory (1865), Jacopo Minore (1890), Jack a minory (1913), and Jack o' Binnorie.

The variants testify to its always being thought of as a name. It was widely disseminated and underwent some rather violent transformations. In two, Jack becomes a woman, in two an Italian, and in the last a Scot. Mother Morey has turned up in the United States as "Mary Morey" in a version published in 1944.[12]

Jamaican *Jack Mandory* would seem most clearly derivable from *Jack a Manory*: loss of weak-stressed "a" and generation of [d] from released [n], common phonetic developments, produce it simply enough. The rhyme with "story" is also confirmed as basic. But the whole verse has undergone a deal of compression or eclipsis to bring it to the point as quickly as possible: " . . . Jack a Nory, . . . my story is done." Yet this kind of compression is not unexampled in Jamaica. As Beckwith has pointed out,[13] the English formula,

> Riddle me this, riddle me that
> Perhaps you can guess this riddle
> And perhaps not

is reduced in Jamaica to,

> Riddle me riddle
> Guess me this riddle
> And perhaps not.

The fact that *Jack a Nory* or *Manory* is English does not entirely remove the possibility of African influence. The English verse gives no hint toward explaining "me no want / choose none;" this is then presumably Jamaican unless further traceable to some African narrative practice.

But the proof of English source comes as a timely warning. The recent enthusiasm to prove African sources for a number of Americanisms has led to some extravagant guesswork.[14] The case of *Jack Mandora* should remind us that the New World Negro is not merely African: he might better be called "Amerafrican," having been profoundly affected by European culture when transplanted to America. His distinction today is due to just this fact, that he blends elements of the two worlds. For linguists it is well to keep in mind that "Black English" is often more English than Black.[15]

Notes

1. Louise Bennett, Dorothy Clarke, Una Wilson, and Others. Kingston 1950.

2. *Transactions of the Jamaica Royal Society of Arts and Agriculture*, New Series, I.66.

3. Walter Jekyll, *Jamaican Song and Story*, London (Nutt). This has texts considerably edited.

4. Last note, page 10.

5. Martha Warren Beckwith, "Jamaica Anancy Stories," *Memoirs of the American Folklore Society*, XVII, New York (Stechert).

6. Elsie Clews Parsons, "Folk-Tales of Andros Island, Bahamas", *Memoirs of the American Folklore Society*, XIII, New York (Stechert) 1918, p. xi et passim.

7. Cassidy, F. G., Macmillan (London) 1961.

8. Cassidy, F. G., and R. B. LePage, Cambridge University Press, 1967.

9. "Some Variants in Concluding Tags in Antillean Folk Tales," *Caribbean Studies* 2.3, 16–25, 1962; and "Additional Notes on Stepping and Bending," *Ibid.* 4.4, 74–76, 1965.

10. Dillard, "Additional Notes. . . . ," 76.

11. Iona and Peter Opie, eds., *Oxford Dictionary of Nursery Rhymes*, Oxford (Clarendon) 1951, No. 260. This verse was used as the "signature" of a British Broadcasting Corporation program which I happened on in 1967. I am indebted to the BBC Reference Library for furnishing me its source.

12. *Nursery Rhymes and Songs*, Racine, Wis. (Whitman). I owe the discovery of this to Mrs. Shelia B. Knee.

13. *Ibid.*, xii.

14. See for example the London *Times*, 19 July, 1969, 9; 23 July, and 25 July, 1969, Letters.

15. See especially Raven I. McDavid, Jr., "Historical, Regional, and Social Variation," *Journal of English Linguistics*, 1, 25–40. 1967.

LITERARY DIALECT IN NELSON ALGREN'S
NEVER COME MORNING

THOMAS J. CRESWELL
Chicago State University

In his novel *Never Come Morning*,[1] Nelson Algren deals with a cast of characters almost exclusively Polish-American. The methods he uses to indicate their Polishness are several. Their surnames, to begin with, serve as clear indicators of their national origin and, in the case of many second-generation individuals, their given names or more frequently their nicknames indicate their at least partial acculturation to the United States: Bonifacy Konstantin, Steffi Rostenkowski, Bruno Lefty Bicek, "Casimir Benkowski from Cortez Street, called Casey by the boys and *Kasimierz* by the girls," Finger Idzikowski, Catfoot Nowogrodski, Punch Drunk Czwartek, Fireball Kodakek, Knothole Chmura, John from the Schlitz Joint, Andy Bogats, Tiger Pultoric. In moments of extreme stress some of the characters lapse into their native or home language. They refer to whiskey as "Polish Pop." They occasionally call each other "Polak." The neighborhood club or gang is called the Polish Warriors at the beginning of the book. Later it becomes the Baldhead True American Social and Athletic Club.

In addition to these means of indicating the Polish-Americanism of his characters, Algren attempts in various ways to suggest their characteristic speech patterns and to contrast them with those of the few characters of non-Polish antecedents who appear in the book.

In one such passage, Bruno Lefty Bicek (who in his short career as a boxer prefers to be known as Lefty Biceps—an interesting example of a fortuitously meaningful Americanization of a foreign name) is in conversation with a determinedly middleclass case worker from a social agency:

"You didn't show up Wednesday morning. Why not?"
"I'm in trainin'. Had to go to bed early 'n sleep late. That was orders."
"Training for *what*? Orders from *whom*?"
"For a fight. From my manager."
"You mean you fight prof*ess*ionally?"
"Uh-huh."

"What do you earn when you fight?"

"I wouldn't pull on a glove for less'n a hunerd."

"How often do you fight, *Mister* Bicek?"

"Ever' chance I get. If I can't get a ring match I pick up a street fight just t' keep in shape. I'm sharp as a razor right now."

This exchange with the case worker suggests nothing about Bruno's second-generation Polish-American status, although it does serve to indicate, or rather to reinforce, since other narrative and descriptive details and the context have already pointed to it, a distinct class difference between Bruno and the case worker. The italicization of *what*, *whom*, and the syllable *fess* in *professionally*, as well as of *Mister* serve to suggest not only a sort of amazed incredulity in the case worker but also the speech patterns of a moderately well-educated American, with no indication of other ethnic background. The additional fillip provided by the proper *whom* serves to intensify the suggestion. Bruno's speech, on the other hand, suggests nothing of Polishness but manages, both by contrast with the speech of the case worker and by the use of more or less conventional literary dialectal elisions, to convey the impression that he is of a lower social status. Just how much lower is not clear.

Sumner Ives has pointed out that "just as the choice of certain dialectal forms can show a difference in social status, so can the selection of other forms give some indication as to the generation to which the character belongs." [2]

A brief example from the speech of Bruno's mother should make clear that Algren attempts to make this distinction. A few moments after Bruno's conversation with the social worker, Bruno hears his ailing first-generation mother call from the back room, asking for a glass of water. After she drinks the water he has brought, she lies back and says, "T'morrow I get up. Do a little work, feel better."

At first glance, and without the background of the story, Mama Bicek's speech might suggest only that of a tired or somewhat laconic middle class American. The only suggestion that it represents something other than the pattern in which such a person might utter these words is the use of a period between *up* and *Do*, and a comma between *work* and *better*. The period highlights the absence of a pronominal subject in the second "sentence." Had it been a comma, the string of predications could have been read as a series. Alone, this curious use of punctuation does not indicate "Polishness," yet it characterizes her speech as different from her son's, less native American in feel. A reading of subsequent speeches by Mama Bicek and other first-generation characters shows that Algren regularly uses as markers of first-generation Polish-American status the three omissions that characterize this brief speech—of pronominal subject, of future tense marker, and of conjunction.

In addition to maintaining a distinction between the speech of first- and second-generation Polish-Americans, Algren uses a number of techniques, discussed below, to distinguish the speech of first-generation Polish-Americans who have lived for some years in the United States from that of two individuals who are identified as greenhorns—relatively recent arrivals.

The foregoing brief examples indicate that the author uses literary dialect to signal differences in social class, national origin, and relative length of acclimatization of his characters. So that the extent of his use of various kinds of available devices can be assessed, it seems useful to discuss features of the dialogue under three headings: grammatical, lexical, and pronunciational.

Grammatical Variants

Two other characters in *Never Come Morning* represent approximately the same degree of acculturation as does Mama Bicek: Bonifacy Konstantin, the Barber, who is a major character, and Mama Rostenkowski, the mother of Steffi.

When Bruno Bicek enters the Widow Rostenkowski's poolroom, she engages him briefly in conversation:

> He entered the widow's poolroom first to make certain that both she and her boy were there instead of upstairs, and bought a five-cent cigar.
> "You work?" Widow Rostenkowski asked hopefully, remembering half-forgotten debts.
> "I'm being managed now, Widow," he explained. "You see, a fella with money back of him is takin' me under his wing."
> The widow appeared puzzled.
> "This is *business*? Fighting is *business*?"
> "Fight business, that's right. I'm a pug now. There's money back of Bruno Lefty now."
> "Is *crooked* business?"
> "Ever' thin's crooked, Widow."

Widow Rostenkowski's "You work?" does not represent anything in the pattern of American English used by native speakers. The closest one might find to this would be "You workin'?" The pattern of "Is *crooked* business?" a query, is an even further departure from normal native speech at any level. True, alone it does not indicate absolutely that she is Polish-American of the first generation, but this pattern, plus her name, plus her milieu, plus the name of her daughter (Steffi) does indicate both her origin and the fact that she must have learned English relatively late in life. This sort of variation from standard grammatical patterns of American English is found almost exclusively in the speech of first-generation characters.

As is frequently the case in the use of literary dialect, the general, all-pervasive pattern of the speech of the second-generation Polish-Americans who constitute a majority of the characters consists largely of what George Krapp has called general "low colloquial." [3]

Jockey, one of the girls at Mama Tomek's sporting house, in discussing Superman, the comic book character, says, "Only how does that sonofabitch fly gets me."

In the speech of other characters occur such "ungrammatical" but none-theless native structures as "Them's Lefty Bicek Helt' Shoes. . . , " "You been here before. . . ," " 'N those jerks who seen you do it—did they give you the dirty eye like you ain't got a right even t' do what you want. . . . "

In addition to such literary representations of general low colloquial speech, however, there are many utterances which mark a departure from the range of grammatical patterns generally available in American English. A rather large group of these utterances may be classified, I think, as sentence patterns *not* characteristic of American speech. Some examples will demonstrate that the patterns vary in a number of ways:

"I should borrow him out some dough he wanted."

This sentence is in response to the query, "What did he want?" Note the unusual placement of the main verb and the use of the expression "borrow him out."

"I couldn't afford."

This occurs in a situation in which the standard pattern calls for an "it" to complete the utterance.

Bonifacy Konstantin, the Barber, provides the largest number of such non-standard patterns in his speech. He is, as has been pointed out above, first-generation, an older man, and perhaps least influenced of all the characters by the speech of Americans not of Polish descent, since his clientele and social circle consist largely of Polish-Americans.

"No more fight. No more borrow."

"How much you pay for such nice haircut?"

Here notice the omission of the article "a" which would occur before "nice" in the speech of a native.

"Price gone up. Is now six bits."

Characteristically, the words "the" and "has" are omitted from the first sentence. "It," the standard expletive, is missing from the second.

"Is forty haircuts, is six bits each, is thirty bucks. . . ."

In this series, again the standard expletive, probably "that," is omitted. This is a distinct reflection of Polish rather than English sentence patterns.

"Tell Mama Tomek come."

Here the infinitive sign is omitted.

"Close door!"

Another example of omission of the article.

"In for kill. Catfoots know. I know. For kill a Greek, what all boyz see. Catfoots know. I know. Catfoots good boy. You like Catfoots?"

In this brief speech can be seen an uninflected verb pattern—no verb has been inflected in any way; an instance of meaningless eye dialect—"boyz"; a mispronunciation—"Catfoots" for "Catfoot", an elision—the words "is a" have been omitted from the utterance "Catfoots good boy."

"You like go home for stay?"

More elision—of the infinitive sign before "go"—and a substitution of "for" for "to" in another infinitive position distinguish this utterance from general low colloquial American English.

Another first-generation character, but of more recent arrival than Bonifacy Konstantin or Widow Rostenkowski, Josie, the greenhorn whore, echoes this last pattern in one of her few speeches:

"I listen for drop sometin'. Nickels. Dimes."

In general, it can be seen that the two large characteristics which Algren has singled out as salient in the dialect of first-generation Polish-Americans are the use of uninflected verb forms and the omission of the "little" words—pronouns, expletives, articles. The second can clearly be traced to the Polish language itself. The first, since it occurs in the speech of many non-native speakers, perhaps can only safely be said to represent unfamiliarity with the language.

There is observable in the speech of all the Polish-American characters, first- and second-generation, a class of variations which might be called additions to the grammar of English.

"I read it all too you."
"Was I scared you. . . ."
"I got butter'n cheese by a place once you'n a pint bottle from whippin' cream. You—whippin' cream."

The use of the appended second person vocative in the way exemplified in these last three speeches is characteristic of the speech of many only partially acculturated Polish-Americans.

The last speech quoted above provides examples of another significant variation—in the use of prepositions—which might be called an addition to English grammar. "By a place" and "from whippin' cream" are substituted for the more usual "at a place" and "of whipping cream." These constructions occur frequently in the speech of both first- and second-generation characters.

Bonifacy Konstantın says, "Come by shop, boyz."

Jockey, another prostitute, says, "When I was in the Walkathon by the Coliseum my girl friend . . . used to get froze stiff in fourteen hun'erd pounds from ice every Tuesday night. . . ."

Casey Benkowski, Bruno's contemporary, says, ". . . let's get half a dog by Rostenkowski's 'n go whorehoppin' afters by Mama Tomek.'

Finger Idzikowski, another contemporary, also uses the expression "by Rostenkowski's."

Bruno Bicek at one point in the story says, "I'm disgusted of myself."

One other tendency which might be described as an addition to the grammar of American English is manifested in the following expressions:

"I'll wait better." (I'd better wait.)
"Just use it on white guys best." (It will be best if you . . .)

All three of these "additions" to the grammar of English—the appended vocative, the substituted preposition, and the misplaced adverb—have their roots in the patterns of the Polish language.

Lexical Variants

Relying, as it seems to, most heavily on the kind of grammatical peculiarities described above to manifest its Polish-American quality, the dialogue of the characters offers, in a selected sample, little that is surprising or "different" in the way of vocabulary. There are a number of items which serve to indicate the social status of the characters rather than their Polish-Americanism:

learn	for	teach
borrow	for	lend
sawbuck	for	ten dollars
Boogie	for	Negro
to ice	for	to knock out (in boxing)

There are a few lexical items which, although not exclusively or incontrovertibly Polishisms, are unusual enough to indicate a departure from the great body of low colloquial American English:

half a dog	for	half a pint (of whiskey)
whorehoppin'	for	visiting a whorehouse
Polish pop	for	whiskey
offsteerin'	for	misleading

(As in "You was offsteerin' me . . .")

A third kind of lexical variation from the standard involves what Krapp referred to when he wrote that mixtures such as German and English or Polish and English are ". . . of interest mainly in the humorous sketch of the vaudeville stage or for occasional comic relief in narrative." [4] These items seem to involve malapropism rather than any tendency which is uniquely Polish:

the dirty eye   for   a dirty look
  (Probably a blend of "a dirty look" and "the evil eye")
psychopathic   for   psychic
  ("That's 'cause I'm psychopathic. I tell what's on their minds.")
Be Aware   for   Beware
  (A backyard sign reads "Be Aware of the Dog.")

Only occasionally does a character lapse into Polish in his speech. Even though some of the Polish expressions are more than single words, perhaps it is as convenient as not to consider the use of Polish as a lexical variant rather than grammatical or pronunciational. On several occasions, minor characters utter the common Polish expletive *Psiakrew*. Josie the greenhorn whore says, on one occasion, "Good *majtek*! Good man! Good lucky!" which can be translated as "Good sailor! He's a good man! He brings good luck."

One Polish proverb is repeated wholly or in part a number of times: "*Grzmoty zabili diabla, diabla zabilia rzyda.*" This translates as "When the thunder kills a devil, a devil kills a jew." It is a saying which the Barber is fond of uttering on occasions in which he is planning to strike back at an individual or at fate for having victimized him. Bruno remembers and repeats the proverb during the crucial moments of his final fight in the ring. It helps him to summon the courage and staying power necessary to defeat his more clever and able opponent.

The term *boobatch*, which can be translated to mean "hick," "hillbilly," "rustic oaf," occurs once. Bruno uses it to describe a middle-aged Polish worker whom he has killed while attempting to rob him. When the immigrant is attacked by Bruno, he frees his mouth from Bruno's hand and shouts "*Mloty bandyta!*" ("Young bandit!").

In anger, during a violent argument, the Barber shouts at Steffi, "*Kurwa! Raiffur! Kurwa! Raiffur!*" He is accurately designating her profession (she works for Mama Tomek) and is suggesting that Bruno, her loved one, is also her protector-procurer.

Only one more instance of the use of Polish occurs—this by Steffi. At the height of intercourse she murmurs, "*Rany boskie. Jestem wniebie!*" ("My Lord. I'm in heaven!")

These last-mentioned three uses of Polish occur in moments of great stress for the speakers, which would suggest that only when moved by strong emotion are partially acculturated individuals likely to revert to their native or home language. Since it occurs, either fully or in part, four times in the book and since it suggests a theme of the novel—the theme of retribution visited upon the weak for wrongs suffered at the hands of the strong—the proverb seems to have a literary rather than a dialectal significance. The other three instances cited seem simply to confirm what the other devices have already strongly asserted—the Polish origins of the characters.

By comparison with the number, kind, and frequency of grammatical variants from English, the lexical variants are almost trifling in total impact. This leads one to suspect that Algren recognized, quite rightly, that the real distinctiveness of American English in comparison to Polish lies in its grammar. It would be most unusual indeed should these immigrants in a large urban community develop a lexicon exclusively theirs. Indeed, he quite rightly assumes that, lexicon being the easiest part of the language to learn, the Polish-Americans would adapt to it most quickly and completely.

Variant Pronunciation

Except in two cases, no attempt is made to suggest differences in pronunciation in the direction of Polishness. The first-generation speakers Josie and Bonifacy Konstantin reeval some pronunciation characteristics which are outside the normal range of American English. Perhaps even a few of these occur in some varieties of native pronunciation. Josie says

Good lucky.	for	Good luck.

(Many Polish words end in a sound much like that in the last syllable of *lucky*.)

I play lipfrog	for	I play leapfrog
wit' t'ings.	for	with things.

The barber consistently says

i-dee	for	idea
t'ing	for	thing
wid	for	with
altogedder	for	altogether
not'ing	for	nothing

What these two lists suggest is that the author made only a very limited attempt to indicate pronunciation differences, even in these two characters who would be most likely to display wide variation from the American pattern. A majority of the examples cited indicate difficulties with the /th/ sound. Only three of the cited words indicate variant vowel sounds. *I-dee*, which suggests a stress on the last syllable rather than a stress on the first, such as might be heard in some American dialects, appears a number of times—only in the speech of the Barber. Josie's *lipfrog* and *lucky* are clearly outside the range of native American pronunciation; *lipfrog*, however, might be found in the speech of non-native-Americans other than Poles.

An examination of many speeches by the book's protagonist, Bruno Bicek, reveals only two items meriting comment. He refers to his "Lefty Bicek Helt' shirt, Lefty Bicek Helt' shoes, and Lefty Bicek Helt' cap." Obviously, this is intended to suggest, although the pattern is not followed in other words containing the /th/ sound, that Lefty still has some vestiges of "Polish" in his speech. We know by his own admission at one point in the story and by his use of two Polish expressions, which have been discussed above, that he can and does on occasion speak Polish. Obviously, this repetition of "t'" is a further attempt to suggest his particular degree of bilingualness.

One other item occurs frequently in his speech. He says "oney" for "only." This pronunciation is probably marginal; that is, it probably occurs even among some varieties of standard English, but is often found in the speech of the young and the relatively uneducated in some areas. It is not "Polish."

In the speech of Steffi, at the beginning of the story, when she is represented as a naive seventeen-year-old who lives a rather cloistered life, there occur three items which, if they are intended to represent her age and relative inexperience, seem to be strangely chosen:

croosical	for	crucial
propitty	for	property
ever'thin'	for	everything

The first is a rather unlikely pronunciation of a word which, whether or not pronounced correctly, seems odd in her otherwise rather limited vocabulary. It is intended, evidently, to suggest her ignorance and unletteredness. The second and third are simply relaxed pronunciations which one might find on occasion in the speech of many Chicagoans.

A final, rather interesting, pronunciation variant is found in the word *hundred*. Bruno pronounces it, as rendered by the author, "hunerd" and, ten pages later, "hunderd." Jockey, one of the girls at Mama Tomek's, also pronounces it "hun'erd." Toward the end of the book, a local ring announcer, national origin not indicated, pronounces it "hunert." All three of these pronunciations occur in general low colloquial.

Never Come Morning abounds, as do many books which deal with characters from lower social strata, with examples of eye dialect:

jollopi	for	jalopy
boyz	for	boys
fer	for	for
'n lay off	for	and lay off
used t'be	for	used to be
ya	for	you
prostitoot	for	prostitute

There are two attempts to indicate pronunciation for which I cannot satisfactorily account:

collyseum	for	coliseum
backerds	for	backwards

The first of these seems to be unlikely in the speech of any Chicagoan, Polish-American or not, who is interested in prizefighting as is the speaker, Finger Idzikowski. The second occurs in the speech of an obscure character, present only in the beginning of the work, a Polish-American called Bibleback. Again, it seems, if interpreted in the only way possible, to indicate a pronunciation highly unlikely in a second generation Chicago-raised Polish-American, even one who works as does Bibleback on the W.P.A.

What all of the evidence suggests is that the author relies only slightly on variant pronunciation to suggest Polishness, using it mainly to indicate class position.

Sensitivity to the Language of Others

The prostitutes who work at Mama Tomek's are strangely sensitive to language. Their sensitivity is, I think, quite effective in a literary way. In addition, the aspects of language to which they show sensitivity are reflective of certain pervasive kinds of social-linguistic behavior.

Tookie, one of the girls, takes out her sense of degradation on her customers by refusing to allow them even the faintest hint of romance, in the literary sense of the term, in their dealings with her. When asked by one customer, "Do you enjoy being a prostitoot?" she replies scornfully, "Prostitute! Prostitute! What a fancy word."

Helen, another of the girls, known by her co-workers as Chiney-Eye Helen, has seen better days and has worked in better houses than Mama Tomek's. Helen considers herself superior to the other girls. She indicates her feelings of superiority, among other ways, in the following exchange:

"Comp'ny askin' for you, Helka," Mama Tomek would tell her gently.
"My name ain't 'Helka,'" the girl would snap; and remain sitting.
"Helen then, Honey, I'm sorry."
"My name ain't Helen."
"What is it, Honey-Sweet?"
"Don't Honey-Sweet me, It's Heléna."
And Mama T. would have to say it just like that: "Heléna."
But when Chiney-Eye Helen was especially cross, her right name was "Heléne."

In a conversation with the Barber, with whom she has been living, Steffi indicates the same kind of sensitivity about her name.
The Barber speaks:

"You not fool wid Lefthander no more, *Stasha*?"
"Don't *Stasha* me. My name is Steffi. . . ."

A few lines later the Barber says

"You like go home for stay?"
"Yes I go home," she told him, falling into his argot, "I go home for stay."

Still further along in the same long conversation this exchange occurs. The Barber again speaks first:

"Don't wor-ry. You not get. Twenty-two-doll-ars."
"Quit talkin' Polish."
"Ain't Polish. Is English."
"By you it sounds Polish."

This passage occurs at a time when she is again angry with the Barber. Obviously, whatever sounds Steffi hears in the foreshortened sentence patterns of the Barber contribute, for her, to a sense of Polishness in his speech. Her last angry remark is particularly touching in that it employs what seems to be a particularly "Polish" expression, "By you."

After further argument, blows, and a violent temporary reconciliation, Steffi says:

"I'll take your goddam coat."
"You not want."
"I want."

She has come full around to her earlier position. She unconsciously echoes his speech patterns again. She is still sensitive to the differentness of his language, but she has surrendered to it.

* * *

All the materials I have quoted from the dialogue in *Never Come Morning*, materials which are representative of the whole body of dialogue in the work, suggest two broad conclusions:

1. The author has relied largely, although not quite exclusively, on grammatical devices in the dialogue to indicate the Polishness of his characters.

2. He has used a combination of grammatical, lexical, and pronunciational techniques to suggest the social class position, especially of the second-generation Polish-Americans.

These findings seem to confirm the accuracy of George Krapp's broad statement of principle seventeen years before the novel was written:

"American dialect literature rests upon a foundation of general informal colloquial speech, locally established by action and setting with its local character confirmed by a slight addition of local practices in speech." [5]

Krapp was here referring to regional dialects, but if for "local" and "locally" we substitute an expression indicating national origin, Krapp's generalization seems to describe accurately Nelson Algren's practice.

Notes

1. Nelson Algren, *Never Come Morning* (New York: Harper and Bros., 1942).

2. Sumner Ives, "Dialect Differentiation in the Stories of Joel Chandler Harris," in *Readings in Applied English Linguistics*, ed. Harold B. Allen (New York: Appleton-Century-Crofts, 1958), p. 414.

3. George Philip Krapp, *The English Language in America* (2 vols; New York: The Century Co., 1925) Vol. I, p. 235.

4. Krapp, *op. cit.*, vol. I, p. 229.

5. Krapp, *op. cit.*, vol. I, p. 243.

LITERARY DIALECT IN MILT GROSS' *NIZE BABY*

LAWRENCE M. DAVIS
Illinois Institute of Technology

In a popular column which appeared in *The New York World* during the 1920's, Mrs. Katz tells Mrs. Feitelbaum that "De baby ate opp all de pills." Mrs. Feitelbaum gets very upset, but then is calmed when Mrs. Katz says that she was *pilling* potatoes, and the baby ate up all the potato pills. To ease the baby's stomach ache, Mrs. Katz runs queek to the medicine cabinet to find the appropriate peels.

If anyone is so culturally deprived as to have never read this and other stories by Milt Gross, he should know that Gross' stories were about Jewish immigrants living in The Bronx during the first decade after World War I. The stories were usually divided into three parts, the first of which was just illustrated. The second part usually involved Morris, on the third floor, beating his son Isidore for some kind of mischief: "So Isidore (SMACK), a dug you bringing into de houze, ha! (SMACK!!!)–." In the third part, Mama rewards the baby for eating all its food: "Nize baby! Itt opp all de farina, so Mamma gonna tell him about de Hare wit de Tuttis." From this third part comes the title of Gross' first extensive collection of dialect stories, *Nize Baby*.[1]

In 1929, Robert Menner praised the literary dialect in *Nize Baby*, saying that Mrs. Feitelbaum's speech reflects "exactly the effect on the ordinary hearer of the Yiddish attempt to pronounce our vowels."[2] Menner seems to confirm the fact that we tend to judge dialect writing in terms of whether or not it "sounds right" to us. That is, if a dialect writer is to be successful, he must present his reader with an illusion of reality. This assumes that the reader already knows, or thinks he knows, what the dialect in question sounds like.

The dialect writer, in this sense, cannot count on as much suspension of disbelief as can other writers. In Hawthorne, we all accept the idea that a man can utter a curse which affects seven generations, but we are not likely to accept the dialect of a Jewish immigrant if he sounds like a Gullah Negro.

Furthermore, the dialect writer must, of course, use the conventional alphabet, with all its drawbacks. In *The Return of Hyman Kaplan*,[3] Leo Rosten points out that one of his characters would probably have said "I hate the brat" for *I ate the bread*, but, because of probable misunderstanding, as well as because of the implications in having a kindly old person say such a thing, Rosten settles for "I ate the brad," and sacrifices some accuracy in the process. Somehow, Milt Gross manages to meet Menner's requirement, giving the illusion of reality within the restrictions of the conventional alphabet, and it would be helpful to examine his technique in greater detail.

One of the major problems posed by Gross' use of literary dialect, a problem common in all such writing, is that of inconsistency. How reassuring it would be if one could find one-to-one correspondences between conventional spellings and dialect spellings. But Gross is not so accommodating. The word *crook*, for example, is sometimes *cruke*, suggesting the pronunciation, [kruk], while at other times, it is *crook*, suggesting the conventional pronunciation, [krʊk].

Because this and similar examples abound in *Nize Baby*, the simplest way to present the phonological aspects of the characters' speech is in tabulary form, so the following tables are divided into three sections: (1) phonological changes indicated by variant spellings, (2) examples of these spellings from *Nize Baby*, and (3) conventional spellings in the book for the same sound, suggesting that the pronunciation of the sound is conventional. In cases where Gross seldom or never attempts dialect spellings, the relevant spaces on the tables are marked "RARE."

Changes	Examples	Regular Spellings
[i>ɪ]	pills (peels)	week, sleeping
	mizzles (measles)	
[ɪ>i]	queek (quick)	did, six
	weenter (winter)	
[e>ɛ, ɪ]	denty (dainty) RARE	baseball, failure
	wickation (vacation) RARE	
[ɛ>æ]	jally fish (jellyfish)	cent, complexion
	tan (ten)	
[æ>ɛ]	abstrect (abstract)	abstract, pants
	plester (plaster)	
[ə>ɔ]	opp (up)	nuts, husband
	stoddy (study)	
[ɚ>ɔi]	woister (worster)	girls, hurt
	goils (girls)	
[ar>a, ɔ]	bok (bark)	harms, card
	homonica (harmonica)	
[u>ʊ]	pull (pool) RARE	shoot, phooey
[u>ui]	cooypons (coupons)	
	Rooybin (Rubin)	
[ʊ>u]	cruke (crook) RARE	crook, wood
[o>ə]	stuns (stones)	hold, elope
	uppened (opened)	

Changes	Examples	Regular Spellings
[or>ə]	reputt (report)	floors
	tuttis (tortoise)	
[ɔ>ə]	tutt (thought)	along, donkeh
	Brunx (Bronx)	
[aʊ>ɔ, a]	donn (down)	out, down
	cron (crown)	
[p>b]	crebs (craps)	swipe
[b>p]	cop (cob)	job
[d>t]	foot (food)	husband
[g>k]	frok (frog)	doing, peeling
[θ>t]	tanks (thanks)	thank
[θ>d]	denks (thanks)	breath
[ð>d]	breeding (breathing)	breathing
[v>f]	fife (five)	five
[v>w]	wcesiting (visiting)	very
[w>v]	svipe (swipe)	swipe
[s>z]	houze (house)	house
[z>s]	gracing (grazing)	business
[s>ts]	tsalesman (salesman)	safe
[dʒ>ʒ]	collision (collegian)	gradually
[ʒ>dʒ]	collegian (collision)	pleasure
[dʒ>tʃ]	cholly (jolly)	just
adds [h]		
between	Coney Highland	
vowels	(Coney Island)	so exhausted

It should be noted here that Gross' technique, for the most part, involves simple substitutions.[4] The tense vowels become lax, and the lax ones tense; the consonants generally become voiceless, or become homorganic affricates or fricatives. But, in each case, the problem of analysis is complicated by the fact that Gross is inconsistent in the way he represents Yiddish-English.[5]

Furthermore, because there are certain patterns in English spelling which can be considered to represent consistently the same sound (i.e. the spelling a-C-e to represent the vowel [e], in *mate*), we can be fairly certain about how Gross wants us to pronounce his dialect spellings. In a few cases, however, a real problem arises. Does the *donn* represent [dan] or [dɔn]? Unfortunately, an analysis of the actual speech of immigrant Jews does not help either, since they use both these pronunciations, as well as the form [daʊn].[6] The simple fact is that *donn* can represent either [dan] or [dɔn]; both pronunciations are possible, and we have no basis for choosing between them.

For sounds which are not readily adaptable to the Yiddish-English dialect, Gross has a tendency to substitute eye dialect. For example, there are only a very few cases in *Nize Baby* where [ɔi] becomes anything else, but Gross frequently uses eye dialect to achieve the illusion of irregularity, as in *loyyer* for *lawyer*.

The syntax employed in *Nize Baby*, like the phonology, is handled inconsistently. That is, though Gross puts many non-standard syntactic patterns in the mouths of his characters, there are many examples of standard sentences as well. The following admittedly incomplete analysis is intended to stress the non-standard aspects of Gross' syntax, and should not be interpreted to mean that there are no standard, regular sentences in the book.

The kinds of games which Gross plays with English syntax can be divided into three major groups. (1) He simply substitutes one word for another in much the same way as he handles the phonological aspect of the dialect; (2) he omits pronouns entirely; and (3) he makes genuine changes in sentence structure. Clearly, these groups tend to overlap, and in any one sentence several devices may occur at the same time.

In the first two groups, involving simple substitutions and omissions, the most common word classes involved are prepositions and pronouns. Gross substitutes (1) *by* for *for*, as in "Was almost by us a calumnity" and "Was quiet by you in de houze lest evening?"; (2) *witt* (*with*) for *of*, as in "Sotch a dope wit a hignorant jenitor wot we got."; (3) *from* for *by* or *of*, as in ". . . a weedow witt a son from de name from Jeck."; (4) *wot* for (*so*) *that*, as in "So Tom gave a wheesper de huss, 'Girryopp.' Wot he gredually ran away, witt de boggy witt all de pipple, wot dey all tombled out in a deetch." (5) *wot dey* or *wot he* for *who*, as in "From a weeked hogre wot he henchanted me" and ". . . it made a tuttle from saven wifes wot dey deesapeared."; (6) omits *it* from construction, as in "What was?" "Was so." and "Now is better."; (7) uses *witt* in parallel lists, as in ". . . was dere a whole cow—witt seextin docks witt fife geeze—witt a willberrel full from cebbidges—witt a heff from peeg yat, witt a whole keg from tsider."

The third kind of syntactic variation in *Nize Baby* involves changes in sentence structure. Once again, Gross is in no sense consistent, but nonetheless he, at the same time, achieves both comedy and apparent verisimilitude. For example, his characters put time adverbials immediately after the verb: "He hed lest week de tonsils cut out." [7] Verb tenses are often non-parallel in cases like "I tut what we'll gonna hev to call a nembulance."; "You promised me you'll gonna change."; "You promised me you'll gonna took it" and many other cases where *gonna* is employed.

Conversely, Gross' characters often employ parallel tenses in sentences where they are not used in English, especially after the verb *did*. For example, "Where deed you was?" "What deed you deed?" "Deed you deed?" Deedn't I deedn't?" "Deed we hed it lest night a peekneck." ". . . he deedn't had no collar in de faze." ". . . I deedn't heard never from a monkeh ranch."

Frequently, also, Mrs. Feitelbaum and friends will put verb phrases before noun phrases, as in "Was sleepery and grizzy de floor."; "Was playing a beeyudiful peectchur." When pronouns are used, the object sometimes precedes the subject and verb, as in "De potato pills he ate." In all constructions involving inversions, the word *it* seems to be entirely optional, if the subject is not a pronoun. Hence, "It geeves a ring de teleaphun" seems to vary freely with "Geeves a ring de telaphun."

Likewise, *it* seems to be optional in constructions, in normal word order, employing a direct object. "So dey hed it one seengle cow" can vary with "Dey hed one single cow" or "One single cow dey hed."

Aside from the phonology and grammar which Gross employs, there are other devices which can be classed under a general rubric—the malapropism. In one of the sections where Morris is beating his son Isidore, this time for breaking a window with an errantly-thrown baseball, part of Morris' monologue runs as follows: "I'll geeve him (SMACK). Dot bum (SMACK). Dot he'll grow opp a respectable poison!!!" (p. 22) Clearly, the spelling of the final word is more than a simple attempt at phonological versimilitude; even though [s] often becomes [z], in examples like "houze", there are enough cases where the shift does not occur. In the case of Morris' speech, however, the spelling tends to comically undercut his whole point.

Similarly, during one of the fairy tales which Mamma tells to nize baby, Pocahontas (spelled correctly, by the way) saves John Smith from her father by threatening to tell "momma what it was going on lest night in the Hell Fay Clob witt you witt dot wemp from a Minnie-Ha-Ha." (p. 89) The chief decides to relent under pressure, and give his blessing: "Blast you mine cheeldren." (p. 90)

There are other more numerous occasions where Gross tends to use humorous malapropisms more-or-less for their own sake, without attempting to approach phonological verisimilitude. In the same Pocahontas story, Nize Baby's mother concludes that John Smith and Pocahontas got married, and "so in a shut time de chiff was a grenpapa from a liddle caboose." (p. 90)

Isidore, of course, is always being whipped for something. On one occasion, when he has thrown a firecracker into a Chinese laundry, Morris doesn't spare the rod, because Morris doesn't want his son to grow up to be a "craptical joker." (p. 53)

In the conversations between Mrs. Feitelbaum and Mrs. Katz, Gross uses phonological shifts to create humorous misunderstandings between the two women:

> Second Floor—Sotch a haxpeerence wot it happened by us lest night, Mrs. Feitelbaum—I'll rimamber it so long wot I'll leeve.
> First Floor—Wot was??
> Second Floor—Hm, don't esk. I fill wick in de knizz.
> First Floor—So wot was???
> Second Floor—De baby swallowed a pan!!
> First Floor—Yi yi yi yi—a pan!—a frying pan, maybe oder a deesh pan?
> Second Floor—No!—a fountain pan!
> . . . .
> First Floor—So in de minntime, wot'll be?
> Second Floor—So in de minntime, we'll write wid a penzil . . . (p. 73)

When Mrs. Katz tells Mrs. Feitelbaum that there was a loud argument between the couple next door when the wife accused the husband of "becoming lately werry infatuated," Mrs. Feitelbaum cannot understand why the lady is complaining. She says, "I weesh wot mine Mowriss would become a liddle more infatuated—Bellive me—he could stand about five pounds more." (p. 41)

The baby swallows pills; potato pills. Stephen Decatur becomes Siffen de caterer. Mrs. Katz son Looy is given a disinfectant so he "shouldn't dewelop an inflection." And, to make a phone call, one character has to call through a "schvitzbud."

Schvitz, in the last example, is incidentally the Yiddish word for *to sweat* or *to perspire*, and is one of the very few Yiddish expressions in *Nize Baby*— an indication that Gross intended his stories to be of interest to Jew and non-Jew as well. This does not mean, however, that one could appreciate *Nize Baby* if he were totally unaware of what Yiddish-English sounds like. But in the case of this dialect particularly, we Americans have been bombarded with comedians like Myron Cohen and others who have made Jewish dialect stories very much a part of American humor. Clearly, if one is familiar with Yiddish-English, either through an appreciation of Myron Cohen's stories, or by an accident of birth, he is more likely to enjoy Gross' humor than is someone who lacks that appreciation or experience.[8]

Perhaps because I do like Myron Cohen's stories, and because I am familiar with Yiddish-English through an accident of birth, I have no wish to deal pedantically from the bottom of the deck to show all the places where Gross' spellings and grammatical structures do not accurately reflect Yiddish-English dialects. Certainly the high number of malapropisms in *Nize Baby* is atypical of Yiddish-English speakers.

The sometimes crude comedy, accurate or inaccurate, is successful, and I am not altogether persuaded that accuracy is, in itself, a sufficient test for the success of literary dialect. Future students of literary dialect might explore this area further, especially with the use of malapropisms. I do know of an old Jewish lady who refers to the Empire State Building as a "sky-scratcher."

Notes

1. (New York, 1925).
2. (New York, 1938, 1959), p. 15.
3. "Popular Phonetics," *AS*, IV (1929), 411. For other examples of literary dialect studies, see the following: Carol Boykin, "Sut's Speech: The Dialect of a 'Nat'ral Borned' Mountaineer," *The Lovinggood Papers* (1965), 36–42; James W. Downer, "The Dialect of the Bigelow Papers," Unpub. disc., Univ. of Michigan, 1958; Sumner Ives, "A Theory of Literary Dialect," *Tulane Studies in English*, (1950); Sumner Ives, "The Phonology of the Uncle Remus Stories," *Publication of the American Dialect Society*. 22 (1954); J. A. Morris, "Gullah in The Novels

of William Gillmore Simms," *American Speech* 22 (1947), 46–53; Eric W. Stock-ton, "Poe's Use of Negro Dialect in 'The Gold Bug'," *Studies in Languages and Linguistics in Honor of Charles C. Fries*, ed. Albert H. Marckwardt (Ann Arbor, 1964); Gary N. Underwood, "Linguistic Realism in *Roderick Random*," *Journal of English and Germanic Philology*. 69 (1970), 32–40.

4. Many of these substitutions are not typical of Yiddish-English speakers. The [s>z], [dʒ>ʒ], [ʒ>dʒ] consonant shifts are exceedingly rare, as are the [i>ɪ], [o>ə] [u>ui], [e>ɪ], vowel shifts. See my "The Phonology of Yiddish-American Speech," Univ. of Chicago Diss., 1967, and "The Stressed Vowels of Yiddish-American English," *PADS* (1967).

5. This inconsistency, incidentally, reflects the actual linguistic behavior of Yiddish-American speakers. See the two studies cited in note 4.

6. "The Phonology of Yiddish-American Speech," p. 45.

7. This and other examples are, of course, a direct result of Yiddish sentence structure's being applied to English. But, because of the numerous standard sentences in *Nize Baby*, it seems fruitless to engage in showing how Gross' syntax reflects Yiddish syntax. The single fact is that the syntax is neither English nor Yiddish when taken *in toto*; it's Grossisch.

8. Gross also depicts non-Jewish dialects with the same success. Cf. the Italian and Cockney dialects, pp. 17–18, and the New York dialect, p. 24.

NOTES ON WEST PENN–OHIO PHONOLOGY

Clyde T. Hankey
Youngstown State University

Two complementary aspects of a principle vigorously enunciated by Raven McDavid are background to the discussion here: the native is his own best and worst informant in a dialect study—unlikely to notice the distinctive idioms of his dialect, but well-situated to assess their systematic relationships. Both aspects of this paradoxical generalization have encouraged and cautioned my examination of what I will for convenience call the West Penn–Ohio (WPO) idiom, both as a native of Pittsburgh and as a resident of Youngstown.

The outer limits of this contiguous core area of West Midland American may conveniently be indexed by the lack of phonemic contrast between [ɑ] and [ɒ], resulting in the homophony of such words as *cot-caught, knotty-naughty,* and *Paul-pall.* The primary phonetic incidence—as noted by Hans Kurath and Raven McDavid, *The Pronunciation of English in the Atlantic States (PEAS)*, pp. 17–18—is [ɒ] generally, [ɑ] in the [-i] and [-u] diphthongs and before [-r]. Secondary occurrence of [ɒ] even in the latter contexts suggests leveling toward narrower allophonic consistency.

Since there are signs that this [ɑ] = [ɒ] phonological feature is spreading locally, it may turn out to be too broad to mark this local idiom, but its place in the WPO phonological system suggests that it will remain the best single descriptive reference to that idiom.

Because it is necessary, for coherence, to choose between complete tabulation of observed WPO usages and an attempt to relate them systematically, I have chosen the latter alternative. Specific citations fall together regularly enough to justify some use of *sporadic* to indicate "not-yet-analyzed currency." And sets of expressions whose relationships must be sought in sociological or semantic rather than more narrowly linguistic domains are frequent in my data, though I will introduce them only to the extent of present relevance.

A. Vowels

Though I am greatly indebted here to the analysis of Kurath and McDavid, *PEAS* (pp. 5–9), and Kurath's *A Phonology and Prosody of Modern English* (pp. 17–20), I will take some liberties of both symbolization and analysis in working from the following scheme of checked and free vowels:

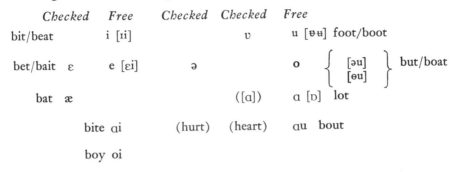

Several considerations make this scheme useful for considering WPO vowel pronunciation:

1. The free vowels /i, e, u, o/, like the diphthongs /ɑi, ɑu, oi, ui/, consistently show either homorganic length (as /i, e, u/, sometimes do) or an outgliding sustension. On the other hand, the typically checked vowels /ɛ, æ/ when free in *yeah* and *bah!* regularly have an ingliding second element [-ə], as does the untypically free /ə/ of *aha!, uh. . .*, and *huh!* (whether nasalized or not) with lengthening.

One effect of this marginally systematic difference seems to be the phonological ambiguity of /ɑ/ as a free or checked vowel. Several aspects of its occurrence in WPO speech readily reflect the conflicting output of the phonemic integrity of /ɑ/ versus (1) the frequency of [ɑ] as a checked allophone and (2) the significance suggested here of [-ə] gliding allophones of "normally" checked vowels. There is, for example, at least a sporadic incidence, among people who also and regularly use [ɒ] in these and similar words, of [ɑə] or [ɑ] in *wash, gosh, God*—sometimes with a peripherally stylistic motivation "considered," or perhaps "pious" for *God*.

2. Back/central and rounded/unrounded contrasts are either sub-systematic or only marginally systematic. Since the range of application of this statement pretty much coincides with the phonemic application of [ɑ = ɒ], the structural implications will be obvious: *hut* and *hurt* differs systematically not in vowel nucleus but by the *r*-consonantism of the second, /hət/ vs. /hərt/; /ə/ is a usually unrounded central-to-back vowel, symmetrical in the system to /ʋ/ and the checked [ɑ] allophone of /ɑ/. Similar observation of the whole or partial centralization of WPO "back" vowels is amply illustrated in Kurath-McDavid, *PEAS* (p. 18 and related synopses).

3. The nuclear vowels of diphthongs are the only source—other than mutually exclusive phones [ə] and [ɵ]—of retained contrast between back-or-rounded and central-or-unrounded vowels for the WPO area. A functional pivot for testing this contrast is the diphthong of *boy*, which always contrasts with that of *buy* though not always with that of *buoy*. In the typical pattern of contrasts for both Youngstown and Pittsburgh focal points of this area, the unrounded nuclei occur in *buy* and *bough* (and, to consider a quasi-diphthongal parallelism, in *bar*), the rounded in *boy* and *buoy* (and *bore*, *boor*). There seem, furthermore, to be only two degrees of height in these diphthongal contrasts. The two usual variant patterns are these:

PATTERN A— *Central/Unrounded* *Back/Rounded* (First variant predominates.)

Higher:		*buoy* /bui/	*boor* /bur/
		[ʋi ∿ ɵi]	[ʋr ∿ ɵr]
Lower: *buy* /bɑi/ *bough* /bɑu/		*boy* /boi/	*bore* /bor/
bar /bɑr/		[ɵi ∿ ɔi ∿ ɒi]	[ɵr ∿ ɔr ∿ ɒr]

PATTERN B— 		*Back/Rounded*

Higher:	*buoy* = *boy* /boi/	*boor* = *bore* /bor/
	[ʋi ∿ ɵi ∿ ɔi]	[ʋr ∿ ɵr ∿ ɔr]
Lower:	*buy* /bɑi/ *bough* /bɑu/	*bar* /bɑr/
	[bɒi] [bɒu]	[bɒr]

A particular individual's pronunciation may show some merging of these patterns, but not in a way that changes the conflict implicit here between phonological system and subsystem—the /ɑ/-/o/ contrast's overtones of central-unrounded versus back-rounded contrasts (Pattern A) against the more simply systematic contrasts (Pattern B, and other phonological circumstances) manifested in terms of low vs mid differences of height.

This subsystematic central (unrounded) versus back (rounded) variation has a peripherally linguistic, and therefore relevant, place in such matters of phonemic incidence as the occurrence of, and disputes about /sɑri/ vs. /sori/ for *sorry*—and similarly for *Laura* (*Lora*, *Lara*), *laurel*, *aural-oral*; this last pair may be /orəl-arəl/, /arəl-orəl/, or homophonous /orəl/ or /arəl/. That is, pronunciations with [ɑ ∿ ɔ] before /r/ are phonologically ambiguous incidences of /ɑ/ and /o/ and will be construed differently—at least on the two very different bases of morphological identification and phonological esthetics. While the pronunciation /sɑri/ seems primarily to exhibit prestige-dialect borrowing, it also satisfies the [ɑ] + /r/ allophonic selection of Pattern A illustrated above. From a different point of view, /sori/ treats *sorry* as a transparent derivation from *sore*. Both motivations for phonemic incidence have a clear place in any WPO idiom. The vocalic selection by post-nuclear /r/ seems significant also to the historical explanation of intrusive /r/ of *wash*, *Washington* /worš, woršɪŋtn̩/ in WPO speech.[1] It would seem from this that the incidence of /ɑ/ or /o/ in this position may be influenced from several different directions.

Somewhat similar but more complex morphophonemic relationships are at work in the WPO variation between /lɑjər/ and /lojər/ for *lawyer* (similarly for *sawyer*). The root *law* is regularly [1ɒ]. Where the idiom permits phonological conditioning across the morpheme boundary, /lɑjər/ may result—contrasting nevertheless with both (1) the monosyllabic /lɑir/ and (2) the (morphologically ordered) disyllabic /lɑiər/ forms of *liar*. (This is not to say that a given pronunciation may not be ambiguous, but rather that the prosodic *freeness* of the vowel of *law* survives the assimilative unrounding toward the following /-j-/.) Where the root form maintains its phonological as well as morphological integrity, however, principles of phonological assimilation internal to both the syllable and the morpheme result in /lojər/. A great many similar factors of the relative ordering with regard to morpheme boundaries, phonological assimilations, and the prosodic suspensions or enhancements of either will appear with WPO usage and perhaps in its differences from other idioms.

4. The preceding discussion will have raised, especially in relation to the /oi/ diphthong, a question of the phonology of /o/. In terms of the variation within WPO speech, it seems most reasonable to regard this as a slightly outgliding phonetic diphthong [ɵu] with a typical mid/central-to-back/ rounded beginning. Chief variants are the typically Pittsburgh [əu] (with some rounding as an occasional feature), back rounded [ɵu] and [ɔu]; the last of these, for some speakers or hearers, marks a prosodic or stlyistic character, perhaps "exclamatory" or "hortatory."

As the first element in the diphthong /oi/, the abbreviated /o/ phoneme maintains a back and/or rounded articulation as a distinctive aspect of its cross-gliding (back-to-front) phonological identity. And it seems consistent with this observation, along with the rest of the preceding discussion, to suggest again that *either or both* back articulation and rounding will characterize the normal identification of the "back" vowels /ʊ, u, o, ɑ/.

5. The suggestion in A3 above of the relevance of prosody to the phonology of *lawyer* and *liar* can apply equally well to a discussion of the /e/ phoneme. Just as *liar* has two regular prosodic variants, one of which is in Western Pennsylvania typically [lɑ⁹r] and homophonous with *lyre*, *payer* has the prosodic variants /peər/ and /pɛr/, the second homophonous with *pair, pear, pare*. The systematic distinction of *liar* and *lyre*, *payer* and *pair* is the direct product of the morphological complexity transparent in /lɑiər/ *liar* and /peər/ *payer* in contrast to the stylistic feature "blur" (popularly, Slurvian) in monosyllabic versions resembling *lyre* and *pair*.[2]

In these and other aspects of phonology, prosody and morphology will exercise considerable control over the systematic character if not the actual articulation of our speech.

6. A rather paradoxical corroboration of the ingliding sustensions of checked vowels, mentioned in A1 above, appears in the presence of a high rather than mid offglide, differently attested in several variant idioms within

as well as outside of WPO speech. Instead of the more regularly current [æə, ɛə, ɪə, ə:, ʊə] allophonic versions of prosodically sustained, hence atypically freed /æ, ɛ, ɪ, ə, ʊ/, there is a systematic but rather randomly distributed appearance of [æɨ, ɛɨ, ɪɨ, əɨ, ʊɨ] in *ash*, *special*, *fish*, *hush*, and *bush*. Two aspects of this phenomenon seem noteworthy:

> (a) The higher offglide shows assimilation to following palatals in the same syllable: The sibilants /š/, /ž/ and stop /-g/ (with front vowels) are the clearest correlates in WPO speech, though other Midland and Southern idioms show similar developments with /-s, -z, -sk, -č, -ǰ, -k/, and there is reason to associate /r/ with this group in considering the incidence of /e/ before intervocalic /r/. (See B5 below.)
>
> (b) The variants [ɛɨ, ɪɨ] regularly coalesce with /e, i/ in these phonetic environments, with the resulting fluctuations and seeming counter-tendencies for /ɛ/ and /e/ in *egg*, *beg*, *leg vague*, *measure*, *pleasure*, and the like. Similar fluctuations exist for /ɪ/ and /i/ in *eagle*, *legal*, *dish*, *wish*, *vision*, and others of that type. In both cases the diphthongization of checked vowels has overtones of social significance, both in (probably older) terms of rural vs. urban, and of unschooled vs. schoolish usage—and perhaps also in still other dimensions.

The relative frequency of this phenomenon in WPO speech seems at a guess to be from greatest to least for /ɛ, ɪ, æ, ʊ, ə/. A comparison of this and other dialects with the same phenomenon would, I suspect, show more clearly both the systematic and geographical ranges of this variation.

7. The assessment of [ʌ] as an allophone of mid-central /ə/ seems desirable on the basis of its predictable occurrence chiefly in the company of velar /1/ (except where /ɛ/, or [ɜ] allophones of /ə/ that may be annexed to /ɛ/ appear, as in *color*, *ulcer*, etc.). Elsewhere, a clearly lower-mid-back vowel (rounded or not) seems frequently to be interpreted as, or annexed to, /ɑ/ ([ɒ]), as in the *un*-prefix, which is sensibly misspelled *on(friendly)* for its sporadic WPO occurrence. (Notice also *PEAS*, Map 88, *nothing* with [ɒ].) Otherwise /ə/ has a wide allophonic range, from [ɐ] to [ɨ] in height, and from front [ɜ] to back [ʌ].

B. Consonants

The system in WPO speech may also reasonably be based on the matrix summarized by Kurath and McDavid, *PEAS*, p. 9:

Labial	*Dental*	*Alveolar*	*Palatal*	*Velar*	*Glottal*
p		t	č	k	
b		d	ǰ	g	
f	θ	s	š		h
v	ð	z	ž		
m		n	l r	ŋ	
w			j(ˀ)		

1. The vertical alignment presented here differs from that in *PEAS* to represent potentially significant peculiarities of WPO phonology. For example, /θ, ð/ are dental fricatives with stop allophones (utterance-initial stressed syllables)—a feature I feel sure is systematically related to the occurrence in some urban idioms of dental stop phonemes in *these* and *those*, and to the fact that contrast is sometimes retained between [ḍoz] *those* and [doz] *doze* in these idioms.

The assignment of /s, z/ as alveolars and /l/, /r/, and /ᶚ/ (the last not really part of WPO phonology) as palatal is altogether the writer's bias. All of these show considerable fluctuation, both by speaker and by phonological context. But like the dorso-velar /r/—which seems, subjectively, to be an Ohio rather than Pennsylvania characteristic—these differences seem not to affect the systematic relevance of the descriptions here.

2. The WPO /r/ seems to be systematically ambiguous. On the one hand, /r/ clearly belongs among the sonorants in (a) its syllabic incidence and (b) its effect on preceding vowels (see B4 below). On the other hand, it shows phonetic symmetry with semivowels /w, j/ and their complementation of postnuclear /-u, -i/. The chief illustration of this latter characteristic has already been noted as the selection of the non-back, unrounded allophone [ɑ, a⌋ in /ɑr/.

3. The normal patterning of /l/ is prevocalic palatal [ḷ], postvocalic velar [ɫ], with both allophones appearing intervocalically. The major separation of idioms seems to be the range of different vowels co-occurring with the intervocalic palatal [ḷ]: [ḷ] only after /i/; [ḷ] between /i, ɪ/ and /i/; [ḷ] between any vowel and /i, ɪ/. These conditions all apply as restrictions upon [ḷ]; intervocalic velar [ɫ] occurs freely throughout WPO speech. In all the idiom variants suggested here there is a potential contrast between *Greeley* [griḷi] and *really* [riəɫi]—especially as an aspect of schoolish usage (see Note 2). In all cases, it seems, the normal velar [ɫ⌊ of root words like *real* and *feel* is sustained by morphological transparency, whereas the intervocalic palatal [ḷ] is within the capacities of WPO phonology, available for stylistic, or other, selections.

That the effective structural contrasts here are vocalic, with incidental variation in /l/ allophones, is especially evident when this interplay between palatal and velar /l/ disappears in that WPO idiom which shows reduction of the /i ≠ ɪ/ contrast before /l/ ([ɫ]) and resulting homophony of *meal*/*mill* and *feel*/*fill*, frequent in the speech of natives of Youngstown and New Castle. Similarly, and especially for New Castle, /u, ʊ/ also do not contrast in this context, so that *pool* = *pull*, and *school* has both /u/ and /ʊ/.

A further aspect of the velarization of /l/, particularly as a Pennsylvania rather than Ohio phenomenon, is the concurrent feature of labialization, so that *feeling* and like forms will have regular articulation variants of the type [fiˠʷɪŋ]. The co-occurrence of features sets *falling* [fɒˠʷɪŋ] apart from *following* [fɒʏ̭əwɪŋ], but not without actual homophony, and regular confusion to those "outside the idiom."

4. Effects similar to the reduction of /i, ɪ/ contrasts before /l/ appear for diphthongs before all the sonorants. These effects are greatest before /l, r/ but prominent also before /m, n/. (Relevant incidences of /ŋ/ are rare if at all current.) Two clear stages of the process appear to be (a) abbreviation of /ɑi/ → [aᵉ, aᵊ] and /ɑu/ → [ɑᵊ, aᵊ]; (b) reduction of /ɑi/–/ɑu/ contrasts in these circumstances. Contrastive sets of at least the following types will be evident:

(1) tire [taᵉr] ≠ tower [taᵊr] ≠ tar [tɑr]
   tile [taᵉɬ] ≠ towel [tɑºɬ] ≠ tall [tɒɬ]
   nine [naᵉn] ≠ noun [naᵊn] ≠ non- [nɒn]
   mime [maᵉm]   ≠   mom [mɒm]

(2) tire [tɑr] = tower [tɑr] ≠ tar [tɑr]
   OR tire [tɑr] ≠ tower [tɑr] = tar [tɑr]
   tile [taɬ] = towel [taɬ] ≠ tall [tɒɬ]
   nine [naᵉn] ≠ noun [naᵊn] ≠ non- [nɒn]
   mime   ≠   mom *as in (1)*

(3) tire [tɑr] = tower [tɑr] = tar [tɑr]
   tile [tɑ<ɬ] = towel [tɑ<ɬ] ≠ tall [tɒɬ]
   Others as above

Similar abbreviations of these diphthongs occur elsewhere—apparently more frequently before voiced or fricative consonants than before voiceless or stop consonants or in open syllables, though for many contexts the incidence of /ɑi/ and /ɑu/ is infrequent or rare enough to make both neat and safe generalization difficult. There is some difference in the occurrence of this diphthong shortening in different parts of the WPO area, but it seems well-established in Pennsylvania and derivative areas of Eastern Ohio, including especially the area south of Youngstown.

A less widely attested but related shortening of /oi/ to [eə] or [ɔə] occurs before [ɬ] (cf. *PEAS*, Map 145: *boiled, spoiled,* and *oil*). The clearest association with a following [ɬ] might suggest that the systematic assignment should be with /i ⌒ ɪ/ and /u ⌒ ʊ/ reductions. But the occurrence more than sporadically of [dʒeᵊn] *join,* [keᵊnɾ] *corner,* and the more frequent [ge:n, geᵊn] *goin'* and ө:ɬ, өᵊɬ] *oil* indicate parallelism to the typically DIPHTHONG + SONORANT abbreviation. (Compare *PEAS*, Map 146, *oyster* for illustration of possibly similar phonology in the morphological reinterpretation /oistɾ/ → /orstɾ/, and its relation to the [ɔə] → [ɔr] suggested in Note 1.)

These diphthongal reductions of contrast and the confusion of free and checked monophthongs (mentioned in A5 above) seem to have comparable results. The recoverability of *lie* + *ing* from [laᵊn] *lyin'* is a significant feature both of its general linguistic character and of the range of phonological forms it shows, whereas [laᵊn] *line = lion* remains "within the grip" of WPO phonology. In all circumstances, furthermore, phonological imitation of morphological necessity— [laiən] for *lion*, [tauər] for *tower*—is a marked aspect of schoolish WPO usage, including the linguistic exaggeration mentioned at the beginning of Note 2.

5. Postvocalic and intervocalic /r/ exhibit distinct but related effects, judging by the incidence of preceding /ɪ ∿ i, e, ε, æ ʊ ∿ u, o, ɑ, ə/. One idiom distinguishes thus:

	V	-r	-r-
ɪ ∿	i:	peer	cheery
e ∿	ε:	pair	cherry, very
	æ:	—	chary, vary
	ə:	purr	hurry
ʊ ∿	u:	poor	Lurie, durable
	o:	pour	lorry, story, adorable
	ɑ:	par	starry

The number of contrasts before postvocalic /r/ is one less than the number before intervocalic /r/. This idiom is one marked by both age and geographical differences. That is, except for Allegheny County (Metropolitan Pittsburg) and eastwards, where the contrast of [æ ≠ ε] + /r/ + VOWEL may be found regardless of age, WPO usage tends to show this contrast only among older people in Ohio and the more western counties of Pennsylvania.

Where /ε/ and /æ/ do not contrast before intervocalic /r/, the prevailing pronunciation pattern is for the words that "could" have /æ/ to show /ε/. But there is a great deal of fluctuation in the case, with such typical incidences as these:

/ɑ/ in *carry*, Harry*, marry*, starry, tarry* "of tar"
/ε/ in *bury, carry, hairy, Harry, marry, Mary, merry, vary*
/ε ∿ e/ in *hairy*, Mary*, vary** (and perhaps others)
/ə/ in *bury, furry*
/ɪ/ in *dearie, merry*.

Of these words, only *dearie, furry, starry*, and *tarry* "of tar" do not appear ever to be pronounced with /æ ∿ ε ∿ e/ in WPO. Those marked here by the asterisk seem legitimately associated with rural and rural-based WPO idioms. The pronunciations with /e/ seem to resemble similar pronunciations of *special, pleasure, measure* as perhaps more rural than not.[3]

The *poor ≠ pour* contrast, [ʊ ≠ o] + /r/, survives more frequently, it would seem, than does the /ε/-/æ/ + /r/ contrast, though in both Western Pennsylvania and Eastern Ohio there are many for whom it does not exist. Just as the contrast of /ε/-/æ/ continues before medial /r/ where it is reduced before terminal /r/, so does the /ʊ/-/o/ contrast: the stressed vowels of *durable* and *adorable* regularly contrast for a great many speakers whose *poor* and *pour* are homophonous. Even where the /ʊ/-/o/ contrast operates systematically, however, its support in frequencies of occurrence will be minimal, with the homophony (freely either /ʊ/ or /o/) of *more/Moore*, *morning/mourning, fore/four, hoe+er/who+er/whore* (prosody permitting—see A5 above), and others. Other than *poor/pour, sure/shore* is the only widely employed contrasting pair I have found, and this functional employment seems to be doomed both by the sometime fashionableness of *sure = shore* and by the reinterpretation of "Ohioan" [šir] as an occurrence of /šər/, as well as by any non-demanding influence from the many speakers who lack the contrast before terminal /r/.

Except for the Pennsylvania variation /ɛ ∿ e/, which occurs as far as I know only with retroflex /r/, it seems not to matter to the variations discussed here which of the two /r/'s occurs.

6. Aside from a trend much wider than WPO for intervocalic /t/ and /d/ to become non-contrastive, comment about these phonemes is largely inseparable from a discussion of the syllabic nasal. The exception to the characteristic medial /d, t/ flap articulation (voiced vs. voiceless when in contrast, otherwise voiced) is the glottalized articulation of these phonemes before a following syllabic /n̩/. For /d/, this consists of glottal closure and release, together marking the transition to the nasal; e.g., *didn't* [dɪd'n̩t]. For /t/, the voiceless stop is co-articulated by alveolar and glottal closure, the release marking the onset of /n̩/, as in *sentence* [sɛnt'n̩s] and *important* [ɪmpórt'n̩t].

As can be inferred from J. S. Kenyon and T. A. Knott, *A Pronouncing Dictionary of American English*, s. v. "didn't," this aspect of pronunciation is much wider than WPO, as is the variant [dɪdənt], which the same entry cites. In addition to continued sporadic [dɪdənt] pronunciations, though, the usage of the Youngstown area shows a striking frequency of yet another pronunciation: [dɪt'n̩t, wʊt'n̩t, kʊt'n̩t] for *didn't, wouldn't, couldn't*—auxiliaries that bring together /-d/ and /n̩t/. Sporadic occurrences, especially among children, of [wʊt'n̩] *wooden* indicate the phonological principle at work here. There are, however, restraints in effect, too, and these seem to be the more frequently operating, with these conditions:

(a) Even where medial /d, t/ have fused generally, the stop, not flap, articulation—and contrast—survives before /n̩/, /d/ being voiced and /t/ showing glottal co-articulation: *wooden* [wʊdn̩], *rotten* [rɒt'n̩].

(b) the reduced, syllabic /n̩t/ alternant of *not* is, like ordinary initial vowels of American English, articulated with an onset of glottal stop release, so that *mightn't* and *oughtn't* have a glottal stop in double phonological function—the closure "belongs" to the /t/, the release to the /n̩/.

(c) Where the medial /d/-/t/ contrast no longer operates, the phonemic incidence regularly reflects phonological assimilation—the voiced flap: *latter* like *ladder*.

(d) The presence of [-'n̩t] in both /dɪdn̩/ and /dɪdn̩t/ strongly suggests the same factor of assimilation—this time by selection of the voiceless stop already partially signaled by the indispensable glottal stop.

(e) Where the glottal stop is not in this way juncturally indispensable, the devoicing of /d/ may not occur, leaving *wooden* [wʊdn̩] and *garden* [gɑrdn̩]. But leveling of the stop + syllabic sequence, [-dn̩ → -t'n̩], is the next phonological step, now sporadic within word boundaries for WPO speech, but perhaps inevitable where it overcomes the morphological counter-tendencies in the word-junctural nature of the change described in conditions (b) and (d).

That the developments discussed here are extensions of medial /d/-/t/ fusion seems also to be indicated by the sporadic occurrence—also clearest among children and young people—of the medial voiced flap /d/ in all the words discussed here: *didn't, wouldn't, wooden, rotten, mightn't, oughtn't, garden*, etc. These exhibit complete leveling like that of /-dn̩ → -tn̩/ but now with the exclusion of syllabic /n̩/ from this idiom: /dɪdənt, wʊdənt, wʊdən, rɑdən/, etc.

7. Except for such tendencies as just noted, the WPO idiom (as well as others) consistently imposes phonological syllabicity on all sonorants in positions of weakest stress after vowel + (one or more) consonant sequences, with considerable variation of the complex relationships involved (as, for example, when two sonorants occur: *children, modern*, [-rn̩ ∿ -r̩n]). Distant relationships show phonetic vocalism, as in *locker* [lɒkər], *toboggan* [təbɒ́gɪn], but these are articulatory accommodations of /lɑkr̩/ and /təbɑ́gn̩/, as the wide subsystematic range of transition vowels—[ɪ,ʊ,ə]—would indicate.

The effect of the distinction between /n̩/ and /ən/ in *button* /bətn̩, bədən/ is to counter the abovementioned uniformity of syllabic /n̩/ by alternant pronunciations differently related to actual phonetic transitions— and differently accommodated by the structure of the idiom, one aspect of which is the extended loss of contrast between medial /d/ and /t/.

8. Like other urban idioms, some urban WPO speech shows [ŋ] only as an allophone of /n/ before /g, k/ in the same syllable or root: *thing, sing*, etc. While the origins of this pronunciation seem clearly to be native to English, its currency suggests survival among ethnic groups whose linguistic antecedents to English were any of a variety of non-Germanic languages, or Yiddish. That is, among speakers of American English without these close ethnic associations, some earlier retention of historical /-g/ in words like *thing* and *sing* must have been a relic of British dialects. Its survival in American English would seem then to be renewed use among speakers in relatively self-conscious ethnic groups of an otherwise increasingly infrequent variant.

Some, especially rural, areas of WPO that have had German-speaking ethnic survivals show a sporadic tendency for historical [-ŋg-] to show up entirely as [-ŋ-] in *finger, hunger, single, shingle, linger*—and in *hungry* and *angry*, where it can also be explained as colloquial assimilation and loss of [g].

The extremes of variation for retained /-ŋg/ seem to be clearly represented by a Youngstowner who has [-ŋg ∿ -ŋɣ] everywhere, including *think* and *sink*, and a native of Westmoreland Co., Pennsylvania who levels terminals to [ŋk ∿ ŋ']: *anything* [ɛnɪθɪŋk].

There is a further sign in WPO speech of either a retained /-g/ or of the tenuous systematic status of terminal [-ŋ]: a widely scattered, more-than-sporadic reinterpretation of [-ɪŋ] *-ing* as [-in]. Since this occurs most frequently in my experience with words like *learning, burning, leaning*, it could be a simple matter of assimilation to the terminal /-n/ of the base. While this is reasonable, there are certainly other factors that influence the occurrence of /in/. The pre-nasal /ɪ/ varies greatly, often toward /i/, enough to be phonologically ambiguous. For some WPO speakers whose usage is the firmly colloquial /lərnɪn, bərnɪn, linɪn/, a functional facsimile of stylish or schoolish /-ɪŋ/ is /-in/. On the other hand, those with only a pre-velar-stop [ŋ] can satisfactorily produce, under whatever social pressure seems to operate here, an acceptable speech modification by substituting /-in/ for /ɪng/, [ɪŋg].

C. Conclusion

The preceding observations do not exhaust relevant generalizations, even on the subjects broached, but they will demonstrate some of the system-wide characteristics of WPO idiom or idioms. Mention of these characteristics seems prerequisite to a description of otherwise apparently isolated usage items.

The implications of some overall features of the idiom extend rather far. For example, labial-velar co-articulation like that mentioned here for /l/ (B4) seems to have a significant potential in Pennsylvania pronunciation, as in the extreme variants [pwit] *put* and [kɵt] *quit* (the first apparently more frequent than the second). Historical doublets like *cud* and *quid*, of course, indicate that the phenomenon is not necessarily local or recent.

And the complex place of nasalization in the syllable and as a phonological segment within the syllable will be pertinent to such observable usages as the pronunciation of *unite* [junáint], or the sometime confusion between *tenet* and *tenant*, or *somatic* and *semantic*, or *predominate* and *predominant*.

But the comments offered here will serve tentatively to introduce further significant characteristics of this areal idiom in relation to overall aspects of American English.

Notes

1. I presume that the explanation for this intrusive /r/ is the obvious one—the false copying of [ɚ] as /r/ in a form of dialect borrowing, perhaps on the basis of this ordinary analogy:

R-less dialect	*Western Pennsylvania*
horse: [hɔəs] ∿ [hɔːs]	[hɔrs]
wash: [waš] ∿ [wɔš] ∿ [wɔːš] ∿ [wɔəš]	[wɔrš]

If such a development does have independent origins in Western Pennsylvania, it seems plausible to look to a continuing Virginian influence in Western Pennsylvania's cultural aspirations long after the actual colonial dominance existed. That such an influence should be incomplete and imperfect suits the social history of the area.

2. One does, at another extreme, encounter the pronunciations /lɑijər/ and /pejər/, phonologically paralleling /lɑjər/ and /lojər/, but with misleading morphological implications, except with humorous intent—that is, to suggest *lie-yer* and *pay-yer*, the first in puns on *lawyer*, the second in similar puns or other linguistic play.

It does seem necessary, though, in reference to serious use of some elaborated pronunciations, to suggest a social category *schoolish* in descriptions of this usage. The obvious historical explanation is *hyperurbanism*, but there are non-historical aspects of usage that make schoolish a useful label—the traditionally prescribed distinction, for example, between *lie* and *lay*, and selection of *well* to replace *good* in "The motor runs. . . . " The observance of such restrictions is relevant to the feel for "elegant" or "studied" usage of other sorts.

For many speakers of the WPO idiom, the *r*-less pronunciation of *wash* is schoolish—a replacement of /worš/ by /wɑš/ [wɑs ∿ wɒs], with consequences that appear at other points in the area's usage. And the many students of Youngstown area schools who distinguish *ant* /ænt/ from *aunt* /ɑnt/, surprising as the latter is as [ɒnt], must be seen not as participating in the "misapprehensions" of hyperurbanism but as individuals responding to the normalizing influences of social forces (here the schools) committed to those language habits.

3. This assessment of /e/ vs /ɛ/ incidence, however, is clearly involved in writer's bias. For natives of Allegheny County (Pittsburgh), and apparently nowhere else in-state or out, the county, river, and derivative names are all /æləgéni/. Natives are thus likely to encounter with surprise the wide use of /æləgéni/—which, if familiar, may seem essentially rural in its nearest "outside" associations.

4. The following words are those to which some pronunciation reference is made; letters and numbers refer to sections and subsections:

adorable B5	cheery B5	fore B5
Allegheny Note 3	cherry B5	four B5
angry B8	children B7	furry B5
ant Note 2	color A7	
ash A6	corner B4	garden B6
aunt Note 2	couldn't B6	God A1
aural A3	cud C	goin' B4
anything B8		gosh A1
	dearie B5	Greeley B3
bah! A1	didn't B6	
bar A3	dish A6	Harry B5
beg A6	doze B1	hairy B5
boor A3	durable B5	hoer B5
bore A3		horse Note 1
bough A3	eagle A6	hunger B8
boy A3	egg A6	hungry B8
burning B8		hurry B5
bush A6	falling B3	hurt A2
buoy A3	feel B3	hush A6
bury B5	feeling B3	hut A2
buy A3	fill B3	
	finger B8	important B6
carry B5	fish A6	
chary B5	following B3	join B4

ladder B6
latter B6
Lara A3
Laura A3
laurel A3
law A3
lawyer A3, A5,
    Note 2
leaning B8
learning B8
leg A6
legal A6
liar A3, A5
    Note 2
line B4
linger B8
lion B4
lyin' B4
lyre A5
locker B7
Lora A3
lorry B5
Lurie B5

marry B5
Mary B5
meal B3
measure A6, B5
merry B5
mightn't B6
mill B3
mime B4
modern B7
mom B4
Moore B5
more B5
morning B5
mourning B5

nine B4
non- B4

not B6
nothing A7
noun B4

oil B4
on(friendly) A7
oral A3
oughtn't B6
oyster B4

pair A5, B5
pare A5
payer A5, Note 2
pear A5
peer B5
pleasure A6, B5
pool B3
poor B5
pour B5
predominant C
predominate C
pull B3
purr B5
put C

quid C
quit C

real B3
really B3
rotten B6

sawyer A3
school B3
semantic C
sentence B6
shingle B8
shore B5
sing B8
single B8
somatic C

sore A3
sorry A3
special A6, B5
starry A5
story B5
sure B5

tall B4
tar B4
tarry B5
tenant C
tenet C
these B1
thing B8
those B1
tile B4
tire B4
toboggan B7
towel B4
tower B4

ulcer A7
un- A7
unite C

vague A6
vary B5
very B5
vision A6

wash A1, A3, Note 1
Washington A3
who-er B5
whore B5
wish A6
wooden B6
wouldn't B6

yeah A1

SECOND DIALECT PEDAGOGY:
HYDRA AND HYBRID

MELVIN HOFFMAN
State University College at Buffalo

In the United States much literature on the language learning problems of the disadvantaged Afro-American has been written in the past few years. Questions have been raised; solutions to problems have been suggested. Little new information will be introduced here. Existing information will be used to support the following contentions:

(1) The literature mentioned contains an implicit non-formalized yet consistent outline which provides guidelines for the development of a new applied linguistic specialty: second dialect pedagogy.

(2) The content and teaching techniques included in the training of a specialist in this area would overlap and yet differ from what is included in the training of specialists in either foreign or native language pedagogy.

(3) Second dialect teaching problems are sufficiently unique to require considerations in application and practice which are unnecessary in other language learning situations.

Sources for the points to be presented in the outline are works of researchers in sociolinguistics and in related disciplines. The discussion of each section of this outline will be followed by a representative quote, in turn followed by references to other authors who make similar or related points. The references, numerous in many instances, are given to substantiate the claim that the outline proposed is more than a mere idiosyncratic construct.

The works, to which I will repeatedly refer, are to the best of my knowledge representative of current thinking in this area. After the outline is presented, support for the above contentions will be drawn from a synthesis of the observations and recommendations of the various authors cited or referred to.

Defining the Problem

I. NONSTANDARD SPEAKERS OF ENGLISH ARE NOT ADEQUATELY TAUGHT BY TRADITIONAL METHODS

A composite paraphrasing of many authors includes these points: Constant correction, admonition, and extensive exposure to formal models have not succeeded in providing written or oral competence in standard English for many Afro-American children with disadvantaged backgrounds.

A contributing factor to this recurrent failure is a misinterpretation on the part of many classroom teachers as to the actual nature of the language problem with which they are confronted. A frequent assessment of the situation is that the pupil is lazy, sloppy, careless, hostile, or indifferent to what the teacher is trying to accomplish. In addition, the child is frequently viewed either as empty of language into whom correct English is to be poured or as speaking a degenerate or disorganized form of English which must be elevated or brought into good order.

An accurate appraisal of the situation includes the following: The pupil is speaking a significantly different language from that of his middle class teachers. This speech is structured and systematic even though it is socially unacceptable in many places and situations. Traditional language teaching procedures fail to distinguish between language differences and value judgements about these differences.

Common results of the failure to properly deal with the second dialect learning situation are: Some pupils become hostile to the learning situation, because they view the denigration of their speech as a personal attack upon their values and way of life. Other pupils are frustrated both because they are taught false and often contradictory information about their speech and because they are continually faced with failure due to their inability to cope with extra, poorly directed, and poorly motivated language-learning tasks.

It is imperative that the speech of the pupil be recognized as patterned, systematic, and fully developed in its sound patterns and grammar as any dialect of English which may enjoy greater social prestige.

Success in overcoming second dialect learning problems depends, to a large extent, upon a realistic and organized pedagogical approach which takes the systematic nature of the pupils' speech into account.

Gladney and Leaverton (1968: 758) state the problem succinctly:

> . . . teachers . . . work tirelessly, if unsuccessfully, to change it using such methods as constant correction, providing a model of standard English and following the various speech activities suggested in many language arts manuals and supplements. Part of our difficulty as educators in effectively coping with this problem of teaching the standard dialect has been a failure to recognize that the child's dialect contains a definite structure and organization and is resistant to change.

Other sources similarly defining the problems are: Bailey (1968: 20), Baratz (1969: 199–200), Brooks (1964: 30), Davis (1966: 93), Goodman (1967: 41), Labov (1967: 141), McDavid (1965: 257), *Nonstandard Dialect* (1967: vii), Shuy (1968: 10), Stewart (1968: 3).

II. IF THE DISADVANTAGED AFRO-AMERICAN PUPIL'S STANDARD LANGUAGE LEARN-
ING PROBLEMS STEM FROM STRUCTURAL DIVERGENCE RATHER THAN DEFI-

CIENCY, STRUCTURAL STUDIES ARE NECESSARY PREREQUISITES TO SUCCESSFUL
CLASSROOM APPLICATIONS:

The linguistic analysis and description of the nonstandard dialect, coupled with a contrastive analysis of the dialect of the pupil and the standard regional dialect to be taught, serves several purposes: More efficient and economical procedures, materials, and techniques become possible. The teacher, armed with a knowledge of the structure of the dialect, is in a position to make meaningful non-value-loaded contrasts between the two dialects, thereby avoiding the creation of unnecessary and defeating conflict. More simply, it is easier to work with rather than against the grain, once the grain is known.

Baratz (1969: 200) is emphatic in her insistence upon structural analysis of the speech of disadvantaged Afro-American pupils prior to their instruction in Standard English:

> It is clear that structural knowledge of non-standard vernacular and the ways it can interfere with learning to speak and read standard English is indispensable to teaching ghetto Negro children.

Others who support this view include: Bailey (1968: 20), Davis (1966: 100), Goodman (1967: 46), Malmstrom (1966–7: 4), McDavid (1966: 258), and Stewart (1964b: 18).

Although there are disagreements concerning the proper description and historical origins[1] of the divergent structures, there is general agreement on the identification of many of the structural differences which underlie the major standard language learning problems of the disadvantaged Afro-American.

An ennumeration of these would fall outside the scope of this discussion, but may be found in the following sources: Bailey (1968: 16–23), Gladney and Leaverton (1968: 759), Labov (1967: 146–63), McDavid (1967: 7–10), Stewart (1964a: 8–11).

III. NATIVE LANGUAGE TEACHING TECHNIQUES ARE INSUFFICIENT FOR HANDLING
THE STANDARD LANGUAGE LEARNING PROBLEMS OF NONSTANDARD SPEAKERS
OF ENGLISH:

Native language teaching methods do not include techniques which deal with pattern interference and pattern conflict. A satisfactory standard language learning situation for the pupils discussed must take structural differences into account.

Foreign language teaching methods include techniques for dealing with structural differences out of obvious necessity. Teaching English as a Foreign Language, as an applied linguistic specialty, is well developed in this country. A natural solution would seem to be the employing of foreign language teaching methods to the teaching of standard English to nonstandard speakers. A noted proponent of this view is McDavid (1964: 7) who states:

The grammatical problems are of such an order that we advance the suggestion—which Mencken had reported before the war and which my wife independently derived from her teaching experience—that in our urban slums and other areas where divergent social dialects exist, we might teach Standard English as a foreign language.

Others term or have come to term (cf. Dillard 1967a and 1967b) the language learning problems of the disadvantaged Afro-American as quasi-foreign language learning problems.

Proponents of this terminology also recommend that foreign language teaching methods be adopted to deal with problems resulting from structural differences between the dialect of the learner and the dialect to be learned. They caution the teacher to remember, however, that the speech of the learner overlaps in many instances with standard English and is closer to standard English than to any foreign language.

Stewart (1964b:10–11) draws this distinction very carefully:

> Although this two-way distinction between native and foreign language teaching has become established in language teaching theory both here and abroad, there is growing evidence that there are certain kinds of teaching and learning situations which do not fall neatly into either category. . . . In pointing out the existence of this kind of language learning problem to English teaching specialists, I once referred to it as a "quasi-foreign language" situation. What I meant by this was that, although the structural correspondences between the language of the learner and the language being taught might, at some linguistic levels (such as their respective vocabularies), be so close that the learner could justifiably be considered as already having a native or near-native command of that aspect of the language being taught, yet there would still be enough differences between the two linguistic systems at other levels (such as in their grammars) to warrant the use of at least some foreign-language teaching procedures.

Others who use the term "quasi-foreign language" include Dillard (1967a:-117) and Malmstrom (1966–7: 2).

Some authors, also recognizing the problem of structural divergence, stress additional considerations. Marckwardt (1964: 152) warns the educator that the use of the term "foreign language" may offend some of the very people whom foreign language pedagogy would benefit. Haugen (1964: 125) rejects the view that the learning situation is a foreign language learning situation. Instead he views the problem as one of changing passive or unconscious bi-dialectals to active conscious ones.

Identifying Unique Aspects of Problems

Such considerations as the foregoing suggest a further search of the literature to attempt to identify more precisely those aspects that distinguish the language learning problems of the disadvantaged Afro-American from those of foreign and native language learners. Three general problem areas stand out:

I. THERE IS EVIDENCE THAT SECOND DIALECT LEARNING IS A MORE DIFFICULT TASK THAN SECOND LANGUAGE LEARNING:

The subtleness of differences in structures between dialects of the same language creates a problem different in degree if not in kind from the problem of second language learning.

Goodman (1967: 41–2) points out that several varieties of classroom English face the child: the teacher's informal speech, the teacher's formal speech, and the stilted language of the texts.

Haugen (1964: 125) suggests that interference may make bidialectalism harder to acquire than bilingualism, since it is generally agreed that it is harder to keep two similar languages apart than two different ones.

Stewart (1968: 3) remarks that similarities between dialects may camouflage functional differences between their linguistic systems.

One of these subtle problems has been termed masking. Masking is a superficial resemblance between two linguistic utterances which misleads an observer into inaccurately identifying and reacting to both as equivalent. Hoffman (1970: 680) discusses this and Stewart (1968: 6) warns:

> . . . if American Negro dialects have evolved in such a way that structural similarities with other dialects of American English (including standard English) are greatest at the superficial word-form level, then it is possible for these similarities to mask any number of grammatical differences between them. And the teacher, concentrating on the more word-form differences is quite likely to miss the grammatical differences in the process—thereby leaving them to persist as apparent malapropisms, awkward turns of phrase, and random "mistakes" in speech and writing.

The traditional pedagogical concentration upon forms and the accompanying disregard for their distribution leads to overcorrection and frustration as by-products of the lack of awareness.

Traditional correction procedures limit emphasized exposure to standard forms to only those occasions when the pupil produces a nonstandard form. This haphazard exposure creates unintended nonstandard forms resulting from overcorrecting. Overcorrections, though inadvertently caused, remain, nevertheless, as socially handicapping as any unacceptable form which is the direct result of structural divergence.

In Hoffman (1970: 679–680) I make several points in this regard: The limiting of emphasized exposure to standard forms to only those occasions when the pupil produces a nonstandard form results in unintended nonstandard collocations such as 'he were' and 'they works.' Not all nonstandard utterances on the part of the pupil indicate a failure either in the teacher's effectiveness or in the pupil's attention. The real failure is the lack of awareness which does not permit the teacher to recognize that nonstandard utterances like 'he were' and 'they works' are of a different order than utterances like 'he work' or 'they was.' The former are attempts to conform to the teacher's expectations by producing the forms taught by the teacher. If a child receives negative sanctions from the teacher, the child is being punished for doing exactly what he has inadvertently been taught to do.

Others concerned with the neglect of attention paid to distribution are: Allen (1964: 218), Gladney and Leaverton (1968: 759), and Hill (1964: 392).

II. UNIQUE SOCIAL PROBLEMS ARE PRESENT TO FURTHER COMPLICATE THE LAN-
GUAGE LEARNING SITUATION.

The motivation for second dialect learning in this country must differ from that required for learning a second language. The chief motivations for language learning are the desire to communicate and the desire to identify oneself with a particular social group. A nonstandard speaker in most cases is readily able to communicate with standard speakers. Further, he may not feel a need to identify himself with the dominant culture.

In *Nonstandard Dialect* (1968: 2), a list of obstacles to proper motivation is presented:

—Self-consciousness about the language of family, friends, community, and socioeconomic class
—Pressures exerted by adolescent peer groups against deviation from their accepted language pattern
—Past censure of pupils' language which they have interpreted as rejection
—Variations in different teachers' language patterns resulting in confusion for pupils needing a standard model
—Past experience with negative correction of isolated items of linguistic behavior instead of positive teaching within a total system

Others concerned with motivation are: Haugen (1964: 125–6), Labov (1964: 94–5), Malmstrom(1966–7: 2–4).

A different approach to motivate second dialect learners has been suggested by some researchers. The value of standard English as a social credential should be made explicit to the student. Brooks (1964: 30) states this as follows:

... should teachers not exploit the tremendous psychological uplift implicit in ... saying ... "I accept you and your language; use it when you need it for communication with your family and friends. But, if you really want to be a successful participant in other areas of American life, why not learn the kind of language accepted and used there."
The teacher must, of course, fit this little speech to the age and mental ability of the pupil but with it he or she may be able to destroy the barrier to communication built up by the usual, unknowingly insensitive rejection.

McQuown (1964: 355–6) expresses a similar view.

Rejection of a person's language is a threat to his self-concept, group identification, and is a major cause of alienation. The child communicates effectively using his language with the people about whom he cares the most. His language permits him to identify with those people, particularly his peers, who are important to him. Rejection of his language constitutes rejection both of himself and of people whom he loves and admires.

Goodman (1967: 40) expresses a similar view and in addition points out the incongruity between the well-meaning adults' treatment of linguistic and non-linguistic differences:

> Ironically, well-meaning adults including teachers who would never intentionally reject a child or any important characteristic of a child such as the clothes he wears or the color of his skin, will immediately and emphatically reject his language. This hurts him far more than other kinds of rejections because it endangers the means which he depends on for communication and self-expression.

The consequences of rejection of the language are stressed by others as well: Brooks (1964: 29), Haugen (1964: 126), McQuown (1964: 356), *Nonstandard Dialect* (1968: 1).

III. QUESTIONS OF POLICY, ETHICS, ETC. FURTHER COMPLICATE THE ALLOCATION OF EFFORT IN SECOND DIALECT PEDAGOGY.

American sociolinguistic concentration is almost exclusively devoted to the disadvantaged Afro-American. Other native speakers in this country beside the Afro-American population encounter structural difficulties in mastering standard English. The techniques of second dialect pedagogy can be profitably employed with these speakers as well. It is primarily the social urgency the has fostered the interest in facilitating language arts programs for Afro-Americans.

Davis (1968: 3) warns that non-Afro-American groups with second dialect learning problems should not be ignored. While admitting that social barriers are less for white Americans with dialect learning problems, he reminds his readers that the problems such dialect differences create can be equally severe for the classroom teacher.

Related considerations may be found among the following: Haugen (1964: 124–5), Marckwardt (1964: 153), *Nonstandard Dialect* (1968: 4).

Since it must be acknowledged that standard English usage and structure is not uniform, the term *standard English* used by either linguist or layman presents certain problems.

Ferguson (1964: 116) addresses himself to considerations of decision making regarding the "standard" to be taught.

It is assumed that English will be the natural medium of instruction. No one has asked whether we should make an effort to teach some kind of Southern standard as our model in certain places in the South or teach some kind of more "General American" standard. Questions like this just haven't been raised. We automatically assume that some kind of unqualified Standard English is right for all over the country. But I think there are several different situations and they might call for different choices under different circumstances.

Goodman (1967: 41) presents his readers with somewhat of a paradox: No dialect of American English has ever achieved the status of a national standard. We have instead a series of regional standards. Yet Americans, ethnocentric in regard to most cultural traits, are more ethnocentric in regard to language. The sanctions brought against those who differ, moreover, can be very severe.

McDavid (1964: 7) indicates that those who are linguistically aware bear a responsibility to make the following more widely known: Standard American English has many varieties, all good. What is regionally different should not be confused with what is socially different. The ability to return to a nonstandard dialect on occasion may be of definite advantage to a person who has mastered a standard dialect of English.

Definitions for standard English vary. Kaplan (1969: 386) uses power as the major criterion:

> In any community, the "standard" dialect may be defined as the speech of that segment of the community which controls the bulk of the wealth and therefore constitutes the dominant power group. By contrast "nonstandard" dialect may be defined as the one or more dialects spoken by the group or groups which do not control wealth or power but which, to one degree or another, aspire to it.

A more usual treatment of standard English may be found in *Nonstandard English* (1967: 1):

> Standard American English . . . is the language pattern that is habitually used—with some regional variations—by most of the educated English-speaking persons in the United States. It is the level of language that facilitates ease of communication in a complex and highly interdependent society.
>
> The speech of a proportion of speakers in any one region, on the other hand, differs from the standard English of that area . . . their lack of command of standard English results both in learning disabilities and career handicaps. . . .

Even if the standard English to be taught were easily agreed upon, such agreement would not solve the problems resulting from the necessity to make decisions among alternatives available in techniques of implementation. Different authors recommend consideration of various alternatives.

Ferguson (1964: 116–7) points out that a very serious choice has to be made: Either the educator should seek to make the nonstandard speaker a functional bidialectal, or the older goal should be followed—the goal of replacing substandard speech with some kind of standard English. According to Ferguson, more than linguistic facts should be brought to bear on the problem. Many matters of more interest to psychologists and sociologists should be more thoroughly researched before this decision is made. Naturally, the choice determines to a great extent what techniques and materials are appropriate for the desired learning situation.

A set of alternatives concerned with the improvement of reading is presented by Goodman (1967: 45–6):

> There seem to be three basic alternatives . . . first . . . to write materials . . . based on their own dialect or rewrite standard materials in their dialect . . . second . . . to teach the children to speak the standard dialect before teaching them to read . . . third . . . to let the children read the standard materials in their own dialect . . . and make it their medium of learning. . . . The only practical alternative I feel is the third one.

Kaplan (1969: 388–9) questions whether linguistic assimilation through teaching mastery of standard English should itself not be considered an alternative open to investigation. Is total standardization desirable if it indeed were even possible?

Marckwardt (1964: 156–7) cautions hesitation. Before deciding important pedagogical issues, more information on dialects must be collected, and a clearer determination of the objectives must be made.

The principal alternatives between which Marckwardt finds it most imperative to decide are, "whether to stimulate the native language-learning process or that which governs our learning of a foreign or second language."

With some variance, the general recommendation of researchers in the field is acceptance of the learner's language either in the learning process, in the end product, or both.

Baratz (1969: 202) in a discussion of reading advocates the use of nonstandard dialect in the initial readers. A difference exists between the child's linguistic system and the linguistic system of the standard reader. There has been success in vernacular teaching around the world. A natural solution is to teach the child reading in his own dialect and then to teach him to read standard English.

Gladney and Leaverton (1968: 759), reporting on an oral language program, state that the learning sequence in teaching standard speech should start with an actual statement made by the child. To insure a systematic approach, only one pattern difference at a time should be focused upon. Nonstandard speech differences, characteristic of the dialect, should be permitted to pass without comment until encountered in the sequence of instruction.

Labov (1967: 164) discusses task differentiation in the teaching of reading. Among others, he reaches the conclusion that ". . . there is no reason why a person cannot learn to read standard English texts quite well in a nonstandard pronunciation."

Shuy (1968: 13) recommends that the original nonstandard dialect be preserved. Situations may exist for the speaker even after he has mastered the standard language where the use of nonstandard speech would be appropriate.

Nonstandard Dialect (1968: 1) takes a positive view of nonstandard dialect both in standard language learning and in retention of its use:

> Teachers should accept the pupils' nonstandard dialect in appropriate situations and build on the language patterns which pupils have been accustomed to using. . . . Standard English dialect thus becomes additive as another available language pattern while the original dialect may still be spoken in situations which the individual considers appropriate.

Synthesis of Problems and Recommendations

For the past few years, many linguists and researchers in related disciplines have addressed themselves to the implementation in the classroom of the results of their research. Fairly explicit and widespread agreement exists in the literature to support the following:

(1) Teachers must abandon prescriptive techniques in teaching standard English to the disadvantaged.

(2) Adequate descriptions of the structure of nonstandard dialects are a necessary prerequisite to the preparation of workable solutions to second dialect learning problems.

(3) Second dialect language learning problems must be distinguished from problems of native language learning.

Differences exist, however, which distinguish second dialect learning from foreign language learning as well as from native language learning. A review of the literature reveals:

(1) The subtleness of differences in structures between dialects of the same language creates a problem different at least in degree if not in kind from the problem of second language learning.

(2) Unique social problems are present which cause the standard language to be rejected by the learner.

(3) Many philosophical and ethical issues complicate the creation and implementation of policy for second dialect pedagogy.

Additional Problems

Other points less explicit or less recurrent occur in the literature as well. I include the following because of their relevance. All are impediments to second dialect learning of a non-linguistic nature.

There is reluctance or refusal of certain sectors of the Afro-American public to admit the problem's existence.

Labov (1966: 143) states:

> It may be difficult to imagine how great are the pressures against the recognition, description or even mention of Negro speech patterns. For various reasons, many teachers, principals, and civil rights leaders wish to

deny that the existence of patterns of Negro speech is a linguistic and social reality in the United States today.

Stewart (1964b:13) provides a possible explanation of this reluctance:

> ... as is quite understandable, many Negroes (particularly educated ones) are somewhat sensitive about any public focus on distinctively Negro behavior, particularly if it happens to be that of lower class Negroes. In some cases, this attitude may stem from a belief that such studies, where unmatched by comparable ones of the behavior of educated Negroes, might well encourage old stereotypes about the American Negro by giving an incomplete picture of the cultural range he represents.

False interpretations of second dialect learning problems are rampant. Stewart (1968: 3) points out one consequence:

> ... because there is obviously some sort of ethnic correlation between pupil success and failure in newly-integrated school situations, the embarrassed educational establishment and the frustrated public enter into a crisis relationship. Some whites charge (privately, at least) that the schools are being given the impossible task of teaching unteachable Negroes. And some Negroes charge (not so privately) that white educators are involved in a conspiracy to deliberately keep Negro children from learning. Parents protest blindly, and school administrators run helter skelter, holding counsels of despair with colleagues who understand the problem no better.

A "credibility gap" exists between the student who has experienced discrimination and the teacher who promises him deferred rewards for linguistic conformity. A good example is provided by Goodman (1967: 45) as follows:

> As one teenager remarked to me, "Ya man, alls I gotta do is walk right and talk right and they gonna make me president of the United States."

This excerpt from McDavid (1969: 45 fn.) speaks for itself:

> In view of the profit in poverty for educational administrators, it should not surprise us that many of the institutions that express no interest in language differences have nevertheless managed to secure substantial grants from governments and foundations for dealing with the problem of the "disadvantaged" though 90% of those problems have to do with the use of language.

Some Fallacies

There are two additional considerations not dealt with extensively in the literature that I wish to include, because they have so much in common with the previous points.

The first I term the *professional white liberal fallacy*. I have heard it expressed by figures with considerable reputation in their respective fields. "We have no right to impose our notions of acceptable language upon people who have already suffered too much from our impositions. Diversity in language as well as in other aspects of our culture should be fostered not restrained." This fallacy is subtle since its proponents frequently support their case on points made by linguists. Among such points are: Social judgments of linguistic acceptability are arbitrary; language varies historically and regionally; the imposition of an alien mode of speech with accompanying negative value judgments on the learner's ideolect is an unhealthy situation; total linguistic conformity is impossible anyway.

Mutually reinforcing this position is what I term the *professional black militant fallacy*. "Why should we learn the white man's language. It has been a vehicle for his oppressions and if we accept it, he will continue to manipulate us through it. We need not accept it as we need not accept his hairstyles or his moral codes. If we must learn a new language, let it be, for example, Swahili, something of ours not his."

Both ignore the following:

1. Standard English can be taught non-prescriptively and can be taught as an addition to, not as a replacement of, one's own speech.

2. Only a person who *is* functionally bidialectal enjoys the *freedom* to choose to reject or accept either dialect, or to use both as the occasion demands. Proponents of the above fallacies seem no more willing to provide the learner with the capability to make his own choices than the prescriptive schoolteacher about whom all complain.

3. Social judgments of linguistic acceptability will not disappear or become less consequential because they are arbitrary.

4. The threat of white domination through language must appear minimal to those former British colonies which have elected to retain English as the national language. A language, like any other tool, can serve the purpose of the user.

Strangely enough, I have heard no proponent of either position who himself lacks command of some regional standard.

Classification of Second Dialect Pedagogy

What is the relation of second dialect pedagogy to native and second language teaching? After distinguishing "quasi-foreign language" pedagogy from both native and foreign language pedagogy, Stewart (1964b:11 fn.) clarifies his position:

> . . . it is not my intention to propose a third category of language teaching, but rather to show that two established categories represent end points on a continuum rather than neat divisions.

The idea of a continuum need not conflict with the development of second dialect pedagogy as an applied linguistic specialty. Figure 1 is a schematic representation of information gathered through a review of the literature.

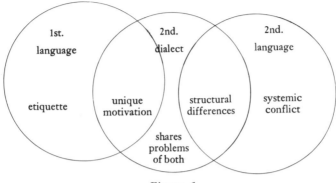

Figure 1

Native language, second dialect, and foreign language teaching are drawn as overlapping positions on a continuum. This is presented from the standpoint of language learning problems in the United States. A regional standard English is assumed as the target language. In the first two cases, the pupil must be persuaded to learn another mode of speech not because he or she will necessarily be better understood, but because social consequences result from lack of mastery. In the second and third cases, structural differences are a barrier that must be overcome.

Second dialect pedagogy may also be looked at in comparison with second dialect learning problems around the world. An excellent treatment of this is found in Ferguson (1964). Ferguson describes in a slightly different order the following:

1. A situation, "diglossia," where a standard language is necessary to learn for formal situations, but is not expected to be used as an ordinary means of communication.

2. A situation where a standard language is necessary to learn, but where one's vernacular is acceptable in an appropriate setting.

3. A situation where one's vernacular is not acceptable in any setting outside one's own social group.

Figure 2 shows a schematic representation of my own based on Ferguson's description. The present situation in the United States is found in the circle on the right.

A review of the literature indicates that to create a successful second dialect learning situation, we must make it more like the learning situation represented in the middle circle than in the situation represented on the right.

Conclusion

I submit that the literature overwhelmingly supports the necessity to establish specialized teacher training programs similar to but differing from training programs in the teaching of English as a second language.

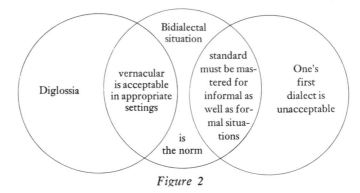

Figure 2

What form should such programs take? At least partial emulation of elements of second language pedagogy seems to be recommended by almost all authors cited. Linguistic tool courses might remain the same. The specialty courses could, however, be in regional and social dialectology drawing upon contrastive dialectology as contrastive language studies are utilized in second language pedagogy. The remainder of such programs could be devoted to courses or more desirably to field experience in schools with disadvantaged Afro-American pupil populations. The purpose of this latter training would be to create an awareness of the necessity to develop solutions to the many non-linguistic problems hindering second dialect learning.

At what type of student should such training be particularly aimed? The literature recommends increasing training at all levels. McDavid (1969) stresses the need to create opportunities for advanced degrees in socio-linguistics. Brooks (1964) emphasizes the need to make the elementary and secondary school teacher aware of the varied and unique problems created by the divergence between the speech of the learner and the speech to be learned. Smith (1968) sees primary grade pedagogy as crucial.

The past few years, I have come into contact with increasing numbers of teachers who are aware of the problems discussed and of the need for special training. A frequent complaint is that there is nowhere to turn for such training. Many institutions, including noted colleges and universities, have nothing to offer teachers seeking such training. When such institutions do offer training in this area, many dedicated teachers are unable to meet the financial and/or admission requirements. Those able to surmount these obstacles are frequently confronted with programs directed heavily to the theoretical and only incidentally to the applied, or with programs including required courses completely irrelevant to the problems with which the teachers are most deeply concerned. A great proportion of teachers must rely almost entirely upon resources available in teacher training institutions, community colleges, and small liberal arts colleges. These, with some notable exceptions, offer little or nothing in this area.

Many teachers, with their new awareness of the need for linguistic sophistication in dealing with the language arts problems of the disadvantaged, have found additional causes for complaint. Frequently brought into question is the linguistic competence of personnel conducting teacher training programs in the area of language arts programs for the disadvantaged. Countless examples have been presented to me of projects, programs, and institutes in both colleges and boards of education with no lingustically trained staff at all.

Linguists do not escape criticism. Common sources of dissatisfaction are linguistic institutes on the language problems of the disadvantaged. Many teachers complain that all too frequently speakers, particularly noted speakers, succeed in creating enthusiasm for second dialect principles and approaches, but have too little to offer in terms of *detailed* applications for *ordinary* classrooms. *Ordinary* refers to classrooms not favored by reduced class size, auxiliary personnel, or special facilities.

Criticisms of this kind suggest that a profitable employment of existing resources might well involve fostering the creation of advanced degree programs in applied second dialect pedagogy to be directed specifically at classroom teachers, existing and potential staff of teacher training institutions, and administrators of language arts activities in the schools.

Such programs, I contend, would conform in principle and in purpose to the mainstream of the recommendations in the current literature. That is, the ultimate aim would be to provide the disadvantaged pupil with a language learning environment which will enable him comfortably to become a functional bidialectal in a manner consistent both with linguistic principle and human dignity.

Sources Cited

Allen, Harold B. "The Linguistic Atlases: Our New Resources." *Readings in Applied English Linguistics.* Ed. Harold B. Allen 2nd. Edition. New York: Appleton-Century Crofts, 1964.

Bailey, Beryl Loftman. "Some Aspects of the Impact of Linguistics on Language Teaching in Disadvantaged Communities." *On the Dialects of Children.* Ed. A. L. Davis. Champaign, Illinois: N.C.T.E., 1968.

Barataz, Joan C. "Linguistic and Cultural Factors in Teaching Reading to Ghetto Children." *Elementary English,* vol. 56 (February, 1969), 199–203.

Brooks, Charlotte K. "Some Approaches to Teaching English as a Second Language." *Nonstandard Speech and the Teaching of English.* Ed. William A. Stewart. Washington D.C.: Center for Applied Linguistics, 1964.

Davis, A. L. "Dialect Research and the Needs of the Schools." *On the Dialects of Children.* Ed. A. L. Davis. Champaign, Illinois: N.C.T.E., 1968.

———, "Social Dialects and Social Change." *The Instructor* (March 1966), 93 and 100.

Dillard, J. L. "The English Teacher and the Language of the Newly Integrated Student." *Teachers College Record,* vol. 69 (November, 1967), 115–120 (cited as 1967a).

———, "Negro Children's Dialect in the Inner City." *The Florida FL Reporter,* (Fall, 1967), 1–4 (cited as 1967b).

Ferguson, Charles. "Teaching Standard Languages to Dialect Speakers." *Social Dialects and Language Learning.* Ed. Roger W. Shuy. Champaign, Illinois: N.C.T.E., 1964.

Gladney, Mildred R. and Leaverton, Lloyd. "A Model for Teaching Standard English to Non-Standard English Speakers." *Elementary English,* vol. 45 (October, 1968), 757–63.

Goodman, Kenneth S. "Dialect Barriers to Reading Comprehension." *Dimensions of Dialect.* Ed. Eldonna L. Evertts. Champaign, Illinois: N.C.T.E., 1967.

Haugen, Einar. "Bilingualism and Bidialectalism." *Social Dialects and Language Learning.* Ed. Roger Shuy. Champaign, Illinois: N.C.T.E., 1964.

Hill, Archibald A. "Correctness and Style in English Composition." *Readings in Applied English Linguistics.* Ed. Harold B. Allen. 2nd. Edition. New York: Appleton-Century Crofts, 1964.

Hoffman, Melvin J. "The Harmful Effects of Traditional Language Arts Teaching Methods when used with Disadvantaged Afro-American Children." *Elementary English,* vol. 47 (May, 1970), 678–683.

Kaplan, Robert B. "On a Note of Protest (In a Minor Key): Bidialectism vs. Bidialectism." *College English,* vol. 30 (February, 1969), 386–389.

Labov, William. "Some Sources of Reading Problems for Negro Speakers of Nonstandard English." *New Directions in Elementary English.* Ed. Alexander Frazier. Champaign, Illinois: N.C.T.E., 1967.

———, "Stages in the Acquisition of Standard English." *Social Dialects and Language Learning.* Ed. Roger Shuy. Champaign, Illinois: N.C.T.E., 1964.

Malmstrom, Jean. "Dialects." *The Florida FL Reporter,* (Winter 1966–7), 1, 2 and 4.

Marckwardt, Albert H. "Review of the Conference." *Social Dialects and Language Learning.* Ed. Roger Shuy. Champaign, Illinois: N.C.T.E., 1964.

McDavid, Raven I. Jr. "American Social Dialects." vol. 26. (January 1965), 254–260.

———, "A Checklist of Significant Features for Discriminating Social Dialects." *Dimensions of Dialect.* Ed. Eldonna L. Evertts. Champaign, Illinois: N.C.T.E., 1967.

———, "Social Dialects and Professional Responsibility." *College English,* vol. 30 (February, 1969), 381–385.

———, "Social Dialects: Cause or Symptom of Social Maladjustment." *Social Dialects and Language Learning.* Ed. Roger Shuy. Champaign, Illinois: N.C.T.E., 1964.

McQuown, Norman A. "Language-Learning from an Anthropological Point of View." *Readings in Applied English Linquistics.* Ed. Harold B. Allen. 2nd. Edition. New York: Appleton-Century Crofts, 1964.

Nonstandard Dialect. New York Board of Education. 1967. Champaign, Illinois: N.C.T.E. 1968.

Shuy, Roger. "Detroit Speech: Systematic or Careless?" *On the Dialects of Children.* Champaign Illinois: N.C.T.E. 1968.

Smith, Henry Lee Jr. "First Things First: Literacy for the Disadvantaged." Appendix 1. *English Morphophonics: Implications for the Teaching of Literacy.* Monograph no. 10 Oneonta: New York State English Council, 1968.

Stewart, William A. "Continuity and Change in American Negro Dialects." *Florida FL Reporter.* (Spring 1968), 1–6.

———, "Foreign Language Teaching Methods in Quasi-Foreign Language Situations." *Non-Standard Speech and the Teaching of English.* Ed. William Stewart. Washington D.C.: Center for Applied Linguistics, 1964 (cited as 1964b).

————, "Sociolinguistic Factors in the History of American Negro Dialects." *Florida FL Reporter* (Spring 1967), 1–4.

————, "Urban Negro Speech: Sociolinguistic Factors Affecting English Teaching." *Social Dialects and Language Learning*. Ed. Roger Shuy. Champaign, Illinois: N.C.T.E., 1964 (cited as 1964a).

Notes

1. Some scholars contend that the chief cause of the differences between nonstandard Afro-American dialects and regional standards is social segregation which has isolated many Afro-Americans from habitual contact with the mainstream of American English. These differences are accounted for as statistically skewed and sometimes archaic features, all or most of which have their origin in some dialect of English.

Other scholars maintain that many differences are the result of a persistent substratum inherited from either an earlier African trade koine or an American slave pidgin.

The argument may be followed in these sources: Bailey (1968: 18), Dillard (1967a: 115–7), Dillard (1967b: 1–3), Labov (1967: 144–5), McDavid (1966: 258 fn.), Stewart (1967: 2–4), and Stewart (1968: 5–6).

THE RECENT HISTORY OF SOME DIALECT MARKERS ON THE ISLAND OF MARTHA'S VINEYARD, MASS.

William Labov
University of Pennsylvania

Thirty years have elapsed since the field workers for the Linguistic Atlas gathered their evidence. In terms of generations, the machinery of reproduction has moved forward by one notch. The children who were learning the English language then are now teaching it, and most of the speakers who were recorded in the Atlas have little to say. The representative citizens located by Guy Lowman and Raven McDavid are now representatively dead and gone, and their children, if they are to be found, are among the oldest inhabitants of their respective bailiwicks.

It is not too soon, then, to ask whether the portrait of the English language drawn by the Atlas is still a good likeness. How many of the old regional markers are still in evidence? More generally, what are the factors that lead to the preservation of some regional markers and the disappearance of others?

The present study is a report on the recent history of the chief lexical markers in the speech of Martha's Vineyard, Massachusetts, with the hope of answering some of these questions. The main body of evidence on the past history of these markers is drawn from the *Linguistic Atlas of New England* (Kurath 1939, 1949); other sources used here are the *Oxford English Dictionary*, the *Dictionary of American English*, and the *Dictionary of Americanisms* (Mathews 1951). Indirect evidence is obtained by statements of present-day informants about past usage. The *English Dialect Dictionary* has been consulted for English sources, and several special glossaries of American fishing terms as well.

Evidence on the recent history of dialect markers on the Vineyard is based on field work in 1961–2, which developed the Atlas questionnaire in greater detail and with specific orientation to this island. Internal differences in Vineyard speech are revealed as well as the overall pattern. Some of the information gathered in this field study was designed to trace the on-going centralization of /ay/ and /aw/ as this sound change responded to social forces (Labov 1963). In this historical study, the main focus will be on time boundaries, and geography will enter only incidentally. The aim is to organize the evidence so that it will bear most directly on the general questions stated above.

1. *The Island of Martha's Vineyard*

The island may be located in respect to the rest of New England on Figure 1. Seen from the air, it is a triangular terrain separated from the southwestern spur of Cape Cod by several miles of open water. It is large enough to appear on any good map of the United States: 150 square miles in all, some 14 miles across the midline.

Separation from the mainland is the all-important element of Vineyard geography: that distance has been preserved in recent times by a ferry toll of eight to ten dollars for a driver and his car. As a result, the island is still an island, and truly insular. Linguistically, it is a good model of a relic area, preserving many archaic features which have disappeared elsewhere—and yet the island has far more intimate contacts with the world at large than downeast Maine or rural Vermont.

Martha's Vineyard differs from Nantucket and many other New England islands in that it has an interior. There are two farm belts: one running across the island from north to south as indicated on Figure 1, and the other smaller region just to the west of Edgartown.

This interior is only farmland in part. Figure 2 shows the island in greater detail: the central region, marked as a state forest, and the marshy region in the south central portion, are largely uninhabited. This makes a partial separation which increases the distance between Edgartown in the east, and Chilmark, on the Southwest corner.

On the coast there are two good harbors: Edgartown and Vineyard Haven, and this region has by far the greatest percentage of the population. The three towns of Vineyard Haven, Oak Bluffs, and Edgartown make up "down island". Beyond these limits we have "up-island": a rural area once devoted entirely to farming and fishing, and now absorbing its share of the summer visitors. The roads running up-island are now hard surface, but this is an improvement of the last few decades.

History of the Population. The Vineyard was settled first in 1642, under a Royal Grant to the first governor, Thomas Mayhew. His direct descendants—along with the Vincents, the Jernegens, the Allens, the Nortons, all now closely related—make up the most characteristic element of the "Yankee" population today.

Some ninety surviving Indians live at Gay Head, the promontory at the southwestern tip of the island; with considerable admixture of Portuguese elements, they represent the last survivors of the original inhabitants. As far as the Indian language is concerned, the last speakers died well before any record could be made by linguists.

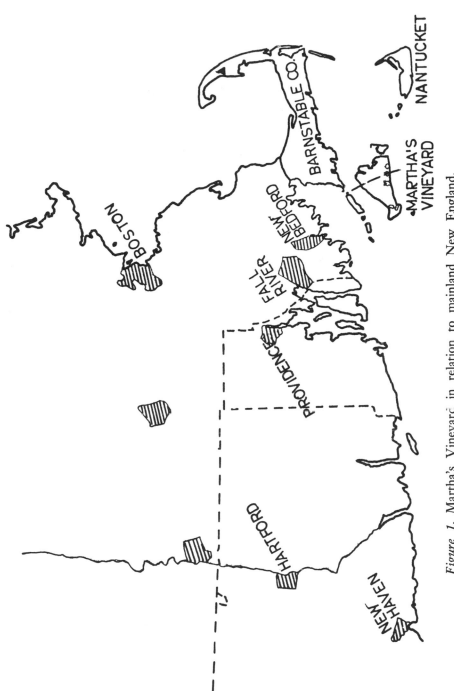

Figure 1. Martha's Vineyard in relation to mainland New England.

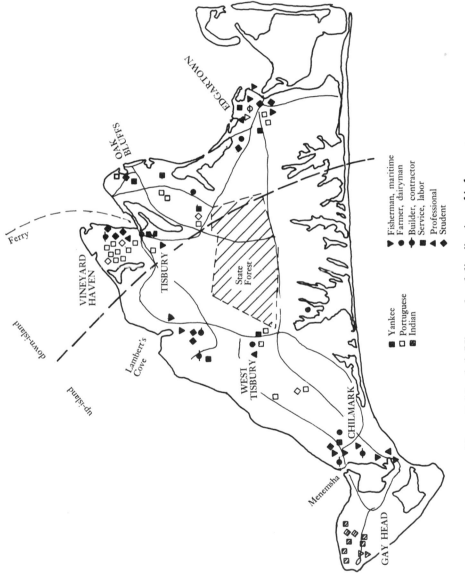

Figure 2. Martha's Vineyard and distribution of informants.

A very considerable part of the island population is of Portuguese descent. The first immigrants arrived in the late 18th century from the Azores, and through the first half of the 19th century from mainland Portugal as well. The more recent influx has been from the Cape Verde islands, especially Brava: darker skinned people who are considered African or "colored" by some Portuguese and by some Americans, especially on the mainland.

The distance between islanders of English and Portuguese descent has decreased rapidly in the 20th century, much more so than on the mainland. Not only has some intermarriage of leading families taken place, but among young people of high school age, social distinctions based on descent have died away almost entirely. A differentiating factor does appear later: a very large percentage of high school graduates of English descent leave the island for further training and mainland careers, but this is not true of those from Portuguese families. As a result, the working population from 20 to 40 is weighted on the Portuguese side.

Second generation Portuguese regularly speak native English with no detectable Portuguese influence. Third generation Portuguese begin to acquire more of the small regional peculiarities of New England and island speech: more so than the down-island children of English descent who plan to leave the Vineyard (Labov 1963).

The economy of Martha's Vineyard has been declining steadily since the death of the whaling industry. The arch type of the Vineyarder in the 19th century was the fisherman-farmer turned whaler, a whaling captain who retired at 28 after five voyages around the world. His great-grandchildren may be making a small living today lobstering and scalloping [up-island], or servicing tourists [down-island]. The farmer or fisherman of the 20th century is faced with a steady rise in transportation cost to the mainland, heavy competition from larger units there, and a sharp downturn in the numbers of fish in the local waters.

The island has become increasingly dependent on tourists, or rather summer visitors, though such developments have been deliberately kept at a slow pace. Still, the entire north shore is blanketed with private estates, and the down-island towns are completely devoted to servicing summer people. The winter population is not much more than 6,000; the summer population is more than 42,000. The richest group of summer people is to be found at Edgartown, where the first exclusive country clubs were founded some years ago.

The social complexity of the Vineyard can be illustrated by the number of dimensions needed to characterize the position of a speaker:

Descent: English, Indian, Portuguese [Azorean or Capeverdean]
Occupation: Fisherman, Farmer, Construction, Service Trades, Professional
Area: down-island, up-island
Status: old family, native, winter resident, summer people

The map of Figure 2 can be sub-divided into seven distinct areas: the three down-island towns, the two farming regions, the fishing village of Menemsha (Chilmark), and the Indian settlement at Gay Head.

In some ways, the farmers are the most conservative in language behavior, as we would expect. They are the most isolated, much more so than the fishermen who travel here and there through the Sound, and over the whole Atlantic Coast at times. The clearest, and most consistent pattern of old-line Vineyard speech was given to me by a farmer, not more than 50 years old, in North Tisbury.

The Chilmarkers are inbred in fact and in speech: here we find the most direct connection with the specifically "Yankee" past. Many islanders refer to a "Chilmark twang", a phrase used to cover nasal intonation, a strong [-ɔ˞] for /r/, and a host of special phrases and mannerisms. This is the area where the fiercely independent pattern of the old Yankee families is most evident and most resistant to the influence of summer people.

But it is at Gay Head that we will find the most archaic patterns of English, since this is the poorest and the most isolated region. The lexical patterns are not so complete or clear as in the Yankee towns, but there are some striking anachronisms which move us further back into lexical history than anywhere else.

It is important to note that up-island units are quite small. The population of Chilmark is under 250, and only 90 Indians live at Gay Head. Therefore family patterns bulk as large as community habits do elsewhere.

This brief review of the island history and geography is essential for our purpose. Though only a few of the lexical items to be discussed will be described in terms of island geography, it is very seldom that a time boundary can be drawn without making allowance for the up-island lag. For example, the 50-year-old farmer mentioned above uses *porch, ell* and *piazza, tempest* and *bonny clabber*, on a par with the oldest living speakers down-island or equivalent to the older Atlas generation of 1932. Again, the word *tempest* is not to be heard from those under fifty in most parts of the island—yet it is still commonly used by youngsters at Gay Head.

It would be convenient if we could apply an automatic correction for the various areas, and say: Age Level 1 at Vineyard Haven equals Level 3 at West Tisbury and Level 5 at Gay Head. Unfortunately, the situation is not quite so neat, for the levelling of some patterns can be very abrupt (especially with the new Regional High School). Nevertheless, we will see that with most of the words there is a constant gradation from down-island to up-island.

2. *Findings of the Linguistic Atlas*

Hans Kurath recognized the importance of Martha's Vineyard as a relic area, and accordingly, four informants were selected from the island for the

LANE. Guy Lowman interviewed a farmer [61] from West Tisbury, a schoolteacher [56] from Chilmark, a farmer [77] outside of Edgartown, and a piano tuner from Edgartown [82].

One may note that these four speakers do not represent a "cross-section" of the population. Only speakers of English descent from the oldest families are included. Three are quite old, and only one of the three down-island towns is represented. But this was an eminently correct procedure from the viewpoint of the Atlas. The purpose was not to provide a sociological document of modern day speech patterns, but to find the underlying pattern which reveals the past linguistic history of the island. And this aim seems to have been directed very successfully at the target.

My own interviews did not contradict anything that Lowman found. They did not find new items contributed to island speech by the other groups: no new Indian or Portuguese words seem to have entered the general vocabulary. To a large extent, the speech of the other groups is a dilution, or a successful adaptation of the speech pattern of the group interviewed by Lowman. It is the immediate matrix from which the speech of the 1960's was formed. The many new items which I am using in this study show an internal elaboration of that pattern.

What is the pattern of Martha's Vineyard? First, the island follows the North in general, and New England in particular. The phonological pattern is that of Eastern New England, with the exception of the retention of /r/:

/ɑ/ and /ɔ/ coalesce in /ɒ/
/or/ contrasts with /ɔr/ [though this is receding]
/hw/ contrasts strongly with /w/

In many lexical items, the Vineyard shares relics with Southeast New England: *tempest* and *whicker*, but not *cade*. Many peculiarities are shared with other recessive areas of New England, such as Cape Ann, downeast Maine, rural Vermont. But in a good many other respects, we find Martha's Vineyard a special area of its own:

[1] final and pre-consonantal /r/ is retained, recorded by Lowman as [ɚ] up-island, and [ə] in Edgartown.

[2] the first vowel in *Mary* is [ɛ], not [e], so that the word is homonymous with *merry*; this merger is regularly associated with *r*-pronunciation above.

[3] a few Vineyard words, such as *belly-gut*, are not found elsewhere in Eastern New England, but appear in the Hudson Valley.

[4] Trade words spreading from Boston, such as *tonic*, have not reached Martha's Vineyard.

[5] Most special Narragansett Bay words, such as *easeworm*, are not found on the Vineyard.

3. Data for the Present Study

The material for the present study of Martha's Vineyard was collected in three visits to the island: August and September of 1961, and January, 1962. Altogether, I interviewed 84 native residents of the island personally, the great majority in their homes. In addition to this, I obtained information from two high school English classes: from ten students in writing, and from twenty orally. Information on the island in general: its history, economy and present social structure, was gathered from many of my informants, but most importantly in conversations with the president of the Chamber of Commerce, the principal of the High School, the editor and staff writer for the *Vineyard Gazette*, selectmen of Chilmark, the town clerk of Edgartown, and a social worker from the Edgartown Boys Club.

The interviews I obtained in my first visit did not include a specific list of lexical items. This was formulated for the second series of interviews—primarily from a review of the individual maps of the LANE. In addition, a list was compiled from two glossaries of maritime words (Colcord 1945; Ashley 1906), though this material did not prove useful for exploring island patterns in general; technical terminology of fishing and boat building will not be presented here.

The purpose of the lexical study was to concentrate on the *variable* items of Martha's Vineyard speech which would reflect the differences within the island. Therefore the questionnaire was modified frequently. If an item showed a consistent positive or negative response, it was dropped. New items brought to my attention by informants were added regularly.

The sample is designed to be representative of various age levels in each community. The great majority of the speakers are males, though in each area there is an interview with a woman as the primary informant. Of the 84 interviews, 41 provide a reasonably complete set of responses to the questionnaire. Data on the most important variable questions was obtained from 40 to 60 informants; on the other hand, some questions which showed a uniform response early in the study were terminated with no more than a dozen replies.

The full form of the questionnaire is given below. Those questions which were used only with informants who had special knowledge in the field are marked with the symbol ø. The most important responses are given in order of age level directly after the question. Minor responses are separated by the symbol ///. The responses in italics or in boldface are of primary interest: if the informant did not volunteer them, their passive use was tested by suggesting the form.

Very often the responses were elicited in general conversation, or by pointing to the object in question, but in most cases the questions were posed as indicated.

4. *The Questionnaire*

WIND AND WATER

1. How would you usually describe the fact that the wind was getting stronger?
   Breezing up, airing up, breezing, breezing on, picking up. /// blowing harder, rising, freshening up, beginning to blow, gusting up, getting gusty, blowing up a gale, springing up, getting windy, it's windier.

2. Wind getting weaker?
   Moderating, diminishing, dying out. /// Flattening out, letting go, declining, dropping off, falling, slacking off, dying down, getting calmer, let up.

3. No wind at all?
   Flat calm, calm, flat ass calm. /// Dead flat calm, oil calm, slick calm, yellow day.

4. What do you call a storm with thunder, lightning, and sheets of rain?
   Tempest [tɛmpɪst]. Thundersquall, squall. Thunderstorm /// electric storm. See Figure 7.

5. A storm coming from the northeast?
   [**nouðistɚ**, nɔrðistɚ, nɔrθistɚ]

Ø 6. If sheets of cloud were gradually covering the whole sky, what would you say was happening?
   [smɪrɪŋ, smɪrɪŋ ʌp]. Clouding up, etc.

Ø 7. A bright spot in the fog as if the sun were trying to break through?
   Fog-eater. (None).

Ø 8. Do you have a word to describe water with a great deal of mud and silt in it?
   [stʌdəld, stʌdlɪ wɒtɚ]. Murky, dirty, etc.

FISH AND FISHING

9. What are the names of the minnows you use for bait, or used to use when you were a boy?
   [mʌmičʌgz] - - - [for many other variants see Fig. 13].
   [čɒksiz, čɒgsiz]. Bait. Sperling. Sand eels. Shiners, silversides. Herring, menhaden, etc.
   [To obtain *mummychug*]: . . the short stubby minnows that are found around the edge of salt marshes? Is a choxie a small cunner? Is there a difference between choxie and mummychug?

10. Is there such a thing as a blackfish? What is it?
    Tautog [tət'ɔːg]. Sea bass. Small whale. **No.**

Ø 11. Is there a difference between squeteague and weakfish?
    [skwɪtiːg] was later called weakfish, then sea trout.

Ø 12. An eel with a silver belly?
    [išɔr, nišɔr], yellow bellied eel.

13. What is a hard clam?
    [koʊhɔg, kwoʊhɔg].

14. The small fish caught for oil? "Menhaden" in New York?
    [poʊgi]. /// Mossbunker, bunker, etc.
    The narrow, flat-nosed fish, called "porgy" in New York?
    [skʌp].

Ø 15. The trash and slime that gets all over the deck when you're cleaning fish?
    [gɪri]. /// Trash, junk, guts, etc.

Ø 16. An anchor made from stone?
    [kɪlɪk, kilɪk].

Ø 17. A "high line" fisherman?
    One who brings in the highest catch. /// A lucky fellow.

Ø 18. Do you ever call a fisherman a "dog"?
    One who goes out in all kinds of weather. /// He's rough.

Ø 19. When you're handlining for cod or halibut, and the fish swallows the hook?
    [poʊkhʌkt].

Ø 20. The notched stick you push down his gullet to get the hook out?
    A muntle. /// Pokestick. Gobstick.

HOUSES

21. The section out in front, with a deck and a roof, but no walls? Where you sit in the summer and rock?
    Piazza. Porch. /// Veranda. See Figure 11.

22. A room added on to the house in back?
    Porch. Ell. Addition. Shed. See Figure 11.

23. A room added on to the side, at right angles?
    Porch. Ell. Wing. /// Sun parlor, porch. See Figure 11.

24. The best room in the house, where company sat on Sundays?
    Parlor.

25. The regular room to sit in the evenings?
    Living room. /// Sitting room.

26. The little room off the kitchen where food is stored?
    Pantry. /// *Buttry.* See Fig. 3.

27. An outdoor privy?
    Backhouse. Outhouse. /// Shithouse. /// Two by four, purvey-or, Aunt Lucy, privilege, little dollie's house, outdoors hut, sacred heart, two-holer, three-holer. See Figure 9.

28. A large chest where clothes are stored on hangers?
    Clothes closet. Closet. Wardrobe.

Ø 29. A room added on above the kitchen or an ell?
    Porch chamber. /// Extra room, bedroom, etc. See Fig. 11.

30. An unfinished room at the top of the house?
    Attic.

31. A summer cottage?
    Camp.

FOOD

32. The pan you fry eggs in?
    Spider. Skillet, Frying pan. /// Fry pan. See Fig. 8.

33. What are the two parts of an egg?
    The white and the [jɛlk, joʊlk, jɔlk, joʊk]. See Fig. 5.

34. Bread baked in the over from flour and yeast?
    Yeast bread. White bread. /// Loaf bread.

35. Baked in the oven out of yellow corn meal?
    Johnny Cake. Corn bread. See Fig. 12.

36. Baked in a large flat cake on the griddle?
    Johnny Cake. Griddle cake, pancake. /// Bannock. See Fig. 12.

37. A dessert made of apples with a crust on top, baked in the oven and served upside down with nutmeg sauce or cream?
    Apple pan dowdy. /// Deep dish apple pie, apple crisp, apple up-side down cake, slump, apple cobbler, apple crunch, apple pot pie.

38. Sour milk so thick you can eat it with a spoon?
    Bonny clabber [boʊni klæpɚ].

39. Cheese made from it?
    Cottage cheese. /// Sour milk cheese.

40. What is a hasslet?
    Don't know.

41. Onions that come up in the spring, with long green shoots and a small
    white bulb?
    [skʌljɪnz, skæljɪnz]. /// Rare-ripe.

42. Carbonated drink that come in bottles?
    Soda. Pop. Soda water. /// Soda pop. Ade. Tonic.

Ø 43. A drink made from ginger and molasses at haying time?
    [swɪčəl]. /// [swænki].

HOUSEHOLD

44. A bag made of very coarse woven stuff?
    Crocus bag. Gunny sack. Burlap bag.

45. A home made cover for cold winter nights?
    Quilt.

46. The container for food scraps and refuse?
    Garbage pail. /// Swill pail.

THE FARM

Ø 47. How did you call in cows from the pasture?
    [kou kou kou. ko ko ko. kwou k͡wou. kɔə kɔə kɔə. /// hɔk hɔk hɔk.
    kʌm bɒs. kmɑn bɒsi]

Ø 48. What do you say to a cow to steady her during milking?
    [sou bɒs]. /// Easy, gal. Steady. [Plays the radio]. Stand still,
    damn it!

Ø 49. Call for pigs?
    [pɪg pɪg pɪg pɪg]. /// šuk šuk šuk. skhɔ̃ɔ̃*]

Ø 50. Enclosure for pigs?
    Pig pen. /// Pig sty. [barn cellar].

Ø 51. Call for chickens?
    [bɪdi bɪdi bɪdi. čɪk čɪk čɪk]. /// [raps pan]. See Fig. 4.

52. A female sheep?
    [juw].

* From an Indian informant who added with a smile, "That's Indian Talk!"

53. A pet lamb? Cade?
    No responses.

Ø 54. A horse and wagon?
    Horse and team.

Ø 55.-59. [Various parts of wagon for attaching harness]:
    Pole or tongue; yoke; cross-bar; evener: whiffletrees.

Ø 60. Left and right hand horses?
    Nigh or near; off. /// [Confused the order].

Ø 61. Storage bin for hay?
    [maʊ]. Loft. /// Bay mow.

Ø 62. A platform for hauling stones?
    Stone drag.

Ø 63. Second crop of hay?
    [raʊən]. /// [roʊən]. Second cut.

Ø 64. Long narrow bin for feeding animals?
    [trɔθ]

CHILDREN

65. Going downhill on a small sled?
    Sliding. /// Coasting. Sledding.

66. Run and jump on the sled face down, go down on your stomach?
    Belly-bump. Belly-flop. /// Belly-gut, -button, -slide, -running it,
    -ride, -bumps. See Figure 10.

67. Taking something small from the kitchen?
    Hooking, swiping, snitching.

68. Getting down as low as you can behind a bush?
    [skʊʊč, skrʊʊč]. Crouch.

69. Board for balancing back and forth?
    See-saw.

PRONUNCIATION

70. Italian: [ɪtæljən]. /// [aɪtæljən].

71. Portuguese: [pɔrtəgi, pɔrčəgiz].

72. Iodine: [aɪodaɪn].

73. Quinine: [kwaɪnaɪn]. /// [kwɪnaɪn].

74. Items noted without direct inquiry:

launch: [læntš]   calm: [ka:m]
coat: [koʊt]   centralization of all
stone: [stoʊn]   /ai/ and /au/ and occasional
road: [roʊd, rəəd]   /ou/ sounds (Labov 1963).
whole: [hoʊl, hʊl]   grammatical points:
boat: [boʊt, bɔət]   *some* as adverb before ad-
both: [boʊθ, bɔəθ]   jective
toad: [təəd]   *so didn't I* for *so did I*
                                        to in *to home*, for *home*

MISCELLANEOUS

75. Main city of a county?
    /// Edgartown. County Seat. Shiretown.

76. Insect that lights up on June evenings?
    Lightning bug, firefly. /// Firebug.

77. Worm that is found in gardens?
    Angleworm, earthworm, nightcrawlers.**

78. Part that collects rain on a house?
    Gutters, gutterspouts.
    Part that brings water down?
    Downspouts. Conductors.

NEW ITEMS

A good many new words appeared in the course of the questionnaire which
may have value as regional markers, but which could not be investigated in
this study:

[jɛm] for "muffin" and [jɛm pæn] for "muffin pan"

[sæmp] for a porridge made of cracked corn.

[boʊl] is a Portuguese word for a very large round flat cake.

[skraɪmi] for "stingy". Still very much in use, apparently.

[θænkjumʌmz] "Thankyoumums". A pile of sand on a dirt road to
help drain the water. The name comes from the motion passengers
made when a car went over the sand piles.

5. *Three modes of analysis.*

The 78 questions listed above would seem to present a formidable task for
the analyst. However, they are not of equal weight, and a limited number will

** There is considerable argument on the Vineyard and elsewhere as to whether
these are the same or different. Nightcrawlers are much larger, and some consider
them a different species altogether.

serve to give us the evidence on the original questions posed. It would be convenient to group the various replies into categories, and there are three useful ways of doing this:

a. By time of use and disappearance, establishing time boundaries for individual items.
b. By complexity of structure, beginning with isolated words, and proceeding to words connected in a linear sequence, those organized in two dimensions, three dimensions, and so on.
c. By their social character, according to the possible reasons for their rise, propagation, and fall.

The first discussion will help to answer the first question raised at the outset. The items which have disappeared or are disappearing will be presented with some information on their past history, in order to gain some perspective on the rate of lexical change.

The second discussion will show the extent to which structural factors in the lexicon influence the survival or semantic shift of certain words. The more complex items will be organized into charts which show the interrelations of the various areas and age levels on the island, and reveal how the mutual relationships of words affect their survival.

The third discussion will provide some broader answers to the second question raised: what factors are associated with language change, or more broadly: what are the causes? and are they still operating?

6. *Times and Orders of Disappearance.*

For this purpose, we will need to establish some arbitrary age levels:

Generation O: now dead: includes Lowman's four informants, since their testimony was given at an earlier time, and does not reflect present influences.
Generation I-A: old people, 75-95, who have lost their physical vigor and are undergoing voluntary retirement.
Generation I-B: older people with grandchildren, 60-75, still in full vigor and with active occupations.
Generation II-A: middle-aged, 45-60, with children in high school or older
Generation II-B: age 30 to 45, with small children
Generation III-A: age 20 to 30, unmarried, or if married, without small children
Generation III-B: age 10 to 20.

A. Non-Existent Forms: *cade*

The word *cade* is one of the clearest examples of a relic word in Southeast

New England. It stems from ME *cad*, "lamb", and is still current in English dialects meaning 'pet lamb'. However, it was not on the Vineyard in Lowman's time, and I have confirmed the fact that there is no trace of it now.

B. Extinct Forms: bannock, buttry, comforter, hasslet, tilting board, whicker, [paɪzn, aɪodijn]

These are words which are known to have existed, from Lowman's records or by indirect evidence from descendants of Vineyard speakers. This latter kind of evidence is remarkably persuasive; informants present clear and vivid recollections of terms their parents or grandparents used. Thus we can record the usage of Generation O who are recently dead, and I have no hesitation in accepting such statements as "My grandmother always said. . . ." Such statements may indeed be more accurate than a person's recollection of what he himself said at that time.

bannock. This is derived from an old Gaelic word for bread, *bannach*; in the OED it dates back to 1000. It is still used in Scotland and the north of England for a large round flat cake of unleavened bread. Bartlett 1848 notes it as a New England word for cakes of Indian meal [corn meal] fried in lard. [The DAE first finds it in America in 1805].

I recorded *bannock* only once: from Mrs. Granville Blaine, an Indian woman 82 years old, one of the most archaic speakers on the island. She volunteered, in speaking of flat cakes of corn meal fried in a spider, that "the old folks called it *bannock*". Others to whom I suggested this word would say they never heard it, or call it a "Scottish word."

We can therefore infer that *bannock* must have become generally extinct on the island before 1900.

buttery [bʌtri]. This was originally "bottle room", a store room for liquor, from OF *boterie*. In this sense it dates from 1389. By the 15th century, it was adapted to its later sense of 'storeroom' generally. It was folk-etymologized to "butter-room", according to my own findings on the Vineyard, and the current spelling given here.

In Lowman's time, this word was fading rapidly. He found only one informant who gave it as a first choice. Yet *pantry*, now the universal replacement, had not yet become general. I found the following evidence from testimony about Generation O:

[bʌtri]   mother of I-A Yankee down-islander
[bʌtri]   father of I-A Yankee up-islander
[bʌtri]   parents of I-B Yankee down-islander
[bʌtri]   great-grandmother of I-B Yankee up-islander
[bʌtəri]   grandmother of I-B Yankee down-islander

Nine other informants remember that the "old folks" used this word. Seven were Gen. I; the two Gen. II were very archaic types. One man of Portuguese descent is included, but of the 4th generation.

We can therefore reconstruct the fact with some certainty that *buttry* was alive until 1930, but died out as Generation O died. It seems to have been fairly evenly distributed throughout the island.

whicker for 'whinny' is considered a Southeast New England word. It was recorded by Lowman, but I only found it as a secondary form when I suggested it. Some informants said that it was used, but it seems effectively dead.

The following five items were recorded by Lowman, from the number of informants indicated, but did not receive any support in my interviews.

hasslet [4] for "liver and lights"
comforter [4] for "quilt"
[paɪzn] [2] for [pɔɪzn]
[aɪədijn] [2] for [aɪodain]
tilting board or *rail* for "see saw" [2]

These regional markers have now been extinguished, or are close to their end, yet we know that they must have been alive in Generation O.

C. Disappearing

Generation I-A

firebug, belly-gut, [jɛlk], [kwɪnaɪn], [aɪtæljən], shiretown, short [ɵ] in [bɵθ], stɵn]

Firebug for "lightning bug" was not given by any of Lowman's informants, but was supplied to me by Mrs. Blaine.

[jɛlk] was recorded only once by Lowman. I obtained five instances, all from archaic inland speakers. See Fig. 5.

belly-gut is one of the most remarkable relics on the Vineyard, and one of a complex set discussed below. De Vere notes *belly-gut* as a corruption of *belly-cutter* in 1872; in *Dialect Notes* I:60, it is noted (in Philadelphia) as *belly-guts*. As far as New England is concerned, *belly-gut* is recorded only on the Vineyard; the nearest similar forms are on the eastern fringes of the Hudson Valley.

I obtained two instances of *belly-gut*, both from Gen. I-A inland figures in Edgartown. We can therefore assume that it disappeared even earlier than *bannock*, since it is a word which is used only in childhood, and it is not likely that these informants used it after they were 20 years old. It must have gone out of use in the early 1890's. See Fig. 10.

The active use of [aɪtæljən] is confined to archaic I-A figures like the older Blaines. However, several I-B informants mentioned that it was an older form they used to hear.

Generation I-B

tempest, hook [for "steal"], crocus bag, rare-ripe, garden sauce [sæs], [bɪdi bɪdi bɪdi], [šuk šuk šuk], swill pail

Tempest (pronounced [tempɪst] with a clear [ɪ]) is one of the best markers of the Southeast New England region. I recorded it myself on the borders of this region in Stonington, Connecticut. In the sense of 'thunderstorm', *tempest* dates back to 1532 according to the OED.

Tempest is still in use on the Vineyard among speakers of Generation I, but only at Gay Head is it actively used by the younger generation. My first contact with the word was during my first interview at Gay Head. I was sitting in a cabin interviewing a younger Indian informant, while rain poured down outside, with lightning and thunder. There was a knock on the door, and an older Indian man wearing oilskins came in: the constable of Gay Head, Jesse Smalley. He had been out on the beach looking for some thieves. My informant asked him if the telephone was safe to use, and Smalley said:

"Well I didn't call before because this tempest was going on."

The other words noted above were all recorded by Lowman. The chicken call [bɪdi bɪdi bɪdi] is worth some note because it was given to me by three I-A's and two I-B's, all of whom had active experience with chicken farming. On the other hand, [čɪk čɪk čɪk] is used by those who do not share this direct contact, but seems to be replacing the first form completely. See Fig. 4.

Lowman recorded [čʊk, čʊg] as a call to pigs: the only related item that I found was [šʊk šʊk šʊk].

Generation II-A

gurry. smurring up. spider. bonny-clabber. sitting room. back-house. [jolk].

Gurry [gɪrɪ] is an Americanism, as the DAE notes, and arose first as a whaling term in 1838: "Gurry and blubber. ." By 1879, Webster listed it in the supplement as meaning the offal of fish as well. It was not an item in the LANE, but is a characteristic regionalism of New Bedford and Martha's Vineyard. Like many specialized fishing terms, *gurry* is commonest in Chilmark, but it is not known to those who have little connection with that area.

The other items noted above were all recorded by Lowman. *Smurry, smur,* or *smurring up* is noted by the OED as an obscure dialectal word meaning 'fine rain or drizzle'. In America, it seems to refer to the formation of clouds that heralds a storm. Like *gurry*, it is centered in Chilmark.

Spider is taken as an Americanism by the DAE in the sense of 'iron frying pan' or 'skillet', sometimes provided with long legs. It dates back to 1790, and is considered by the LANE as an important marker of the Northern region. Lowman recorded three uses of this term, and it is known to everyone on the island, but its active use is pretty well confined to II-A and older. See Figure 8 for its interrelations.

Bonny-clabber [boʊni klæpɚ] is dated by the DAE to 1731, going back to the Anglo-Irish in 1631, from Gael. *bainne clabair*, sour thick milk. As this sour milk is not easily made for pasteurized milk, the material itself is not to be found except where cows are kept, and even then, it is rare. On the island, *bonny clabber* was especially popular for cooking, making pancakes; some people fed it to the pigs.

[jolk] or [jɔlk] is discussed in detail below; see Figure 5.

Backhouse is another Americanism, noted by the DAE first in Webster 1847; it goes back to England for its use as any outdoor structure in the rear of the house. Like any word involved with excrement, it shows the rapid shifting associated with taboos. See Figure 9 for its relations with *outhouse*, and other items. Various humorous local forms are shown following question 27. For those over fifty, *backhouse* cannot be used freely in mixed company, and it is quoted with smiles and knowing looks that are hard for younger people to understand. It follows the usual pattern of euphemisms that become tainted themselves, are stigmatized, and finally repressed.

Generation II-B

belly-bump. belly-flop. nigh-off, whiffletree, pole, yoke, evener.

Belly-bump and *belly-flop* are Americanisms, recorded by the DAE under *belly-bumbo, -bumps, -bunt, -flumps, -bunk, -buster, -flop, -flounder, -gutter, -plumper, -whack* and *-whopper*. *Belly-gut* is listed separately. The first good reference for these terms dates back to 1855.

On Martha's Vineyard, Lowman recorded only one case of "belly-bump". For the proliferation of these terms on the island, see question 66, and for their interrelations as a whole, see Figure 10.

The words concerning horse and wagon gear all follow the outline of the LANE. Consistent and complete information on them can be obtained from a number of farmers over 40, and some of the items themselves can still be seen in the barns. "Nigh" or "near" and "off" are well known, but are becoming confused in Generation II-A and B.

Generation III-A

piazza, verandah, ell. skillet.

The first three words are part of a very complex history which is illustrated in Figure 11. They are all somewhat outmoded at this point, through it is hard to say whether later generations will revive them.

Piazza [piæzə] was originally adapted from Italian, meaning an open square in the center of a town, where we now use *plaza*. In 1583 we find the first reference in this sense, and later in the 17th century it was extended to mean a colonnade in front of a building. In the 18th century, the word came to mean a *verandah* in the United States—that is, a wide open porch. The DAE first records the word used in this sense in America in 1699.

Verandah was taken from Portuguese via Indian about the same time, in 1711, and the two words have been in competition in America ever since. *Porch* dates back to 1290 in England, in the sense of a covered approachway or vestibule, adapted from Latin *porticus*. About 1832, according to the DAE, this word was used in America to mean *verandah* also, giving three words in direct competition.

We don't know at what time *porch* was taken over in America in its New England regional sense of an addition to a house, particularly the kitchen ell in back, but in the 19th century it began to compete in this sense with its other use. Finally, we find the word *portico* in use on the Vineyard in Lowman's time meaning '*verandah*', though this word is now extinct. The internal relations of all these terms may be seen in Figure 11.

The meaning of *porch* as an additional room is not recorded in the DAE, DA or the OED, but was clearly noted in Atlas records. None of these sources noted the remarkable remnant *porch chamber* or *porch room*, which was used on the Vineyard long after *porch* had been switched to mean the open structure in front. A *porch chamber* is a room built over the kitchen in the back of the house.

For the relations involving *skillet*, see Figure 8.

D. Items Receding and Limited Geographically

apple pan dowdy, belly bump, piazza, studdled, smurry, tempest, [læntš]

Most of these items are confined to up-island areas, particularly Chilmark and Gay Head. They have been listed as items now disappearing, for that is true enough in most parts of the island. At the same time, these are the most useful words for establishing geographical patterns of language on the island. See Figure 10.

studdled or *studdly* meaning 'dirty [water]' is the prize exhibit of a Vineyard word collector. It did not appear in the LANE, but is well established and recognized in the up-island areas of the Vineyard, especially Chilmark and Gay Head. The OED reports it only once, in 1852, but Wright's EDD has a number of records in Berks, Hampshire, Wiltshire: "to stir up so as to make thick and muddy".

I have recorded "studdled" in seven cases in Chilmark, and "studdly" [stʌdli] as the form used in Gay Head.

apple pan dowdy is an Americanism of unknown origin, according to the DAE. It first appears in 1830 as "pan dowdy", and is described in 1895 as "a compote of apples, with several layers of pastry made from rye meal, baked in a deep earthern dish and eaten with milk." A menu for this dish appeared in the *New York Post* of November 2, 1961 (p. 48): the "dowdying" is said to be an extra mincing operation performed half way through the baking. This is not done on the Vineyard; as made by Mrs. Donald Poole of Chilmark, apple pan dowdy is baked with a crust on top only, then turned upside down on the plate, and topped with nutmeg sauce. [Thick clotted cream is said to be preferred when cows are nearby.] A number of modern terms are given as equivalents by down-islanders [see question 37].

E. Still Current

There is a sizeable body of regional markers which remain fairly constant on the island as a whole, to the extent that speakers are familiar with the lexical area in question:

> breezing up, calm or flat calm or flat ass calm, moderating, squall, scup, pogy, tautog
> gutter, gutterspout, camp
> pigpen, [ko ko ko], [soʊ bɒs], rowen, hay mow
> quilt, soda, [skʌljɪnz]
> sliding

We have another body of words which are still common, but which oscillate between alternate forms:

> [kohɔg ~ kwohɔg]
> mummychug ~ choxie [see Fig. 13]
> Johnny cake ~ corn bread ~ griddle cake ~ pancake
> angleworm ~ nightcrawler
> blackfish ~ tautog or sea bass

At the same time, we must recognize the great increase in the use of standardized non-regional terms on the island:

> porch, wing, pantry
> quilt
> ewe [jʊ], [gidæp], [čɪk čɪk čɪk]
> earthworm
> thunderstorm

This list might be extended indefinitely, from one lexical area to another; the list of regionalisms can be increased, but not without some difficulty.

F. New Items

In the course of this study, a number of new items appeared, which could not be investigated in the questionnaire. Some have already been listed above. There are also a number of phrases and grammatical constructions which are regional markers common in rural eastern New England. Some are old, but are being strongly reinforced in the third generation, as with *some* used as an intensifying adverb before adjectives:

> He was some tickled.
> You ought to try those fried clams. Boy! They're some good!
> That wind was blowing some hard.

In this usage of 'very much', the word is not described in the OED or DAE except as independent predicate. However, the EDD gives a number of examples of *some* used in this way.

like-a-that: a Chilmark form

a-going: participles preceded by *a-* are common in many rural areas, but seem to be flourishing on the Vineyard.

finest kind: meaning "O.K. Swell. Good job." Said to be used in downeast Maine.

away: meaning off-island. Known humorously as "America".

so didn't I for *so did I*. This is said to have originated in Generation III in Edgartown; it is now widespread among young people from 12 to 25. From my own experience at the High School, I know that *so didn't I* has become general enough to be stigmatized by teachers, and a point of local humor. More recent observations show that it is not at all limited to the Vineyard: it is found in other areas of Massachusetts and is quite general in southeastern Maine. In Brunswick, Maine, I have recorded *so don't I* in the natural conversation of adolescent boys.

to is used in areas where we would omit it altogether, and as the familiar alternant of *at*: "He was to home". "That was on to the rock."

7. *First Conclusions*

Our original impressions of the linguistic situation on the Vineyard is that most of the regional markers are disappearing—that they are vanishing and leaving in their place a thoroughly standard speech. I believe that careful examination of the facts will show that this is an illusion.

Generation by generation, there has been no sudden jump in the number of dialect markers which are eliminated. Generation O has left some evidence of the terms which it abandoned: this dates back to the 1890's, long before the standardizing influence of radio and television. The distribution of the other items through several age levels is quite uniform. There is evidence that the process of dialect marker decay is fairly steady.

To begin to count and calculate in years and items would be a fallacy, for there is nothing exhaustive about our method of selecting items. These markers are the ones that came to the attention of Hans Kurath, or to my attention in the course of this study. No one can estimate the number of regional markers which have not been examined.

The steadiness of this process of extinction may be taken as a warrant for a uniformitarian doctrine of dialectology; as far as this one area is concerned, we can say that the forces which are operating today are the same *in kind* as those which operated in 1890. If we take a sudden view of the differences between the usage of 1890 (reflected in Kurath's questionnaire) and 1960, we are startled by the loss of so many items. But as a rule we don't reflect on how many generations have intervened. How heavily is this process weighted on the side of extinction? How many new forms are arising to take the place of the old? This is a hard question to answer, because the new markers are so much harder to perceive. But there are some indications that the reverse current exists, perhaps not so strong as the movement towards extinction.

First of all, note that many of our disappearing markers are not so old after all. True, some date back to the 16th century, or earlier, but many are 18th century innovations, and many more have their sources in the 19th century. The special uses of *porch* as 'kitchen' probably do not antedate 1800 by very much: we know that *verandah* and *piazza* began about 1700, in the sense of modern "porch", and *porch* itself is first recorded in its modern sense in 1832. Therefore the present structure is not an old, old pattern which is suddenly decaying, but rather one that has been in constant flux ever since the country was settled.

The words in the *belly-bump* category are 19th century innovations, as far as we know, and it was only fifty years after *belly-gut* was brought in that it went out. *Backhouse* is not very old either, and from our knowledge of the history of euphemisms, we know that it too must have begun its career from polite to rude to old-fashioned to extinction, not long after it reached the Vineyard.

It is also important to note that many of these regional markers belong to very unstable semantic fields, which will be explored further in later pages.

The case of *soda* is very revealing. In Generation I-A the word was still new in the sense of carbonated drink, and we get such forms as *ade*, *switchel*, and other non-carbonated drinks supplied by the very old folks from up-island. Here was a regionalism in the process of formation, and its future history is that of resistance to the Boston trade word *tonic*. To many Vineyarders, *tonic* still means a patent medicine.

Some of the new markers that are growing up have been noted in the pages above. However, there is much more that might be done in this field, exploring the equivalents of Vineyard terms for short order sandwiches, soda fountain specialties, and other categories which vary regionally throughout the country.

8. *Lexical Structures*

We will now take up the interrelations of the dialect markers themselves, in order to illustrate the internal structure of the semantic systems, and the influences which words exert on each other in their progressive rise and fall.

A. *Isolates*

A certain small percentage of markers which disappear are isolated words: they die away and are replaced by nothing. This may be merely an intermission before another term arises; or the items described may no longer be in existence, or the aspect of nature described may no longer count. The last is certainly the case with *fog-eater*. The OED places this in 1867 as a synonym of *fog-dog* and *fog-bow*, which referred either to the lower end of a rainbow or a bright patch in the fog. *Fog-eater* seems to live at Edgartown for a few seafaring II-A men, but it is being extinguished without a replacement.

A similar situation is to be found with all the horse-bearing equipment: *whiffletrees, evener, yoke, cross-bar.* These now form a semantic complex, and they are not isolates: but the last one to go will seem to be an isolate. Perhaps a similar situation exists with *stone drag, garden sauce, swill pail,* and so on. All of these are cases are examples of words referring to customs and objects no longer in use.

The case of an intermission may be found with *shiretown*. This is being replaced by the name of the town itself, *Edgartown*, for many people, but perhaps *county seat* will fill the gap before long.

B. *Linear Series*

It is normal for an extinct word to have a replacement, and be succeeded in time by another word. These cases hardly need diagramming, but will serve to contrast with the complexity of those in the next category. In Figures 3–6, the vertical axis represents age level; the horizontal axis the proportion of speakers who use the form. Down-island usage is placed to the right; up-island to the left.

A simple linear series is that of
buttery : : pantry.
As shown in Figure 3, the word *pantry* has become universal and is the only active word in this area. This is not entirely expected, because most houses don't have pantries any more, and I would expect this word to begin to disintegrate. But it hasn't done so, and Figure 3 is the result.

The next case is that of calls to chickens:
bɪdi bɪdi bɪdi : : čɪk čɪk čɪk
The replacement has been fairly abrupt: those who know something about chickens say the first, while modern people who are more or less amateurs say the second. This represents a break in tradition which has accelerated the change.

The succession in pronunciation of *yolk* is one step more complicated:
[jɛɫk : : joɫk ~ jɔɫk : : jouk]
Phonetically, the step from a dark [ɫ] to a high back vowel is only the loss of one feature; this succession is phonetically motivated by the velar nature of the /1/ as well as standardization from the outside.

Most speakers are quite unconscious of this variation around them. Mr. and Mrs. Blaine answered the question simultaneously: he said [joɫk] and she said [jɛɫk] but neither realized the other had said anything different. Another interesting case is that of a middle aged unmarried woman who had lived all her life with her father, now 92. He said [jɛɫk]; she said [jɛɫk], but added, "I guess it should be [joɫk]." They both were quite isolated from modern day changes.

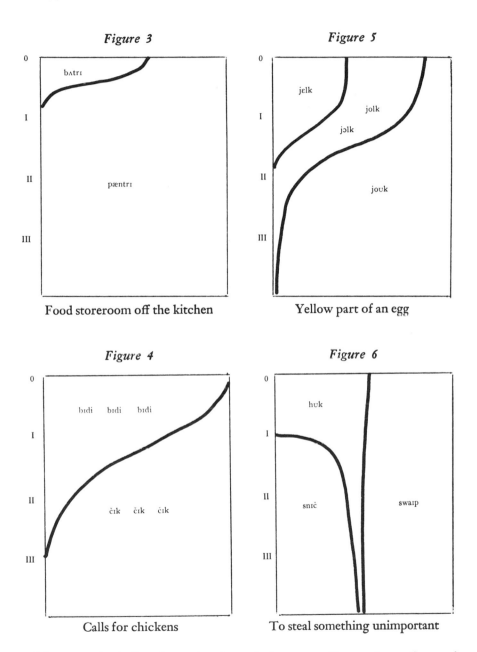

Figure 3

0

bʌtrɪ

I

II   pæntrɪ

III

Food storeroom off the kitchen

Figure 5

0

jɛlk

jolk

I

jɔlk

II

joʊk

III

Yellow part of an egg

Figure 4

0

bɪdi   bɪdi   bɪdi

I

II   čɪk   čɪk   čɪk

III

Calls for chickens

Figure 6

0

hʊk

I

II   snɪč   swaɪp

III

To steal something unimportant

The case of *snitch* and associated words for petty thievery is another such case. The general term *swipe* continues in use, while *snitch* replaces *hook*:

hook → snitch

s   w   i   p   e

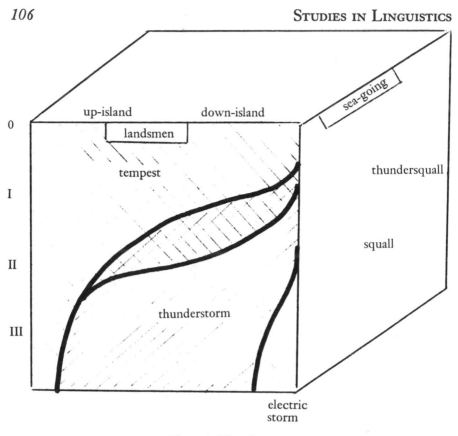

Figure 7. Thunderstorm

C. *Two-Dimensional Structures*

The next series shows items located in a more complex field. *Tempest* and the other words for 'thunderstorm' present a comparatively straightforward case, as shown in Figure 7. On the front plane is shown the terminology used by landsmen; sea-going usage is indicated at right-angles to this. Again, the vertical dimension represents the usage of age levels, and up-island is oriented to the left, down-island to the right. *Tempest* is preserved as an up-island term in the youngest generation, though it was once quite general. We thus have

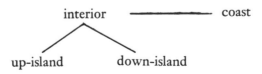

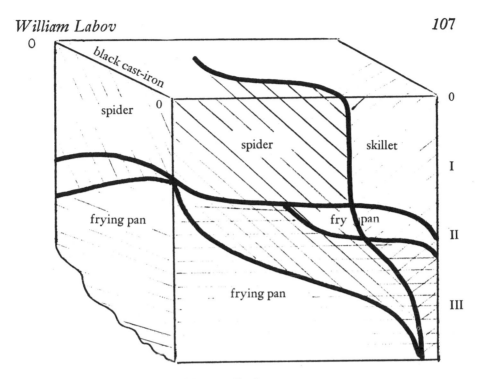

Figure 8. Frying pan

By 'interior', I mean to indicate those speakers who are not completely oriented towards the sea by occupation and inclination. The alternating between *thundersquall* and *squall* is not entirely a case of free variation: younger speakers seem to favor *squall*. On the landsmen's side, *thunderstorm* has generally replaced *tempest*, except for some up-island speakers and for some down-island speakers who refer to *electric storm*.

Figure 8 shows words for 'frying pan'. The third dimension is used here to distinguish between the lighter-weighted modern utensil and the older heavy black cast-iron pan. The oldest form of the cast-iron pan had three legs, and for several of the most archaic informants, the item with three legs is the *spider*. But for most speakers, the terms *spider* and *skillet* are homonyms— unless they are actually confronted with the heavy black-iron pan, when they show less tendency to use the term *skillet*. Eventually, the standard term *frying pan* replaces both *spider* and *skillet*, though the intermediate form *fry pan* appears in the II-A generation.

The two horizontal dimensions of Figure 9 refer not to the referent, but the social situation in which the terms for 'outdoor latrine' are used. In this sense, Figure 9 resembles Figure 7 more than 8. Yet the situation represented in Figure 9 does not show divided usage show much as the stylistic shift which is within the competence of speakers at each level: thus each speaker is expected to know two terms and use them appropriately. The polite term

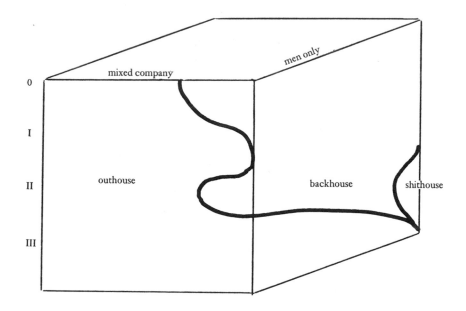

Figure 9. An outdoor latrine

is shown on the front panel; at right angles to this, the more direct term used among men only. In the course of historical development, terms move from polite usage to impolite: that is, their association with excrement leads to "pejoration". This is the case with *backhouse*, originally a euphemism for the relatively constant *shithouse* and other older terms. As *backhouse* became stigmatized, it was replaced by *outhouse*. The process seems to have come to an end, however, as the item itself is no longer a major piece of apparatus in social arrangements. Question 27 lists a number of examples of other terms which illustrate the rich local humor that clusters around this semantic field.

D. *Three-Dimensional Structures*

Figure 10 shows graphically the internal relations of the terms for a 'down-hill sled ride'. The front panel is divided into up-island and down-island usage, as with Figure 7. In this case, the geographical differentiation is quite sharp: *belly-bump* seems to have been strictly up-island. The older term *belly-gut* is the original down-island term, also found up-island in the oldest generation; we see this giving way to *belly-bump* up-island and *belly-flop* down-island. In the third generation, we see the sudden switch of semantic field: the denotation of *belly-flop* moves to the area of diving into the water, and there is no term at all left for a face-down sled ride. This switch coincides with a similar shift which we find over the United States, almost without respect to the actual term being used: it represents the most striking influence of a

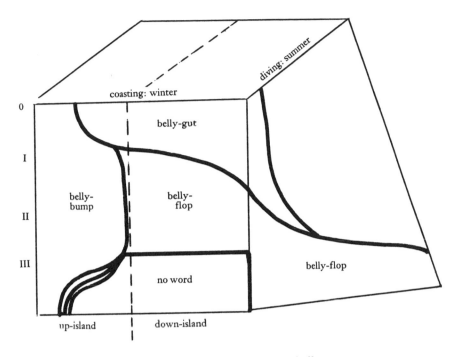

Figure 10. Going down on your belly

cultural influence on language independent of formal features. Perhaps the term *belly-bump* is the most notable exception to the general trend: as compared to *belly-smash, -gut, -flop, -whick,* etc., *belly-bump* may preserve some association with the sensation of hitting an uneven terrain, sometimes deliberately constructed in the run to add to the fun.

This shift of usage illustrates another general principle associated with regional markers: the terms of pre-adolescent usage change without successive generations being aware of it. Parents do not know what terms their children use for their local games and oral legislation: they are quite surprised when children answer that there is no word for coasting on your stomach: "Just sliding".

The term *sliding* is itself a New England regional term, as opposed to Midland *sleigh-riding,* which can only mean a ride in a horse-drawn sleigh for most New Englanders. *Sledding* is the more general New England form, but *sliding* is uniform on the Vineyard as the general term for riding down hill on a small sled. The vowel is unusual in that it shows an extremely centralized form of [əⁱ], even for speakers who do not usually show this phonetic variant (Labov 1963). In fact, the vowel is so obscure that it is difficult to be sure if some speakers are saying *sledding* or *sliding,* which may reflect the mechanism of the shift.

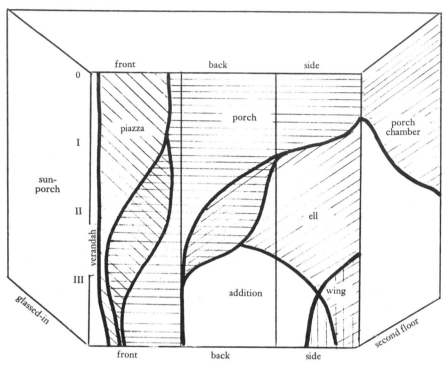

Figure 11. Peripheral additions to a house

　　As noted above, the term *belly-gut* is part of an older stratum which is also found in the Hudson Valley. *Belly-flop* is a mainland importation replacing *belly-gut*, and obviously has more influence down-island as with other mainland forms. The area of uncertainty in the up-island column in the third generation refers to a proliferation of terms such as *belly-ride, belly-button, belly-slide,* and *belly-running it* among up-island youngsters. With this evidence, we may want to point to the continued cultural importance of sledding up-island as the basis for the survival of the terms, rather than the semantic associations of *belly-bump.* There is a Belly-Bump Hill in Chilmark.

E. *Four-Dimensional Structures.*

　　The cases of 'Johnny cake' and 'porch' will show us lexical and semantic fields of greater complexity than those considered above. Terms for the peripheral additions to a house are illustrated in Figure 11: this represents a semantic area which is unstable in most English dialects, and in other languages as well. The foreign languages which are preserved in the United States for several generations usually show loan words for such items as these, which reflect the instability of the cultural situation in the background. We can see such shifting in *buttery - pantry, backhouse - outhouse,* and it also appears in *parlor - living room - sitting room, closet - clothes press,* and *lumber room - attic.* On the other hand, we do not find such alternations for

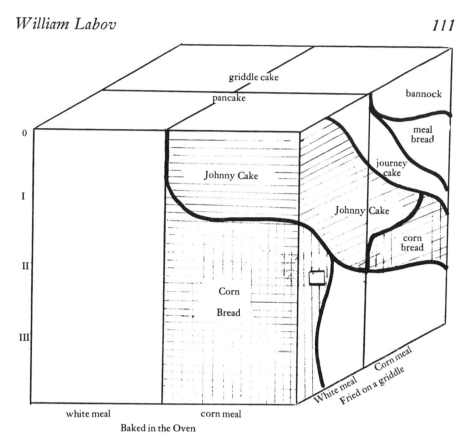

Figure 12. Johnny Cake and corn bread

'bedroom' and 'kitchen', since rooms for sleeping and preparing food are invariant parts of a house in our culture.

The maximum instability appears in the terms for peripheral additions to a house as shown in Figure 11. Three categories of additions are shown on the front panel: structures added to the front, back, and side of the house. As subsidiary dimensions we have the structures indicated on the left side panel: glassed-in additions; and second-story additions on the right panel.

The term *porch* appears as the general word for additions to the back or side of the house in the oldest generations; only a small minority use *porch* for a front addition in its most general application today. We then observe a gradual shift, with mixed usage in Generation II, until *porch* is well established as the term for a front-of-the-house structure in Generation III. *Porch* replaces *piazza*, which is the overwhelming choice of Generation O and I speakers for a front addition. In Generation IB we see the beginning of an alternation between *piazza* and *porch*, which continues through Generation II, and finally *piazza* all but disappears for the youngest speakers. The term *verandah* preserves a small number of adherents among the older Vineyarders, and has actually gained ground slightly in the third generation.

When *porch* shifted its sense, it left a gap which was filled at first by *ell* for an addition to the side of a house, and for the back as well. In Generation II, we see that *porch* is no longer used at all for the side of the house, and it alternates with *ell* for a back addition. In Generation IIB, *porch* is so strongly attached to the front of the house that it is no longer used for a back addition at all; but neither is *ell* thought of as suitable for this, and the simple term *addition* is preferred. In the third generation, *addition* spreads at the expense of *ell*, and a new term for a side addition appears, *wing*. One might consider that the image associated with *ell* strongly suggests a side addition, so that its use as an addition to the back gave way before its original meaning. In other words, *ell* was extended to indicate a back addition only because *porch* was shifting its meaning, and sometimes was needed to fill the gap, but the extension was only temporary.

Finally, we can observe that the term *porch chamber* survived well into Generation II to indicate a room built over the kitchen. With the view offered us by Figure 11, we can readily understand how this term originated and what it means. But informants who had lost the original meaning of *porch* found it difficult to understand the origin of their own term, *porch chamber*.

The movements of *piazza*, *porch*, and *ell* show the internal structure of the lexicon, in which the pressure to avoid homonymy within a restricted denotational system acts as a powerful determinant of linguistic change. If we consider that the primary factor in the change was the obsolescence of *piazza*, then the whole process may be thought of as a "drag chain". But if we think of the influence of the standardized term *porch* for 'front addition', then we can think of *porch* pushing *piazza* out and dragging *ell* behind it.

One unifying feature is the use of *sun porch* for a glassed-in enclosure. Sun porches are generally on the side of a house, and so this term mediates between the use of *porch* for a front addition, and its older status as a back and side addition to a house.

The terms for corn meal cakes baked in the oven or fried on a griddle present an even more complex set of components. Figure 12 utilizes the front panel of our display for items baked in the oven, and the vertical dimension as usual to indicate developments through age levels. The third dimension refers to items fried on a griddle. Each of the horizontal dimensions is divided into two sections for items made from white (wheat) meal, and those made from yellow (corn) meal. We could further discriminate the use of flour from the use of meal; on the top of the diagram, the terms *griddle cake* and *pancake* are used to indicate this more modern aspect of the question. Other considerations such as the use of milk vs. water, or the addition of an egg, will not be pursued here, except to indicate that this is a rich area for componential analysis.

The prevailing usage on Martha's Vineyard is to equate *Johnny cake* with *corn bread*. *Johnny cake* is the older term, and it was used more widely to indicate something baked in a deep pan in the oven than a flat cake fried on the griddle. *Johnny cake* is essentially baked out of Indian meal, directly opposed to the Rhode Island sense of a *Johnny cake* which is a made out of white meal and baked on the griddle. Rhode Island white meal is sold on the Vineyard in a few stores for people who have adopted this standard. For them, anything made of corn meal is *corn bread*, in the oven or on the griddle. Others feel that *Johnny cake* must be made of corn meal, even on the griddle: this sense is indicated in Generations I and II. However, a corn meal cake baked on a griddle was originally a *bannock*, a term which disappeared early in this development, giving way to *meal bread, journey cake, Johnny cake*, and finally *corn bread*.

For the younger generation, *Johnny cake* and *corn bread* continue to be used for a meal cake baked in the oven. But meal is no longer used for pan cakes, and the more general terms *griddle cake* and *pancake* are normal in Generation III.

F. *Fractionation*

In this study, many cases of semantic and formal diversification or "fractionation" were observed. The case of *breezing up* (Question 1) shows how substitutes which have no clearly established tradition can proliferate in an almost random pattern: *airing up, breezing, breezing on, picking up, freshening up, gusting up, springing up*, and so on. Those familiar with boats and the sea use one or two terms: those who are not usually have no term at all, and supply such periphrastic forms as "getting windier". A similar situation exists with the substitutes for *apple pan dowdy* (Question 37). The original item has one name: the latter substitutes are unlimited.

A proliferation of alternates can often be observed in terms which have their origin in Indian languages. Most of them were originally long, unanalyzable morphemes which did not fit into the canonical form of English words. A clear-cut case is that of the fish *skuppaug* (Stenotomos argyrops), a commercial food fish that grows up to a foot and a half, found in the Atlantic waters from Cape Cod south. The name is derived from Narragansett *mishcùp*, plural *mishcùppaûog*.

This term was broken into two parts:*

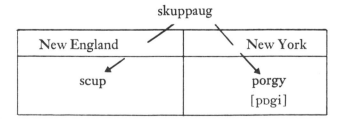

It is understandable that the term would be shortened, but why did it split in this way? Why did New England take the first half and the middle Atlantic

---

* or perhaps we could say that *scup* was derived from the singular.

states the second? The answer is quite plainly due to the pressure to avoid homonymy: indeed, it is an even clearer case than the example of *gattus* cited so often from Bloomfield's presentation of Gillieron's work. (Bloomfield 1933:397). There is another fish in these waters generally known as the *menhaden* (Brevoortia tyrannus), a smaller commercial fish used for fertilizer and oil. *Menhaden* is another Narragansett term, known from Rhode Island southward. But in New England, the fish is known as the *pogy* (from an Algonquian name). This is altogether too close to *porgy* for a clear distinction to be maintained, especially when we consider that the only difference is that of vowel height. The *skuppaug* etymology shows that *porgy* was originally r-less, and the spelling *r* is a classic hypercorrection.* Whenever the *o* in *pogie* is shortened, we may get a low vowel not far from *porgy* [pɒgi]. Map 233 of the LANE shows that its editors were not unaware of this situation, since *porgy-scup* and *pogie-menhaden* were mapped together. The general distribution of the two sets is obvious:

New England	New York W. Connecticut
scup	porgy
pogie	menhaden

But a detailed examination of the map shows that the pressure to avoid homonymy leads to much more precise results than this. Figure 13 shows the distribution of these four terms in Eastern Connecticut, Rhode Island, and Cape Cod, with the eastern tip of Long Island, Block Island, Martha's Vineyard and Nantucket included. The westernmost of the four isoglosses is that of *scup*, which is found as a second choice in the eastern margin of Connecticut, up to the Thames River. Beyond this point, we have only one isolated mention of *scup* as a second choice from an informant on Long Island Sound.

The easternmost isogloss is that of *menhaden*, which extends to Rhode Island and Nantucket; it is found as a second choice at several points on Cape Cod and the Vineyard as well. Thus the two terms which do *not* show any possibility of homonymy overlap considerably, leaving a sizeable region in the center where a *pogie* is also known as *menhaden*, and a *porgy* is also known as a *scup*. But the two isoglosses of concern to us here—*pogie* and *porgy*—show no such overlap. They run side by side through Connecticut and Long Island, and diverge only for one point: Block Island. There are only two points on the entire map where an empty circle is joined with a solid triangle, indicating that the lexicon of those speakers include *pogie* and *porgy*. Both are

---

* There is also a short -o form *poggy*. The *r* form *porgy* falls together with the original name of another fish, derived by metathesis from L. *pagrus*.

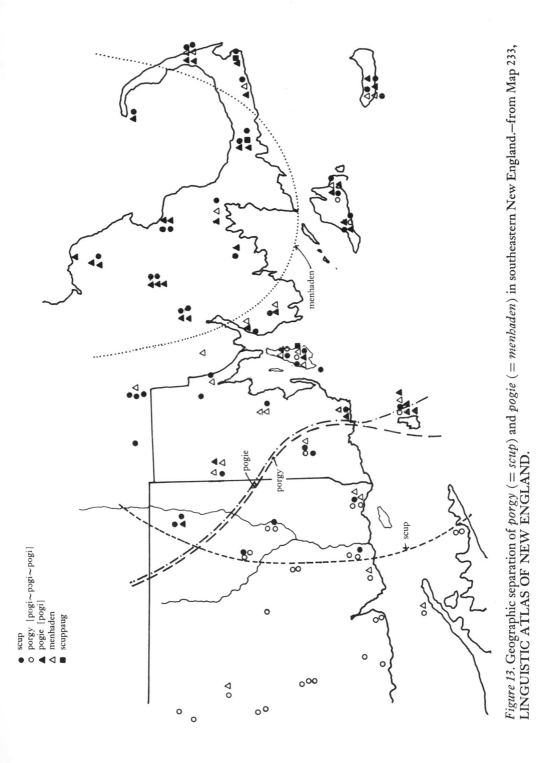

Figure 13. Geographic separation of *porgy* (= *scup*) and *pogie* (= *menhaden*) in southeastern New England.—from Map 233, LINGUISTIC ATLAS OF NEW ENGLAND.

islanders: one on Block Island, who gave *porgy* as his first choice and *pogie* as his second, and the other at Edgartown on the Vineyard, who gave both of these terms. Aside from these, there are no other cases where the both terms were supplied by one speaker, even in response to a suggestion.

The picture is even sharper than this, for the area where *scup* passes the *pogie-porgy* line includes second choices for *scup*; if we draw a line for primary *scup* choices, it coincides almost exactly with the *pogie-porgy* line. The overall situation may be summed up as follows: west of the critical bundle, *porgy* and *menhaden* are the primary terms, with a small scattering of *scup* as an alternant for *porgy*; east of that line, *scup* and *pogy* are used, with *menhaden* alternating with *pogie* for some distance. Only two islanders allow the two terms *pogie* and *porgy* in a single system.

Among my informants, no one departed from the New England pattern of *scup* and *pogie*, except to add *bunker* and *mossbunker* for the latter.

The word *quahaug* shows oscillation, perhaps because of the preservation of the original spelling. On the Vineyard, there is oscillation between [kwohɔg] and [kohɔg]. Aside from a slight bias in favor of down-island for the former, there is free variation between speakers. Individual speakers seem to choose one or the other variant and stay with it.

Another fish name, the *squeteague* [skwɪtiːg], suffered from a different kind of linguistic pathology. The name seems to have discouraged sales among consumers, and it was changed to *weakfish* in the thirties. It seems a poor choice to hindsight, and the commercial standing of this fish did not improve as a matter of fact. But when the name was changed to *sea trout*, it began to sell and the demand has not yet slackened.

A fourth kind of variation is shown by the *tautog*, normally [təˈtɔːg]. *Blackfish* has been used as an alternant, but *blackfish* also means 'sea bass', 'rock bass', and refers to a member of the whale family as well. The original Narragansett word was *tautau*, plural *tautauog*, which is literally translated as 'blackfish'.

The outstanding example of fractionation can be seen in the name for a small brown, minnow-like fish: the killifish *Fundulus heteroclitus*. It is known locally by many variants derived from Narragansett *Moamitteaug*; the oldest and widest known form appears to be *mummychug*, an authentic Americanism according to the DAE.

Mummychugs are caught in fresh water streams, mostly by children; it is essentially a landlubber's bait. The name itself combines a number of features which would lead to shortening and fractionation: it is altogether too long for an English morpheme, and there is no obvious folk etymology; the *chug* suggests nothing useful in English; and it is seldom written down, subject to rapid modification in the pre-literate practice of the children who use the word most often. Figure 14 shows the result of this fractionation: an array which uses almost every possible permutation of the original word. We can

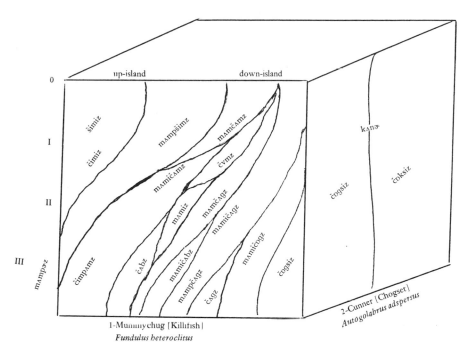

Figure 14. Killifish and cunner

see this development more clearly from the linguistic point of view in the following table:

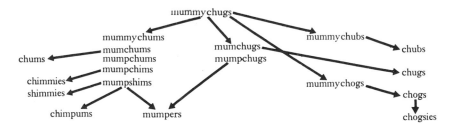

These nineteen variants are produced by a series of simple sound changes: nasalization, vowel reduction and deletion, epenthetic consonant, and then abrupt fractionation to produce the up-island forms such as *shimmies*. The down-island variants were produced by a different kind of vowel shift and experimentation with the place of articulation of the final consonant. One of the end-results, *chogsies*, was an unfortunate direction for sound change to take. There is another fish, somewhat larger, that is found around the ocean docks: the cunner, *Autogolabrus adspersus*. Its Pequot name was *chochokesit*, which was reduced to *chogset*. The common colloquial form is either *chogsie* or *choxie*: [čɒgzi, čɒksi]. We have already seen that one of the end results of the evolution of *mummychug* was *chogsie*. The fish are not well enough known to adults to avoid confusion, so that we now find quite a few islanders willing to state that a *chogsie* and a *mummychug*—or a *choxie* and a *mummy-chug*—are really the same fish.

We can conclude this discussion of structural factors in the development of this regional vocabulary by noting that there is ample evidence that such pressures exist. Structural forces to avoid homonymy and to fill gaps are exerted upon the lexicon, and provide explanations as to why certain developments took place in the direction they did—or even at the places that they did. But on the whole, we find that such pressures need strong reinforcement from the most favorable extra-linguistic forces. Two commercial fish, of considerable importance to fishermen, cannot both have the same name. But two unimportant bait-fish, hardly known to most adults, can very easily develop the same name. There is a strong parallel to the findings of our work on sound change, where it appears that structural factors are weak forces in linguistic evolution which can be over-ridden in the most surprising way (Labov 1966). But they are constant and everpresent in daily interaction, so that in the long run, most important distinctions of the language are preserved by one means or another.

9. *Causes of Extinction*

We can now return to the final question raised in our introduction: the external factors which lead to the disappearance of regional markers. Enough information has been accumulated so that we should be able to sum up the history of the lexical markers on Martha's Vineyard in terms of some general causes of linguistic change. Though there may be counter-currents, it must be admitted that most of the important markers are disappearing. For example, if we take the initial set of isoglosses used by Kurath in the *Word Geography*:

Martha's Vineyard alone:	belly-gut
As part of SENE:	whicker
	tempest
	cade
As part of ENE:	bonny clabber
	sour milk cheese
	hasslet
As part of the North:	spider
	buttry
	teeterboard

we find that they are all gone. Why?

A. *Technological Change*

Simple change of material conditions is a larger factor in the elimination of these words. *Buttery* was associated with the fact that butter was kept in that room. When butter went into the icebox, *pantry* was given that much more help in replacing the older term. *Bonny clabber* cannot be made from pasteurized milk: its extinction was certain from the time that pasteurization became standard. *Sour milk cheese* went with it, yielding to the standard "cottage cheese".

The competition between *backhouse* and *outhouse* was settled by indoor plumbing. As the heavy black cast-iron *spider* went out of fashion, the need for a distinction between *spider* and *skillet* was gone. Behind this change lay the general loss of any use for legs on a cooking instrument.

Meal is no longer cheaper than flour. Even the poorest of us can cook or bake with flour, and therefore *samp* and *bannock* left us, and *Johnny cake* was tossed into the oven along with *corn bread*. A whole range of fishing and farming terms have been made obsolete by technological change: rather than attempt to list them all, I will indicate the areas.

Anything to do with horses as draft animals is obsolete: therefore *whiffle-trees, pole, evener, yoke, nigh, off* and others are gone. Cows are quieted by radio music: and *so bossie* is heard much less often. Animals are seldom called: chickens are kept in poultry runs which allow very little wandering (our only poultryman on the Vineyard never calls his); there aren't enough horses left to call; and so with pigs and sheep.

The words associated with sport or semi-commercial fishing are still alive, but a great many technical fishing terms are naturally gone.

Swichel is no longer to be found cooling in the well: instead, there is *soda* in the icebox. But if we want to make our older informants happy, we need only ask them about *swichel* and so stir up pleasant memories.

B. *Social Change*

This is a more powerful factor than simple technological change, for it affects many more linguistic situations. Whether the diminishing farm population may be taken as one or the other is not important, since technological change cannot occur without social change. But the disappearance of *yeast bread, apple pan dowdy, hasslet,* and *garden sauce* reflects a changing attitude towards the kitchen and the garden. There is nothing preventing people from growing their own small vegetables, baking their own bread, but for various economic and ideological reasons they do not do so.

Houses are now simpler than they used to be, not for any technical reason, but because the family unit is smaller. So the rapid shifts of *parlor, sitting room, porch, piazza, ell, porch chamber,* may be attributed in part to the construction of houses for small nuclear families rather than grafting additions on to accommodate the extending extended family.

These are all expressions of the more pervading force of standardization, which is conveyed through all the media of mass communication. It is too well documented to discuss here, but we can sum up many lexical changes under this heading: the preference for

cottage cheese	over	sour milk cheese
griddle cake	over	pancake
soda	over	pop
[joʊk]	over	[jɛlk]
porch	over	piazza
thunderstorm	over	tempest

are typical examples of a much larger list. Many of these items have been accounted for elsewhere in our discussion; we must expect that at least one of these causes is operating at all times, and it is only a concatenation of several factors which will lead to the change.

Linguists like to find internal linguistic motivation in language change. The cases of *belly-flop*, *yolk*, *mummychug-choxie*, *pogy-scup*, are all good examples. But the social change from emphasis on sledding to swimming is the major factor behind the shift of *belly-flop*; *yolk* is undergoing standardization; *mummychug* is at the mercy of children's language; only the behavior of *pogy* and *scup* can be explained solely in terms of linguistic interference.

If we now attempt to balance these forces against those which resist linguistic change, we might say that the *form* of conservatism which encourages the retention of old linguistic forms is somewhat different in nature from what it used to be.

The older form of conservatism was largely unconscious of any disturbing factors. People said *bannock* because people always said *bannock*: what else was there to say? This attitude is characteristic of many I-A informants, who are surprised to hear that there is any other way to say *yolk* besides [jɛłk].

All but the oldest speakers on the Vineyard know that the standard word for 'porch' is *porch*. If they continue to say *piazza*, it is not due to an automatic inheritance of the past, but rather a conscious preference for the older world. The older unconscious regional marker may now be giving way to a consciously marked rural stereotype. We can reasonably expect that resistance to standardizing forces will play a role in the development of our language in the future. How conscious this resistance is will vary according to the aspect of language affected, and the strength of the dominant culture. If we expect to find divergence, we are more likely to succeed than if we assume that language is becoming more and more uniform everywhere. In any case, it is not likely that the subject matter of dialectology will disappear.

References

Ashley, Clifford W. 1906. *The Yankee Whaler*. Cambridge: Riverside Press.

Colcord, Joanna C. 1945. *Sea Language Comes Ashore*. New York: Maritime Press.

Kurath, Hans. 1939. *The Linguistic Atlas of New England* [LANE]. Providence: Brown University.

——. 1949. *A Word Geography of the Eastern United States*. Ann Arbor: University of Michigan Press.

Labov, William. 1963. "The Social Motivation of a Sound Change". *Word* 19:273–309.

——. 1966. *The Social Stratification of English in New York City*. Washington, D.C.: Center for Applied Linguistics.

Mathews, M. *Dictionary of Americanisms*.

BLACK SPEECH, WHITE SPEECH, AND THE AL SMITH SYNDROME

LEE PEDERSON
Emory University

When Raven I. McDavid, Jr., spoke at Emory University in February, 1969, he characterized the field-oriented methods of linguistic geography in terms of "the Al Smith syndrome, with the insistence on looking at the actual record regardless of the eloquence of the case," after stating more specifically:

> The first lesson the dialectologist learns is to be data oriented. Now this is an unfashionable attitude today, when in some quarters *data* is a more obscene four-letter word than any of those that have been publicized by the playful children of Berkeley. We will concede that it is desirable to have the most elegant theoretical analysis that our best scholars are capable of; we will equally concede that there are certain advantages in working spider-wise out of one's own vitals and not undergoing the troublesome chores of finding live informants and interviewing them. Nevertheless, as I once reminded Arch Hill, data must not be buried in an elegant symmetry. If the theory will not accommodate the data, then the theory must be modified in some way, or a new theory must be devised.[1]

Although a recently completed investigation of rural speech in Northern Georgia has not produced data to challenge or threaten contemporary theories of language, its evidence does suggest a reconsideration of several other issues in current discussions of American English social dialects.[2] More important than those considerations, however, is its provision of a record to be looked at, a synchronic view of black and white speech in a rural Southern setting.

Given the limitations described in "Dialect Patterns in Rural Northern Georgia," one can readily identify three regional dialect areas in the territory north of the Fall Line Hills on the basis of white folk speech: a variety of Up-country Lower Southern (commonly identified as "Plantation Southern") distinguishes the southern-most extremes of the territory, a variety of South Midland speech (better known as "Mountain Speech" or "Hill Southern") prevails in the north, and an extremely mixed transition dialect, centered in the valley of the Chattahoochee River, separates the speech of the principal areas.[3]

Within that regional context three social dialects were consistently investigated—lowerclass and uneducated blacks and whites, as well as middleclass and better educated whites.[4] And even within that partially developed social construct, the distribution of phonological, grammatical, and lexical forms here reflects the complexity of these rural societies and recommends a more thoughtful approach to the question of racially designated social dialects. Social composition and inter-personal relationships vary considerably across this territory. In some mountain communities—for example, Chatsworth (A2), Blue Ridge(A3), and Rabun Gap(A5)—participation in the activities of the dominant culture by blacks is an economic necessity because, if for no other reason,[5] it is not feasible to offer separate facilities for a limited number of students. Elsewhere in the mountains, the blacks are totally segregated, territorially as well as socially, as in the agricultural community of Bean Creek (A4) in White County. Similarly, in the transition area, patterns of residence vary from community to community, and in the areas which preserve vestiges of the old plantation system, as in Loganville(C4) and Monticello(D4), a social structure endures which is unlike anything found in either the Chattahoochee Valley or the mountains.[6]

Within a situation such as this one, conventional discussions of black speech simply do not stand up. Not a single recurrent pronunciation of a phoneme, distribution of an allomorph, or incidence of a grammatical form or lexical item was restricted to black speech, and those are the criteria usually advanced by those who describe "Black English." Statistical descriptions of the segmental data and systematic analyses of the paralinguistic phenomena would be a much more useful basis for discriminating speech differences along racial lines,[7] but these are neither the terms nor the techniques with which racially identified social dialects are usually discussed.

Another misdirected habit of mind in some pedagogically oriented discussions of American English concerns the use of the terms "Non-Standard English" and "black speech" without carefully formulated complemental statements which describe the structure of "Standard English" and "white speech." To equate "black speech" with "Non-Standard English" may well be the predictable result of limited experience, where an investigator's tacit assumptions concerning "Standard English" contrast with observed data which happen to represent the speech of Negroes and which the investigator has not found in the speech of Caucasians, but to speak glibly of "black speech" in this way does not advance understanding.[8]

A different interpretation of those terms is necessary in the mountain community of Blue Ridge(A3), where the speech of the lone black informant contrasts sharply with the forms used by three whites.[9] Although the black informant(BI), with her eighth-grade education and her occupation as a domestic, was ranked in the lowest socioeconomic class, her choice of verb forms was regularly more consistent with the expected usage of educated speech than were the responses of the comparably educated(WI), the slightly better educated(WII), or the best educated(WIII) white informants interviewed in Blue Ridge. A comparison of their responses in 12 situations—six verbs in the simple past(P) and the past participial (PP) forms—is suggestive of these habits:

		eat				*climb*	
	P	PP			P	PP	
BI	ate	has been eaten		BI	climbed	has been climbed	
WI	eat/it/	has been ate		WI	clim/klɪm/	has been clim/klɪm/	
WII	eaten	has been eaten		WII	climb	has been climbed	
WIII	et/ɛt/	has been et/ɛt/		WIII	clum/klʌm/	has been clum/klʌm/	

		do				*ride*	
	P	PP			P	PP	
BI	did	has been done		BI	rode	has been ridden	
WI	done	has been done		WI	rode	has been rode	
WII	done	has been done		WII	rode	has been rode	
WIII	done	has been done		WIII	rode	has been rode	

		ring				*grow*	
	P	PP			P	PP	
BI	rang	has been rung		BI	grew	has been grown	
WI	rung	has been rung		WI	grew	has been grown	
WII	rung	has been rung		WII	growed	has been grown	
WIII	rang	has been rung		WIII	growed	has been growed	

A *black versus white* dichotomy here results in educated usage, or "Standard English," emerging in this set as the distinctive feature of "Blue Ridge Black English." This is probably the result of the informant's not having participated in the affairs of the rural white folk culture enough to have assimilated regional verb morphology, not having a sufficiently large black folk community present to reinforce other forms, but having worked and lived in the company of cultivated whites.

Where blacks are clearly segregated in the mountains and transition areas—for example, the community of approximately 75 families at Bean Creek(A4) near Helen—the distinctiveness of their speech is, for the most part, determined by features which have wide currency among blacks and whites in the plantation area. These transplanted regionalisms include: the loss of postvocalic /-r/ in tautosyllabic environments, a palatal diphthong [ɜɪ] or a rounded monophthong [ɞ] for /ɜ/ in *birds* and similar words, a distinction among the vowels in *Mary* /e/, *marry* /æ/, and *merry* /ɛ/, the simplification of some verb forms, the deletion of other verb forms, and a number of regional vocabulary items, such as *lightwood* /laitɪd/ for resinous kindling wood, *snap beans* for stringbeans, *baits* for worms, *crocus sack* or *crocus bag* for burlap sack or bag, *battercakes* for pancakes, and *press peach* or *plum peach* for clingstone peach, instead of the more usual *fat pine, green beans, redworms*, *tow sack*, *flitters*, and *cling peach* in the mountain areas where South Midland speech prevails.

Other features of black speech in the mountain and transition areas are shared by black and white uneducated informants throughout rural Northern Georgia, and, especially in the plantation area, these forms also occur in cultivated white speech, so they cannot be properly designated as folk forms. These include several phonemic problems, such as the substitution of /t,d,f,v,s/ for /θ, ð/, the simplification of postvocalic consonant clusters, *hand* (or, more simply, *han*) for *hands*, the loss of postvocalic stop consonants, e.g., /g/ in *dog* (usually replaced by a lengthened diphthong [dɔ·ᵛ] or [dɒ·ᵛ]), as well as grammatical features, such as uninflected verb forms, *he do* for *he does*, and the so-called "zero copula," *he dead* for *he is dead*. All of these recessive forms are more common in uneducated black speech than among the other social varieties isolated in the survey, but their incidence is by no means restricted to that group or even to the plantation area.

Another group of features recurrent in black speech is best identified as relics. *Hit* for *it* occurred in 21 of 25 communities, everywhere except in communities fairly close to Atlanta and Athens. In the north, however, it is most common among poor whites and in the south, among poor blacks. That form, like other relics found in rural Northern Georgia, such as *mought* /maut/ for *might*, *holp* for *helped*, *narrow* (rhyming with *borrow* instead of *arrow*), and *point* (homophonous with *pint*), is a survival from an earlier stage of the English language, and the durability of such pronunciations suggests the regional and social isolation of the speakers, as well as the habitual force of folk speech.

In the plantation area, the relationships between educated and uneducated speech are much more complicated than in the mountains, as the distribution of certain forms among the Loganville(C4) informants suggests. Situated in the center of the Piedmont Plateau(the particular area of which is designated as the Midland Slope) and midway between Atlanta and Athens, Loganville has shared the cultural history of a region which includes Upcountry South Carolina and all of Northern Georgia south of the Blue Ridge and Appalachian Mountains. In this respect, a consideration of the small community of approximately 1,300 residents complements McDavid's discussions of South Carolina speech in general and Greenville speech in particular.[10]

The Loganville informants include a retired black domestic(BI), a black housewife whose husband is a retired farmer(BII), a retired white textile mill worker(WI), and a retired white school teacher(WII), and all four women bear family names which were found in Walton County at least 15 years before Loganville was organized in 1844.[11] As in any unilingual community of this size, the four Loganville idiolects share a common linguistic system, for without such phonological, grammatical, and lexical agreement, communication would be impossible. Furthermore, the dialect differences themselves are rarely unique, even within the context of Loganville speech as represented by these four ladies, but the points of agreement, the dialectal concordances, found here reveal a distribution and reflect a social organization which are radically different from the expected patterns in the urban North.

Three basic patterns of distribution recur: 1) features shared by both black informants(BI, BII) and the cultivated white informant(WII), 2) features shared by both black informants(BI, BII) and the uncultivated white informant(WI), and 3) features shared by the black(BI) and white(WI) uncultivated informants, and these are found within each of the subsystems of the language, at the phonetic level, at the phonemic level, at the grammatical level, and at the lexical level.

Phonetic Patterns:

1) BI, BII, and WII

/ɛ/ in *bread*		/au/ in *cloud*		/ɜ/ in *birds*	
BIɛᵊ	ɛ¹WI	BIau	æɵWI	BIɜɪ	ɚWI
BIIɛᵊ	ɛᵊWII	BIIau	auWII	BIIɜɪ	ɜɪWII

2) BI, BII, and WI

/ʌ/ in *mush*		/æ/ in *pancakes*		/l/ in *bullfrog*	
BIɤ	ɤWI	BIæ̃	æ̃WI	BIɯ	ɯWI
BIIɤ	ʌWII	BIIæ̃	æɛWII	BIIɯ	lWII

3) BI and WI; BII and WII

/i/ in *field*		/ɪ/ in *wrist*		/ai/ in *nineteen*	
BIiᵊ	iᵊWI	BIiᵊ	iᵊWI	BIa	aWI
BIIiᵛi	iᵛiWII	BIIɪ	ɪWII	BIIaɪ	aɪWII

Phonemic Patterns:

1) BI, BII, and WII

/hw/ ~ /w/ in *white*		V + /r/ in *ear*		V + /r/ in *hair*	
BI hw	w WI	BI ɪə	ɛə WI	BI æə	ær WI
BII hw	hw WII	BII ɪə	ɪə WII	BII æə	æə WII

V + /r/ in *fire*		V + /r/ in *car*		V + /r/ in *Mary*	
BI aɪə	ɔr WI	BI ɐ	ɔr WI	BI er	ɛr WI
BII aɪə	aɪə WII	BII ɐ	ɐ WII	BII er	er WII

2) BI, BII, and WI

/ð/~/d/ in *the*		/ʌ/~/a/ in *thumb*		/r/ in *April*	
BI d	d WI	BI a	a WI	BI -pl	-pl WI
BII d	ð WII	BII a	ʌ WII	BII -pl	-prl WII

3) BI and WI; BII and WII

/v/~/b/ in *seven*		/æ/ ~ /e/ in *can't*		/l/ in *help*	
BI b	b WI	BI e	e WI	BI hɛp	hɛp WI
BII v	v WII	BII æ	æ WII	BII hɛlp	hɛlp WII

Grammatical patterns:

1) BI, BII, and WII

3rd singular pronoun *it~bit*

BI it	hit WI
BII it	it WII

past tense of *dive dived~div* /dɪv/

BI dived	div WI
BII dived	dived WII

past tense of *take took~tuk* /tʌk/

BI took	tuk WI
BIItook	took WII

past tense of *ride rode~rid* /rɪd/

BI rode	rid WI
BII rode	rode WII

2) BI, BII, and WI

plural of *nest nests~nestis* /-ɪz/

BI nestis	nestis WI
BIInestis	nestis WII

negative form of *do* (3rd sing.) *doesn't~don't*

BI don't	don't WI
BII don't	doesn't WII

past tense of *grow grew~growed*

BI growed	growed WI
BII growed	grew WII

past participle of *ride ridden~rode*

BI rode	rode WI
BII rode	ridden WII

3) BI and WI

past tense of *drag dragged~drug*

BI drug	drug WI
BII dragged	dragged WII

past tense of *rise rose~riz* /rɪz/

BI riz	riz WI
BIIrose	rose WII

past participle of *drink drunk~drinken*

BI drinken	drinken WI
BIIdrunk	drunk WII

Lexical Patterns:

1) BI, BII, and WII

heavy cloth sack

BI crocus sack	burlap sack WI
BIIcrocus sack	crocus sack WII

when the sun disappears

BI sunset	sundown WI
BII sunset	sunset WII

turnip tops

BI sallit	sallit WI
BIIsallit	greens WII

2) BI, BII, and WI

clingstone peach

BI plum peach	plum peach WI
BIIplum peach	cling peach WII

woodpecker

BI peckerwood	peckerwood WI
BII peckerwood	woodpecker WII

suspenders
BI galluses   galluses WI
BIIgalluses   suspenders WII

bread cooked in the ashes
  of a fire
BI ash cake   ash cake WI
BIIash cake   pone WII

3) BI and WI
man's chest
BI breast   breast WI
BII chest   chest WII

similar appearance (facial)
BI favors   favors WI
BII favors   resembles WII

lowlying farm land
BI bottoms   bottoms WI
BII bottoms   river bed WII

midwife
BI granny woman   granny woman WI
BII midwife   midwife WII

small frog
BI tree frog   tree frog WI
BIItree frog   *no term* WII

sick to one's stomach
BI at the   at the WI
BII at the   at his WII

corn eaten on the cob
BI roasting ears   roasting ears WI
BII boiled corn   corn o/t cob WII

There were, of course, isolated instances of pronunciation, grammatical usage, and vocabulary items which occurred only in the speech of one or the other of the black informants; *e.g.*, BI had *mantleboard* where WI had *fireboard* and WII and BII had *mantlepiece*, and BII had *cow pen* where BI, WI, and WII had *lot*, but these were exceptions which did not contribute to larger patterns. Moreover, the form *mantleboard* in the speech of BI is emblematic of the pivotal position of the black folk speaker in the Loganville dialectal and social structure. The form which seems to blend *mantlepiece* and *fireboard* suggests the central position of the speaker, sharing some language and experience with the better educated white as well as the lesser educated white but living as a member of the black caste. In this respect, well documented by the participation of BI in every set of the patterns listed above, it could be better argued that her speech is most representative of the community, more nearly normative than that of any other of the idiolects observed in Loganville.

And, in Loganville, as in every other community investigated in the survey, there are points of difference where black speech is distinguished from one or another variety of white speech, but these differences do not reveal a homogeneous black dialect, a variety of speech to be called "Black English." Since the basis of dialectal distinctiveness is differing cultural experience and since it is hard to imagine a cultural force more powerful than the caste barrier, a contrast between black and white speech is certainly to be expected. There is, however, another aspect of that same principle which also needs to be considered. A common black dialect in the plantation area, the mountains, and the transition belt would require a contant cultural experience in all these places. This implies not only membership in a common caste, which surely is the case, but also the existence of a common neighboring culture, which just as surely is not the case. Since the regional dialects are demonstrably different in the three areas, the basic patterns of black and white speech are not structured in the same way in Blue Ridge, Bean Creek, and Loganville. Furthermore, the relationships between blacks and whites differ as sharply as the speech patterns, so the composition of social dialects cannot be expected to develop in the same way in Bean Creek and Loganville. Such an assumption might have validity when considering patterns of residence in the urban North, where the ghetto cultures of Chicago and Detroit, according to some observers, differ in name only, but that situation is simply not the one found in the part of the rural South represented by the Northern Georgia sample. Here smaller numbers of people and widely different patterns of speech, social organization, and community interaction preclude such broad generalizations as those which underlie racially-designated social dialects.

Although that conclusion offers small promise of establishing a neat pattern for language pathologists concerned with black speech, white speech, and non-standard English, the methods used in Northern Georgia provide a basis for an initial step in that direction. Some expectation is held out for getting closer to the sociolinguistic realities by accepting the facts and accommodating them in the discussion in accordance with the symptoms which have characterized the work of Alfred E. Smith and Raven I. McDavid, Jr. In a study of a phenomenon as complicated as speech—which is the product and property of creatures as complicated as human beings—to expect or promise more than this at this time is to demonstrate another set of symptoms, which comprise a much less salutary syndrome.

Notes

1. Raven I. McDavid, Jr., "Dialectology: Where Linguistics Meets the People," *Emory University Quarterly* 23(1967), 213–214.

2. *Rural Northern Georgia* includes the territory from the northern border of the state (Tennessee in the northwest and North Carolina in the northeast) to the Fall Line Hills in the southwest (a few miles north of La Grange) and across those hills and the Louisville Plateau in the southeast (a few miles south of Augusta). This area of approximately 27,000 square miles is represented here by 25 communities with rural populations (*i.e.*, under 2,500 in the U. S. Census of 1960). These places were selected in a system of 30-mile grids, which are regionally characterized as South Midland (SM) or Upcountry Lower Southern (ULS) dialect areas and which are identified in Map 1, "Communities of Rural Northern Georgia." In each community four informants were interviewed, 100 native residents of 25 rural places, and these informants, with a median age of 72, are distinguished by racial caste, Black and White, and, in this report, as lesser and better educated, although the conventional Atlas designations of I(folk), II(common), and III(cultivated) speech provide the basic classification in the Dialect Survey of Rural Georgia. A supplementary social index, August B. Hollingshead's Two-Factor Index of Social Position (Yale University, mimeographed) is also used to characterize the informants.

The aims and methods of the Dialect Survey of Rural Georgia are briefly summarized in "Dialect Patterns in Rural Northern Georgia" in a forthcoming publication of *Zeitschrift für Mundartforschung* and in "Southern Speech and the LAGS Project" in *Orbis*, 20(1971), 79–89 and more elaborately by several staff members, *e.g.*, Howard G. Dunlap, "Dialect Investigation in Atlanta and Rural Georgia" at the joint meeting of the Speech Association of America and the American Dialect Society, Chicago, 1968; Grace S. Rueter, "Progress in the Dialect Survey of Rural Georgia" at the Linguistics Section of SAMLA, Jacksonville, 1968; Lee Pederson, "Problems in Southern Regional Dialect Study" at the ADS Section of NCTE, Washington, D.C., 1969.

In "Dialect Patterns in Rural Northern Georgia" the distribution of nine classic markers of South Midland and Upcountry Lower Southern dialects indicates the impossibility of establishing dialect boundaries in the area without recognizing social factors. The incidence of Upcountry Lower Southern features deep in South Midland territory in the speech of many uneducated blacks and several better educated whites suggests that conventional dialect demarcation reflects the usage of white folk speech and that, under these circumstances, patterns can be identified with much greater assurance that can *dialect areas* in the usual sense of the term.

Another consideration for current discussions of American social dialects is presented in "Obstruent Consonants in Rural Northern Georgia" in a forthcoming publication of the University of Minnesota Press, which recommends phonemic descriptions that are sensitive to the regional and social variants of consonants, as well as vowels, as a necessary preliminary procedure in grammatical analysis. This is particularly important in the investigation of grammatical patterns in the speech of Southerners, which is certainly not "General American" and which seems to be one of the primary sources of those social dialects which concern students of dialect in the urban centers of the North.

Finally, two further suggestions are offered in "Southern Speech and the LAGS Project": 1) a considerable amount of substantial research in Southern speech has been done already and much of this is being ignored, and 2) a considerable amount of research in Southern speech remains to be done, and this fact is also being ignored by some who generalize about an area which, for the most part, has never been systematically investigated.

3. Map 2, "Dialect Areas of Rural Northern Georgia" indicates the dialect boundaries suggested by Raven I. McDavid, Jr., and Virginia McDavid in "Regional Linguistic Atlases in the United States" *Orbis* 5(1956), which combines the extrapolations of McDavid's work in South Carolina and the boundaries established there with his and Lowman's research in Georgia. In addition to those boundaries(Lines A & B on Map2), a third boundary suggested by Wood on the basis of his postal survey(reported in Gordon R. Wood, "Dialect Contours in the Southern States," *American Speech* 38(1963) is marked by Line C on the map. All these have been substantially confirmed in the current survey. McDavid's lines mark the southern extreme of the South Midland territory and the northern extreme of the Upcountry Lower Southern territory with a wide transition area separating them. Wood's line suggests a division of the transition area into essentially South Midland and essentially Upcountry Lower Southern regions and indicates that boundary by the valley of the Chattahoochee River.

4. There were not many well-educated blacks over age 65 to be found in most of those rural communities, so that probable fourth social group was not represented in a consistent way across the entire area. All better educated blacks who did participate in the interviews were retired teachers in the transition and Upcountry Lower Southern areas, and their speech in both sectors were regularly much closer to that of the educated variety of Upcountry Lower Southern white speech than of any other regional or social type.

5. There are, of course, other reasons. In addition to the egalitarianism which has always characterized the world view of the Southern Highlanders and which explains their mixed reactions to American social and political problems from 1860 to the present, there is also the fact that these mountaineers were never a monolithic social group. See J. C. Campbell, *The Southern Highlander and His Home* (1921); H. Kephart, *Our Southern Highlanders* (1913); J. W. Hatcher, "Appalachian America" in W. T. Couch, ed., *Culture in the South* (1934), 374–402. Hatcher notes: "Despite the emphasis of various authors—and especially that of John C. Campbell in *The Southern Highlander and His Home*—upon the fact of the existence of various social classes in the mountains, it seems to have made little or no impression upon the public. Certain salient characteristics, usually those of the most repressed class, have been selected, generalized, and presented as those of the typical mountaineer. This appraisal has been accepted, emotional response has been made to it, and as no differences are seen among Negroes or people of another culture by this public, so there is none among the mountain people." An excellent summary of research since World War II is found in J. Kenneth Moreland, "Anthropology and the Study of Culture, Society, and Community in the South" in E. T. Thompson, ed., *Perspectives on the South: Agenda for Research* (1967), 125–145.

6. The social composition and historical processes peculiar to the plantation areas in rural Northern Georgia are reflected in the dialect patterns which are remarkably similar to those described by McDavid in "Postvocalic -r in South Carolina: A Social Analysis," *American Speech* 23 (1948), 194–203.

7. This point is nicely made by McDavid (1967), 216–17: "Again, with the question of the racially different 'deep structure' of the English of Negroes and that of whites. If one juxtaposes the English of uneducated Negroes from the Chicago South Side and that of the gold-encrusted suburbs of the North Shore, one might plausibly make this assumption. Still, one recognizes that there have been all kinds of patterns of Negro-white association, even under slavery, that there are millions of poor WASPS without an economic sting, and that there are different regional styles in the amount of relaxation permitted in the informal discourse of the educated. The uninflected third singular, such as *he do*, the finite *be*, and the use of *done* as a perfective auxiliary (as 'I done told you that three times'), are very common in Negro speech, and perhaps statistically much more common than in the speech of whites. This would not be surprising, when one is aware of the cultural lag of the South with respect to the rest of the nation, or of the Southern Negro with respect to his white counterpart. But every study in depth, when Southern whites—and particularly Southern poor whites—are brought into the calculations, suggests that the racial differences are statistical rather than typological."

8. McDavid (1967), 217: "With all respect for the aspirations of Negroes and their need for group identity—to say nothing for simplifying a pedagogical approach—it is no ultimate favor to them, and is a short-changing of the poor white with similar problems, to assert the simplistic statement."

9. Only one informant over 65 could be located in Blue Ridge to represent black speech. In several South Georgia communities, it has been necessary to interview three blacks where poor or better educated whites were not to be found.

10. In addition to McDavid(1948), see Raven I. McDavid, Jr., "Dialect Differences and Social Differences in an Urban Society," in William Bright, ed., *Sociolinguistics: Proceedings of the UCLA Sociolinguistic Conference, 1964*(1966), 72–83. In that essay McDavid contrasts "Greenville: A Microcosm" with "Chicago: A Macrocosm" and indicates the same kinds of phenomena observed here in the "Mini-Microcosm" of Loganville.

11. Anita B. Sams, *Wayfarers in Walton* (1967), esp., "Pioneer Residents," 49–53.

Map 1: Communities in Rural Northern Georgia

SMC*		ULSC**	
A1	Ringgold	B6	Nuberg
A2	Chatsworth	C4	Loganville
A3	Blue Ridge	C5	Lexington
A4	Helen	C6	Middleton
A5	Rabun Gap	C7	Lincolnton
B1	Menlo	DI	Franklin
B2	Cassville	D2	Turin
B3	Jasper	D3	Flippen
B4	Oakwood	D4	Monticello
B5	Carnesville	D5	Penfield
C1	Felton	D6	Warrenton
C2	Dallas	D7	Appling
C3	Alpharetta		

*South Midland Communities
**Upcountry Lower Southern Communities

Map 2: Dialect Areas in Rural Northern Georgia

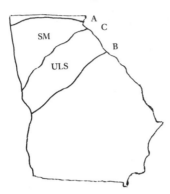

SM is the South Midland Area according to the Dialect Survey of Rural Georgia (1968-)

ULS is the Upcountry Lower Southern Area according to the Dialect Survey of Rural Georgia (1968-)

Line A: Southern boundary of South Midland Area suggested by McDavid and McDavid (1956)

Line B: Northern boundary of Upcountry Lower Southern Area suggested by McDavid and McDavid (1956)

Lince C: Division of Transition Area suggested by Wood (1963)

PROBLEMS OF ENGLISH SPEECH MIXTURE IN CALIFORNIA AND NEVADA

CARROLL E. REED, *University of Massachusetts*
DAVID W. REED, *Northwestern University*

Twenty years ago efforts were first made to develop a Linguistic Atlas of the Pacific Coast (that was twenty years after the beginning of the Linguistic Atlas of the United States). David Reed directed the work in California and Nevada, where check sheets and field records were completed within a few years, and Carroll Reed started the work in the Pacific Northwest, where check sheets were soon completed for Washington, Oregon, and Idaho, and a number of field records were made in Washington and Idaho. Only two field records have been made in Oregon, one by each of us.

In previous reports we have described the provenience and distribution of certain dialectically significant vocabulary items. In addition to this, the pronunciation of English in the Pacific Northwest has also been treated. Three doctoral dissertations have been written, based on Atlas material: David DeCamp, *The Pronunciation of English in San Francisco* (University of California, Berkeley, 1953); Fred H. Brengelman, *The Native American English Spoken in the Puget Sound Area* (University of Washington, 1957); and Elizabeth S. Bright, *A Word Geography of California and Nevada* (University of California, Berkeley, 1967).

Since so much of the work still remains in archives, it seems appropriate for us to present at this time at least a brief description of what these archives have to offer. Especially interesting, of course, is the possibility of comparing information contained in both sets of data, one from the Pacific Northwest, the other from California and Nevada.

It has been observed that the English of Idaho and Washington is characterized, to a high degree, as "Northern" speech, whereas Oregon shows more "Midland" features. California seems to have more Midland traits than Washington or Idaho, but less than Oregon. While such a statement reflects the general nature of settlement on the Pacific Coast, it fails to account sufficiently for the transplanting and specific distribution of eastern dialect features; moreover, it does not take into consideration those dialect elements that are purely of local origin.

The westward migration of people in the 19th century and the early 20th century took similar paths: the Oregon Trail, the California Trail, and even the Butterfield Overland Mail originated in Iowa and Missouri. Most of the early settlers who came overland were born in these and nearby states, notably Illinois and Ohio. By far the largest single group of people were the New Yorkers who, along with residents of Maine and Massachusetts, made their way westward by sea.

In the Pacific Northwest there was a lively trade in furs; agriculture flourished; lumbering and fishing became profitable industries; supplies and facilities were provided for the transient hordes impelled by Alaska gold fever, and various local mining operations were established (in silver, coal, and lead, for example). Water was plentiful, both from rivers and from rain, and settlements were extended progressively along lines of access from urban centers to rural resources. This general pattern was disturbed only by massive industrialization in a few port areas after World War I.

While California and Nevada were largely agricultural states, it was the recurrent impetus of mineral discoveries that was responsible for the changing tides of early settlement. Until the beginning of the 20th century, the bulk of California's population was centered in San Francisco, which was the hub of civilization for settlers in the Sacramento and San Joaquin Valleys, and for would-be gold miners on the way to Nevada or Alaska. In the 20th century, however, southern California began to accelerate in growth, following the increasing availability of water, and the Los Angeles area soon became one of the world's most populated centers. As the railroads and highways developed, routes of access were shifted, sometimes rather radically. The tide of people seeking pay-dirt receded; and, where population pressure changed its directions, residual sectors lapsed into obscurity. All these factors constituting the ebb and flow of California settlement were then enormously complicated by the concentrated development of certain agricultural products, such as oranges, apples, avocados, walnuts, olives, cattle, and cotton.

Throughout all the Pacific Coast areas, natural facilities and natural barriers influenced the development of population and the incumbent speech patterns. Non-English elements came into the language most notably in the Spanish of southern California, but also, to some degree, in the French of the Pacific Northwest. The heavy German settlements in early days left few linguistic traces, and the influence of Scandinavian appears to have been equally light.

In connection with the maps that follow, it will be noted first that the Pacific Northwest is separated from California and Nevada by rugged terrain. Chains of mountains constituting the Coast Range and, further inland, the Cascades-Sierra Nevadas regulate the moisture fall, and widely different latitudes are related, from north to south, to increasing temperatures, evaporation, and dryness. The Sacramento and San Joaquin Valleys are flat, fertile, and moistened by small rivers and irrigation canals; they enjoy mild temperatures and a long growing season.

The land east of the Cascades-Sierra Nevadas is dry, frequently desert. In the Pacific Northwest it can be suitable for grazing or the raising of fruit and hard wheat. Most of eastern Oregon is sparsely populated. The same is true of Nevada, and much of eastern California is wasteland.

Southern California, cut off by mountains to the north, is much dryer and warmer than most of the valley in northern California, and is especially suitable for winter crops. Northern and southern California have their focal centers in the cities of San Francisco and Los Angeles, respectively.

In Linguistic Atlas check sheets and field records, a relatively high number of informants were polled in these important urban centers; otherwise, the gathering of data has been more or less uniform throughout all areas.

Maps 1–4 below illustrate the distribution of northern trace forms in the Pacific States, and it will be noted that previous observations are here confirmed. Folk terms for the dragonfly are more accurately depicted in moist areas, although definitions may also be adjusted in those places where the insect is rare. Nevertheless, this "Northern" term has its greatest relative concentration in northern Washington and Idaho, in eastern Idaho, in the San Francisco Bay Area, and in the Sacramento Valley.

A much more limited, but similar distribution is to be seen for the word *stoop* on Map 2, and again for the term *Dutch cheese* on Map 3, as well as for *johnny cake* on Map 4. The participation of California and Nevada in the use of such forms is relatively feeble, and distributions there are less predictable than in the Northwest because of the complicated settlement patterns described above. While San Francisco and its derivative sectors throughout the Sacramento Valley were settled in the early days by people from Northern dialect areas, various Midland groups soon followed, and clusters of divergent dialect speakers came to be located next to one another.

Nevada has been settled largely from California, first in response to gold discoveries, later as an extension of agricultural interests in the Sacramento Valley. The early seeding of Northern forms in Nevada is less significant than the initial planting in adjacent sections of California and is thus frequently obscured by the Midland influence of a later era.

Southern California shows a curious overlay of Northern and Midland forms, a situation occasioned also by successive waves of settlement involving the simultaneous arrival of diverse elements by sea as well as by land routes. Both San Bernardino and Riverside were founded by Northern speakers, and the descendants of these pioneers seem to have perpetuated their Northern characteristics up to the present day. In the course of time, other groups came from both Midland and Southern areas (including Oklahoma, Arkansas, and Texas), and their traces are also unmistakable in the speech of this area. Los Angeles itself is heavily represented by people from New York and its

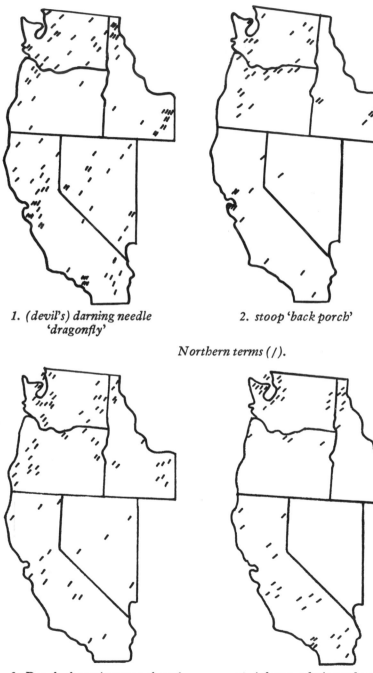

1. (devil's) darning needle
'dragonfly'

2. stoop 'back porch'

Northern terms (/).

3. Dutch cheese 'cottage cheese'

4. johnny cake 'corn bread'

Northern terms (/).

neighboring States, as well as by those from areas further south, so that it shares too in the retention of trace forms from both Northern and Midland areas.

The Midland folk words for the dragonfly, *snake feeder* and *snake doctor,* seen on Map 11, reflect most accurately the prominent areas of early Midland settlement. These are supported also by occurrences of the term *dog irons* for andirons (see Map 10), and *(barn) lot* for barnyard (see Map 9). Because of conditions peculiar to stock raising in the dry lands, however, the Spanish term *corral* has replaced other synonyms for barnyard, especially in California, Nevada, and Idaho, so that the trace forms are diminished accordingly. Similarly, the widespread use of a fire grate has all but eliminated andirons and their designations in approximately the same areas; hence, the diminution of *(barn) lot* here in contrast to the more conservative areas of western Oregon and southwestern Washington.

Other Midland terms of relatively high frequency in all areas are *roasting ears* for corn-on-the-cob (see Map 5) *piece (meal)* (*or piecing*) for a snack between meals (see Map 6), and *smearcase* for cottage cheese (see Map 7). The fact that the word *piece(meal)* follows regular Midland patterns is remarkable in view of its low prevalence in the eastern United States. On the other hand, the expression *quarter till* (eleven), which is widely used in the eastern Midlands, is drastically restricted in California and Nevada, even though well represented in the Pacific Northwest. The high occurence of *quarter to* in all the Pacific States except Oregon reflects the strong use of this form in most areas of the East Coast: it is nearly as common as *quarter of* in the North, and is the only alternative to *quarter till* in the Midland and the South.

Of surprisingly strong occurrence in California is the word *mosquito hawk* for the dragonfly (see Map 12), which is generally known as a Southern term. Otherwise, Southern speech is poorly represented in all areas.

Maps 13 through 20 have information pertaining to California and Nevada alone. Isoglosses on Maps 13 and 14 are adapted from the work of Elizabeth Bright[1]. They show the outward limitations of usage for certain terms in Northern California. The distribution of *chesterfield* for sofa (which stops short of the northern tier of counties in California and Nevada) has been attributed to the commercial thrust of San Francisco, some enterprising dealers, and the effective delivery of San Francisco newspapers. The provenance of *shiners* for minnows, *burial/burying ground* for cemetery, and *public school* for grammar school, is still unknown, but their isoglosses here illustrate something of the speech continuity in Northern California and Nevada.

Maps 15 - 18 show some of the unique contours of urban areas. A commercial term for flat, spirally formed sweet rolls is *butterhorns* in San Francisco and *snails* in Los Angeles as well as in other areas (*butterhorns* are most common in Washington, *snails* in Oregon).

5. *roasting ear 'corn on the cob'*   6. *piece(meal), piecing 'snack'*

Midland terms (ᵥ)

7. *smearcase 'cottage cheese'*   8. *quarter till 'quarter of'*

Midland terms (ᵥ)

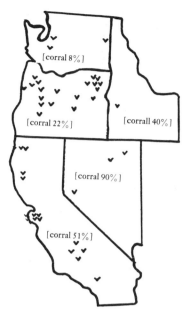

9. *(barn) lot 'barnyard'*

10. *dogirons 'andirons'*

Midland terms (v)

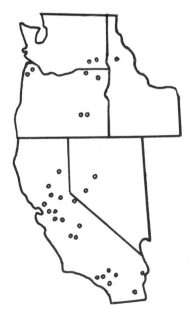

11. v *snake doctor 'dragonfly'*

ʌ *snake feeder*

Midland terms (v   ʌ).

12. *mosquito hawk 'dragon fly'*

Southern term (o).

13. -o-o-*shiners* '*minnows*'
------*chesterfield* '*sofa*'
(*northern limits*)

14. ------*burial/burying ground*
-o-o-*public school*

15. *butterhorns* '*sweet rolls*'
(otherwise: *snails*)

16. [wăs]
(otherwise: [wɒš])

17. put it *on!* [an]
(otherwise: [ɒn])

18. eggs [ɛ]
(otherwise: [eᴵ/ɛᴵ/e])

In the matter of pronunciation, certain items are common to both cities: the use of a low unrounded vowel in the words *wash* or *on* (see Maps 16 and 17), and the use of a simple open [ɛ] in words like egg, rather than a higher mid-front vowel or a diphthong (see Map 18).

The localization of certain common phenomena and the application of different terms for the same is illustrated by words for a warm dry/moist wind, called a *chinook* in the Northwest and in Nevada, and a *Santa Ana* (or *Santana*) in southern California. Adoption of the Spanish terms is typical in the latter area, particularly with items of topography, ranching, or food. Map 20 indicates the area where *arroyo* is used in reference to a large dry gully. Although many Spanish loans are widely current throughout the West,

19. (dry) warm wind

    I chinook

    II Santa Ana

20. arroyo 'dry wash gully'

    (Spanish loan-word)

the use of this term corresponds to the primary area of Spanish influence in California. Continued use of the Spanish language, particularly in southern California, adds a special dimension to the speech patterns of the Southwest. At the same time it promises to complicate once more the developing historical effects of what has here been described as an ebbing and flowing of diverse populations with consequent mixtures of English in California and Nevada.

Notes

1. All items have been checked carefully in the archives of the Linguistic Atlas of California and Nevada, located at the University of California in Berkeley.

SOCIAL DIALECT AND EMPLOYABILITY: SOME PITFALLS OF GOOD INTENTIONS

Roger W. Shuy

Georgetown University

The importance of language in relating to one's fellow employees was never more clear to me than it was back in the days when I was working my way through college on a six to midnight general labor job at the Firestone Tire and Rubber Company. My particular duty was to produce a certain kind of tire tread on a machine which engaged a crew of five other men. My pay was based on how much we as a crew produced in a given evening while my fellow workers were paid at a constant hourly rate, regardless of what we produced. As a graduate student in English, my role was obviously precarious from the perspective of the other members of my crew, all high school drop-outs at best. Whatever else could be deduced from the situation, it was clear beyond words that it behooved me to speak the language of my audience. Since my paycheck was at their mercy, it was obvious that the speech of an English major simply would not do on the assembly line. This was not a new situation for me, however, for almost all males who grew up in working class communities can probably remember their adolescent need to speak with masculinity, particularly if there was any question whatsoever about their physical prowess, their ability as athletes, or if they were tortured by the anomaly of a relatively late development of facial hair and a deeper voice. Masculinity, they discovered, could be expressed by a choice of vocabulary, grammar, and pronunciation even after their bodies had unceremoniously failed them.

Thus we can see here two legitimate evidences of a need to speak something other than "school-room-English" at work in a society which at least outwardly claims that its values are to be placed on entirely different forms. It cannot be denied that a man must adjust to the social needs of his environment, particularly if he gains physically or psychologically from that adjustment. The good intention of the school frequently causes the boy to produce standard English, not realizing what the ramification of such usage might be in an entirely different context. The school might consider itself a failure, furthermore, if it produced graduate students in English who say "bring them crates over here," despite the fact that such a locution might seem more appropriate in the factory than "bring those crates over here" or the hyper-standard, "gentlemen would you kindly convey these containers to this portion of the edifice." Such good intentions generally are characterized by tunnel vision, failing to recognize the complexity or multitude of the forces which constantly operate in a person's life.

Although our attention here is to be directed to the employee-employer relationship rather than to the teacher-pupil context, we can benefit greatly from what we see in the schools, for they often provide a kind of microcosm of business and industry, especially with regard to attitudes toward language. Several of the attitudes of schools toward spoken language may be listed as follows:

1. Speech is an important criterion for job opportunity.
2. There is one best form of English which should be spoken at all times.
3. A person's language use reflects his logic and intelligence.
4. Non-standard speech should be eradicated.
5. The person who succeeds in the world is the one whose language is clearly understood and pleasant.

There are many other such maxims which might be added to this list, but these will suffice to provide a framework for our examination of personnel practices with respect to selecting, training, and promoting employees.

Speech and Employability

It is not a well guarded secret that the schools have had very few sources of motivation to cause students to want to speak standard English. One classic motivation has been that of pleasing the teacher, obtaining a tangible or abstract reward from the instructor. This might be called a contiguous, or short-range motivation. Its long range counterpart requires the student to project into the misty future, seeking out the abstraction of his potential life work as the motivation for learning acceptable schoolroom English. Usually at the onset of junior high school (or earlier) students are barraged with statements about the importance of learning standard English if ever they are to make something of their lives.

The question some of us who are interested in language attitudes have been asking is as follows, "Is speech really an important criterion in employ-ability?" In an effort to answer this question we produced a tape recording of 16 samples of Washington, D.C. Negro male adults and teenagers from the complete range of socioeconomic status groups in the city. The tape included two adult (21-55) and two teen age (14-17) speakers to represent each of four social classes. The passages chosen for the study were taken from the discourse section of the interview conducted as a part of the Washington

Dialect Study. The passages selected for the tape were based on two criteria: 1) the linguistic features in the passage should represent the particular social group of the informant 2) the passage should be as culturally unmarked as possible, since we wanted the people who listened to the tapes to react solely on the basis of linguistic criteria.

This tape was played individually to 16 persons who actually do the hiring for various Washington employers. These people represent approximately 40,000 jobs of all sorts in this area. Nine of the 16 employers claimed that on the basis of the speech sample which they heard they considered all 16 men employable.

These nine people represented employment in the hotel, telephone, dry-cleaning, baking, lumber, drug, and newspaper businesses. Representatives of a large department store and a printing business found only one person unemployable while employers from a men's clothing store, another printing company, the telephone company and a large automotive repair business found three of the taped speakers unemployable.

On the whole, the reactions of these employers to the taped speech samples were fairly consonant with the idea generally perpetrated by the classrooms of America, namely, that speech is directly proportionate to employability. Of the four lower working-class tape speech samples, the representative of the men's clothing store picked two as unemployable. The other two he would hire as porters, or as receiving-room workers with no public contact. The other employers gave comparable answers.

On the other hand, when asked to comment in writing on the extent to which they are influenced by the speech of a prospective employee, many employers denied that any such influence took place. The representative of one of Washington's largest hotels, in fact, observed "I would say that speech plays a relatively minor part in hiring an employee . . . general presentation, knowledge and appearance weigh most heavily." Likewise the employment supervisor of a large chain drug company which employs 9000 Washingtonians observed that the most important speech criterion for his employees is that they be "able to express themselfs [sic] in a way that is understood by our customers." The only employers who expressed much interest in speech as a criterion for selection were, predictably, those from the telephone company and the men's clothing store and, much less predictably, the one in the automotive repair business.

The general liberality of our employers when asked to comment on the significance of a job applicant's speech may have resulted from their attempt to bend over backward toward utter fairness, perhaps even a bit defensively. This liberality was generally not so evident, however, in a follow-up study in which the same employers were asked to rank each speaker on the same tape by job categories. Seven job categories were established, ranging from the highest (doctor, professor, architect) to the lowest (laborer, janitor, busboy). The professional, well educated speakers of the highest actual category were consistently ranked in the fourth and fifth categories(salesmen, police-men, mechanics), indicating a general unwillingness to believe that such persons could be as highly placed as they actually were.

What, then, are we to say about the importance of speech as a criterion for job opportunity? It appears that it operates differently on different points of a continuum of awareness. Most of the employers in our study consciously denied that speech is a consideration but they unconsciously reacted with amazing uniformity in assigning jobs on the basis of very few linguistic clues. The better jobs invariably went to the standard speakers. Those who were judged unemployable were invariably those with a lesser degree of standard English. One might say that employers seem better able *to use* linguistic clues as a criterion for employment than they are *to talk about them*. This is not at all surprising to linguists who have been working in this area for it is also generally true of English teachers, especially those with little or no training in the nature of the English language.

Although this generally uniform ability to assign jobs from the clues pro-vided by a small sample of speech seems encouraging, there are a number of pitfalls which many of our Washington employers illustrate. One employer, for example, observed that speech tells ". . . an unmistakable story about a person's background, training and mental altertness." We may agree that speech reveals interesting information about his geographical origins, his social status, his education, and even his race. But in no way can it be con-sidered a useful index to his mental alertness or intelligence. In his recent article on the logic of nonstandard English, William Labov (1969) puts to sleep for good the widely held but totally erroneous notion that nonstandard speech is a signal of mental inadequacy. For far too many years now the general public and the schools have assumed the position currently espoused by Carl Bereiter, who observes: ". . . the language of culturally deprived children . . . is not merely an under-developed version of standard English, but is a basically non-logical mode of expressive behavior." (1966) In order to overcome this illogicality and underdevelopment, this psychologist urges teachers to proceed as though the children have no language at all and to train children to speak in fully explicit formal language. The absurdity of these admonitions becomes evident when we examine the solutions to the illogicality and underdevelopment. Bereiter argues for unelliptical responses to questions (for example, *The squirrel is in the tree* is preferred over *in the tree*) as though, somehow, the full unelliptical form is the well developed and logical version from which all other versions diverge. Current linguistics clearly argues that the semantics of each of these sentences is the same and that there are only superficial surface structure differences between them. In his recent overview of the assumptions of linguists who work with social dialects, Walt Wolfram observed: "All languages are equally capable of conceptuali-zation and expressing logical propositions, but the particular mode . . . for conceptualizing may differ drastically between language systems. The linguist, therefore, assumes that different surface forms for expression have nothing to do with the underlying logic of a sentence." (1970, p. 11) It is safe to assert that linguists are unanimous in this position.

In clear terms of the relationship of a person's use of language and employability, then, it can be concluded that it is dangerous to infer anything about a speaker's logic or intelligence on the basis of his use of the language. Far more revealing might be the person's social status, his education, or his geographical origins. Furthermore, however tempting it may be to use a prospective employee's non-standard grammar, pronunciation, and vocabulary as a sign of his motivation or trainability, chances are that all one can accurately infer is that the candidate has grown up in a non-standard English speaking environment.

Clear evidence of how dangerous it can be for the non-linguistically sensitized employment manager to speculate about the clues language provides may be found in the previously cited study of Washington employers. The vice president of one of the city's largest dry cleaning companies, for example, expressed a theory that the efficiency of his truck drivers is directly related to their speech tempo. It is of some interest, also, that this gentleman himself speaks at a very rapid rate, suggesting, perhaps, that he has either a personal or cultural bias against people unlike himself, at least with regard to speech tempo. Regardless of the source of his feeling, however, he is convinced that his drivers who speak slowly take longer to deliver their goods and, for whatever it is worth, they take too much time, as he put it, "commuting with customers" [sic].

Another employment manager's observations about language also seem to be widely held. After listening to our tape recorded speech samples, this department store executive expressed the opinion that the people who came into his office had much worse speech than any of the samples on the tape (our tape, of course, contained samples from *all* levels of Washington society) and that he couldn't hire many people because they couldn't make themselves well enough understood to give any pertinent information to the interviewer.

Linguists who have worked with educators have faced this situation for many years. Teachers bitterly complain that their students have a very limited vocabulary. They assume, quite wrongly, that the lack of vocabulary used in school settings is equivalent to lack of overall vocabulary. Teachers also indicate little or no understanding of the slum child's grammar, often paying great heed to features which are actually of little consequence in terms of social stigmatization. Many are utterly unaware of what sociolinguistic research has indicated about the relative importance of grammatical features in social stigmatization as opposed to non-standard pronunciations. That is, they fail to understand that English speakers tend to tolerate or accept pronunciation differences much more than grammatical variations. If teachers fail to respond to these clues, how can we expect employment managers to do so? For they, like teachers, hear English spoken in very specialized and, in some ways, tense situations. A person seeking employment, like a school child, is apt to be guarded, nervous, and timid in an obviously intimidating situation. Employment interviewers, like teachers, are apt to forget how used to their jobs they have become. They are apt to forget that their subjects are not at all used to such interviewing or that they are aware of being judged at all times. The child in the first grade soon learns that the point of the game of education is to be wrong as seldom as possible and to be right as often as possible. He may determine, quite properly, that his best defense is a retreat into silence. If the teacher corrects his speech enough times when he responds with the right answer, the child may logically assume that his answer is really wrong or quite possibly, that this school-business doesn't make a whole lot of sense anyway.

It is not difficult to translate the school setting to the employment interview. The setting of the employment office is undoubtedly as intimidating as many American classrooms manage to be. If a prospective employee appears to have a limited vocabulary, it may be for the same reason that some first graders appear to be "non-verbal." Our department store employment manager listened to tape recorded speech which was elicited under considerably less tense circumstances. Consequently he could easily conclude that the people who come into his office have much worse speech than those on the taped sample. It is reasonable to expect the employment manager to react in exactly the same way that many teachers do, placing the blame for the communication breakdown squarely on the job seeker. Linguists and anthropologists long ago discovered that the blame may well stem from their own lack of sensitivity to the whole situation. One of the cardinal tenets of current sociolinguistic research is to clearly define the speech context and to elicit different styles of language by manipulating the situation. We know, for example, that almost everyone has a range of linguistic formality which can be triggered by changing the speech contexts. A person may exhibit speech which comes closest to standard English norms in his oral reading. It is slightly less standard in the recitation of word lists or in single word responses to questions. His speech may become less and less standard as the contexts move first toward the speech used with peer-group, then casual speech and, perhaps most nonstandard of all, toward the intimate speech of those who know each other so well that there is no need to put on one's best linguistic armor.

One last example of the dangers involved in speculating about language without a clear understanding of everything involved may be seen in the observation of a personnel assistant at a Washington printing company. Having noted that many residents of the area have difficulty producing the sounds represented by the letters *r* and *l*, she opined that this is a direct result of brain damage induced by overdoses of paregoric given to local children in order to keep them quiet. The wonders of medical science never cease.

Speech and Training Programs

For several decades commercial organizations have stressed the importance of appropriate speech for their employees to the extent that in-service training has been recommended, though not frequently attempted. Several programs for such training have recently come to our attention. Under contract with the U.S. Department of Labor, several faculty members at St. Mary's Dominican College in New Orleans, for example, developed an adult education program called *Business English: A Second Language for Vocational Use* which, although it says in the foreword that it does *not* favor the eradication of a person's home dialect, proceeds to try to do just that.

Why is it that it has taken such programs so long to learn that a simple statement in the foreword is not sufficient to clear the air and make learning a second dialect possible? The commitment to the equality and legitimacy of both language systems (that is, the one used at home as well as the one used in school) is a commitment to a different sort of program than one would concoct if the desire were merely to eradicate home speech patterns. Recent research on the speech of people who are considered in some circles the most nonstandard of all nonstandard English speakers clearly demonstrates that these people are capable of producing all of the non-stigmatized counterparts of their own stigmatized speech features, if the researcher is patient enough, as well as non-intimidating and resourceful. Speakers of non-standard English do not lack the ability to produce standard English pronunciations and grammatical forms. In fact they *do* produce them in certain styles and in certain contexts, as the figures on frequency distribution clearly indicate in the recent sociolinguistic research done in New York, Detroit and Washington. Put simply, a program to teach standard English to speakers of non-standard English should not assume that these people are learning to produce pronunciations or grammatical forms that they do not know. They already know them. What they lack is the ability to develop their control in selecting between these standard and non-standard pronunciations and grammatical forms. This simple fact is the one most frequently overlooked in programs developed for training speakers of one dialect to learn another. Realization of this principle will cause the materials in question to take on an almost entirely different dimension than they otherwise would have taken. Drills which would be perfectly appropriate for the acquisition of a new and unknown language are not necessarily appropriate for learning to control two known dialects of the same language. The former requires sensitivity primarily to linguistic forms; the latter requires sensitivity primarily to the relationship between linguistic forms and various well-defined social contexts. Until programs developed to teach standard English realize this principle they will continue to spin their wheels with only incidental or short range learning as their products.

Any training program which sets the stage very clearly concerning the social appropriateness of different variants of the same grammatical features, must still do more, however. Again let us take a clue from the pitfalls of good intentions illustrated daily in our public schools. Thousands of well meaning English teachers in this country are humbled daily by the speech of their prize students once the final bell has rung. Their almost constant lament is that although the children may ultimately produce standard English in the class-room, they forget it the minute they get outside the school. Sometimes, in fact, they even use their non-standard right on the school grounds. Thus, scores of teachers sit in the loneliness of their after school paper-grading, with a sense of despair and failure.

We would say to these teachers, don't despair. There is something ludicrous about the prospect of expecting teen-age boys to use standard English in the football huddle. There is little reason to expect fist fights to be conducted with impeccable grammar and little reason to expect teen-age girls to maintain school English in their interminable telephone conversations.

Thus, a training program in industry might expect the same sort of reactions. Even if the program is sound, well taught, and taken by reasonably teachable employees, there is still no reason to expect these employees to speak standard English in the cafeteria or at the water-cooler. What I am saying is that the expectations of the program should be specified to the contexts where such speech is judged appropriate. But there is no reason to expect it, or even desire it, elsewhere. If a bank teller can produce English which does not embarrass the bank in all his public contacts, there is no reason to expect him to produce it in the men's room. Human nature argues against it. At least for a while (and perhaps permanently) he may prefer to preserve his other identity more or less the way it was before he came to work for you. And, of course, outside of the bank, there is no reason to expect him to either talk past or down to people that he knows intimately and loves. Employee training programs in standard English, therefore, should set contextual goals and not be discouraged if the rub-off on other contexts is not immediate or great.

One area largely overlooked in speech training programs would focus, not on the speech of the employees, but in developing sensitivity to the speech of customers. Although telephone companies have been known to place considerable attention on developing consistent telephone-operator standards of diction and usage, I know of no program devised to train, for example, standard English speaking operators to understand the non-standard English of many of their customers. And while we are at it, why not train employment managers to understand the utterances of the people who come to them seeking employment? And for those who are developing some sort of program for non-standard English speakers, one might hope for some training which would enable them to address themselves to the most important features (see Fasold and Wolfram, 1970), so that we could avoid the trivia of teaching adults to produce an [1] in words like *solve* (*Business Speech*, p. 118) when there are so many really stigmatized features to worry about.

Another area which has received only scant attention in employee training relates a person's oral language to his ability to read and write. Although our focus here is clearly on speech, one must at least mention that reading is increasingly thought of as a language processing phenomenon these days and that there is considerable reason to suspect that interference to the development of reading skills may come from the relative lack of correspondence between a person's everyday speech and the language system of the written page. Likewise, there is reason to suspect that a person's oral language has a direct relationship to his representation of that language on paper. For example, a recent informal investigation of the written compositions of college freshmen from inner-city Detroit revealed that approximately 45% of their misspellings and unacceptable grammatical forms were directly relatable to interference from the phonology and grammar of their everyday spoken English.

In short, training programs in standard English for employees should not busy themselves in eradicating non-standard English but should, instead, teach employees to make appropriate choices in the appropriate contexts, realizing that non-standard forms are also appropriate in certain contexts. Despite his protests to the contrary, I seriously doubt that our employment manager at the Washington automotive repair company is realistic in expecting his mechanics to produce standard English. Chances are that not even his most snooty customers expect it. Training programs should recognize that employees have a number of different contexts where different language systems are possible, even necessary.

Speech and Promotion

Recently I was asked by a lawyer to testify in a court trial involving a police officer who was refused promotion on the grounds that he was unable to pass a test on English usage which had been given as part of the promotion requirements. Stories of this sort have long circulated in the education world, the most notorious of which usually involve the former New York State requirement that prospective teachers be able to produce British received pronunciation.

Perhaps the best thing that can be said about the use of such tests for the purposes of employee promotion is that it is a case of the blind leading the blind. Those who are most adamant for the usefulness of such measures are almost always those who know the least about the features selected for such tests. Linguists will undoubtedly agree that currently no good test of non-standardness exists. The whole area of language testing, particularly as it relates to social varieties of English, is currently under very careful scrutiny. Many of us are relatively convinced, for example, that standardized tests to measure reading skills severely penalize the non-mainstream, non-middle, non-silent American. And, of course, New York State's measurement of its future teachers' ability to articulate British English has long been the source of amusement to those who found the test totally irrelevant. College entrance examinations have a long history asking such questions as, "Which is right: the garage is behind the house *or* the garage is in back of the house?"

If the experience of the Detroit Head Start School teachers is any indication, it is very difficult for non-linguists to identify the features which characterize non-standard speech anyway. There is even less reason to suspect that we can use such features to construct a fair test upon which to base employee promotions. As an example of how difficult it is to produce a culture-fair test question let me cite the experiment conducted by John Connelly in West Virginia. By changing the word *mongrel* to *cur dog*, on the Iowa Test of Basic Skills, he increased the reading ability of a group of white children by three months (personal correspondence).

Since a person's command of standard English in no way indicates his logical prowess or his integrity, we must wonder about what relevance a test of such qualities might have for promotion, even if it were possible to suddenly build one. Chances are the supervisor will have a number of other more clear-cut indices for promotion at his disposal. Of course he may want to take an employee's ability to use the language into consideration in some way. What we argue for is fairness in doing so. He should know that language variation is a normal and acceptable thing. He should know the difference between socially stigmatized speech and other non-stigmatized variations. He should understand that after all these many years, our country is showing signs of pluralism as opposed to melting-potism and that many people continue to claim their own variety of English as part of their group identity and that refusal to ambiguate this identity is not a sign of stupidity, maliciousness, or even rebelliousness. Employers who offer such speech programs may be advised that it is best to make them optional rather than required. After all, even IBM executives are now allowed to wear colored shirts to the office.

Conclusion

The good intentions of employers run the risk of paralleling the good intentions of the American education system unless they are careful to avoid some of the pitfalls noted in this paper. Speech appears to be an important criterion for job opportunity, despite protestations to the contrary from employers. Speech reveals a great deal about a person, but practically nothing about his intelligence or use of logic. Employers should be especially wary of inferring personality traits from the speech of employees. The *context* of the employee's speech must be carefully considered in any judgment related to it, for the employment interview is constructed to bring out the worst in a potential employee's language usage. Training programs geared to help speakers of non-standard English should differentiate between learning to control standard and non-standard English from learning a new dialect. The former situation is the one that obtains even though the latter is the approach most frequently taken in available materials. In any case, there is no need to spend time eradicating a language system which may come in handy in the employee's relationship with his friends and family. Promotion will be at least partly related to an employee's ability to make himself understood and appreciated through his speech, but promotion tests have not succeeded in measuring the quality that, at present, comes better through intuition or a feel for language.

Those of us in the field of sociolinguistics do not pretend to have all the answers to the problems of hiring, training, and promoting employees. But we wish to point out that many of these problems seem to be related to language. We get this information first from the employers themselves, either directly or indirectly, and second, from the logical extension of problems observed in teacher-student relationships with which we have been working. If our successes in dealing with the schools until fairly recently have been relatively unspectacular, it may be borne in mind that even Disraeli had to make over 300 speeches to persuade Great Britain to accept the electoral reform of 1867. It is hoped that in business and industry the sailing will be smoother, primarily because of their greater sensitivity to the problem and their distinct advantage of *not* having a contrary and wrong headed tradition to overcome before a positive and workable program can be set up. In our brief contacts with industrial programs, we have been impressed with this sensitivity and intuitive turning to the most productive approaches and attitudes. Couple this with the sort of information about language and language teaching which linguists can provide and there is considerable reason for optimism. Employers who are accurately sensitive to the importance of the language dimension in hiring, training, and promotion will discover a tool of great usefulness, both from the view of their own successful use of personnel talent and also from the view of the employees' own sense of identity and dignity. In this, linguists genially and genuinely encourage the cooperation of industry, business, government and foundations.. Perhaps no aspect of our humanity is as obvious as our language—or as little understood and utilized as a resource. Such an awareness may contribute significantly to the history of social relations, self-development and economic efficiency so that historians of the 1970's may not have to say of us, as Brogan wrote of the third French Republic, that it was ". . . a people . . . which had astonished the world in every field of achievement . . . yet failed to find institutions that . . . gave them a political way of life worthy of their genius, their courage, and their legitimate hopes."

Bibliography

Bereiter, Carl, et al. "An academically oriented pre-school for culturally deprived children," in Fred M. Hechinger (ed.) *Pre-School Education Today.* New York: Doubleday, 1966.

Business Speech: A Second Language for Vocational Use. New Orleans: St. Mary's Dominican College, n.d.

Fasold, Ralph and Walt Wolfram, "Some Linguistic Features of Negro Dialect" in Ralph Fasold and Roger Shuy (eds.) *Teaching Standard English in the Inner City*, Washington, D.C.: Center for Applied Linguistics, 1970.

Labov, William. *The Social Stratification of English in New York City.* Washington, D.C.: Center for Applied Linguistics, 1966.

Shuy, Roger, Joan Baratz, and Walt Wolfram. *Sociolinguistic Factors in Speech Identification.* National Institutes of Mental Health Project No. MH-15048-01, 1969.

Wolfram, Walter. "Social Dialects from a Linguistic Perspective," in R. Shuy (compiler) *Sociolinguistics: A Crossdisciplinary Perspective.* Washington: Center for Applied Linguistics, 1971.

_____. *A Sociolinguistic Description of Detroit Negro Speech.* Washington, D.C.: Center for Applied Linguistics, 1969.

THE MORPHOPHONE AND ENGLISH DIALECTS

HENRY LEE SMITH, JR.
State University of New York at Buffalo

It is with the greatest pleasure that I submit this paper for publication in this collection to honor my old friend and colleague, Raven McDavid. I had thought I might offer either a paper on a more limited topic having to do with the morphophonic status of /h/ and of /+/ and the other junctures, or one on a reconsideration of Old English prosody. The more I thought about it, however, the more I became convinced that this paper was far more appropriate for inclusion in this collection since it had to do with matters that have always been of primary concern to both McDavid and me. In addition, nowhere else have I given so detailed an account of my most recent thinking concerning the phonological basis—phonetic and phonemic—for the morphophone.

The treatment, particularly at the beginning of the paper, will doubtless seem unnecessarily elementary to the specialist, and for this I apologize in advance. For some who are perhaps not so well acquainted with what is being more and more frequently referred to as *aspectual linguistics*—the term is George L. Trager's—the development may not seem quite so overly simple. Also, many of the examples and the tables may strike those who have read other things I have published on the morphophone as being more than a little familiar. Even so, I feel that this particular treatment is most appropriate for inclusion here and welcome the opportunity to present it. I will begin, then, with a rather elementary, but, I feel, essential statement of my theoretical position.

All human languages are alike in that they can be seen to be the same kinds of structured *systems*: systems of arbitrary vocal symbols through which men *interact* and therefore *communicate* in terms of their common cultural experiences and expectancies. Language is a part of culture, a system of culture unique in that all the other systems comprising the culture are reflected and transmitted through language. In fact, by far the larger part of what we learn, we learn through and by language. But language itself must be learned by each human being as part of the process of his enculturation and socialization. The linguistic system he learns has often been called a code, and this code is shared by all others constituting the *speech community* and the society into which he has been born. Examination and analysis indicate that all the learned and shared linguistic systems used by human beings have in common a unique aspect of structuring which seems to require a special kind of learning exhibited only by human beings. That is, languages are so structured that the learner has to respond to the same linguistic event at two or more levels at once and in such a way that he assigns different significances to the same event when that event is seen at different levels. To put it another way, he must learn that two events which are the same on one level may have a quite different significance on another, and, conversely, he must be able to see that events different at one level may be equivalent at another. As an example, the final sound in the word *left*, when in the phrase *my left*, is identical to the final sound in *left* in the sentence *I left*. The learner of English, however, has to become aware that a different grammatical significance, the past tense of leave, is carried by the *t*-sound in *I left*, while the same sound in *my left* is simply the last sound of the noun *left*. To illustrate the converse, when *difference* in sounds is reacted to as carrying the *same* grammatical significance, we can make *I left* versus *I lef'*, when the *t*-sound has been lost absolutely, though the word so pronounced still signals the past tense owing to the vowel change heard between *leave* and *lef'*. Only human languages show this basic dichotomy between *phonology* (sound structure) and *grammar*: no other modality of human or animal communication is so structured, and to learn what is significant and what is not significant, what constitutes *contrast* and what constitutes *equivalence* at the various levels of organization of language, requires a kind of learning that is uniquely human, differing in kind, not just in degree, from all other learning. Finally, through his uniquely structured linguistic systems man is able to impart meaning to the things and events in his environment, including features and aspects of his language itself, and largely through language he is able to comprehend meanings imparted by others.

Complexly structured as languages are and uniquely equipped as human beings are to learn them, language behavior is essentially habitual behavior, and great pressure is exerted on the individual to conform to the lingiustic norms shared by those of his speeh community. Even so, complete uniformity in speech behavior never exists, and linguistic systems, like all other systems of culture, are subject to gradual and inevitable change. When we add to this the fact that man's history can be seen to be punctuated by migrations resulting in almost complete and continued separation of sizable groups from the main body of speakers of a language, it is not hard to see how dialects emerge and how, ultimately, new languages are formed. The principal explanation of regional dialects, then, is easily seen in settlement history, but it is actually harder to explain the long-continuing similarities that can be observed between the speech of totally separated groups. This persistence is partly owing to the fact that language is learned so thoroughly, so early, and so largely below the level of awareness, but in some measure the slow rate of change can be attributed to the nature of linguistic systems themselves, and to how they are learned, used and reacted to by their speakers. It is almost as though we were partners to an agreement to consider certain aspects of our language inviolate, but to permit a quite wide range of diversity in other areas. For instance, such contrasts as that between the initial sounds in *pen* and *ten* are not to be tampered with, but whether the speaker pronounces *pen* so as to rhyme with his pronunciation of *pin* is seen as a matter of far less consequence. When human beings, by virtue of their unique brains and their unique conditioning, learn their native languages, they learn not only the structuring of their own dialects, but *internalize*, so to speak, the *overall pattern* of the language, through which, by a sort of *calibration*, linguistic forms different in certain features from those they have learned are seen to be equivalent to the ones they are accustomed to. Contrast *versus* equivalence, then, lies at the center of the study of dialect and language.

In order to determine the most basic and fundamental distinctions between *significant* and *non-significant*, between *contrastive* and *non-contrastive* events, the linguist has traditionally concerned himself first with the *segmentable* speech-sounds, or *phones*, which comprise the stream of speech as uttered and perceived. These phones are real events in the real world, and their sequences and arrangements constitute the ultimate embodiment, the *actualization* of language. But as the atom can be seen to be composed of sub-atomic particles, the phone can be seen as a "bundle" of *articulation features*. These articulation features have to do mainly with the *manner* of articulation and with the place of articulation. For example, the initial sounds in *pen* and *ten*, *pin* and *tin* are alike in exhibiting the same manner of articulation; they are *stops*. They differ, however, in the place where the stoppage is instituted; the *p*-sounds are made by stopping the air by a coming together of both lips, while *t*-sounds' stoppage is made by the apex of the tongue contacting the alveolar ridge. Initial *p*-sounds and *t*-sounds, of course, share other features in common; both are *voiceless*, both are *fortis*, and both are *aspirated*. In contrast, the initial *b*- and *d*- sounds in *Ben* and *den*, *bin* and *din*, though also characterized, respectively, as bilabial and alveolar stops, are *voiced* (at least partially), *lenis*, and *unaspirated*. Through these different initial sounds *contrasts* are established, and *sounds we react to as the same* also furnish the basis of contrasts in medial and final positions—*pip*, *pit*; *bib*, *bid*; *latter*, *ladder*; *flappy*, *flabby*, etc. In clusters with *s* preceding, *p* and *t* also make contrasts, as in *span* vs. *Stan*; *b* and *d* do not occur in clusters with *s* nor with its voiced partner, *z*. Careful listening can establish the fact that though the initial, medial, and final occurrences, respectively, of the *p* and *t*, *b* and *d*-sounds are *phonetically similar*, they are by no means identical. For example, *final p's and t's are unreleased*; no puff of breath regularly accompanies their articulation, and the medial *b*'s and *d*'s, unlike the initial and final varieties, are fully vocied. But even more striking are the differences between the initial occurrences of *p* and *t* and those following *s*, since in these situations the *p*'s and *t*'s are not only unaspirated but are also lenis rather than fortis. Thus the only feature of articulation that distinguishes them from the lenis, unaspirated *b*'s and *d*'s is their voicelessness; all varieties of *b* and *d* are at least paritally voiced.

We have been seeing that all sounds of a certain type—illustrated above by the bilabial and alveolar stops—show the same kinds of predictable, positionally determined, non-contrastive variants. This fact is referred to as *pattern congruity*, and what we have used in the preceding paragraph demonstrates that contrasts are actually established by families or *classes* of sounds whose members are phonetically similar, non-contrastively distributed, and congruently patterned. These contrast-making classes of sounds are, of course, the *phonemes*, and the members of the classes we have been examining are the *allophones* of the phonemes. When speaking, we react to the phoneme *as a whole* as a contrast-making entity and not to the non-significantly different though phonetically similar allophones. The allophones, though, must be learned, and their nature and composition are binding on all native speakers. They are learned, however, below the level of awareness, and we are not conscious of the non-significant differences between them. Rather each speaker identifies each perceived allophone as a member of its phoneme, and contrasts are thus made at the level of the phoneme and not at the level of the allophone. For analyst and speaker alike, each identified phone is assigned to one phoneme class and to *only* one in each dialect of a language, and every contrast of any kind made at any time by any native speaker of a language must be accounted for in the inventory of phonemes for that language as a whole. Though it is true that from the point of view of linguistic analysis the phoneme can be seen as a *construct* of the analyst, as an abstraction, even as a fiction, we must not lose sight of the fact that to speaker and hearer the phoneme has a psychological reality, since ultimately all contrasts are made through phonemes.

Though the process of identification of allophones and of their assignment to phonemes takes place below the level of awareness, this is not the case for for *diaphones* of a phoneme. Diaphones are phones seen as members of a phoneme that are characteristic of one dialect but not necessarily of another. For example, the alveolar phone one hears medially in many pronunciations of *latter, waiter, water, butter, bottle*, etc., is often *voiced* rather than voiceless, but, unlike the voiced *d*-phone in *ladder, wader*, etc., it is *fortis* rather than lenis. This fact can be determined by hearing that the vowel phone preceding the alveolar consonant in *latter, waiter* is not prolonged, as is the case when a *d*-phone follows, e.g. *ladder, wader*, etc. In distributional situations when *l*'s or *n*'s follow *t*'s, or in cases where a *t*-phone is generally heard in final position, e.g. *bottle, mountain, thought*, many dialects have a *glottal* rather than an alveolar stop, the effect often being described as "swallowing the *t*." But in all these cases, the native speaker, having internalized the phonemic pattern of the language as a whole—the *phonemic inventory*—identifies diaphones of the *t*-phoneme that may be different from his own as equivalent of those selected by his dialect. The inventory of consonant phonemes for English as a whole follows:

TABLE I

p		t			k
b		d			g
				č (*ch* in 'church')	
				j (*j* and *dge* in 'judge')	
f θ (*th* in 'thin')		s		š (*sh* in 'shin')	
v ð (*th* in 'then')		z		ž (*s* in 'measure')	
m			n		ŋ *ng* in 'sing',
			l	r	but *ng* spells ŋg in *finger*')

Note: Symbols for phonemes are conventionally enclosed in slant lines— /p/, /t/, /k/; symbols for phones are enclosed in brackets—[p'-], [sp-], [-p ⌐].

In establishing the phonemes of the inventory and in assigning phones to phoneme classes, the linguist follows the two principles already mentioned: first, every contrast of any kind made at any time by any native speaker must be accounted for by a phoneme in the inventory, and, second, every identified phone in each dialect or idiolect must be assigned to one phoneme class, and to only one. Situations may arise that at first seem to contradict these principles; for example, in the case of the phonemic assignment of the *velar nasal* phone, [ŋ], heard in *think* and *finger*, and usually associated with the letters "ng". When speaker A contrasts *lawn* and *long* through occurrences of *final* [-n] and final [-ŋ], respectively, quite obviously the linguist must establish two different phonemes, /n/ and /ŋ/, to account for the situation. Such speakers also usually show medial contrasts made by occurrences of the velar nasal, [-ŋ-], as against a sequence of the velar nasal followed by the *velar stop*, [g], as in *longer* 'one who longs' with [-ŋ-] alone, and *longer*, the comparative of the adjective, in the sequence [-ŋg-]. The phonemic assignments here would be, respectively, to /-ŋ-/ and /-ŋg-/. Now many speakers contrast *lawn* and *long*, *sin* and *sing* not by [-n] vs. [-ŋ], but by [-n] vs the sequence [-ŋg], and also have no medial contrast between [-ŋ-] and [-ŋg-], but show only medial [-ŋg-] for both *longer* (n.) and *longer* (adj.), *singer* and *finger*, *wringer* and *linger*, etc. These speakers, however, like those of the dialect of speaker A, show only the velar nasal, [ŋ], in *think*, *ink*, etc., which leads to the conclusion that all speakers of English, regardless of dialect, can have only the velar nasal when a velar stop, [k] or [g], follows, since speakers of both dialect A and dialect B show [ŋk] and [ŋg]. But the phonemic assignment of the [ŋ] phones will differ between the two dialects; for dialect A, all [ŋ]'s will be assigned to the phoneme /ŋ/, but for dialect B, there is no necessity of a separate /ŋ/ phoneme, since [ŋ] *by itself* never contrasts with [n], as is the case in dialect A. Therefore, [ŋ] in dialect B is assigned to the phoneme /n/ of the inventory and the dialect is said to lack the phoneme [ŋ], which, of course, is a necessary member of the inventory, in order to handle the contrasts of dialect A. The principle forbidding the assignment of the same phone to two phonemes is not abrogated, since this principle applies only to individual dialects, not to the language as a whole. Put another way, [ŋ] is assigned only to /ŋ/ in dialect A and only to /n/ in dialect B. The [ŋ] of /n/ in dialect B is termed a *dia-allophone* rather than an *allophone* of the phoneme, since the occurrence of this positionally determined variant is limited to the speakers of certain dialects and is not binding on all the speakers of the language. Thus we have three kinds of membership in a phoneme class: first, *allophones*, positionally determined variants binding on all speakers of a language, second, *dia-allophones*, positionally determined variants binding only on the speakers of certain dialects, and, third, *diaphones*, positional variants that are generally more characteristic of specific dialects but that may be *selected* at any time by the speakers of any dialect.[1]

In addition to the twenty-one consonant phonemes, there are three "glide-like" phonemes, /y/, /w/, and /h/, which are called *semi-vowels* and which do double duty. That is, their allophones function like those of consonant phonemes when they precede vowels—e.g. *ye, yea; we, way; he, hay; you, yo-yo; woo, woe; who, hoe, hah, haw*—but "mirror images" of the initial sounds occur after "short" vowel sounds to form what have been traditionally called "long vowels" and "diphthongs." To understand the structuring of these *complex nuclei*, we must first identify some of the *simple* vowel nuclei in the inventory and determine the real meaning of "vowel length" in English.

To begin with, nearly all speakers use contrasting simple vowel phonemes in *pit, pet, pat, put, putt, pot*, and, in addition to these six, northern Middle Western speakers show a seventh contrasting simple vowel in *caught* vs *cot, taut* vs *tot, wrought* vs. *rot*, etc. Though the tongue is low in the mouth in the pronunciation of all the words, the back rather than the center portion is slightly tensened for the vowels in *caught, taught*, etc., and their articulation is accompanied by a slight but clearly perceptible rounding of the lips. In contrast, the vowels in *pot, tot, cot*, etc., are completely unrounded and considerably *fronted*. An eighth simple vowel must be placed in the inventory since the majority of English speakers *at times* makes a four-way contrast between the vowels in *gist* (as in *pit*), *jest* (as in *pet*), *just* (adj.) as in *putt*, and *just* (adv.). The contrast-making vowel in the last word is also heard as the first vowel in many pronunciations of *children*, and under *weak* stress occurs as the vowel in the plural ending in such cases as *matches, horses, judges*. It can be heard quite clearly in these dialects in such *minimal pairs* as *roses* vs *Rosa's*, where the latter word has, under weak stress, a *mid-central* vowel, like that of *putt* or *but*, rather than the *high central* vowel we have been identifying which occurs in the final syllable of *roses*.

There still is one more simple vowel that must be added to the inventory, since, particularly in New England, many speakers use a "short *o*-sound" in *coat, road, home, whole*, so as to make these words sound to speakers of other dialects much like words with mid-central vowels in them, that is, like *cut, bud, hum, hull*. But the New Englander's vowel is pronounced with the tongue farther back, and is accompanied by clearly perceptible lip-rounding. It is, therefore, clearly in contrast with the mid-central vowels he, too, has in *cut, bud, hum,* and *hull*. The New Englander also shows no regular occurrence of the low, central, *unrounded* vowel as heard in most American and Canadian dialects in *pot, cot, lot*, etc., but uses the low, back, *rounded* vowel, identified in the Chicagoan's pronunciation of *caught* and *thought*, for both *cot* and *caught, tot* and *taught, caller* and *collar*, etc., and thus makes no contrast between the two sets of words. This low, back, rounded vowel also occurs in most dialects in Great Britain in the words *pot, tot, cot*, etc., but, as we shall see, with *complex* rather than with a simple nucleus. Table II immediately below arranges all nine of the simple vowels in the inventory in terms of tongue position—whether high and to the front, low and to the center, etc.— and gives symbols for each of the phonemes.

TABLE II

	Front	Center	Back (with lip-rounding)
High	/i/ *pit*	/ɨ/ *just*, adv.	/u/ *put*
Mid	/e/ *pet*	/ə/ *putt, just*, adj.	/o/ *coat, home* [N.E.]
Low	/æ/ *pat*	/a/ *pot*	/ɔ/ *pot, cot* [N.E. and G.B.]
			caught [northern Mid-West]

The principal allophones of the simple vowel phonemes are statable in terms of automatic, predictable, positionally-determined and, hence, non-contrastive *vowel length*. This non-significant prolongation is in direct proportion to the degree of "lenisness" of the following consonants. Thus the absolutely shortest vowels are heard where the most fortis of all the consonants, the voiceless stops, follow, while the considerably more lenis voiced stops are seen to prolong preceding vowels by an amount we can, for convenience, designate as one *mora*. Thus the vowel phone in *bib* is one *mora* longer than that in *pip*, the vowel in *pig* one *mora* longer than the one in *pick*, etc. The nasals [m], [n], [ŋ] and the [r] and [l] sounds also lengthen preceding vowels by one *mora*, but the more fortis voiceless *spirant* phones, [f], [θ], [s], [š], cause only a half *mora* prolongation. The voiced spirant phones, [v], [ð], [z], [ž], cause lengthening of a *mora* and a half, as in *have* and *has*, indicating that in English, voiced sounds are regularly more lenis than their voiceless counterparts. The purely automatic, *allophonic*, nature of vowel length in English is further, and quite dramatically, demonstrated when we realize that the vowels we may have always thought of as *long* are, when followed by *voiceless* stops, actually *shorter* by half a *mora* than so-called *short* vowels followed by *voiced* stops, and a full *mora* shorter than so-called short vowels followed by voiced *spirants*. Thus the vowel nucleus in *peek* is a half *mora* shorter than that of *pig*, and a full *mora* shorter than the one in *his*; *fate* is a half *mora* shorter than *fed*, and a full *mora* shorter than *fez*; *slope* is a half *mora* shorter than *slob*, and a full *mora* shorter than *Oz*, etc. But when the so-called long vowels are followed by voiced stops and voiced spirants, the nuclei are prolonged by the expected one *mora* and one and one-half *morae*, respectively, so that the nuclei in *fade* and *faze* are, respectively, one *mora* and one *mora* and a half longer than the nucleus in *fate*; *babe* and *bathe* are one *mora* and one and a half *morae* longer than *tape*, etc.

We must realize, however, that the so-called long vowels and diphthongs are one-half *mora* longer than the so-called short vowels when each type is followed by the same consonants. Thus *feet* is one-half *mora* longer than *fit*, *bead* is one-half *mora* longer than *bid*, and *he's* one-half *mora* longer than *his*. The longest vowel nuclei of all, fully two and one-half *morae* longer than simple vowel nuclei followed by voiceless stops, are heard when a "long vowel" or "diphthong" is followed by no consonant at all, as in *see, say, sigh, Sioux, sew, sow* (n.), *law, Pa*. The data we have been examining indicate that there must be phones of one-half *mora* in duration present in the "long" vowel nuclei which are not present in the short vowel nuclei. That these phones are *glides* following simple vowel nuclei can quite clearly be perceived if we slowly pronounce words like those in the list immediately above. In *see, say, sigh*, the front of the tongue can be felt and seen to rise and travel farther front in the mouth from a starting vowel-position slightly, but perceptibly, lower and farther back. Also, during this glide to a higher and fronter position, there is a noticeable increase in the *tenseness* of the muscles in front of the tongue. In the second set of three words, the tongue moves farther back and higher, with an increase of tenseness and lip-rounding during the articulation of the two segments of each of the complex nuclei. In each set of words, the height of the tongue at the termination of the glides is determined by the position of the tongue at the start, so that the higher the starting point, the higher the tongue at the termination, and the lower the starting point, the lower the tongue-height at the completion of the pronunciation of the nucleus. Thus we end up with a higher tongue position when we say *see* and *Sioux* than when we say *sigh* and *sow* (n.), while the tongue-height is somewhere between these two positions at the termination of nuclei in *say* and *sew*. Each set of these post-vocalic glides, then, can be seen to comprise phonetically similar, postionally determined, non-contrastive *allophones* of two contrasting *phonemes*, which in every respect are mirror images of the *prevocalic* glides occurring in *ye, woo; yea, woe*, etc. That is, these prevocalic glides duplicate *in reverse* what we saw in the case of the post-vocalic glides in *ye, woo*, etc., since the pre-vocalic glides *start* from positions that are, respectively, higher and farther front and higher and farther back than the tongue positions of the following simple vowel. Also, the starting points of the initial glides are positionally determined by the tongue-position of the following simple vowel in a manner exactly the reverse of the situation in respect to the post-vocalic glides. Thus the pre- and post-vocalic glides constitute phonetically similar, non-contrastively distributed, congruently patterned *allophones* of the contrasting semi-vowel phonemes, /y/ and /w/. Words like *ye* and *yea*, *woo* and *woe* are thus analyzed as having three phonemes—initial semi-vowels, simple vowels and final semi-vowels—with the simple vowel, final semi-vowel sequence constituting the *complex nuclei*, i.e., /iy/, /ey/; /uw/, /ow/. Thus we have the following phonemic structurings: *ye*, /yiy/; *yea*, /yey/; *you*, /yuw/; *yo-yo*, /yow-yow/; *woo* /wuw/; *woe*, /wow/; *wow*, /waw/; *way*, /wey/; *why*, /(h)way/; *see*, /siy/; *say*, /sey/; *sigh*, /say/; *Sioux*, /suw/; *sew*, /sow/; *sow*, /saw/.

The third semi-vowel, heard in *law* and *Pa*, is identified as a glide to the center of the mouth, with no increase in tenseness, from a preceding simple vowel, and the tongue ends up quite close to the position for the mid-central vowels heard in *putt* and *Rosa* when the preceding short vowel is a mid vowel. However, if the preceding vowel is high, the tongue ends up higher than the mid-central position, and if the simple vowel in the nucleus is low, the tongue ends up lower than the mid-central position. Thus the allophones of this post-vocalic phoneme are positionally determined in a manner similar to that of the post-vocalic allophones of /y/ and /w/, and, like /y/ and /w/, this phoneme, when occurring post-vocalically, contributes to a complex nucleus one half *mora* longer than corresponding simple nuclei. For example, the center glides heard in the words *caught, laud, pause*, as pronounced by most Englishmen and most eastern Americans south of New England, occur in nuclei exactly half a *mora* longer than those heard in their pronunciations of *cot, god, Oz*. Also, words like *paw*, Pa; *saw, hah*, where no consonant follows the nuclei, are pronounced with nuclei two and a half *morae* longer than those in *pit, pet*, etc., as was the case with the nuclei in *ye, woo*, etc.

There is, then, a striking similarity in the patterning of all three post-vocalic glides, and therefore, we would expect to find an initial, mirror image partner to the center glide. Now the only pre-vocalic phones that can be linked with the allophones of the post-vocalic center glide phoneme are those we associate with the letter *h*, since initial *h*-phones can be seen to be articulated with the tongue in very different positions in the mouth depending upon the tongue position of the following vowel. Thus the tongue-position used in articulating the initial *h*-phone in *he* is dramatically different from the one occurring in *hall* or *hah*, and the differences are similar to the differences heard in the *post*-vocalic glides occurring in the words *fear* and *far* as pronounced by Londoners and New Yorkers. True, the initial *h*-phones are voiceless and *spirantal*, that is, accompanied by *friction noise*, features generally absent in the articulation of the post-vocalic center glides, and this fact has led some linguists to set up two defectively distributed *h*-like phonemes, one initial and one final, or to see the post-vocalic glides as members of a *phoneme of length* and assign the initial *h*-phones to a phoneme /h/ which occurs only initially. Both of these solutions abrogate the principle of *parsimony* in scientific description and can be arrived at only by failing to take into account the congruent patterning displayed by all three glides, and by failing to see vowel length as wholly *phonetic*, and hence non-contrastive and non-phonemic. Furthermore, no linguist hesitates to assign the voiceless, spirantal *r*-phone occurring after [t] in *tree, tray, try* to the same /r/ phoneme to which he assigns the fully voiced, non-spirantal *r*-phone in *Rhee, ray, rye*. Finally, it is interesting to note that many speakers in southern Wisconsin have a diaphone of the final, post-vocalic center glide in words like *Pa, hah,* which is characterized by ending up voiceless and with friction noise! All evidence, then points to one phoneme, /h/, with the characteristic pre- and post-vocalic allophones we have been discussing.

In forming complex nuclei, each of the three semi-vowels can follow each of the nine simple vowels to give a total of twenty-seven, and in Table III, below, the most frequently occurring complex nuclei have been circled. Of the circled nuclei, /iy/, /ey/, /ay/, /uw/, /ow/ and /aw/ have already been exemplified,

TABLE III

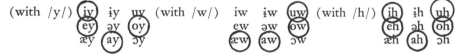

(with /y/) iy iy uy (with /w/) iw iw uw (with /h/) ih ih uh
ey əy oy ew əw ow eh əh oh
æy ay ɔy æw aw ɔw æh ah ɔh

and /oy/ occurs most frequently in *boy, toy,* etc., while /æw/ occurs in *cow, now, out* in large numbers of dialects rather than /aw/, which is principally heard in northern Middle Western dialects close to the Canadian border. The words *paw* and *Pa* and others like them show /oh/ in contrast with /ah/ in the Central Atlantic Seaborad (C.A.S.), but /ɔh/ vs /ah/ in the northern Middle West (N.M.W.). In most Canadian dialects and in the northern United States west of Nebraska and the Dakotas, there is no contrast between *paw* and *Pa*, with /ah/ occurring in both words. In the C.A.S., /ih/ occurs before /r/ in *peer, fear,* etc., /uh/ before /r/ in *poor,* /oh/ before /r/ in *pour,* and /eh/ before /r/ in *pair*. Regularly in this dialect, complex nuclei with /h/ occur in monosyllabic words, when /r/ or /r/ plus a consonant follows a stressed vowel, so we hear *girl, first, fur; Carl, parsed, far,* as /gə́hrl/, /fə́hrst/, /fə́hr/; /káhrl/, /páhrst/, /fáhr/. In the case of dissyllabic words with /r/, /ah/ contrasts with /a/ in such pairs as *sari* /sáhriy/ vs *sorry* /sáriy/, and /a/ vs /ah/ furnishes the basis for the contrast in monosyllabic words with /m/ as *bomb* /bám/ vs. *balm* /báhm/. This simple vs complex nucleus contrast is also heard in *bother* /báðɨr/ vs *father* /fáhðɨr/, though *rather* may be pronounced with four different nuclei, two simple and two complex—/ráðɨr/, /rǽðɨr/, /ráhðɨr/, /rǽhðɨr/.

In contrast to the situation described above, /h/ almost never occurs before /r/ in N.M.W. dialects, and we hear /pír/, /púr/, /pór/, /pér/; /gɨ́rl/, /fɨ́rst/, /fɨ́r/; /kárl/, /párst/, /fár/; /sáriy/, /sáriy/. Also no simple vs complex nucleus distinction occurs in the other examples cited above, and we find /bám/ for both *bomb* and *balm*, and /báðɨr/ for *bother* and /fáðɨr/ for *father*. In fact, the only place /h/ *does* occur in these dialects is finally in such words as *paw* and *Pa*, /pɔ́h/ and /páh/, since a *stressed* vowel in English must be followed either by a consonant or a semi-vowel, though under *weak* stress any one of the nine simple vowels may occur finally, as, for example, in /síti/ rather than /sítiy/ for *city*, as heard in Great Britain and in many dialects in the southeast of the United States. In coastal New England, we find many speakers using complex nuclei with /y/ and /w/ followed by a syllable consisting of /ə/ in *peer*, /píyə/; *pair*, /péyə/; *poor*, /púwə/; *pour*, /pówə/, while Southern Coastal speakers frequently show /píhə/, /péhə/ /púhə/, /póhə/ for these words, with /póhə/ often occuring for both *poor* and *pour*. The dialects of quite an extended area in the southeastern part of the country, ranging from northwestern Mississippi through southern and eastern Tennessee (Chattanooga) including northwestern and north central Georgia (Carrollton-Atlanta), show interesting pronunciations of *fire* and *pyre,* with the four variant forms /fáyɨr/, /fáyə/ /fǽyə/, /fǽhə/ having been recorded for the first word of the pair, and /páhɨr/, /pǽhr/, /páhə/ for the second. Quite often, more than one of the above forms might occur in the same idiolect. In Philadelphia, Baltimore and Washington *fire* and *pyre* rhyme, being heard as /fáyɨr/, /páyɨr/; /fáyə/, /páyə/; or /fáhr/, /páhr/, with the last pair of pronunciations often regarded as non-standard. In these cities standard speakers often use either /áhr/ or /ǽwɨr/ for *our*, but only /ǽwɨr/ for *hour*, while non-standard speakers may use /ǽhr/ for both *our* and *hour*, /pǽhr/ for *power* vs the standard speaker's /pǽwɨr/, etc. Also standard and non-standard speakers alike contrast *can* (v.), /kǽn/ and *can* (n.), /kéhn/; *bomb*, /bám/ and *balm*, /báhm/; *hurry*, /hɨ́riy/ and *furry*, /fɨ́hriy/.

When we take these dialect variations into account and note further such strikingly different pronunciations as /láwst/ (northern Alabama), /lóhst/ (New York City) /lɔ́st/ (Chicago), for *lost*; /háws/ (Cleveland), /hǽws/, (Philadelphia), /hɔ́ws/ (Toronto), /héws/ (Richmond), for *house*, and /mériy/ (Milwaukee), /mǽriy/ (Gary, Indiana), /méhriy/ (Baltimore), /méyriy/ (Charlottesville, Virginia), for *Mary*, it becomes apparent that there must be some way in which speakers of different dialects immediately sense the equivalence between the occurrences of quite different phonemes in what they recognize to be the same words. The level at which this *calibration* is achieved is the level of the *morphophone*, and within this level there are to be seen different gradations, so to speak, at which speakers differentiate between contrast and equivalence. From one point of view, the morphophone can be seen as a sort of "holding company" or "super family" of different phonemes which are *non-contrasting in the same words*, but, from another point of view, it must be seen as a *unit* of the language *as a whole* which, *as a unit*, furnishes the basis for "higher order" or "higher level" *contrasts*. To put it in technical language, the morphophone is the *basic unit* of the morpheme, and morphophones are *expressed* by phonemes. Thus phonemes remain the *ultimate* units of everything that gets said in a language, but different phonemes and phoneme sequences may be assigned to the same morphophone units. Again, like the phoneme, the morphophone is more than a "mere construct of the analyst," since its "psychological reality" is amply demonstrated when we realize how quickly and unerringly speakers are enabled to suppress, so to speak, the contrast-making aspect of different phonemes in favor of reacting to these as non-contrasting expressions of higher level, language-wide contrast-making units. For example, the words *house* and *out* contain the same morphophone unit for *all* speakers of *all* dialects of English though the unit may be expressed by four different non-contrasting phoneme sequences or *variants*—e.g. /áw/, /ǽw/, /ɔ́w/, /éw/. We can symbolize this unit by aw. and note how it contrasts with another unit, heard in *gross* and *oat*, which will be represented by ow. This latter unit is expressed as /ɔ́w/ in Philadelphia, as /éw/ by some speakers in London, and as /ów/ generally in the northern United States and in Canada. Thus /ɔ́w/ and /éw/ are members, or variants, of *two* contrasting morphophone units, aw. and ow., with /ɔ́w/ of ow. occurring in *oat* in Philadelphia and contrasting in that dialect with /ǽw/ of aw. in *out*, while in Toronto, /ɔ́w/ is the regular expression of aw. in *out*, and *oat* contrasts there through the /ów/ expression of ow. In London all three expressions, or *variants*, of ow. occur, so we hear /ówt/, /ɔ́wt/, /éwt/ for *oat* in contrast with either /áw/ or /ǽw/ of aw. in *out*. Thus, though there may be *overlapping variants* of morphophone units, each dialect always preserves the *morphophonic* contrast, and each morphophone unit always has at least one variant that it shares with no other unit, as is the case with /ów/ of ow. and with /áw/ and /ǽw/ of aw. Our present-day writing system is based principally on the graphic representation of morphophone units, not of phonemes, and hence the digraphs <ou> and <oa> stand, respectively, for the units aw. and ow., and each reader responds to the graphic symbolizations by giving the phonemic expressions of the morphophones which are characteristic of his dialect or idiolect.

In order to arrive at the inventory of *vocalic* morphophone units for English as a whole, it is convenient to start with a single idiolect and to elicit, first, contrasts made by vowel phonemes in what is termed *pristine environment*; that is, where the contrasting vowels occur in monosyllabic words ending in [-pˀ], [-tˀ], [-kˀ]; /-p/, /-t/, /-k/. Such an environment assures us that the phonetic *actualization* of each vowel nucleus is one that is unaffected in any way, but particularly in regard to length, by the following consonants. Contrasts occurring in pristine enviroment in any idiolect are termed *primary contrasts*, and each such contrast must be accounted for by a separate morphophone unit in the inventory for the language as a whole. The phonemes through which these contrasts are made in each dialect are called the *principal variants* (of the morphophone units) for that dialect, and all the principal variants occurring in all the dialects constitute the *pure variants* of each morphophone unit of the language. Thus /áw/, /ǽw/, /ɔ́w/, /éw/ constitute the pure variants of the unit aw., since each of these expressions occurs as the principal variant of the unit in one or more dialects.

With my own idiolect as a basis, fifteen vocalic morphophone units are established for the language as shown in Table IV, where the units are numbered as well as symbolized by letters followed by periods in order to minimize the confusion that may arise between phoneme and morphophone.

TABLE IV

1. i. /pít/ 'pit'		4. u. /pút/ 'put'
2. e. /pét/ 'pet'	7. ə. /pɔ́t/ 'putt'	5. o. /kóht/ 'caught'
3. æ. /pǽt/ 'pat'		6. a. /pát/ 'pot'
- - - - - - - - - -	- - - - - - - - - - -	- - - - - - - - - - -
8. iy. /píyt/ 'peat'	14. yuw. /byúwt/ 'beaut'	11. uw. /búwt/ 'boot'
9. ey. /péyt/ 'pate'	15. oy. /hóyt/ 'Hoyt'	12. ow. /bówt/ 'boat'
10. ay. /báyt/ 'bite'		13. aw. /bǽwt/ 'bout'

The dotted line separates the units that will be termed *short* from those that will be designated *long*, the difference being that the long units are always and only expressed by complex phonemic nuclei, though short units may be expressed by *either* complex or simple nuclei. The principal variant /óh/ in my dialect for the short unit o. (5.) is an example, as is the Western New Yorker's principal variant /éh/ of æ. (3.), where we hear /héht/, /béhk/ for *hat* and *back*, rather than the Baltimorean's (/hǽt/, /bǽk/, etc. Also in my dialect, /ɨ/ and /ɔ/ never occur in pristine environment and thus never form the basis of primary contrasts, though /ɨ/ frequently occurs in free variations with /í/ as in /jɨ́st/, /jíst/ 'gist', and with /ə/ as in /jɨ́st/, /jə́st/ 'just' (adv.). Similarly, /ɔ/ (with *tertiary* rather than *primary* stress) occurs in free variation in the idiolect with /òh/ in 'alcohol'— /ǽlkəhɔl/, /ǽlkə-hòhl/, and with /à/ in 'Nujol'—/núwjɔl/, núwjàl/. This leads to the conclusion that here /ɨ/ and /ɔ/ are each variants of *two* morphophone units, with /ɨ/ being assignable to both 1. i. and 7. ə., and /ɔ/ to both 5.o. and 6.a. The contrasts made in such situations are termed *tertiary contrasts*, the criteria for such contrasts being 1) that the phonemes making the contrasts never occur in pristine environment and hence never constitute principal variants, 2) that the phonemes making the contrasts be assignable *within the idiolect* to two morphophone units, and 3) that the phonemes be in free variation with those constituting the principal variants of each of the two units.

No dialect of English has more than fifteen vocalic morphophone units in pristine environment to which the thirty-six phonemic nuclei in the overall pattern of the language are to be assigned, and some have only fourteen units. These are the dialects that make no contrast between *cot* and *caught*, etc., but show either /ɔ/ in free variation with /ɔh/ in *both* sets of words (N.E.), or /á/ freely varying with /áh/ in both (Canada). In these cases, the different phonemic expressions are analyzed as the principal *co-variants* of the same unit, 5.o. But in many Canadian dialects, e.g. Toronto, an obligatory contrast occurs between /á(h)/ and /óh/ when /r/ follows, so that we hear /á(h)r/ in *are*, *far*, *car*, etc., vs /óhr/ in *or*, *for*, *core*, etc. Quite similarly, many speakers in and around Boston contrast /ɔ/ and /óh/ when /n/ follows, as in *John* /jɔn/ vs *on* /óhn/. These contrasts are as binding on the speakers as are the primary contrasts of the dialects, but since they do not occur in pristine environment, they are termed *secondary contrasts*. Since in the cases just examined /óh/ expressed the contrasts in both dialects, we will symbolize this secondary contrast-making unit oh. and number it 5ᵃ.

In the United States and Canada, only the dialects in the northern and southern Central Atlantic Seaboard regularly show a secondary contrast between 3.æ. and a second secondary unit which we will write eh. (3.ᵃ). This secondary unit is usually expressed /éh/ below the fortieth parallel and /ǽh/ above that line, so that we hear /kǽn/ *can* (v.), with æ. vs. /kéhn/, /kǽehn/ *can* (n.) with eh.; /hǽv/ *have*, with æ. vs. /héhv/, /hǽehv/ *halve*, with eh., etc. In Great Britain, the so-called "broad *a*" is to be taken as the /ah/ expression of this unit as heard in /páhs/ *pass*, /gráhs/ *grass* vs. /gǽs/ *gas*, /mǽs/ *mass*, with æ. It is also in the C.A.S. that the third secondary unit, ah. (6ᵃ.), expressed as /áh/, is heard in contrast with /á/ of 6.a. Thus we have /bám/ *bomb* (6.a.) vs /báhm/ *balm* (6ᵃ. ah.), /kán/ *Conn* (6.a.) vs /káhn/ *Kahn* (6ᵃ. ah.), /sáriy/ *sorry* (6.a.) vs /sáhriy/ *sari* (6ᵃ. ah.), /báðɨr/ *bother* (6.a.) vs /fáhðɨr/ *father* (6ᵃ. ah.). In these dialects, then /ǽ/ of æ. is in contrast with /á/ of a. and with /éh/, /ǽh/ of eh.; /á/ of a. is in contrast with /ǽ/ of æ. and /áh/ of ah.; and /éh/, /ǽ/ of eh. are in contrast with /áh/ of ah. In Great Britain, however, the /áh/, /ǽh/ of *balm, father*, etc. are not assigned to ah. but rather to er., since there is no contrast between /áh/, /ǽh/, on the one hand, and /éh/, on the other and, consequently, no basis for setting up the unit ah. in contrast to eh.

The phonemic nuclei we have been so far assigning to morphophone units and seeing as the expression of these units as they form primary, secondary, and tertiary contrasts are of a type we can call *free* or *pure variants*, since all of the contrasts occur in identical phonological surroundings. We have already noted, though, that between dialects and even *within* dialects, equivalent forms such as /fáyɨr/, /fáhr/ occur for *fire*, /púwə/, /púhr/ for *poor*;

that is, nuclei ending in /h/ calibrate with nuclei ending in /y/ or /w/. Taking both types of nuclei as expressions of the units ay. and uw., respectively, the nuclei ending with /h/ can be said to be variants *conditioned* by the following /r/. This kind of conditioning is called *smoothing*, and other examples of smoothing by /r/ are: /píhr/ *peer* (iy.), /péhr/ *pair* (ey.), /kyúhr/ *cure* (yuw.), /póhr/ *pour* (ow.), /áhr/, /ǽhr/ *our* (aw.). Smoothing also occurs before /l/, as in /péhl/ *pail* (ey.), /áhl/ *I'll* (ay.), /óhl/ *oil* (oy.), /púhl/ *pool* (uw.). In Ontario and in most other parts of Canada /ǽw/ is the conditioned variant of aw. when voiced stops or spirants follow, as in /lǽwd/ *loud*, /hǽwz/ *house* (v.) while, it will be remembered, /ɔ́w/ is the principal variant of aw. as heard in /ɔ́wt/, /hɔ́ws/ for *out, house*. A similar conditioning occurs in Tidewater Virginia, where one hears /lǽwd/ and /hǽwz/ beside /éwt/ and /héws/. In Canada /ɔ́y/ is the principal variant for ay. and, in a manner parallel to the conditioning by voiced stops and spirants of the variants of aw., one hears /áy/ of this unit when voiced consonants follow as /tɔ́yt/ *tight* vs. /táyd/ *tide*; /nɔ́ys/ *nice* vs. /sáyz/ *size*. A following /š/ contributes in some southern Middle Western dialects to the *lengthening* by the addition of /y/ to the expressions of the short vocalic units i., e., æ., u., o.—e.g. /fíyš/ *fish*, /méyš/ *mesh*, /ǽyš/ *ash*, /púyš/ *push*, /wóyš/ *wash*—and though expressed as complex nuclei, the forms are reacted to within the dialect as containing short, not long, vocalic units.[2] Following /d/ and /g/ in many Southern and "near Southern" dialects also lengthen the expressions of e. and as in /héyd/ *head*, /léyg/ *leg*, /bǽyg/ *bag*, and the voiceless spirants /s/, /f/ and the nasal /n/ lengthen the expression of æ. to /ǽy/ quite generally in the South East—/pǽys/ *pass*, /hǽyf/ *half*, /mǽy(ɨ)n/ *man*. In my dialect, since only /éh/ occurs before /nt/, /sp/, /st/, /sk/ as in *can't* /kéhnt/, *clasp* /kléhsp/, *past* /péhst/, *task* /téhsk/, the /éh/ is taken as a conditioned variant of 3.æ. rather than as the /éh/ expression of 3ª.eh. . A similar assignment is given the New Yorker's /ǽh/ and the Londoner's /áh/, since in those dialects, too, there are no /ǽ/ vs /ǽh/ or /áh/ occurrences when these consonants follow. The nucleus /éh/, then, is both a *principal* variant (as in Western New York) and a *conditioned* variant of 3.æ, and also one of the variants of 3ª.eh., as well as being the result of smoothing by /r/ of unit 9.ey., as in /péhr/ *pair*, /méhriy/ *Mary*. Whenever and wherever it occurs, cultivated speakers are careful to avoid *actualizing* the nucleus by an overly raised, tensed and nasalized first segment, since such a diaphone seems to be universally frowned upon. In order to avoid the "inelegant" diaphone, some speakers "over-correct" to the amusing extent of even putting a "broad *a*" in *ham sandwich*, to give /háhm|sáhndwič/.

The systematic, non-contrasting, phonemically different but *equivalent* expressions we have been examining above as pure or conditioned variants of the same morphophone units constitute sub-morphophonic, *diaphonemic selections*, and a summary presentation of these with the eighteen vocalic morphophone units in the overall pattern of English—primary and secondary units; short and long—is given in Table V below.

TABLE V

VOCALIC MORPHOPHONE UNITS

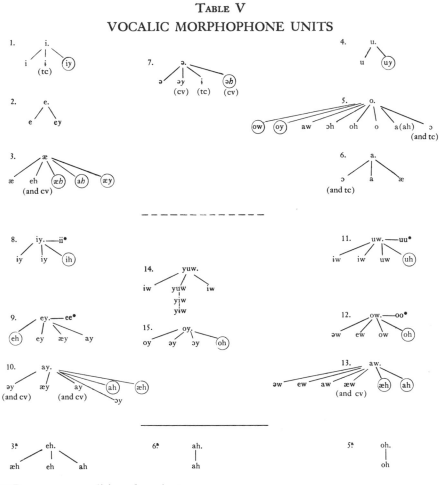

N.B.   cv = conditioned variant
         tc = tertiary contrast
         Phonemic variants which are circled are conditionėd variants only. Those which are uncircled are principal variants or form tertiary contrasts where indicated.

The principal variants so marked occur mainly in N.E. England. But dialects differ as well in having equivalents formed through the selection of different morphophone units *as units* which are non-contrasting in the same words. These correspondences are termed *diamorphophonic selections.* For example, if the same speaker pronounces *get* as /gít/, but everywhere else has the expected /é/ of e., as in /wét/ *wet,* /pép/ *pep,* /nék/ *neck,* we cannot analyze the /í/ in *get* as either a pure or conditioned variant of e., since it occurs in pristine environment, and since, quite obviously, the principal variant of e. in the dialect is /é/. Rather we must say that there is a *substitution* of morphophone i. for morphophone e. here, and that in the dialect there is an *interchange* between i. and e.. These morphophones are also in interchange in my dialect, but not in pristine environment, since I pronounce *milk* as /mélk/ but *silk*, *bilk*, etc., as /sílk/, /bílk/, etc. Here the substitution is in the reverse direction, with e. being substituted for i. There are seventeen such substitutions of short units for short units in the language, and such pairs as /krík/ beside /kríyk/, for *creek*, /kúp/ beside /kúwp/, for *coop* indicate another type of substitution, termed *shortening*, where the short units are substituted for long units. In the two examples just given, i. was substituted for iy. (i.←iy.) and u. for uw. (u. ← uw.). Further examples of shortening are: e. ← ey. /əgén/, /əgéyn/ *again*; o. ← ow. /hól/ vs /hówl/ *whole*; e. ← iy. /lévɨr/ vs /líyvɨr/ *lever*; æ. ← ey. /ræsɨn/ vs /réysɨn/ *ration*. i. ← ay. /dínɨstiy/ vs /dáynɨstiy/ *dynasty*; a. ←ow. /prágrɨs/ vs /prówgrɨs/ *progress*; ə. ← ow. /kəvirt/ vs /kówvɨrt/ *covert*. Finally, there are substitutions between long units—ay. ← iy. /áyðɨr/ vs. /íyðɨr/ *either*; aw. ← uw. /ráwt/ vs. /rúwt/ *route*; iy. ← ey. /dríyn/ vs. /dréyn/ *drain*; uw. ← ow. /lúwm/ vs. /lówm/ *loam*; ow. ← uw. /póhr/ vs. /púhr/ *poor*; /móhr/ vs. /múhr/ *Moore*; uw. ← yuw. /núw/ vs. /nyúw/ *new*; ay. ← oy. /ráyl/ vs. /róyl/ *roil*.[3]

At the level of the morphophone, there are twenty-one consonantal and three semi-vocalic units which are expressed by the twenty-one consonant phonemes and the three semi-vowels although there is not complete one-to-one correspondence between phoneme and morphophone. For instance, the /š/ in *fish* and the initial and final /č/'s in *church* are assigned to the š. and č. morphophones, respectively, but the /š/ in *issue* and the /č/ in *pasture* are taken as *portmanteau* phonemes which are the results of the coalescence of /-sy-/ and /-ty-/, respectively, since careful (or overly careful) speakers pronounce these words /ísyùw/ and /pǽstyùwr/ rather than /íšuw/ and /pǽsčɨr/ or /péhsčɨr/. The morphophone structuring of the items is, respectively, i.s.yuw. and p.æ.s.t.yuw.r. Like the vocalic morphophones, consonantal morphophones also show substitutions. These are of two major types, *voiced-voiceless pairs* and *homarticulate pairs*. Examples of *voiced-voiceless* pairs are: ð. ← θ. in *with*, v. ← f. in *effervescent*, z. ← s. in *blouse*, d. ← t. in *congratulate*, g. ← k. in *exit*; examples of *homarticulate pairs* are: *stops* t. ← k. in /bǽt/ for /bǽk/, *back*; *spirant-stop* θ. ← t. in /dráwθ/, /dráwt/, *drouth*, *drought*; d. ← ð. in /díyz/ for /ðíyz/, *these*; d. ← z. in /bídnis/ for /bíznis/, *business*; t. ← θ. in /wít/ for /wíθ/, *with*; b. ← v. in /gəbmɨnt/ for /gəvmɨnt/, *government*; *spirants* f. ← θ. in /nóhrf/ for /nóhrθ/, *north*; θ. ← f. in /tróhθ/ for /tróhf/, *trough*; š. ← s. in /nɨgówšiyèyt/ for /nɨgówsiyèyt/, *negotiate*; *nasals* n. ← m. in /kənfɨrt/ for /kəmfɨrt/, *comfort*; m. ← n. in /sébɨm/ for /sévɨn/, *seven*; *nasal-lateral* l. ← n. in /čímliy/ for /čímniy/, *chimney*; *spirant-affricate* č. ← s. in /rénč/ for /réns, ríns/, *rinse*.[4]

Two other kinds of systematic morphophonic *alternations* occur, *alterations* and *replacements*. Since alterations[5], limited to the vocalics, as in *divine*, *divinity*, *extreme*, *extremity*, are binding on all speakers of the language, they need not detain us, but replacements are of considerable interest to the student of dialects.[6] Both vocalic and consonantal replacements occur in the environment of morphophones seen in *paradigmatic* and *derivational* morphemes. For example, in *freeze, frozen*, iy. is replaced by ow. (iy. → ow.) in the environment of -n., expressed as /in/, of the past participle suffix, and in *foul, filth*, aw. → i. in the environment of -θ.-, a noun-deriving ending. In such cases as *ride, rode*, the linguist posits a *zero morphophone*, Ø., as constituting the ending of the past tense, and the ay. → ow. replacement is seen going on in that environment. Non-standard speakers throughout the English-speaking world quite frequently fail to show the ə. →ey. replacement for the past tense of *come*, using /kəm/ for both present and past tenses. In *knife, knives*, we have a replacement of f. by v. in the environment of -z. of the plural ending, and this consonantal replacement occurs almost everywhere English is spoken. The s. → z. replacement in *house, houses*, however, does not occur in the speech of large numbers of speakers in metropolitan areas along the eastern Great Lakes. Though in *louse, lousy*, nearly all speakers have s. → z. in the environment of the adjective-deriving ending, -y.-, few have the replacement in *mousey*, the adjective derived from *mouse*. This s. → z. replacement is almost universal in the adjective *greasy*, from *grease* (n.), in dialects east of the Mississippi and south of the parallel 40°, and almost totally absent north of this line. Similarly, the s. → z. replacement occurs in the speech of southerners in the environment of the -Ø.- of the verb-deriving ending in *grease* from the noun *grease*, and we hear /gríyz/ rather than /gríys/. It is the southerner, too, who has the z. ← s. *substitution* in *blouse*, but this alternation is distinguished from the homophonous *replacement* heard in *grease* (v.), since *blouse*, the *name form* or "subject case" of a noun, has no ending, paradigmatic or derivational, occurring after it.

Just as the "*grease, greasy* line" forms the basis of a clear-cut division between northern and southern speakers, so the famous triad *merry, marry, Mary* distinguishes speakers east of the crests of the Allegheny Mountains from those to the west. In the southern C.A.S., for example, we hear *merry* as /mériy/ of m.é.r.y., *mary* as /mǽriy/ of m.ǽ.r.y., and *Mary* as /méhriy/ of m.éy.r.y. In Chicago, all three words show /mériy/ of m.é.r.y.. To account for the vowel in *marry*, we see the substitution e. ← æ., and *Mary* shows the substitution (shortening) e. ← ey.. In Gary, Indiana, many speakers have the shortening æ. ← ey. in *Mary*, to give /mǽriy/, and some older generation speakers in Virginia and New England still have /éy/ of the ey. in *Mary*, *vary, fairy*, etc. In Philadelphia many speakers show the substitution ə. ← e. in *merry*, to give /məriy/, and speakers in Buffalo give either /mériy/ *or* /méhriy/ for each of the three words. Their pronunciations of the three words as /mériy/ are accounted for as were the occurrences in the Chicago dialect, but the occurrences with /éh/ require separate explanations. Starting with /méhriy/ for *Mary*, we can assume the smoothing of ey., as is the case with the C.A.S. speakers, while the /éh/ in the pronunciation of *marry* can be taken simply as an occurrence of the principal variant of the morphophone æ., which is regularly /éh/ for this dialect. Finally, the /éh/ in *merry* can be seen as a lengthened expression of e., since in this dialect, before /r/, /h/ varies freely with its absence, as in /sáriy/, /sáhriy/; /sɔ́riy/, /sɔ́hriy/, all for *sorry*, and with /sáriy/ and /sáhriy/ occurring as well for *sari*.⁷

The two levels of phoneme and morphophone, finally, offer a far more refined and objective method of distinguishing between *dialect* and *language*, that is, of designating two closely related speech forms as dialects of a single language or as constituting separate languages. The criterion of mutual intelligibility, which heretofore has been the one principally invoked in making these decisions, is quite obviously not accurate enough when we see speakers of different languages "understanding" each other and find speakers of one dialect of a language asserting another dialect of the same language to be incomprehensible. Criteria based on similarity and difference in vocabulary, so often made the major basis for dialect differentiation, can now be correlated with a far more accurate criterion based on the selection and expression of objectively established morphophone units. If the basis for calibration between seemingly disparate forms is clearly demonstrable, we are dealing with dialects of the same language, but if no such calibration can be achieved, the evidence would indicate two or more separate languages. Therefore, we now have at hand the knowledge necessary for a more complete understanding of regional dialects and those correlated with socioeconomic factors and to see more clearly the relationships between them. Such knowledge cannot help but be of immeasurable assistance in understanding the nature of numerous social problems stemming from language difference.

Notes

1. Since writing this, I have become convinced that it is more accurate to assign the /ŋ/ phones occurring in any dialect to the /ŋ/ phoneme in the phonemic inventory of the language as a whole, and to handle the differences noted between dialects A and B at the *morphophonic* rather than at the phonemic level. So seen, dialect B does not lack an /ŋ/ phoneme, but an ŋ. morphophone. Thus dialect A's *singer* is /síŋir/ of s.í.ŋ.r., from *sing*, /síŋ/ of s.í.ŋ. in contrast with *finger*, /fíŋgir/ of f.í.ŋ.g.r.; *longer* (noun) is /lóhŋir/ of l.ó.ŋ.r. from *long* (v.), /lóhŋ/ of l.ó.ŋ. in contrast with *longer* (adj.) /lóhŋgir/ of l.ó.ŋ.g.r. from *long* (adj.), /lóhŋ/ of l.ó.ŋ.. Dialect B, however, with no ŋ. morphophone, shows /síng/ of s.í.n.g. for *sing* and /lóhng/ of l.ó.n.g. for both *long* (v.) and *long* (adj.). Consequently, no contrast will occur between *longer* (n.) and *longer* (adj.), with both showing /lóhngir/ of l.ó.n.g.r. and medially only /-ng-/ of -n.g.- will occur in both *singer* and *finger* as /síngir/ and /fíngir/. The /ŋ/ phoneme of dialect B is thus seen as a *conditioned expression* of the morphophone n., occurring as the result of the following velar nasal stop, since all speakers of English must have a velar nasal

when a velar stop follows. Therefore, both dialects A and B show /íŋk/ and θíŋk/ for *ink* and *think*, and for *both* dialects the /ŋ/ is taken as a conditioned expression of the morphophone n., even though dialect A has a contrast-making ŋ. morphophone. Conditioned expressions are seen as different from *conditioned variants* (p. 171) since the latter are not binding even on all speakers of a dialect, whereas the former are binding on all speakers of the language.

2. In such cases, the /y/ is said to be *excrescent*, the term being used for non-morphophonically based phonemes that are binding on speakers of a dialect, but not on all speakers of a language. Excrescent phonemes are underlined in writing, italicized in print.

3. For a more complete tabulation, see my monograph, *English Morphophonics: Implications for the Teaching of Literacy*, Monograph No. 10, New York State English Council, 1968.

4. *English Morphophonics*, pp. 57–8.

5. *Ibid.*, pp. 74–7. I now see such cases as opa*que*, opa*c*ity as the result of morphophonic changes in *French*, not English.

6. *Ibid.*, 78–85.

7. Where *within* a dialect a non-morphophonically based phoneme varies freely with its absence, it is said to be *epenthetic*, and is enclosed in parentheses—e.g. /sá(h)riy/.

SHORTENING THE LONG CONVERSATIONAL DIALECT INTERVIEW

WILLIAM R. VAN RIPER
Louisiana State University

In the course of the fieldwork for the Linguistic Atlas of Oklahoma[1], a method of interviewing was developed which shortened the time required of the informant for a lengthy interview slanted toward conversational responses, yet which did not slight the interview by reducing the number of items or by hurrying the informant. The method is an adaptation of that used for the Linguistic Atlas of the United States and Canada as taught by Hans Kurath and Raven I. McDavid, Jr. It places great emphasis on conversation in the early part of the interview and relies upon a tape recorder to pick up the informant's responses. It is a method which is particularly useful when the informant is used only in sessions of two or three hours each and when the fieldworker has sufficient time to work with the tape recording after each session.

From the outset of the Oklahoma Atlas project it was decided that every interview would be recorded not only in alphabetical phonetic notation but also with a tape recorder. Informants were to be interviewed on their home ground, interviews were to be as informal as possible, and responses were to be secured for approximately one thousand worksheet items. The questioning and conversation which brought forth and included the responses, all extraneous noise, conversations, and what-have-you were to be taped. Only things which were personal and private or which might be either embarrassing or derogatory to the informant were to be avoided in taping in their entirety. Although there was some apprehension at first that prospective informants might refuse to be interviewed in the presence of a tape recorder, these fears probably had little basis in fact.[2]

The interviewing method was to be the one common to Atlas interviews which sort the worksheet items by subject matter and which aim at conversational style.[3] Whenever possible, the informant was encouraged to talk about experiences associated with the general areas of concern—illnesses, work, relationships with other people, leisure activities, childhood recollections, and other things as they applied. It was the primary job of the field-worker during the interview to direct the conversation so that useful responses would be forthcoming and to record these responses. The tape recording was intended to be auxiliary to the phonetic notation made by the fieldworker during the interview. Its primary purposes were to provide a check on the interviewing technique of the fieldworker and on the accuracy of his alphabetical recording, to furnish a record of speech features which are difficult to transcribe in rapid, connected speech, and to add the context in which the informant gave his responses. The tapes were to be preserved so that each interview would be on record in totality.

After the first few interviews it became apparent that the tape recording could provide more assistance than was being asked of it. Although it could not duplicate the interview by giving a visual image of such things as lip rounding and gesture, it did provide a surprisingly accurate record of the interview.[4] Usually the microphone was closer to the informant's lips than was the ear of the fieldworker, with the consequence that sound of slight volume was recorded on the tape whereas it was frequently missed by the fieldworker. Of greater significance, however, were the number of pertinent responses which sometimes came in bursts so rapid that the fieldworker would be hard pressed to record any great number of them accurately in phonetic notation, and the fact that some responses slipped by unrecorded. Not only was the informant giving more responses than the fieldworker was recording, he was also giving more than the fieldworker was noticing.[5] It was apparent that when the fieldworker tried to record more than several of these in succession, he ran the risk of allowing the interview to get away from him: whereas the informant had been talking about something which he found interesting and informative, his interest frequently waned if the fieldworker busied himself with pencil and paper and did not participate actively in the conversation about these matters, or else it took another direction which would lead only circuitously to other items on the topic toward which the fieldworker had been pointing the conversation.

A decision was made to change the interviewing technique for those interviews in which the informant would be available for only two or three hours at a session and to keep the interview flowing smoothly even if this meant that the fieldworker might not have time to write down all the responses which he recognized. If he was unable to write down the response accurately, he was to make a check beside the item in the worksheets so that he would be reminded that he had a response for it, and if there were no nearby indication of the location of the response on the tape, then he was to jot down the number on the recorder's digital counter which corresponded to this portion of the tape. Thus the response could be located, played back, and entered in the worksheets in phonetic notation after the day's interviewing.[6]

After more interviews had been made and more experience gained, this technique was extended to include responses for items which might be a considerable distance ahead in the worksheets. The fieldworker was to jot these down as quickly as he could in the margin of the page upon which he was working and enter the counter number. If he could use phonetic notation it was to his advantage, but if the interview was moving rapidly he was to use any notation possible and add the phonetic notation after the interviewing session.

The final revision of the technique came about rather late in the course of the interviewing. By this time the fieldworker was thoroughly familiar with his recording equipment, he had the worksheet items and their locations firmly in mind, and he had a good understanding of where responses for each of them could normally be found most easily in the course of visiting through the interview with the informant. While the fieldworker directed the conversation, he noted responses as they appeared, using phonetic notation whenever possible, but he placed more reliance upon the tape recording than he had in earlier interviews. To secure the maximum number of conversational responses, he encouraged the informant to talk, and to talk about things pertinent to the interview. He did not want the informant at this point to regard the interview as mainly a question and answer procedure. Although the fieldworker asked questions to clarify some of the informant's responses as they went along, he did not interrupt a conversation to elicit a response for the next item on the worksheet, but instead passed it by, marking it to indicate an omission. The response for the omitted item would then be added either during or after the present session, or else after the remaining pages of the workbook had been filled.

The interviewing process went like this.

After the fieldworker had located a suitable informant, explained the purpose of the study, requested permission to use a tape recorder, and secured consent to an interview which would take place in several sessions of several hours each, the fieldworker could then set up his recording equipment and proceed with the interview.

The tape recorder was placed on the floor beside the fieldworker, but to the side away from the informant in a position which would permit the fieldworker to see the counter numbers readily while still not making the presence of the machine conspicuous. The microphone on its wooden and cork pedestal was usually placed between and slightly in front of the informant and the fieldworker, either on the fieldworker's briefcase or on a table or some other elevated object.[7] While he was setting up the equipment, the fieldworker chatted about the function of the parts and the location of the microphone, turned on the machine, and kept up his casual conversation. Informants generally were silent through all of this, so the fieldworker would ask a direct question to elicit a reply, and while the informant answered he would check the signal strength on his recorder and adjust the volume so that the informant's voice would be recorded clearly. Then he would turn away from the recorder, face the informant, and begin to visit with him about the locality, his residence, his occupation, and other things relevant to the interview. In the early part of the interview, he attempted to maneuver the conversation so that the informant would talk about various subjects dealing with worksheet items, intruding with direct questions only to stimulate or steer the conversation, or else to gather further information about certain responses. He made every effort to encourage the informant to talk, and he worked to direct this into the most useful channels.

The fieldworker had to be constantly alert for the responses which he was seeking, since these would not occur in the order in which they appeared in his worksheets. When he identified one, he either entered it in its proper place on the page before him, or he made note of it in the margin of the worksheet so that it could be entered on the appropriate page later. He also kept this response in mind so that he would not spend time trying to elicit it again if it was called for in the worksheets before the interviewing session had ended. If the response occurred more than a short time after he had had occasion to write down the number on the digital counter, he wrote down the number which appeared during the response.

After each session with the informant, the fieldworker not only followed the normal procedure of reviewing his worksheet entries, but he also worked with the tape which had been recorded at the last session. After he had left the informant, he transferred the marginal notations to their proper places in the worksheets, entering the cross reference to the page on which the response had first been entered, and on that page a cross reference to the page where the item was called for in the worksheets. It was important to enter the response in its proper place before the next interviewing session so that the fieldworker would not spend time trying to elicit it again; it was equally important to cross-list the page on which the response was first noted so that it could easily be found at a particular place on a particular reel of tape. Then the fieldworker played back the tape, listening carefully for responses which he had missed during the interview and entering them in phonetic notation in their proper places in the worksheets. He also entered the phonetic notation for those responses which he had noted in the page margins during the interview, and in addition compared suspicious transcriptions made during the session with what he heard on the tape, being alert for any discrepancies which he might wish to investigate at the next interviewing session.

In the following session or sessions, the fieldworker made greater use of indirect and then direct questioning as the stock of items awaiting responses became smaller. Finally, when the informant and the fieldworker had worked through the worksheets, the fieldworker turned back to the first page and then leafed through the worksheets again, eliciting responses for only those items which were still marked to indicate that a response had not been noted for them. If the fieldworker had made a list of these after every session and then had worked through the list during the next session, his task at this point was that much easier. When he came to the end of the worksheets the second time, he checked the informant vita to make certain that it was complete and in accord with what he had heard in the interview, closed the workbook, and told the informant that they had finished it. However, he left the recorder on and continued the conversation for a few minutes so that he would have a record of the informant's reaction to having finished and an indication of whether the informant's speech changed in any distinguishable respects after the workbook had been closed and the interviewing obligation presumably met. If the informant had been reserved and careful with his speech during the interview, it generally became apparent at this point when the informant relaxed, lowered his guard, and changed his linguistic style or code.

This approach generally has worked best when the interviewing sessions have been relatively short, between two and three hours, but the length depends upon the informant's time and the fieldworker's ability during the session to remember what responses the informant has already given. If he cannot keep these in mind, he cannot direct the conversation most effectively and he may waste time. Then, too, the yield of pertinent responses from the informant's directed conversation is greatest in the early part of the interview when there are still many responses to be recorded and while the fieldworker can most easily recall which ones he has already heard. As responses are added and the workbook fills, the emphasis shifts and he concentrates more on specific items for which he still needs responses. Eventually, he will resort to indirect and then direct questioning to complete the interview.

This method has proven useful in reducing the amount of time required of informants under certain conditions, while at the same time yielding a large number of conversational responses, but these advantages are gained at the cost of placing an added burden upon the fieldworker. For the informant, the interviewing session consists only of that time during which he is conversing in the fieldworker's presence, but for the fieldworker, the time spent personally with the informant is only a small part of the interviewing total. The hardest work comes afterward when the tape must be examined for missed responses and checked for omitted transcriptions. The fieldworker may derive a greater amount of pleasure from an interview with an informant who can give as much time as the fieldworker desires for leisurely sessions, who will give natural responses systematically, and who will allow them to be written down unhurriedly. Unfortunately, not all dialect interviews can be conducted under such circumstances.

Notes

1. Fieldwork for fifty interviews began in 1960 and was completed in 1963. The work was supported by grants from the Oklahoma State University Research Foundation.

2. Since one of the requirements for an informant was that he would allow the interview to be recorded on tape, only likely candidates were approached. Consequently, there is little evidence of how the use of a tape recorder actually did limit the choice of informants. Of those who initially consented, only three refused to continue after the first session—two because they "saw no use to it" and one, in a hilly region of poor soil and small agriculture, because the fieldworker appeared to show too much interest in what crops were grown, especially corn.

The reason offered for most of the refusals to participate was that the interview would take too much time, but as the interviewing method discussed here developed, the fieldworker could ask for less time from busy prospective informants and as a result the number of refusals for this reason decreased.

3. Hans Kurath and others, *Handbook of the Linguistic Geography of New England* (Providence, R.I., 1939), on pages 48–50 presents a list of the instructions for field practice given to the fieldworkers of the *Linguistic Atlas of New England*, and on pages 147–148 discusses the arrangement of the items on the worksheets used for that project and the practices of the fieldworkers in regard to this arrangement.

4. Rex Wilson, in 1956, as a result of fieldwork done in Canada, pointed out that the tape recorder could be a valuable tool to the fieldworker by allowing him more opportunity to concentrate on the interviewing procedure itself and thereby reduce the amount of "dead" time during the interview. The fieldwork for the Linguistic Atlas of Oklahoma has only confirmed his observation. See his "The Implications of Tape Recording in the Field of Dialect Geography," *Journal of the Canadian Lingiustic Association* II, i (1956), 17–21.

5. Fieldworkers conducting Atlas-type interviews have long made good use of the unsolicited responses which are given by the informant in conversation. Kurath, *Handbook*, p. 147, calls attention to the "inevitably recurring verb forms, adverbs, conjunctions, exclamations and idioms" and makes the point that these can be observed while the informant is off guard. Raven I. McDavid, Jr., in "Tape Recording in Dialect Geography: A Cautionary Note," *Journal of the Canadian Linguistic Association* III, i (1957), 3–8, points out, among other things, the tape recorder's especial merit in picking up such forms from the informant's conversation.

One informant for the Oklahoma Atlas used the following responses, all called for in the worksheets, in a period of thirty-five seconds: *bottom* (land), *creek*, *rock, water, mother, carry, kettle, washing, wash, bushes*, and *things*. The fieldworker who could record all of these accurately in phonetic notation while still keeping the interview moving smoothly would have to be exceptionally talented and alert.

6. Relying upon the tape recorder to make the initial record involves an obvious risk. If for any reason the informant's responses are not recorded or are not recorded clearly, that portion of the interview will have been wasted. If the portion is extensive, the informant may refuse to repeat that part or even refuse to continue the inteview. At the very least, time is lost.

7. This position served adequately with the equipment used on this project. Other investigators, placing different emphasis on such things as the amount of time necessary to prepare the informant for the interview, achievement of the best possible clarity and quality of recorded sound, or the naturalness of the informant in the situation, may use different positions. Eberhard Zwirner in "A Guide to Linguistic Tape Recording," *New Trends in Linguistic Research*, Council for Cultural Co-operation of the Council of Europe (Strasbourg, 1963), 9–47, on page 33 advocates placing the microphone "20–25 cm from the speaker's

mouth" to achieve the best reception. William J. Samarin in *Field Linguistics: A Guide to Linguistic Fieldwork* (New York, 1967), on page 99 suggests placing the microphone "around 8 inches from the speaker's mouth and about 4 to 6 inches down." The microphone was farther away from the Oklahoma informants, usually between two and three feet. While this position did not allow the clarity of one nearer the informant, it did usually permit some sort of partial concealment of the microphone so that it would not continue to call more attention to itself than was necessary. Nonetheless, one prospective informant did begin the interview by staring straight at the microphone and talking in his best declamatory style until he was stopped by the surprised fieldworker.

A lavalier microphone might be used successfully with some informants, although the time spent for them to become accustomed to wearing the microphone with its attached cord could possibly cancel the advantage that the equipment gives in reducing the time with an informant. Of course, the clarity of reception which such microphones might offer and the possibility of using two with a stereophonic recorder to permit the fieldworker and informant to have separate sound tracks, either of which could be reduced or increased in volume in playback, could make them highly attractive tools to use in an interview where time is not a consideration.

REGIONAL VERB FORMS IN SOUTHERN ENGLAND

WOLFGANG VIERECK
Johannes Gutenberg University (Mainz)

The important problem of the interrelationship between regional British and American English and of the origins of the latter has, because of lack of data, been tackled only sparingly in the past.[1] Since we are now fortunate in having available more evidence of twentieth-century British English dialects,[2] more studies can and, hopefully, will be launched in this wide area. We have chosen here the relatively small field of verb morphology within which, as the table below reveals, we had to limit ourselves again for practical reasons.[3] When in 1953 Atwood published his careful interpretative study of the verb forms in the Eastern United States, making use of the field records of the *Linguistic Atlas of New England* (published under the editorship of Hans Kurath between 1939 and 1943) and of the *Linguistic Atlas of the Middle and South Atlantic States* (now being published by Raven I. McDavid, Jr., as editor-in-chief), he wrote:

> Our knowledge of the present-day distribution of dialect features in England is far from complete, and our knowledge of Early Modern English dialects is extremely limited. To argue from present-day distribution that a certain form must have been brought to an American colony from a certain area of England is risky and neglects the possibility that many forms may have become obsolete in certain areas in the course of two or three hundred years. Such a study should be undertaken only after many cautions and much historical research, and preferably only after a complete survey of England on Linguistic Atlas lines.[4]

With Lowman's material and the *Basic Material* of the *Survey of English Dialects* [*SED*] being accessible now, much has been done to increase our knowledge of the dissemination of modern dialectal features in England. Yet Atwood's plea for the need for historical research—linguistic and emigratory—can only be repeated. Although beginnings have been made, no doubt much remains to be done here, both in England and the United States, before we reach firm conclusions in the problem concerning us.

The following table shows, in alphabetical order, all past tense and past participle forms of verbs occurring in Eugen Dieth and Harold Orton, *A Questionnaire for a Linguistic Atlas of England* (Leeds, 1952, rev.ed.1962), in G. S. Lowman, Jr., and Hans Kurath, *Worksheets for Southern England* (1937), and in Atwood's study. Auxiliaries have not been included in the table. It gives a complete picture of what can presently be done in the field of comparative verb morphology. From this it follows that verbs occurring only in the *Worksheets* used in the American Atlas, i.e. in Atwood's study, and not in either the Dieth-Orton *Questionnaire* or the Lowman-Kurath *Worksheets* have been excluded from this list.[5]

Dieth-Orton *Questionnaire* (references are to the numbering in the *Questionnaire* and the *Worksheets*)	Lowman-Kurath *Worksheets*	Atwood (numbers refer to pages)
ate VI.5.11	ate 28.2	ate 12–13; Fig. 9
began VII.6.23	began 53.5	began 6, 42
– –	bitten 19.4	bitten 6
broken IX.3.5	– –	broken 7, 41, 43
– –	brought 15.5	brought 7, 42
caught IX.3.8	caught 52.3	caught 8, 38, 41–42; Fig. 4
came IX.3.4	came 53.7	came 9
– –	climbed 50.1	climbed 3,8–9;Fig.5
– –	dived 49.6	dived 9,41; Fig.6
– –	drank 28.6	drank 10–11; Fig.7
– –	dreamed 50.6	dreamed 10,41,44
– –	drove 6.5	drove 11–12; Fig.8
– –	drowned 49.7	drowned 12
drunk VI.13.11	drunk 28.7	drunk 11,43
eaten VI.5.11	eaten 28.3	eaten 13
– –	fitted 15.6	fitted 14,41
– –	froze 4.3	froze 14; Fig.11
– –	gave 53.4	gave 15
grew IX.3.9	grew 37.7	grew 15–16
– –	grown 37.8	grown 15–16
– –	kneeled 50.3	kneeled 17,41
knew VI.5.17	– –	knew 17,41,42
– –	lay 50.5	lay 18
– –	ran 53.6	ran 20,41,42,44
– –	ridden 20.2	ridden 19; Fig.15
– –	rose 2.5	rose 19–20; Fig.16
– –	sat 29.3	sat 21
saw VIII.2.5	saw 53.8	saw 20,40,41,42,43; Fig.17
stole VIII.7.5	– –	stole 22,44
– –	swam 49.5	swam 23,41,42
– –	sweated 43.6	sweated 22,40,41,44
taken IX.3.7	taken 43.4	taken 24,43
taught III.13.17	– –	taught 24,41,42

Dieth-Orton *Questionnaire*	Lowman-Kurath *Worksheets*	Atwood
--	threw 18.3	threw 24–25,38,41,42
took IX.3.7	--	took 23–24,40,41,43 Fig.19,30
--	torn 54.1	torn 24,41,44
--	woke 50.7	woke 25,44
--	worn 42.6	worn 25,38,41,43
--	written 52.7	written 26,42,43

The table reveals the limited comparability of the items included in the Dieth-Orton *Questionnaire* with those of the American Atlas (only 14 out of 39). Furthermore, Francis draws our attention to an important point: "Many of the verb forms which show interesting regional distribution in the United States were not included in the English survey. Nor were the contexts in which the forms were sought always comparable semantically and grammatically." [6] Here Lowman's material is of specific importance since he used a specially prepared version of the *Worksheets* employed in the Atlantic States.[7] Consequently, all of Lowman's morphological items are also discussed in Atwood's study.[8] Their results are furthermore strictly comparable on the same speech level since they were sought in the same context. Only five of Atwood's items are not included in Lowman's *Worksheets*, but the results on England have been made available through the *SED*. The table above also shows that nine items in Lowman's *Worksheets* are identical to those in the *Questionnaire* compiled by Dieth and Orton. Since about one generation lies between these two investigations, a comparison of these data reveals the linguistic change, above all, the influence of Standard English, that may have taken place in the meantime. It is evident that this aspect can have important consequences for the problem which we are here concerned with (a point already made by Atwood in the quotation cited at the beginning of this paper). It is a pity that the morphological evidence provided by Joseph Wright in his *English Dialect Dictionary* (1898–1905) cannot, in many cases, be interpreted unequivocally and thus was used only sparingly.

Despite the great comparability of the data of the American Atlas with Lowman's results, it is important to stress the difference in method of these two projects. As is well known, the American Atlas investigated not only regional dialects but also class dialects by interviewing three different types of informants (called I, II, and III) at two different age levels, thus doing justice to the fact that there is not one canonized form of educated speech in the United States as there is in England. Since Standard British English is sufficiently well described there was further reason to dispense with the investigation of class dialects in the projects carried out in England. However, since a comparison is only valid at the same level of speech, we are thus confined to comparing Lowman's data only with those of the American informants belonging to Type I A = "Little formal education, little reading and restricted social contacts; Aged, and/or regarded by the field worker as old-fashioned." [9] Like Lowman, the *SED* is concerned with folk speech only. Consequently, the results of these two projects are strictly comparable.[10]

Before discussing a few examples to illustrate some patterns in the regional distribution of uneducated speech in the two countries, the following general remarks must be premised. During the Middle English period we observe—apart from some leveling of inflections and the weakening of verb endings—considerable losses among the strong verbs, a tendency which continued in subsequent centuries.

> Some thirty [strong verbs] became obsolete in the course of Middle English, and an equal number, which were still in use in the sixteenth and seventeenth centuries, finally died out except in the dialects, often after they had passed over to the weak conjugation or had developed weak forms alongside the strong. Today more than half of the Old English strong verbs have disappeared completely from the standard language.[11]

Although negligible in comparison with the loss of strong verbs, the opposite possibility, i.e. originally weak verbs developing new strong forms, is also manifest in a few cases. Furthermore, those strong verbs that survived have only rarely come down to us in the forms representing a normal development from Old English. Instead they have yielded to various processes of leveling and analogical change. Thus it can justifiably be said that almost every strong verb and some of the weak verbs, too, have an interesting history of their own, which is hardly apparent any more, judging from the present-day forms in the standard language, but which is still reflected to a large extent in the dialects as will be seen on the following eight maps. The diachronic point of view provides, therefore, above all an explanation of the various forms still current in present-day dialects.

Map I shows the various preterite forms of the verb *begin* in Southern England as recorded by Lowman in the context "He *began* to talk".

Since vowel leveling between the preterite singular and the preterite plural did not follow a uniform pattern, two alternative past tense forms were used in this verb in the 16th century, one with *a* (going back to the Old English preterite singular *began*, strong verb Class III) and the other with *u* (going back to the Old English preterite plural *begunnon*). *Begun* as past tense was widespread in the 16th and 17th centuries and current until the early 19th century. Then its use was discontinued and *began* gained priority, being now the only preterite form in the standard language. But this is not so in the dialects, where *begun* (/ʊ~ʌ/) was still almost universal as past tense at the end of the thirties of this century. Standard English *began* (/æ/) occurred three times in the vicinity of London and in northern Kent, furthermore in Huntingdonshire, northern Norfolk, and northeast Suffolk. The uninflected *begin* was recorded only twice in two separate areas (in Norfolk and in Devon).

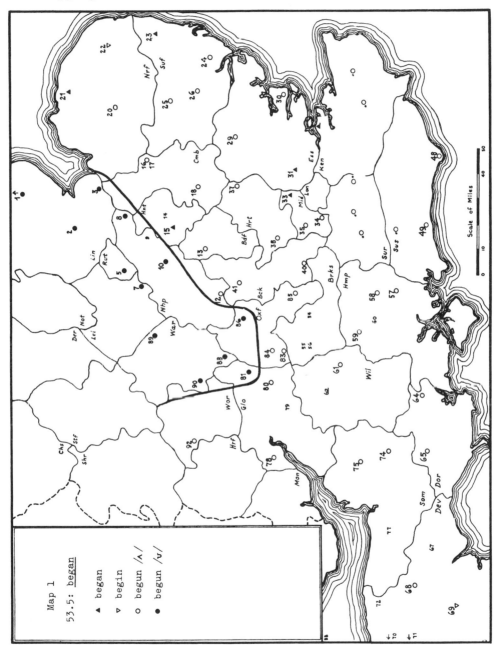

Map 1

53.5: <u>began</u>

▲ began

▽ begin

○ begun /ʌ/

● begun /ʊ/

Although we are here concerned with morphology, one interesting phonological feature must be pointed out on this map, viz. the clear-cut /ʊ/–/ʌ/ isogloss. South of a line running between Lincolnshire, Northamptonshire, and Huntingdonshire in the East down to northern Oxfordshire, northeastern Gloucestershire, and Warwickshire in the West Middle English /u/ (*begunnen*)

> was gradually unrounded and lowered . . . during the latter part of the 16. century, except in certain positions. . . . Since A[merican] E[nglish] is in substantial agreement with B[ritish] E[nglish] in the incidence of /ʌ/, this process must have been completed before the first American colonies were planted.[12]

North of this line Middle English /u/ remained /ʊ/. (On Map 2, *ran*, this phonological isogloss is exactly identical.)

A comparison with the *SED* results reveals a considerable increase of Standard English *began* forms within the last twenty-five years. This remains remarkable even if we allow for the fact that Lowman's Survey is rather wide-meshed and that in the Southwest there are no records available for almost half the localities. Thus some instances of *began* may have escaped Lowman. South of the Thames *began* forms (/æ/) even outnumber those of *begun* (/ʌ/) at a ratio of over 2:1. This is also true of parts of the northern Midlands (Norfolk, Rutland, Leicestershire), whereas in the southern Midlands *begun* still strongly predominates. "The intermingling of forms indicates a competition in uneducated rural speech between the Standard English form *began* and the leveled form *begun*."[13] Provided that the trend indicated through this comparison continues at this rapid pace, *begun* as past tense will be completely erased also from the dialects before long and be replaced by Standard English *began*. The number of occurrences of *begin*—still widely separated—increased slightly. This may be due to the greater number of localities investigated by the *SED*.

In the Eastern United States "the frequency of the preterite forms cannot be determined because a rather large number of informants in all areas choose the verb *commence*, and a number of others use the preterite of *start*."[14] Wherever the verb *begin* was used, it is interesting to note that there is not a single occurrence of *began* as past tense in Type I speech. According to Atwood, *begun* (always with /ʌ/) occurs in about half the communities in New England and in a little less than that in most other areas. *Begin* is rather common in the South Atlantic States but quite rare elsewhere.

Map 2 records the responses for the preterite *ran* obtained in the context "He *ran* ashore".

The leveling process of the various forms of the verb *run* (Old English *rinnan*, strong verb Class III) is somewhat different from that of the preceding verb. Here also the present tense is affected. Around 1550 *run* became the dominating form in the present and established itself in the standard language. The vowel resulted from leveling from forms in which *u* was original, viz.

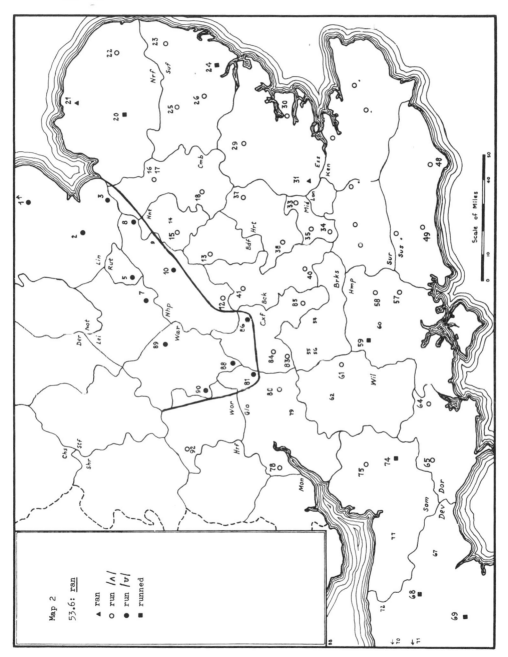

Map 2

53.6: ran

▲ ran
○ run /ʌ/
● run /ʊ/
■ runned

the preterite plural and the past participle. In the preterite two alternative forms existed alongside each other: *ran* (going back to the Old English preterite singular *ran*) and *run* (going back to the Old English preterite plural *runnon*). (See *began*.) *Run*, however, died out as a preterite form at the beginning of the 17th century; *ran* became the only form and remained so in the standard language up to the present day.

Although *run* went out of use as a past tense form two centuries earlier than *begun*, it survived to the same extent in dialectal English. As the map shows, *run* (/ʊ∼ʌ/) was used practically universally at the time when Lowman carried out his investigations. *Ran* (/æ/) occurred only twice, once near London and once in northern Norfolk. Unfortunately, the *SED* lacks comparable information. Thus it cannot be determined whether the influence of Standard English *ran*, if any, parallels that of *began*. (The incidence of /ʌ/ and /ʊ/ in *run* is exactly identical with that in *begun*; see the isogloss on the map, which, however, must again remain incomplete in the West.)

For the Atlantic Seaboard Atwood notes that north and east of the Merrimack as well as south of the Potomac *run* (always with /ʌ/) is almost universal in uneducated speech. *Ran* predominates in eastern New York and northern New Jersey. In the remainder of the Middle Atlantic States the use of *run* ranges from two thirds (in Pennsylvania) to over nine tenths (in West Virginia) of Type I informants.[15]

Map 3 shows two preterite forms of the verb *sweat* to be in use in dialectal English in Southern England. They were recorded in the context "He *sweated* hard".

Sweat, a weak verb belonging to Class I in Old English, had originally a long stem vowel, which, however, was shortened in the preterite and the past participle because of syncope of the suffix vowel and the resulting consonant cluster. In this verb, the short stem vowel was later also adopted in the present tense, so that all three tense forms were completely identical. To keep a distinction, the preterite (and the past participle) added -*ed*, thus conforming to the pattern of the weak conjugation. These forms became fully accepted, and indeed predominant, in Standard British English, where *sweat* as preterite and past participle is now obsolete. In the United States, however, educated usage differs somewhat, which, in turn, shows no perceptible variation from popular usage.

In England the distributional pattern of *sweat* and *sweated* is clear-cut in folk speech; it is somewhat less so in the Eastern United States. In the mother country, the area in which the inflected, etymologically unjustified form *sweated* occurs in the eastern parts of the East Midlands is well marked on the map. (Outside this area there is only one further instance of *sweated* in northern Sussex.) Elsewhere in Southern England the uninflected *sweat* is universal.

Unfortunately, the past tense of this verb was not specifically asked for by the *SED*.

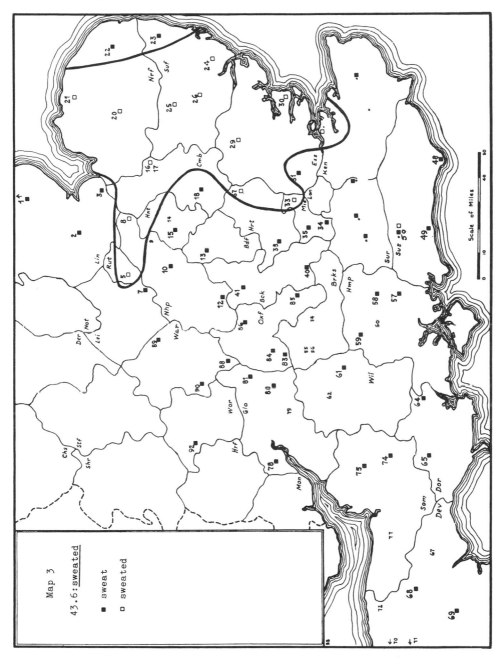

Map 3

43.6: sweated

■ sweat

□ sweated

In the entire Northern area of the Eastern United States (New England, New York, northern New Jersey, and the northern half of Pennsylvania) *sweat* is practically universal.

> Beginning in c[entral] Pa., the inflected form *sweated* . . . becomes increasingly frequent as one moves southward. It predominates in Md. (two thirds use it) and N.C. (four fifths use it), whereas in Va. and S.C. *sweat* and *sweated* are about equally common.[16]

Map 4 shows the various forms of the past participle of the verb *take* as recorded in the following context "Haven't you *taken* your medicine yet?"

One of the few verbs that belonged to Class VI of the strong verbs in Old English and that did not change in the course of history to the weak conjugation is *take*. Yet it must be noted that as early as the 14th century *take* had weak as well as strong forms in the preterite and the past participle (*taked*). The weak forms, however, did not survive in the standard language nor in the dialects.

In folk speech the leveled *took* is used as past participle almost everywhere in Southern England. In most areas it is the only response offered. In the eastern portions of the East Midlands, however, Standard English *taken* is about as common as *took*. Moreover, there is one occurrence of the hybrid *tooked* (in Devon).

The *SED* investigated both the preterite and the past participle of *take*. For the past participle its results reveal in the East Midlands a spreading of Standard *taken* only in Leicestershire, Rutland, and Northamptonshire. Elsewhere in this area the situation has remained unchanged. Also in other parts Standard English influence has only been slight in this case. Thus the *SED* records now a few scattered occurrences of *taken* in Gloucestershire, Oxfordshire, Kent, and Sussex. The strong predominance of the leveled form *took* in the West Midlands and the Southern Counties has not been broken. *Tooked* kept its ground. The *SED* still records it in Devon and Dorset.

In the Eastern United States[17] *taken* is practically universal in Type I speech throughout New England and the Middle Atlantic States as far south as the Pennsylvania-Maryland boundary. South of it it is still common. In the South Midland and the South *took* also occurs, but only infrequently. The past participles *take* and *takened*, both recorded, though rarely, in the United States, do not show up at all in England. On the other hand, *tooked*—as past participle recorded only in the extreme Southwest of England—does not seem to have been carried across the Ocean.

Map 5 shows the past participle forms of the verb *tear* as recorded in the context "The road was all *torn* up".

In Old English *tear* belonged to Class IV of the strong verbs (*teran*). In this verb, which had a short *e* in the present tense, *o* begins to appear in the preterite already in early Middle English, probably due to vowel leveling with the past participle. *Tore* became the usual form from about 1600. Standard English *torn* represents a regular development of the Old English form.

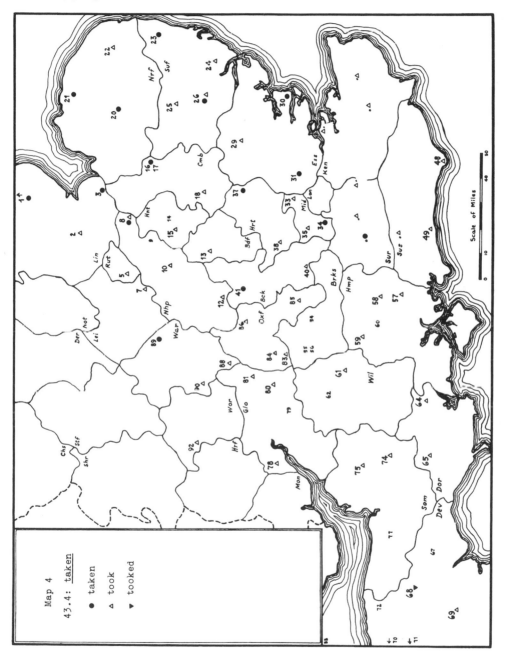

Map 4
43.4: <u>taken</u>

● taken
△ took
▼ tooked

In the 14th century, *tear*, like so many other verbs, had developed weak forms (*teared*) alongside the strong forms. The weak forms, however, in this case did not survive in the standard language, but still show up in the dialects.

In dialectal English *tore* is frequently leveled with the past participle. As such it is practically universal in the East Midlands, occurs sporadically in the West Midlands, and predominates in the Southeast (including Hampshire). There are a few scattered occurrences of Standard *torn* in the East Midlands. This form is somewhat more frequent in the extreme Southeast of England. Three informants in the West (one each in Oxfordshire, Somerset, and Devon) use the hybrid *tored* as past participle. Although records are lacking for a number of localities especially in the Southwest, it can still be inferred from the offered responses that the weak form *teared* strongly predominates in an area west of a line running from between Warwickshire and Northamptonshire—excluding southern Warwickshire and including most of Oxfordshire—down to the eastern county boundary of Dorset. The line on the map, which unfortunately must remain incomplete in the North, marks the eastern limit of the weak *teared*.

Comparable data are lacking in the *SED*.

In the Eastern United States *tore* heavily predominates in Type I speech in northeast New England, whereas in south and west New England as well as in east New York and northern New Jersey *torn* out-numbers the occurrences of *tore* by far. Elsewhere in the Middle Atlantic States and, above all, in the whole South Atlantic States *tore* is almost universally used by Type I informants. Two West Virginia informants and one Virginia informant (Negro) gave *tored*.[18] There is not a single instance of *teared* in the entire Atlantic Seaboard area.

Map 6 shows the distribution of the preterite forms of the verbs *wake* and *waken* as recorded in the context "I *woke* up early". Through their merging in Middle English several verbs contributed in form and meaning to Modern English *wake(n)*: Old English *wæcnan* (strong verb Class VI, also with weak forms in the preterite and the past participle), *wæcnian* (weak verb Class II), and *wacian* (weak verb Class II). The strong forms (preterite *wok*, past participle *waken*) disappeared in early Modern English. During the 17th century new strong forms arose—preterite *woke*, past participle *woken*, which, obviously, cannot go back to the Old English forms, but must have been formed in analogy, possibly with *break*. In Standard English *woke* (and *woken*) became gradually accepted, whereas in the dialects weak forms are still current in large areas today.

In the eastern parts of the East Midlands (East Anglia, Essex, Cambridgeshire, east Hertfordshire, and Middlesex) Standard *woke* is universal. It is nearly so in the extreme Southeast. In the West Midlands *woke* occurs as often as the weak form *waked*, which, in turn, dominates in the western portions of the East Midlands and in the Southwest (including Hampshire). The hybrid *woked* is used sparingly (once in west Oxfordshire and once in south

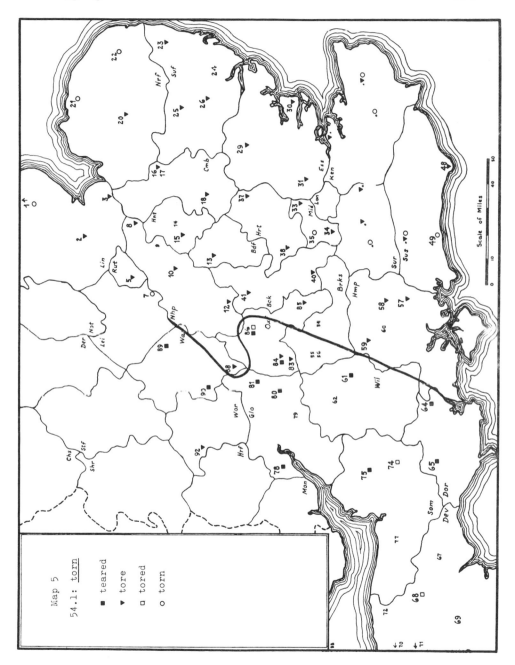

Map 5

54.1: <u>torn</u>

- ■ teared
- ▼ tore
- ▢ tored
- ○ torn

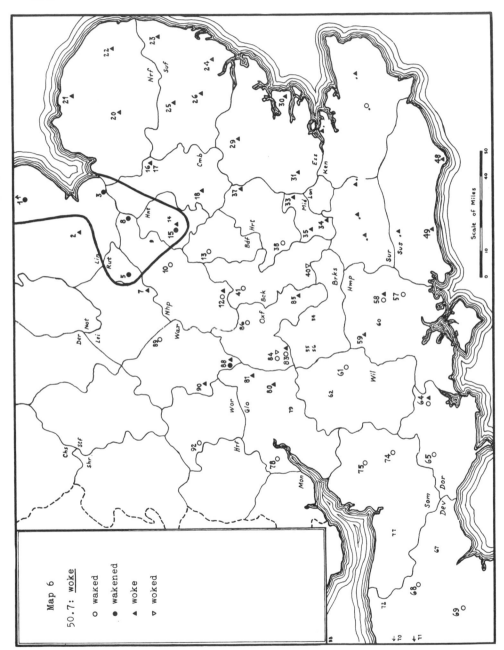

Map 6

50.7: woke

o waxed
• wakened
▲ woke
▽ woked

Buckinghamshire), whereas *wakened* occurs in a small, neatly defined area consisting of eastern Lincolnshire, Rutland, northern Northhamptonshire, and Huntingdonshire—see the line on the map—and was furthermore recorded once in southern Warwickshire.

Here again the *SED* lacks comparable material so that possible and possibly increasing Standard English influence cannot be assessed.

In the Eastern United States *woke* is being used by Type I informants almost everywhere, however with differing frequency. It is very common in western New England, New York, and the entire Midland area and occurs less frequently in eastern New England and throughout the South, but is still predominant there. *Waked* is recorded most often in North Carolina, where it is used by about half of the Type I informants. Going north, its occurrence gradually diminishes. It is regarded as the older form and is becoming substituted for *woke*. *Wakened* is used sporadically in folk speech in the North and the Midland but not in the South. It occurs in some contiguous communities in central Pennsylvania and the upper Ohio Valley.[19] *Woked* as well as *woken* and *wake* are noted a few times in isolation. The two forms mentioned last have, according to Lowman, no counterpart in the mother country.

Map 7 presents the past participle forms of the verb *wear* as recorded in the context "He is *worn* out".

Wear, a weak verb belonging to Class I in Old English (*werian*, past tense *werede*, past participle *wered*), changed from the weak to the strong conjugation on the analogy of Old English strong verbs of Class IV, like *bear*, *swear*, *tear*. This change began in the 14th century but did not become established before the 16th century. In all the verbs mentioned above the strong forms won out in Standard English. The weak form *weared*, still current in present-day folk speech, represents an etymologically correct development, whereas in *tear* (Map 5) the weak form (*teared*) is due to a later addition and therefore etymologically unjustified.

In dialectal English *wore* (a leveling of the past tense with the past participle) is practically universal in the entire East Midlands, occurs much less frequently in the extreme Southeast (Surrey, Sussex, Kent), and only six times in the whole western area (West Midlands and Southwest, including Hampshire). There are a few scattering instances of Standard *worn* in the East Midlands. This form, however, occurs about equally as often as *wore* in the extreme Southeast, but is almost non-existent in the entire West. Heavily predominating in this area is the weak form *weared*. The line on the map—unfortunately incomplete in the North—marks the eastern limit of this form. Compared with the occurrences of *teared* forms on Map 5, this line runs a little further to the east and includes the whole of Oxfordshire as well as Hampshire. *Wored* is used by two informants within the *weared* area.

In the *SED* this item was not systematically asked for. (*Weared out* and

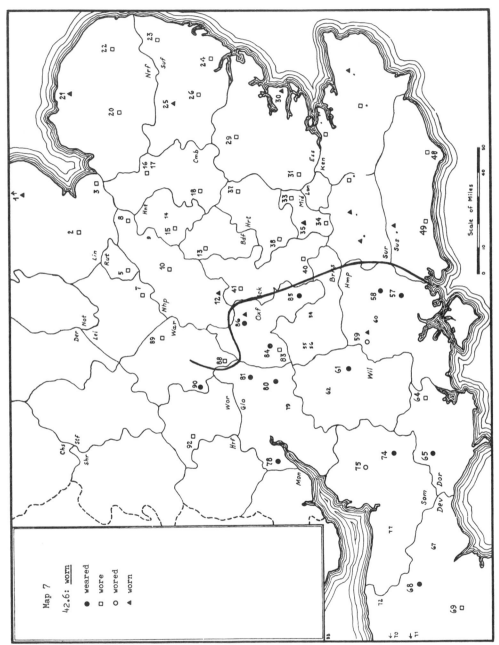

Map 7

42.6: WORN

● weared
□ wore
○ wored
▲ worn

worn out were offered a few times as responses to question VI.13.8: *exhausted*.)

In the Eastern United States the standard *worn* predominates in Type I speech in southern New England, New York, and the northern two thirds of New Jersey, but it is considerably limited elsewhere by the variant *wore*.

> *Wore* . . . is used in n.e.N.Eng. by about three fourths of the Type I A informants. . . . In s.N.Eng., e.N.Y., and n.N.J. *wore* is given by less than one third of the Type I informants; elsewhere in the M.A.S. and the S.A.S. its frequency in this group varies from about two thirds (Pa.) to more than nine tenths (N.C.).[20]

As is the case with *teared*, here again the weak form *weared*, which is regularly used in a large area in the mother country, is not to be encountered in the United States.

Map 8 shows the distribution of the various past participle forms of the verb *write* as recorded in the context "I have *written* to him".

In Old English *write* belonged to Class I of the strong verbs. During the 16th century the preterite and the past participle were leveled. *Wrote*, however, was current as an alternative past participle only until the 18th century, when, in the standard language, *written* finally supplanted it. Yet in dialectal English *wrote* is still widely used today.

In the entire area of investigation Standard *written* was offered only five times, scattered in the East (in Lincolnshire, Suffolk, Buckinghamshire, and Surrey). As the line on the map reveals, *writ* is concentrated in the central Midlands (in southern Lincolnshire, Northamptonshire, southern Warwickshire, Oxfordshire, southern Buckinghamshire, Bedfordshire, Huntingdonshire, Cambridgeshire, and northern Essex). Since the survey is rather wide-meshed, the *writ* area could be indicated only roughly. Outside this area *writ* occurs only three times in separate parts of the country (in east Norfolk, east Hampshire, and east Wiltshire). *Wrote* is almost regularly used in the whole South, the remaining West Midlands, and the eastern parts of the East Midlands; it occurs only twice in the *writ* area.

Unfortunately, the *SED* furnishes no comparable material.

In New England *wrote* and *written* occur in folk speech about equally as often. Elsewhere in the Eastern United States *wrote* strongly predominates in Type I, the proportions ranging from about three fifths in New York to well over nine tenths in North Carolina. The occurrence of *written* is thus considerably limited outside of New England. *Writ* is used a few times in the Merrimack Valley and elsewhere in northeastern New England and occurs furthermore in four or five contiguous communities in central West Virginia.[21]

In this paper we have discussed the preterite and past participle forms of only a few verbs which are interesting also from a diachronic point of view. To Francis' examples of verb forms that show a significant regional distribu-

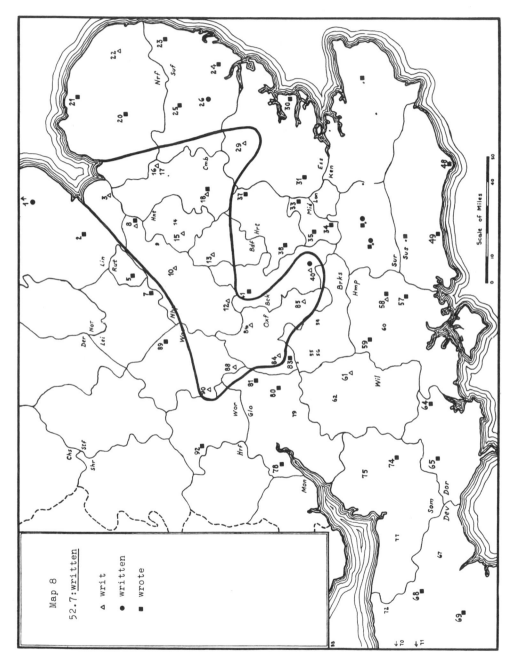

Map 8

52.7: written

△ writ

● written

■ wrote

tion on both sides of the Atlantic tempting enough to draw conclusions we can add, among others, *sweat/sweated, wakened,* and *writ*.[22] But we have refrained from drawing conclusions, since in the light of more historical linguistic evidence which is so badly needed—especially from the Colonial period—our conclusions may later appear somewhat hasty. It is surprising that forms like *teared* and *weared,* though covering wide areas in Southern England (see Maps 5 and 7), were not recorded in any part of the Eastern United States. They either did not go to America at all, or have died out there. The present-day distributional patterns are striking in variety. To correlate them with sufficient historical evidence still remains a task of the future.

Notes

1. The treatment of phonetic (and phonemic) features on both sides of the Atlantic has received absolute priority and can therefore be excepted from this dictum. See Hans Kurath and Raven I. McDavid, Jr., *The Pronunciation of English in the Atlantic States.* Studies in American English 3 (Ann Arbor, 1961); Hans Kurath, *A Phonology and Prosody of Modern English* (Heidelberg and Ann Arbor, 1964); Hans Kurath, "British Sources of Selected Features of American Pronunciation: Problems and Methods," *In Honour of Daniel Jones: Papers contributed on the occasion of his eightieth birthday, 12th September, 1961,* ed. by D. Abercrombie *et al.* (London, 1964), 146–155; Hans Kurath, "Some Aspects of Atlantic Seaboard English considered in their Connections with British English", *Communications et Rapports du Premier Congrès International de Dialectologie Générale,* 3me partie, Fasc.IX (Louvain and Brussels, 1965), 236–240. Kurath, "Contributions of British Folk Speech to American Pronunciation." *Studies in Honour of Harold Orton: Leeds Studies in English* NS II (1969), 129–134. Lowman's Survey, mentioned in footnote 2, furnished the phonetic data in England. Using Lowman's materials, Kurath has completed a study of the phonology of the Southern British Dialects that will appear in *Publications of the American Dialect Society.* The only comparison of lexical items in England and the United States available so far is that by W.Nelson Francis, "Some Dialect Isoglosses in England," *American Speech* 34 (1959), 243–250. In several cases we were able to correct this study in our book mentioned in the following footnote.

2. The publication of the *Basic Material* of the *Survey of English Dialects* for the whole of England is completed now. See Harold Orton, *Survey of English Dialects* (A): *Introduction* (Leeds, 1962); Harold Orton and Wilfrid J. Halliday (eds.), *Survey of English Dialects* (B): *Basic Material.* Vol.I: *The Six Northern Counties and the Isle of Man.* Part I (Leeds, 1962), Parts II and III (Leeds, 1963); Harold Orton and Philip M.Tilling (eds.), Vol.II: *The East Midland Counties and East Anglia.* Part I (Leeds, 1969), Parts II and III (Leeds, 1970); Harold Orton and Michael V. Barry (eds.), Vol. III: *The West Midland Counties.* Part I (Leeds, 1969), Parts II and III (Leeds, 1970); Harold Orton and Martyn F. Wakelin (eds.), Vol.IV: *The Southern Counties.* Parts I and II (Leeds, 1967), Part III (Leeds, 1968). Furthermore we have edited the lexical and grammatical material of Guy S.Lowman's Survey which he carried out in Southern England in 1937–38: Wolfgang Viereck, *Lexikalische und grammatische Ergebnisse des Lowman Survey von Mittel-und Südengland* (Munich, 1972). See also Wolfgang Viereck, "Guy S. Lowman's Contribution to British English Dialectology," *Transactions of the Yorkshire Dialect Society* Part 68, Vol.12 (1968), 32–39. This

is the appropriate place to thank Professor McDavid and Professor Kurath most cordially for entrusting me the material. I owe a special gratitude to Professor Mc-David with whom I worked in 1966–67 in Chicago under a Research Fellowship granted to me by the American Council of Learned Societies and from whose criticism I have greatly profited.

3. To our knowledge only one study deals with verb morphology in the way here suggested: W. Nelson Francis, "Some Dialectal Verb Forms in England," *Orbis* 10 (1961), 1–14. As in his lexical article, Francis here also draws on the results of the *SED*. His discusses the following verbs: *began, came, caught, drunk, grew, knew,* and *saw.*

4. E. Bagby Atwood, *A Survey of Verb Forms in the Eastern United States.* Studies in American English 2 (Ann Arbor, 1953), p.42, fn.18. Also quoted by Francis in "Some Dialectal Verb Forms in England", *Orbis* 10 (1961), p.1. In the United States we have a second important interpretative study dealing with verb morphology, which is modeled on Atwood's work: Virginia G. McDavid, *Verb Forms of the North Central States and Upper Midwest.* Ph.D.Thesis, University of Minnesota, 1956. It is available on microfilm.

5. The following verbs are included only in the *Questionnaire* compiled by Dieth and Orton: *broke, burnt, caught* p.p., *crept* p.t. and p.p., *died, found* p.t. and p.p., *given, gone, heard* p.t., *made* p.t. and p.p., *put* p.t. and p.p., *reached* p.t. and p.p., *rode, spoke, spoken, stolen, tried,* and *went.* Only in the United States the following tense forms of verbs were investigated: *asked, blew, boiled, burst, drew, fought, hanged, heard* p.p., *helped* p.t. and p.p., *knitted, pleaded, rang, shrank, swelled,* and *swollen.* As can be concluded there was enough room to increase the comparability of the data.

6. Francis, "Some Dialectal Verb Forms in England," *Orbis* 10 (1961), p.2.

7. Hans Kurath and Guy S. Lowman, Jr., *Worksheets for Southern England* (based upon the Worksheets of New England and of the South Atlantic States) (1937) [typewritten].

8. As the maps show, Lowman covered only the South and great parts of the Midlands, areas from which most of the early New England settlers came. Recent research, however, disclosed a strikingly great number of emigrants—already in the 17th century—from regions in England not covered by Lowman. See Mildred Campbell, "Social Origins of Some Early Americans," *Seventeenth-Century America: Essays in Colonial History,* ed.James Morton Smith (Chapel Hill, 1959), 63–89. Much more research is needed in this field.

9. Hans Kurath *et al., Handbook of the Linguistic Geography of New England* (Providence, R.I., 1939, 2nd print. 1954), p.44.

10. For detailed information on the different methodology of the various American and British Linguistic Atlases see Wolfgang Viereck, "Britische und amerikanische Sprachatlanten," *Zeitschrift für Dialektologie und Linguistik.* 38, No. 2, 1971. This article is dedicated to Prof. Hans Kurath on the occasion of his eightieth birthday.

11. Albert C. Baugh, *A History of the English Language,* 2nd ed. (New York, 1957), p.195. See also pp.196–199.

12. Hans Kurath, *A Phonology and Prosody of Modern English* (Heidelberg, 1964), p.94.

13. Francis, "Some Dialectal Verb Forms in England," *Orbis* 10, 1961), p.2.

14. Atwood, *op.cit.,* p.6. In the regional classification of the Eastern United States Atwood follows Kurath's *Word Geography of the Eastern United States.* Studies in American English 1 (Ann Arbor, 1949, 2nd print.1966). See Atwood, *op.cit.,* p.3.

15. Atwood, *op.cit*.p.20. Lowman noted six scattered instances of *runned*—two in East Anglia and four in the Southwest. This form was not recorded in the Eastern United States.

16. Atwood, *op.cit.*, p.22. As pointed out already, this is true of the speech of Types I, II, and III informants.

17. See Atwood, *op.cit.*, p.23 f.

18. Atwood, *op.cit.*, p.24.

19. Atwood, *op.cit.*, p.25.

20. Atwood, *op.cit.*,p.25. *Wored* does not occur in the United States.

21. Atwood, *op.cit.*, p.26.

22. All of Lowman's morphological items as documented in the table above are, with the exception of the eight verbs dealt with here, discussed in our book mentioned in footnote 2. Lowman's data are compared with Atwood's of the Atlantic Seaboard and, wherever possible, with those of the *SED*. As a result, quite a few verb forms reveal significant distributional patterns in England and the United States.

A LOOK AT THE DIRECT QUESTION

Juanita V. Williamson
LeMoyne-Owen College

In the past decade there has appeared an increasing number of manuals for teachers, articles, and monographs dealing with the speech of black Americans. These usually treat a number of structures found in the black American's speech and show how they diverge from those found in standard English as spoken by the white American.

One of the structures frequently discussed is the direct question. In two teacher-oriented manuals published by the boards of education of Chicago and New York, two cities in which there are large black populations, it is indicated that black speakers do not use the inverted order in yes/no questions as do white speakers of standard English. In *Psycholinguistics Oral Language Program: A Bi-dialectal Approach* (Chicago Board of Education, 1968) such sentences as

> Your mother pretty? (p. 16)
> They getting up? (p. 35)
> You want to go to the bathroom? (p. 128)

are considered "Everyday Talk," a euphemistic phrase meaning the speech of black persons; and such sentences as

> Is your mother pretty?
> Are they getting up?
> Do you want to go to the bathroom?

are considered "School Talk," or standard English. In *Nonstandard Dialect*[1] (New York Board of Education and the National Council of Teachers of English, 1968) it is stated that non-standard speakers "must learn to transform 'He fixes that?' to 'Does he fix that?'" (p. 9)

Susan Houston, Walter Wolfram, and Ralph Fasold, who are among those who have joined a growing number of linguists studying the speech of black Americans, say that the black American forms his wh-questions differently from the white standard speaker. In "A Sociolinguistic Consideration of the

Black English of Children in Northern Florida" (*Language*, December, 1969, pp. 599–607) Houston says that "Black English in the so-called wh-question does not invert word order or add a 'do' transformation before forming the question." Wolfram and Fasold in "Reading Materials for Speakers of Black English" (in Baratz and Shuy, *Teaching Black Children to Read*, Center for Applied Linguistics, 1969) state that "Sentences which would have a pre-posed verbal auxiliary in Standard English due to the formation of a content question generally have no auxiliary at all in the corresponding Black English. For example, the 'do' which would appear in the Standard English equivalent of questions like 'What you mean by nothing?' is absent for this reason." (p. 152)

It would seem, therefore, from the statements made in the manuals that yes/no questions without the auxiliary in initial position do not occur in standard English. It would also appear from the statements made by Houston, Wolfram, and Fasold that wh-questions without the auxiliary also do not occur in standard English.

Grammar books tend to treat these structures very briefly. A great many, whether their orientation is traditional, structural, or transformational, mention only that the inverted order does occur in the question. Some do indicate that the normal statement pattern may also occur with a rising final contour. A few, among them *The Structure of American English* by W. Nelson Francis (New York, 1958), include material on spoken English. Francis points out (p. 385) that the auxiliary may be omitted in the yes/no question in standard English and gives the following examples:

(Are) you going?
(Does) he like cooking?
(Is) he going to come?

Of particular interest is Dwight Bolinger's study, *Interrogative Structures of American English* (Publication of the American Dialect Society, No 28, 1957), a study for which Bolinger himself was his chief informant. He states that the auxiliary may be omitted in yes/no questions as in "She buy many things like this?", "They gone already?" (p. 38) and "Anybody here?", "Any money in the drawer?" (p. 39). He also states that it may be omitted in the wh-question as in "Why you got to go?" (p. 124).

In my files on the speech of white Americans, there is a growing number of examples of both the yes/no question and the wh-question, used by both standard and non-standard speakers, in which the auxiliary is omitted. Most of the examples are from southern speech, for I am particularly interested in the speech of the South, but there are examples from other areas also. The material in the files comes from three sources: the dialogue in fictional works, speech as recorded in newspapers, and the speech of individuals recorded as they were speaking.

Yes/no questions in which *be*, *do*, and *have* are omitted occur in the speech of poorly educated characters in Erskine Caldwell's *Tobacco Road*,[2] William Faulkner's "Spotted Horses," Carson McCullers' *The Heart Is a Lonely Hunter*, Flannery O'Connor's "The Life You Save May Be Your Own" and *Wise Blood*, John Steinbeck's *Grapes of Wrath*, Eudora Welty's "The Hitch Hikers," and Robert Penn Warren's *All The King's Men*. All these deal with the southern scene. Examples from these are given below:

> "You the boss?"
>> *Grapes of Wrath*, p. 157
> "You from here?"
>> "The Life You Save May Be Your Own," p. 498
> "You sick, Mike?"
>> "The Hitch Hikers", p. 898
> "You going to let me drive all the time?"
>> *Tobacco Road*, p. 93
> "You hunting something?"
>> *Wise Blood*, p.84.
> "Ma, you scared again?"
>> *Grapes of Wrath*, p. 108
> "You ever have any strikes here?"
>> *The Heart Is a Lonely Hunter*, p.53.
> "You and Flem have some trouble back yonder?"
>> "Spotted Horses," p. 5
> "You ladies drive?"
>> "The Life You Save May Be Your Own," p. 498
> "You seen the boss?" he asked.
>> *All the King's Men*, p.418

The auxiliaries are omitted in the speech of middle class educated characters in Shirley Jackson's "The Lottery", Harper Lee's *To Kill a Mockingbird*, Sinclair Lewis's *Babbitt*, Arthur Miller's *Death of a Salesman*, J. D. Salinger's *The Catcher in the Rye*, Anne Tyler's *If Morning Ever Comes*, and Thornton Wilder's *Our Town*. Only two of these, *To Kill a Mockingbird* and *If Morning Ever Comes*, are set in the South. All the others, except "The Lottery," which has no precise locale, take place in the Northeast or Midwest. Typical examples are

> "He over his grippe yet?"
>> *The Catcher in the Rye*, p. 6
> "That you?"
>> *If Morning Ever Comes*, p. 3
> "Everything clear?"
>> "The Lottery," p. 235
> "You willing to come down?"
>> *Babbitt*, p. 43

"You makin fun of me again, Mr. Finch?"
    To Kill a Mockingbird, p. 109
"You set now, boy?"
    Death of a Salesman, p. 397
"You know that?"
    The Catcher in the Rye, p. 50
"The paper have any mistakes in it?"
    Our Town, p. 119
"Old Man Warner make it?"
    "The Lottery," p. 237
"You had lunch yet?" I asked her.
    The Catcher in the Rye, p. 207
"You ever thought of that?"
    If Morning Ever Comes, p. 33
"Somebody been sick, Doc?"
    Our Town, p. 6

The wh-question in which there is no auxiliary occurs in the speech of poorly educated white characters in *All the King's Men*, *Grapes of Wrath*, *The Heart Is a Lonely Hunter*, *Wise Blood*, Erskine Caldwell's *Tragic Ground*, Marjorie Kinnan Rawlings' "South Sea Under," Katherine Anne Porter's "Noon Wine," and Robert Penn Warren's "Blackberry Winter," all set in the South:

"What you studyin', Py-tee?"
    "South Moon Under", p. 7
"What you looking at?"
    "Blackberry Winter," p. 729
"How much you fixing to gouge outta me?"
    "Noon Wine," p. 109
'Where it all happen?"
    Tragic Ground, p. 88
'What we owe you for this here con-rod and piston?"
    Grapes of Wrath, 160
"How you feel this morning?"
    The Heart Is a Lonely Hunter, p. 206
"What you seen?"
    Wise Blood, p. 63
"How you been making out?"
    All The King's Men, p. 315
"What you boys been up to?"
    "Noon Wine," p. 111

Educated characters may also omit the auxiliary in wh-questions. The following examples are taken from *If Morning Ever Comes*, *To Kill a*

Mockingbird, Babbitt, The Catcher in the Rye, and David Westheimer's *Days of Wine and Roses*. Only the first two are set in the South. It is of interest to note that the structure also occurs in William Golding's *Lord of the Flies*, a British novel.

> "What time you going to lunch?"
>   *Babbitt*, p. 44
> "What you wanting to see her for?"
>   *If Morning Ever Comes*, p. 82
> "What we going to do?"
>   *Lord of the Flies*, p. 115
> "What you think Mama's going to say?"
>   *If Morning Ever Comes*, p. 82
> "What you say?"
>   *Lord of the Flies*, p. 143
> "Whenja get here?"
>   *The Catcher in the Rye*, p. 163
> "How many witnesses you got?"
>   *To Kill a Mockingbird*, p. 174
> "How the hell you been?"
>   *Days of Wine and Roses*, p. 4
> "What you been doing that makes you so glum?"
>   *If Morning Ever Comes*, p. 91

Yes/no questions and wh-questions without auxiliaries occur in the recorded speech found in the two Memphis, Tennessee newspapers, *The Commercial Appeal* (*CA*) and *The Memphis Press Scimitar* (*MPS*). The structures are also found in comic strips, cartoons, and advertisements.

Examples of the yes/no question:

> "You partial, Coach?"
>   Reporter, *CA* 6/6/69
> "This your house?" the reporter asked.
>   *CA* 12/3/68
> "You game, Sandy?"
>   "Little Orphan Annie," comic strip, 4/29/69
> "You coming to the Crusade?"
>   Nationally known evangelist, *MPS* 6/12/69
> "You interested in some slightly used Wallace bumper stickers?"
>   Man in Memphis' City Hall, *CA* 11/10/68
> "You going nuts or something?" asked the secretary of defense.
>   *MPS* 11/22/67
> "You call this a plush office?"
>   Southerner, former presidential candidate, *CA* 11/7/69

"You think there aren't a whole lot of people who don't like to come in off the water?"

Sports writer, *MPS* 1/25/69

"Anything happen while I was out?"

"Eb and Flo," comic strip, 4/24/69

"You been watching 'The Brotherhood'?"

New York lawyer, *CA* 3/12/69

"Hey, Alf? You seen my tube of shampoo?"

"The Drop Outs," comic strip, 7/3/69

Examples of the wh-question:

"What you doing here?" he asked. "What you doing here?" the other countered.

Two Alabama legislators in a casino in Freeport *CA* 9/19/69

"Where you gonna put it?"

Bank advertisement on Memphis bus, 4/70

"How many thousands you reckon that is?"

Columnist, *MPS* 1/4/70

"Where you been?"

"There Ought to Be a Law," cartoon, 8/28/69

"How long you been out?" the general (Eisenhower) wanted to know.

Reprint of a column, *CA* 3/3/69

"Where you been keeping yourself?"

Tennessee legislator, *CA* 2/19/69

The following were recorded as the speakers were talking.
Examples of the yes/no question:

"This one of them?"

Conductor on a train

"You busy?"

Clerk in a department store, Memphis

"You going to where?"

Man in a North Carolina department store

"You going to address it?"

Clerk in a North Carolina department store

"You ever wreck a bus?"

Woman on Greyhound bus in Alabama

"You know her?"

Clerk in Memphis department store

"You all have Globe (discount department store) in Chicago?"

Young Memphis surburbanite

"You ever drove up here?"

Woman in Georgia

"You ever been on a trip?"

Airlines Clerk, Memphis

"Daddy already left?"
Well educated young man in North Carolina

Examples of the wh-question:

"Who y'all?"
Bus driver, Tennessean
"Where you going?"
Bus driver, Tennessean
"Where you living now?"
Greyhound bus driver, in Tennessee
"Where you get these?"
College student, Chicagoan
"How much they charge?"
College teacher, Tennessean
"How long you been gone?"
Memphis surburbanite
"What you reckoned?"
Greyhound bus driver, in North Carolina

Descriptions of the black American's speech which indicate that the omission of *be*, *do*, or *have* in the direct question is found in the speech of the black person but not in standard English do not take into consideration actual American usage. Speakers of American English have here, as in so many instances, an option. Programs for our schools based upon a misinterpretation of the facts can lead at best to a new prescriptivism, hurtful to black and white alike. At worst it can lead to a type of racism which may be unintentional but none the less is to be deplored. It is of this that Raven I. McDavid, Jr. wrote in "Dialect Study and English Education": [3]

> It is in the matter of social dialects, however, that there is properly the greatest interest at this time. It is unfortunately directed almost intensively at the speech of the disadvantaged Negroes in our northern slums—I say "unfortunately" not because their problems are not acute, or their numbers large, but because this focus is likely to become a racist one, with certain features singled out and emphasized as features of "Negro speech" although the specific details may be found clustering in the same way in many varieties of white Anglo-Saxon Protestant Gentile English....

It is important that we not overlook the fact that speakers of standard English often have a variety of structures from which to choose. Whenever the speech of any American is compared to standard English, those choices should not be ignored.

Notes

1. There is no statement in *Non-Standard English* which indicates who the non-standard speakers described are. The manual, however, is based on William Labov's paper submitted to the New York City Board of Education for aid in

the preparation of a manual for language arts, grades 9-12. The purpose of the paper, "Some Suggestions for Teaching Standard English to Speakers of Non-Standard Dialects," available through ERIC Documentation Reproduction Service, was to present informantion on "Negro Dialects." Many of the examples used in *Non-Standard English* are found in this paper.

2. Fictional works from which material is quoted in this paper are:

Erskine Caldwell, *Tobacco Road* (New York: Signet Books, 1932).

——— *Tragic Ground* (New York: Signet Books, 1932).

William Faulkner, "Spotted Horses", in *Three Famous Short Stories by William Faulkner* (New York: Vintage Books, 1951).

William Golding, *Lord of the Flies* (New York: Capricorn Books, 1954).

Shirley Jackson, "The Lottery", in *The Scope of Fiction*, ed. Cleanth Brooks and Robert Penn Warren (New York: Appleton-Century-Crofts, Inc., 1960).

Harper Lee, *To Kill a Mockingbird* (New York: J. P. Lippincott Co., 1960).

Sinclair Lewis, *Babbitt* (New York: Signet Books, 1922).

Carson McCullers, *The Heart Is a Lonley Hunter* (New York: Bantam Books, 1940).

Arthur Miller, *Death of a Salesman*, in A *Quarto of Modern Literature* ed. Leonard Brown (New York: Charles Scribner's Sons, 1965).

Flannery O'Connor, "The Life You Save May Be Your Own," in *Literature*, ed. by Walter Blair et al. (Atlanta: Scott-Foresman and Company, 1959).

———, *Wise Blood* (New York: Farrar Straus and Cudahy, 1949).

Katherine Anne Porter, "Noon Wine", in *An Approach to Literature*, ed. Cleanth Brooks et al. New York: Meredith Publishing Company, 1964).

Majorie Kinnan Rawlings, "South Sea Under," in *The Marjorie Rawlings Reader*, ed. Julia Bigham (New York: Charles Scribner's Sons 1956).

J. D. Salinger, *The Catcher in the Rye* (New York: Bantam Books, 1951).

John Steinbeck, *Grapes of Wrath* (New York: The Viking Press, 1939).

Anne Tyler, *If Morning Ever Comes* (New York: Bantam Books, 1934).

Robert Penn Warren, "Blackberry Winter," in *Pattern of Writing*, ed. Robert Doremus et al. (New York: Henry Holt and Company, Inc., 1950).

Eudora Welty, "The Hitch Hikers," in *Literature of the South*, ed, Thomas Young et al. (Atlanta: Scott, Foresman and Company, 1952).

Thornton Wilder, *Our Town* (New York: Pocket Books, Inc., 1938).

3. In *New Trends in English Education* ed. David Stryker (Champaign, Ill., National Council of Teachers of English, 1966), pp. 43–52.

FROM POSTULATES TO PROCEDURES IN THE INTERPRETATION OF SPELLINGS

H. Rex Wilson
University of Western Ontario

The use of "naive" or "occasional" spellings is a time-honored means of retrieving past pronunciation. The evidence derived from the aberrations of keepers of records in past centuries is especially attractive because of its plausibility to the unintiated, especially when it is used impressionistically, as has too often been the case. How careless or naive interpretations can be was revealed to me as I sought guidance in my first investigation into what I prefer to call "aberrant" spellings, a term better suited to my underlying assumption about the nature of the spellings under study. My discoveries are by no means "all my own work." I have been greatly assisted by the timely appearance of Edward A. Stephenson's "On the Interpretation of Occasional Spellings," [1] which appears to be the first call for order and sanity in the interpretation of aberrant spellings since Zachrisson's brief comments in *Pronunciation of English Vowels 1400–1700*.[2]

The examples used in this paper are drawn from my own study in progress of the spellings in an eighteenth century Massachusetts journal. The journal was kept by Abijah Willard, a 31-year-old Captain in the New England forces which took Fort Beauséjour in 1755 and later carried out the expulsion of the Acadians from the region and the destruction of their villages. Abijah Willard was born in Lancaster, Mass., and lived in that vicinity until the Revolutionary War, when his choice of sides resulted in emigration to New Brunswick. The manuscript of this journal and an accompanying orderly book, which is continued to cover the period of Willard's service with Amherst in 1759 at Fort Edward and Lake George, is held by the Henry E. Huntington Library and Art Gallery in San Marino, California. The library has provided me with a complete photocopy of the manuscript, but citation in this paper will be from the *Journal* only, which is available in print as edited by Dr. Clarence Webster for the New Brunswick Historical Society.[3] In keeping with Stephenson's strictures against the use of printed versions of old records I will not place in evidence any items in which I suspect Webster erred in the interpretation of the handwriting. The diary contains entries, some extensive, some of only a line, for every day from April 9, 1755 to January 6, 1756—91 closely-written pages in the MS and 63 in print.[4]

Postulates

My starting point in developing procedures for the interpretation of aberrant spellings is Stephenson's second postulate, "Spellings should be classified according to carefully formulated definitions of classes of spellings." [5] His first postulate, that spellings should be taken from original manuscripts seems so axiomatic that it should not need to be stated, but the examples he gives[6] amply demonstrate the need to tell interpreters that "it should be obvious . . . that a text transmitted only from writer to linguist is preferable . . . to a text transmitted from writer to editor to printer to linguist." [7] His third and fourth postulates need some reinterpretation.

There is a fifth postulate not stated in Stephenson's article but implicit in the way he handles his evidence in his doctoral dissertation[8] and in his discussion of the evaluation of omissions of letters.[9] Weight should be given to the number of times an aberrant spelling occurs; one occurrence is worthless. We all make slips of the pen, some of them wildly improbable. Anything can happen once—if it happens twice we may need to take it seriously and the oftener it happens the more convincing it gets. Perhaps eventually we may be able to form a statistical scale for the evaluation of the evidence on the basis of frequency. For the moment frequency has only the status of a rule of thumb which will protect the interpretation from the suspicions raised by Orbeck's procedure[10] of recording only the first occurrence of a form. The frequency of a given misspelling in relation to the number of conventional spellings is a matter for future study.

Naive But Not a Completely Innocent

The basic assumption in the interpretation of spellings is that alphabets are at least crudely phonemic. A second assumption is that, however they may have learned to spell, all spellers are at least subliminally aware of a system of phoneme-grapheme correspondence. A third assumption rests upon the fact that this correspondence in English is not complete and therefore revealing slips may occur where conventional spelling does not correspond with an individual's pronunciation. All slips are not equally revealing. Perhaps most of them reveal only that someone has blundered. A careful sifting of the meaningful from the meaningless is a necessary preliminary to the drawing of phonological conclusions from misspelling. The application of Stephenson's second postulate will provide the sieve.

Non-meaningful spellings may be described under the following heads (the examples are from Abijah Willard's journal):

1. Haplological—
   The dropping of a letter.   attempt—attept
2. Dittographic—
   Repetition, echoing, or
   anticipation of letters.   hours—hourers
3. Excrescent—
   Addition of letters, most
   notably final 'e'.   officer—officere
4. Morphological—
   Endings added without
   observing combining rule.   fired—fireed
5. Suppletive—
   Related morphological
   form substituted.   stamp—stampt

The types capable of revealing some degree of phonological significance are:

6. Graphemic—
   Substitution of a member of   happens—hoppens
   a different grapheme.
7. Allographic—
   Substitution of an allograph
   of the same grapheme;   meat—meete
   a) inverse spelling;   water—warter
   b) omission.   regulars—regulas
8. Logographic—
   Substitution of a homophone.   waylay—weigh ley
9. Name—
   Use of a letter with the value
   of its name in the alphabet.   rained—rand
10. Sandhi—
    Reflection of word juncture
    assimilations.   marched to—march to

Problems in Classification

The classification of misspellings is not always simple. The process must be carried out with great care, and if there is any bias it should be toward withholding the item. (But never toward discarding it, for further studies or collateral evidence may give doubtful items relevance.)

A compelling case for inclusion under a specific type is always necessary. It is easy to have a heart too soon made glad, especially when some pet theory might be supported by one interpretation. As a Canadian dialectologist, I have a special interest in the development of ME ou, so such apparent graphemic substitutions as *abote* and *abute* are very tempting. Obviously they show a stage in the development of ME ou parallel to the present state in much of Canadian English. Or this would be obvious except for the fact that these could equally well be the result of scribal haplology; each type has one half of the grapheme. *Abute* occurs only once and is easily dismissed but *abote occurs* eight times. *Carose* and *hosees* (houses) also occur once each. The decision must be a Scotch verdict and these items should be noted and put away until the time when collateral evidence is considered.

The usefulness of the various categories of significant spelling varies greatly. The most helpful are 6. Graphemic and, for vowels, 9. Name. Substitutions of 'o' for 'a' fifteen times in nine words (*called, camp, cannon, captain, chaplain, clams, clapped, commanded, happens*) suggest an articulation farther back than we expect today. The use of 'i' for 'oi' thirteen times in four words (*disappointed, hoisted, point, spoiled*) is compelling evidence for a different diphthong than is in use today in the English of educated North Americans.

Type 7. Allographic spellings are largely corroborative of the identity of sounds within certain groups, while 8. Logographic spellings may be compared with rhymes in their usefulness. Type 10. Sandhi spellings have a special, if minor, usefulness in revealing features occurring at word juncture, one of the few types of evidence that gets us beyond some gross information about the unit phonemes (or paraphonemes).

In evaluating spellings from the pre-typewriter era we are of course, faced with the need to apply the non-linguistic arts of the palaeographer. The validity of my comments on the substitution of 'o' for 'a' is strongly dependent on the interpretation of the linking stroke between the supposed 'o' and the following letter. With the exception of 'clams' all the words cited are represented by other writings which are clearly 'a'. The ligatures of 'called' and 'Captain' (one occurrence each with apparent 'o') may be ambiguous.

The facts of articulatory phonetics, too, are a resource to assist in the evaluation of a spelling as significant. Orbeck's rejection of *crambery* as a mere "scribal approximation" [11] is a classic example of failure to use this resource. I happened to review this rejection on a day when I had just seen this form on a luncheon menu. I suspect that this very plausible assimilation occurs in my own speech.

System vs. Lapses From System

The term 'system' in the discussion of aberrant spellings must be used with caution or the diffidence of Orbeck (". . . the systems, if we may call them such, of the various scribes. . . .") [12] Diarists, and other record keepers have "learned their letters" within the graphemic system of their speech community. Their lapses from the conventional system are valuable only when analyzed in terms of the underlying common system. Even John Bate, described by Harold Whitehall as a ". . . kind of unintentional Yankee Orm . . . ," [13] used his letters from time to time in the conventional way, sometimes producing whole conventional words!

It is because of the centrality of contrast to the study of spelling that I prefer the term 'aberrant'. These contrasts may be fairly consistent, as appears to be the case with Bate, or they may be somewhat scattered as would seem the case with Abijah Willard; frequent in the case of Bate, or in the minority as with Willard. As long as there are enough of a given type of spelling for it to be taken seriously, it is the direction in which it points phonetically, along with the directions of alternate aberrant spellings for the same class of sound, that counts.

The Stressed Vowels of Abijah Willard

As illustrations of the way we may examine aberrant spellings, I offer the following brief preliminary sketch of Abijah Williard's writing of stressed vowels and the treatment of historic 'r' between vowel and consonant and finally. I hope the low percentage of truly significant spellings will not set the art back seriously.

'a'

In the published *Journal* Abijah Willard writes 'a' for other spellings of stressed vowels 43 times in 14 words. Twenty-five of these occurrences are in seven words where [e] would be expected today. These, then, are 'name' spellings, and serve as an indicator of the degree of faithfulness of Willard's 'transcription', they reveal nothing surprising about the sound system of the dialect nor about any individual word.

Of the remaining 'a' writings 'wather' occurs 10 times, but any assumptions at this point would be hasty. Might this represent [e], as we have seen it used, or [æ] on the assumption that it is allographic? It could be haplological. The number of occurrences is impressive, but for almost every day from April 9, 1755 to January 6, 1756 Abipah Willard made a weather report. The problem of frequency enters the picture here.

The form *stra berys* occurs once. In view of Willard's apparent use of 'o' for low-back vowel types, this is probably merely a haplology.

'a+r'

The remaining 'a' spellings all occur before 'r'. Two occurrences of *'desart'* (v.) are linked in spelling with *'garls'* (2) and *gard*, interesting in themselves and in connection with the discussion of 'r'.

'ay'

This writing occurs just once (*rayleed*) and suggests a fronting of [æ] but interpretation must be held in abeyance. (Intrusions are rare in Willard's spellings).

'e'

Simple 'e' spellings in the Journal present a special palaeographical problem. While moderately sprawling, Willard's hand is usually clear. One irritating exception is the lack of differentiation of small 'e' and 'i'. Although there are 'e's' that have clear loops or a broadening suggesting a compressed loop, the majority might very well be undotted 'i's'. Webster in the printed text interprets an expected small 'i' as 'e' 19 times in 12 words. I am not that confident after examining my copy of the manuscript. Caution would suggest ignoring these as unreliable, but Williard's capital 'I' and 'E' are unmistakable and he gives us 'Endians" twice and 'Envaleeds' once. Clearly some of those undotted 'i's' may well be 'e's'. The puzzle must be attempted, but solution may have to wait upon a chance to examine the manuscript—and possibly the employment of expert assistance. However, examination of the four 'e' interpretations for 'village' yields one unequivocal 'e'. Willard appears to have had a lowering or centralizing of 'short i' but the strength of the evidence cannot be assessed at this time.

Not all the 22 confirmed and apparent substitutions of 'e' for 'i' represent 'short i'. Three occurrences of 'e' in 'obliged' are noted by Webster. Of these, one is fully convincing.

Used with its 'name' value, 'e' occurs for 'ee', 'ei', and 'e . . . e' 12 times in five words.

It occurs suggestively once for 'a' in 'lamentation', and 'ey' in 'they' three times, presumably haplological.

'ea'

Willard writes 'ea' eight times for the 'a' of *detach*. This substitution occurs only in this word. It appears to be an allographic substitution. Except for failing to drop final 'e' in adding inflectional endings, Willard does not intrude extra vowels. Perhaps this offers a converse for the 'a' of 'plasing'. Along with the use of 'e' for 'ea' in *ahead, breast, pleasant,* and *weather* suggests a fairly close grouping in the low front region of later [i], [ε], [æ], and perhaps some wavering in pronunciation.

This writing is used once each in *sleds* (semi-logographic *-lead*) *here* (logographic), *seemed, steered, pieces.*

'ee'

Willard writes 'ee' for 'e' once each in *best, where,* and *well* (suspected false doubling of 'e' for 'l') *kept, met* (suppletive morphological forms).

This writing occurs in varying strengths for *neat, peas* (3) *meat* (4), *preached, wheat* (2), *stream, team* (7). For 'ey' it occurs once, in *keys.*

'eea'

One curious notation, 'eea' for 'ea' in *beat* looks like a momentary indecision over allographs which produced a composite.

'ei'

An apparent logographic spelling which persists in one word is 'ei' for 'e . . . e' in *there* (34 times).

'ew'

As an alternate for 'ieu' 'ew' occurs once each in the words *lieu* and *lieutenant*, interesting data for the history of the second word, if not for the plonological system.[14] This spelling occurs once also for *ue* in blue.

'eigh'

The previously cited logographic *weigh* occurs twice in *waylay*.

'ey'

The same word on one occasion has -*ley*.

'i'

The spelling 'i' substitutes for nine different spellings 39 times in 13 words. It occurs sixteen times with its name value as a substitute for 'i . . . e' in *miles* and once again (though possibly influenced by the following ending) for 'y' in *crying*. A large proportion of the sample is suggestive in the substitution of 'i' for 'oi' *disappointed* (2), *hoisted* (4), *point* (5), *spoiled* (2) (Total, 13 occurrences.)

The remaining nine occurrences are in *been*, which also occurs five times with 'e'.

'ia'

Willard uses 'ia' once for 'ie' in *siege*.

'ie'

The spelling 'ie' occurs once for 'ee' in *weeks*. This is a true 'ie'; the 'i' is dotted.

'ieu'

A partial converse of the 'ew' for 'lieu' in lieutenant is the three occurrences of 'lieu' for 'iew' in *view*, and *review* (2).

'o'

An apparent haplological 'o' appears for both the modern [ʊ] and [u] six times (*schooner, soon,* (2) *took, look, wooden*). As noted it also occurs eight times for *about* and once each for *carouse, houses, journey, encourage.*

In eight words it occurs 13 times for 'a' where modern [æ] might be expected. These might in some cases be 'a's' with high ligatures, but by inspection they appear to be typical 'o's'. All occur before nasals and/or bilabials: *camp* (2) *cannon* (3), *captain, chaplain* (2), *clams, clapped, commanded, happens* (2). Place names along with other proper names, have not been included in the first stage of my work, but it is notable that the town of Annapolis (Annapolis Royal, Nova Scotia) is spelled ten times with 'o' for medial 'a'. Further, 'o' appears for 'a' in *called*, while the apparent misspelling 'molosas' approaches Sheridan's 'molosses' [mo'lɔsɪz]. Clearly in these words the vowel was somewhat retracted from its present position.

'o . . . e'

Allographic spellings in 'o . . . e' appear in *only, uproar* (2), *own*, and *going.* There are three occurrences in *abroad.*

'oo'

In three words 'o' is doubled, *fort, sober, who.* In the last case it may be allographic, the others appear just to be slips. It occurs twice for *lose* and once for *moved*, both allographic: and may be similarly interpreted in *shoes.*

'ou'

In *soldiers,* 'ou' appears 30 times, and is presumably logographic.

'ow'

In *saw* (pret.) the 'aw' is clearly written 'ow' in three cases. It occurs once as well in *houses* and once in *broke*, and once for the 'ough' in *through.*

'oy'

Join and *rejoicing* (3) have 'oy' for 'oi'.

'u'

For 'o' representing a mid-central vowel 'u' is often substituted: *come* (3), *done* (2), *some* (35), *tone* (2). The single appearance of this spelling in *bombs* suggests Walker's pronunciation (but not Sheridan's).

This spelling seems to appear once for 'oi' in *soiled*, but the spelling *sulled* may represent *sullied*, which fits the context as well.

And then there is my favorite *abute* for *about*—which occurs only once.

Enough appears as *anuff* twice, and *rough* as *ruff* twice. Far is rendered as *fur* twice.

'u . . . e'

The writing 'u . . . e' occurs three times in *pursuits*, and once in *few.*

'y'

Tried is rendered as *tryed* once, a morphologically influenced misspelling.

'ye'

In *lye* 'ye' represents 'ie'.
In *tryell* it represents 'ia'.

Evidences of R-Loss

Abijah Willard was raised in the heart of a noted 'r-less' area, but most of the time his spellings show 'r' where residents of his area do not ordinarily pronounce them. However in *are, boarded, fort* (2), *marched, marsh, number, orders, party, quarters, regulars* (4), *returned, warm,* and *weather,* he omits 'r' between vowel and consonant or finally. Further, it is inserted in *Chignecto* (*Chekenector*), *rapid* (*rapard*), *wages* (*wagers*), and *water* (*warter*) (2). The secret is out: r-loss was a feature of Lancaster pronunciation in the second quarter of the eighteenth century.[15]

"Assay" of Aberrant Spellings

At first glance a document written by an unconventional speller may look excitingly rich, but this will often prove illusory, since misspellings call attention to themselves, especially for anyone who is looking for them. The proportion of aberrant spellings to orthodox spellings will vary from document to document, but their existence and consistency are the important facts.

In the *Journal* under consideration here there are approximately 13,000 words which yield 352 interesting spellings of vowels in 134 words. Of these between 51 and 68 (depending on the ultimate decision on the i/e spellings) should be discarded as mere slips of the pen or be reserved for consideration in the event of repetition in the *Orderly Book* or in comparison with the practice of contemporary scribes in the area. (Three diaries of Abijah's father Samuel have been preserved.)[16] Of the remaining plausible respelled words, between 51 and 68 (once again depending on the final disposal of the i/e spellings) suggest interesting features of the distribution of vowels in the speech of the Lancaster area in the second quarter of the eighteenth century. The remainder merely illustrate an unconscious restructuring of the graphemic system. At least 80% of Willard's respellings of vowels, then, seem to be reliable representations of linguistic facts. This would seem reassuring, but as yet no rule had been established. On the other hand a maximum of .52% of Abijah Willard's words reveal vowel spellings of interest to the historical linguist. Is the game worth the candle?

That's a good question, especially when we consider that the mere excerpting of this relatively brief document took approximately 48 hours, usually in not more than two-hour blocks. Such drudgery, attractive in the past, fortunately, to generations of monkishly devoted philologers, is no longer necessary. The next step is to find means, or adapt existing means, of storing such materials and retrieving only the relevant items by computer. When we can simply 'ask the swami' to produce the renditions we want from a given document, the valuable evidence which lies half ridden in the records of earlier periods will become available in profusion.

The Use of Collateral Evidence

I have deferred reference to Stephenson's third and fourth postulates because the third looks shockingly wrong-headed, while the fourth implies a principle which, if applied to the third, would bring it into line with the rigor he seeks. "Interpretations should be in accord with the information provided by historical phonology." [17] When I first read that statement of the third postulate my immediate reaction was, "If this is so, then we are like small boys doing sums to match the answers in the back of the book." That this is not the intent of this postulate is suggested by the rather different statement of the same postulate on p.46 as: "checking these interpretations against the rules and common occurrences of historical phonology and finding justification therein for the interpretations. . . ." His own independent championing of the forms *linning* and *lining*[18] as representing in his materials a hyper-correct pronunciation rather than the conventional assumption of an inverse spelling further suggests that my initial interpretation of the third postulate is incorrect.

The object of the interpretation of aberrant spellings from the past is to get some clues concerning earlier language features. To assume the necessity to conform to the previously known "facts" about the historical development of the English language is to fall victim to the unified stream fallacy of language development. Admittedly, strong evidence is needed to refute, or find exceptions to, "reputable theory"; but we must be willing to stand up for our findings.

The fourth postulate implies precisely the right attitude: "Interpretations should be reviewed in the light of all the collateral evidence available." [19] "Reviewed" is just the right word and implies that interpretations should be worked out in two stages, the internal evaluation of the evidence and a re-evaluation in the light of collateral evidence, historical as well as geographical. Indeed all types of studies of earlier pronunciation should be carried out in the sort of framework outlined by Helge Kökeritz in 1961 when he recommended the integration of a wide range of resources in the study of earlier English pronunciation: orthoepic testimony, spellings, rhymes and stress patterns in verse, and puns.[20] To these I would add the study of dialect literature and, for the recent past, early phonograph recordings.

Collateral Evidence in The Present Instance

Collateral evidence is of two types, historical and current. The historical evidence is most readily used when it has been collated and set forth in scholarly works such as Wyld's *A History of Modern Colloquial English*[21] but individual studies limited rather strictly as to time and place must be considered, such as Orbeck's *Early New England Pronunciation*, which can be evaluated and compared with results obtained in a study in progress. While more difficult to use, these studies are a protection against ". . . sound-laws that have become firmly codified by now that it almost impossible to repudiate some of them despite conclusive evidence of their inaccuracy." [22] We should re-examine historical phonology in the light of our findings, though no single study should be expected to possess the power of conclusive refutation. The cumulative effect of many such studies might develop this power, however. But this cumulative effect will not be achieved if each study in turn is fudged to conform to the doctrine.

Current evidence is drawn from modern dialect surveys, which often reveal conservative dialects, particularly in relic areas where the earlier usages of an area under consideration may have been preserved and may shed light on evidence from spellings which does not conform to current practice in the area from which the scribe came. One such work, which also has a foot under the historical classification, is Joseph Wright's *English Dialect Grammar*.[23] Since its collections were made in the last quarter of the nineteenth century, some parts of this material must represent speech characteristics of the second quarter of the century at least, although the amateur status of the field workers makes is impossible to regard any single item as narrowly accurate.

A comparison of some of the more unusual indications of Abijah Willard's spelling with reports by Wyld and Wright and the evidence of the *Linguistic Atlas of New England*[24] and the items reported for the South of England and the South Midlands in *The Pronunciation of English in the Atlantic States*[25] may be helpful.

'a+r'

Willard's *desart* (v.) (2) reflects a familiar feature for which Wyld cites Queen Elizabeth as a witness and in other words runs it back to the late fifteenth century.

The two occurrences of *garls* find a parallel in reports by Wright of this word with low-central to low-back vowels in Northamptonshire, Shropshire, Oxfordshire, Bedfordshire, Sussex, Devon, and Hertfordshire. These citations, incidentally, are all r-less. These facts, plus the evidence for r-loss cited, suggest the borrowing of 'ar' to represent a type of 'long a' (cf. *gard*), and I am emboldened to use this scanty evidence thus reinforced to suggest a paraphonemic transcription of the words as ⌿dəza:t⌿, ⌿ga:lz⌿, and ⌿ga:d⌿.

Some light on Willard's repeated writing of 'ea' for 'a' in *detach* is shed by Wyld's citation of Cooper[27], (1685) who has [e:] in *teach*[28] (210), while the 'a' of 'plasing' is also assumed by Wyld to be [e:] on the basis of rhyme in Lady Mary Wortley[29] (211) which he sees as competing form in this period. The 'e' for 'ea' writing may parallel Isaac Watts' rhyme *made-head*[30]. Paraphonemically we may have here ⌿date:č⌿, ⌿ple:zɪn⌿[31]; ⌿ahe:d⌿ and ⌿sle:dz⌿.

'o'

A good deal of light can be shed from several sources on the curious writing of 'o' for 'a' in *cannon, captain, chaplain, clams, clapped, commanded, happens*. LANE (Map 151) notes [haˆmə] (*hammer*) for 207 Stirling, a part of Lancaster. Wright finds low-central, to low-back types for *clap* in Staffordshire and Northumberland, Durham, Cumberland, and Westmorland.

Wright's reports of *hammer* with these types of articulation are spread literally the length of the island, while Lowman recorded them pretty generally in his area. All of these were in competition with [æ] types. It is possible that Willard is here offering fairly substantial evidence of a backed articulation suspected by Orbeck. He cites only two items with 'o', *gronted*, and *plonting*, noting that evidence is 'scant'.[32]

What We Can Learn From Aberrant Spellings

The resources of spelling interpretation will vary from document to document, but it would seem possible to supplement the resources of one document with evidence from others of approximately the same time and place so that a reasonably complete picture of the segmental phonemes (or paraphonemes, if we are to be cautious) might be obtained. In piecing together evidence from a number of sources each document must be described in its own terms. Note Orbeck's dismissal of this principle: "In my study of the naive forms of the town records I have made no attempt, for reasons which will become obvious as we proceed, to consider the systems, if we may call them such, of the various scribes separately. There are differences, of course, between scribe and scribe, but these differences are not vital here."[33] Perhaps, in view of the fact that the records of one town will form a continuum with each scribe the product of only slightly varying conditions, Orbeck may have been justified, but I would not like to put the evidence drawn from John Bate's ledger into the same pot with that from Abijah Willard's journal.

They are two very different kettles of fish and they must be kept apart to reveal their own particular combinations of ingredients.

The search for evidence of suprasegmentals in aberrant spellings cannot, of course, be expected to be very rewarding, but the possibility of some sort of meaningful patterning should be kept in mind. Might a wildly improbable vowel in a stressed position be evidence of weak stress? Do compounds written as separate words indicate secondary or even stress rather than no stress for one member? Willard's *after noon* (16), *day light, fair well, fore noon* (6) *in to* (5), *my self, sun down* (2), *sun rise, sun sett, sun shine, to morrow* (5) *under stood, up rore, weigh laid*, are tempting.

As I was excerpting the *Journal* I was reminded by these writings of the diction of a Vermonter born and raised, now in her eighties, who startled me when I first knew her by the improbable phrase *after words* occurring in her speech. After a time I learned to correct this automatically to *afterwards* but the stress pattern remained impressed on my memory. LANE notes the occurrence in New England of level stress or initial or final stress in contrast with usage outside the area for *forenoon* (Map 77) and *almost* (Map 714). *Sunset* (Map 74) is noted as having the second member "sometimes very weakly stressed." *Sunrise* (Map 73) has no comment on stress. All the words listed might conceivably have once had this 'even' stress. There is only one other word in the *Journal* which is divided, *a clock* (o'clock) (2), which is presumably written on the analogy of article plus noun.

Such indications as this are probably rare in the study of aberrant spellings, but they should be kept in mind. It may be that the way a scribe divides his words may be as valuable as any alternation of alphabetic symbol.

Notes

1. Edward A. Stephenson, "On the Interpretation of Occasional Spellings," *Publication of the American Dialect Society*, Number 48 (November 1967).

2. R.E. Zachrisson, *Pronunciation of English Vowels 1400–1700* (Göteborg, 1913).

3. *Journal of Abijah Willard 1755*, ed. J.C. Webster, New Brunswick Historical Society, No. 13.

4. Two other journals have survived from this expedition, one by a battalion commander, Col. John Winslow of Marshfield, and one by another Marshfield man, John Thomas, a surgeon. Neither of these men is strikingly conventional in his spelling. Analysis of their journals should enlarge our perspective of eighteenth century Massachusetts speech. Indeed, if the Orbeck materials were reworked with the guidance of the same postulates, we could have a three-point chronological sampling of two important localities, for Lancaster, which was settled at least in part from Watertown, gives us an 18th century check on the Orbeck Watertown and Groton materials, and Marshfield represents the Plymouth colony. The records of *The Linguistic Atlas of New England* complete the picture.

5. Stephenson, p. 33.

6. *Ibid.*, pp. 34 and 35.

7. *Ibid.*, p. 35.

8. Edward A. Stephenson, *Early North Carolina Pronunciation,* University of North Carolina Doctoral Dissertation, 1958.

9. Stephenson, "On the Interpretation of Occasional Spellings," p. 38.

10. Anders Orbeck, *Early New England Pronunciation* (Ann Arbor, 1927), p. 18.

11. *Ibid.,* p. 9.

12. *Ibid.,* p. 10.

13. Harold Whitehall, "The Orthography of John Bate of Sharon, Connecticut (1700–1784)," *American Speech,* XXII, No. 1, pt. 2. (1947).

14. Thomas Sheridan, A.M., *A Complete Dictionary of the English Language* (Second Edition), (London, 1789). Gives [1ɪf-].

John Walker, *A Critical Pronouncing Dictionary* (London, 1791), Scolar Press Facsimile, No. 117. Gives [lɛv-]

15. That is, the period during which Willard's speech characteristics developed.

16. Burr Angle and Richard Venezky, *A Report on the Materials in the Hanley English Language Collections at the University of Wisconsin,* Department of English, University of Wisconsin, Madison, Wisconsin, 1968 (Mimeographed), Part II, Appendixes, p. 27:
"...MSS in Mass. Archives..."

17. Stephenson, "On the Interpretation of Occasional Spellings," p. 33.

18. *Ibid.,* p. 41.

19. *Ibid.,* p. 33.

20. Helge Kökeritz, Review of E.J. Dobson, *English Pronunciation 1500–1700, Language* XXXVII (1961), 150–151.

21. Henry Cecil Wyld, *A History of Modern Colloquial English* (Oxford, 1936).

22. Kökeritz, p. 160.

23. Joseph Wright, *The English Dialect Grammar* (Oxford, 1905).

24. Hans Kurath and Others, *Linguistic Atlas of New England* (Three Volumes and a Handbook), Providence, R.I., 1939.

25. Hans Kurath and Raven I. McDavid, Jr., *The Pronunciation of English in the Atlantic States* (Ann Arbor, 1961).

26. Wyld, p. 219.

27. Charles Cooper, *Grammatica Anglicana* (1685).

28. Wyld, p. 210.

29. *Ibid.,* p. 211.

30. Isaac Watts, "Jesus shall reign where'er the sun ...," Stanza 2.

31. /ʌnʌ/ assumed only on the basis of reference to 'pudden pinte', May 15, 1755.

32. Orbeck, p. 22.

33. *Ibid.,* p. 2.

STRUCTURE OF LANGUAGE

THE BEHAVIORAL COMPONENTS OF A TWO-WAY CONVERSATION

WILLIAM M. AUSTIN

Illinois Institute of Technology

The Modalities of Communication

Perhaps the simplest model of a communicational interchange is the A-B-X triangle where A and B are communicating about something, X, as,

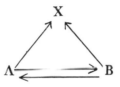

(Newcomb, 1953). This diagram, whatever satisfaction it, or complifications of it, might offer psychologically, is simplistic for human communication. In the interchange A: "How-do-you-do, a fine day isn't it?" B: "Yes, a beautiful day." it would be rather naive to assume that X = "weather". A and B are simply giving verbal tokens of mutual awareness. X need not be "out there" —trees, rocks, waves, mountains, or love, honor, dignity, despair—but institutional, social or internal states that are being communicated. At any rate, if all communicational interchange has a content, even if that content may be zero, it is a constant and need not be noted, much less diagramed, at all. So we are left simply with A and B communicating with each other. But how? If language alone is involved we would have an exchange of letters, memoranda, or telegrams, or an information exchange between two computers. Human communication normally occurs on four levels, or modalities, simultaneously and these are embedded in a spatial matrix which in itself constitutes a form of communication.

Communication is coeval with living organisms. If language can be considered to be the *definiens* of the species Homo sapiens, then communication has the same relation to organic life. All interchanges of information are based on the senses and progressed from the more simple to the more complex as these senses developed from the primitive tactile (with at first only two signals, pleasure/pain) through the gustatory, olfactory, visual, and finally, commencing with the inner ear of the fishes, the auditory. The five-sense classification might seem quaint and inadequate to modern psychologists but it is quite sufficient for the sensory receptors of communicative stimuli. Most of the placental mammals employ five modalities of communicative behavior: the tactile (a better term is "haptic"), gustatory, olfactory, kinesic (visual reception) and paralinguistic (aural reception), but with differing emphasis. The dog, for example, is more centered on the gustatory and olfactory than the cat, who is more sensitive to the kinesic (the feline "stare"). Man not only uses the audio-vocal tract for paralanguage as do other species, but has added the all-important, duality-principled modality of language.

In general communication two of the modalities have become relatively unimportant for man, although here there is some cultural variation. The most intimate of all, the gustatory ("it was so close I could almost taste it"), is used only in sexual interchanges. Olfaction in America and Europe is also, by and large, involved with sexual signaling, although in some cultures, e.g. with the Arabs (cf. Hall, 1959), smell is a normal feature of communicative behavior. In this paper these two levels of signaling will be ignored. For one thing, there is an almost non-existence of relevant material (the psychologists' sensory testing is largely irrelevant here). For another, particularly in the latter area, there is a serious lack of lexical parameters, at least in English. This would not be true in Totonac, for example, for which Eugene Nida (1949) lists nineteen different "smell" words derived from eight stems.

The four basic systems of human communication can be summarized as follows:

Stimulus	Reception	System
articulated vocal tract	aural	language
non-articulated vocal tract	aural	paralanguage
body movement	visual	kinesics
pressure	tactile	haptics

On paralanguage see Austin (1965, 1970), Trager (1958), Pittenger and Smith (1957), and Smith (1969). On kinesics see Birdwhistell (1952, 1966). On haptics see Austin (1970), and Frank (1957). On the proxemic settings for these systems see Hall (1959, 1966).

Formal Non-two-way Conversations

When General Douglas MacArthur met with President Truman on Wake Island in October, 1950 it was said to be the first two-way conversation the former had had in fifteen years. A two-way conversation or interchange must be both formally (institutionally) and informally (psychologically) based. A non-two-way interchange may be formally or informally based. The most glaring example of the former is, of course, the military, a highly "institutionalized" set-up where everyone knows exactly how to "talk up" and "talk down." This extends to the other three systems as well and no formal instruction is given or received. This out-of-awareness learning is a by-product (perhaps the most important by-product) of basic training. The haptic non-two-way signalings are clear. The handshake must be initiated by the higher-ranked to the lower. The double handshake (two hands touching one—gratitude, confidence, "warmth") is very markedly a superior-to-inferior interchange. The hand on the shoulder is another such instance. When the institution allows a two-way communication, in the army between two sergeants, two majors and so forth, though tenure in rank may be a factor, the handshake, shoulder-touch may be reciprocally initiated.

The same holds true for kinesics. The standing and sitting posture of the lower-ranked is more rigid than that of the higher, the spine is stiffer, there is no sprawl or leg-cross while sitting. The lower-ranked's chin is normally tilted higher, the lids are wide open, the eye focus more direct, certainly no eye wandering. This pattern is repeated in the paralinguistic modality. The lower-ranked's voice pitch tends to be higher (markedly so in the German army of World Wars I and II) and the lingual set is more clear. The higher-ranked's voice set may be lower, the lingual set more slurred. The language signals are more obvious, having been learned in-awareness. *Sir*, generally with a rising intonation, marks the address of the enlisted man to an officer. It is also used between lower-ranked and higher-ranked officers, but here with falling intonation. The supra-segmental contours are also involved. A simple interchange between, say, a sergeant and a major, would be "How are you, sir?" with 22|33|| and "I'm fine, sergeant, how are you?" with 22|22|231. In general terms, rising intonation (equates with higher pitch, clearer enunciation, more rigid body stance, no touch, in the other systems) versus falling intonation (equates with lower pitch, less careful enunciation, more relaxed body set, and the potentiality of touch).

A similar situation, although somewhat more relaxed, prevails in another sub-culture, that of medicine and the hospital. The up and down talk is quite noticeable between such hierarchies as student-nurse, nurse, head-nurse, and intern, doctor, and chief-of-staff. Non-two-way conversations, of course, both reflect and solidify existing social and institutional structures and mitigate against change. It is little wonder that the American Medical Association is noted for its conservatism. The world of business is still less rigorously hierarchized than that of medicine, but two-way interchanges hardly exist between office-boy and executive. Inhibitions against two-way interchanges are proxemically reinforced by the desk, the one behind the desk having an edge in an unequal exchange (which is sometimes obviated by the other party's standing, or sitting on the desk). The larger and more expensive the desk, the greater the conversation gap. This not always good business and is avoided in some offices with chairs and sofas arranged around a low coffee table (see Hall, 1957, 1966). Of all our institutions the academic is the most relaxed in this respect, although two-way conversations between student and teacher can generally not be maintained for long, nor between instructors and full professors. In both of these cases age is as much a factor as rank.

In society at large it would be otiose to mention the many instances of non-two-way interchanges. Many languages have built-in inhibitors, such as the *tu/vous* of French, the *tu/usted* of Spanish, the *tu/lei* of Italian, the *du/Sie* of German, and so forth. Attempts at obviating social interchange inequalities have not always been successful. Mussolini tried to institute *voi* as the only term for 'you' but the more "democratic" post-war Italy immediately reverted to the *tu/lei* distinction. A similar attempt at equality was the Soviet Russian insertion of "comrade" before all titles, but its very omnipresence rendered it meaningless (what is totally predictable does not exist). But some vestiges of the less communicating past are gone from most modern societies. The English laborer no longer doffs his hat in the presence of gentry nor do East European peasants drop to their knees at the passing of nobility, the most primitive and powerful barrier to a two-way exchange.

Informal Non-Two-Way Conversations

While the above represent largely institutionally imposed inequalities, informal (internally directed, psychological) non-two-way exchanges are more indicative of distance than inequality. We all, and some more than others, sometimes wear masks and this game people play, which is not in Eric Berne's popular book, is called "Who am I?". We become accustomed to this in early childhood when we are told to behave in certain ways with strangers, visiting relatives, ministers, school teachers. The "goodie-goodie" little girl, who may be essentially a holy terror ("house devil, street saint") learns early the protective value of a mask. This disguise may require deviations from the base line from grammar, often dialect, through phonology and paralanguage (pitch overly high or low, tempo overly fast or slow, overly nasal or oral, and so forth), hand movement, lid closure, body set, and proxemic placing. Deviations from the norm entail a certain amount of discomfort and cannot be endured constantly. In the previous system various safety devices, such as "recess," "at ease," "relaxation," "coffee break," "martini lunch" are institutionally built-in. Here one can simply return to the base line or withdraw.

The need to present ourselves sometimes as other than we are is as old as mankind and as necessary as dreams. There are elements of this in primitive dance and ritual, masks and body paint, the *mardi-gras*, charades and the theater, with masks in ancient Greece and grease paint today. An informal non-two-way interchange is often the modus in early stages of courtship where the language may be too careful (or too lax), the pitch too low (or too high), the laugh too loud (or too restrained), the eyes too open (or too closed) and females have long had the advantage of the fan. These devices set up distance, but not insurmountable ones ("I'm hard to get, therefore valuable"). Another informal non-two-way communicative ploy is mimicking. In the United States northern men, on meeting southern girls, often use an imitation southern accent (however fake or inaccurate the imitation might be is of no relevance here). If the imitation continues too long the man obviously is trying to avoid a two-way conversation and succeeds. In modern western marriages two-way conversations between the partners are the norm, though this has not always been the case. But even in the best regulated of households non-two-way interludes are sometimes necessary. If the partners are not in phase the reaction is generally one of anger ("don't shout," "get that tone out of your voice"). If in phase, a friendly bantering or "kidding" will result. A friend of mine for over thirty-five years maintains this relationship almost constantly with his wife, children, in-laws, and friends. He needs distance, or does not like himself without his mask.

Informal, as well as formal, non-two-way interchanges are formidable barriers in the communication between Blacks and Whites in the United States. The American Negro has long worn a mask, the "Uncle Tom", not to mention the linguistic non-two-way *ma'am* and *suh*. Even in well-integrated situations where the language modality may be two-way, the other modalities may not. The result can be loosely called "strained."

A Two-way Conversation

A two-way conversation, both formally and informally structured, is when communication is at its maximum, when we are being most ourselves, when we adhere to our base lines in all modalities simultaneously. The base line does not require long study to calibrate. We determine the 231 of a sentence pitch contour instantly, no matter what the tonal variation might be, and Chinese peasants have no difficulty in calibrating a tone that might be octaves apart (or fractions thereof) in two speakers. Statistical investigation is of no use here. The human science is one of pattern recognitions. Two way conversations are easiest between members of the same sex (unless special factors are involved), the same age group, and the same social position. The loneliest are those who can do this the least, for example the President of the United States.

Being oneself and communicating optimally is of course desirable, but not always. There are formal restrictions for the safety and order of society and informal ones for the health and sanity of the individual. Nothing is

total for always. The patterning of two-way and non-two-way exchanges
may be summarized as follows:

Formally (Institutionally) Structured
Non-two-way Communication

linguistic		base line
paralinguistic		base line
kinesic		base line
haptic		base line

Informally (Psychologically) Structured
Non-two-way Communication

linguistic		base line
paralinguistic		base line
kinesic		base line
haptic		base line

Formally and Informally Structured
Two-way Communication

linguistic		base line
paralinguistic		base line
kinesic		base line
haptic		base line

References

Austin, William M., "Some Social Aspects of Paralanguage," *Canadian Journal of Linguistics*, 11, pp. 31–39 (1965); "Non-verbal Communication," Davis, A. L., ed. *Culture, Class and Language Variety: A Resource Book for Teachers.*

Berne, Eric, *Games People Play* (1964).

Birdwhistell, Ray L., *An Introduction to Kinesics* (1952); "Some Relations Between American Kinesics and Spoken American English" in Smith, A. G., *Communication and Culture*, pp. 182–189 (1966).

Davis, Alva L. ed., *Culture, Class and Language Variety: A Resource Book for Teachers*, (1971).

Frank, Lawrence K., "Tactile Communication," in *Genetic Psychology Monographs*, 56, pp. 209–255 (1957), reprinted in A. G. Smith, above.

Hall, Edward T., *The Silent Language* (1957); *The Hidden Dimension*, (1966).

Newcomb, Theodore M., "An Approach to the Study of Communicative Acts," in *Psychological Review*, 60, 393–404 (1953), reprinted in A. G. Smith, above.

Nida, Eugene, *Morphology*, 2nd ed. p. 158 (1949).

Pittenger, Robert E. and Smith, Henry L., Jr., "A Basis for Some Contributions of Linguistics to Psychiatry," *Psychiatry* 20, pp. 61–78 (1957).

Smith, Alfred G. ed., *Communication and Culture* (1966).

Smith, Henry Lee, Jr., "Language and the Total System of Communication," in Hill, Archibald A., ed. *Linguistics Today* pp. 89–102 (1969).

Trager, George L., "Paralanguage: A First Approximation," *Studies in Linguistics*, 13, pp. 1–12 (1958).

THE PHONEMIC SEGMENTS OF AN EDMONTON IDIOLECT

WALTER S. AVIS
Royal Military College of Canada

During the past century or so, some 200 writings having reference to Canadian English have appeared in print, most of them since 1950.[1] For the most part, the writers have been concerned with the speech of certain regions or with usages typical of Canadian English, especially as contrasted with usage in the United States and/or the United Kingdom. Because too few of the authors and even fewer of their readers were knowledgeable about linguistics, vocabulary has received the most attention. For the same reason, phonology has received relatively little, except for occasional references to specific features, which were often described in terms imprecise and naive.

In recent years, however, at least three attempts to describe varieties of Canadian pronunciation in organized linguistic terms have been published in the *Journal of the Canadian Linguistic Association*.[2] The present paper is a somewhat tardy contribution to this series: a phonemic analysis of a speech sample recorded at Edmonton, Alberta, in 1959.

The informant, whose parents had immigrated to Alberta from Ontario early in the present century, was born and educated in Edmonton, where he graduated from the University of Alberta. At the time of the interview, he had been working for some years as a reporter with the *Edmonton Journal*. In matters of language he was alert to the social demands for acceptable usage and somewhat inclined to remark "faults" in the speech of others. There was, however, little evidence of affectation or preciousness in his speech, which was typical of Edmontonians in his age group and at his level of education. In his pronunciation I observed no Briticisms or Americanisms that might not have been expected among other speakers of "General Canadian." [3]

This phonemic description is based on a taped reading of some 700 words, specially composed to provide a suitable corpus for the study of Canadian English pronunciation. Moreover, the taped materials were checked and augmented during a subsequent interview with the informant. Suprasegmental features, whether considered phonemic or not, are not treated here although three levels of stress are indicated for polysyllabic words. In general, the phonemic interpretation of the data follows the procedures I learned from Professors Kurath, Pike, Fries, and McDavid at the University of Michigan, an approach I have found pragmatically useful in describing regional varieties of English.[4]

Vowels and Diphthongs

Although the informant's speech was transcribed in narrow notation, the phonetic samples presented here will be substantially broader. There seems little point in complicating the typographical problems where allophonic variation is commonplace in North American English. Accordingly, the consistent difference in length between vowels preceding voiceless consonants and those occurring elsewhere is ignored except where regionally significant allophones which also exhibit a difference in quality are concerned, as with the phoneme /au/, actualized as [aᵘ] in *loud* and as [əᵘ] in *shout*. Other systematic variations of length which occur under certain prosodic conditions, such as stress-and-intonation contours, have also been ignored. Again, the unstable and subphonemic inglides that sometimes follow checked vowels are noted only occasionally; such ingliding diphthongs—as opposed to upgliding types—occur only sporadically and appear to be conditioned by the phonetic environment and prosodic factors. Shift signs, it should be added, are used sparingly in this paper. Because the incidence of the vowels is a matter of some interest, I have included among my examples certain words which illustrate typically Canadian pronunciations. Finally, I have, whereever I deemed it informative, inserted notes within the text, this course being chosen in preference to that of multiplying footnotes.

In this idiolect there are 14 vowel phonemes—four /ɪ, ɛ, æ, ʊ/ checked monophthongs (occurring in preconsonantal position only), six /i, e, ɑ, ə, o, u/ free monophthongs (occurring in both preconsonantal and word-final position), and four free diphthongs /ai, au, ɔɪ, iu/. These phonemes may be schematically arranged as follows:

```
              iu     ʊ    u
    i    ɪ                o
    e      ɛ      ə
             æ     ɑ
    ai          au        ɔi
```

The most striking feature of this inventory is the absence of a phoneme /ɔ/, which, as is usual in General Canadian idiolects, has coalesced with /ɑ/.[5] For convenience in cross-referring, the vowel phonemes described hereunder are numbered 1 to 14.

1. /i/ (free) is normally actualized as a high-front unround diphthong,

beginning somewhat low and lax and gliding rapidly to higher and tenser tongue position, [ɪˠ]~[iˠ], as in creek /krik/, *guarantee* /ˌgærən'ti/, *tree* /tri/, *lever* /'livər/, and *beef, feet, wheat,* etc. Before /l/ in *wheel* an ingliding allophone occurs, [iᴵ ᶜ]. In weakly stressed syllables a monophthong may occur [iˠ]~[i ᶜ], as in *greasy* /'grisi/, *pretty* /'prɪti/, *Tuesday* /'tiuzdi/, and *beyond* /bɪ'jɑnd/.

2. /ɪ/ (checked) is normally actualized as a lax, lower-high-front, unround monophthong, [ɪ]~[ɪ ᶜ], as in *inner* /'ɪnər/, *lilies, little, milk, window*. A somewhat centered allophone, [ɪ ᶜ], occurs in *Williams* and *busy*, and a non-syllabic inglide is sometimes evident before /g/, as in *pig* [pɪᵊg]. Before /r/ the allophone is somewhat higher than the norm, [ɪˆ]~[iˠ], as in *near* /nɪr/. The phone [ɪ]—which often appears in checked position in unstressed syllables—is here interpreted as an allophone of /ɪ/, as in *spirit* /'spɪrɪt/, *oranges* /'orɪnjɪz/, *building* /'bɪldɪŋ/, parents /'pɛrɪnts/, *decided* /dɪ'saidɪd/, and because /bɪ'kɑz/.[6]

3. /e/ (free) is normally actualized as a tense, unround diphthong beginning in mid-front position and gliding upward toward high front, [eᴵ], as in *take* /tek/, *vase* /vez/, *granary, tomatoes, today, haymow*.

4. /ɛ/ (checked) is normally actualized as a lax, lower-mid-front, unround monophthong, [ɛ]~[ɛˆ], as in *egg* /ɛg/, *elm* /ɛlm/, *already, center, Quebec* /kwə'bɛk/, *threshing*. Before /r/ a somewhat lower allophone, [ɛˠ]~[ɛ ᶜ], occurs, as in *Mary* and *merry* /'mɛri/, *hairy* /'hɛri/, *care, cherry, dairy, Ontario, stairs*.

5. /æ/ (checked) is normally actualized as a low-front, unround, slightly tense monophthong, [æ]~[æ ᶜ], as in *aunt* /ænt/, *answer, danced; after* /'æftər/, *rafter; calves* /kævz/, *half; rather* /'ræðər/, *path; grass* /græs/, *glass, pasture; garage* /gə'ræʒ/; *ashcan* /'æšˌkæn/, *pan, stamping, matters,* etc. A non-syllabic inglide often occurs before /g/, as in *bag* [bæᵊg] and *flags*. Before /r/ the allophones vary from [æˠ] to [æˆ], as in *Harry* /'hæri/, *marry* /'mæri/, *marrows* /'mæroz/, *barrel* /'bærəl/, *guarantee* /ˌgærən'ti/. The phone in *sat* [sɛ ᶜ t] is somewhat arbitrarily interpreted as /æ/.

6. /ɑ/ (free) is normally actualized as a lax, low-central, unround monophthong, [ɑ], but has a wide range of allophones difficult to attribute to specific environments, [aᶜ ~ɑˆ ~ɑᶜ ~ɑˆ~ ɑᶜ ~ɒᶜ], as in *shone* /šɑn/, *gone, haunted, job, odds, broad, caught* or *cot* /kɑt/, *brought* /brɑt/, *thought* /θɑt/, *daughter, father, small, stall, want, watch, water, wash, sausages, coffee, across, lilac* /'lailɑk/. In certain positions under prosodic influence non-syllabic inglides occur: [dɑg] but also [dɑᵊg], [pɑm] but also [kɑᵊm], [smɑl] but also [wɑᵊl], [wɑʃ] but also [skwɑᵊʃ]; the forms [strɑᵊ] and ['ɑˈmənz] occurs for *straw* and *almonds* respectively. Before /r/ the allophones [a~aᶜ ~ɑ ᶜ] occur, the norm being noticeably fronted, as in *barnyard* ['baᶜ ɚnˌjaɚd], i.e., /'bɑrnˌjɑrd/, *khaki* ['kaɚki], i.e., /'kɑrki/, *bark, car, far, garden, large, marsh, Martha.*[7]

7. /o/ (free) is normally actualized as a tense, round diphthong, begin-

ning in mid-front position and gliding upward toward high back, [oᵁ] ~ [c ' ᵁ], as in *coat* /kot/, *clothes* /kloz/, *collie* /'koli/, *almost, both, low, mauve, posts, road, stone, thrown, whole, won't.* Under certain prosodic conditions, the upglide is very slight or lacking entirely, [oᵒˇ] ~ [o], as in *grocery, don't, coat of paint;* a similar tendency toward monophthongization is evident under weak stress, as in *window, tomatoes, marrows.* Before /r/ the allophones [ɔˇ] ~ [oˇ] occur, as in *horse* and *hoarse* /hors/, *morn* and *mourn* /morn/, *door, floor, porch, worn.*⁸

8. /ʊ/ (checked) is normally actualized as lax, lower-high-front, round monophthong, [ʊ] ~ [ʊ '], as in *butcher* / 'bʊčər/, *could* /kʊd/, *foot, good, pushing, stood.* Before /r/ a lowered, retracted allophone occurs, [ʊ '], as in *poor* /pʊr/ and *sure* /šʊr/.

9. /u/ (free) is normally actualized as a high-back, round diphthong, beginning somewhat low and lax and gliding rapidly to a higher and tenser tongue position, [ʊˇᵘ] ~ [uˇᵘ] ~ [u ' ᵘ], as in *cool* /kul/, *do* and *due* /du/, *food, hoop, hoot, roof, root* and *route* /rut/, *shoe, slough* /slu/, *soot* /sut/, *stewing, suit, tube, manure* /mə'nur/. In the sequence /ju/ a somewhat centered monophthong occurs, [u '] [u '], as in *genuine* /'jɛnju,wain/, *using* /'juzɪŋ/.⁹

10. /ə/ (free) is normally a central, unround monophthong and has five distinctive allophones:

(a) a retracted and lower centrál lax monophthong which occurs only under stress in checked position, [ʌ] ~ [ʌ '] ~ [ʌ '], as in *butter* /'bətər/, *gums* /gəmz/, *junk, mother, rough, son, under, was* /wəz/, *because* /bɪ'kəz/.

(b) a mid-central, lax monophthong which occurs in both free and checked position in unstressed syllables only, [ə] ~ [əˇ], as in *Edmonton* /'ɛdməntən/, *Quebec* /kwə'bɛk/, *Toronto* /tə'rɑnto/, *about* /ə'baut/, *again* /ə'gɛn/, *barrel* /'bærəl/, *stables* /'stebəlz/, *vegetables* /'vɛjtəbəlz/, *Martha* /'mɑrθə/. The raised variant of this allophone probably occurs in free variation with [ɪ '] (ascribed to /ɪ/ in No. 2 above) in certain unstressed closed syllables, as in *chicken* /čɪkən/, *garden* /'gɑrdən/, *haunted* /'hɑntəd/, *sherbet* /'šərbət/, as opposed to *blanket, bushes, decided, oranges, sausages, spirit,* all of which were recorded with an allophone of /ɪ/ in the final unstressed syllable.¹⁰

(c) a mid-central unround monophthong articulated with lateral constriction of the tongue ("*r*-coloring"), occurring in both free and checked positions in stressed syllables only, [ɝ]. This composite vocoid is here interpreted as the phonemic sequence /ər/, as in *burlap* /'bərlæp/, *girl* /gərl/, *squirrels* /skwərlz/, *syrup* /'sərɪp/, *work* /wərk/.

(d) a mid-central monophthong similar in description to [ɝ], its stressed counterpart; this constricted allophone, [ɚ], occurs in both free and checked position in unstressed syllables only, as in *butcher* /'bʊčər/, *either* /'aiðər/, *flowers* /'flauərz/, *water* /'wɑtər/; *were* stressed is [wɝ], unstressed is [wə]: both are phonemically /wər/.

(e) the syllabic feature of [l̩] and [n̩], as in *bristles* /'brɪsəlz/, *little* /'lɪtəl/, *mountain* /'mauntən/.

11. /iu/ (free) is normally a rising diphthong having a lax, unround, high-central onset and gliding toward a tense, round, high-back second element that is usually quite fronted, [ɪuˈ] [ɪʉˈ] [ɪʉ], as in *few* /fiu/, *nephew* /'nɛfiu/, *new* /niu/, *Tuesday* /'tiuzdi/. Following alveolar stops and nasals, usage is somewhat unsettled with this speaker, some words having /iu/, as in *new* and *Tuesday*, others having /u/, as in *due*, *stewing*, and *tubes*. After /s/ and /l/ only /u/ occurs, as in *suit* and *slough*; *new suit* for this speaker is /ˌniu 'sut/.[11]

It must be admitted that the setting up of /iu/ as phonemically distinct from the sequence /ju/ is somewhat arbitrary since the latter is probably substitutable wherever the former occurs. Yet the phonetic quality of both the first and the second elements of /ju/ in *using*, *you*, *genuine* and of /iu/ in *few*, *new*, *Tuesday* are so strikingly dissimilar in this idiolect that their separation seems pragmatically reasonable.

12. /ai/ (free) is a falling, upgliding diphthong having two conspicuous allophones:

(a) an unround diphthong normally actualized with an open low-front beginning followed by a fast upglide toward high-front position, [aᴵ]~[aᶦ] [aˆᴵ] [a ˈᴵ], etc.; this allophone occurs word finally and before voiced sounds, as in *dry* /drai/, *either* /'aiðər/, *fine*, *idea*, *genuine*, *lilac*, *nine*, *while* /hwail/. A somewhat higher onset is evident before /r/ in *tires* and *tired*, namely, [aˆ ˈᴵ].[12]

(b) an unround, very fast diphthong normally actualized with a mid-central beginning, often lowered and fronted, followed by a slight upglide toward high-front or advanced high-central position, [əᴵ]~ [əˆᴵ]~[ɐ ˈᴵ], etc. This allophone occurs only in checked position before voiceless consonants, as in *height* /hait/, *knife*, *night*, *white* /hwait/, *wipe*.[13]

13. /au/ (free) is a falling, upgliding diphthong having two conspicuous allophones:

(a) a diphthong normally actualized with an open, low-front, unround beginning followed by a fast upglide toward high-back, round position, [aᵁ]~[a ˈ ᵒˆ]~[ɑˈ ᵁ], etc.; this allophone occurs word finally and before voiced sounds, as in *mow* /mau/, *our* /aur/, *owls*, *found*, *flowers* /'flauərz/, *mountain*.[14]

(b) a very fast diphthong normally actualized with a mid-central beginning, often lowered and fronted, followed by a slight upglide toward high-back, round position, [əᵁ]~[əˆᵁ]~ [ɐˆᵁ]~[ɐ ˈᵁ], etc.; this allophone occurs only in checked position before voiceless consonants, in *about* /ə'baut/, *drought* /draut/, *house* /haus/, *out*, *shout*.[15]

14. /ɔi/ (free) a falling, upgliding diphthong normally actualized with a lowered mid-central, round beginning followed by a fast upglide toward high-front position, [ɔ^ɪ] ~ [ɔˆ^ɪ], etc., as in *oil* /ɔil/, *boy* /bɔi/.[16]

On the whole, the consonant phonemes of North American English are fairly stable and their allophones predictable. It should therefore be sufficient here to present a traditional chart for those of the idiolect under examination and to add a few notes concerning the phonemes that have allophones meriting special attention. On the following chart, the phonemes are arranged according to the type of sound, the point of articulation, and the state of the glottis during the articulation of the typical allophones:

	bi-labial vl vd	labio-dental vl vd	dental vl vd	alveolar vl vd	palatal vl vd	velar vl vd	glottal vl
stops	p b			t d		k g	
fricatives		f v	θ ð	s z	š ž		h
affricates					č ǰ		
nasals	m			n		ŋ	
lateral				l			
glides				r	j	w	

It will be seen from the foregoing chart that [tʃ] and dӡ] are interpreted as the unit phonemes /č/ and /ǰ/ respectively.[17] Moreover, /h/ is interpreted as a voiceless glottal fricative and /r/, /j/, and /w/ as voiced glides, the last shown as a velar although it has a no less significant bilabial feature. As remarked above, the allophones of most of the consonants are just what might be expected in North American English: /h/ has a voiced allophone that occurs intervocalically preceding a stressed syllable, as in *perhaps*; /l/ has "light" and "dark" allophones according to position, the former occurring before front vowels word-initially, the latter elsewhere. Characteristically, /θ/ and /ð/ are dental, not interdental, fricatives. The voiceless stops /p, t, k/ are strongly aspirated word-initially before vowels, except in certain clusters, /sp, st, sk/, where they are devoiced, lenis allophones; in word-final position the occlusion of these stops may or may not be released, much more often not.

Since /t/ has a wider range of conditioned variants than most consonants, a sketch of its allophones will be given here:

(a) an aspirated allophone, [tʰ], occurs in word-initial position before vowels, as in *teeth* /tiθ/ and *town* /taun/.

(b) an unreleased allophone, [t˘] occurs word-finally in free variation with released [tᴸ] as in *route* /rut/, and *soot* /sut/; the former type is, however, much more frequent.

(c) a lenis allophone, [ḑ], occurs in the cluster /st/ in prevocalic position, as in *stone*. In word-final position, the /t/ of this cluster is normally released, as in *rust* /rəst/ and *post* /post/.

(d) a voiced, fortis allophone, [t̬] occurs intervocalically following a stressed vowel, as in *butter* /ˈbətər/, *daughter*, *little*, *matter*, *shutting*, and *tomatoes*. Probably because this allophone remains fortis, the preceding vowel retains its relative brevity as characteristic of vowels before voiceless stops; thus *matter* retains the short vowel of *mat* as opposed to the half-long vowel of *mad*. Furthermore, *shouting* retains the characteristic diphthong of *shout* [ʃaʊt] as opposed to that of *loud* [laʊd], confirming that this consonant allophone belongs to /t/, at least in this idiolect.[18]

(e) the flap [ɾ] occurs between /n/ and a following unstressed vowel, as in *haunted* /'hauntəd/, *center* /'sɛntər/, and *Toronto* /tə'ranto/.

(f) the glottal stop [ʔ] occurs in such words as *mountain* ['ma ʾᵘnʔn̩] and *cotton* ['katʔn̩], where homorganic alveolar sequences are involved. In both cases, however, a simultaneous [ʔ] articulation is probable.[19]

(g) an excrescent stop in the homorganic sequence of such words as *dance* /dænts/, *fence* /fɛnts/, and *rinse* /rɪnts/.[20]

The phoneme /r/ also has an unusual number of allophones in this idiolect, none of them unfamiliar to students of American English. These allophones fall into two groups: (a) those occurring in prevocalic position, and (b) those occurring in the postvocalic position:

(a) i. the norm is a frictionless glide, [r], as in *rafters* and *rough*.

ii. a glide having friction, [ɹ], which occurs after /d/, as in *drought* and *dry*, and after /t/, as in *trough* and *try*, this type being devoiced, [ɹ̥]. Similar devoiced allophones occur after the other voiceless stops, as in *pry* and *across*.

iii. a trill may occur after /θ/, especially when the word is uttered with emphasis, as in *three* and *thrill*; this allophone is devoiced, [r̥], and is in free variation with the devoiced fricative type mentioned above.

(b) i. in the final unstressed syllable of *father* and *mother*, the allophone is a clearly audible component of the syllabic, which is articulated with lateral constriction and, sometimes, slight retroflection of the tongue, [ɚ]. Under stress, in such words as *Perth*, *sherbet*, and *were*, the articulation is virtually identical, this composite vowel being phonetically transcribed [ɝ]. The vowels in question have already been treated under No. 10 above, where [ɚ] and [ɝ] are analysed as /ər/, unstressed and stressed respectively.

ii. in the stressed syllables of such words as *far* [faɚ], /far/, *door*, *hear*, *poor*, *sure*, /r/, is actualized as a nonsyllabic constricted offglide, the tongue tension coloring the preceding vowel.[21]

iii. the same allophone, [ɚ] occurs in preconsonantal position in such words as *barn* [ba ʾɚn], /barn/, *border*, *dark*, *horses*, *tires*.

iv. in intervocalic position, /r/ is actualized as a frictionless glide, the tongue constriction usually coloring the preceding vowel, as in *Harry* /'hæri/, *dairy*, *hairy*, *Mary*.[22].

Two other matters related to the consonants of this idiolect remain to be commented on. First, the words *with* and *without* occur with /θ/ and not /ð/; a more extensive sample might have shown the speaker's usage to be unsettled, as is often the case among Canadians. Second, such words as *wheat* and *white* begin with what is interpreted to be the cluster /hw/, which was consistently used by this speaker in words bearing full stress. In *which*, the word being used under light sentence stress, the /h/ did not occur; in *while*, also used under light sentence stress, the initial fricative was audible, but only just. The tendency for /h/ to fade or disappear entirely in unstressed syllables is widely attested in English. Many speakers of General Canadian, however, use /hw/ or /w/ as free variants in such words as *whale*, *wheat*, *wheel*, and *white*, that is, in words normally bearing full stress.

This attempt to describe the vowel phonemes and some of the more significant allophones of the consonant phonemes might well be concluded with a few comments relating usage in this idiolect to the general usage in what I have referred to as General Canadian (GC). The following systematic characteristics of this idiolect are typical of GC (the cross-reference being to the numbered vowels and the consonants treated above):

1. No /ɔ/ phoneme occurs (see Nos. 6, 7, 14).
2. /i/, /e/, /o/, /u/ are actualized as upgliding diphthongs (see Nos. 1, 3, 7, 9).
3. /ai/ /au/, /ɔi/ have distinctive centralized allophones before voiceless consonants (see Nos. 12, 13, 14).
4. /iu/~/ju/~/u/ are unsettled following alveolars, /u/ predominating for this speaker. (Usage in GC is much divided and unsettled because of the prestige factor of /iu/~/ju/; see No. 11).
5. /u/ is usual in *coop*, *roof*, *root*, etc. (This speaker's pronunciation of *soot* /sut/ is, however, atypical of GC, though it is seemingly frequent in the West: see Nos. 8, 9).
6. /ɛ/ is used in *Mary* and *merry* but /æ/ in *marry*; *hairy* and *Harry* are also distinguished by this speaker. (Usage in GC seems to be much divided with respect to such sets; it seems probable that the last-mentioned pair are falling together, at least among the young, and especially in the West. See Nos. 3, 4, 5).
7. /o/ is common to *horse*, *hoarse*, *morning*, *mourning* (see No. 7).
8. /ɪ/, usually [ɪ] types, predominates over /ə/, that is, [ə^] in medial unstressed position (see Nos. 2, 10).
9. /r/ prevocalic is actualized as a glide, preconsonantal as a tongue-constricted feature superimposed on the accompanying vowel and/or as a nonsyllabic tongue-constricted offglide: [ɚ], [ɚ], or [ɚ] (see No. 10 under "Vowels" and /r/ under "Consonants").
10. /t/ occurs intervocalically as a voiced, fortis allophone, [t̬]; in certain other voiced environments following a stressed syllable, /t/ occurs as a flap or glottal stop (see "consonants" under /t/).[28]

11. /t/ is regularly excrescent in *dance, fence, rinse,* etc., and /k/ is excrescent in *length, strength.*

12. /hw/ is constant under full stress in *wheat, while, white,* etc., the fricative tending to disappear as stress decreases, as in unstressed *which* /wɪč/. (Usage is both unsettled and divided for such words in GC, especially among the educated.)

13. The incidence of the phonemes in certain individual words also reveals the GC character of this informant's speech:

almonds /ˈɑmɔndz/	lever /ˈlivər/	syrup /ˈsərɪp/
blouse /blauz/	nephew /ˈnɛfiu/	tomato /təˈmeto/
clothes /kloz/	Quebec /kwəˈbɛk/	vase /vez/
creek /krik/	route /rut/	won't /wont/
drought /draut/	schedule /ˈskɛjəl/	
greasy /ˈgrisi/	shone /šɑn/	
height /hait/	squirrel /skwərl/	

Other variants are, of course, heard from speakers of GC for these words, some regional (as for *drought, lever, Quebec, won't*), others social (as for *clothes, creek, height, route, schedule, squirrel, syrup, tomato, vase*); a few of those listed, however, are highly stable in Canada; *greasy, nephew, shone.*

14. Certain other individual items in this idiolect are examples of words for which there is a great deal of divided usage:[24]

again /əˈgɛn/ vs. /əˈgen/	genuine /ˈǰenjuˌain/ vs. /-ɪn/
been /bɪn/ vs. /bin/	granary /ˈgrenɑri/ vs. /ˈgrænəri/
collie /ˈkoli/ vs. /ˈkɑli/	lilac /ˈlailɑk/ vs. /ˈlailək/
either /ˈiðər/ vs. /ˈaiðər/	slough /slu/ vs. /slau/
garage /gəˈræž/ vs. /gəˈrɑž/ or /gəˈræj/	were /wər/ vs. /wɛr/

Here again the explanation for the variant is sometimes regional, as with *slough,* /slu/ being a distinctive Prairie usage and /slau/ a form used west of the Rockies and east of the Lakehead, where it is a book-word for many. Such forms as /əˈgen/, /bin/, and /wɛr/ are probably recessive though they are often classed as distinctive Canadian pronounciations.[25]

The foregoing treatment is admittedly sketchy, a shortcoming that is in part due to the limitations of the corpus and in part to the limitations of the author. It is, however, high time that some attempt was being made to add to the limited amount of information available in published form to students of language, especially those interested in Canadian English.

Notes

1. See Walter S. Avis, *Bibliography of Writings on Canadian English: 1857–1965* (Toronto: Gage, 1965). This listing is updated in the Canadian English section of "Linguistica Canadiana"—a cumulative bibliography appearing in the

Canadian Journal of Linguistics (*CJL*), formerly called the *Journal of the Canadian Linguistic Association* (*JCLA*)—*CJL*, 15:1 (Fall, 1969).

2. R.J. Gregg, "Notes on the Pronunciation of Canadian English as Spoken in Vancouver, B.C.," *JCLA* 3 (1957), 20–6; see also Gregg's "Neutralism and Fusion of Vocalic Phonemes in Canadian English as Spoken in the Vancouver Area," *ibid.*, 78–83. P.D. Drysdale, "A First approach to Newfoundland Phonemes," *JCLA*, 5 (1959), 25–34. Walter Lehn, "Vowel Contrasts in a Saskatchewan English Dialect." *JCLA*, 5 (1959), 90–8. This journal is now called the *Canadian Journal of Linguistics* (*CJL*).

3. The term *General Canadian*, which has been in use for over 30 years, refers to that variety of English heard generally from Ontario westward, especially among the urban educated class. Closely related to the "Northern American" speech of adjacent regions of the United States, General Canadian has its roots in old Upper Canada, doubtless in the Toronto area of influence. It is the prestige dialect throughout most of Canada and is the variety of speech most commonly heard on the national network of the Canadian Broadcasting Corporation as well as on the commercial CTV network and, with some regional variations, on most local stations. See my "The English Language in Canada: A Report," *Current Trends in Linguistics*, Vol. 10, now in preparation.

4. This approach, which involves the unitary as opposed to the binary interpretation of diphthongal vowels, is expounded at some length in Hans Kurath and Raven I. McDavid, Jr., *The Pronunciation of English in the Atlantic States* (Ann Arbor: University of Michigan Press, 1961), pp. 3–9.

5. Kurath and McDavid's Type IV: Western Pennsylvania (*op. cit.*, p. 7) also lacks /ɔ/. There is no great significance in the fact that Type IV includes /ʌ/, which is lacking above; I have simply interpreted [ʌ] and [ə] as allophones of /ə/, the conditioning factor being stress, as described at No. 10 below.

6. I see no point in setting up "barred *i*" as a phoneme when /ɪ/, itself a checked vowel, is available; in any case, my corpus does not include the items required to establish the contrast. It is probable that this speaker's usage with respect to [ɪ] and [ə] in checked position is somewhat unsettled. Nevertheless, the higher phone dominated in closed syllables (see No. 10 below). It might be noted that his idiolect has /ɪ/ in *been* [bɪ ' n] whether stressed or not. Furthermore, nasalization of vowels is not strongly evident, being slightly noticeable in *pint* and *paint*.

7. This fronted allophone before /r/, as in [faˤ], is one of the distinctive features of General Canadian although it is obscured by the phonemic representation /ɑr/ adopted here. Some speakers of General Canadian (but not this one) have a three-way contrast in the series *bam* [bæm], *balm* [bam], and *bomb* [bɑm] and/or in *lather* ['læðɚ], *rather* ['raðɚ], and *father* ['faðɚ], a situation which permits the setting up of three low phonemes /æ/, /a/, and /ɑ/. In such idiolects (of which mine is one), the representations /far/, /barn/, etc. are possible and call due attention to the fronted nature of the vowel in such words. This characteristic fronting is also a feature of the initial element in upgliding diphthongs of [raᵘnd] and [raɪnd], for which see Nos. 12 and 13 below. In passing, I might point out that many Western Canadians use this fronted phone in *guarantee* [ˌgarən'ti], that is, /a/; this speaker, however, uses /æ/, as pointed out in No. 5 above.

8. For the interpretation of the unitary diphthong of /bɔi/ see No. 14 below.

9. For a note on the variation /u/ ~ /ju/ ~ /iu/ after alveolars, see No. 11.

10. To group [ɪ] and [ə] as allophones of /ə/, as is sometimes done, seems quite unsatisfactory, for they are often significant diaphones regionally; moreover, there are significant social restrictions since ['soᵘfɪ] and ['kænədɪ] for *sofa* and *Canada* are old-fashioned and rural variants of the current ['soᵘfə] and ['kænədə], that is, /'sofə/ and /'kænədə/.

11. Unsettled and divided usage is characteristic of General Canadian for this class of words, partly because the /iu/ variants are learned as prestige forms by many. However, it is highly unusual for the substitution of /iu/ for /u/ to be made consistently throughout the class, many speakers saying /'tiuzdi/ but /'studənt/, /diuk/ but /dun/, and even /diu/ *dew* but /du/ *due* (or vice versa). A by-product of this process is that many such switchers commonly use the hyperurbanisms /niun/ for *noon* and /tiu/ for *two* and/or too. See my "Speech Differences Along the Ontario-United States Border: III, Pronunciation," *JCLA*, 2 (October 1956), 48–49.

12. A unique variant occurs in *tiger* (*lilies*) ['tæ ˈɪɡɚ], which is pretty close to—and may well be—/'tægər/, a form that has been observed in other Canadian idiolects.

13. Although the evidence in the data is scarce, it seems possible that this allophone occurs also at times before clusters of a liquid or nasal plus a voiceless stop; in this corpus *pint* is [pɐɪnt]. See fn. 14.

14. The word *mountain* has a diphthong with a somewhat higher onset than usual, [aˈʊ], which suggests that the allophone described in (b) may occur at times before liquids and nasals plus a voiceless stop, especially /nt/, as in *count, fount, mount*, etc. See fn. 13.

15. The "fast" diphthongs [əɪ] and [əʊ] before voiceless consonants are characteristic of (but not peculiar to) General Canadian. Persons unfamiliar with the sound often claim that Canadians pronounce *out* [ut] as many Scots do. Indeed, the Scottish influence on Canadian speech has been strong for over a century and a half, so that there may well be a connection.

16. The instances of this phoneme in the corpus are too few to draw any conclusions, but I nevertheless believe that there is an allophonic distribution-pattern similar to that for /ai/ and /au/. Judging from my own idiolect, I would say that /ɔi/ before voiceles consonants and the cluster /nt/ would be actualized with a much fronted beginning, that is, as [ɵɪ], which might be expected in such words as *quoit, Boyce*, and *point*, as opposed to *annoyed, boys*, and *joined*, which have [ɔɪ]. I would like to add here that the falling diphthongs /ai/, /au/, and /ɔi/ are symbolized as they are for a reason. The second element is significant primarily in terms of the direction taken by the upglide and not in terms of the terminal point. Moreover, since the quality of the onset is regionally significant, I have used symbols which most clearly identify the nature of the initial elements. On the other hand, my opting for the unitary interpretation of diphthongs has obscured the General Canadian distinction between the vowels of *loud* and *lout*, *ride* and *write*, and *boys* and *Boyce* at the phonemic level.

17. See the discussion of this interpretation in Kurath and McDavid, *op. cit.*, p. 9.

18. This question was discussed thirty years ago by Martin Joos in "A Phonological Dilemma in Canadian English," *Language*, 18 (1942), 141–144.

19. The glottal allophone does not occur in this idiolect in the word *Edmonton* ['ɛdməntən], the previous syllable not being stressed.

20. By the same token, *length* is /'lɛŋkθ/ on the one occasion it occurs in this corpus. I might add that the variant /lɛnθ/ is often heard in Canada, no doubt reflecting Scots influence.

21. I regret that the question as to whether or not *flower* and *flour* have two syllables or one must remain unanswered, even though I have transcribed *flowers* as /'flauərz/ under No. 14 above.

22. *Hurry* and *furry* do not happen to occur in the corpus. If they did, one might expect ['hɜri] and ['fɜri], with *r*-coloring evident in the mid-central vowel; the allophone [ɜ] in this position in this idiolect never has the quality of [ʌ] in *gum* or *mud*. Phonemically, these words are transcribed as /'həri/ and /'fəri/; compare,

for example, *squirrel* /skwərl/ and *syrup* /ˈsərɪp/ as pronounced by this speaker. I suspect that all attempts to symbolize the allophones of North American /r/ accurately are more or less arbitrary.

23. Such pronunciations are often castigated as "sloppy articulation." Nevertheless, they are commonplace even in the speech of those whose tertiary response is hostile. A recent and related development is the spread of the form [kənˌgrædʒəˈleʃn̩z] for *congratulations*; this displacement of voiceless /č/ with voiced /ǰ/ seems commonest among the young. The word was not recorded for the present informant.

24. The first variant in each set is that used in the idiolect under examination.

25. Numerous variant forms not included in this corpus are characteristic of, or at least commonplace in, Canadian English, that is, GC, for example, the systematic occurrence of /i/ in *anti-, semi-, multi-,* etc.; of /-iz/ in *Chinese, Japanese, Javanese,* etc.; of /æ/ in *Czechoslovakia, Java, Yugoslavia, Viet Nam,* etc: of /iu/ /ju/ in *avenue, revenue,* etc.; of /ail/ in *crocodile, docile, reptile,* etc. (but not at all consistently in *fertile* or *missile*); of /o/ in *process, progress,* etc. (where the /ɑ/ variant is now common and probably spreading). The following pronunciations of specific items are too widespread in GC to be ignored: *arctic* /ˈɑrtɪk/, *columnist* /ˈkɑləmɪst/, *figure* /ˈfɪgər/, *suggest* /səˈǰɛst/, *vehicle* /ˈviɪkəl/. It might be added that few of the variants in use are the cause of much hostile response by the guardians of the language; however, *arctic* /ˈɑrtɪk/ and *genuine* /ˈǰɛnjəˌwain/ still must be classed as social shibboleths.

FREQUENCIES OF SOME SENTENCE CONNECTORS

WILLIAM CARD
Chicago State University

The vehicle for this investigation of the frequencies of sentence connectors[1] was a class in advanced rhetoric whose members were all teachers in the schools of Chicago and suburbs and most of whom were candidates for Master of Arts in English.[2] I wanted to free them from dependence on the handbooks by giving them some experience in the techniques of investigation in rhetoric and style.

I had already noted that some mediocre and poor writers are given to overheavy rhetoric; I had thought that some handbooks, whether intentionally or not, tended to encourage such rhetoric and that some high school teachers followed the handbooks in this respect because it was easy to teach. And, always optimistic, I hoped that if this study was published it might be noticed by some handbook writers. But of course this is a very slim hope: they go on and on copying each other and developing the same points, some good, some bad.

The corpus was partly determined by the fact that I had selected Leo Hamalian and Edmond L. Volpe's *Essays of Our Time [I]* (New York: McGraw-Hill, 1960) as the textbook for the course. Some essays were eliminated because some members of the class dropped out after the meeting in which we divided the corpus among the class members. Later we eliminated those that were translations or that were written by authors not native speakers of English. We also eliminated those that had a preponderance of conversation and two that were eccentric in style—those by e.e. cummings and Henry Miller. Since our corpus had to be small, we wanted to make it representative of a normal expository style rather than of several possible styles.

I list here the full names of the authors, the titles of their essays (for the light they throw on subject matter) and the dates of first publication where given by Hamalian and Volpe:

William Barrett, "Modern Art," 1958.

Percy Bridgman, "Science and Common Sense," 1954.
Roger Burlingame, "The Analyst's Couch," 1959.
Bruce Catton, "The Great American Game," 1959.
Agnes DeMille, "Milk of Paradise."
Jerome Ellison, "Are We Making a Playground out of College?" 1959.
Louis Finkelstein, "The Businessman's Moral Failure," 1958.
Geoffrey Gorer, "Success and the Dollar," 1948.
Aldous Huxley, "Mother," 1952.
Julian Huxley, "What Do We Know about Love," 1955.
John Keats, "The Call of the Open Road," 1958.
Russell Lynes, "Teen-agers in the Looking Glass," 1959.
Ronald Melzack, "The Personal Pain," 1958.
Vance Packard, "The Packaged Soul?" 1957.
I. I. Rabi, "Scientist and Humanist," 1956.
David Riesman, "Books: Gunpowder of the Mind," 1957.
Elmo Roper, "Roadblocks to Bookbuying," 1958.
Bertrand Russell, "The Good Life," 1957.
Shunzo Sakamaki, "Zen and Intuited Knowledge," 1959.
Ian Stevenson, "The Uncomfortable Facts about Extrasensory Perception,"
    1959.
Dylan Thomas, "A Visit to America," 1954.
Stephen Ullman, "The Prism of Language," 1954.

John Keats is a contemporary journalist.

In the tabulation, British and American writers were counted separately to show up any national differences that might exist. Only a few minor ones appeared, and these I leave to the reader to study out for himself.

In these essays we undertook to count all those words and phrases which implied the existence of a previous sentence without which the full meaning of the sentence at hand could not be understood. This definition includes, obviously, personal prepositions whose antecedents lie in a previous sentence, but counting these was postponed till later on the supposition that counting too many things at one time leads to errors. Seeking the author's own style, we did not count connectors of either kind in quoted material.

Such rhetorical devices as the repetition of key words, the use of synonyms for important words, and parallel structures in successive sentences also serve to connect sentences into clusters but were excluded from the study to make it more manageable.

In the second stage, the count of personal pronouns,[3] we did not count two sentences that had antecedents in previous sentences but that included "postcedents" in themselves. We did not count "nonreferent *it*" (it is raining), "situational *it*" (it seems to me), or "anticipatory *it*" (It is easy to please John). We did not count "participatory *we*" (We now turn to the topic

TABLE 1

AMERICAN WRITERS

	W	S	C	P	S/C	S/P	S/P+C
Barrett	6280	208	81	34	2.6	6.1	1.8
Bridgman	6627	227	108	5	2.1	45.4	2.1
Burlingame	2675	140	40	36	3.5	3.9	1.8
Catton	3660	113	40	45	2.8	2.5	1.3
DeMille	5871	299	108	126	2.8	2.4	1.3
Ellison	4659	219	59	40	3.7	5.5	2.2
Finkelstein	3616	171	34	73	5.0	2.3	1.6
Keats	5891	230	75	63	3.0	3.8	1.7
Lynes	2340	104	27	73	3.9	1.4	1.0
Packard	2427	110	30	24	3.7	4.6	1.7
Rabi	3356	159	38	40	4.2	4.0	2.0
Riesman	5106	123	53	12	2.3	10.3	1.9
Roper	6395	203	66	67	3.1	3.0	1.5
Sakamaki	1198	42	19	5	2.2	8.4	1.7
Stevenson	4803	220	99	58	2.2	3.8	1.4
Subtotals or means	64,904	2568	877	701	2.6	3.7	1.6

BRITISH WRITERS

	W	S	C	P	S/C	S/P	S/P+C
Gorer	4123	123	42	13	2.9	10.9	2.2
A. Huxley	3038	125	31	37	4.0	3.4	1.8
J. Huxley	6523	243	119	58	2.0	4.2	1.4
Melzack	2560	111	59	37	1.9	3.0	1.2
Russell	2226	104	43	8	2.4	13.0	2.0
Thomas	1831	48	22	63	2.2	0.8	0.6
Ullman	2410	98	37	25	2.6	3.9	1.6
Subtotals or means	22,711	852	353	241	2.4	3.5	1.4
Totals or means	87,615	3420	1230	942	2.8	3.6	1.6

Abbreviations: W, words; S, sentences; C, connective words and phrases; P, connective pronouns

of . . .), in which the author seems to include the reader in the decision-making process. *We* was counted only when its referents were explicitly defined in a previous sentence. Here is an example:

> The problems to which I have addressed myself are not particularly American. The same condition exists in England, France, and indeed in all other countries. From my observation we are perhaps better off than most. Our American colleges and universities, since they are fairly recent and are rapidly expanding, have not settled into complacency.—I. I. Rabi (p. 259)

There were only nine such cases in all. (Of course under *we* are included all the similar instances of *us, our, ours,* and *ourselves,* and likewise for the other pronouns.)

In this first section of my discussion of the data, I will deal with the single words and lump American and British frequencies together.

Personal pronouns account for 942 instances of sentence connection. (This is not equivalent to 942 connected sentences, since many sentences contained two or more pronouns with antecedents in a preceding sentence.) This is of a total of 2174 sentence connectors and constitutes about 43.4 percent of the total.[4]

This, that, these, and *those* account for 390 additional connections. Words of similar syntax—i.e those that can be either adjectival or nominal, such as *such, other, same, any, another, latter, more, many, both, each, either, former, similar,* and others—account for another 120 cases. The total of 510 of these two groups constitutes about 23.5 percent of all connectors. Throwing them in with the personal pronouns, the three groups constitute about 66.9 percent of all connectors in the corpus, or just about exactly two-thirds. They may be said to be *grammatical* connectors, as distinct from the adverbial connectors, which state relations of time, order, place, manner, etc. or make logical connections.

Confronted with such facts, handbooks and teachers of composition might reconsider their canons of criticism in the marking of student themes.

I turn now to those words that make connections but not grammatical connections between sentences. The coordinating conjunctions (*and, but, yet, for, or, nor, so*) account for 290 instances or just under 13.3 percent of all connectors. About 8.5 percent of the sentences in the corpus begin with a coordinating conjunction—very close to the 8.75 percent reported by Francis Christensen in a study of a corpus of 2000 sentences from ten expository writers.[5]

There are several points ot be made in this connection.

Quite a few handbooks do not admit to seven coordinating conjunctions. *So* and *yet* are the two most commonly left off the lists. (It is true that these two can be preceded by *and,* whereas the others displace each other.) Some oldfashioned handbooks even say that *so* must be preceded by a semicolon when it heads an independent clause, which is certainly a curious rule. In our American frequency count, *yet* stands at 20, ahead of *for* (12) and *or* (8); the latter the books do not dispute. *So* stands at 7, but only 4 American instances and one British were appearances as a coordinating conjunction. *Nor* is at 5, with no British instances. None of the handbooks give nearly as much attention to these words as sentence connectors as they do to conjunctive adverbs, which are only half as frequent.

Many college students and even graduates think they should not begin a sentence with *and* or *but,* though one out of fifteen sentences in our com-

TABLE 2

FREQUENCY LIST OF CONNECTIVE WORDS

	Am	Br		Am	Br
this	213	70	hence	2	1
but	101	45	likewise	2	–
these	58	24	moreover	2	1
and	48	40	obviously	2	–
however	27	15	similar	2	–
such	26	11	which	2	–
then	25	8	withal	2	–
here	23	5	accordingly	1	–
yet	20	5	actually	1	–
that	18	3	all	1	–
indeed	17	9	analogously	1	–
thus	15	8	as	1	1
now	14	–	briefly	1	–
other(s)	13	6	consequently	1	1
for	12	–	equally	1	–
also	10	9	few	1	–
therefore	10	3	finally	1	2
same	9	9	foregoing	1	–
or	8	1	last	1	–
nevertheless	8	1	less	1	1
contrary	7	1	like	1	–
so	7	4	neither	1	–
any	6	–	nowadays	1	–
first	5	1	O	1	–
nor	5	–	oh	1	–
today	5	1	one	1	2
another	4	2	only	1	–
furthermore	4	1	otherwise	1	–
latter	4	1	perhaps	1	–
more	4	2	similarly	1	2
rather	4	1	still	1	1
second	4	–	subsequently	1	–
there	4	1	therein	1	–
instead	3	1	third	1	–
many	3	–	though	1	–
maybe	3	1	whereupon	1	–
meanwhile	3	1	well	1	–
next	3	–	some	–	2
those	3	1	besides	–	1
too	3	3	conversely	–	1
again	2	4	further	–	1
both	2	–	incidentally	–	1
each	2	2	secondly	–	1
either	2	–	two	–	1
former	2	–	when	–	1

bined corpus was so initiated. Prohibitions of initial *and* and *but* begin in grade school, where the overabundance of initial *and*s is a problem for the teacher. I have suggested to some of my students who teach in those grades that they might try saying—instead of "Never begin a sentence with *and*"—"Don't begin any more sentences with *and* this semester, and next semester ask your teacher if you may when it seems to be specially fitting."

Noting that the British writers in our corpus use *and* more freely than the Americans represented, I suggested to my class that instruction in the English schools might differ on this point. But a student born in England dissented: "They were always dinning it in our ears."

After coordinating conjunctions, the next largest group of connectors is the one traditionally called conjunctive adverbs, words like *however, indeed, thus, therefore, nevertheless, furthermore, rather, instead, hence, moreover,* etc., constituting 158 instances in our corpus, or about 7.3 percent of all connectors. Included with conjunctive adverbs are a dozen or so adverbs of manner like *obviously, similarly,* and others occurring only once each.

There are some points of interest here.

Among college students quite a few mediocre writers are given to overuse of conjunctive adverbs, especially in contexts where the content is rather slight; e.g., "I stayed home to study; however, I didn't get much done." Themes of 300 words with five or six *howevers* from such writers are not uncommon, though the word turns up only once in every 2000 words in our corpus. This suggests that some high school and college teachers are solving the problems of teaching continuity and transitions by oversimple means.

For some time before this investigation was begun I had had a notion that the handbooks paid too much attention to the type of sentence in which a first independent clause is followed by a semicolon, a conjunctive adverb, and a second independent clause. Some handbooks do not actually advise students to write such sentences but do give them such prominence in illustrations of how to avoid the comma fault or comma splice as to amount to an invitation to write them.

I made a special check through our corpus to find out how often such sentences appeared. I found only three indubitable cases. The fourth depended on the classification of *here*. These are the sentences:

> Knowledge and love are both indefinitely extensible; therefore, however good a life may be, a better life can be imagined.—Russell (p. 136)

> In other cases it is far less intense; indeed it would seem likely that all altruistic emotion is a sort of overflow of parental feeling, or sometimes a sublimation of it.—Russell (p. 137)

> To rise in such a way, these upstarts do not need to acquire the stern discipline typical for the print-oriented person; rather, they need the same equipment American children have who go about in Davy Crockett suits—a

willingness, often quite passive and unstrenuous, to let fancy roam at the dictates of the mass media.—David Riesman (p. 34)

In the Middle East, where the movies and radio arrived ahead of the book, there is no such balance—though I suppose Turkey comes paradoxically closest, where Kemal Ataturk detached the young from even the literate old by imposing the Roman script; here the print-oriented are not simply the students of the Koran but are up-to-date and Westernized.—David Riesman (p. 36)

Depending on how you wish to classify *here*, this is just over or just under one sentence per thousand of those in our corpus for this sentence-type so fondly treated by so many teachers.

Coming back to other connectors, the only remaining sizeable group are the adverbs of time, order, or place, like *then, here, how, today, there, meanwhile, again*. These constitute 101 instances and about 4.7 percent of all connectors.

Another 73 instances or 3.4 percent of the total I will call miscellaneous. They include *also, contrary, so* when it is not a coordinating conjunction, *too, first, second, maybe, similar, which, withal, less,* and others that occur only once.

Of the 19 instances of *also* reported here, only 2 appeared initially in the sentence (and both in the American corpus). But initial *also* appears quite frequently in student writing. I used to tell my classes in composition not to use *also* as a sentence connector. When they asked me why, I told them it was amateurish.

That *amateurish* is not too strong a word will be evident from three examples of student writing kindly supplied by a colleague:

The successful student is one that has a goal for himself. Also, he has good study habits.

One will find enthusiasm about projects he is able to perform. Also he will not be impressed by the material gains of other persons.

Most high schools offer business courses that prepare students for making a living. Also, good secretaries are needed in all fields.

Fortunately for me, none of the students I called amateurish ever thought to reply, "We *are* amateurs. Why should you expect us to write like professionals?" But I have adopted a safer ploy. Now I say, "Some of my graduate students have counted the frequency of initial *also* in professional writing. It turns up once in 44,000 words. You have used it once. Write 44,000 words and then you may use it again." (I do not include in these strictures "inverting *also*" [Also to be considered is . . .])

I asked some of my classes why they began sentences with *also*, and they told me they did it because their teachers had told them not to begin a sentence with *and*.

TABLE 3

FREQUENCY LIST OF CONNECTIVE PHRASES

	Am	Br		Am	Br
of course	12	5	on the one hand	1	–
in fact	10	2	so much for . . .	1	–
for example	9	6	so much the better	1	–
for instance	6	4	suffice it to say	1	–
in short	3	–	to begin with	1	–
to be sure	3	–	to give one example	1	–
for one thing	2	1	to take two . . . examples	1	–
on the other hand	2	1	what I have just . . .	1	–
after all	1	–	what is more	1	2
ah yes	1	–	as we have seen	–	2
as a result	1	1	as a consequence	–	1
as follows	1	–	at least	–	1
as it is	1	–	at once	–	1
as I have just . . .	1	–	by the way	–	1
even so	1	–	later on	–	1
in addition	1	–	needless to say	–	1
in contrast	1	–	that is	–	1
in general	1	1	to phrase it briefly	–	1
in particular	1	–			

To conclude, the 100 phrases cited in Table 3 constitute another 4.6 percent of all connectors counted.

I should point out that the number of phrases has been reduced in the tally. Wherever the connective element of a phrase could be reduced to a single word, the word was tallied and the phrase dropped. Thus instances of "on the contrary" were tallied as instances of *contrary*. The motive here was the desire to make possible an economical presentation of the data in the handout for the oral presentation of the paper, since the phrases which occur only once would be numerous and would require a good deal of space.[6] Because of this procedure, Tables 2 and 3 cannot be used to show the relative frequency of phrase connectives compared to one-word connectors. If one were interested in teaching English as a second language, he would wish to proceed in a different fashion.

Notes

1. I got the idea for this count in the course of reading Viola Waterhouse, "Independent and Dependent Sentences," *International Journal of American Linguistics*, 29 (January 1963), 45–54.

2. I am grateful to Paul H. Black, Maizie R. Ellis, Margaret K. Fiedler, Patrick J. Finn, Thaddeus W. Lenart, Lucia L. Long, Bernice J. Miller, Milton Rocklin, Vivienne S. Schechtman, Eleanor G. Schwab, Florence T. Stein, and Irene Swarz for their assistance in this project. It should be understood that I checked all results and am alone responsible for the final figures.

3. Connective pronouns in seven essays—those by Bridgman, J. Huxley, Keats, Lynes, Melzack, Stevenson, and Russell—were counted by students and checked

by me. The rest of the counts, which may not be as accurate as the earlier ones, were made by me in the course of preparing this paper for publication.

4. The percents here given are slide-rule approximations rounded to one decimal. They total 100.2 because of rounding. There are other minor errors: the total of connectors in the British corpus is one greater in Table 1 than it is in Tables 2 and 3; the total for the American corpus is 3 fewer than the totals in Tables 1 and 2. These minor discrepancies obviously do not affect the percents.

5. *Notes Toward a New Rhetoric: Six Essays for Teachers,* (New York: Harper and Roe, 1967), p. 46.

6. An early version of this paper was read at the 1965 meeting of the Linguistics section of the Midwest Modern Language Association at Illinois State University at Normal. By a happy coincidence, the chairman of the meeting was Raven I. McDavid, Jr.

PORT-ROYAL LINGUISTICS

LÉON DOSTERT
Occidental College

BOŻENA DOSTERT
California Institute of Technology

A common pitfall of the historian is to look at the past with the eyes of the present. If he is a thesis-historian with a particular truth-view he is often brought to subjective selective procedures in which specific incidents or data are magnified or neglected in terms of his espoused theses. Michelet and Marx are cases in point. In the study of the movement of ideas or of the development of a particular discipline the pitfall is the greater, since the restraint of the more data-based taxonomic approach is less compelling.

In his quest for antecedents foretelling, and thus strengthening, his positions and conclusions in current linguistic theory and technique, Professor Noam Chomsky has the unquestioned merit of having stimulated a renewed interest in the Port-Royal *Grammar*.[1] His *Cartesian Linguistics*[2] undoubtedly contributed to the reproduction of the *Grammaire générale et raisonnée* (hereafter the *Grammar*), as well as of the English translation of 1753, *A General and Rational Grammar*.[3] Thus what is characterized in the Preface as "ce petit Traité" is now readily available. Its reproduction will help bring closer a goal defined in *Cartesian Linguistics*:

> The important problem is to determine the exact nature of "the capital of ideas" accumulated in the premodern period, to evaluate the contemporary significance of this contribution, and to find ways to exploit it for advancing the study of language. (p. 3).

Given the scope of the *Grammar*, which is clearly one of the best and most comprehensive premodern Western European treatises on grammar, it is not possible to present fully in a short paper the ideas and formulations contained in it, even though its 40,000 words cover less than 150 pages. However, any reader of *Cartesian Linguistics* must have realized that the *Grammar* contained more than the part (Chapter IX, *Du Pronom appellé Relatif*) containing the well-known, and unfortunately often singly quoted sentence, "Dieu invisible a créé le monde visible." The *Grammar* does deal with many additional points of particular interest to 20th century linguistics. We will return to these later.

The significance of the Port-Royal *Grammar* may be more accurately evaluated if the "Port-Royal" part of its name is given brief consideration and if some of the circumstances which led to its publication are recalled.

The long and virulent Jansenist[4] controversy over the problem of "efficacious" divine grace, construed by some as deterministic, and the concept of human free will, was to have wide reverberations in the history of 17th century France. It was a factor in the Fronde insurrection preceding by a few years the personal reign of Louis XIV in 1661. It involved the major political and religious figures of the period from the King, the Queen Mother, the Prime Minister, Cardinal Mazarin to the humblest sisters and pensionnaires in the cloister of Port-Royal–de–Paris and Port-Royal des Champs. It brought Pascal to conversion to its doctrine and to the writing of his celebrated *Provinciales.*

More related to our concern here, the intellectual leader of the Port-Royal group, Antoine Arnauld, Le Grand Arnauld, decided to challenge the Jesuits in their field of predilection: the teaching of the young, and the Port-Royal publications became the source of basic educational reforms.

And so it was that the Petites Ecoles were established and that dom Claude Lancelot came to write pedagogical grammars of Greek, Latin, Italian, and Spanish, "plutost par recontre que par mon choix," as he tells us in the opening words of the Preface (rather indeed by chance, than from any choice of my own).

One thing leading to another, and the "Grammaires de diverses Langues" having been widely accepted and become known as the "Méthodes de Port-Royal" (in the preceding century, Montaigne gave us the "méthode directe" for Latin!), they attracted the attention of Le Grand Arnauld and his participation in the development of a general grammar. That the initial objective was pedagogical is made clear by repeated allusions to the "Grammaires de diverses Langues" in the Port-Royal *Grammar*, e.g., "Voyez Nou. Meth. Latine." (p 34). But there is corroboration in an unexpected source.

No less a personage than Jean Racine (1639-1699) spent his most formative years from 1654-1657 at the Port-Royal schools—la maison des Granges—which really became his family. Racine was soon a brilliant student of Greek and Latin under the tutelage of Claude Lancelot. In the *Abrégé de l'Histoire de Port-Royal*[5] published from a manuscript revised for publication by his son Jean-Baptiste, Racine refers to the pedagogical competition between Jansenists and Jesuits, and to the "méthodes de Port-Royal."

Ajoutez qu'à toutes ces querelles de religion il se joignit encore entre les jésuites et les écrivains de Port-Royal une pique de gens de lettres. Les jésuites s'étaient vus longtemps en possession du premier rang dans les lettres . . . Il leur était donc sensible de se voir dépossédés de ce premier rang, et de cette vogue par de nouveaux-venus . . . Ils eurent même peur durant quelque temps que le Port-Royal ne leur enlevât l'éducation de la jeunesse, c'est-à-dire ne tarît leur crédit dans sa source . . . Quelques personnes de qualité avaient résolu de mettre plusieurs (de leurs enfants) ensemble sous la conduite de gens choises. Ils avaient pris là-dessus conseil de M. Arnauld et de quelques ecclésiastiques de ses amis; et on leur avait donné des maîtres tels qu'ils les pouvaient souhaiter. Ces maîtres n'étaient pas des hommes ordinaires. Il suffit de dire que l'un d'entre eux était le célèbre M. Nicole.[6] *Un autre était ce même M. Lancelot à qui l'on doit les nouvelles méthodes grecque et latine si connues sous de nom de* METHODES DE PORT-ROYAL. *M. Arnauld de dédaignait pas de travailler lui-même à l'instruction de cette jeunesse par des ouvrages très utiles: et c'est ce qui a donné naissance aux excellents livres de la* LOGIQUE, *de la* GEOMETRIE *et de la* GRAMMAIRE GENERALE. (*ital. ours*) (pp. 49–51, *passim.*)

[To all these religious quarrels there was added between the Jesuits and the writers of Port-Royal a tiff such as occurs among men of letters. For a long time the Jesuits found themselves in a leading position in literature. . . . They were thus sensitive at seeing themselves lose this leading position and vogue to upstarts. . . . They even feared for a while that Port-Royal might take from them the education of the young, thus drying up their status at its very springhead. . . . A few persons of distinction had decided to put several (of their children) together under the guidance of select persons. They had sought the advice of M. Arnauld on this matter and of a few of his ecclesiastical friends, and they were given teachers as capable as they could have wished. These teachers were no ordinary men. It suffices to say that one among them was the famous M. Nicole.[6] *Another was the same M. Lancelot to whom are owed the new methods for Greek and Latin so well known under the name of* PORT-ROYAL METHODS. *M. Arnauld did not consider it beneath him to work himself in the teaching of these young people through the most useful publications: and this is what brought into being the excellent volumes on* LOGIC, GEOMETRY *and* GENERAL GRAMMAR.] (*Tr. ours*)

We have quoted Racine at some length to clarify the significant and not merely conventional *Preface* of the *Grammar*. Lancelot tells us there that he was brought by chance rather than by choice to write grammar manuals for the teaching of the classical languages, as well as Italian and Spanish. Thus the initial aim of the Port-Royalists was to provide what we would, unfortunately, call "teaching materials." He adds that, having encountered difficulties, he discussed them as they arose with "un de mes Amis," obviously Antoine Arnauld. Arnauld was not a "grammairien," for Lancelot states plainly in the *Preface* that his friend "ne (s'était) jamais appliqué à cete sorte de science" (was unpracticed in this field of knowledge. *Tr. ours*). Nor did Arnauld, we are told, participate in the actual writing of the *Grammar*.

In the course of his consultations with Arnauld, Lancelot became aware of the revealing character of his views, for neither the classical nor the more recent grammarians had shown such novel or precise insight on the true foundations of the "art of speaking."

Et mes questions mesme ont été cause qu'il a fait diverses réflexions sur les vrais fondemens de l'Art de parler, dont m'ayant entretenu dans la conversation, je les trouvay si solides que je fis conscience de les laisser perdre n'ayant rien vu dans les anciens Grammairiens, ny dans les nouveaux, qui fust plus curieux ou plus juste sur cette matière. C'est pourquoi j'obtins encore de la bonté qu'il a pour moy, qu'il me les dictast à des heures perduës et ainsi les ayant recueillies et mises en ordre, j'en ai fait ce petit Traité (p. 3).

[My consulting him upon these difficulties was the cause of his making various reflexions on the art of speaking* which he was pleased to impart to me in conversation, and I found them so very solid, that I scrupled to deprive posterity of them, having never met with anything more curious or more exact upon the subject, either among the ancient or modern grammarians. As he had a great kindness for me, I prevailed on him to dictate those reflexions to me at his leisure hours; and having collected and digested them, I have ventured to send them abroad in the present form.]**

The French original has "ce petit Traité." Modesty was still in flower . . .

It is clear that the early pedagogical aim was now replaced by a concern to preserve the significant and revealing insights for the study of language expressed by Arnauld in the course of the conversations. We may be forgiven for noting in passing the low esteem in which the work of predecessors and contemporaries is held in contrast to the new enlightenment!

The concluding lines of the *Preface* are not without current significance in view of the controversy over the "native speaker."

. . . . si la parole est un des plus grands avantages de l'homme, ce ne doit pas estre une chose méprisable de posseder cét avantage avec toute la perfection qui convient à l'homme, qui es de n'en avoir pas seulement l'usage, mais d'en penestrer aussi les raisons, et de faire par science ce que les autres font seulement par coustume. (p. 4)

[If speech is one of the greatest advantages of man, surely it is no contemptible thing to possess this advantage in its full extent, which consists not only in having the use of it, but in understanding its nature, and in doing by knowledge what others do only by custom.]

It would seem that the Port-Royal authors distinguish between a speaker who uses a language only by habit, and one who has the additional knowledge of its grammar. Whether both are "native speakers" is not, for obvious reasons, indicated.

The *Grammar* is divided into two parts. Part I deals with "letters and characters in writing" (six chapters, twenty pages) and Part II (twenty-four chapters, one hundred twenty-two pages) with the "principles and reasons on which the various forms of the signification of words are founded." The descriptions of both parts are fundamental understatements. Without yielding to the temptation of looking at the past with the eyes of the present, Part I and the beginning of Part II can be considered as an inchoate formulation of the phonemic principle.[7] Part II can be seen in a broad sense as a

* Not really an accurate rendition of "art de parler" as it is used in the *Grammar*. It does not refer to rhetoric. It means, rather, the "acquired skill of speech."
** The 1753 English text represents an exceedingly free translation, as can readily be seen by comparison with the original French.

treatment of syntax which suggests the notion of "deep structure." It also contains examples of "surface structure" analysis which intuitively anticipate Fries' substitution frames formulas.

The Foreword defines the respective scopes of Parts I and II. Part I will deal with the material nature of language signs, Part II with their "signification, *viz.* the manner in which men make use of them to express their thoughts."

> "Grammar is the art of speaking. Speaking is to explain our thoughts by signs, which men have invented for this purpose. Experience has shewn that the most convenient signs are sounds, and the voice." (p. 1)

Language thus is seen primarily as spoken. The function of language signs is to express thoughts. The Saussurian duality signifiant/signifié has an obvious precursor in this statement.

In seeking a reasoned explanation, not of any necessity "Cartesian," the *Grammar* notes that oral sounds are "transient" and that therefore "other signs have been devised, in order to render them durable and visible, which are the characters made use of in writing. . . . " This is a clear recognition of the "secondary" nature of written language signs.

Whether sounds or writing, the signs may be considered in their form ("in their own nature as sounds and characters") or in their function, which is that of signification; i.e., "the manner in which men make use of them to express their thoughts." This reinforces the concepts of signs and content, and also of "nature and functions." [8]

The very brief but significant first chapter of Part I deals with the vowels of French, omitting the nasal vowels. It underscores the inadequacy of graphemic vowel representations in French (a, e. i, o, u,) and analyzes and describes them "according to the various openings of the mouth." Disregarding length, "from where arises a considerable variety in the sound," the inventory of vowels considered as "simple sounds" reaches the total of ten listed thus: "a, é, è, i, o, ô, eu, ou, u, e muet," the last being described as "what the Hebrews call the *scheva*."

Proceeding with a similarly taxonomic inventory, the *Grammar* considers consonants as "sons simples." There is a comparative table listing the consonants under 1) "Latines et vulgaires," 2) "Grecques" and 3) "Hebraïques," with brief commentaries on comparative or contrastive features among the "principal languages." The "vulgaires" contains comparisons among French, Italian, and Spanish. The short chapter, in essence, represents in an obviously (to us) naive manner, an attempt at comparative phonology. The technique is non-synchronic, and non-diachronic. Since the factor of time is disregarded in the analysis, the procedure may be termed *achronic*.

Chapter III consists of two pages on syllables, described as "complete sounds" consisting of one or more letters, and Chapter IV treats "of words as sounds, and likewise of accents." Words are simply "what is pronounced and written separately." But "what is most remarkable in the pronunciation of words is the accent, which is a raising of the voice on one of the syllables of the word, after which the voice is necessarily lowered," the first being the "acute accent," the second "grave." The reader is referred to what has been said on the accents of the Greeks and Latins in the Nouvelles Methodes. "The Hebrews have many accents which some believe to have been used long ago in their music, and several of which have now the same use as our periods and commas." This is at least moving in the direction of stress, pitch, and juncture. The chapter concludes by distinguishing between "natural" accents and what are called "accens de Rhetoriques"—clearly, stress and intonation.

Chapter V—letters considered as characters—stresses that initially characters were meant to represent sound only, but nevertheless "men often go from the characters to the very thing that is signified."

If characters are viewed only as representations of sounds the imperfections of the writing systems are obvious. An ideal writing system, in effect a phonemic transcription, would have observed the following "choses": 1) nothing is written that is not pronounced; 2) nothing is pronounced that is not written; 3) each character marks only one sound, either "simple or double"; 4) a given sound is not to be represented by different characters.

An ideal system of sound-to-written sign having been noted and the vagaries of spelling in natural languages recognized, nevertheless conventional spelling is not without some advantages. One of them is that it sometimes shows etymology or historical development. This point is not without interest to any one who has devoted some time to the study of the *Sound Pattern of English*.[9] Another point of definite interest is the vague awareness of the authors of what we would call *phonological syntax* in the preceding chapter when dealing with the "rhetorical accent" and here with what they consider the value of capital letters.

The problem of spelling reform is realistically discussed in terms of the persistence of "custom." Even "Emperor Claudius with all his authority could not introduce a new character." If Bernard Shaw and Colonel McCormick had but read the *Grammar*!

For no discernible reason, Part I ends with a rather zealous two-page description of a "new method of learning easily to read in all sorts of languages." The *Grammar* repeatedly sends the reader to consult one or the other of the nouvelles méthodes for language teaching, but for reading we have here rather a brief prospectus suggesting that: "il en faudroit faire un petit traitté a part" (It should be written in the form of a short separate treatise. *Tr. ours*), in which the information would be given so that it would be used for all languages. The main point the chapter makes, and many school systems are still to discover it, is that *naming* the letters of the alphabet in the initial phase of reading only confuses the learner, since the name is not the sound. So children should learn letters "par le nom de leur prononciation," or by their sound or "natural" value; thus the consonants as their articulation and "e muet." One has the feeling that Le Grand Arnauld must have been weary or indifferent when Lancelot came up with this new method. It is hard to think that here he obtained "de la bonté qu'il a pour moy, qu'il me les dictast à des heures perduës."

The first chapter of Part II poses the philosophical foundations of Chapter IX, which has been interpreted as revealing the "Cartesian" quality of the *Grammar* and as announcing the concept of "deep structure." Having considered language in its material nature in Part I, the authors are now ready to study it as "spiritual" (mental). In keeping (in point 3) with scholastic tradition of reasoning from effect to cause, language: 1) is one of the "greatest advantages of man"; 2) places him "above all other animals"; and 3) is one of the most convincing "proofs of his rationality."

But far more important, and hitherto unnoted in current linguistic discussions, is the recognition, long before Humboldt, of the principle of the use of restricted finite means for infinite use in language production. The first and very significant passage must be studied in its entirety.

> Il nous reste à examiner ce qu'elle [la parole] [10] a de spirituel, qui fait l'un des plus grands avantages de l'homme au dessus des autres animaux, et qui est une des plus grandes preuves de sa raison. *C'est l'usage que nous en faisons pour signifier nos pensées, et cette invention merveilleuse de composer de 25 ou 30 sons cette infinie varieté de mots, qui n'ayant rien de semblable en eux-mesmes, à ce qui se passe dans notre esprit, ne laissent pas d'en découvrir aux autres tout le secret*, et de faire entendre à ceux qui n'y peuvent pénétrer, tout ce que nous concevons, et tous les divers mouvements de notre âme. (p. 27).

> [There now remains for us to examine the abstract nature of speech, which constitutes one of the greatest advantages of man above other animals, and which is one of the greatest proofs of his rationality. *This is the use we make of speech to express our thoughts, and that marvellous inventiveness of composing out of 25 or 30 sounds the infinite variety of words which having no resemblance in themselves to what takes place in our mind, nevertheless uncover its hidden content to others*, and to communicate to those who cannot see in our minds, all that we think and all that we feel.] (*Tr. and ital. ours*)

In a few lines the premodern authors of the *Grammar* have dealt with or at least alluded to a number of modern concerns in linguistics: 1) the dichotomy "langue"/"parole"; 2) the human specificity of language; 3) mind and language; 4) the Humboldt view that "a language makes infinite use of finite means" [11]; 5) the arbitrariness of language signs; and 6) language as communication.

Chapter I of Part II is of basic importance to the "raisonnée" of the French title, for it deals with "what passes in the mind, (which) is necessary to comprehend the foundations of grammar." Philosophers generally teach that there are "three operations of the mind"; *perception* (or conception), *judgment* and *reasoning*. The first may be purely intellectual, such as the concepts of duration or existence, or "corporeal" such as imagining a square or a dog. Judgment is to affirm or deny something about what one conceives, thus the two concepts "earth" and "roundness" permit the judgment "the earth (subject) is round (attribute)."* The third operation is when by reasoning, a third judgment is inferred from two preceding ones: e.g. 1) Virtue is commendable, 2) Patience is a virtue, 3) Patience is commendable. This is of course the Aristotelian syllogism in its basic formulation and had been taught by the scholastics for centuries.

The *Grammar* observes that, in his use of language, man nearly always expresses judgment on what he conceives, and this is called "proposition," which of necessity is made up of subject and attribute. But there must be related to this the conjunctions, disjunctions, and the like operations of the mind as much as the other emotions of the soul, such as desires, commands, interrogations, etc. "Thus the most general distinction of words must be this, that some signify the objects, and others the form or manner of our thoughts; tho' it frequently happens that they do not signify the manner alone (separately) but in conjunction with the object." In the first group, the *Grammar* lists nouns, pronouns, participles, prepositions and adverbs; in the second, verbs, conjunctions and interjections.

Nouns are divided as substantives and adjectives, in terms of the traditional philosophical distinction between substance and accident. The nominalization of adjectives (le blanc, le noir); the derivation of nouns from adjectives (human; humanité); the use of "accidentals" as substantives (peintre, soldat) are discussed. Proper nouns are those referring to "idées singulières" (Socrates, Paris) and "appellatifs ou generaux" those signifying "des idées communes." Common nouns are divided on the basis of "singulier et plurier", with a discussion of individual or universal singularity, total or partial plurality; duality (Greek); "natural" or class duality (Hebrew) eyes, scissors; proper name plurality: Caesars, Platos (their infrastructure: all persons who may be like them). Even though common nouns " ought, it seems, by their nature to have always a plural number," this is followed by a brief statement on bulk nouns; e.g., gold, silver, which are always singular.

The origin of genders is ingeniously accounted for, "Now men have made themselves the first subject of their consideration, and upon observing a very remarkable difference, which is that of the two sexes, they have thought proper to vary the nouns adjective, by giving them different terminations, as they applied to men and women. . . ." The general agreement of the adjectives is explained thus: "For as these same adjectives might have been attributed to other things besides men and women, they were obliged to give them one or the other of the terminations." This is not the only passage where "rational" seems to yield to rationalization. And the authors' frustra-

---

* Interestingly, the same example is used by Sweet for the same purpose in his *New English Grammar*, Part I, Introduction, p. 6, which appeared in 1892.

tion is even more obvious when they note that some things happen in language "through mere caprice, and without any other reason than the influence of custom", *viz*, Lat. arbor (f)—Fr. arbre (m).

Chapters VI, VII and VIII deal respectively with cases, articles and pronouns. The functions of terminations which are "to express relations and are called cases, from the Latin *cadere*, to fall, being as it were the different falls of a word."

Continuing concern for generality and logicality brings the authors inescapably to explain why cases in language must be explained, thus making, so to speak, an early case for cases. (Chapter VI).

> True it is, they observe, that Greek and Latin are perhaps the only languages in which some nouns have properly cases. Nevertheless there are very few which have not some sort of cases in their pronouns, and as without that it would be difficult to have a right understanding of the connexion of discourse commonly called construction, it seems almost necessary for the knowledge of any language whatever to know what is meant by these cases. We shall endeavor to explain them with as much perspecuity as possible.[13]

There are a number of incisive explanations indeed. The nominative is seen as the base from which cases are made by changing its ending. Its principal use is to be placed before the verb to be the subject of the proposition. The deletion of the article before common nouns marks the ablative in French. The attempted logical explanation of the genitive is relatively lengthy and confused; the Latin ablative is useful in that it contributes to clearer explanation of pronouns. It is also useful to "give" the ablative case to Greek, "always similar to the dative, since this preserves a greater analogy between the two languages, which are usually learned together."

The teacher takes over from the grammarian.

The articles (Chapter VII) are considered to have been invented "in almost all languages" to reduce the ambiguity of common nouns, which is also the explanation for the singular and plural. The contracted forms *du*, *des*, *au*, *aux* are seen as markers respectively for the genitive and dative in French. *Des* and *de* also are described as the plural forms of the indefinite article. But the authors recognize that it is difficult to explain how the articles resolve the ambiguity of nouns "because the practice is not alike in all languages that have articles." And in respect to the use of the article with proper nouns, which "signify a single and determined thing" and thus need no clarification, the *Grammar* reluctantly comes to the admission that in language "custom and reason often differ."

The discussion of personal and possessive pronouns in Chapter VIII attributes their "invention" to the fact that "it would have been troublesome to always repeat the name nouns" in discourse. The concept of first, second and third person is analyzed, as well as "reciprocal" pronouns and the matters of number, gender and case in personal pronouns. Problems in the use of personal pronouns in personalization of inanimate things are reviewed and the rule described. But again Lancelot is brought to write: "I am not ignorant, that this rule is liable to exceptions." These are listed at length and then the author concludes that "There may still be some other difficulties raised or objection to this rule." In current parlance, one could invoke variance rules.

It is in Chapter IX that the idea of deep structure is said to be developed. This chapter, "of the pronoun called relative," underscores that this pronoun shares with other pronouns the function of replacing nouns, but additionally has a distinct and particular function, in that the proposition "into which it enters (which may be called incidental) may be part of the subject, or the attribute of another proposition which we may call principal." The explanation of the structure of propositions given in Chapter I is recalled. Propositions may be simple, "God is good," or complex, "An *able* magistrate is a *useful* man to the Republic." A proposition may contain more than one term in subject and attribute, and still be simple, thus: "The valor of Achilles was the cause of the taking of Troy," where two nouns—one governing the other—enter in the subject and in the attribute.

Now we come to the type of propositions containing several terms in the subject or attribute and which enfold, *at least in our mind* several affirmations which can be expressed as propositions. "Thus when I say: *Invisible God created the visible world*, three judgments occur in my mind which are enclosed in this proposition. For I judge: 1. *that God is invisible*, 2. *that he created the world*, 3. *that the world is visible*." The unexpressed proposition in our mind may sometimes be actually exprsesed, "*and therein consists the use of the relative*" (ital. ours). Then the same example is reduced to the terms: *God who is invisible has created the world which is visible*. So, what is distinct and particular to the relative is that the proposition in which it enters may be part of the subject or of the attribute of another proposition. Thus the two uses of the relative are seen as pronoun and conjunction, which serves to explain several problems which have perplexed the "Grammairiens." The *Grammar* points to a similar use of the relative to join two propositions together in Hebrew, and of the *que* in French in such constructions as: *je suppose que vous serez sage*.

Thus it is clear that in demonstrating a specific function of the relative pronoun *qui*, and in showing how an implicit incidental part of the subject or attribute can be made explicit, the *Grammar* delved into deep structure, very much like Sedaine's philosopher—*sans le savoir*. This does not obviously minimize the significance of the event. .

Chapter X is a rather long discussion on another use of the relative *qui* and the rule made known by Vaugelas that a "relative may not occur after a noun without article." The *Grammar* shows that a noun can be "determined" by factors other than the presence of the article, and nine of them are discussed in belabored detail. The only significant part of the chapter comes at the very end in the discussion of usage.

> There is a norm which those who undertake to write of a living language ought to always remember: namely that the forms of speech authorized by a general and uncontested practice, ought to be looked upon as legitimate, though they be contrary to the rules and analogy of the languages: but that they ought not to be alleged with a view of contesting the rules and perplexing the analogy, nor of drawing inferences to authorize other phrases and expressions not sufficiently established by custom. So that to regard nothing else but the irregularities of custom, without observing this maxim, is the way to render a language uncertain, and to leave it without principles by which it might be ascertained.

In more current terms, general practice and usage should be the aim of linguistics as a field of rational inquiry, rather than "the irregularities of custom."

The preposition, whose function "is to express the relations which things have to one another" is the subject of a few remarks, the most important of which is to note the lack of consistency in the use of prepositions, for:

> No one language has followed on the subject of prepositions what reason seems to require, which is that one relation should be marked only by one preposition, and that the same preposition should mark no more than one relation.

The nominal use of *dedans, dehors, dessus,* and *dessous* is noted in passing. The next chapter on adverbs, notes that they were invented "to shorten discourse" and derive their name from the fact that they are "generally formed with the verb to modify and determine the action."

So far the *Grammar* in its Part II has "explained those words which signify the objects of our thoughts." In dealing with verbs "we come now to treat of those which signify the manner of thinking, namely verbs, and also interjections and conjunctions."

Ten chapters (54 pages) are devoted to the discussion of verbs, one to conjunctions and interjections, the last chapter concludes with a discussion of what it calls syntax: "la construction des mots ensemble" (the way words are formed in sequences. *Tr. ours*).

After reviewing, and discarding, various definitions of "verb" by other writers, the *Grammar* arrives at the following: 1) "*A word which signifies affirmation, with the designation of person, number and time.*" This is considered adequate only for the "substantive" verb (être). For other verbs, since they differ because of the "union which men have made of affirmation with some attribute," more is required; 2) *A word which signifies the affirmation of some attribute, with designation of person, number and time.* The verb *to be* then is the verb of affirmation, the "substantive" verb. Other verbs contain affirmation, and carry a supplementary or accidental or adjectival attribute. This seems to be a non-Cartesian view, since Descartes resorts to the accidental attribute of his *thinking* to demonstrate evidentially the substantive fact of his *being*. This view of the authors of the *Grammar* is closer to that of scholastic teaching,[17] namely that the awareness of one's own existence is immediately, i.e. non-mediately or directly, evident. In this view it is *o* in *cogito* which affirms consciousness of self-existence, not *cogit*. This concept is further revealed in Chapter XVII (XVIII in the English translation) dealing with adjectival verbs, which combine attribute.

> with the signification common to all verbs which is that of affirmation. . . we even see that the substantive verb *sum, I am* is frequently adjective by reason that instead of being taken to signify the affirmation simply, it is joined to the most general of all attributes which is *being*, as when I say: *I think, therefore I am, I am* signifies *sum ens, I am a being, a thing*; *I exist* signifies also *sum existens, I am, I exist.*

This would seem to cast some doubt on the depth of Port-Royal's "Cartesianism".

In the relatively lengthy discussions of verbs (active, passive, neuter; tenses, numbers, modes; infinitive, subjunctive, imperative; participles, gerunds, supines; auxiliaries) the major point of current interest is the discussions of the nominal functions of the infinitive and participles. When the infinitive "retains the affirmation, it functions as a verb, (but) very often it loses it and becomes a noun; *le manger, je veux manger*" (ChXVI; XVII of Eng. Tr.). Chapter XVIII (XX of the English version) starts with the plain statement: "Participles are real nouns adjectives," i.e. real nouns.

A critical analysis of the *Grammar* would require a monograph equal to its own volume. Our discussion had to be cursory. It focused only on the points which we considered of current interest. In characterizing the *Grammar* as "one of the intellectual landmarks of the seventeenth century" the prefatory note of the 1968 Scolar Press reproduction may be exaggerating. But certain it is that, although indebted to a number of earlier works in the field, the Port-Royal treatise reveals innovative and significant insight in the study of language.

The contemporaneous interest in language is attested to in many ways: the foundation of the Académie Française; Descartes' view of language as distinguishing man from beast; the widely read *Remarques sur la langue francaise*; Boileau's *Art Poétique*; Molière's *Bourgeois Gentilhomme* ("Vos beaux yeux, belle marquise . . . ") and *Les Femmes Savantes*; the Salons and Préciosité, etc.; and we have seen that there were other than purely scholarly aims in the Port-Royal publications in language.

The *Grammar* represents an incisive, if only partial, approach to descriptive phonology; it approximates the formulation of the phonemic principle if only in its analysis of the French oral vowels; it strikingly points to inventiveness in human use of language; it seeks what may well be considered contextual analysis for the establishment of functional rather than categorized parts of speech; it approaches the concept of deep and surface structure, and, in a way, the process of transformational analysis. In terms of method, it is partly traditionalist and by its own title rationalist, and to a notable extent broadly descriptivist. Its occasional categorism and naiveté do not eclipse its remarkable insight on language, both theoretically and descriptively. Who can foretell how some of our current "definitive" views on language will be seen three centuries hence, assuming the temporal continuity, not the metaphysical infinity, of man's existence on earth?

Notes

1. Name generally given to *Grammaire générale et raisonnée*, chez Pierre Le Petit, Paris MDCLX. The authors are known to have been Claude Lancelot and Antoine Arnauld, both members of the *solitaires* of Port Royal, Arnauld being the leader of the group. We have used the reproduction of the French text, and most of the quotations in English are from the translation of the 1753 reproduction, both by The Scolar Press Limited, Menston, England, 1967 and 1968 respectively.

2. *Cartesian Linguistics, A Chapter in the History of Rationalist Thought*, Harper & Row, New York and London, 1966.

3. Attributed to Thomas Nugent.

4. From Jansenism (doctrine of Bishop Jansen [Jansenius] 1585–1638), the name given to a religious doctrine primarily concerned with ethics, which evoked the writings of St. Augustine in support of its rigorous and austere morality. The chief religious opponents of the Jansenists were the Jesuits, whom Pascal attacked in the sharp and witty satire of his *Provinciales* for their alleged casuistical tolerance in ethical doctrine.

5. Jean Racine, *Abrégé de l'Histoire de Port-Royal*, Paris, 1908, A. Gazier, editor.

6. Pierre Nicole, a precocious and gifted scholar, was one of the brilliant stars in the Port-Royal constellation. He made major contributions to the development of the Petites Écoles and their innovative pedagogy. Racine was among his pupils. In association with Arnauld he wrote the well-known Port-Royal *Logique*, and independently his scholarly but readable *Essais de morale*. He was the major source of Pascal's information on the abstract and doctrinal aspect of the *Provinciales*.

7. Louis Meigredt (c. 1510–c. 1560) had taken some steps toward that goal. See George Raymond Shipman, *The Vowel Phonemes of Meigret*, Monograph Series on Languages and Linguistics, No. 3, Washington, D. C., Georgetown University Press, 1953.

8. The important work, still largely ignored by linguists, by Brice Parain, *Recherches sur la nature et les fonctions du language*, Gallimard Paris, 1942, follows broadly the same lines of reasoning, but in much greater depth and in modern terms.

9. Noam Chomsky and Morris Halle, *The Sound Pattern of English*, Harper & Row, 1968.

10. N.B. La *parole*, not la *langue*.

11. Quoted by Chomsky, *Aspects of the Theory of Syntax* (p. V), M.I.T. Press, 1965 (no specific reference given).

12. The prefatory note in the Scolar Press reproduction of the *Grammar* states that: "The impact of the Port Royal works on grammar, logic and rhetoric was soon felt throughout Europe. . . . The importance of the Port Royal grammar as one of the intellectual landmarks of the seventeenth century has long been acknowledged . . ." The partial list of republications suggests the possibility of access to the *Grammar* to scholars in at least the period covered. Paris, 1662, 2nd ed.; 1676, 3rd; 1679, 4th; 1709, 5th; Amsterdam, 1703; Paris, 1754, 1768, 1769, 1803, 1830, 1845.

13. Rationalization of cases here brings to mind the words of a Belgian missionary in the Congo some fifteen years ago who readily acknowledged that his Ki Congo manual for language training of Congolese troops had been cast in the mold of Latin grammar. He was convinced that this was a more rational and explicit procedure than those of "les simples méthodes de description," which "explain" nothing.

14. There are two chapters in the *Grammar* numbered IX. It is the initial IX which is discussed in *Cartesian Linguistics* as arriving at the concept of "deep structure."

15. The 1753 (Nugent) translation inserts here: "which I don't remember ever to have been observed." This discrepancy, along with other minor ones, suggests that Nugent may have based his translation on a later edition than that of 1660.

16. Jules-César Scaliger (1484–1558), soldier turned physician, then philologist and polemist, author of *De causis linguae latinae* (1540). He is presumably one of the "grammairiens," ancient or modern, who seem to be for the Port Royalist scholars in languages something akin to the "descriptivists" in the eyes of some writers in twentieth century linguistics. Vaugelas, the author of the then widely read *Remarques sur la langue française* (1647) did not escape the occasional barbs of the *Grammar*. But these are aimed not at his work on the lexicon or stylistics of French, but at his much weaker efforts in its grammar. For Vaugelas, the arbiter of language was *usage*, not "what people speak" or the competence/performance of an ideal speaker-hearer; but usage of a very real elite. The *Grammar* clearly accepts the same norm.

17. Arnauld was at one time a member of the Sorbonne Faculty of Theology.

A PILOT STUDY IN APPLIED LINGUISTICS

PAUL L. GARVIN
State University of New York at Buffalo

This paper reports on a pilot study designed to explore the possibility of transforming a research method which has been applied in semantic analysis into an educational technique suited for the teaching of the comprehension of explanatory reading materials, such as elementary science texts.

1. Description of Predication-Typing as a Research Tool

The method of predication-typing was developed for use in research on the semantic structure of English technical discourse (Garvin, Brewer and Mathiot, 1967). It is a form of directed paraphrasing, that is, paraphrasing performed by a subject under the direction of an analyst.[1] The application of this method is based on the assumption that paraphrase is one of the operationally tractable manifestations of linguistic meaning and therefore suitable for the use as a method of empirical semantic research. The technique of predication-typing consists in requesting a subject, or subjects, to paraphrase the sentences of a selected text by using a number of prescribed schemata called predication types. The sentence which is to be paraphrased is called the "original statement"; the sentence resulting from the paraphrase is called the "resultant statement." The predication types represent a mandatory format for wording the paraphrases that are to be performed upon the sentences of the text. They all fit into the basic format, "A is in some way a function of B"; examples of some of the predication types used in previous research are "A is based on B," "A is followed by B." This paraphrasing format has been designed to be adaptable to impersonal expository style such as is found in technical literature. Sentences which did not lend themselves to predication-typing were considered "nonpredications" and so indicated in the record. An example of the use of a predication type for paraphrasing is the following:

"After this discovery, extensive additional research was initiated."

This sentence would be paraphrased using the schema "A is followed by B" to read:

> "This discovery was followed by the initiation of extensive additional research."

In the predication-typing research conducted so far, each time a sentence was paraphrased, subjects were asked to underline that word or words within the original sentence which prompted them to select a particular predication type. This underlined form was called the cue form. In the sample sentence cited previously, the word "after" was the cue form prompting the selection of the schema "A is followed by B."

A total of 33 predication types was used as paraphrasing schemata in the research. This list was chosen intuitively on the basis of an inspection of text. It is shown in Table 1. A corpus of 7500 sentences was paraphrased (predication-typed) by a small number of subjects. The record of this predication-typing activity served as the basis for a preliminary analysis of the semantic system of connective elements in English as represented by the cue forms recorded in the course of predication-typing.

2. *Adaptation of Predication-Typing to Educational Purposes*

The conversion of this research method into an educational technique is suggested on the basis of the generally recognized significance of paraphrasing as a technique for teaching reading comprehension. It is further based on the assumption that a directed form of paraphrasing is significantly superior to undirected paraphrasing, because it achieves greater control over the learner's behavior and hence has a higher likelihood of achieving the behavioral objectives of the educational process.

The research on predication-typing has shown the suitability of this method for purposes of paraphrasing technical discourse. The impersonal format used in predication-typing is particularly well suited to the explanatory style of writing, which is geared towards the description of relations between concepts rather than the narration of actions by people. Since this is an area in which reading comprehension encounters the greatest difficulties, experimentation with new educational techniques seems justified.

To test the suitability of predication-typing for purposes of teaching reading comprehension, a pilot study was performed by the author[2] in which the method of predication-typing was applied to an explanatory text designed for elementary readers. The pilot study is discussed in the subsequent section.

TABLE 1
LIST OF PREDICATION TYPES USED IN SEMANTIC RESEARCH

Symbol	Predication Type	Paraphrasing Schema
A	Statement of accompanying circumstance	A is accompanied by B

TABLE 1 (Cont'd)

Symbol	Predication Type	Paraphrasing Schema
Ac	Statement of acquisition	A is acquired by B
B	Indication of basic relation	A is based on B
C	Statement of causation	A is due to B
Cm	Statement of computation	A is computed for B
Cn	Statement of concern	A concerns B
Cp	Statement of comparability	A is comparable to B
Cs	Indication of constituency	A constitutes B
D	Descriptive statement	A has a property of B
Df	Definition	A is defined as B
Dm	Demonstration	A is shown by means of B
E	Description of equipment	A is provided with B
Ef	Indication of effect	A affects B
Ex	Explanatory statement	A is accounted for by B
F	Statement of succession	A is followed by B
I	Indication of insertion	A is placed into B
L	Indication of location	A is found in B
M	Indication of measurement	A is measured by means of B
Ma	Description of movement away	A moves away from B
O	Indication of origin	A stems from B
P	Indication of possibility	A allows for B
Pf	Description of performance	A is accomplished by means of B
R	Statement of established result	A has been established as B
Re	Indication of replacement	A is replaced by B
Rm	Description of result of motion	A arrives at B
Rp	Statement of represented condition	A is presented as B
Rq	Indication of requirement	A requires B
S	Assertion of adequacy	A satisfies the conditions for B
Su	Indication of superiority	A exceeds B
T	Statement of passage	A passes through B
U	Description of use	A is used for B
V	Indication of co-variance	A varies with B
Va	Statement of value	A has the value of B

3. Pilot Study in Predication-Typing for Educational Purposes

The sample text selected for this pilot study was *The Little Golden Book of Helicopters*, by Carl Memling (Golden Press, New York, 1959).[3] It was paraphrased in its entirety by the method of predication-typing, using a set of paraphrasing schemata developed in the course of the study. These are shown in Table 2. The record of this activity is shown in Table 3.

Note that the purpose of the pilot study was to explore the applicability of the techniques of predication-typing to elementary explanatory text, rather than to develop a set of paraphrasing schemata for immediate use in elementary instruction. It is expected that for use in the classroom the paraphrasing schemata will have to be further modified in line with educational principles.

The following tentative conclusions can be drawn from this pilot study:

(1) The technique of predication-typing is well suited for the directed paraphrasing of elementary explanatory texts. Of a total of fifty-four sentences of the sample text, only six did not lend themselves to predication-typing and had to be recorded as nonpredications. As can be seen from the record, most of these sentences are not explanatory in nature.

(2) With regard to the individual sentences of the text, the result of paraphrase by predication-typing appears to be a clearer and more systematic indication of the meaning of each sentence: an inspection of the resultant statement shows that most of the sentences of the text serve to describe the properties of helicopters and characterize their uses. It may be expected that the kind of information revealed by predication-typing will be an important contributing factor in reading comprehension.

(3) With regard to the text as a whole, predication-typing seems to reveal the extent to which a particular text is clearly structured. Thus, the sample text seems to concentrate in the beginning on descriptive statements, the bulk of the text consists of descriptions of use, and the end is characterized by nonpredications which are interpreted as nonexplanatory passages—probably intended by the author to bring the subject matter closer to the reader's life. Note that the descriptive statements and descriptions of use are interrupted by other predication types, which may be ascribed (at least in part) to the author's desire for variety in the presentation of content.

TABLE 2

LIST OF PREDICATION TYPES USED IN PILOT STUDY

Symbol	Predication Type	Paraphrasing Schema
Cs	Indication of constituency	A constitutes B
D	Descriptive statement	A has the property of B
E	Indication of event*	A takes place in B
$\overline{\text{E}}$	Negative indication of event*	A does not pake place in B
E(?)	Interrogative indication of event*	Does A take place in B?
F	Statement of succession	A is followed by B
L	Indication of location	A is found in/on B
N	Naming statement*	A is called B
Pf	Description of performance	A is accomplished by means of B

TABLE 3 (Cont'd)

Symbol	Predication Type	Paraphrasing Schema
Re	Indication of replacement	A is replaced by B
Rm	Description of result of motion	A arrives at B
Rq	Indication of requirement	A requires B
$\overline{\text{Rq}}$	Negative indication of requirement	A does not require B
Rs	Statement of result*	A results in B
U	Description of use	A is used for B
O	Nonpredication	– –

* These predication-types were newly introduced for purposes of the pilot study.

TABLE 3

RECORD OF PREDICATION-TYPING

Sample Text: *The Little Golden Book of Helicopters*, by Carl Memling, Golden Press, New York, 1959.

Original Statement	Predication Type	Resultant Statement
On a busy street in a busy city stands a tall narrow building	L	A tall narrow building is found on a busy street in a busy city.
There is a small yellow circle on the roof of the building.	L	A small yellow circle is found on the roof of the building.
Could an airplane ever land inside that small circle? Could it?	E(?)	Could the landing of an airplane take place inside that small circle?
A regular airplane couldn't land there.	$\overline{\text{E}}$	The landing of a regular airplane couldn't take place there.
A regular airplane comes down fast and at a slant.	D	A regular airplane has the property of coming down fast and at a slant.
It rolls along the ground after it lands.	D	It has the property of rolling along the ground after it lands.
Regular airplanes need long runways for take-offs and landings.	Rq	The take-offs and landings of regular airplanes require long runways.
They need airports.	Rq	They require airports.
But this is a special kind of airplane.	Cs	This constitutes a special kind of airplane.

TABLE 3 (Cont'd)

Original Statement	Predication Type	Resultant Statement
This is a helicopter.	N	This is called a helicopter.
A helicopter can come down *very slowly*—and *straight down*, instead of at a slant.	D	A helicopter has the property of coming down very slowly—and straight down, instead of at a slant.
A helicopter can *stand still in mid-air*—it can even *move backwards*!	D	A helicopter has the property of standing still in mid-air and even of moving backwards.
A helicopter lands lightly on its skids, right inside the circle, and the pilot steps out.	F	A helicopter's light landing on its skids, right inside the circle, is followed by the pilot stepping out.
Even your very own back-yard could serve as a heliport for a helicopter, just as the small yellow circle on the roof of the tall building on the busy street in the busy city is a heliport.	Cs	Even your very own back-yard constitutes a heliport for a helicopter, just as the small yellow circle on the roof of the tall building on the busy street in the busy city constitutes a heliport.
What has no wings, but can fly through the sky? A helicopter!	D	A helicopter has the property of having no wings but being able to fly through the sky.
We call them: whirlybirds, egg beaters, flying wind-mills, and choppers.	N	They are called whirlybirds, egg beaters, flying windmills, and choppers.
We use them as: ambu-lances, trucks, buses, letter carriers, lifeguards, and cowboys.	U	They are used for ambulance duty, trucking, bussing, mail delivery, lifeguard duty, and work on the range.
A Marine helicopter comes whirring down from the sky, to the rescue.	U	A Marine helicopter is used for rescue.
When a soldier is hurt, a helicopter is the ambulance that carries him from the battlefield back to the hospital.	U	A helicopter is used for carrying the wounded soldier back from the battlefield to the hospital.
Soldiers use big helicopters as buses.	U	Big helicopters are used for bussing soldiers.
Instead of having to climb up to the top of the steep mountain, the soldiers fly up.	Re	Climbing up to the top of the steep mountain is re-placed by flying up.

TABLE 3 (Cont'd)

Original Statement	Predication Type	Resultant Statement
Only a helicopter could land up there on the narrow peak.	D	Only a helicopter has the property of landing up there on the narrow peak.
The big guns are carried up to the peak by the flying trucks that look like egg beaters.	U	The big trucks that look like egg beaters are used for carrying the big guns up to the peak.
The Coast Guard uses helicopters.	U	Helicopters are used for Coast Guard duty.
The helicopters patrol the waters near the coast, on the lookout for boats in trouble.	U	The helicopters are used for patrolling the waters near the coast on the look-out for boats in trouble.
They swoop down swiftly to the rescue when trouble strikes.	F	Trouble striking is followed by their swooping down swiftly to the rescue.
Helicopters string telephone wires over high mountains.	U	Helicopters are used for stringing telephone wires over high mountains.
The wire unwinds slowly from the humming reel, and is laid across the tree tops.	F	The slow unwinding of the wire from the humming reel is followed by laying it across the tree tops.
Now people will be able to talk to each other across the high mountain.	Rs	This results in people being able to talk to each other across the high mountain.
Farmers use helicopters, too.	U	Helicopters are used for farming.
To fight weeds and bugs, the farmers use the flying wind-mills to spray the crops with poison dust.	U	The flying windmills are used for spraying the crops with poison dust to fight weeds and bugs.
Helicopters are letter carriers.	U	Helicopters are used for mail delivery.
Airmail letters that arrive at the big airport no longer have to wait for trucks on wheels.	$\overline{\text{Rq}}$	The delivery of airmail letters arriving at the big airport no longer requires waiting for trucks on wheels.
Helicopters fly them swiftly from the big airport to the small post offices.	U	Helicopters are used for flying them swiftly from the big airport to the small post offices.

TABLE 3 (Cont'd)

Original Statement	Predication Type	Resultant Statement
Policemen use helicopters.	U	Helicopters are used for police work.
For watching the highways, for patrolling the beaches, for finding lost people, policemen use helicopters all the time.	U	Helicopters are used all the time for watching the highways, for patrolling the beaches, for finding lost people.
Even cowboys use helicopters.	U	Helicopters are used even for work on the range.
This cowboy is herding stray cattle out of the brush by darting down at them with his trusty whirlybird.	U	This trusty whirlybird is used for herding stray cattle out of the brush.
And even some fathers use helicopters.	Ø	
Instead of taking a train to the office, they fly by helicopter.	U	Helicopters are used for flying to the office.
They fly straight to the middle of the busy city.	Rm	They arrive at the middle of the city.
They land on a small yellow circle on the roof of a tall building—and their office is only minutes away.	E	Their landing takes place on a small yellow circle on the roof of a tall building, only minutes away from their office.
Some fathers use helicopters for pleasure trips.	U	Helicopters are used for pleasure trips.
They take the whole family along, and everybody has a wonderful time.	Rs	Taking the whole family along results in everybody having a wonderful time.
The big propeller on the top of the helicopter is called the rotor.	N	Same
As it whirls around, it chops at the air and pulls the helicopter through the sky.	Pf	Pulling the helicopter through the sky is accomplished by means of its whirling around and chopping at the air.
The pilot uses a control stick to change the tilt of the rotor.	U	The control stick is used for changing the tilt of the rotor.
The rotor tilts and the helicopter goes forward or backward or right or left.	F	The tilting of the rotor is followed by the helicopter going forward or backward or right or left.

TABLE 3 (Cont'd)

Original Statement	Predication Type	Resultant Statement
New helicopters are being built all the time.	Ø	
Bigger ones than ever before.	Ø	
And smaller ones than ever before.	Ø	
Some helicopters are so small that they can fit inside a garage.	D	Some helicopters have the property of fitting inside a garage.
Wouldn't it be fun if one day your father, or the father of one of your friends, rolled up his garage door—and there was a brand-new helicopter inside?	Ø	
Then, if anyone asked—"Who can fly through the sky, sitting inside something that has no wings?" the answer would be—YOU!	Ø	

Notes

1. This is to be differentiated from active paraphrasing, which the analyst himself performs, and undirected paraphrasing, where the subject is at liberty to paraphrase as he wishes.

2. This study was conducted while the author was at the Bunker-Ramo Corporation.

3. Reproduced by permission.

Reference Cited

Garvin, Paul L., Jocelyn Brewer and Madeleine Mathiot, *Predication-Typing: A Pilot Study in Semantic Analysis.* Language Monograph No. 27 (Language 43:2 pt. 2, 1967).

JURY TESTING IN ANALYSIS OF CONTEMPORARY LANGUAGE

ARCHIBALD A. HILL
University of Texas at Austin

At the 1969 meeting of the Lingiustic Society of America, William Labov presented a paper describing a state of affairs in New York pronunciation of American English, which must be commoner than usually realized. Words such as *sauce* and *source* were presented in normal, non-minimal sentence pairs. The words were then studied on the spectrograph and shown to be overlapping, in that some uttcrances of the pair were alike, though other utterances were not. The informants were then asked about their own pronunciations, and intcrestingly enough, their replies were uncertain. I have no criticism of Professor Labov's procedure, which was designed to throw light on sound-change, and does so importantly. Yet I do not think that such a procedure does full justice to the system of sounds available for distinction-making in the speech of New Yorkers.

In the early days of phonemic theory it was naively supposed that all sounds available for distinctions would be automatically recognized by the speakers who used them. Professor Labov's investigations ought to destroy any remnants of such naiveté. My own experience is that whenever a distinction is undergoing neutralization, or has little function in distinction-making, speakers can be quite uncertain about their own usage. Typical replies are (with failure to recognize the all-or-none quality of contrast) 'I guess they sound pretty near alike' or 'I don't notice much difference.' It is also quite easy for a speaker to believe that he makes distinction which he does not. All through my student days I believed that I made a distinction between *Mary* (proper name) and *merry* (Merry Christmas). I do not, though it is true that in exaggeratedly careful speech I can introduce an artificial difference. Such mythical distinctions are often based on spelling, as mine probably was, but they can also be based on failure to observe difference between one's own speech and that of a model. One of my best students, observing that I make a distinction between such forms as *kitty* and *kiddie* on the basis of a flapped consonant in the first, and a normally closed consonant in the second, and being able to distinguish my pronunciations with complete accuracy, assumed he made the same distinction. Years later, when he ran his own speech through a spectrograph, he found that the two forms were alike in his speech, unless he introduced an artificial distinction like my *Mary:merry*.

There is only one way for the analyst to thread his way through such difficulties. It is by extensive use of the jury test, which in phonology must be in the narrower form of a discrimination test. This test is a test of a jury's ability to recognize each of two sentences in which a suspected pair of sounds are the only possible distinguishing feature. Suppose, for instance, that we wish to know whether a speaker from Texas distinguishes between /i/ and /e/ before the dental nasal. If the jury can properly identify each of the two sentences 'John picked up a pin,' and 'John picked up a pen,' when our speaker pronounces them, then the speaker makes the distinction, and the opposition is not neutralized.

There are limitations on the usefulness of the test, and on the ways in which it should be set up, if the best results are to be achieved. Care must be taken to be sure that the presented sentences are in normal, undistorted speech. In an informal experiment which was for me a convincing demonstration of the usefulness of the method, I was myself the speaker, and the jury was a group of linguist friends. The sentences were 'It's under a tack' and 'It's under attack.' I knew that in isolation *attack* and *a tack* were alike, so that I expected the sentences to be indistinguishable. I secured natural pronunciation by visualizing a pile of bills tacked down on a desk for the first, and a group of men storming a fort for the second. That is, I directed my attention away from the sounds and towards the semantic content of each sentence. Further, at the suggestion of Martin Joos, who was one of the jury, I randomized the sequence by pronouncing the two sentences in accord with the toss of a coin. I was astonished to find that my jury distinguished the two sentences with regularity, so that there was no possibility of denying that I had pronounced them differently. I now know of the difference, of course, and can not recover the skepticism with which I entered the experiment.[1]

It is revealing, also, that it took some discussion among the members of the jury to decide on what the difference was. In phonetic terms, the /r/ in *under attack* was longer than the other one. The elongation was the phenomenon that I would now call a syllabic separator, and that used to be called a plus juncture.

The uncertainties we experienced in identifying the difference after we had proved its existence are usual and to be expected. Thus in the most extensive and sophisticated use of the jury test for identification in phonology that I know of, that by Ilse Lehiste in *An Acoustic-Phonetic Study of Internal Open Juncture*,[2] it is not possible to argue against her conclusions when she says that such forms as *grade A* and *grey day* are auditorially distinguishable, since her jury of native speakers identified the two forms correctly. Yet in interpretation of what the significant differences are, discussion is quite possible. To me, for instance, it does not seem satisfactory to assign the 'internal open juncture' to the feature of greater length in a post-pausal /t/, though I have no intention of discussing the matter here.

It is also true that the discrimination test is only a one-way street. It can not be assumed that failure to identify a pair of suspected utterances proves that they are indeed the same. The failure may be due to a lack of familiarity with a given distinction on the part of the jury members. I once gave the pair *That's tough* and *That stuff* to a class some of whom had a non-English background. I can prove without doubt that the two forms are identifiable, but my particular class both failed to identify correctly, and maintained positively that the two utterances were the same. Negative evidence, in the form of failure to identify, can at most lead the analyst to suspect that forms are identical, it can not prove it. When identity is thus suspected, the analyst should go to the machine, and I think that it is in such situations that the machine gives its greatest service. Miss Lehiste, for instance, was able to show that a pair her juries had been unable to identify, *a board* and *aboard*, were indeed identical. The machine is much more useful in checking suspected sameness than it is in identifying the distinctive features of two forms which have been shown, by discrimination, to be different. For example, after I have shown *that's tough* and *that stuff* to be different because identifiable, the spectrograph will show me a conglomeration of differences—in the length of the two /t/s, in their aspiration and release, and in the length of the preceding vowel, not to mention whatever differences may exist in the two /s/s. The assignment of the distinctive features, as always, is a structural decision, to be taken only in relation to the emerging pattern found in all other sounds. It is not a simple matter of pointing out what difference or differences are most prominent. The prominent differences are cues, certainly, but cues and distinctive features are not necessarily the same.

There are other results, besides correct identification and failure to identify, which can occur. One is unimportant, except that it must be allowed for and understood. Mistakes can occur, both in the jury's identification, and in the informant's presentation of the forms. It is therefore not necessary to demand one hundred percent accuracy in a discrimination test. If the jury's identifications are significantly better than could be expected by chance, the difference is proved. If there is doubt that the results are 'significantly better than chance,' the analyst should fall back on his statistically trained colleagues, since they have developed excellent techniques for measuring the significance of such results.

A final type of result is much less common, and is more interesting. Occasionally, at least when the jury is made up of one person only, the identifications may be symmetrically transposed. I once tried a pair of sentences involving my fourth grade of stress on my colleague, the late Bagby Atwood. The pair were 'We have twenty new Mexican students,' and 'We have twenty New Mexican students.' Professor Atwood identified all my Mexican students as New Mexican, and vice versa. There was no denying that I had made a difference, and equally, no denying that the difference was foreign, at least in these sentences, to his speech. The fact was that a great many of the distinctions which I make in the minor grades of stress were foreign to him, but the mere fact that he could identify (even though wrongly) argues that the distinction was present in his speech somewhere.

Before I leave jury testing in matters of phonology, I can say a word about the use of test sentences on a simpler, same-different basis. That is, a pair of minimally different (or possibly minimally different) sentences can be given to a jury in randomly chosen pairs of sames and differents. The test is not so reliable as the discrimination test, in finding contrasts. Often a jury can be led to notice unimportant differences between successive utterances of the same sentence, as when a jury comes to hear that one version of a sentence explodes a final stop, and another does not. The same-different test is phonologically useful only in a situation quite different from analysis; namely, foreign-language teaching. When a foreign distinction has been fully established and explained for the class, the same-different test is a useful stage in teaching the distinction, though even here the same-different testing should be followed by discrimination testing.

I have often maintained that linguists do not make enough use of jury testing, which it seems to me should be the foundation of almost all theoretical constructs on every level of language. I can cite an example, to me startling, of an instance in which a phonological statement was vitiated for lack of use of the test. The statement is from the 'Guide to Pronunciation' in *Webster's Third.*

> Some observers who grant the levelling of the consonants in pairs like *ladder:latter* insist that the pair are nevertheless distinct in that the vowel preceding the consonant is longer for the *d(d)* than for the *t(t)* word. We have not been sufficiently convinced of such a distinction to show it.[3]

Either the distinction exists (as I am sure it does) or it does not. The jury test would have settled the matter, though only to shift it to the more abstract ground of whether the distinctive features should be assigned to the consonant or to the vowel. *Webster's* was not justified in dismissing a distinction, necessarily an all-or-none difference, on the ground of the mere uncertainty of the analyst.

I have described the same-different test as less useful in phonology than the discrimination test. In another level of language, however, the same-different test is the principal tool. This is in semantic distinction. I have described its use on this level in the Presidential Address to the 1969 meeting of the Linguistic Society of America,[4] and will only summarize here. A pair of like-sounding forms, whether of differing etymology like *compound* (mixture) and *compound* (enclosure), or of the same etymology like *ground* (surface of the earth) and *ground* (wire) are different words if they can be shown to identify different sentences. The basic assumption is that a word is composed of its sequential sounds, its intonation pattern, and its semantic content. Also, words differentiate sentences just as sounds differentiate words. For the two instances of *ground*, a test sentence might be 'Even the ground was burned.' The sentence can then be put in a larger pair of contexts, such as

'It was a terrible forest fire. *Even the ground was burned.*"

and

'Every part of the wiring of the motor was destroyed by fire. *Even the ground was burned.*'

It must be made clear that it is only the identical material of the two longer utterances that is being tested. If the jury answers that the two utterances of the tested material are different sentences, then the two instances of *ground* are different words. I believe that such a testing procedure holds out hope for segmenting the meaning of words in a way analogous to the discovery by the structuralists of the thirties that they could segment the continuum of sounds.

The last area in which jury testing is useful is in testing the application of rules, to see whether they result in grammatical or ungrammatical sentences. The test as here used constitutes a third type of test, the good-bad test, differing from both discrimination tests in phonology, and some-different tests in semantics.

In a discussion begun some years ago in *Word*, I objected to the rather cavalier statements made about ungrammaticality by Noam Chomsky in *Syntactic Structures*. I was objecting to two things, one of which is a simple matter of confusion, but the second of which is still unresolved.[5] The confusion lies in the fact that the average adult speaker uses the term ungrammatical for several things, such as the use of a low-prestige form like *ain't*, and analogical departures from normal usage for some special effect, like 'What do you mean he's coming man? He's a *come* man.' The second, and more important difficulty is that grammaticality was said (apparently rightly) by Chomsky to be gradient. If gradient, instead of all-or-none, it is difficult to see how it can be made the criterion for an all-or-none rejection test. Once more we face the linguists' special problem of the segmentation of a continuum.

The difficulty is real, and still faces transformational-generative analysts. I have recently seen some of the early draft of a dissertation on comparative structures in English. The author complains that speakers of English seem to be uncertain about accepting or rejecting any kind of deviation from the simplest type of comparative sentence. 'John is taller than Bill' is always accepted, but 'John is taller than Bill·is taller than Jack' produces a doubtful response. I would propose two ways of handling such real difficulties.

The first is by a properly designed good-bad test. To be useful, the test must

consist in application of a previously identified process to previously identified material. Neither the process nor the material can be allowed to vary in
identity. A typical, though obvious, example of such a test is the following:

> Test sentence: *The chauffeur drives the car.*
> Question: Is it all right to change this into *The car is driven by the
> chauffeur?*
> Second test sentence: *The chauffeur is driving the car.*
> Question: Is it all right to change this into *The car is driving by the
> chauffeur?*

The reason for concern about the identity of the items is made plain by the
phrase *by the chauffeur.* In the second sentence it clearly indicates the actor.
If the fourth sentence were merely tossed out without a contextual build-up,
the phrase might be taken to mean 'alongside the chauffeur,' in which case
the sentence might be taken to be grammatical. If shifts in identity are not
prevented, a jury is certain to follow the normal human tendency, and supply
a meaning and an imagined context which makes the sentence sensible and
acceptable. If, for instance, one asks an informant whether 'John electrified
the Church' is grammatical, an informant could certainly be expected to
understand the sentence as meaning "John supplied electricity to the church
building,' or that he astonished the totality of the clergy, not that he astonished the church building, or that he supplied the totality of clergymen
with electric wiring.

Careful testing should remove a large part of the confusion in measurement of grammaticality, but since gradience is real, it will not remove it all.
There is no difficulty, of course, with the sentences which are one hundred
percent grammatical, since these will be accepted by any jury. They may
be quite trivial and unlikely to occur in normal conversation, like the sentence
'Horses don't build nests.' Trival or not, they remain acceptable. The only
way I know of handling gradience is to make the rule that whenever a test
sentence is rejected by more than some arbitrarily chosen percentage of
juries, then it must be taken to be ungrammatical. Such a procedure would
have two advantages, I believe. The more important one is that it would
remove a great deal of the uncertainty that lingers in analytical statements,
where one of the commonest audience reactions is to quarrel about the
grammaticality of sentences generated by a set of rules. The other is that
it might remove some of the strangeness that pervades many of the sentences
used as examples in syntactic analysis. For me, at any rate, even the well
known 'the boy hit the ball' is slightly strange, since the definite articles would
not be used in normal conversation.

I can close this discussion of discrimination tests, same-different tests, and
good-bad tests by returning to the point at which I began. If some New
Yorkers pronounce *sauce* and *source* in such a way that the two words are
sometimes alike, and sometimes different, an experiment could be designed

which would show conclusively whether any functional load still persists in the differing pronunciations, or whether the differing pronunciations have become genuine free variants. The test sentence could be 'It's the source that matters,' and 'It's the sauce that matters.' Each would be put into a larger context which would suggest one meaning or the other to the informants. There should then be several recordings of each of the full contexts. From these the test sentences should be selected, and then run through the spectrograph. From the sentences spectrographically studied, the identical pronunciations of *source* and *sauce* should be rejected. The remaining sentences, those minimal pairs in which the two words were different, should then be played back for the informants. If the informants could discriminate, the two pronunciations would still be functional, no matter whether or not they were mere relics. If the two forms could not be discriminated, they would then be free variants, and the experiment would have the interesting result of for once defining a free variant experimentally.

Notes

1. The experiment is described in a brief article, 'The audibility of / + /,' in the *Journal of the Canadian Linguistic Association,* 5 (1959), 81–82.

2. *Phonetica,* 5 (1960), Supplement.

3. Edward Artin in *Webster's Third New International Dictionary,* Springfield, (1961), page 41a, col. 2.

4. "Laymen, Lexicographers, and Linguists." *Language,* 46(1970), 245–247.

5. 'Grammaticality,' *Word* 17 (1961) 1–10. The article and Chomsky's reply ('Some Methodological Remarks on Generative Grammar') can be found conveniently in *Reading in Applied English Linguistics,* ed. Harold B. Allen, New York, 2nd ed., (1964), 163–192. Chomsky discusses several quite different articles; the part of his essay which is relevant to mine is on pp. 181–183.

KIOWA AND ENGLISH PRONOUNS:
CONTRASTIVE MORPHO-SEMANTICS

EDITH CROWELL TRAGER–JOHNSON
University of California, Santa Barbara and
San José State University

Since it does not seem wise to reach for universals lightly, the topic of this paper is quite circumscribed. It deals with the personal pronominal elements, both their morphology and their semantic structure, of English and Kiowa. First there will be set forth a possible set of semantic features for at least the surface structure of English personal pronouns; then the rather unusual and complex sets of Kiowa pronouns will be presented, along with a hypothesis about a simple set of features. Finally, it is hoped that some viable suggestions can be made about rethinking pronominal systems in general.

The morphological attributes of English pronouns have been analyzed by Trager and Hill and referred to by Lees (v. References). Table I shows the usual array, using the label Nominative for the subject forms, Accusative for the object forms, and Genitive for the two possessives. It has been observed that final /y,w/ is a sign of the Nom, /m/ a sign of the Acc, /y,r/ or /s~z/ of the possessive adjective, to use a traditional term, and /n/ or /z/ of the other possessive.

Raven I. McDavid's work has influenced many successive waves of students in linguistics, especially in the area of American English dialectology. Let me refer to just one of his many varied contributions, the very special fourth edition of Mencken (McDavid, 1963). There, in the passage on the pronoun in the section called The Common Speech, there are listed the following forms in addition to those listed in Table 1: *yous, you-all, you-uns, mongstye* and the corresponding possessives *you-all's, you-unses, mongstye's* as well as the other possesives in /n/, *yourn, hisn, hern, ourn*, and *theirn*. All of these forms fit into the semantic structure analysis that will be attempted below.

It should be clear from an examination of Table 2 that only the surface-most levels are being dealt with. I say "levels" because in marking the first and second person pronouns as plus or minus masculine [± masc], there is reference to units of discourse longer than one sentence since gender is not marked within a single sentence in English except for third person. Furthermore, let us say for the sake of argument that Fillmore is right when he says that nominative, accusative, and genitive are all surface cases. "Case forms are assigned to English pronouns relatively late in the grammar" and "the relation 'subject' . . . is now seen exclusively as a surface-structure phenomenon." He is persuasive when he makes a case for the universality of his deep cases (Agentive, Instrumental, Dative, Factitive, Locative, Objective, and others yet undiscovered) and for his "view that conversion to genitive is a matter of the surface structure," a reflex of his deep Dative (Fillmore, 1968). Nevertheless, the forms of the English pronouns in Table 1 can be said to have both syntactic features (set up as N=Noun Phrase, acc= accusative, and gen=genitive) as well as semantic features which specify number, person, and gender. Thus three features specify the surface case forms and six semantic features account for the nine different columns of pronouns. These nine features economically account for the thirty-six pronouns.

TABLE 1

FORMS OF ENGLISH PRONOUNS								
	1S	2S	3SM - F - N			1P	3P	2S	WH
Nominative	ay	yuw	hiy	šiy	it	wiy	ðey	ðaw	huw
Accusative	miy	↑	him	hər	↑	əs	ðem	ðiy	huw(m)
Genitive Det.	may	yur	hiz	↑	its	awr	ðer	ðay	huwz
Genitive N	mayn	yurz	↑	hərz	↑	awrz	ðerz	ðayn	↑

TABLE 2

SYNTACTIC FEATURES			
[+N] (=nom, acc, gen. N)		[−N]	(=gen. det.)
[+acc] (=acc)		[−acc]	(=nom, gen. N)
[+gen] (=gen. det., gen. N)		[−gen]	(=nom, acc)

SEMANTIC FEATURES			
[+plur]	(=plural)	[−plur]	(=singular)
[+spkr]	(=speaker)	[−spkr]	(=2, 3)
[+hrer]	(=hearer)	[−hrer]	(=1, 3) } persons
[+topc]	(=topic)	[−topc]	(=1, 2)
[+humn]	(=human)	[−humn]	(=neuter)
[+masc]	(=masculine)	[−masc]	(=feminine)

TABLE 3

	N	acc	poss	plur	spkr	hrer	topc	humn	masc
EXAMPLES									
I	+	−	−	−	+	−	−	+	±
me	+	+	−	−	+	−	−	+	±
my	−	−	+	−	+	−	−	+	±
mine	+	−	+	−	+	−	−	+	±
your	−	−	+	±	−	+	−	+	±
theirs	+	−	+	+	−	−	+	±	±
us	+	+	−	+	+	±	±	+	±
him	+	+	−	−	−	−	+	+	+
she	+	−	−	−	−	−	+	+	−
it	+	±	−	−	−	−	+	−	O

In Table 2, the plus and minus values of these features are listed with explanatory material in parentheses. Table 3 takes some of the pronouns and, in classificatory matrix forms, shows how they would be specified in terms of the features in Table 2. Thus, for instance, 'your' has both plus and minus in the 'plural' column since it is both singular and plural; 'theirs' has both plus and minus in the 'human' and 'masculine' columns because there is no gender distinction in the third person plural. (Freeman, 1970, and C.D. Johnson, personal communication, were helpful in this formulation although in no way responsible for its weaknesses).

It is interesting to note that although English does not have inclusive and exclusive *we*, unlike Kiowa and many other languages, we can distinguish between those two uses of *we* as well as the global *we* and also *I* by using just three features, as shown below; 'plural' is not necessary for Table 4.

TABLE 4

	speaker	hearer	topic
we (global)	+	+	+
we (inclusive)	+	+	−
we (exclusive)	+	−	+
I	+	−	−

Were we to expand our list of semantic features to includes other well-known Indo-European pronoun systems, we would have to cover forms like the singular-familiar second person *tú* of Spanish, as well as *vos* and *usted(es)* along with *ellos* and *ellas*; the dual of Classical Greek; the intricacies of Swedish pronouns of address and many others. If we then turned to Semitic, we would add gender distinctions in the second person pronouns, both singular and plural.

In *Language*, R. B. Jones reviewed Cooke's *Pronominal Reference in Thai, Burmese and Vietnamese* (Jones, 1970). He notes that three primary semantic features have been proposed indicating addressee status (± superior) and speaker attitude (± intimate, ± nonrestraint). He suggests that, because of certain co-occurrences of those features, the analysis could be simplified to one primary feature (± deference), with secondary modifications. Other factors that occur throughout Asia, says Jones, are age, kin status, and social rank.

We need to know about all of this, and much more besides, but obviously no universal base for pronouns will be arrived at by mere expansion of a list of characteristics, nor yet by introspection. It is not yet clear exactly how we should proceed but perhaps the presentation of the Kiowa pronominal system that is to follow will at least add another dimension to our thinking about pronouns.

Although I had not read Martin Buber's *I and Thou* (Buber, 1958) until quite recently when urged to do so by some students to whom I had presented some aspects of the system of Kiowa pronouns, I found that on his early pages, he had, unkowingly, written a poetic introduction to that system. "The primary words are not isolated words, but combined words. The one primary word is the combination I-Thou. The other primary word is the combination I-It . . . the I of the primary word I-Thou is a different I from that of the primary word I-It." Such is the case for a great many more relationships in Kiowa.

Kiowa is a language spoken in Oklahoma by about two thousand speakers of various degrees of bilingualism. It is most closely related to the Tanoan languages, such as Taos, spoken in the Rio Grande valley pueblos of New Mexico (Trager, G., 1942). It seems reasonable to say that Kiowa-Tanoan and Uto-Aztecan are related and probable that they constitute the Azteco-Tanoan group of languages (Hale, 1967).

Both Taos and Kiowa have a set of pronominal verb prefixes which co-occur and interact in a fairly intricate way with the noun classes and their suffixes. Kiowa, while it may not be unique, exhibits an unusually tight interlocking of its morphophonemic and semantic structures. It is possibly unusual enough to jog us out of a certain amount of complacency about pronouns and perhaps pronominalization, although pronominalization per se is not dealt with here.

There is an excellent reason in the case of Kiowa for beginning a discussion of its pronominal system with a statement about its phonological system.

Table 5 shows the twenty-two consonants of Kiowa, fifteen of which involve stopping. There are four series of stops and affricates—plain, aspirated, glottalized and voiced—and a glottal stop, along with the two frica-tives, two nasals and three resonants. (cf. Zwicky on Nez Perce vowels.) As will be shown below, the pronominal system employs only /b, d, g, m, ny/.

Table 6 shows the six vowel qualities of Kiowa. Again, a limited selection of the total inventory of long, short, oral, and nasal vowels occurs in the pronouns. Only three of the non-high short vowels appear—/eaɔ/ and their nasalized equivalents. As you will see, the voiced stops /b, d/ alternate, not surprisingly, with /m, n/; /g/, however, alternates with /y/ in analogous en-vironments, so that it is tempting to posit an /ŋ/ underlying the /y/.

My field work in Kiowa yielded far more data on nouns than on prono-minal elements but in the course of writing it up, I made extensive use of Harrington's exhaustive treatment of the verb prefixes that constitute almost the whole of the pronominal system (Harrington, 1928). Merrifield's re-formulation made thirty years later seems even more involuted (Merrifield, 1959). Surprisingly, it appears rather often to be based on translation mean-ing. This seems almost forgivable, however, once you are aware, first, of the complexity of the semantic structure of Kiowa pronouns and, second, of the almost total disparity between that structure and those of a variety of more familiar languages. It is even more understandable that Harrington would make use of the concepts familiar to scholars from the various American Indian languages known about at that time. There is, in particular, the dual-plural distinction which turns out to be valid for Kiowa; there is also the inclusive-exclusive distinction which may not be relevant at all.

In any case, Harrington had six complicated charts of pronominal forms: 1-subjective series; 2-transitive series; 3-reflexive series; 4-subjective-referential series; 5-transitive-referential series; 6-reflexive-referential series. Because of an enormous amount of overlap and redundancy, it has been pos-sible to condense the majority of these forms into Tables 7 and 8.

The categories used by Harrington are first person singular inclusive and exclusive (1s, i, e), second person singular, dual and plural (2s, d, p), and third person singular, dual, and three kinds of 'plural' (3s, d, pA, pB, pC), major animate, minor animate, and collective. The object categories differ from the subject ones in having a first duo-plural (1dp) rather than the inclusive-exclusive distinction, but this difference may turn out to be merely terminological. Note that Table 7 is partial because the various so-called third person plurals are omitted from the 'object' axis.

Table 8 includes forms that are called referential but which by someone other than Harrington might be called indirect object forms, benefactives, or something else. At any rate he uses 'referential' for forms which occur in situations in which X does Y "with references to Z." We will return to this point to question it and also to question the validity of the terms 'subject' and 'object.' After working through the hundreds of Harrington's forms and dozens of his categories and noticing certain recurrent partials while checking my own data, Harrington's charts, and Merrifield's definitions, I decided it would be wise to put aside all these analyses and simply observe the forms of the pronominal prefixes.

The first thing that became clear was that some pronouns consisted just of an oral or a nasal vowel of one of three qualities, /a e ɔ/. Others had an initial consonant, one of a limited stock of six, either /b d g/ or /m n y/. Still others might begin with zero or one of those six consonants and end in either /t/ or /n/. It also emerged that the final consonant was /t/ if the vowel was oral, /n/ if it was nasal. Furthermore, if the vowel was nasal, and there was an initial consonant, it too was one of the nasals /m, n/ or /y/. It began to seem that nasalization was a kind of prosodic feature.

Table 9 shows by the presence of an *x* just which combinations of vowels and consonants appear in the pronominal verb prefixes of Kiowa and specifies their co-occurrence. Note that the set /b d g/ is comlementarily distributed with the set /m n y/ with respect to the oral and nasal vowels. Notice also the systematic gaps: missing are *da, *dat and *ge, *get and the corresponding nasal sequences *nã(n), *yẽ(n). For these gaps it has proven possible to find a semantic explanation.

Table 10 pulls together this information in a slightly different way and shows us that, with /a/ or /ã/, you find the labials and the velars; with /e/ and /ẽ/, the labials and dentals; with /ɔ/ and /ɔ̃/, all three categories of stops occur, except for the mysteriously absent /y ɔ̃-n/.

It began to emerge that it was not unlikely that each segment of the one, two, or three-part prefix, when compared to the tabulations of translation-meaning, was a morpheme. Table 11 helps clarify this. There, capital B is used as a morphophonemic symbol for /b/ and /m/, capital D for /d/ and /n/, and G for /g/ and /y/. As suggested earlier, it seems possible that the underlying representation of this /y/ might be /ŋ/. Actually, some modern Kiowa /y/'s are a reflex of Proto-Kiowa-Tanoan *w; (Trager and Trager, 1959) but those that enter into the alternation with /g/ may well go back to a velar nasal (C. Douglas Johnson, personal communication). Evidence would have to be sought anew elsewhere in the language. In Table 10, again, the upper case vowel letters represent both the nasal and oral vowels of each of the three qualities; T represents /t/ and /n/.

The scope of this paper does not permit me to spell out the labors involved in working out the close relationship between the phonological structure of the pronominal prefixes and the semantic structure of their referents. It is relevant, however, that the noun classes have suffixes which can be written GƆ, BƆ, DƆ, and that helped lead to the conclusion shown in Table 11. There is also determiner concord of a sort that reinforced the main hunch that it would be better to jettison completely the traditional categories in which so much of our thinking about pronouns has been done.

For instance, subject and object do not even seem to be valid concepts in Kiowa. Instead, I should like to hypothesize that there are two interactors which could be called, rather awkwardly, Interactor A and Interactor B. This implies that if in our English translation we have a "2d subject" and a "1p object," we will have in Kiowa the identical prefix with a situation in which there is the seeming reverse, a "1p subject" and a "2d object"—and so on for other categories of interaction. There may be an interactional pronoun where there is an intransitive verb in English, furthermore—like Buber's I-It, expanded. That is, for something like 'I walk' there might be the prefix for interaction 1s/3pC, showing that 'I' am interacting with an inanimate entity. Clearly, it was tempting to use *phonosememe* instead of *morphophoneme*.

The details of my hypothesis, which naturally needs testing in the field, are set forth in Table 12. If you look under Sememe 1, you see that an initial /g/ or /y/ means that the Interactors are singular or plural, that is, *non-dual*; an initial /b/ or /m/ means that they are dual or plural, that is, *non-singular*; and an initial /d/ or /n/ signals that they are singular or dual, that is, *non-plural*.

Sememe 2 seems to clarify Sememe 1. If the vowel is A, it specifies *plural*; if E, it specifies *dual*; if Ɔ, it specifies *indefinite*, which I shall have to leave undefined. Internal evidence for the validity of this hypothesis lies in the systematic gaps noted above. GE and DA do not occur because they would be paradoxical, since G means non-dual and E dual, and since D means non-plural and A plural.

Sememe 3 is either Ø or T, i.e. /t/ or /n/. It is possible, since the final consonant occurs chiefly in the referential series of pronouns with 3dp "objects" that we should say that Sememe 3 signals *non-singular referent*.

Two other points that do not appear in the chart but which should be checked in the field are these: does the lack of an initial consonant signal a third person interactor or yet something else; does the presence of nasality throughout the pronoun mean something like symmetry of interaction, between two dual interactors for instance. These seem to be reasonable possibilities.

If Kiowa, then, does indeed have the semantic features of [singular, dual, plural, indefinite, interactor A, interactor B, referent, symmetry], there is almost no point of comparison with the surface semantic features of English pronouns. Perhaps we have not even begun to systematize the possibilities of the semantic structure of the pronoun systems of the various language families. I suspect that this sort of thing runs in families, language families, and that if we keep in mind the possibility of various kinds of interaction, of a dynamic semantic structure rather than the familiar static categories of person, number, gender, and case, we may discover pronominal phenomena which we have not yet imagined.

TABLE 5

KIOWA CONSONANTS					
	Labial	Dental	Palatal	Velar	Glottal
Stops	p	t	c	k	ʔ
and	pʰ	tʰ		kʰ	
Affricates	pʾ	tʾ	cʾ	kʾ	
	b	d		g	
Fricatives		s			
		z			
Nasals	m	n			
Resonants		l	y		h

TABLE 6

KIOWA VOWELS		
i	u	[+ high]
e	o	[− high, − low]
a	ɔ	[+ low]

[− back]   [+ back]

All vowels occur ± length and ± nasalazation

Charts of Pronominal Prefixes
(adapted from Harrington)

TABLE 7

PARTIAL TABLE OF SUBJECT PRONOUNS								
Object Subject	Ø	1s	1dp	2s	2d	2p	3s	3d
1s	a	de	ēm	ēm	mɔ̃	bɔ	yãn	nẽn
1i	ba	– –	be	– –	– –	– –	ba	bet
1e	e	– –	et	gɔ	mɔ̃	bɔ	e	et
2s	ēm	e	dɔ	be	– –	– –	a	mẽn
2d	mã	mã	dɔ	– –	mẽ	– –	mã	mẽn
2p	ba	ba	dɔ		– –	be	be	bet
3s	Ø	ẽ	dɔ	gɔ	mɔ̃	ba	Ø	ẽ
3d	e	ẽ	dɔ	gɔ	mɔ̃	ba	ẽ	ẽn
3pA	ã~Ø	a	dɔ	gɔ	mɔ̃	ba	e	et
3pB	e~Ø	e	dɔ	gɔ	mɔ̃	ba	e	et
3pC	ga	Ø	Ø	gɔ	mɔ̃	ba	Ø	Ø

TABLE 8

PARTIAL TABLE OF SUBJECT-REFERENTIAL PRONOUNS

	3s	3d	3pA	3pB	3pC
1s/2s	ga	nẽn	nẽn	gɔ	yãn
2d	mɔ̃	mẽn	mɔ̃n/mẽn	mɔ̃n	mãn
2p	bɔ	bet	bɔt/bet	bɔt	---
1p/2s	gɔ	det	det	gɔt	gat
2d	mɔ̃	mẽn	mɔ̃n/mẽn	mɔ̃n	mãn
1i/2p	bɔ	---	bet	---	---
3	baʔa	bedeʔe	←→	bɔdɔʔɔ	baga
3d	mẽ	mẽn	mẽn	mẽn	mẽn
3pA	ba	bet	be	bet	bat

TABLE 9

FORM OF KIOWA VERB PREFIXES

(C_1) V (C_2)

C_1 \ V (C_2)	a	e	ɔ	at	et	ɔt	ã	ẽ	ɔ̃	ãn	ẽn	ɔ̃n
Ø	x	x	x		x			x		x	x	x
b	x	x	x	x	x	x	–	–	–	–	–	–
d	–	x	x	–	x	x	–	–	–	–	–	–
g	x	–	x	x	–	x	–	–	–	–	–	–
m	–	–	–	–	–	–	x	x	x	x	x	x
n	–	–	–	–	–	–	x	x	–	x	x	x
y	–	–	–	–	–	–	x	–	–	x	–	–

TABLE 10

DISTRIBUTIONS OF SEGMENTS OF VERBS PREFIXES

Segment 1 (C_1)	Segment 2 (V)	Segment 3 (C_2)
Ø, b, g	a	t, Ø
Ø, m, y	ã	n, Ø
Ø, b, d	e	t, Ø
Ø, m, n	ẽ	n, Ø
Ø, b, d, g	ɔ	t, Ø
Ø, m, n	ɔ̃	n, Ø

TABLE 11

UNDERLYING FORMS OF VERB PREFIXES		
Morphophoneme 1	Morphophoneme 2	Morphophoneme 3
Ø, B, G	A	T, Ø
Ø, B, D	E	T, Ø
Ø, B, D, G	Ɔ	T, Ø

TABLE 12

SEMANTIC FEATURES OF KIOWA PRONOUNS		
Sememe 1 (Interactor A or B)	Sememe 2 (Interactor B or A)	Sememe 3 (Singularity of Referent)
G non-dual	A plural	Ø singular referent
B non-singular	E dual	T non-sing. referent
D non-plural	Ɔ indefinite	

References

Buber, Martin (1958), *I and Thou*, second edition. New York, Charles Scribner's Sons.

Crowell, Edith (1949), "A Preliminary Report on Kiowa Structure." *International Journal of American Linguistics*, XV, 163–7.

Fillmore, Charles J. (1968), "The Case for Case." *Universals in Linguistic Theory*, ed. by E. Bach and R. T. Harms. New York; Holt, Rinehart and Winston, Inc. pp. 15, 17, 24, 50.

Freeman, Michael (1970), "Systematic Morphological Change as Reflected in the Evolution of the French Pronouns." Ph.D. thesis (in preparation). University of California, Santa Barbara.

Hale, Kenneth (1967), "Toward a Reconstruction of Kiowa-Tanoan Phonology." *International Journal of American Linguistics*, 33:2, 112–20.

Harrington, John Peabody (1928), *Vocabulary of the Kiowa Language*. Bureau of American Ethnology, Bulletin 84.

Hill, Archibald A. (1958), *Introduction to Linguistic Structures*. New York, Harcourt, Brace.

Jones, Robert B. (1970), Review of Joseph R. Cooke, Pronominal Reference in Thai, Burmese, and Vietnamese. *Language*, Vol. 46, No. 1, 214–7.

Lees, Robert B. and E. S. Klima (1963), "Rules for English Pronominalization." *Language*, 39, 17–28.

McDavid, Raven I., Jr. (1963), Editor and annotator of H. L. Mencken, *The American Language*, fourth edition. New York, Alfred A. Knopf. 543–4.

Merrifield, William R. (1959), "The Kiowa Verb Prefix." *International Journal of American Linguistics*, 25, 168–76.

Trager, Edith Crowell (1960), "The Kiowa Language: A Grammatical Study." Unpublished Ph.D. dissertation, University of Pennsylvania.

Trager, George L. (1942), "Historical Phonology of the Tiwa Languages." *Studies in Linguistics*, Occasional Papers, No. 3. Norman, Oklahoma, Battenburg Press.

Trager, George L. and Edith C. (1959), "Kiowa and Tanoan." *American Anthropologist*, 51:1078–83.

Zwicky, Arnold M. (1970), "Greek-Letter Variables and the Sanskrit *ruki* Class." *Linguistic Inquiry*, 1:4, 551.

A SYSTEM OF ENGLISH PHONEMES

KEMP MALONE

Johns Hopkins University

I

We mark the beginning of civilization (as against barbarism) by the rise of writing systems, and these in the nature of the case reflect analyses of the utterances of speech. Such analyses in terms of meaning led to logographic systems, exemplified in the logograms of Chinese. Further analysis in terms of sound brought into being the syllabaries and alphabets of antiquity and one of these, the Latin alphabet, came into use for writing English as early as the seventh century of our era, when the English people by their conversion to Christianity were drawn into the orbit of Mediterranean culture. In ordinary writing we use this alphabet still, and an expanded form of it, the International Phonetic Alphabet (IPA for short), made for transcribing all languages, often serves in professional linguistic works to write English, though commonly with more or less modification. Thus, Hans Kurath and his fellows in their Linguistic Atlas of the United States and Canada, Kenyon and Knott in their Pronouncing Dictionary of American English, and Daniel Jones in his English Pronouncing Dictionary used modified forms of IPA for their transcriptions.

Unlike these are the respellings for pronunciation traditional for dictionaries and other books brought out to meet the needs of the general public. Here the letters commonly keep values they have in conventional orthography, the inconsistencies and deficiencies of which are removed by regularization, dropping of silent letters, and use of special digraphs, diacritics, and other marks. Thus, *vain*, *vane*, and *vein* all become 'van' in the third edition (1961) of the Merriam-Webster New International Dictionary of the English Language (3NID), since in our English tradition of respelling for pronunciation the vowel heard in these words is so written wherever it occurs. Again, in this tradition a digraph 'zh' (modeled on 'sh') stands for the vibrant fricative heard in *beige*, *occasion*, *measure*, *azure* etc. It is also traditional to keep the digraph 'th' in words where it stands for a fricative, its two fricative values being distinguished variously; in 3NID the vibrant value is shown by underscoring, the surd one by want of a mark. The letters *q* and *x* are not used in the respellings and *c* occurs only in the digraph 'ch', which represents the palatalized dental surd affricate heard in *church* etc.

But things are not always so simple. Thus, the letter *y*, which seldom has consonantal value in ordinary writing, is restricted to this value in traditional respelling, with the further restriction to cases where it comes before the sonant (i.e. main sound)[1] of its syllable, as in *yet* and *lawyer*; moreover, if it is thought of as combined with this sonant to make a rising diphthong, as in *you*, *Yule* etc., this is commonly respelled (u), though the respelling (yoo) also occurs. In cases where consonantal *y* follows the sonant of its syllable, as in *boy*, and wherever *y* represents a sonant, as in *hymn*, *why*, and *myrtle*, it is commonly replaced by (i), (ī), or (û) as the case may be. Taken as a whole, the traditional respellings give a transcription far from phonemic. The many departures from the tradition found in 3NID make the system more confusing to the layman without satisfying the professional linguist; see my paper in *Studies . . . in Honour of Margaret Schlauch* (Warsaw, 1966).[2]

Somewhere between IPA and traditional respelling comes the system of transcription found in the NED and its abridgement the Shorter Oxford. A major feature of this system (see Shorter Oxford, p. ix) is the recognition of the primary or ideal value of the many vowels that undergo obscuration or reduction in unstressed positions, but which at any time may revert to their full quality, as in rhetorical utterance, in singing, and in cases of deliberate or affected precision. A breve or dot, set over the "full-quality" symbol, marks this fluctuation between real and ideal. Two obscured or reduced types are distinguished: a middle-of-the-mouth type, as in the first syllable of *about*, *confess*, *together* etc. and the second syllable of *human*, *moment*, *unity* etc.; and a palatal type, as in the first syllable of *befool*, *rely*, the second of *bullet*, *illness*, *bounteous*. The former type "tends" toward the schwa of the phoneticians, the symbol for which is actually used in a good many Oxford transcriptions (e.g. the last syllable of *bounteous* and *purpose*); presumably the editors thought of (ə) as standing for an obscure rather than an obscured sound. They did not recognize a rounded type; contrast Daniel Jones, whose symbol for it is [o], as in *obey* [o'bei] and *fellow* ['felo].[8]

The term reversion carries with it a diachronic approach, one proper enough, of course, in a work entitled A New English Dictionary on Historical Principles, but I find it hard to believe that the sound symbolized by *a* in *about* and *human* ever reverts to anything else, unless perhaps at a spelling-bee: e.g. "h-u hu [xu], m-a-n man [mæn], human." One might fancy that the Oxford's transcription (hiū•măn) reflects a system in which all members of a given gradation have the same symbol, but the transcriptions (æ) and (ē¹) for the *a* of *humanity* and *humane* show that the editors had no thought of such a system.[4] Again, their (ĕ) in *moment*, uttered as a palatal, does not strike me as rhetorical, deliberately or affectedly precise, or the like. If I ever heard it (I never have) I should take it for dialectal, but of course things may have been otherwise in the 19th century, when the NED system of transcription was set up.

Jones recognizes rounded variants of the [ə] he gives for the *o* in *confess* and *together* and distinguishes between them, transcribing [kon] but [tu]. In so doing he departs (as I think) from broad transcription; his unstressed [o] and [u] belong to the same phoneme, best described as the rounded counterpart of [ə]. The NED editors make a like (though not the same) distinction, misled by their theory of reversion. Since in standard English the *con-* and *to-* of these words are regularly without stress irrespective of style, what we have here is simply a variation between [ə] and its rounded counterpart. As to the *i* of *unity* etc., in my own speech it has a palatal value oftener than not, though the value [ə] is also familiar to my tongue and ears. So far as I can tell, the variation is free, and the palatal variant, since like its alternative it takes no stress, necessarily differs in quality from the *i* of *pity* etc. A syllable that has never been stressed (compare Latin *unitas*) cannot well revert to a stressed state. At most one may speak here of reversion to palatal quality. For words like unity the Oxford's symbol (ĭ) tells us in truth, though not in intention, that it stands for either of two sound-effects (commonly called phonemes) which in other settings make an opposition, witness the minimal pair *serif* vs. *seraph*. This two-value symbol answers to the dotted schwa sign of 3NID, a device for saving space, as the 3NID editor duly points out (p. 34*a*). It would have been well had the NED editors so justified their (ĭ) but they thought of what they were doing in other terms.[5]

The NED also has the schwa sign, printed in smaller type and set high, though not above the minim line, for "the vowel-element developed between i, e, . . . etc. and r, . . . ; the modern southern development of (uᵊ) to (oᵊ) . . . is not admitted, nor the monophthongal pronunciation in words like *door*, i.e. (dǫɹ) as opposed to (doᵊɹ)." [6] Daniel Jones, however, not only admits but gives first place to the monophthong and the Random House Dictionary (RHD for short) recognizes only monophthongal pronunciation here, the schwa sign being conspicuous by its absence.[7] From childhood I have been familiar with an r-less and schwa-less [do] for *door* and the like for *four*, *floor* etc., but at home and at school we were taken to task if we left out the schwa (the r was another matter) and shamed into habitual use of the diphthong; not till I was grown did I learn that in England many perfectly respectable people left schwa out and (more shocking still) made no distinction between *door* and *daw*, *floor* and *flaw* etc. The professional linguist must of course go by the facts of usage, but I still get a certain satisfaction from the refusal of the NED editors to recognize that a monophthong in words like *door* was admissible.

Another important feature of the NED transcription system is the device for distinguishing close and open quality in vowels otherwise given the same symbol: italic type marks a close vowel, roman the corresponding open one. Examples: (pūl) for *pool* but (pūᵊɹ) for *poor* and (pul) for *pull*; (bōᵘn) for *bon*e but (bōᵊɹ) for *boar* and *bore*; (sǫɹt) for *sort* and (gǫt) for *got* but (bǭt) for *bought*, (wǭɹt) for *wart* and (wǫt) for *watt*; (bɪn) for *bean* but (bɪᵊɹ) for *beer* and (bin) for *bin*; (pēⁱn) for *pain* and *pane* but (pēᵊɹ) for *pair* and *pare* and (pen) for *pen*; (pö) for French *peu* but (köln) for German *Köln*. For the vowel of *cut* etc. an upside-down italic a is used but for that of *calm* etc. the *a* is roman and upright. The IPA symbol for the vowel of *cut* and the like is [ʌ] but some phoneticians have [a] instead and I cannot say why the NED editors thought it needful to invert the italic symbol. They take the vowel of *fur* etc. for the long of their (*ʋ*), that of *fir* etc. for the long of their (ə), a distinction foreign to me and, I think, to most native speakers. The distinction they make between (ǫ) and (o) is also unfamiliar to me, long and short alike.

The Oxford distinguishes between close and open quality not only in stressed but also in unstressed syllables, witness the minimal pair *levee* (le•vi) vs. *levy* (le•vi), but Daniel Jones has ['levi] for both and in 3NID and RHD too the words are made homophones. The distinction the Oxford makes seems to be one that no longer holds. On the other hand, RHD with its minimal pair *candied* (kan'dēd) vs. *candid* (kan'did) makes a distinction between close and open quality in weak syllables not recognized by the Oxford or Jones. (The macron, the traditional mark of long quantity, serves in both RHD and 3NID to mark quality, an unhappy device, baffling to the general.) The 3NID entry *candied* gives no respelling for pronunciation but from the entry *candy* ('kandē, -di) we are entitled to infer recognition of the variant pronunciations (-dēd) and (-did) for the weak syllable of *candied*. From the 3NID entry *candid* we learn that here too (unlike RHD) variant pronunciations of the weak syllable are recognized: (-did) and (-dəd). That is, 3NID takes into account not only the speakers for whom *candied* and *candid* make a minimal pair but also the ones for whom these words are homophones. In my own speech they are not distinguished and the same holds, I think, of most native speakers. But how do those who distinguish them do so? If we go by 3NID they may make the distinction in three ways: (-dēd) vs. (-did), (-dēd) vs. (-dəd), and (-did) vs. (-dəd). In my Studies . . . of 1959 (p. 266, fn. 35) I accepted (-dēd) as widely heard, in America at least, and gave a historical explanation of it, but I have come to doubt more and more that many or indeed any speakers have it and I now think that the ones who make the distinction do so by opposing schwa to its palatal counterpart, sounds symbolized in 3NID by (ə) and (i). Such speakers may well have advanced allophones of both phonemes.[8]

It remains true that in singing, riming, and other settings a weak syllable may take stress (i.e. become more or less strong), a change that necessarily affects the syllabic structure, but such changes need not be taken (as the NED editors take them) for reversions to earlier norms. We have to do, rather, with gradation (see fn. 4 above): the sonant proper to the weak syllable is replaced by one proper to a strong syllable. Thus, in "I said *de*serve, not *reserve*" the italicized syllables, normally weak, are strong by contrastive stress and their sonants accordingly take a strong grade of the gradations they belong to.[9] In ordinary writing, as we have seen, the grades of some gradations are distinguished, those of others are not, whereas in phonetic writing one would expect them all to be distinguished, since they all differ in quality. Here traditional English phonetics fails most markedly when it comes to palatal gradation. Thus, Daniel Jones has ['timid] for *timid* and [ti'miditi] for *timidity* and the Oxford with its (ti•mid) and (timi•dĭti) does little better. Obviously the first syllable of these words takes a strong grade in the adj., a weak one in the noun, and the second syllable has things the other way, but the symbols for the sounds do not bring this out and the difference in grade must be shown by a supplementary device. Contrast Jones's ['sʌmən] and the Oxford's (sɒ •mən) for *summon*, where the stress mark, though given by *Systemzwang*, is needless. In 3NID, which makes more of differences in sonantal quality, palatal gradation is better handled, though the presentation leaves something to be desired.

In general, the NED transcription system is most open to question in its treatment of weak syllables, witness *handle* (hæ•nd'l) but *sandal* (sæ•ndăl), *diary* (dəi•ări) but *fiery* (fəiᵊ•ri), *at om* (æ•təm) but *dictum* (di•ktɐm), *famine* (fæ•min) but *women* (wi•mĕn).[10] And the great weakness common to the systems taken up above is their failure to recognize and provide for the fundamental difference in structure between strong and weak (i.e. stressed and unstressed) syllables in English. The sonant of an English strong syllable is regularly a vowel; that of a weak syllable, a sonorant (i.e. a liquid, nasal, or semivowel), otherwise known as a resonant. I have dealt at some length with this matter in my *Studies . . . of 1959* (pp. 263 ff.) and see no need of repeating myself here. It will be enough to say that the system for phonemic transcription of English given below takes the structural difference between strong and weak syllables fully into account.

II

The phonemes of English, in terms of their behavior as members of a syllable, fall into three groups: vowels, sonorants, and obstruents.[11] I will begin with the vowels, distinguishing close and open ones (or tense and lax ones, if you will) by printing the close kind in roman, the open kind in italic type (NED has it the other way). I take up first the tergals, i.e. the vowels made by approaching more or less closely tongue-root and tergum (back wall of pharynx).[12] Tergal articulations divide the oro-pharyngeal cavity into a long upper resonance chamber, stretching from teeth to tergum, and a small lower chamber, the nether part of the pharynx. I distinguish four vowels so made: a close spread /a/ as in *calm*, an open spread /*a*/ as in *cut*, close rounded /ɔ/ as in *caught*, and an open rounded /*ɔ*/ as in *cot*. These distinctions are the ones I make in my own speech, but many speakers have no /ɔ/, using /a/ instead, and others do not distinguish /ɔ/ from /ɒ/, having a rounded phoneme that I hear as open rather than close. Yet other speakers make a distinction between short and long that is phonemic for the close spread vowel, as in the minimal pair *bomb* /bam/ vs. *balm* /bām/. The tergal spread vowels occur in two allophonic types, which I distinguish as simple tergals and tergotectals. The latter are marked by a secondary articulation in which the tongue-stem makes a slight approach to the roof of the mouth (tectum), thus lessening a bit the depth of the upper resonance chamber. Many New Englanders have the tergo-tectal /a/, many southerners the tergo-tectal /*a*/.

Moving with the breath-stream we come next to the velar vowels, in making which the tongue-stem approaches more or less closely the soft palate (velum) and thereby divides the oro-pharyngal cavity into two resonance chambers, one to the back, the other to the front. All the vowels so made are rounded. Many New Englanders have four: a higher close /u/ as in *fool*, a higher open /*u*/ as in *full*, a lower close /o/ as in *hole*, and a lower open /*o*/ as in *whole*. But in the speech of nearly everybody else /*o*/ is wanting and we leave it out of account in our system of English phonemes. The lower close vowel has allophones ending with an up-glide, whence the [ou] of the phoneticians.[13]

Opposed to the velar vowels are the palatals, all of which are spread. In making them the tongue-stem approaches the hard palate, thereby dividing the oro-pharyngal cavity into two resonance chambers very unequal in size: a big back chamber and a small front one. I distinguish five phonemes so made: a high close /i/ as in *marine*, a high open /*i*/ as in *chin*; a mid close /e/ as in *veil*, a mid open /*e*/ as in *bet*; and a low /æ/ with close and open allophones, as in *fare* and *fat*. The mid close vowel has allophones ending with an up-glide, whence the [ei] of the phoneticians.[13] The close allophonic type of /æ/ occurs only as the first member of a diphthong; see below.

The vowel heard in *sir*, *surf* and the like is neither velar (back) nor palatal (front); it is made in the middle of the mouth and is best described as medial. It occurs in two main allophonic types: simple and rhotacized. Kenyon accordingly has two symbols for the vowel, a distinction proper enough in phonetic but out of place in phonemic transcription. The IPA symbol for this vowel agrees in shape with the Russian equivalent of Greek zeta but is to be taken as a stylized open form of the schwa sign. I used the IPA symbol as late as my paper in the Schlauch festschrift of 1966, but I have come to feel it more fitting to represent the vowel with /ɹ/; that is, an r upside down.[14]

Finally, standard English has two glide vowels: an upward-moving one symbolized with crossed v or inverted small-capital a, as in *bough*, *bout* /bʌ, bʌt/, and a forward-moving one symbolized with y, as in *buy*, *bite* /by, byt/. Such a phoneme differs from a simple vowel in that during its utterance the shape of its resonance chambers is steadily changing in a set pattern of movement. The limits of a given pattern are ill defined and variable, so much so that in some allophones the glide is hard to tell from a simple vowel. And since the movement is gradual, without division into two parts by a shift (contrast the two-phoneme word *by* with the three-phoneme word *boy*), the usual analysis of /ɤ/ and /y/ as two-member sequences, symbolized with [au] or [aw] and [ai] or [aj], does violence to the phonetic facts and falsifies the phonemic picture. The distinctive thing about these phonemes is the glide effect, which differentiates them from simple vowels on the one hand and diphthongs on the other.[15]

From vowels we go to semivowels. In ordinary English writing the two are not systematically distinguished, the same set of symbols (viz., the letters a,e,i,o,u,w,y) serving for both, but in phonemic transcription, of course, we need a special character for each of the three semivocalic phonemes of the language. I use /w/ for the rounded or labio-velar one, as in *willow, queen, suave, choir, obey, piano* /wɪlm, kwin, swav, kwyər, wbe, pɪænw/;[16] the schwa sign for the neutral or tectal one, as in *fairy, awake, solemn, beautifully, wisdom, circus* /fæərɪ, əwek, sɔləm, bɪutəfllɪ, wɪzdəm, sɪkəs/; and dot-less or small-capital i for the spread or palatal one, as in *yearly, cubic, you, holy, eunuch, bullet, courage* /ɪiərlɪ,[17] kɪubɪk/, ɪu, holɪ, ɪunək, bʊlɪt, kɑrɪj/.[18] The labio-velar /w/ serves as weak grade of rounded, the palatal /ɪ/ as weak grade of spread vowels; the tectal /ə/, as weak or reduced grade of vowels in general. But of course a semivowel may occur on its own, so to speak; that is, without belonging to a gradation.

Like the other sonorants, a semivowel may serve as sonant of a weak syllable; witness the unstressed syllables of the words italicized in the paragraph above. If such a syllable has two semivowels, as in *onion, penguin, undulate* /ʌnɪən, peŋgwɪn, ʌndɪwlet/, the first of these is consonantal, the second sonantal. In *Bedouin* /bedwwɪn/ the first /w/ is sonantal (ending its syllable), the second consonantal (heading its syllable); similarly *carrion* /kærɪɪən/ and the like. In strong syllables a semivowel stands next to the vowel of its syllable, making with this vowel a rising or falling diphthong. Whether rising (semivowel plus vowel) or falling (vowel plus semivowel), a diphthong is a sequence of two phonemes and differs from a glide vowel, as we saw above. But oftener than not the linguists make no such distinction. Thus, *diphthong* is defined in 3NID as

> a gliding monosyllabic speech item that starts at or near the articulatory position for one vowel and moves to or toward the position for another . . . and that is usually indicated in phonetic transcription by two symbols representing often only approximately the beginning and ending limits of the glide. . . .

Here a diphthong as a whole is called a glide, though in the entry *glide* (noun 3b) we are told otherwise: "*specif*: the less prominent vowel or sound like a vowel in the articulation of two consecutive vowel sounds unequal in prominence. . . . " (The example given is *y* in *yell*.) In this definition the scope of the term "glide" is clearly restricted to the subordinate part of the diphthong; that is, to the semivowel. But a semivowel is not a glide, as we have seen.

The writer of the definition of *diphthong* in the New World Dictionary of 1953 really gives two definitions:

> a complex sound made by gliding continuously from the position for one vowel to that for another within the same syllable. . . . In many languages, diphthongs can be interpreted and phonetically written as a vowel followed by a semivowel (glide). . . .

The first of these two definitions does not fit a diphthong but would do for the glide vowels /ʌ/ and /y/ if the limits of the glide were not identified (as unhappily they are) with definite vowel positions; here 3NID is more cautious. The adj. "complex" is misleading where it stands but would not be if limited to the alternative definition. This alternative is restricted to falling diphthongs but otherwise agrees with the traditional sense of the word (see fn. 6 above) if taken without the "(glide)" tacked on at the end. It is noteworthy, besides, that this parenthetical addition goes contrary to the same dictionary's definition of *semivowel*, viz. "a vowel used as a consonant."

I will take up one more dictionary definition of *diphthong*, that given in RHD:

> an unsegmentable, gliding speech sound varying continuously in phonetic quality but held to be a single sound or phoneme and identified by its apparent beginning and ending sound, as the *oi*-sound of *toy* or *boil*, or the *ch*-sound of *chip*.

Here the definition proper ("an . . . phoneme") fits not diphthongs but the glide vowels /ʌ/ and /y/. The examples are another matter: the "*oi*-sound" is no glide but a sequence of two sharply distinguished phonemes, the vowel /ɔ/ and the semivowel /ɪ/; and the "*ch*-sound" (Kenyon's consonantal diphthong) is clearly segmentable into stop and fricative and the phoneticians write it accordingly, though the phonemicists commonly (and rightly, I think) reckon it a unit phoneme.

Of the rising diphthongs of English, only /ɪu/ as in *you, few, feud* is often given the diphthongal name and many restrict the scope of the term to the falling kind. The latter end with /ɪ/ or /ə/. Most speakers have three falling diphthongs with /ɪ/ for semivowel: /uɪ oɪ ɔɪ,/ as in *ruin, Cohen, coin* /ruɪn koɪn kɔɪn/; but many New Yorkers and not a few other Americans have /ɹɪ/ as in *bird* /bɹɪd/ etc. for fourth /ɪ/-diphthong and a fifth such diphthong /aɪ/ as in *large* /laɪj/ occurs in the speech of Georgians and perhaps elsewhere.[19] Diphthongs ending in /ə/ fall into three groups: those headed by back vowels (tergals or velars), as in *cruel, boa, hoary* /kruəl kruəl boə hoərɪ hɔərɪ/; by front vowels, as in *peon, really, Graham, hairy* /piən riəlɪ greəm hæərɪ; and by glide vowels, as in *towel, tower, dial, dire* /tʌəl tʌər dyəl dyər/. (For *aisle* /yəl/ and the like see below.) Daniel Jones (l.c.)

gives the diphthongal name to six of these /ə/-diphthongs but does not recognize /uə/ and /iə/; his [uə iə] are my/*uə iə*/. Furthermore, unlike the Oxford, he does not reckon diphthongal the sequences having a glide vowel for first member. Thus, he transcribes *our* and *ire* with ['auə] and ['aiə], his stress mark showing that he thought them disyllabic words, whereas the Oxford, which gives no stress mark here, shows thereby that its editors thought the words monosyllabic.

Semivowels are made like vowels, though they have their own way of behaving. The other sonorants, which behave like the semivowels, are made otherwise. The two liquids, /l/ and /r/, are traditionally so called; the name reflects the fact that in Latin they had a clear, frictionless sound. English /r/ has fricative allophones, as we shall see, but the old term is convenient and has held its own. In making both phonemes the front part of the tongue articulates against the dentum (i.e. prepalatal region of tectum along with upper gums and teeth). In /l/ the front end of the tongue presses against the dentum and the breath gets out over the sides of the tongue, whence the name lateral. In /r/ the tongue is drawn back a bit and the sides of its front part press against the dentum; its front edge is raised but lax, with room left for the breath to escape over it without making audible friction except in certain sequences taken up below.

The lateral liquid occurs in three allophonic types: dark (or hollow), middling, and clear. Sonantal /l/, as in *needle* /nidl/, is regularly dark. Consonantal /l/ is commonly clear or middling when it heads a syllable or ends a pre-sonantal sequence, as in *lie, sly* /ly sly/. Elsewhere it is commonly dark, but most speakers have a middling /l/ after tauto-syllabic /y/ or /ɔɪ/, as in *aisle, wild, boil, boiled* /yl wyld bɔɪl bɔɪld/. The speakers who here too have dark /l/ typically make this the second member of a sequence /əl/; hence /yəl wəyld/ etc., with diphthongal /yə/, and /bɔɪəl bɔɪəld/, with disyllabic pronunciation. The dark /l/ is made with a secondary articulation of the tongue-stem that divides the oro-pharyngal cavity into two resonant chambers, the back chamber reaching from tergum to velum, the front one from velum to dentum; a channel varying in depth links the two chambers. This articulation is slight in the middling, absent in the clear type; the latter thus has only one resonance chamber, stretching from tergum to dentum. Words like *needling* may be disyllabic, with clear consonantal /l/, or trisyllabic, with dark sonantal /l/ ending the penult and clear consonantal /l/ heading the ultima: /nidlɪŋ/ or /nidllɪŋ/. Here the syllabic boundaries are obvious. In my own speech they are equally so in words like *billy, oily* /hɪlɪ ɔɪlɪ/, where /l/ is clear and therefore pre-sonantal, and for speakers with dark /l/ this ends its syllable. Minimal pairs like disyllabic *peddling* /pedlɪŋ/ vs. trisyllabic *pedaling* /pedllɪŋ/ show that presence vs. absence of sonantal /l/ may have a phonemic function, serving to distinguish one word from another.

The frontal liquid, like the lateral one, falls into allophonic types. Three such types are commonly distinguished: an open one as described above, the usual articulation; a fricative, heard in presonantal /dr, tr/, as in *dry, try*; and a reduced trill, heard between vowel and semivowel, as in *very*, and after a spread dental fricative, as in *southron, three* /saðrən, þri/. In American speech the trill between vowel and semivowel is seldom heard, the usual open articulation occurring here too. Contrariwise, in some forms of English (e.g. Scots) the trilled type is or may be heard in all settings.

Many American and most British speakers have only pre-sonantal /r/; where post-sonantal /r/ occurs in "r-keeping" speech, "r-droppers" have either /ə/ or nothing. Thus, with such speakers *heart* /hart/ takes shape as /haət/ or simply /hat/. Words that traditionally end in [r] take variant forms for r-droppers, who may be r-keepers in liaison, witness the utterance *There it is* [ðæərɪtiz], where the liquid heads the second syllable. But such variation between presence and absence of /r/ is only a particular case of the general rule: /r/ is present in liaison because it is pre-sonantal, a syllable-heading phoneme. The same explanation holds for the medial /r/ of *parity*, *ferry* and a multitude of other words: the r-droppers have it because it comes before its sonant, and such words fall into syllables accordingly. Like the other sonorants /r/ may be sonantal in weak syllables: thus, medial /r/ in *wonderful* /wandrfl/, final /r/ in *wonder* /wandr/. Here again the r-droppers have /ə/ except in liaison. In words like *wondering* both /ər/ and /rr/ are heard, seemingly in free variation. The first /r/ of the latter is sonantal (ending its syllable), the second /r/ consonantal (heading its syllable). Compare disyllabic *wondrous*, where the standing sequence /dr/ heads the ultima.

Of the sonorants I take up the nasals last because they lead naturally to the stops, the obstruents *par excellence*. In method of formation, indeed, the nasals of English might well be called obstruents, but in terms of their behavior in syllables they belong to the sonorants and I am presenting our phonemic system in syllabic terms. One makes nasals proper (as against oro-nasals) by blocking the passage through the mouth and driving the breath-stream out the nose. The chief resonance chamber for the articulation is accordingly the nasal cavity, ranging above the tectum and including the nostrils. Below this the oro-pharyngal cavity makes a secondary resonance chamber stretching from the tergum to the point at which the oral passage is blocked. In English /ŋ/, as in *dung* /daŋ/, the tongue-stem blocks this passage at the tectum; in /n/, as in *dun* /dan/, the front end of the tongue does the blocking at the dentum; and in /m/, as in *dumb* /dam/, the lips block the passage. The three nasals of English are therefore distinguished as tectal, dental, and labial. In strong syllables, as in the examples just given, the nasals are always consonantal; in weak ones they may be sonantal, as in the phrase "back and forth" /bækŋ foərþ/, where *and* is enclitic, and in such words as *button* /batn/ and *open* /opm/. In *weakening, buttoning, opening* /wikŋniŋ, batnniŋ, opmnɪŋ/ and the like the first nasal is sonantal (ending its syllable), the second and third are consonantal (heading and ending their syllable). The minimal pair *ordinance* /ɔədnnəns/ vs. *ordnance* /ɔədnəns/, as I pronounce these words, exemplifies the distinguishing of one word from another by presence vs. absence of a sonantal nasal.

The vowels and sonorants are all vibrants in ordinary speech; that is, all are made with vibration of the vocal cords. In whispered speech they are all surds; that is, made without such vibration. It follows that the distinction between vibrant and surd has a stylistic rather than a phonemic function in these speech-sounds. In obstruents, however, the distinction is commonly phonemic; that is, nearly all these phonemes fall into pairs, one member of which in ordinary speech is vibrant, the other surd. Obstruents differ from vowels and sonorants also in that they always have a consonantal function in the structure of the syllable. In taking them up I begin with the stops,[20] which are made with oral stoppage like nasals but differ from these by having nasal stoppage too, the velum being raised enough to keep the breath-stream from entering the nasal cavity. Answering to the nasals /ŋ,n,m/ are the paired stops /g,k; d,t; b,p/, the first member of each pair being vibrant, the second surd. Tectal examples: *gag, cook* /gæg, kʌk/; dentals: *dud, tot* /dad, tɔt/; labials: *bib, pip* /bɪb, pɪp/. English also has a pair of palatalized dental onset stops /j,c/ with no corresponding nasal.[21] Vibrant examples: *judge, gem* /jaj, jem/; surds: *cello, each, itch* /celw, ic, ic/.

Made like the onset stops but without stoppage are the fricative pair /ž,š/. Vibrant examples: *vision, rouge* /vižən, ruž/; surds: *ship, bush* /šip, buš/. For the matching pair made at the dentum and not palatalized I keep the usual unmarked symbols /z,s/. Vibrant examples: *zone, rose* /zon, roz/; surds: *soup, loose* /sup, lus/. Both these fricative pairs give a rough acoustic effect. English has, besides, a pair of smooth dental fricatives: vibrant /ð/ as in *then, loathe* /ðen, loð/ and surd /þ/ as in *thin, loath* /þin, loþ/. These phonemes are made with tongue edge spread at upper teeth. The corresponding labio-dental fricative pair /v,f/, as in *vat* (vibrant) and *fat* (surd), may also be reckoned smooth.

The fricative phonemes remain, two of which, the palatal /x/ as in *hew, hue* /xu/, *human* /xumən/ and the labial /q/ as in *wheel, why* /qil, qy/, have an obstruent function in the flow of speech and are here classified accordingly. (The phoneticians reckon them the surd equivalents of /ı/ and /w/.) [22] The third fricative, the breathing /h/, as in *he, high* /hi, hy/, makes a class of its own (but see fn. 11). Between vibrants /h/ may itself be vibrant, as in *mohair* and *prehistoric*; otherwise it is surd. Apart from this surdness it agrees in articulation with the vowel or semivowel that comes next after it. Like the other fricatives it is always consonantal and like /q/ and /x/ it always heads its syllable. It tends to be dropped in weak syllables, as in the antepenult of *prehistoric*; in weak forms of words like *he, his, him, her*, loss of /h/ is regular.

So much for the phonemes proper, or primary phonemes, as Bloomfield called them.[23] In the flow of speech these typically occur as members of an utterance made up of one or more syllables, and with such an utterance go patterns of stress and pitch. Since in English the strong syllables are already marked by having a vowel, the weak ones by having a sonorant for sonant, and since many if not most words with two or more strong syllables take the main stress on the first of these (i.e. have a "regular" stress-pattern), a special stress-mark is needed only for words that take the main stress on a strong syllable other than the first. In the present system of English phonemes the acute accent, set over the vowel, marks such a main stress, e.g. in *melancholia* /melənkólɪɪə/ as against *melancholy* /melənkɔlɪ/, the stress-pattern of which is brought out by the transcription as it stands. In some utterances a grave as well as an acute accent-mark is needed to show the stress-pattern; e.g. in "Alcohólic consolàtion is better than none," where the pattern subordinates the penult of the noun to that of the adj., a feature shown in transcription by marking the adj. with an acute, the noun with a grave, accent on the third syllable.

The transition from one phoneme to the next in an utterance may or may not need a marker. If the two phonemes belong to the same morpheme the transition serves to join them and may reasonably be called a junction or juncture. Here no marker is needed and in phonemic as in conventional script the process of joining is shown by setting the alphabetic symbols in immediate sequence. If the transition is from one morpheme to the next within a higher unit of meaning it remains a juncture when made within a syllable, as in plural forms like *weeks* [wiks] or contractions like *won't* [wont] and *let's* [lets]. Again, the transition is a joining, not a parting, in plurals like *roses* [rozɪz], derivatives like *bigotry* [bigətrɪ], and utterances like *Here it is* [hɪərɪtiz.], in which syllables and morphemes overlap. In phonetic writing this kind of juncture likewise takes no marker but in phonemic notation I note it with the marker ͯ where possible.[24]

When we put an utterance into conventional written form we commonly mark only the transitions that serve to part rather than to join.[25] In particular, we divide most utterances into words by spacing and some words into morphemes by hyphenation. Such devices befit phonemic writing too and have the further advantage of being familiar.[26] In using them, however, one sometimes finds it needful to depart from tradition. The adverbial phrase *at all*, for instance, in phonemic terms takes shape as one word, occurring in two variants, /ətɔl/ and /ət-ɔl/; in the first variant /t/ heads, in the second it ends, its syllable.

Spacing and the hyphen are boundary markers for words and morphemes. A break within an utterance may also be phonemic. Here are two utterances that differ in meaning by virtue of a break in the one, the lack of a break in the other:

> They murdered the witness, who knew too much.
> They murdered the witness who knew too much.

With such a break goes a characteristic pitch-pattern. In conventional writing a comma is the usual marker for break or pause within a sentence or vocule[27] and it may so serve in phonemic writing too. Likewise in both kinds of writing the period, the question-mark, and the exclamation point symbolize halt (i.e. the end of an utterance) and a characteristic pitch-pattern goes with each kind of halt. In my Studies . . . of 1959 (pp. 241 ff.) I dealt briefly with pitch; here it must suffice to say that in phonemic as against phonetic script, given the four markers / , . ? ! /, one for break and three for halt, no special markers for pitch are needed. As I noted above (see fn. 4), phonemic transcription does a good job of roughing out the pronunciation but sets aside as allophonic many features brought out in phonetic (narrow) transcription. The early Greek alphabet and its offshoots reflect thinking in phonemic, not in phonetic terms and our 20th-century phonemicists were in effect reviving and refining an approach which the rise of 19th-century phonetics had made unfashionable.

By way of summary I give a tabulation of the 42 phonemes proper:

vowels: tergal a *a*   medial ɹ glide y ɤ sonorants:
           ɔ ɔ   palatal i *i*   semivowels w ə ɪ
velar u *u*   e *e*   liquids   l r
       o   æ   nasals   ŋ n m
obstruents: rough fricatives ž š ; z s
            smooth fricatives x ; ð þ ; v f ; q   breathing: h
            stops g k ; j c ; d t ; b p

Besides these, as we have seen, utterances take stress and pitch patterns and their phonemes and phonemic sequences (morphemes etc.) are joined and parted in various ways symbolized by the markers set out above: for stress, the acute and grave accent marks; for morphemic juncture, ɤ; for shead, spacing to mark word boundaries and the hyphen to mark morphemic boundaries within a word; for break, a comma; for halt, a period, a question-mark, and an exclamation point.

The present paper on English phonemes and the much longer one in my *Studies . . . of 1959* differ markedly in approach and scope but agree where they overlap and are to be taken as complementary treatments of the theme. It is a particular pleasure to me to contribute my new look at an old subject to this volume, got out in honor of a longtime friend and fellow-southerner.

Notes

1. This sense of *sonant* (in which it is opposed to *consonant*) is traditional in European grammatical writings, witness *passim* K. Luick's *Historische Grammatik der englischen Sprache*, and it is duly entered in some American dictionaries, e.g. the *Random House Dictionary* (1966) and the College Edition (1953) of *Webster's New World Dictionary* (see the entries *consonant* and *sonant* and p. xx of Harold Whitehall's prefatory essay on the English language), but the opposition *sonant* vs. *consonant* is wanting in the Oxford and in 3NID, though implied in the Oxford's definition of *diphthong*, for which see fn. 6 below.

2. Unhappily the misprint "with" for "without" on p. 240, line 17 of my paper

makes nonsense of the passage in which it occurs.

3. Jones also gives the variants ['əbei] and ['felə], without rounding, and [ou'bei] and ['felou], with "full quality"; the latter are doubtless cases of spelling-pronunciation, not of reversion. See the entry *-ow* in Kenyon and Knott, and my Studies . . . in Current Speech (Copenhagen, 1959), pp. 235 f.

4. As everybody knows, the *a* of our conventional orthography symbolizes the gradation found in the second syllable of *human, humanist, humane, humanity* etc. and parallels occur in many other word-groups, but such symbols have other values besides and many gradations go without symbolization. Thus, each grade of the gradation found in *sing, sang, sung, song* has a symbol but the gradation as such is not symbolized. A system of transcription based on gradation and like features would give us a notation that might be deep (the term now fashionable) but would need a supplementary system of pointing (compare the Semitic alphabet) to mark the grades. Latter-day nominalists who in theory reject phonemes need not in practice give up broad (i.e. phonemic) transcription, since this does a good job roughing out the pronunciation. A fully narrow transcription would be one in terms of distinctive features, a method which Otto Jespersen pioneered in his Analphabetic Notation and which I elaborated in my Numerical Notation, set out in my *Phonology of Modern Icelandic* (1923) and there applied to a longish conversation.

5. Compare their special symbols for the "divergent pronunciations of the vowels of such words as *fast, bath* and *cough, lost, soft*" (p. ix), symbols which they used "to indicate that such local or individual varieties exist," not to save space.

6. Note the Oxford's traditional definition of *diphthong*: "A union of two vowels pronounced in one syllable; the combination of a sonantal with a con-sonantal vowel." In more modern terms the definition might be phrased thus: a tautosyllabic two-phoneme sequence of which one member is a vowel, the other a semivowel. For the distinction between diphthong and glide vowel see below.

7. But RHD gives diphthongal pronunciation in *tire* etc., though not in *tyrant* etc., where [r] heads its syllable. We are told (p. xxxii) that the raised schwa sign "occurs . . . in accented syllables between $\bar{\imath}$ and *r* to show diphthongal quality, as in *fire* (fi³r) *hire* (hī³r)". Here the "long i" is rightly treated as a vowel. (On p. xxvii it is called a diphthong and the raised schwa sign is said to show triphthongal quality.) Contrast RHD's (our, ou'ər) for *hour*, where the pronunciation put first is schwa-less and the one put second has an ordinary schwa sign (not a raised one) and is reckoned disyllabic. In fact, of course, saying *hour* or the like with an [r] not preceded by schwa constitutes a phonetic feat of which few native speakers of English are capable, and such a pronunciation would normally mark the speaker a foreigner. For more discussion see below.

8. An "advanced" allophone of this (ə) is better described as slightly palatalized; of this (i), as slightly less open.

9. Such a graduation may be traditional, witness this riming couplet from the old hymn "Veni Emmanuel":

> Make safe the way that leads on high
> And close the path to misery,

where the weak grade normal for the syllable *-ry* is replaced by the strong one needed for the rime with *high*. The 19th-century hymn "Onward, Christian Soldiers" shows another strong grade of the same gradation in the following:

> At the sign of triumph
> Satan's host doth flee;
> Oh, then, Christian soldiers,
> On to victory!

10. Note in particular that sonantal [l] is recognized in *handle* but not in *sandal*, and that the *a* of *diary* is taken as sonantal but the *e* of *fiery* as consonantal. See fnn. 6 and 7 above.

11. But the breathing /h/ is in a class by itself, unless one reckons it (as some do) a glottal obstruent. L. Bloomfield in his book *Language* (1933), p. 121, wrongly (as I think) makes /r/ an exception to the general rule that sonorants are always consonantal in strong syllables.

12. For these terms, which I introduced some fifty years ago, see my paper in the journal *Language* 38 (1962).142 ff.

13. As I pointed out in my *Studies . . . of 1959* (p. 239), such off-glides may be present or absent and are therefore features to be ignored in phonemic as opposed to phonetic transcription.

14. In the NED entry R we are told that (ɹ) symbolizes "an ə-sound," but in the transcriptions this sound is never the sonant of its syllable and my /ɹ/, which is always sonantal, differs fundamentally in function from the (ɹ) of NED.

15. For further discussion see my paper in *Mélanges Mossé* (Paris, 1959) and my *Studies . . . of 1959*, pp. 238 f., 244 ff. In the latter I used w, not crossed v or inverted small-capital a, for the upward-moving glide vowel, but I now feel that this departure from custom was perhaps too radical and in the present paper /w/ has its traditional value as the symbol for the labio-velar semivowel, though in some ways small-capital u would be more suitable for this semivowel.

16. In *willow* and the like the *o* may be taken as a way of marking the following *w* sonantal in function.

17. Some analysts deny the existence of /ə/ before tautosyllabic /r/, going on the theory that the schwa-like sound heard before the /r/ is only a feature of that phoneme. But see my *Studies . . . of 1959*, p. 245.

18. In traditional British phonetics (following A. M. Bell of Visible Speech fame) consonantal /w/ and /ɪ/ are termed glides, but we have no reason to think that the start of *wet, watt* or *yet, yacht* is any more of a glide than is the start of *let, lot* or *net, not* or the like, and the movement from the first to the second phoneme in all these words is clearly a shift, not a glide. In the nature of the case a transition from semivowel to vowel is less marked than one from liquid, nasal, or obstruent to vowel, where the difference in articulation is greater, but this fact does not make a semivowel a glide. In has also been argued that consonantal /w/ and /ɪ/ must be glides because they cannot be prolonged, but in fact it is easy to hold them indefinitely in their typical position, as the reader can see for himself by doing so, and some languages have long palatal and labial consonants of this type. In sum, calling /w/ and /ɪ/ glides goes contrary to sound phonetic analysis and cannot reasonably be upheld. The old semivocalic name for them is right.

19. See further my *Studies . . . 1959*, p. 244 (with fn. 19) and note that though Daniel Jones recognizes five, [i]-diphthongs, two of these, [ei] and [ai], answer to my /e/ and /y/, and for my [ɪɪ] and /aɪ/ he has simple vowels. We thus have only three diphthongs of this type in common: his [ui, oi, ɔi] answer to my /uɪ, oɪ, ɔɪ/. Moreover, the example for [oi] which he gives (Dict., 4th ed., p. xxv) is not a true diphthong: the *o* and the *i* of *going* belong to different syllables!

20. The term "stop" is the usual one in this country but Daniel Jones and other British phoneticians have "plosive" instead, though recognizing that the stoppage need not end with an explosion. It seldom so ends, indeed, in ordinary English speech. Before a vowel the release may·be slow enough for the breath to be heard escaping, an effect called aspiration, as in *tool*; or the release may be quicker, as in *stool*, so that no such effect is readily heard; in neither case is the release properly described as explosive. Before other phonemes, the release takes place in a variety

of ways that need not be taken up here; it will be enough to note that in words like *pity* or *matter*, where /t/ comes before a sonantal sonorant, it may undergo lenition in American speech, with loose stoppage (or a mere approach to stoppage) and a touch of vibrancy. The homorganic stop /d/ seemingly does not undergo lenition; contrast *center* with *cinder* and *latter* with *ladder*. Before a halt or a pause there may be no release as part of the articulation; the velum falls to permit ordinary breathing but the other organs may stay where they were for the time being. This is most likely to happen with the labial, least likely with the tectal stops.

21. An onset stop is so called because made with stoppage in its first phase only; it is more commonly called an affricate, being named in terms of its second phase, which is fricative.

22. Some linguists deny /x/ and /q/ the status of unit phonemes, taking them for two-phoneme sequences (or "clusters," to quote their misnomer) with /h/ for first member and the palatal or labio-velar semivowel (as the case may be) for second; in the present system of transcription, /hɪ/ and /hw/.

23. Instead of Bloomfield's primary and secondary, many linguists speak of segmental and suprasegmental phonemes, ignoring the fact that all phonemes are segmental (i.e. make a segment in the flow of speech).

24. Hence /wikⅠs, woⅠnt, letⅠs, bigətꞮri, hiərꟾɪtꟾiz/. But it would be possible to say *bigotry* without overlapping; see the discussion of /tr/ vs. /t-r/ in my *Studies . . . of 1959*, pp. 240 f. In the slang utterance *I get you* [y gecw] the overlap becomes fusion and /c/, the fusion-product, belonging to both morphemes as it does, incorporates the juncture. Here and in other cases the marker ꟾ for morphemic junction cannot be used. On various problems connected with overlap see E. Standop in *Anglia* 81 (1963) and my paper in the *International Journal of American Linguistics*, Vol. 28, No. 2, Part IV (April 1962).

25. For such a transition the term "juncture" is manifestly a misnomer and I call it "shead" (an early form of *shed* in its old sense of separation); see my *Studies . . . of 1959*, p. 251, fn. 31. A. A. Hill in his review of the book (*Language* 36.247) saw fit to greet *shead* with a jest but I still take it seriously, believing as I do that in professional work, more than elsewhere, misleading or otherwise inaccurate terms are harmful. For this reason I deplore calling glide vowels diphthongs, semivowels glides, tectals gutturals, stops plosives, sequences clusters, etc., and distinguishing patent consonants from stops by calling them continuants (as if stops were never long).

26. In my *Studies . . . of 1959*, pp. 240 ff., the use of spacing to separate words was left out of the picture except in a passage discussing the opposition *a name* /ənem/ vs. *an aim* /ən-em/, where *a* but not *an* was deemed proclitic, a distinction that I no longer make, though it is phonetically defensible. In the present system I write the opposition thus: /əꟾem/ vs. /ənꟾem/.

27. A vocule (Latin *vocula* 'little speech') in my terminology is an utterance lacking the grammatical structure of a sentence: e.g. What?

PATTERNED PHONEMIC DISLOCATION IN A FOUR-YEAR-OLD CHILD

Francis Lee Utley

The Ohio State University

The evidence on which this paper is based was recorded from the speech of my son Philip, during a period extending from his fortieth to his seventieth month of age—roughly his fourth and part of his fifth years.[1] If the judgement of the father is to be trusted, Philip was a normal child in every respect. This data is presented because it seems to reveal a pattern of spontaneous and patterned sound-shifting analogous for a time to what we call isolative sound-change in historical phonology. Most studies of children's language have concentrated on morphological, syntactic, and lexical matters.[2] What work has been done on child phonetics has been largely confined to consonantal substitutions,[3] since it is in these articulatory positions where physiological infantilism or loss (of teeth, for instance) leads to the most notable phonetic "lapses."

Here the recorded material is of a series of contiguous vowel-phonemes, involving only central and front vowels. High-front and back vowels appear to have been free from dislocation. The data is scanty, and it may suffer from selection, but in that event the election has managed to highlight the unusual phenomenon, and it may therefore be a legitimate and heuristic spur to future more systematic observation by other students. The data was recorded many years ago, in 1944, and it therefore suffers from the lack of certain modern sophistications of hypothesis and observations, most notably attention to distinctive features.[4] Most deplorable is the lack of what would have appeared as Philip's norm before, during, and after the observed dislocation. Nevertheless, the data is certainly worth reproduction and commentary.[5]

(1) Mid-central unround lowered and retracted /ə/ becomes lower lower mid-front /e/—/breðər/ *brother*; /kreč/ *crutch*; / "debəl it' ep/ *double it up*; / 'wilyə" jest "waš" miy/ *Will you just wash me* (an impatient utterance—apparently his mother was doing other things as well).

(2) Low-central unround /a/ shifts in two directions:
   (a) it becomes the diphthong /æw/ : /æwliv/ *olive*

(b) it becomes lower mid-front /e/: /wešt/ *washed*.

(3) Low-front unround /æ/ becomes low-central unround /a/: /'bad' flay/ *bad fly*; /'sandi/ *Sandy* (a cat); /ant/ *aunt*; confusion of *mop* and *map*.

(4) Lower mid-front unround /e/ shifts in two directions:

(a) it becomes lower high-front /i/:/yistər'di/ yesterday; /yis/ *yes*; /dris/ *dress*; / ay bit/ *I bet* /din/ *den*; /ig/ *egg*; / min layk "mint ən leydiz' down:/ *Men like mint and ladies don't;* / 'towni "bidəl 'wint: ðə "has' pid l/ *Tony Biddle went to the hospital.*

(b) it becomes low-front unround /æ/: /yæs/ *yes*; /'ælis/ *Ellis* confused with *Alice*; /'hwær iz hæl/ *Where is Hal?* confused with *Where is hell?*; / "æs' huks/ *S-hooks.*

(5) Mid front (/ey/ rarely becomes high-front /iy/: /giym/ *game.*

Casual as it is, this evidence seems significant for two reasons. First, it involves true leaps, not minor variations or gradual shifts, the slight heightening or lowering of a vowel which Jespersen, Herzog, and others[6] assumed to be the extent of a child's "faulty imitation," but a direct displacement of one vowel phoneme by another. Second, these shifts took place in a set of contiguous phonemes, and involved therefore a temporary dislocation of the whole phonemic pattern, analogous though of course not equivalent to such a major linguistic phenomenon as the Great Vowel Shift of Old and Middle English. Three questions raised by the data deserve discussion:

(1) Are these changes or "substitutions" more properly described as isolative or as combinatory?

(2) Are they phonemic?

(3) What was their cause?

To the first question we may answer that, within the bounds of a synchronic study such as this one, the vowel-shifts are parallel to the isolative changes of, say OE *mona* to Late ME *moon*, rather than to a combinatory change like the lowering of EME /uw/ to /u/ before lip and teeth consonants—compare *roof, hoop, broom*. Certain of the dislocations, such as that from /e/ to /i/, might have been encouraged by surrounding consonantal sounds. The dentals /s/ and /n/ might account for /yistərdi/, /dris/ and /din/. Against this we have the parallel shift in /ig/ for *egg*. Hypernormal correction, rather than phonological accommodation, seems responsible for the reverse movement, the lowering of /e/ to /æ/ in /yæs/ and /hæl/. Similarly, the shift of /æ/ to /a/ in /sandi/ and /ant/ might be ascribed to the following nasal, but its appearance in /bad flay/ cannot be so explained. The odd pronunciation of /æwliv/ for *olive*, on the other hand, is certainly a combinatory change influenced by the /l/, and perhaps does not belong in this report at all except to protect the writer from the charge of suppressing contrary evidence. Despite these reservations, we still seem to be in the presence of a contiguous and patterned set of variations, which are a little more than fortuitous or "free." [7]

Whether these changes are to be called "phonemic" or not depends on a number of considerations. Despite recent attacks on a long-favored term, we will assume that the phonetic-phonemic or type-token distinction has not been wholly transformed and liquidated. If we accept the term *isolative* we are not likely to worry too much about the term *phonemic*. Yet we have been reminded that phonemic change demands a permanent change of pattern, a "functional change," to be properly compared to the major shifts of linguistic history.[8] Carroll seems doubtful whether we can properly speak of phonemes in an idiolect.[9] The exact nature of the leaps would be better understood were our evidence a part of a full record from the first months of infancy,[10] such as those provided by Leopold and Velten.[11] A complete record means just that—a record of every speech sound uttered by a child from the time the obstetrician spanks his bottom. Observation of this perfection is clearly hard to achieve, though we could approach it if we used a sophisticated program and machinery. While there is such a glaring gap in our evidence, it is absurd to declare that we have "enough data," whatever the state of our theory. Yet, in default of perfection, it may be profitable to cite one more fragment of the evidence we have in favor of phonemic "dislocation"—the conflict of homonyms resulting from the new identity of /pin/ and /pen/, /bet/ and /bit/, *Hell* and *Hal*, *map* and *mop*, *Ellis* and *Alice*. For himself Philip created a causal explanation of sexual psychology out of one magnificent pun: / "min 'layk "mint n "laydiz "down:/. His parents were severely embarassed by another confusion—when he lowered the first vowel in his pronunciation of "S-hooks," a device on his gymnasium set, in front of guests. The confusion of homonyms, so subtle a factor in general semantic change, is usually cleared up in the child by the parental norm, consciously and unconsciously applied.

Questions of terminology aside, our third problem is to seek a cause for these patterned changes. Phonetic causation is a notable area of disagreement and frustration. Perhaps one might be in a favored position when one is studying a single dynamic idiolect, since there is some control over raw data, and one is not in the presence of statistical abstraction. Presumably one normative cause would be imitation of the speech of the two parents—in this case Inland Northern and Southwestern New England. The father was born in Wisconsin from a family with New England, New York, and Austrian ancestry (the latter his mother's provenience, but she died before he was three). Most of his youth was spent in Southern California and Northern Michigan. The mother was born and raised in that part of Western Massachusetts, the Berkshires, which is sufficiently far west of the Connecticut River[12] to have produced a speech-pattern diverging very little from that of the father. Hence no major bi-dialectical conflict is known to have been present in the home environment. The mother may have influenced one "dislocation," the pronunciation of *aunt* as /ant/. This is her sole "broad a" in the usual sense of that term. It is a fossil survival from her schoolteachers, who told her she must distinguish in pronunciation between the insect and the female relative. Contrast pattern or phonemic fission by binaries, so well described by Jakobson as a preferred generative hypothesis of the development of vowel-pattern among children,[13] also played a part in the /a/~/æ/ alternation, since there was a period in this child's infancy when he used a single vowel for low-front unround and low-central unround. The two phonemes were thus once undifferentiated, and a cell-division took place; the occasional low-central for low-front vowel may be a relic of this change.

Assuming the parents' fairly uniform speech as the major models for Philip's formative imitation, most observers would explain vowel-shifts of this sort as "contamination" from other children or adults who speak a dialect diverging from that of the parents. Leonard Bloomfield has stated the common view: "children are especially imitative in their first contacts outside the immediate family circle." [14] We need not deny that a child's or an adult's speech is a remarkably composite matter. Yet too much can be made of this easy explanation, which almost implies a conscious desire on the part of the child to imitate the novel and the non-parental, or, even more profoundly, it suggests an unconscious revolt of some kind. We play here on the edge of stereotyped explanations, more Freudian or less sophisticated. Particularly common is the ascription of lexical divergence to imitation outside the family circle—the use of swear-words, for instance. At a later date Philip's mother exhibited a natural impulse to blame precocious profanity on association with a neighboring child whose social antecedents were different from our own. In all honesty this provenience cannot be accepted by the father, who, proper in all other respects, has a habit of hitting his thumb with a hammer every time he tries to drive in a nail, and of giving out with the emotionally fitting but socially improper interjections. Our cited evidence may even suggest that Philip achieved certain off-color morphemes spontaneously and unaware of what he was doing. In his phonology the extramural explanation remains tempting, nevertheless, since Columbus, Ohio, is near enough to Kentucky and the Midlands to allow a shift from /brəš/ to /breš/ as a normal result of dialect proximity. In later years Philip and his brother Scott, now school-children, frequently were "corrected" by the parents, who found the boys' use of the South Midland /æw/ in place of their own /aw/ in *house* or *cow* objectionable. Indeed, Columbus is said to be bisected by the traditional North and South Midland isogloss—Route 40. McDavid places it in the Northern West Virginia extension.[15] Yet it must be insisted that during this period Philip had no outside contacts which would merit such an explanation, whether they be neighbors, the little-used radio, or the Berkshire grandparents, the only ones alive. And we shall see that other factors may have been involved in the fronting of the mid-central /ə/. Similarly, the cat's name, /'sandi/, "sounded Scotch" to the neighbors who owned the cat. Their name was McNiven, and they liked the explanation. Despite their name, these neighbors, who provided a baby-sitter, showed no significant departures from their own dialectical norms, which were formed in Wisconsin and in Northern Indiana, and which did not center the low-front vowel.

These remarks are not meant to confute the importance of non-parental influence in the development of children's speech, but merely to correct in this single case the common habit of overestimating this element—often for purposes of social snobbery, when one wishes to deny the "lapses" of one's children as the result of unfortunate outside contact. Here the outside influence came later; both brothers had a non-indigenous /pɔnd/ for what the parents would have called /pand/; it was always confined to a special kind of small lake they encountered on visits to Cape Cod and other parts of Massachusetts. Certainly there are other important triggers for the mechanism of patterned change of the kind we are discussion. One such factor lies within the bosom of the family itself. Though the two parents are representative of a Southwest New England–Inland Northern norm, careful study would no doubt show minute shifts, the slight fronting or heightening or lowering of certain of these vowels in the parents, affecting Philip's patterned shift. These minute departures from an acoustical norm could be the stimulus for more exaggerated directional shifts on the part of a keen-eared childish imitator.[16] At times the father has witnesed in himself a slightly less retracted version of /ɚ/ than is ordinarily attributed to his region. It is for this reason that one regrets that a full contemporary record of the parents was not made during Philip's fourth year. Jespersen has warned us against assuming too greatly a fixity for one person, even in adult life:

> Everyone thinks that he talks today just as he did yesterday, and, of course, he does so in nearly every point. But no one knows if he pronounces his mother-tongue in every respect in the same manner as he did twenty years ago. . . . It is not enough for one man to alter his pronunciation, many must co-operate [for major sound-change]. . . . As regards those little gradual shiftings of sound which take place in spite of . . . conservative influence, changes in which the sound and the articulation alter simultaneously, I cannot see that the transmission of the language to a new generation need exert any essential influence: we may imagine them being brought about equally well in a society which for hundreds of years consisted of the same adults who never died and had no issue.[17]

We must never forget that our phonetic records are selective, and our phonemic systems selective abstractions—generalizations of individual and community speech patterns in terms of a mere segment of time and of society. As we theorize we are always in danger of reification.[18] Saussureans and Bloomfieldians, and no doubt other more favored modern schools, often reify unblushingly and with pride—we badly need a proper study of how these selectings differ from the exhaustive and real continuum. Dealing as we just have with the factor of non-parental influence on speech we are apt to consider the family itself as a stable environment, assaulted by outside influences. Relatively speaking this is so, but parents may betray, as we have seen, minute variations in phones, and if we were to compare formal and informal situations we would find even greater variation. But the intra-familial environment contains still another variable. We say that two children born to the same parents have the same environment. This statement is a form of pragmatic imprecision, which holds in many situations well enough so that it is not subject to criticism. Yet the first temporal environment of the second child, one sibling plus two parents, is certainly different from that of the first child, two parents alone. We catch a glimpse of this variable in action when we observe two contrasting schemes of phonetic fission in Philip and his younger brother Scott. Both of them long harbored two pairs of phonemes which we describe as voiced and voiceless apico-alveolar fricatives and voiced and voiceles fronto-alveolar fricatives /s z š ž/. But their points of articulation were different. Philip said /'saks en 'suwz/ for *socks and shoes*; Scott, perhaps as the result of his brother's being corrected and reacting hypernormally, said /'šakš ən 'šuwž/. Both, we remind ourselves, had the same parents.[19]

We have listed several factors which might have helped trigger Philip's patterned vowel-shifts: the intrusion of strangers into the family environment, minute variations and contrasts within the family environment, combinatory changes from phonetic accommodation, and relics of the child's earlier phonemic fission. With further evidence at our disposal we might discuss the factors of homonymic conflict and of relative frequency. The chain-reaction set up by the dislocation of an original /e/ becoming /æ/ may well have led to a surfeit of that phoneme, which would have been relieved by a further displacement of /æ/ to the retracted /a/, already favored by fission memory. Similarly we have the correction or hyper-correction of the /i/ which results from the dislocation of normal /e/. Influenced by parental norms, one assumes, it moved back down again to the /æ/ position. Here we see a small "leap silently 'corrected' or cancelled by the consensus of usage." [20]

Our observation of this remarkable infantile departure from adult norms leads us inevitably to propose one of the vexed questions of historical linguistics—what influence the child has on adult speech and on diachronic sound-change. Bloomfield, for instance, remarked that the difficulty in attributing sound-change to imperfections in children's learning of language consists in the fact that childish imperfections is a permanent antecedent condition, whereas sound-change is sporadic.[21] But is not this the very juncture we seek between diachronic and synchronic patterns? Perhaps a distinction should be made between the "permanent antecedent condition" of physiological incapacity in the child, such as the lisp from loss of teeth or the loss of *r*-constriction from lack of trained tongue-control or musculature, and less regularly conditioned changes like those we have been observing. Though Jespersen has two valuable chapters on "The Influence of the Child on Linguistic Development," he is also restrained in his conclusions.[22] He concedes that the child has considerable influence on lexicon, and some on syntax. Leaps of all kinds, semantic, syntactic, and lexical, he is willing to ascribe to the child's influence. But gradual changes must be due to adults, or to adult and child taken together with no possibility of distinction. With Herman Paul as authority he terms phonetic changes gradual, and dismisses them almost wholly from consideration, except as they produce linguistic splitting or differentiation in meaning. He cites the British distinction "I take /'medsin/ but I study /'medisin/." [23] Wyld objects to the theories of Darmesteter and Passy, who attributed sound-change to childish "faulty imitation," with the following comment: "It is not explained how it comes about that all of the children of the same generation make approximately the same mistakes." [24] He has a different view of the evidence from Bloomfield, and we may counter him with the remark that children cannot make all the same mistakes, but that the sound-change which sticks in the future will be a resultant of a myriad various changes in various individuals, coming together, cancelling out, and producing a final abstractional fixity or "phoneme."

Velten has warned us against phylogenetic explanations—against the tempting theory that the ontogeny of infant speech recapitulates diachronic sound-change, the phylogeny of the dialect group or race. Ullmann, with his earlier Saussurean views, distinguishes between the leaps of *parole* and the gradual changes of *langue*; "What is gradual in certain types of semantic [may we read phonetic?] change is not the *innovation* itself, only its crystallization, dissemination, and eventual acceptance." [26] The general skittishness of scientists in the presence of "leaps" is probably due to unconscious memory of the Linnean axiom, *Natura non facit saltus*, the steady application of which was so profitable in the development of biology, geology, and cosmology, as in literary and linguistic history.[27] Given the full continuum of individual speech in groups, with cancellation and cross-purpose in variable time and space, the leaps can be filled in; there are no gaps or chasms, and all is plenitude, a notion we have not abandoned with the Middle Ages. Yet an atomistic and strictly generative view of the data would not ignore the relatively startling leaps which each individual at some time in his life might manifest. As Jakobson insists, the child is truly creative in language.[28]

With Bloomfield we may admit that childish "slips" are permanent, or rather perennial—fixed radiation rather than stroboscopic light, whereas diachronic sound-change is a set of sporadic phenomena. Yet the results are always patterned, and it remains to be seen whether extended clinical observation might not reveal a fairly consistent set of forces in a number of children studied synchronically from one dialect area. Wyld's charge that consistent mistakes among children of the same generation, adding up to an identifiable result, has not been proved, was a wise answer to those who were claiming too much. But it was merely a remark of controversy, which was made to sound like an ultimate limitation of knowledge, rather than a gap in our past and present knowledge. Such is the peril of theory which rests itself only on the data already in and available. Even Jespersen, as master of observation so great that recent Cartesians seem to find themselves content with his collections in spite of their age and their confinement to Great Britain, can be supplemented. For his phonetic gradualism, true in a Linnean sense, fails to take into account the mutations which an individual can produce, and which, without strict recording, can be lost to history. In Lehmann's terminology, Philip's leaps are primary rather than secondary splits.[29] Considered abstractly as the final results of a balanced series of isolative changes, helped along by dialectical interchange, combinatory change, relative frequency, free variation and the like, the process seems gradual enough. But closer synchronous study, properly undertaken, might discover the quanta of many startling leaps within the frame.

Sapir has chastened us for leaving out of account "the humble child, who is laboriously orienting himself in the world of his society, yet is not, in the normal case, sacrificing his forthright psychological status as a significant ego. . . ." [30] The context is anthropological, but linguistics is a part of anthropology. Carroll has proposed for such a study teams "of linguists and psychologists and sound engineers." [31] Our own record is casual, and its conclusions highly tentative. The parallelism to the Great Vowel Shift is only analogous, for the changes in that massive transformation of the phonemic system of English proceeded in a different direction,[32] and over a long period of time—it is one of the most useful and yet most drastic abstractions in all of linguistics. Perhaps the greatest error of all is to assume that it is over.[33]

Further analysis of the points raised in this paper would be greatly enhanced by a consistent and collaborative series of clinical studies. Some of these might be conducted in orphanages, day-care nurseries, and other institutions where proper linguistic observers could use organized and controlled observation. Since such institutions set up environmental conditions which are deviant from those of the normal family, such studies should further enlist the enthusiasm of a corps of young linguists, studying according to group practice their own children. Ideally both parents should be trained as observers, to make the records more ample and more valid, and their own speech patterns should be carefully recorded, probably by another couple working reciprocally with them. As Bloomfield said, "Almost nothing is known about child language because observers report what the child says, but not what it has heard." [34] Useful data, as I hope this paper shows, can be gathered in isolation, but the true leap in observation needed is likely to be collaborative. Such work should be planned and guided as skillfully as has been that of the Linguistic Atlas of America, though it might well be confined to one or two contrasting regions from that project. Surely it would greatly supplement the findings of the Atlas on the phonetic level, and probably on others as well. Can we properly abstract a description of speech from one informant at one time of his life? Must we not have records of the progress of many representative speakers from infancy to old age before we can really arrive at sound conclusions with regard to present speech, its lengthy past, and its infinite future? As Antoine Grégoire said, children surely deserve as much attention as wasps and ants.[35]

Notes

1. Several studies have been made of four-year olds, but they show little evidence of this kind of patterned shift: Florence Mateer, "The Vocabulary of a Four Year Old Boy," *The Pedagogical Seminary*, XV (1908), 63–73; C.F. Voegelin and Sidney Adams, "A Phonetic Study of Young Children's Speech," *The Journal of Experimental Education*, III (1934), 107–108; L. Sprague de Camp, "Learning to Talk," *American Speech*, XXI (1946), 23–28; Ephraim Cross, "Some Features of the Phonology of a Four-Year-Old Boy," *Word*, VI (1950), 137–140; John B. Brannon, "A Comparison of Syntactic Structures in the Speech of Three-Year-Old and Four-Year-Old Children," *Language and Speech*, XI (1968), 171–181. It is a special pleasure to dedicate this essay to Raven McDavid, who saved the State of Ohio for the Linguistic Atlas. He loves children, and shares neither the common preconception that the older linguists are without merit nor the impatient theoretical view that the data is all in.

2. For the literature, in addition to that cited in note 1, see Werner F. Leopold, *Bibliography of Child Language* (Evanston, 1952); H.L. Mencken, *Supplement II: The American Language* (New York, 1948), p. 351; Leopold, "The Study of Child Language and Infant Bilingualism," *Word*, IX (1948), 1–17; the valuable pioneer study of James Sully, *Studies of Childhood* (New York, 1896), pp. 133–190; Sol Saporta and Jarvis R. Bastian, ed., *Psycholinguistics: A Book of Readings*, pp. 331–375.

3. See for instance Cross, *Word*, VI (1950), 137–140, and the bulk of the literature.

4. Roman Jakobson, C.G.M. Fant, and Morris Halle, *Preliminaries to Speech Analysis: The Distinctive Features and their Correlates* (Cambridge, Mass., 1965); Jakobson, *Selected Writings* I ('S'Gravenhage, 1962), pp. 449–504; Noam Chomsky and Morris Halle, *The Sound Pattern of English* (New York, 1968), pp. 64–69, 164–166, 335–340, 400–435. There is an anticipation of his later views in Jakobson's *Kindersprache* (1942), which I cite here as *Child Language, Aphasia and Phonological Universals* (The Hague, 1968); see pp. 13–15, 49–57.

5. Terminology and symbols here and elsewhere in the paper are from W. Nelson Francis and Raven I. McDavid, *The Structure of American English* (New York, 1958—reprint of 1954).

6. Otto Jespersen, *Language* (London, 1933—reprint of 1922), pp. 161–168. See titles in note 23.

7. The fullest study, before Leopold, of a child's language is that of Antoine Grégoire, *L'apprentisage du langage*, 2 vols. (Liège, 1937). He finds some contiguous dislocations in pure vowels in a two-year-old child (pp. 268–271), and a later correction of Walloon vowels to French (pp. 350–351). O.C. Irwin, in L. Kaiser, *Manual of Phonetics* (Amsterdam, 1957), pp. 416–422, finds variables in an individual child to be race, sex, sibling influence, occupational status of parents, general intelligence, and deprivation of speech stimulus (as in an orphanage). Jakobson, *Child Language*, p. 15, found "a kind of sound-change" in individual Russian and English children. See H.V. Velten, "The Growth of Patterns in Infant Language," *Language*, XIX (1943), 288–290; Charles F. Hockett, *A Course in Modern Linguistics* (New York, 1958), pp. 358–359; Charles F. Fries and Kenneth L. Pike, "Coexistent Phonemic Systems," *Language*, XXV (1949), 29–50; Harry

Hoijer, "Linguistics and Culture Change," *Language*, XXIV (1948), 339. These studies all have valuable information for us, but none provides a dislocation of the kind we are discussing in this paper.

8. John T. Waterman, *Perspectives in Linguistics* (Chicago, 1963), p. 75; Hockett, *Course*, pp. 444–445; John B. Carroll, *The Study of Language* (Cambridge, Mass., 1953), p. 236.

9. See Carroll, cited in last note.

10. For an earlier record of Philip in the babbling stage see Appendix.

11. Werner F. Leopold, *Speech Development of a Bilingual Child: A Linguist's Record* II (Evanston, 1947); Velten, *Language*, XIX (1943), 281–292; for other good phonetic studies see Yuen Ren Chao, "The Cantian Idiolect," in Walter J. Fischel, ed., *Semitic and Oriental Studies: A Volume Presented to William Popper* (Berkeley, 1951), pp. 27–44.

12. Hans Kurath et al., *Handbook of the Linguistic Geography of New England* (Providence, 1939), pp. 99, 200–201; Hans Kurath and Raven McDavid, *The Pronunciation of English in the Atlantic States* (Ann Arbor, 1961), pp. 15–16; Francis and McDavid, pp. 516–519.

13. The classic statement is in Jackson, *Child Language*, see especially pp. 14–15, 27–31, 51–57, 73–81. See also Francis and and McDavid, pp. 544–549; Velten, p. 282; Hockett, *Course*, pp. 358–359; Grégoire, I, 217–219; Pelio Fronzaroli, *Il linguaggio dei bambino* (Bologna, 1957), pp. 124–131; Leopold, *Speech Development*, pp. 1–3; Leopold, "Patterning in Children's Language Learning," *Language Learning*, V (1953-54), 1–14; de Camp, *American Speech*, XXI (1946), 23–28 (note his skepticism on excessive attempts to find phonetic symmetry). Another example of fission in Philip's speech was free variation between /š/ and /č/ in *share* and *chair*, *sherry* and *cherry*, *shin* and *chin*, *shoe* and *chew*. Perhaps the "voiced t" of *shudder* and *shutter* and of /has pidəl/ in the evidence cited in the text involves a similar phenomenon.

14. Bloomfield, *Language* (New York, 1933), p. 512.

15. Francis and McDavid, p. 580 (map).

16. Hockett, *Course*, p. 358. Kenneth Pike, *Phonemics* (Ann Arbor, 1947), p. 66, cites experiments of Martin Joos which reveal the subtle balance of interchange between child and adult.

17. Jespersen, *Language*, p. 166.

18. See Eugene A. Nida, "The Identification of Morphemes," *Language*, XXIV (1948), 342; David G. Mandelbaum, ed., *Selected Writings of Edward Sapir in Language, Culture, and Personality* (Berkeley, 1949), p. 579; Clyde Kluckhohn, *Navaho Witchcraft* (Cambridge, Mass., 1944), pp. 46–47.

19. See Leopold, *Speech Development*, where Hildegard, the major informant, is constantly compared to her younger sister Karla. See also Charles Hockett, "Age-Grading and Linguistic Continuity," *Language*, XXVI (1950), 449–451, where the mechanism of continuity is said to be within the childhood peer groups (a phenomenon common also in the study of children's rhymes).

20. Sapir, *Language*, pp. 158, 160.

21. Bloomfield, *Language*, p. 386.

22. Jespersen, *Language*, pp. 161–188.

23. Pages 166–167. John S. Kenyon, *American Pronunciation*, 8th edn. (Ann Arbor, 1940), pp. 12, 35, dropped the statement that analogical change was sudden and phonological gradual between the second and the eighth edition. For other statements of the gradual position see Edgar H. Sturtevant, *An Introduction to Linguistic Science* (New Haven, 1947), pp. 75–76; Jakobson, *Child Language*, p. 18; Hockett, *Course*, pp. 361, 392, 439; de Camp, pp. 27–28; G.L. Brook, *A History of the English Language* (London, 1956), p. 71; Janet Aiken, *Why English Sounds*

Change (New York, 1958), p. 118; Albert C. Baugh, *A History of the English Language* (New York, 1935), p. 20.

24. Henry C. Wyld, *Studies in English Rhymes from Surrey to Pope* (New York, 1924), p. 43; *The Historical Study of the Mother Tongue* (London, 1928), p. 84.

25. Velten, p. 282; Angela Zincanella, "L'evoluzione del linguaggio umano del punto di vista ontogenetico," *Atti dell' Accademia della Scienze de Ferrara*, XXVIII (1950–51), 73–99; Sapir, *Language*, pp. 165, 194; Jakobson, *Child Language, pp.* 13–15; Franz Boas, *General Anthropology* (Boston, 1938), p. 666.

26. Stephen Ullmann, *Principles of Semantics* (Glasgow, 1951), p. 180. See Eugene A. Nida, *Linguistic Interludes* (Glendale, Calif., 1944), p. 119.

27. For its use see Max Lerner, *The Mind and Faith of Justice Holmes* (Boston, 1943), p. 378; René Wellek, *The Rise of English Literary History* (Chapel, Hill, N.C., 1941), p. 38; Burton Stevenson, *The Macmillan Book of Proverbs, Maxims, and Famous Phrases* (New York, 1965—reprint of 1948), p. 1661 (first instance dated 1613 A.D.).

28. *Child Language*, pp. 15–16.

29. Winfred P. Lehmann, *Historical Linguistics: An Introduction* (New York, 1962), pp. 157–159.

30. Mandelbaum, pp. 193, 596; see Melville Herskovits, *Man and his Works* (New York, 1948), pp. 583–584; Sapir, *Language*, p. 165.

31. Carroll, *Study of Language*, pp. 51, 100–101.

32. When Albert Marckwardt first heard this paper he stressed this point.

33. See C.M. Lotspeich, "The Cause of Long Vowel Changes in English," *JEGP*, XX (1921), 208–212; John S. Kenyon, *A Guide to Pronunciation* (Springfield, Mass., 1934), pp. xliii, xlvi and *passim*; Arthur J. Bronstein, "Trends in American Pronunciation," *Quarterly Journal of Speech*, XXVIII (1942), 452–456. Sometimes the shifts have not proceeded properly. A class of mine, thoroughly American, was once surprised when I asked a Glasgovian student of Irish extraction to give the modern equivalent of Chaucer's vowels in *bird:byrd*, *word*, and *erthe*, and she replied /bird/, /word/ and /erθ/, all with the proper trilled r's and the proper vowels, which would have pleased Chaucer.

34. *Language*, p. 512.

35. See Leopold, *Speech Development*, p. viii.

Appendix (Note 10)

Certain notes taken on April 15, 1941, during Philip's twelfth month (he was born May 7, 1940) may be appended here as an example of the kind of observations possible in the late babbling stage (SR = sounds recognized, SU = sounds uttered with apparent meaning, MF = mother's identification, perhaps fanciful at times). During the babbling stage he made most consonants by chance. Many of them were lengthened: /p b t d č j; the bilabial fricatives φ and β; k xm R m m: : : :, 1 (*rare*) f v θ ð s z z z w/. The affricates /ts dz/ were also common. Vowels, largely dominated /a/, were commonly in combination /i iy e æ a ə u uw/. There were many reduplications:

/ga' ga/ /gə''a/ /gyé:/ (with heavily accented final vowel, usued for general recognition, pleasure. /ga/ the most frequent sound).

/kçiiy/ (SU *kitty*, indicating pleasure over food, since cup, bib and dish all had "kitties" or animals on them).

/tuw''ə/ /ta ta/ /ča ča/ (MF *thank you*).

/da:da/ and /dæy dæy dæy/ (a general utility sound used to indicate pleasure or against ennui, but spoken so often in return by mother in anticipation of father that it appears by this time to be SU. Certainly SR in "Where's dada?")

/"filip/ (SR when uttered as especially stressed, with lengthening: /"hwe;;rz "fi"lip/ (usually wins a gurgle or a laugh, whether the speaker is in sight or not; perhaps especially when not. No sign of the "morpheme" in Philip himself.)

(open the) *door* SR. (take off your) *socks* SR

straining grunt /" ə : : : : : : :/ is often responsed to by bowel movement—SR?

/gɔi gɔi/ (often repeated in long series, very frequent, made with fingers in mouth and apparently a variant of /ga/ with tongue depression because of fingers. Since this sound was often made with the "snuggle ducky," a straight jacket popular in those days which later became the sleep-inducing equivalent of a security blanket, it came to stand for that object in the family, hence later SR.)

/w:a uw wa/ (repeated, and made like last "word" with finger in mouth).

Mother says she has heard /gu' ga/ *good god* MF.

/m:a m:a/ (rarely made, to mother's desperation, although once or twice finer pointing has made it SR with head turned to mother. This failure with regard to a very important person comes from the fact that the calls for the mother are manifold, and not like the carefully taught /da da/. Loud squalls with breath holding = desire for food, response to pain, desire for attention, and are usually answered, and thus become SU with complete understanding. Sighs (pharyngeal fricatives) indicate ennui, but apparently also pleasure. Cries taper into little moans, as if too tired to go on, when mere attention-getting cries are ignored.)

/ba ba be/ ∼/ ba ba bæ/ with heavy plosion—MF *baby*.

/bwəo bwəo/ made with fingers manipulating lips.

How big, with species stress on /"bi : : : : g/ SR very well about eleven months of age. He clasps and raises hands above head, even without the original parental gesture being imitated. "Bye-bye" and "paddycake" seem to elicit the same response, but /haw"bi : : : : g/ is the master stimulus. Later "paddycake" begins to be distinguished, with Philip pounding on a flat surface.

Long uvular fricatives /y : : : : : : : / are indicative of pleasure, or sounds to drive away ennui.

Occasional trilled or flapped /r/ carried on at length.

/s : : : : i/ MF says it is "see," but this is not certain. When an object is recognized with pleasure, Philip says /sssssssssss/.

/gu'/ MF *good*. Perhaps has become SU because so often made by parents to encourage eating.

For some time embarrassed little cough used by child to obtain attention; it seems to be directly datable to first cold in tenth month.

/gm/ MF *gum*. /fwi/ MF *fooey?*

/"məm "məm "mə/ and /"mnəm "mnəm "mnəm/ expressions of pleasure when food is in mouth.

SOME SOCIOLINGUISTIC FACTORS IN THE DEVELOPMENT OF ENGLISH

JOSEF VACHEK

Czechoslovak Academy of Sciences (Prague)

One of the points in which the conception of language development as formulated by the linguistic school of Prague basically differed from the conception voiced by the Copenhagen glossematicists and from that voiced by the Yale group was that the Prague scholars never backed an exclusively immanentist character of this development. Thus, already R. Jakobson (1929), though insisting on the primary part being played in this development by 'immanent laws' of phonological development, admits that some aspects of this development can only be accounted for "par l'analyse des rapports entre le système de la langue et les autres systèmes conjugués d'ordre social et géographique" (p. 96). Similar ideas could be found in the writings of other members of the pre-war Prague school (see, e.g., B. Havránek 1931).

More recently, one of our own post-war papers (J. Vachek 1962) was devoted to the problem of the interplay of external and internal factors in language development; in it we arrived at the conclusion that the operation of the external factors in this development cannot be left out of account, even if the systemic exigencies of the concerned language exercise the right of control over the external influence with which that language is faced (p. 448). This conception follows quite naturally from the functionalist approach of the Prague school: the primary function of language is, undoubtedly, to serve the needs and wants of the community using it; since, however, this community does not live in a vacuum, due attention must also be paid to the circumstances (social, economic, political, etc.) under which the operation of language is taking place. If, then, 'sociolinguistics' means the study of social implications of the phenomena of language,[1] it is clear that the Prague linguists had been aware of at least some of the basic issues belonging under the heading of sociolinguistics, and that they had been so long before the heading itself came to be coined.

From what has been said above it clearly follows that, although the external circumstances certainly do constitute a non-negligible factor in language development, their part is hierarchically subordinated to that which is played in this development by the specific exigencies of the given language system. Certainly one could not subscribe to the opinion of those scholars who believe that it is only the external factors which are responsible for the obvious facts that languages change at all (such opinion was voiced, e.g., by N. Y. Marr, cf. I. I. Mescaninov 1950, p. 40). Already R. Jakobson (1929) duly pointed out that "l'explication hétéronome de l'évolution phonologique n'est pas en mesure de remplacer l'explication immanente, elle ne peut que la compléter" (p. 96). The suggested hierarchical relationship of the factors influencing language development is certainly most important, since even today this relationship is not always seen clearly.[2]

However, more important than aprioristic theoretical speculations appear to be, at least in the present stage of research, detailed analyses of some concrete situations in which the "systematic covariance of linguistic and social structures" (to use Bright's formulation) can be convincingly demonstrated. A number of such concrete specimens were presented in the course of the last five years or so (e.g., in the volume prefaced by Bright's paper just referred to above). Of special interest, however, are some points of the development of concrete languages which had defied all attempts at a truly adequate explanation until sociolinguistic considerations were brought to bear on them. In the present paper we want to point out, as briefly as possible, two such points found in the development of English.

One of them is concerned with the development of the Middle English phoneme /ę̄/, especially with regard to that of /ẹ̄/, its closest neighbor in the ME system of long vowel phonemes. As is commonly known, the two ē-vowels represented in ME two distinctly separate phonemes, exactly as their velar counterparts, representing the ME phonemes /ǭ/ and /ọ̄/. In Modern English, however, the two palatal vowel phonemes have merged into one, while the two velar vowel phonemes continue to be kept apart (cf. ME *del*, *lēpen*: *fēlen*, *dēp*—ModE merged /di:l/, /li:p/, /fi:l/, /di:p/, as opposed to ME *stōn*: *spōn*—ModE /stəun/ : /spu:n/, where no merger has occurred).

The question that emerges here is why the development of the two palatal long vowels was not parallel to that of their velar opposite numbers. Also the process of the coalescence of the two palatal vowels presents some interesting features which shall be discussed here first. According to the older view (see Joseph Wright and E. M. Wright, 1924) the original ME ę̄ was narrowed, by the end of the 15th century, to ẹ̄. This should have happened (within the well-known complex of changes termed the 'Great Vowel Shift'[3]) soon after the original ME ẹ̄-vowel had been narrowed to ī. Perfectly parallel to this was, of course, the narrowing of the original ME ǭ *to* ọ̄, soon after the original ME ọ̄ had been narrowed to ū. Here, however, the parallel development of the palatal and velar vowels comes to a stop. The new ẹ̄-vowel, according to the traditional view, persisted in this quality until the latter half of the 17th century, when it was to be narrowed still further, to *ī* (and so to become merged with the *ī*-vowel which had developed from the original ME *ẹ̄*). In the velar region of the ME long systems of vowel phonemes, as already pointed out, no such merger has taken place: the original ME *ǭ*, which in the 15th century (and probably earlier) had been narrowed to *ọ*, came to be diphthongized into *ou*, Present Day English /əu/, not merging with *ū* which had arisen through the narrowing of the original ME *ō*.

While the traditional Neogrammarian approach represented by the Wrights was content with describing the *how* of the process (to use the phraseology of A. Juilland 1967), Karl Luick (1914) was the first scholar to seriously tackle the question of the *why* of that process. He dealt with the changes affecting ME *ẹ̄* with constant regard for other changes included in the complex of the Great Vowel Shift, particularly those changes that had affected the original ME *ǭ* (already referred to above) and especially the original ME *ā*. As is well known, the latter vowel changed into *ẹ̄*, probably in the latter half of the 16th century; about a century later this *ẹ̄* was to be narrowed to *ẹ̄* which, by the end of the 18th century, was to be diphthongized into *ei* (cf. ME *lādi, māken*—ModE /leidi/, /meik/).

So much for the bare facts of the development. Luick's explanation of these facts was very ingenious, and showed remarkable insight into the structural situation of the Early ModE phonological system. With constant regard for the situation obtaining in ModE local dialects, he argued that the original ME *ā*, by its palatalization into *ẹ̄*, had to 'drive' the original ME *ẹ̄* to become narrowed. As a result of this 'fronting' of the original ME *ā*-vowel, its systemic position in the phonological pattern was to become substantially changed: by its fronting to *ẹ̄* it ceased to be a vowel phoneme neutral with regard to the opposition palatal vs velar, and joined the palatal series. Luick points out that by its change into *ẹ̄* the original *ā*-vowel was to become a systemic counterpart of the original ME *ọ*. Consequently, Luick argues, the original ME *ẹ̄*-vowel was to become isolated in the phonological system and had to find its new place in it. The said situation can be demonstrated by the following scheme, showing the state of things before the change of ME *ā > ẹ̄*:

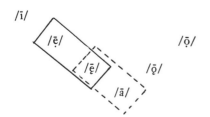

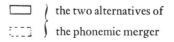

} the two alternatives of
} the phonemic merger

Luick shows that this reintegration of the original *e*-vowel into the system could be effected by choosing one of two possible alternatives: the original ME *ẹ̄* either merged with the original ME *ẹ̄* (and, together with it, to be later still further narrowed to [i:], or else, merged with the original ME $\bar{a}$ (and, together with it, to be later diphthongized to [ei]). The former case was chosen in a large majority of words containing the original $\bar{e}$; the latter course in three words only: *break*, *great* and *yea*. This other course was common in some dialects which, in Luick's opinion, may have influenced the Standard English development of these three expressions. In any case, the merger was to reestablish the balance in the system of Early ModE vowel phonemes. After the merger both the palatal and the velar series contained three items each, whereas before the redressal the palatal series had contained one item more than its velar counterpart.

Luick's explanation, as presented here above, might fully satisfy a structuralistically-minded specialist in the historical development of English. And yet it does not seem to cover all the aspects of this most interesting and most complex process. The scholar who was to become aware of such unexplained aspects and to point them out was the Oxford linguist Henry Cecil Wyld (1914). A careful examination of all available materials led him to the conclusion that some evidence for the pronunciation of ME $\bar{e}$ as $\bar{\imath}$ points to a much earlier date than was formerly believed. Thus, already in the latter half of the 15th century one finds spellings like *hylen* (for *hēlen* 'to heal'); later, in the 16th century, *bryke* and *spyken* (for *brēken* and *spēken*). There is, of course, also clear evidence for the persistence of the older, $\bar{e}$-type of pronunciation. In the 17th century the $\bar{\imath}$-type of pronunciation was to score a decisive victory, with instances of the type *break*, *great*, *yea* being perhaps the only surviving specimens of the older, receding type. (But even Wyld does not fully dismiss the possibility of their dialectal provenience.)

The conclusion that Wyld drew from such facts was that one is faced here with two different class pronunciations which were coexisting for almost two centuries: the type $\bar{e}$ was characteristic of the upper, the type $\bar{\imath}$ of the lower classes (This is in full conformity with the fact that many early writers on pronunciation classify this latter type as socially inferior.) If, then, $\bar{\imath}$ finally superseded $\bar{e}$, this, in Wyld's view, should not be regarded as another sound-change but rather as a result of the lower class pronunciation's ousting that of the upper classes. And it is at this point that the sociolinguistic factor comes in; it will be seen, moreover, that this factor played a decisive role in the process of the phonological development of English in the Early Modern period. A simple reflection will prove this.

If one examines the given phonological process in some detail, it will be easily discovered that Wyld's theory of the coexistence of at least two class dialects can be profitably combined with the structuralistically conceived explanation of the process given by Luick. Clearly, there had been some structural difficulties with the original ME $\bar{e}$-vowel, and there were two available ways to eliminate such difficulties. If the ultimately adopted solution to the problem was the one characteristic of the usage of the lower classes, this might be mechanically explained away as due to the greater biological strength of a section of a population gradually penetrating into the positions formerly held by the members of the rival upper class. It is well known, however, that the ascending lower classes usually do their utmost to conform to the speech habits of that class into which they want to penetrate; thus, the purely mechanical explanation will not do. Obviously, deeper motives than merely mechanical ones were at play.

If we try to discover these deeper motives, we discover that, from a purely communicative viewpoint, the solution chosen by the lower class was to prove more profitable than the alternative preferred by the upper class dialect. It becomes clear that although the merger of the original ME vowels $\bar{\ell}$ and $\bar{e}$ duly resulted in some increase of homonyms in the language, the other merger, that of the original ME $\bar{a}$ and $\bar{\ell}$, would have necessarily resulted in a still greater increase, because with ME $\bar{a}$ were also to be merged the original ME diphthongs *ai* and *ei*. Thus it appears that the lower classes excelled over the upper ones not only by greater biological vitality but also by the unconscious linguistic instinct that led them to adopt the safer and the more profitable of the two alternatives, despite the 'natural' attractiveness of the speech habits of the upper classes for the lower ones.

The said conclusion again underlines the necessity of establishing the due hierarchy of inner and outer factors in language development—the hierarchy insisted upon in our earlier paper (Vachek 1962). It is always the exigencies of the system of language which have the last say; i.e., which exercise the right of control over the external factors and of course give free way to the operation of those factors which satisfy those exigencies (or, at least, do not contradict them). In the concrete case under discussion, the exigencies of the system not only prevented the acceptance of the course enforced by the upper classes, but even, rather unexpectedly, made that course unattractive to the speech habits of the lower classes; moreover, the progressive features of the course ultimately adopted by the lower classes were to make that course the most functionally commendable, and thus highly acceptable not only to the lower class speakers themselves but also to the collective instinct of the much wider community of the speakers of the Early ModE standard. In other words, the usual hierarchy of class differences in language, classifying the upper class habits as more commendable than those of the lower class, came to be reevaluated in exactly the opposite sense, in view of the structural and functional superiority of the lower class habits in this particular point.

So much for the first of the two points of Early ModE development in which sociolinguistic factors played an important part. The other of the two points is concerned with the phonic differentiation of what is now called the General American (GA) standard of English from the Southern British Standard, and with the historical situation in which this differentiation came to be established.

It has long been realized that what is now called the GA standard of English represents, at least on its phonic level, a stage of development distinctly older than the one represented by the present-day Southern British (SB) standard. This was usually explained, at least in part, by the fact that the streams of settlers coming into the New World from Britain were bringing along with them that pronunciation which was then typical of their mother country. In Britain this pronunciation was to become subjected to further development, while in the New World it was to remain virtually stationary. To some extent, the conservative character of the GA type of pronunciation was also accounted for by the local provenience of some groups of new settlers (e.g., by the Northern Irish provenience of some compact groups that were coming to America between 1730 and 1775 etc.).

The main problem appears to be the fixing of that period of development of English which appears to be 'reflected' by the GA standard as spoken in the USA at present. The question has been tackled by many scholars; here we want to mention, as briefly as possible, a solution which appears particularly interesting from the sociolinguistic point-of-view. It may be found in a short but important monograph by the late Swedish scholar Eilert Ekwall (1946). In his opinion, the available data drawn both from the history of the language and from its present-day phonic structure suggest the following solution of the given problem: It appears probable that the present state of the GA type of pronunciation reflects, roughly, the state of SB pronunciation at the time of the outbreak of hostilities between the mother country and the thirteen Atlantic colonies. This answer to our question may have sounded rather surprising at first because scholars had been inclined to identify the state of modern GA pronunciation rather with that of Jacobean English, i.e. of the period in which great masses of settlers started their colonization of the trans-Atlantic coast. But one must admit that Ekwall's arguments sound fairly reasonable.

Ekwell argues that up to the time of the revolution itself the English language of the British colonies in North America was virtually the same as that (mainly Southern English) in the mother country. It should be realized, he says, that until the outburst of hostilities the said colonies had been regularly administered through officials sent from England. These officials were undoubtedly regarded as typical, model representatives of the mother country in matters of behavior, of good taste, of the current fashion in dressing, and, last but not least, also in the manner of speaking. In all these points the behavior of those officials was very naturally regarded as something like *dernier cri*, i.e. taken for something that should be imitated by the colonists and their families who, quite understandably, did not want to stay behind the latest development taking place in the mother country. Here again the sociolinguistic factor, the deliberate effort of the colonists to keep abreast of the speech habits of the mother country, can account for the ability of the colonists to keep pace, until a certain moment, with the language development taking place in England. But the most interesting aspect of this sociolinguistic situation was yet to come, and it was during that later stage that relationship between the SB and GA standards developed which was to persist for almost two centuries, down to the present-day.

The aspect we have in mind was to emerge when, after a protracted war, the colonial revolt achieved its final victory. During the hostilities, of course, the contact with the mother country was interrupted, and only after the war could it be re-established. The curious thing, however, was that this re-establishment was not to result in some renewed effort at the adaptation of the GA standard to the pronunciation ypical of the SB speakers. On the contrary, the GA type of pronunciation (which today is used by the overwhelming majority of American English speakers) was to become virtually stationary, and so more and more different from the SB type of pronunciation, admittedly regarded as a kind of model pronunciation of English in the European geographical zone. If one asks for the reason for this rather surprising development—and this question was not particularly formulated even by Ekwall himself—the answer can again only be formulated in sociolinguistic terms. After the victorious war, the American attitude towards the British ways and customs came to be basically altered. A new national and political consciousness was taking shape. In this new social and political atmosphere it was no longer felt necessary to conform to the British models; on the contrary, it was deemed essential to become as differentiated from them as was possible under the given circumstances. In other words, the deviations of the American speech habits from those of the British speakers, which before the outbreak of war had been negative markers, were to become positive markers when the war was over. This attitudinal change regarding objectively the same phonic differences was exclusively due to sociolinguistic factors, and it can thus be pinpointed as a specimen instance of the operation of such factors in the course of language development.

It should also be noted that in this latter case the hierarchy of the operation of internal and external factors influencing the development of language was duly preserved, because the establishment, and even underlining, of the specific features of American English served a specific functional purpose. Shortly after World War II, Karel Horálek, one of the members of the Prague school, pointed out (1948) the existence in language communities of a specific function of language, analogous to the function of the national costume in many ethnic communities. It is called by Horálek 'la fonction de la structure des fonctions de la langue,' and its basic idea is the function of a certain integrality, different from the mere sum of the components of which that structure consists (p. 43). Every speaking community positively appreciates its language (dialect etc.) precisely because of the presence in it of this specific integrality, signalled by some structural deviations from other, allied structures. It is for this reason that when, in modern times, a new literary language becomes established, it is regularly based on that local dialect which exhibits markedly different features from those of the literary language in which that dialect originally belonged, as if to justify the functional necessity of the literary language's just arising. (This could be illustrated by a number of examples of the newly formed literary languages within the Slavonic geographical zone in the course of the nineteenth and twentieth centuries.) No wonder, therefore, that with the growing self-consciousness of the trans-Atlantic colonists, and with the increasing tendency to express this selfconsciousness in linguistic terms, all features of their language which markedly differed from the corresponding features of British English were to be reevaluated as particularly welcome, as evidence of the specific character of the 'function of the structure of functions' of the colonists' language.

It appears then that the sociolinguistic factors may indeed play quite an important role in language development. It should only be stressed that their place in this development must be assessed with due regard to the hierarchy of the external and internal factors cooperating in this development. And it has been again shown here that in this hierarchy the decisive role always belongs to the internal, not to the external factors.

Notes

1. According to William Bright (1966) the task of the sociolinguist is "to show the systemic covariance of linguistic structure and social structure—and perhaps even to show a causal relationship in one direction or the other" (p. 11).
2. See, e.g., Alphonse Juilland (1967), whose diagnosis of the causes of the too static nature of the (mainly American) linguistic research during the first post-war decade is most adequate. On the other hand, the perspective drawn by Juilland from the (again mainly American) research done in the following decade appears to be less convincing (see, e.g., J. Vachek 1964). In any case, the part played by the external factors, though certainly important, does not appear to be put into proper hierarchy in Juilland's otherwise very penetrating and stimulating paper.
3. For the phonological explanation of the English Great Vowel Shift see B. Trnka 1969, J. Vachek 1965.

Bibliography

Bright, W. "The Dimensions of Sociolinguistics." *Sociolinguistics*. Proceedings of the UCLA Sociolinguistic Conference, The Hague, 1964 pp. 11–15.
Ekwall, E. *American and British Pronunciation*. Uppsala. 1946.
Havránek, B. Contribution to discussion. *Travaux du Cercle Linguistique de Prague*, 4, 1931 p. 304.
Horálek, K. "La fonction de la 'structure des fonctions' de la langue." *Recueil Linguistique de Bratislava* 1, 1948, pp. 39–43. Reprinted in J. Vachek (ed.): *A Prague School Reader in Linguistics*, Bloomington, 1964, pp. 421–425.
Juilland, A. "Perspectives du structuralisme évolutif." Word 23, 1967, pp. 350–361.
Luick, K. *Historische Grammatik der englischen Sprache*. Leipzig 1914–40.
Mescaninov, I. I. Prazské prednásky o jazyce (*Prague Lectures on Language*). Prague, 1950.
Trnka, B. "A Phonemic Aspect of the Great Vowel Shift." *Mélanges de lin-*

guistique et de philologie F. Mossé in memoriam. Paris, 1959, pp. 440–443.

Vachek, J. "On the Interplay of External and Internal Factors in the Development of Language." *Lingua* 11, 1962, pp. 433–448.

Vachek, J. "On Some Basic Principles of 'Classical' Phonology." *Zeitschrift fur Phonetik* . . . 17, 1964 pp. 409–431.

Vachek, J. "The English Great Vowel Shift Again." *Prague Studies in English* 11, 1965, pp. 3–13.

Wright, J., Wright, E. M. *An Elementary Historical New English Grammar.* Oxford, 1924.

Wyld, H. C. *A History of Modern Colloquial English.* London, 1914.

THOUGHTS ABOUT *THINK ABOUT* AND ITS PARALLELS

GORDON R. WOOD
Southern Illinois University

For years it has been obvious that in English sentences *about* and other prepositions are linked with words like *thoughts* in one way and with those like *think* in another. This difference has appeared in prescriptive grammars; there linguistic intuition has shown itself in the comments that prepositions join sets of nouns and pronouns, and in the prescription against ending a sentence with a preposition. Better to write *something about which to think* than *something to think about.* Scholarly grammars, on the other hand, have noticed some differences between the noun and verb sequences, and have sought to describe the observed patterns; thus, intuition has long since led grammarians to the conclusion that the functions of *about* and other members of the preposition list are different in these settings.[1]

If these things are so, then why should we return to a topic in grammar and syntax which has furnished both prescription and description enough? My main reason is that it raises some difficult problems for the new transformational grammarian, and may indeed lead to some rethinking of the position taken in *Syntactic Structures* (1957) that "grammar is autonomous and independent of meaning. . . ."[2] If *prepositions*, or whatever the technical term will be, function as a part of those hypothetical segments of structure called *noun phrase* and *verb phrase*, then how does anyone determine their place in the formulation of grammatical sentences? Here I simply wish to explore a range of verb-preposition combinations and leave to professional grammarians the statement of God's truth.

One aspect of that truth is that some verbs accept prepositions while others do not combine with them under any circumstances. At least that is so in my dialect of English; others with other dialects will have to judge for themselves. No one will have to look far to find examples of differences in dialectal choice. Literary criticism, for example, is an elegant and edited dialect. Within its conventions I find this verb-preposition sequence: "The first step was to sort out the words of [*Webster*] 2 into a hundred and nine categories."[3] In my dialect *sort into* is sufficient, and *sort out into* is redundant. To turn from print to speech, the presence of *of* generally serves to distinguish *hear it* from *hear of it*, *know it* from *know of it*, and so on; some speakers distinguish *feel it* from *feel of it*, while others consider that the verb *feel* cannot be followed by *of* at all, though they will ordinarily accept the nominal sequence *the feel of it*.

My interest in this problem of verb and preposition relationships was aroused by the presence of *think about* as a part of a sentence generated in a specific generative formulation. The pertinent article, Rosenbaum's on phrase structure principles (1967), is a display of the construction and application of grammar rules that lead to "a compelling account of a wide range of English complex sentence phenomena." [4] The specific details are these:

(27) b.   VP   →   V PP

      c.   PP   →   PREP NP

(28) In part:

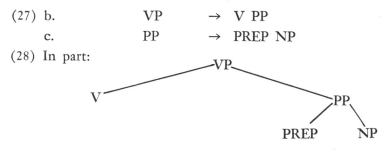

(29)   [V [PREP [DET N S] . . .

(33)   [[thinks] V [[about] PREP [[the] DET [idea] N . . .

Illustrative sentences show that these rules will lead to active, passive, and so-called pseudo-cleft patterns.

(30) *Everyone thinks about the idea that misery loves company.*

(31) *The idea that misery loves company is thought about by everyone.*

(32) *What everyone thinks about is the idea that misery loves company.*[5]

If we replace the dummy portion of the structure with *it*, we gain by having a shorter set of test sentences. And surely there is no loss of elegance in *It is thought about by everyone* or *What everyone thinks about is it*.

When *Syntactic Structures* appeared in 1957, one could simply introduce a preposition if a sentence formula needed it to flesh out that formula. *By* turned up without any grammatical label to account for its appearance; the surface structure of passives needed such a word and it was at hand. Under the newer formulation the presence of a given preposition arises from decoding PREP. One assumes that this decoding will give the same word list that would arise from decoding *Prt.* in *Syntactic Structures* where a "large number of productive subconstructions of *V*" is said to "deserve some mention." [6] The evidence is a list there containing *bring in, call up*, and *drive away*.

The newer formulation VP→ V PP leaves us in doubt about the procedures for decoding. If it says that *all* verb phrases are to be rewritten as a sequence of any verb followed by any preposition, that is nonsense. The verb *turn*, for instance, must function in some senses without a following preposition; in other instances it will permit a prepositional sequence like *turn on it*; and in still others it will require that *it* must fall between the two verb elements—*turn it on*. In a Biblical context, position and exclusion or inclusion of *on* could give three different meanings, the last of which is "to induce a psychedelic experience." We are advised not to cast pearls before swine lest "they turn and rend you." It could be rephrased as *turn on you* and keep the original sense, but not *turn you*. And if it were put as *turn you on*, then swine would be given as a new stimulus for those who wish to expand their minds.

Similar indications of shift in meaning and in possible combinations can be illustrated by *drink* and *do*. *They are drinking it* and *they are doing it* do not mean the same as *they are drinking it in* and *they are doing it over* (in "They are doing over one of the brownstone houses"). And *they are drinking in it* and *they are doing over it* have still other meanings as well as functional relationships. Compare the latter with *they are fussing over it* and the unlikely *they are fussing it over*. Or consider the range of possibilities in *you can run out of your shorts but you can't run out of corn flakes*. *Run your shorts* is unlikely except when we add something similar to *through the wringer*. *Run out of* with *shorts* can mean "race in the nude or in some other garment," "go so fast as to lose one's shorts," or in this context "be devoid of." If *corn flakes* is the name of a town, then *run out of* can mean "under the sponsorship of" or "from a point of departure"; here it means "exhaust the supply of." But in no one of these instances can *shorts* or *corn flakes* be placed immediately after *run* as the last element in a sentence.

As for transitive verbs that accept no preposition at all under any imaginable circumstances, the difficulty is being sure that most of the likely circumstances have been tested. *Rend*, for instance, looks as though it would not combine with *about, out of,* or *on*. Yet there is the lurking suspicion that *rend you up* is possible on analogy to *tear you up*. At the other end of the scale is the relative ease or difficulty with which members of the full preposition list will link with a preceding verb. *Up with* readily links to *put*: *they will not put up with it*. It also links with *turn* though perhaps the sense and grammar are not the same in *turn up with the money* and *turn up with the measles*. But *up with* does not seem to me to form an acceptable verb pattern with *think, believe, hear, worry, batter,* and so on.

If Rosenbaum's notation means that one or more verbs can be linked in some fashion with a following preposition, and I guess this is what the formula does mean, the problem still remains of deciding how to state this possibility. Included in the how is both the placing of PREP in the grammar tree or some other scheme of display, and the use of the evidence of meaning as a guide in syntactic formulas. Hints abound, but I will cite two; the first from a traditional scholarly grammar of English, the second from *Syntactic Structures*.

Traditional linguistics had noted that among other things the preposition could serve to convert "the intransitive into a transitive" in some instances, a generative procedure as it were; and generative grammar has raised the point that this particle could be one of the "so-called 'grammatically functioning' morphemes." [7] From the examples in the present essay given, it is clear that the particle or preposition is a part of the verb element; when it is absent the sense is changed for those verbs that accept prepositions. It further seems likely that gradations between prepositional functions and verb functions must be recognized in a grammar of English—*turn on a dime, turn on you, turn you on.* The matter of position, relationship, and sense indicates that a semantic choice has to be incorporated in that grammar at the very deepest levels of structural formulation.

At one time it was held that the notion that "grammar is based on meaning" was misguided.[8] If that position is still held, then perhaps these remarks on *think about* could lead to better formulations of the problem of grammar construction. Clearly a large number of English verbs have a prepositional variant. The choice to include or exclude the variant must be noted as a grammatical signal each time a verb is used. This is true for all verbs since even those that exclude all prepositions must be generated by a syntax that indicates this exclusion as a part of the verbal substance. And these choices are inextricably linked with meaning. Or to put it another way VP at its inception must include an expression of this choice. That Rosenbaum's article did not include this element is neither here nor there; the relation between verb and preposition was incidental to the course of developing a larger argument. What is important for the design of a grammar of current English is that the structural characteristics of deep grammar must accommodate a variable based on meaning which will allow a range of choices between no preposition and selected prepositions. Then somewhere between the deepest structure and the surface sentence, other variables will be called into play which either restrict the preposition to one place in the sentence or which allow for a choice of either of two places. It is a grammatical-syntactical thought to think about.

Notes

1. Representative illustrations of traditional and structural analyses respectively are in George O. Curme, *English Grammar* (College Outline Series), New York, 1947; Barbara M.H. Strang, *Modern English Structure*, New York, 1965.

2. Noam Chomsky's "purely negative discussion of the possibility of finding semantic foundations for syntactic theory" is the substance of Chapter 9, *Syntactic Structures*, The Hague, 1957; present citations are from the 1966 printing. I cite *Syntactic Structures* because it is a familiar starting point and because it embodies the notion of separation of meaning and grammar. For an indication of developments which tend to combine the study of meaning and grammar, see James D. McCawley, "The Role of Semantics in Grammar," *Universals in Linguistic Theory*, eds. Emmon Bach and Robert T. Harms, New York, 1968.

3. From a review by Dwight MacDonald in *The New Yorker*, March 10, 1962, pp. 130–60. In the same article are *meshed gears with, refer back to, go down the*

drain, and *softening up* to illustrate that in McDonald's words "English, like other languages, is beautiful when properly used. . . ."

4. Peter S. Rosenbaum, "Phrase Structure Principles in English Complex Sentence Formation," *Journal of Linguistics*, III (1967), 103. Roderick A. Jacobs and Peter S. Rosenbaum examine prepositions and particles, distinguishing between them in *English Transformational Grammar*, Waltham, Mass., 1968, noting (p. 103) that their representation in deep structure "has not yet been resolved by grammarians." With regard to the problem of meaning, they note (p. 18) "For now, it is important simply to recognize that the deep structure of a sentence or constituent provides an explicit account of the meaning of the sentence or constituent, a meaning which is not contained in any *explicit* way in the surface structure." They and I may be saying the same thing about the functions of meaning as a part of an analysis or invention of grammatical relationships. On the other hand, prayer and meditation on that last set of remarks has brought me no assurance that mere mortals can understand it.

5. Rosenbaum (1967), p. 108; the parenthetical numbering is that of the article.

6. Chomsky, p. 75. Extensive tables of verb-preposition (or verb-particle) combinations begin on p. 445 in Anna H. Live, "The Discontinuous Verb in English," *Word* (1965), 428–51.

7. Curme (1947), p. 29; Chomsky (1957), p. 104; Strang (1965), pp. 156–7. The last of these, a description of patterns of verb-particle sequence, can be written and tested as a set of generative rules if one is so inclined.

8. Chomsky (1957), pp. 92 ff., plus a forest of internal cross references. It is evident that some researchers who consider themselves transformational-generative grammarians have found that semantics and syntax go hand in hand. At the same time it is not equally clear that surface syntax is viewed as having an impact on the presentation of deep syntax that I suggest here.

HISTORY OF LANGUAGE

A LINGUISTIC ALMANAC(K)
FOR RAVEN I. McDAVID, JR.
BORN OCTOBER 16, 1911

Audrey R. Duckert
University of Massachusetts

October 16 in History

It is a most remarkable coincidence that Noah Webster was born on October 16, 1758. Raven McDavid also shares his birthdate and the sign of Libra with Oscar Wilde (1854) and Eugene O'Neill (1888). So much for the zodiac.

Louis XVI and Marie Antoinette were guillotined in Paris October 16, 1793. Miscellaneous events listed over the past ten years in the *Old Farmer's Almanac(k)* include the "first U. S. modern hotel"—the Tremont in Boston (1829), Hurricane Hazel (1954) and "Gallus Day," mentioned from 1967 onwards and accompanied by cryptic notes like "dry *gallus*, dry spring." The *Dictionary of American English* and the *Dictionary of Americanisms* have no entry for such a day, but their entries at *gallus* and *gallows* indicate a shock of corn or grain; a hint, perhaps, at a variation on the Harvest Home.

The Cardiff Giant, one of the monumental hoaxes of our times, was "revealed" on October 16, 1889. An entertaining account of it appears in Curtis MacDougall's book *Hoaxes*, wherein is also detailed the funny-sad "bathtub hoax" that H. L. Mencken started as a joke when his future abridger and editor was just past his sixth birthday.

October 16, 1911, as a Day and as a Landmark in the History of the English Language

It would have been fun and highly appropriate to have gathered newspapers of that day from all the major dialect regions of the country to compare them with their present-day counterparts, but that must wait for the McDavid Diamond Jubilee in 1986, when Halley's Comet will also appear. (It is true that Queen Victoria celebrated her Diamond Jubilee after 60 years of reign, but Webster's *Third* notes 75 as well as 60.) For the present, then, a survey of *The New York Times* for the date in 1911 and 1969 will have to do.

On Monday, October 16, 1911, the sun rose in New York at 6:11 and set at 5:20. The *Times* had twenty pages and cost one cent. The weather was fair, but the next day might be unsettled, with local rainstorms and moderate winds. On page 13 the weather in the "Cotton and Grain States" which included the Carolinas, was "... fair Monday; Tuesday fair ... "

It might be observed that this was the heyday of the muckrakers and of a tradition of free-swinging journalism, and that today's *Times* may have a different definition of what news is fit to print—and on what page—than it did then. From page 1, this brief excerpt from a story with ethnic labels that would surely make Theodore Bernstein *et al* cringe:

Three Story House Stolen

Four Italians, three men and a woman, were arrested yesterday at Woodhaven, L.I., charged with carting away, in sections, a three-story frame house, said to be owned by a Polish priest who lives in Brooklyn. . . .

Another ethnic reference in an article which would be unthinkable in today's *Times* appears on page 2.

Find Mrs. Belmont's Annoyer is Dead

. . . Dr. Jackala was a Finn and had established a large practice here. . . . It came out that Dr. Jackala was a graduate of the University of Washington and of Chicago University. . . .

Further from page 1:

Robbers Hold Up Car Near Fort Lee

[The story makes clear that it was a trolley car.] . . . Within the car were a dozen excited men, and in a corner several women bent over Edward Sweike of Jersey City Heights, using their handkerchiefs and petticoats to stanch the blood flowing from a wound in the head. . . .

The word *stanch* is also still spelled thus by the *Times* in the adjective sense (a *stanch* supporter); *Webster's Third*, presumably on the basis of usage frequency, treats the verb at an entry headed **stanch** *also* **staunch** and the adjective at **staunch** *also* **stanch**. It would be interesting to know how the *Times* editorial staff pronounce the adjective.

Train Wreck Kills Seven in the West

[a Missouri Pacific passenger train collided with a fast freight near Omaha] . . . among the victims were an eight-year old girl named Wisterian Rowtmann and unidentified colored woman. . .

Another page 1 story, unaccompanied by either a picture or any racial identification, raises a question because of the language:

Ran Away to See the Giants

Bloomfield, N.J. Oct. 15—"If I didn't see de game, I see'd New York," said John Ward, the nine-year-old son of Herkimer Ward of Bloomfield early today when he reached his home after tramping to and from the Polo Grounds in hopes of witnessing the championship game yesterday . . [He had put his quarter in his stocking to avoid pickpockets.] . . . . "But de man wouldn't let me in for a quarter," said the boy almost tearfully.

The Giants, of course, have long since left the Polo Grounds, and the *Times* has largely abandoned attempts at conveying anything more than the substantive content with its quotations. Though I lack positive evidence, I strongly suspect that such dark and menacing things as double negatives and *ain't*, to say nothing of cuss words and subject-verb disagreements are edited out of most quotations from ordinary people. Given the Amos and Andy style of *de* and *see'd*, the reader can only speculate about John Ward's race, but he is unlikely to see anything similar in the *Times* these days.

Even more incredible is the wording of a story on page 20, under the head: "Woman Beats Off a Negro" which says, in part, " . . . Tonight a large posse is searching for the negro [lower case] and he will be lynched if caught." The matter-of-factness is downright bone-chilling. Page 1 of the 1969 issue described the previous day's anti-war demonstrations: " . . . Blue collar workers and Negroes [capital] did not participate in great numbers. . . . " And on the same page, in an account of Bishop Sheen's resignation from Rochester: " . . . 'I move too fast,' he said, alluding to his concern with the conditions of slum blacks. . . . " [lower case].

While the subject of the incongruous is before us, another page 1 story for October 16, 1911 might be considered. It may seem a pity to delete parts of it, but the *Times* is available on microfilm in many libraries and can be checked.

GIRL A SUICIDE FOR LOVE
Avis Linnell Ends Life on Reading Of
Cambridge Minister's Engagement

Boston, Oct. 15. Avis Linnell, a 19-year old student at the Conservatory of Music committed suicide by taking cyanide of potassium last night in her room at the Boston Young Women's Christian Association. . . . . when the door was burst open, the girl was dead on the floor, with a copy of the *Cambridge Chronicle*, which contained the announcement, within a few feet of her body.

Not only would such a story—from Boston of all places—find no place on any page of today's *Times*, its language would have been much condensed even if it had happened to a person so prominent as to require full details. YWCA has become standard; specifics such as cyanide of potassium and the *Cambridge Chronicle* would be replaced by 'poison' and 'a local newspaper' and we'd never have known that the poor girl had been out shopping for items for her trousseau, since she and the young clergyman had been engaged. The fact that the young man could not be reached for comment does have an abiding ring to it.

Prominent people do get put into a different category. Their privacy is at once more and less honored. In the current *Times*, Society editor Charlotte

Curtis uses detail in a totally devastating way—witness her report on the Washington gala a few years ago at which the twenty-fifth anniversary of the National Gallery of Art was celebrated and Mrs. Mellon Bruce's Balenciaga gown wouldn't stay fastened in the back. The language of the general news stories is sparer these days; it is, paradoxically, at once more precise and less specific. Detail can easily have the effect of leading the reader or listener away from the main point.

Still on that monumental page 1, a movement calling itself "Man and Religion Forward" announced a series of 8-day campaigns in 74 large cities, and the article said ". . . The cities to be campaigned are in Canada as well as the United States." This transitive use of *campaign* is scantily attested. *OED* labels its one citation a nonce use and presumably includes it only because it comes from Sterne's *Sentimental Journey* (1778): 'An old soldier . . *campaigned* and worn out to death in the service.' *OED Supp* offers no further information; *Webster's Third* enters one transitive sense restrictively defined as 'to race (a horse) in a series of major races.' The sole citation in *DA*, defined as 'to exploit' and labeled *Rare* has also to do with horses and may not be as general as the definition implies. The citation, dated March 28, 1888 is from the *Boston Globe* and reads: "The new owner sold the steed for 800 dollars to James Gray . . . who after *campaigning* him on the track for a couple of years . . . sold him to Bonner." In these times when functional change has become a way of language life and when *campaign* is such a common word, it does indeed seem odd that this usage has not extended. Given the citations, it would not seem tactful to apply the word to a religious campaign.

Two notes of historical interest reported on page 1: William Jennings Bryan, the silver tongued cross-of-gold orator finally conceded he would never be president. The *Chronicle* reported from London that there were persistent rumors that the Home Secretary, Winston Spencer Churchill, would succeed Augustine Birrell as Chief Secretary for Ireland. [The rumors were false; Birrell remained in the post until 1916, and Churchill became First Lord of the Admiralty. This may have changed the course of history. It is always hard to say.]

Advertising begins on page 2 of the 1911 *Times*, advocating Sanatogen for the nerves and offering accommodations at the Hotel St. Regis at 5th and 55th: Single room without bath $3; suites consisting of parlor, bedroom, and bath, $10 upward. But just as the vocabulary of this decade is exploding with space terminology, so did the burgeoning field of aeronautics take over in the years just before World War I. Witness: "Naval Apprentice Seaman Daniel A. Mackney has perfected a hydro-aeroplane. He hopes to begin flights next spring. . . . Mackney will be the first naval aviator in the ranks." *OED Supplement* cites *hydro-aeroplane* between the years 1909 and 1928 and then label it *Disused*. The contraption was a far cry from today's *hydroplane*, but it's interesting to note the return of a shorter form of the same basic compound. Aeroplane is, to be sure, *plane* in today's *Times*, having arrived by way of *airplane*. *Aviator*, cited in the *Supplement* from 1896 on, has now largely been replaced by *pilot* which would have implied rivers and harbors in 1911.

The Packard Motor Company hired space on page 3 to proclaim ". . . The first motor truck to cross the continent entirely under its own power. Left New York July 8, reached San Francisco August 24." *Motor* was a necessary modifier then, just as it was in the early days of *motor cars*. *Truck* was long established in the American language for hauling conveyances that were not self-propelled; *DA*'s earliest citation is dated 1805 and comes from the journals of Lewis and Clark.

Also on page 3:

> Lynn, Mass. Oct. 15 — For the second time within a week the shoe manu-facturers of Lynn adopted a resolution to-night rejecting the proposition of the Knights of Labor Shoe Cutters for an eight-hour day. [7–4 with an hour off at noon.] The resolution says that the eight-hour day "would impose too great a hardship on the manufacturers. . ." The cutters would be notified that their services were not required and a lockout would follow.

And in 1969 on page 1 of the *Times*, the United Shoe Workers of America were endorsing a moratorium against the Vietnam war. *Lockout* is recorded by *OED* from 1860 but, curiously, it is not noted in the *Supp* and the last citation in the main text in 1863. *DAE* chronicles it up through 1908.

An irate letter writer deplores Sunday revels:

> I wonder Almighty God didn't shift the earthquake from San Francisco to the Atlantic Coast and bury Newport. . . . In that resort, Pompeii, Sodom, or Gomorrah called Newport . . . last summer the revelry was on Saturday night and it lasted until Monday morning. The men would come down Saturday night and the dances, pow-wows, and revels started then. They marched the streets Sunday morning at 3 o'clock in their paraphernalia of dancing, and there were women smoking cigarettes and drinking.

OED documents *pow-wow* from 1812 on, showing its extension from the Indian gathering to "any meeting compared to an Indian conference . . . e.g. a friendly consultation, or a merry-making; a 'palaver' of any kind." We may be coming full cycle on this one. An article by Calvin Trillin in the April 18, 1970 *New Yorker* describes a Saturday night Indian pow-wow in Los Angeles: "As the word is used offscreen in Los Angeles, a powow is not a discussion but a social event in which Indians in traditional costumes dance around a drum." But getting back to 1911, the horror of women smoking cigarettes and drinking is so shattering that it is best to turn the page and not comment.

Player pianos seem to have consumed the greatest amount of advertising space, but a small and singularly unprepossessing ad from the Schlitz brew-eries should not go unnoticed, since the product has been nectar to linguists since time began:

> We use the costliest materials—we age Schlitz for months to prevent biliousness—it will not ferment in your stomach.

Biliousness, in case anyone is remotely interested, has been with the language since De Quincey's *Confessions*, according to OED. Shades of everything from Lysistrata to Women's Liberation, on page 6:

URGES MARRIAGE STRIKE
Emma Goldman Tells East Side Girls to Wait For Better Times

Emma Goldman, the anarchist leader, started the first of a series of talks to east siders in Yiddish yesterday....

What a language-poor time that was, when we consider the wide choice now available: *dissident, militant, protester,* and the ever-serviceable *communist,* which did not even appear in the 1911 *Times.* Her sins were doubtless compounded by the fact that she did not use English but spoke in the language her audience understood. Theodore Roosevelt was later to say that there was room for only one language in America—the English language—and the country must not become a polyglot boarding house; but New York in 1911 seems to have been more realistic and more tolerant. Witness this account of a political campaign:

East Side Yearns For Alderman Louie
"Wireless" Zeltner Says So Himself
And If He Doesn't Know, Who Does?

... "Besides these pictures which will be hanged in every window nearly in the east side," he said, "I am going to make a personal appeal myself, taking the stump in Yiddish and English every night, beginning next week.... "And anyhow, Alderman Zeltner will right away recommend to the Public Service Commission that all car lines should have to give a 3-cent fare during rush hours," he announced....

"Wireless" Zeltner must have been a joy to contemporary connoisseurs of campaign oratory. The headline seems to imply that the *Times* is not taking the candidate seriously; it would be unlikely today. *Car lines* and *rush hours* as used here are Americanisms recorded from 1898 when the rush hour as we now know it would have been unimaginable.

Gilding the lily (from page 9):

Robert W. De Forest, President of the Charity Organization Society, has added his vote at the budget exhibit in favor of the changing of the name of Blackwell's Island to Hospital Park or some other which will remove the stigma which the long association with the county prison has created.

An article in the *Times Magazine* for Sunday, March 1, 1970, describes a proposed New Town to be built on this island; it was followed by a letter from Harmon H. Goldstone, Chairman of the Landmarks Preservation Commission, printed on March 16:

... Place names are a part of a shared past and, as pointed out in a recent letter, they deserve respect. Like landmarks, they lend a sense of continuity to the shifting scence.

And there are pitfalls in impulsive changes. In 1921 the 235-year-old name of Blackwell's Island was changed to Welfare Island in an effort to sweeten the odor of a prison scandal. Now that the place is to be rebuilt with fine new parks and handsome housing, who will want to say he lives "on welfare"?

The latest word, but surely not the last, comes in a *Times* editorial on April 12, 1970, the 25th anniversary of the death of Franklin Delano Roosevelt. Regretting the lack of an appropriate Roosevelt memorial in New York City, it suggested that Welfare Island be renamed in his honor.

Page 9 of the 1911 *Times* states that the " . . . blind poor to the number of 544 will receive this morning their allowance from the Department of Public Charities. . . . "; and page 9 of the 1969 *Times* announces the appointment of " . . . a taskforce on the problems of the physically handicapped. . . . " The blind poor have probably become the visually handicapped and economically disadvantaged; it comes as no surprise that Frank Campbell advertised under the rubric of *undertaker* in 1911 and is now The Funeral Chapel. It is probably only a matter of time until these euphemisms, like their predecessors, wear thin at the elbows and bring us too close to the truth. Creating new ones is a real challenge to the future; perhaps the substitution of numbers which, unlike words, have not yet acquired connotations, is the answer.

There'll always be an adman, and one of his wiles will always be the transferred use of contemporary language in an effort to convey the immediacy of his product: Thus, in 1911:

> Are you a coal-bill aviator? Does the annual struggle to keep your coal-bills down serve to keep you "up in the air" financially?

And in 1969, *passim.*: "Find it in Bonwit's Espresso Shop," "The turtleneck . . . is a real comer," "Pantsuit message, delivered in orlon."

The following used car ad from page 12 in 1911 may serve as an index of the spate of innovations in the language that came from the automotive age:

> Speedwell 1911 four-passenger semi-racer with toy tonneau: used only 4 months: perfect condition: extraordinary equipment includes top, windshield, shock absorbers, motor-driven tire pump, 2 extra Firestone demountable rims, extra shoes and tubes, speedometer, slipcovers, pigskin upholstery and klaxon. . . .

Shock absorbers is first noted in the *OED Supp* in 1916, and *klaxon* in 1914, though *DA*'s first citation for klaxon is 1910. But the real surprise is *windshield*, which is not in *OED* or *OED, Supp*, nor is it in *DAE*. *DA*'s first citation for it is from the *Saturday Evening Post* for December 24, 1927, making the antedating an amazing 16 years. Oddly enough, the term does appear in the supplementary matter in my 1916 printing of the *Century Dictionary and Cyclopedia* with a quotation from—of all places—the *Encyclopædia Britannica*. It is not in my 1916 printing of *Webster's New International*.

On the same page is an utterly baffling ad for Ye Olde Watchman whiskey which says " . . . After 100 years of experiment, the non-refillable bottle has at last been perfected. . . . " The bottle pictured appears to be an ordinary bottle, and one wonders at the semantic instability evidenced by non-refillable. Surely if it was capable of being filled once. . . .

The 1911 Classified Section lists real estate For Sale or To Let; in 1969 it is left to the reader to decide from the context whether he is renting or buying. *Apartment* is the operative word in 1911; *flat* occurs, but *tenement* does not. Currently, the variety of apartments would fill a page; representative are: *studio, penthouse, terrace, professional, luxury, luxury doorman, bachelor, executive, brownstone*, and—believe it or not—*walkup*. Houses are generally houses in current ads, but two sub-categories are Farms and Country *Homes* and Vacation and Leisure *Homes*. In 1911 a "commuter's farm" in New Jersey is advertised for sale—60 acres and one mile to the depot—; in 1969, the depot has become the *station*, and a clothing ad is aimed at men who "commute" to Florida.

I have tried to show a representative few of the changes that have taken place within 60 years of the English language. Obvious innovations (television, dacron, and the like) have been passed without comment; for it is the language as a reflection of the society that uses it that invites most interesting speculation. From a corpus of ordinary language such as a large daily newspaper provides, a way of life emerges. One small example, again from advertising: nearly an entire page of the classified section in 1911 was headed "Boarders Wanted" and in the entire paper there was not one single ad for a restaurant; in 1969 restaurants advertised, but no one sought boarders.

The salient fact that emerges, strengthened and renewed, from this excursion is that the English language is indeed a living thing, and that its changes, both in nature and use, are the surest signs of its vitality. Change balanced by an inner stability—even as evidenced by the abiding phenomenon of the euphemism—results in the enduring wonder of the language.

ANGLICIZED FORMS OF PROPER NAMES: A REPORT ON A QUESTIONNAIRE FILLED OUT BY STUDENTS AT YOUNGSTOWN STATE UNIVERSITY

KARL W. DYKEMA
Youngstown State University

The naturalization of foreign names is as inevitable as the naturalization of other foreign words because the foreign terms can be expressed only through the repertory of phonemes of the speaker. Except in the very rare instances where the speaker also controls the phonemes of the foreign language, he uses the vowels, consonants, and intonation patterns which seem to his ear most closely to approximate those he hears in the native pronunciation of the word he is trying to say in his own language. Or, especially in the case of names, what he sees in the conventional foreign spelling.

Names, unless they are those of important places or persons, occur only infrequently in the general use of a language. On the rare occasions when we are called upon to say such names, we have no established spoken usage to guide us. If the owner of the name is present, we can ask him to pronounce it; if not, we do the best we can from its transcription. Sometimes, at least according to the testimony of some of the questionnaires I worked with, we impose our pronunciation in spite of the presence of the owner of the name. What this paper attempts to do it to describe some of the ways in which the non-English names of college students have been Anglicized. The necessity of substituting English phonemes for foreign ones is certainly a primary factor; but it will become apparent that a good many other forces play an important part in altering the names.

The conclusions are based on the responses to a questionnaire to which several hundred students at Youngstown State University responded some years ago. The questions asked are listed in Table 1. The useful, or at least the interesting, responses were relatively few, and some generalizations on this disappointing fact should perhaps be attempted. Evidently there was either a great deal of reticence or a great deal of ignorance among the students and their informants. The ignorance was probably in many instances the basis for the reticence. In a few cases a parent or grandparent had been persuaded to write his name in the original alphabet, and the transcription was obviously faulty. In other cases the information supplied was incorrect (I. 1, 2, & 3). One student attributed his name of *Miller* to an identical German form, which is hardly credible; another gave an incorrect source for the name *Baker*, whereas her uncle told me the name came from the corresponding German noun; and the third example was explained in this statement: "Because the American pronunciation gradually changed the 'ch' sound in my name to an 's', it became 'Rosselli'." Evidently the student assumes that *ch* in Italian is pronounced as it is in English. Probably for every one of these older people who did provide shaky evidence there were a dozen others who were so aware of their uncertainty that they refused to put it in written form.

But it is also apparent that a vast number of Americans of recent foreign extraction are only too anxious to forget their provenience. At least they profess to know nothing of their less immediate antecedents and to have no interest in their family names. The few whose names I have had a chance to ask specific questions about seem generally to have been genuinely ignorant and amazed that anyone should be interested in the matter. They seem to want to shed every particle of their un-American heritage, including the considerable command they often have of another language. (I may ask, for instance, a student with an Italian name, if he knows any foreign language, and he will usually answer that he studied French or Latin or Spanish in high school. He will not volunteer the information that Italian is spoken at home, and only when asked will he confess deprecatingly that he can follow a conversation in Italian quite easily. Yet most such students have never made any effort to read the language and seem to consider their control of it as worthless.)

There are exceptions to this attitude, of course, as the following comments show (II. 1, 2, 3, 4, & 5):

1. In the old country my great grandfather was Elias Kassis. His son, my grandfather, was the first immigrant of our family to this country. His name was Michael. In order to signify who he was, he came to be known as Michael, son of Elias—or in short Michael Elias. Thus my last name—Elias.

2. The name originally was something like Ēshtinich. Difficulty in American pronunciation caused Dad Istnick to have it changed legally to Istnick. (Incidentally, Dad and Mom Istnick are both dead. Since all the six children were born and reared here and broke with the traditions of the old country, about six different versions have been given us as to original spelling etc. No one is any longer positive. Probably, the only one who would really know would be a remaining cousin in Yugoslavia, but contact with him the past three years has been lost.)

Another interesting observation is that when the name was being changed, the name Kabol or Cabol (something like that was suggested since names representing the father's trade were often taken). I guess the family trade had been tailoring and Cabol was the word for tailor. For one reason or another that name was rejected and Istnick used.

3. The name in Slovak and Hungarian means "grower of apples." Originally spelled either Almasi or Almasy in the Old Country, the main part of the name *almas* signified the actual translation. However, according to the Slavic

tongues, *I* or *Y* at the end of a name signifies wealth and social position. It is believed that a Count Almasy, seen in Yugoslavia two years ago, is a direct descendant of the Almasy family that lived in Hungary and Czechoslavokia for hundreds of years, and to which my father's grandparents were related. It was in Almasy Castle, just outside Budapest, that Josef Cardinal Mindzenty was held prisoner by the Communists just prior to his death.

4. There has been no change in the spelling of our name. It is just pronounced according to English phonetics. Our name is used in Germany as a first, last, and middle name; it is a title (like a baron, small title). It can be found on many Renaissance paintings by Holbein. It is a very common name in Germany. Many important people through German history have had the name.

5. The name was originally spelled Leonard in Ireland. The family went to Alsace-Lorraine, then occupied by Germany. When writing in English they spelled the name Leonard and when writing in German they spelled it Lehnerd. Both spellings continued when they came to this country until my great uncle entered college. He was then asked to use either one spelling or the other and the family chose the German spelling—Lehnerd.

Perhaps before presenting any more testimony I should comment on the reliability of the evidence. The students seem to have answered the questions as honestly as they could; there appeared to be no instances of manufactured evidence. But the material already presented makes clear that these are not expert witnesses. To be quite sure about the statements they made would require an individual investigation of each questionnaire.

I have classified the Anglicizing of foreign names into about a dozen catagories, some of them not very clearly defined, others somewhat overlapping. The first, transliteration, I shall not attempt to discuss because of the obvious typographical difficulties. There were several responses which gave the original name in Russian, Greek, Arabic, or Chinese characters, often with interesting comments.

The next group is a small one and puzzling (III. 1). The explanation reads: "The German H at that time resembled the English S and this brought about the change." The time is not stated. Probably he is referring to German script, but I don't see how the confusion would arise.

Naturalization papers establish a legal spelling for an immigrant's name, and apparently alterations in spelling often occur in them (IV). The comments on the second and third are: "The immigration people spelled it this way to get my father's pronunciation."

An error was made in the naturalization papers in 1920, the officials made the error and told my father to leave the spelling as they had written it. The papers were filled out when the error was noticed; therefore, they would not change it.

Often the spelling of a name is somewhat simplified, usually to have it conform more nearly to American practice (V. 1), or to help in pronunciation. Only two comments seems worth quoting here (V. 2): " 'DZ' difficult to pronounce in English." "My husband's grandfather's American sponsor unknowingly dropped the 'ch' in spelling his name."

Schoolteachers and employers, being in positions of authority, can impose arbitrary spelling on the names of their pupils and employees, and at least in the past must have done so fairly often. Here are a few of the many examples and comments (VI. 1): "First employed in a Pennsylvania coal mine, the timekeeper entered the name as Colson, and the spelling was carried as such . . . until naturalization." "My grandfather received his first American paycheck with the name spelled *Mozzillo* instead of *Muzzillo*; this spelling was retained thereafter." "When my father was young he was advised by his teacher to add another 't' to his last name since the pronunciation was not too clear with only one 't'." "For ease in pronunciation this was done by one of my elementary teachers." "My father's teacher in grade school started the spelling of Lawrence in the family." "Klenotich was changed to Klenotic by Carnegie Steel for convenience in pronunciation." "In Europe his name was pronounced Mlynar, which meant a miller who grinds flour. When my grandfather came to the United States and the children started school, the school teacher could not pronounce it, so she changed it to Maliner."

Related to the preceding category are those spellings which attempt a phonetically more accurate transcription for English of the sounds in the original language (VII. 1). The comments on three of these deserve quotation (VII. 2): "The Slovak 'ž', pronounced as the 'z' in azure, is very uncommon in English, so it was changed to the hard English 'z'. The Slovak 'c', pronounced as 'ts', was changed to the English 'ts'." "When my grandfather . . . came to America some important man asked him his name and he replied, 'Petrisin.' The man asked, 'Peterson'? My grandfather said yes and it has been Peterson ever since." "My father got tired of hearing so many people mispronounce our family name so in the 1920s he had it changed to Chick."

Sometimes the change in spelling is confessedly to avoid recognition of the name as foreign. Here are two frank avowals (VIII. 1): "My grandfather took the 'i' off the end of 'Penotti'. He wanted to make the name American instead of Italian." "During the first World War many German people Anglicized their names to avoid persecution in the United States."

Translation would seem to be a fairly obvious method of establishing an English-sounding name, but only a few examples turned up on the questionnaire. No doubt the legal problem of naturalization would be an impediment here. The first two examples (IX. 1) are attested on the questionnaire; Mr. Stoneburner, however, merely stated that his ancestor came from Germany.

Since some foreign names are appreciably longer than English ones, we might expect them to be shortened. Several Russian and Greek ones, which I have not discussed because they involve transliteration, show much shortening. Of the first two listed (X. 1), a Polish and an Italian one, *August* was explained as more convenient, *Squillo* as more convenient to pronounce. The other two had a practical justification (X. 2): "Because Stall is easier to pronounce; it was to be used as the name of a store." "Lazarovitz couldn't be fitted comfortably on a store sign."

Some of the alternatives already cited may have seemed pretty arbitrary, so this next category, which I label arbitrary alterations, may seem an artificial one (XI. 1). The comment on the second seems a little mysterious: "I had my name changed legally in Mercer County Court House on the advice of a close professional friend."

The last category I call simplification, but again it is not sharply differentiated from some of the others (XII. 1). The comments on these changes merely state that they were for the sake of simplification.

I shall conclude with four unclassifiable quotations, each of which shows a rather surprisingly different interest in the family name. "(XIII. 1) They were a family of the lower aristocracy. The girls married beneath them socially and when they came to this country the elegant 'Von' was dropped." The reference of the last *they* is presumably to *family*. "(XIII. 2) Many times people spell *our* name Moderelli like other people do with the same name as ours. Our name is Modarelli and not Moderelli." The comment on XIII. 3 is rather involved; as I unravel it, it comes to this: The greatgrandfather was named Morten Boë; the grandfather was christened Theodore Boë, but because he was the son of Morten he decided to call himself Mortenson, and that is now the family name. Finally there is this sample of playing fast and loose with names: "(XIII. 4) According to Dad, at the time he and his six brothers were old enough to get factory jobs, there was a company ruling not to employ 'hunkies' or anyone related to someone already employed there. An uncle of his had them change their names and got jobs for all seven of them in his department at a manufacturing plant in Erie, Pennsylvania."

TABLE 1

QUESTIONNAIRE

We are making a study of the Americanization of non-English proper names, and we need your help. Many of us in this community inherit our family names from ancestors who came from Europe or other parts of the world, not from England. These names were usually hard to pronounce in English; therefore they had to be altered. Sometimes they couldn't even be written in the English alphabet because the original language used another system of writing.

What we should like you to do is to take this form home with you and fill it out with the help of your parents or grandparents or of other relatives. Some of the questions may be a bit puzzling, but do the best you can with them. When you have completed the form, return it to your Communication instructor.

TABLE 1 (Cont'd)

1. Your name, spelled as you would sign it on a check or other legal document:

Last Name	First Name	Middle Name or Names

2. How you pronounce your last name: _____
Use any method you like to show the pronunciation. We suggest the symbols on the first page of your *American College Dictionary* (the tan page at the very front) or on page xxvii of that dictionary. Be sure to use accent marks to show which syllables are stressed; this is very important.

3. Your family name as it was written by that ancestor of yours who brought it to this country. This should be spelled as it was in the old country and should be written in the alphabet used in the old country; that is, a Greek name should be written in Greek symbols, a Russion one in Russian symbols, etc. If you don't write this alphabet, get a relative to do it for you.

4. The country that this ancestor came from _____.
Since there have been a good many changes of names of countries in the last fifty years, give the name the country had when your ancestor left it, the approximate date when he left, and the present name of the country; for example: Serbia, 1912, now Yugoslavia.

5. If the Americanization of your family name has caused a substantial change in it and you know the reason for it and care to describe it, please give an account of it below.

TABLE 2

CATEGORIES OF ANGLICIZING

In what follows ":" means "derived from".
I. Incorrect attribution.
  1. Miller:Miller (German, Mueller)
  2. Baker:Bacher (German, Bäcker)
  3. Rosselli:Rochelle
II. Strong interest in foreign source.
  1. Elias Kassis; Michael Elias (from Lebanon)
  2. Eshtinich; Istnick; Kabol or Cabol
  3. Almasi or Almasy
  4. Ulrich, pronounced All rich
  5. Leonard, Lehnerd
III. Confusion of English and German letters.
  1. Rasor:Rahor
IV. Naturalization paper alterations.
  1. Erickson:Erikson
  2. Nemetz:Niemiec
  3. Berndt:Berendt

TABLE 2 (Cont'd)

V. Spelling simplifications.
1. Beringer:Behringer; Baltes:Baltess; Slaby:Slabej; Lucas:Lukač; Bobovnik:Bobovnyik; Ritz:Hritz; Fisher:Fischer
2. Durek:Dzurek; Swartzbeck:Schwartzbeck

VI. Teachers' and employers' changes
1. Colson:Colacino; Mozzillo:Muzzilo; Brott:Brot; Boncila:Bancilă; Lawrence:Lorenc or Lorencz; Klenotic:Klenotich; Maliner: Mlynar

VII. English respelling to approximate the original pronunciation.
1. Myers:Meiers; Mihalko:Michalko; Sicafuse:Ziegenfuss; Yanik: Janik;Cook:Couco;Langosh:Langoš
2. Zetts:Zec; Peterson:Petrišin; Chick:Cicco

VIII. Respelling to obscure foreign source.
1. Penott:Penotti; Shelar:Schelar

IX. Translation.
1. Williams:Guglielmo; Joseph:DiGiuseppe
2. Stoneburner: [Steinbrenner]

X. Shortening for convenience.
1. August:Augustnowicz; Squillo:Squillociotti
2. Stall:Asztalnak; Lazar:Lazarovitz

XI. Arbitrary alterations.
1. Poidmore:Poidimani; Marsh:Marosecevich

XII. Simplification.
1. Cardille:Quadagno; Rabek:Wyrobek; Trieff:Trivfu

XIII. Unclassifiable
1. Conrad:Von Conrade
2. Modarelli; not Moderelli
3. Mortenson:Morten Boë
4. Rogers, Reed, Ryder, Busch:Rydzewski

RELICS OF ENGLISH FOLK SPEECH
IN AMERICAN ENGLISH

Hans Kurath
University of Michigan

The transplantation of English from the British Isles to America began at a time when the literary language was already highly standardized. In cultivated speech even the spoken word was highly standardized in its phonemic structure and in the lexical incidence of the phonemes. When the influx of Englishmen and Scots into the colonies was temporarily halted by the Revolution, the written word of Great Britain continued to influence American usage in morphology, syntax, and spelling.

The establishment of cultivated British usage on the American continent was a highly complicated process. Most of the early settlers were unlettered and, coming from various parts of the British Isles, spoke a variety of English dialects, or regional varieties of Standard English, in their homes. Thrown together in the several colonies, they gradually abandoned regional features in favor of the cultivated usage of leading families and British officials. This trend toward uniformity in the several colonial centers, strung out from New England to South Carolina, created regional varieties of cultivated English that underlie present usage.

In American folk speech, phonological regionalisms of English survive in considerable numbers, usually restricted to certain subareas, They are especially common when usage in Standard British English (SBE) was unsettled during the period of colonization or when a feature deviating from SBE was widely current in English folk speech, and hence spoken by many of the settlers.

The ten regional survivals discussed below can be regarded as symptomatic of the recession of hundreds of English dialect features imported during the settlement period. Our record of modern folk usage in America and in southern England provides the basis for suggesting their probable history in linguistic and in sociocultural terms. With two exceptions, the evidence for the items presented here is given in H. Kurath and R. I. McDavid, Jr., *The Pronunciation of English in the Atlantic States* (PEAS).

American dialect areas referred to in the discussion are set off on map 2 of PEAS.

On the accompanying sketch map, diagnostic heteroglossic lines indicate the dialectal structure of the southern part of England.

West of line *A-1* postvocalic /r/ is preserved, to the east it has shifted to unsyllabic [ə], as in *here, fair, four, poor.*

West of line *A-2* the long ME *u* has shifted to [au], east of it to [æu~ɛu], as in *down, house.*

Between lines *A-1* and *A-2* lies a transition zone between the Western and the Eastern dialect areas.

In *apple, cat, sack, man* the ME short *a* appears as [a] to the west of line *B*, as [æ] to the east of it.

East of line *C* the ME long open vowel *ǭ* has shifted to [uᵊ~u], as in *road, stone.*

North of line *D* the ME short *u* survives as rounded [u], to the south it was unrounded to [ʌ], as in *come, hundred.*

Lines *A-1* and *A-2* separate the West from the East, line *C* sets off East Anglia, line *D* the North Midland. These subareas of England will be referred to in the discussion of the ten items treated below.

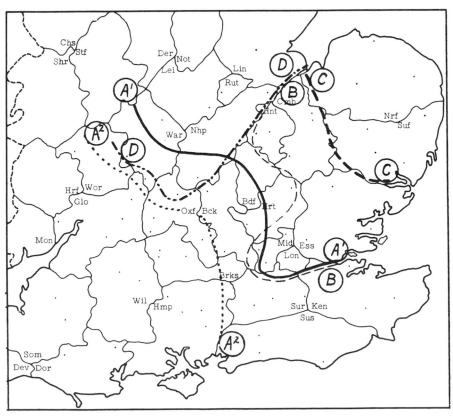

again

In the Eastern States *again* rimes either with *pen*, with *pin*, or with *pain* [PEAS: 131 and maps 60-61]. In speech of the cultured and the middle class, the /ɛ/ of *pen* predominates, in folk speech the /ɪ/ of *pin*. The relative frequency of /ɛ/ and /ɪ/ varies regionally, especially in the middle group.

The type of *again* with the vowel of *pain* has a most unusual dissemination, both geographically and socially. In folk speech it occurs not infrequently in highly conservative areas: in the upper Connecticut valley, on Long Island Sound, and on Albemarle Sound in North Carolina. In cultivated speech the incidence of /e/ is erratic. Only 1 in 12 cultured speakers, scattered from New England to Georgia (from Boston to Atlanta), actually uses it.

In English folk speech, the type of /əgɪn/ is regular in the eastern counties (from Sussex to Norfolk) and the type of /əgɛn/ in the central counties (from Hampshire to Northampton and beyond). The variant riming with *pain* is exceedingly rare and the instances are scattered, which points to importation from SBE.

In SBE usage has always wavered between /əgen/ and /əgen/. Shakespeare rimed the word with *brain*, *vain*, etc., occasionally also with *men*, *pen* [Kökeritz 1935]. John Walker [1797] recognized only /əgen/. Daniel Jones [1927] reports /əgen/ as predominant but not general.

In AE the predominant type /əgɛn/ must be regarded as an English folk pronunciation, supported during the Colonial period by SBE usage. The type of /əgɪn/ was brought over from the eastern counties of England. In cultivated speech, /əgen/ may well be a recent importation from SBE, supported by the spelling *again*; but in folk speech along the conservative Atlantic coast its history is obscure.

It is a curious fact that the pronunciation /əgen/ of SBE has no basis in the folk speech of southern England. On the other hand, it is a normal descendant of ME *again* in stressed position.

bristle

In the New England settlement area, and only there, *bristle* has the vowel /ʌ/ of *brush* in folk speech. In rural northern New England this pronunciation has rather general currency among the middle class as well [PEAS: 130 and map 59]. The dissemination pattern of this pronunciation is so striking that *brustle* can serve as a 'tracer' of the migration of New Englanders into the Great Lakes area and into East Jersey.

In English folk speech the type of *brustle* is current in three separate areas: along the North Sea from Essex to Lincolnshire, in coastal Sussex, and in Dorset-Somerset. With the exceptions of these peripheral counties, the folk speech of southern England now shares the type of *bristle* with SBE.

In ME both *i* and *u* were current, as the spellings show [MED, OD]; but by c1400 *bristle* became the usual spelling, showing the early adoption of /ɪ/ in literary English.

Since both /ɪ/ and /ʌ/ are still current in English folk speech, we must assume that both pronunciations were used to some extent in all the American colonies. The survival of /ʌ/ in New England can probably be attributed to a high percentage of settlers from the eastern counties of England. The complete elimination of /ʌ/ in the South, including the conservative coastal districts, is rather surprising. The predominance of settlers from the extensive /ɪ/ pronouncing parts of England, supported by literary English, may account for this development.

bulge

In a large and solid area extending from the eastern shore of Chesapeake Bay through Virginia into the upcountry of the Carolinas, the words *bulge* and *bulk* have the rounded vowel /ʊ/ of *bull, full* [PEAS: 144 and map 84]. Here this pronunciation is current on all social levels, though on the periphery cultured speakers tend to adopt the unrounded vowel /ʌ/ of the adjoining areas. The American North and North Midland as well as the coastal plain of the Carolinas and Georgia regularly have the unrounded /ʌ/, thus conforming to SBE.

In English folk speech rounded /ʊ/ in *bulge* is largely confined to the North Midland, where ME short *u* survives in all positions, as in *hundred, come, luck*, etc. Scattered relics of /ʊ/ farther south indicate that it was formerly more widely disseminated and has probably receded under the influence of SBE. This inference is supported by the currency of /ʊ/ in such large sections of America. That rounded /ʊ/ should survive in *bulge* and *bulk* as well as in *bull* is surely not surprising, since it is flanked by the same consonants.

There can hardly be any doubt that both /ʌ/ and /ʊ/ were originally current to some extent in all the American colonies and that the present uniformity in the several sections of the Atlantic States developed in the course of time by oral communication. In this case the spelling is no guide.

It is of interest to observe in passing that the rather widely used English variants [bæʊǧ ~ bəʊǧ] from earlier [būǧ <bulǧ] are not attested in AE. The same is true of the variants [šæʊd- ~ šəud-] of *shoulder*.

father

In all varieties of AE, *father* has a low vowel, ranging phonically from low-front [aˑ] in eastern New England to low-back-round [ɒˑ] in western Pennsylvania [PEAS: 112 and map 32]. The most wide-spread variants are low-central [ɑ•] and low-back-unround [ɒ•]. In the areas that lack post-vocalic /r/, *father* rimes with *farther*, as in SBE, elsewhere with *bother*.

In English folk speech low-front [a• ~ a] predominates all the way from Kent to Yorkshire. But there are some regional variants: [ɑ• ~ ɒ•] in the Home Counties, as in SBE; [æ ~ æ•] in Sommerset-Devon and coastal Sussex; [e•ə ~ ɛ•ə] in Oxford-Warwick-Worcester-Gloucester, and beside the usual [a] in Yorkshire-Lancashire [Orton 869].

The regional variant [e•ə~ɛ•ə] is the normal reflex of ME long *ā* of the uninflected form *fader*. All other variants are derived from the ME short *a* of the inflected forms.

The normal reflexes of ME short *a* appear in English folk speech in such words as (1) *apple, hammer* and (2) *glass, bath*. The southwest of England as well as the North Midland and the North have [a ~ a•] in both sets; and so also in *father*. The eastern counties from the Thames to the Wash have [æ] in *apple, hammer* and [a•~ɑ•] in *glass, bath*. In this area *father* has the vowel of *glass, bath* and rimes with *farther*, whence also in SBE. This development of ME short *a* appears in SBE also in *rather, lather*; but *gather* has [æ]. For attempts to explain this feature see O. Jespersen [1922:308] and K. Luick [1929:708].

In AE, where *gather, lather* and—with some exceptions—*rather* have the same vowel as *ladder, matter*, the low vowel [a•~ɑ•~ɒ•~ɒ•] in *father* is exceptional. Was it imported from SBE as a prestige pronunciation? The fact that the low vowel appears in *rather* chiefly in the cultivated speech of urban centers along the Atlantic seaboard—Boston, New York City, Philadelphia, Baltimore and Charleston—suggests this possibility [PEAS: maps 72–73]. However, the radically different dissemination pattern of the low vowel in *father* is against this interpretation.

A different view of the universal currency of the low vowel in *father* seems more probable, surprising as it may seem. As pointed out above, a low vowel predominates in English folk speech from Kent to Yorkshire and westward to Devonshire, and is regular in Scotland. Why could it not survive in the American family, where it has been in daily use from the very beginning? Along the Atlantic seaboard it could be supported by SBE, but the American inland usually escapes this cultural influence. It is not unlikely that the common nursery words *pa* and *ma* favored the preservation of the low vowel in *father*.

gums

Cultivated AE agrees with SBE in having the vowel /ʌ/ of *sun* in the word *gums*, and this pronunciation also has general currency in folk speech throughout the South and the Midland. In New England, one the other hand, the vowel /u/ of *doom* predominates in folk speech and has been carried westward into Upstate New York and adjoining parts of Pennsylvania. Beside /u/, the vowel /ʊ/ of *full* is widely used in eastern New England [PEAS: 144 and map 85].

This New Englandism seems surprising. And yet, it is the /ʌ/ of SBE that is exceptional, since this word had a long close ǭ in ME (OE *gōma*) and might be expected to rime with *bloom, doom, loom*. The sixteenth century spellings *gomme, gumme* show that this deviation from the norm is of early date.

Other deviant reflexes of ME close ǭ appear in SBE *blood, flood* and *good, room*. Underlying these inconsistencies is the great regional diversity in the phonic reflexes of ME ǭ in English folk speech.

home, loam, goal

In AE the long open ǭ of ME is normally represented by the free vowel /o/ whose phonic character varies regionally from [oʊ ~ ɜʊ] to [oˑ ~ oᵊ], as in *ago, coat* [PEAS: 106 and maps 20-21].

All of these phonic reflexes of ME ǭ have their counterparts in the folk speech of England: [oˑə ~ oə] in the southern counties (Devon to Sussex) and [oʊ ~ ɜʊ] in the Home Counties (whence also in SBE). In addition, [uˑə ~ uə] is current in some of the western counties (Buckingham-Oxford-Wiltshire), [ʊᵊ] in East Anglia, [oᵊ] in the North Midland.

It is a striking fact that in AE upgliding [oʊ] predominates, although in English folk speech this phonic type is confined to a rather small area—evidence of the pervasive influence of SBE on the pronunciation of AE.

Clear survival of a regional English folk pronunciation is to be seen in the short checked vowel /ə/ of New England folk speech in such words as *coat, stone, whole*, which is in contrast with the diphthongal free /o/ of *ago, grown* [PEAS: 157-8 and map 30]. The regional and the social dissemination of checked /ə/ as well as its lexical incidence show that it is being replaced by free /o/ of *ago* [Avis 1961].

The British source of the New England /ə/ seems to be the [oᵊ] of the counties of Essex-Cambridge-Lincoln, which is phonically similar to the [ʊᵊ ~ ʊ] of Norfolk-Suffolk. The latter survives in eastern Virginia in the word *home*, in northern New England in *loam* [PEAS: maps 123-4].

Deviating from the normal reflex /o/ of ME open ǭ, the words *goal* (in children's games) and the farm word *loam* have the free vowel /u/ of *do* in the folk speech of New England and its western settlements. In *loam* /u/ occurs also in the North Midland (Pennsylvania-West Virginia) [PEAS: maps 122, 124]. The source of these deviations is apparently to be sought in the phonic reflex [uˑə ~ uə] of ME open ǭ in the counties of Buckingham-Oxford-Wiltshire.

nephew

In America *nephew* almost universally has the voiceless fricative /f/, which matches the pseudo-learned Latinate spelling *ph* (cp. Latin *nepotem*) that gradually replaced the earlier spelling *v* from the sixteenth century onward. Relics of /v/ survive only along the Atlantic coast, especially in New England, along Chesapeake Bay, in northeastern North Carolina, and in South Carolina [PEAS: 176 and map 169]. In these old and conservative areas the oral tradition is strong.

In the folk speech of England, /v/ and /f/ exhibit a remarkably clear areal pattern. The original French /v/ is universal in the south—from Kent-Essex to Hampshire-Gloucester—and greatly predominates in the northern counties, except for Lancashire and the West Riding of Yorkshire [Orton 881]. The spelling pronunciation /f/ occupies the North Midland and East Anglia and extends northward into the industrial areas of Lancashire and Yorkshire. These three separate belts of relatively uniform usage have obviously come into being since the sixteenth century.

SBE agrees with the folk speech of the southern counties of England in preserving the /v/ of Old French *neveu*, adopted c1300.

In view of this fact and the extensive currency of /v/ in the folk speech of England it is rather surprising that the spelling pronunciation /f/ has become almost universal in AE. Is *nephew* a 'book word', taught in the schools and read in the literature? If so, what is the familiar expression? Does one usually say *my brother's boy, my sister's son*?

radish

In the Eastern United States, *radish* rather generally has the vowel of *red* in folk speech, and this pronunciation is not uncommon among the middle class from Pennsylvania southward [PEAS: 140 and map 76]. On the other hand, the vowel /æ/ of *bat* is nearly universal in cultivated speech and is replacing the /ɛ/, as the social and age dissemination of the variants shows. Both pronunciations were obviously brought over from England during the settlement.

In English folk speech, *radish* has the vowel /ɛ/ in the eastern counties north of the Thames and [a ~ æ] south of it and in the southwestern counties. The boundary between the two areas is remarkably sharp, and usage within the two areas strikingly uniform.

One might expect SBE to conform to the usage of the Home Counties, but it has /æ/. The spelling with *a* in literary English from c1400 onward shows that this usage is old; but *e* spellings compete with *a* as late as c1650. John Walker's comment [1797] that 'this word is commonly, but corruptly, pronounced as if written *Reddish*' suggests that SBE usage was not yet settled in his day.

As far as AE is concerned, the gradual replacement of /ɛ/ by /æ/ in *radish* is prompted by the spelling taught in the schools rather than by SBE. In this 'homely' word the folk pronunciation with /ɛ/ will long endure.

shut

In two areas of the Eastern States *shut* has the vowel /ɛ/ of *bet* in folk speech: the South and South Midland, and northern New England [PEAS: 146 and map 90].

In English folk speech /ɛ/ predominates in the eastern counties from Middlesex-Essex to Norfolk. It occurs also with some frequency in the south-western counties. Elsewhere /ʌ/ is common, and the historically corresponding /ʊ/ is regular in the North Midland and the northern counties [Orton 995].

It is a striking fact that SBE shares the type of ME *shutten* with the North Midland and the North, thus deviating from the folk usage of the southeastern counties, which reflects the ME *shetten* of Chaucer and Gower. Was the type of *shet* abandoned in SBE because it overlapped with variants of the word for 'defecate'? The type of ME *shitten*, a normal reflex of OE *scyttan*, was apparently given up by c1600 for this very reason.

American cultivated and middle class usage fully agrees with SBE in which /ʌ/ had been fully established by 1600.

wound 'injury'

In New England folk speech, *wound* rimes with *round*, and scattered instances of /au/ occur in other parts of the Eastern States [PEAS: 156 and map 117].

In England the diphthong /au/ in *wound* is largely confined to East Anglia (Norfolk-Suffolk-Cambridge), but scattered instances occur also in the most westerly counties.

Off-hand one would be inclined to trace the New England /au/ directly to East Anglian folk speech, but the story is more complicated.

In SBE the diphthong /au/ was current in *wound* as late as the eighteenth century, when it was finally superseded by /u/. Shakespeare rimed *wound* with *round, sound* [Kökeritz 1953]. John Walker [1797] records '*woond* or *wound*' and comments as follows: 'The first pronunciation of this word, though generally received among the polite world, is certainly a capricious novelty'. After advocating the rejection of *oo* on historical grounds, he concludes: 'But where is the man bold enough to risk the imputation of vulgarity by such an expulsion?'

The emergence of the /u/ of *woo* in *wound* is indeed an anomaly in SBE. It is the only word in which /u/ occurs before /nd/, a fact that unmistakably points to importation. But what is the source? Can it be the Northern [uˑ] attested before /nd/ in *round* [Orton 978] ? Is it an adaptation of the North Midland /ʊ/ in *hundred*? One thing is clear: it has no basis in the folk speech of southern England, where ME long *ū* yields [au~æu~ɐu~əu] and ME short *u* becomes /ʌ/.

If the origin of this pronunciation in SBE remains unclear, its diffusion into the folk speech of southern England and its establishment in American English testifies to the pervasive influence of SBE. In England only conservative East Anglia and parts of Worcester-Gloucester-Devon have preserved the normal reflex [ɐu ~ əu] of ME *ū* in this word. In America conservative New England is the only area in which /au/ survives with some frequency. It is possible that East Anglian usage underlies this phenomenon.

Bibliography

Avis, W. S., "The 'New England Short o' : A Recessive Phoneme." Language 1961. 37:544–58.

Jespersen, O., *A Modern English Grammar*, part I. Heidelberg, 1909.

Jones, D., *An English Pronouncing Dictionary*. London, 1927.

Kökeritz, H., *Shakespeare's Pronunciation*. New Haven, 1953.

Kurath, H., *British Sources of Selected Features of American Pronunciation: Problems and Methods*. In Honor of Daniel Jones, ed. D. Abercrombie. London 1964. pp. 146–55.

Kurath, H., *Contributions of British Folk Speech to American Pronunciation*. Leeds Studies in English, 1970.

Kurath, H. and R.I. McDavid, Jr., *The Pronunciation of English in the Atlantic States*. Ann Arbor, 1961.

Lowman, G.S., Jr., *Sampling Survey of the Southern Counties of England*, 1936. [Collections of the LA of the USA.]

Luick, K., *Historische Grammatik der englischen Sprache*. Leipzig, 1914–29.

Orton, H. and W. J. Halliday, *Survey of English Dialects: The Six Northern Counties*. Leeds, 1962–3.

PEAS, see Kurath and McDavid.

Walker, J., *A Critical Pronouncing Dictionary and Expositor of the English Language*. London, 1797.

PRESCRIPTIVISM, PSYCHOLOGY, AND *THAT* DICTIONARY

ROSEMARY M. LAUGHLIN
Mundelein College

The 1969 Summer issue of *Horizon*, resplendent in green and gold binding with a handsome Gaugin detail on the cover, incongruously showed on one of its inside pages a cartoon where a mischievous moustached devil sat perusing *Webster's Dictionary* while a benign, sage-like angel (replete with halo) next to him contemplated *The American Heritage Dictionary*! The text accompanying the cartoon announced the appearance of *The American Heritage Dictionary*,[1] and though it was calm and rational in presenting its arguments for the prescriptive principle informing the work, there were occasional if subtle barbs against *Webster's Third New International Dictionary* (*Webster III*) that—along with the cartoon—recalled to the reader the great extended furor over lexicography and linguistics in the 1960's.

It was, in fact, early in 1962 that Dwight Macdonald issued his charge and rallying cry by paraphrasing Johnson and Shakespeare. "Things have changed," he wrote. "Lexicographers may still be drudges, but they are certainly not harmless. They have untuned the string, made a sop of the solid structure of English, and encouraged the language to eat up himself." [2] The astonishing fact was that Macdonald's accusations of anarchy, permissiveness, and nihilism on the part of the editors of *Webster III* were echoed by numerous other critics and reviewers in newspapers, popular magazines and periodicals—to such an extent that the reaction quickly became a phenomenon called the Webster War or the Webster Affair, and lasted in varying degrees of intensity for an entire decade. It remains to be seen whether the new *Heritage* will rekindle critical fires in the 1970's.

The volleys of the critics angry with *Webster III* seemed to be aimed chiefly at four things: (1) the admittance without stern restrictive labels of certain words formerly considered grammatical solecisms or slang (e.g., *hugeous, egghead, double-dome, finalize, everybody wants their lunch*), (2) a multitude of citations from mid-twentieth century personages who were not recognized authors or representatives of a cultured world (e.g., Willie

Mays, Art Linkletter, Ethel Merman), (3) failure to include encyclopedic matter (e.g., information about Mark Twain or the Virgin Mary), (4) the meaning of the publishers' motto "Supreme Authority" used by the Merriam-Webster company for over a century. Almost invariably the critics claimed that the cause of the corruption was the science of Structural Linguistics whose principles the editors held.[3]

Further details of the furor over *Webster III* will not be elaborated here since they have already been chronicled by James Sledd and Wilma Ebbitt in *Dictionaries and THAT Dictionary*.[4] Sledd and Ebbitt called the Webster Affair "one of the most striking episodes in the history of lexicography," [5] and they are right. Throughout the English-speaking world the uproar called English teachers and trainers of English teachers to an accounting for the conceptions of language they have tenaciously clung to since the eighteenth century when certain gentlemen—faced with problems of grammatical and orthographic uniformity brought by mass printing, imbued with the taste of the age for system and regularity, and convinced that the language had reached a Golden Age of perfection that must be preserved at all costs—fitted English to a Procrustean bed of Latin grammar and laid down arbitrary rules on points of speech.[6]

During the nineteenth century influential purists like Richard Grant White and Edward Sherman Gould insistently urged educated Americans to accept the concept of cultivated non-changing British English and to admit no word as standard that did not have the pedigree of British origin (Indian words such as *papoose*, *squash* etc. and borrowings from other languages were to be considered as foreign usages and preferably italicized in writing). Zealous and often linguistically insecure schoolteachers (whom Mencken irreverently dubbed "milk-maids armed with hickory sticks") did their best to put these notions into practice. If students ignored the rules in their own speech once they were out of the classroom, they at least paid lip-service to what they had been taught.[7] It took American linguists and H.L. Mencken in the twentieth century to proclaim the fresh and colorful speech of America in its infinite variety not only acceptable but desirable; but their liberal attitudes, however, trickled slowly—despite the practical work of men like Charles Fries in new grammar books—into accepted grammar on the schoolroom level where it was taught.

That *Webster III* conflicted with traditional concepts of language and sorely discomfited those who believed in them was evidenced by the heated reaction of educated men in many different fields, who wrote or read comments about the new dictionary in their professional journals. Hence, the collective reaction quickly reached the proportions of a social and psychological as well as a linguistic phenomenon. If it is to be understood as fully as possible in these three aspects it is evident that something beyond a chronicling—even one as brilliant as the Sledd and Ebbitt casebook—is needed. This essay attempts to provide at least part of a fuller understanding by presenting basically two things: (1) a view of lexicographical criticism in nineteenth and twentieth-century American magazines, newspapers and journals, in order to see whether there are underlying causes (i.e., repeated demands by critics and reviewers that the dictionary provide prescriptive language authority) that can explain the reactions in the 1960's, or whether, on the contrary, there is no clear progression toward the outbreak against *Webster III*; (2) a study of attitudes that views the critics' responses in the cultural atmosphere of the late 1950's and early 1960's, and in relation to what psychologists have discovered about personal needs for authority.

Lexicographical Criticism of the Past

To facilitate a historical survey of critical views it is convenient to divide the development of American lexicography into three periods. The first of these is from 1798 when the first American dictionary was published (by Samuel Johnson, Jr., no relation to Dr. Samuel Johnson) to 1864, the end of the first great Dictionary War. During this period the United States took the lead in English lexicography with Noah Webster's *An American Dictionary of the English Language* (first published in 1828 with revised editions in 1847 and 1864) and Joseph Worcester's *A Comprehensive Pronouncing and Explanatory Dictionary of the English Language* (first appeared in 1830, with revisions and title changes in 1835, 1846, and 1860; in 1846 it was called *A Universal and Critical Dictionary of the English Language*, and in 1860 *A Dictionary of the English Language*). The rivalry that grew between the Webster and Worcester dictionaries was initially started by the aging Webster who, fearing his reputation threatened, issued charges of plagiarism against Worcester. Publishers on both sides fanned the flames of battle by issuing pamphlets and encouraging treatment of the controversy in newspapers and journals. The different spellings and pronunciations offered and recommended by Webster and Worcester were the chief points of contention.[8] When the debate finally ended as the Civil War began, the Webster dictionaries (Merriam-Webster since 1847) were commercially victorious chiefly because the popularity of Webster's *American Spelling Book* had made the name a household word, partly because of the death of Joseph Worcester in 1865, and partly because of the merit of the Merriam product from 1864 onward.[9]

As for the general development of attitudes in lexicographical criticism, one notes first of all that the feelings of American critics towards American usages moved from dependence on Britain—particularly by veneration of Dr. Johnson's *Dictionary* in its updated editions, and of British orthoepists like Walker and Sheridan—during the first three decades to increasingly self-confident independence, especially after the appearance in 1828 of the *American Dictionary*. As independence grew stronger, the hopes of purists for an

American Academy changed from active planning to nostalgic longing. In this period, too, there was keen interest in etymological information; though Noah Webster's Tower of Babel theories were generally recognized as inaccurate, the critics were, for that, eagerly receptive to the work of the German linguists and philologists as it became known. Certainly one of the most interesting facts about the criticism of the time was that the great majority of writers were very much familiar with the tradition of English Lexicography. Nearly all of them who had reviews over a page in length summarized the history and principles of lexicography from Johnson to Webster. Whether they were liberals or purists, their knowledge of background shows that they were qualified to choose the preference they did.

The second division of time in the history of American lexicography—from 1864 to 1909—might best be called the Transition Era. While the limelight returned to England and focused on *The Oxford Dictionary* (begun in 1858, with the first volume appearing in 1884), American lexicographers were not idle. Following the trend of earlier Webster and Worcester dictionaries towards the inclusion of encyclopedic material, and utilizing the method of current popular British encyclopedic dictionaries, the great encyclopedic lexicon *The Century Dictionary* appeared in six volumes between 1889 and 1891. Funk and Wagnalls' *A Standard Dictionary of the English Language* (1893–94) and Merriam's *Webster's International Dictionary* (1890) both made their debut; along with the first modern collegiate, Merriam's *A Collegiate Dictionary* (1898) they cemented the trend towards a one-volume work crammed with cyclopedic information, and arranged and type-set for efficient utility.

In the critical reviews of these dictionaries there was general enthusiastic acceptance, with difference of opinion arising only with regard to inclusion or exclusion, as the case might be, of certain simplified spellings recommended by the Spelling Reform Association, and to occasional words where British vowels or accentuation were preferred to American alternatives. The most striking similarity the reviews have is the expression of delight that new dictionaries unallied to Worcester or Webster appeared.[10] Typical of these was the review in the *Atlantic Monthly* stating that

> the great energy displayed in the making of dictionaries and encyclopedias is having its result in an emancipation of the people from the tyranny of the dictionary. The habit has grown up in America of referring to the dictionary as final authority. . . . As long as there was only one dictionary, or at the most two, it was quite possible, as the phrase goes, to swear by Webster or by Worcester, as the case might be. But the more dictionaries there are in the field, the thinner is the film of authority, and it is not impossible that both the makers of dictionaries and the users of them will come to agree that these books are records and not rulers.[11]

The third period in the development of the American dictionary might well be called the Age of the Collegiates. To be sure, the unabridged dictionaries became bigger and better, but by 1961 necessarily quite limited to lexical information on account of the snowballing vocabulary of the twentieth century, especially in science and technology. The beginning of the period is marked by the appearance of *Webster's New International Dictionary* in 1909. Its second edition (referred to here as *Webster II*) came out in 1934, an enormous book laden with encyclopedic matter; but *Webster III* in 1961 clearly showed that the "Definitive Unabridged" must severely curtail its encyclopedic material, appendixes, and gazetteer in order to remain the single volume that the American market unqualifiedly demands.

The inclusion of encyclopedic matter was assumed in abbreviated form by the lexical newcomer of the era, the collegiate, the sophisticated successor to the countless school and spelling dictionaries of the nineteenth century.[12] With the junior collegiates, the Thorndike-Century school dictionaries, a revolutionary lexicographical achievement was made: a vocabulary based on scientific word counts called frequency lists. When the word-count technique was adapted to the senior collegiates as it quickly was, it meant that the well-educated reader would be able to find the word he wanted, and have other kinds of practical and historical information at his fingertips as well—all at a reasonable price (five to eight dollars, whereas the unabridged dictionary cost about forty).

The tone of lexicographical criticism was never more benign than during this period preceding 1961. Critical treatment of the collegiates consisted mainly in comparing the virtues of one with the others, and the unabridged works were most consistently praised for their ability to keep up-to-date in the recording of both scientific vocabulary and contemporary locutions including slang. The principle of descriptivism used by the editors was clearly understood and praised by the reviewers. Typically, in 1910, a reviewer for *Life* declared that since "words by writers like Henry James and Walter Pater find lodgment in the lexicon, so should the words of O. Henry's cowboys, if the dictionary is to be thorough and comprehensive." [13] A review in the New York *Sun* about *Webster's New International* read:

> Their [the editors'] aim has been to make the dictionary not a mere standard of literary acceptance but a register of all English terms that are in use and need to be explained. While this may put an end to the worship of the dictionary as the arbiter of what is right and wrong use, it adds immensely to its practical utility and in explaining whatever words puzzle the persons who consult it.[14]

It was a rare reviewer who did object to the principle of including current slang; in fact, I could find none in the reviews of *Webster II*.[15] There was one feature, however, that consistently received negative criticism in this period— the outmoded pronunciation keys used by Merriam and Funk and Wagnalls in their unabridged dictionaries. Kemp Malone found the height of irony in the fact that the introductory matter of *Webster II* contained a brilliant essay by J.S. Kenyon arguing the superiority of the International Phonetic Association Key, while the old confusing Merriam symbols were all that were offered in the dictionary itself.[16] But such exasperation that might be found in Malone's comments did not even remotely resemble the disgust and outrage of the later critics who clucked that "the moral permissiveness now on the wane in child-rearing, has caught up with the dictionary makers," [17] or that *like* used as a conjunction was "a symptom of general decay in values," and an indication that "we are robbing ourselves of all righteous indignation against evil." [18]

The Cultural and Psychological Aspects of Prescriptivism

Preliminary to any discussion of the vehemently expressed desires for prescriptivism as the formative principle of the largest unabridged dictionary, several statements should be made about the dictionary as prescriptive authority in the United States in the past. The first of these is that the policy of the major American lexicographers following Noah Webster[19] has been without exception to make dictionaries on descriptive principles; the influence of *The New English Dictionary* has insured that it would always remain so. This policy is stated in the preface of each dictionary. For example, there was Chauncey Goodrich's rejection of Webster's "reformed" spellings and pronunciations (except, of course, those that had achieved some degree of usage, and these were listed as variants) in the first *American Dictionary* published by the Merriam Brothers. There was William Dwight Whitney's plan in the *Century Dictionary* to present all the facts that could be ascertained about a term to the reader, who should then use the word guided by his own judgment alone. There was F. Sturgis Allen's refusal to include in the first *New International* simplified spellings insufficiently sanctioned by usage. Clarence Barnhart typified the lexicographer's attitude well when he wrote in the introduction to *The American College Dictionary*:

> No dictionary founded on the methods of modern scholarship can prescribe as to usage; it can only inform on the basis of the fact of usage. . . . It is not the function of the dictionary-maker to tell you how to speak, any more than it is the function of the map-maker to move rivers or re-arrange mountains or fill in lakes.[20]

The second conclusion is that despite the lexicographers' policy of descriptivism, for the vast majority of Americans the dictionary is regarded as the arbiter and authority of language usage. Circumstances in the United States have conspired to make and keep this so. In the first place, there has always been a mobile society from the founding of the Republic until the present; a man is free to rise to a higher socioeconomic state by virtue of his ability and ingenuity to amass money in a free-enterprise system. In any society when this mobility is possible there will be a need by people on the move[21] for an authority to define the proprieties of social behavior for the class level that has recently been achieved or that is the object of aspiration. Since pronunciation and usage of language are perhaps the most obvious and "foolproof" marks—in a way that dress is not—of social class in the United States,[22] the dictionary has become against its own nature an authority and arbiter. Furthermore, there is no language Academy in the United States to assume the role of arbiter as there is in certain countries like France, Spain, and Italy.

In the second place, the training of English teachers was cast in a mold in the eighteenth and nineteenth centuries, a mold not yet entirely broken. It was shaped by the belief that English grammar should be based on Latin grammar and by English usage rigidly patterned on points arbitrarily decided in the eighteenth century (e.g., that split infinitives, double negatives, and double superlatives ["the most unkindest cut"] were incorrect, or that there were complex grammatic distinctions between *shall* and *will*). It was a mold readily accepted in the beginning by the new training institutions and young teachers because, as in England, order and regularity were the preference and taste of the age, and also because it furnished a hold on security and certainty in a rude new country where even survival itself was often unassured on the frontier. This attitude towards grammar and usage (it might be called the mentality of authority) quickly became part of the conventional wisdom on every level of the educational structure, and conventional wisdom is one of the hardest things to relinquish in any area. In the early twentieth century this attitude was strengthened by the German scare of World War I. The use and study of German were anathema in the United States; naturally, then, American students and teachers were not exposed as a result of study to the more liberal attitudes of German linguists and grammarians towards language. The modern foreign languages primarily taught in the schools were French, Italian, and Spanish; these were languages that had Academies. Those who studied them became used to the idea of an ultimate language arbiter; if they studied beyond the elementary level they became aware that the dictionaries they used were prescribed by the Academy.[23] It was easy and natural, then, to think of English dictionaries as having the same kind of authority; and because courses on the history and structure of English were rarely required, students and prospective teachers were left unaware of the differences in the natures of English and the Romance languages with Academies. The teachers perpetuated their notions by passing them on to their students. Just several years before the outbreak of the critics against *Webster III*, James Hulbert confirmed this when he stated:

> What I am trying to get at is that throughout our school life and to some extent afterwards, we are so constantly being impressed with the idea of correctness, primarily in spelling (for the irregularities of spelling compel everyone to work at that intensely and for a long time), but also in grammar and pronunciation, that we are likely to feel that all aspects of English are hedged about with rules of right and wrong.[24]

A third reason for the dictionary's image of prescriptive authority for the American people goes back to the middle of the nineteenth century when the heated Webster-Worcester controversy polarized feelings and forced people to take sides. The prevailing attitude was that if Webster was correct then Worcester wasn't, and vice versa; in short, what most people wanted settled for them was merely "Who is the best Authority?" Webster ultimately won; it was not only his dictionary but his *American Spelling Book*, ubiquitous and familiar, that enabled the aura of authority to settle upon his name. The Merriam Company quickly capitalized on the association of authority with their product by adopting the motto "The Supreme Authority" for advertising purposes. Furthermore, it was not long before other dictionary-makers by the score were trying to cash in on that association by using "Webster" somehow in the titles of their works.

The third major statement or conclusion is a startling one in view of what has just been said. It is that despite the very strong belief in the dictionary as prescriptive authority on the part of the majority of people in the United States, there has been a general development in the attitudes of dictionary reviewers and critics towards an understanding and acceptance of the descriptive nature of the dictionary. The record from 1798 to 1961, very briefly capsuled here but fully documented elsewhere,[25] is the basis for this statement. It can be inferred that perhaps one of the most logical reasons for this is that the majority of reviewers were responsible critics who made sure that they knew something of the history and nature of lexicography before they presumed to judge the particular work at hand. As has already been noted, the familiarity of the great majority of nineteenth-century critics with the history of lexicography was strikingly apparent from summaries that were almost invariably included for the benefit of the reader. And in the first Dictionary War, as long as Noah Webster was inculcating his reforms, the serious reviewers in the established periodicals (as opposed to the inflammatory pamphleteers and newspaper journalists) favored Worcester precisely because he attempted to follow descriptive principles rather than private theories.

Using these statements or conclusions, then, as a basis, an answer can be made to the question initially posed in this essay: Is there a progression in American lexicographical criticism of the past towards the outbreak made by many critics against *Webster III* in 1961? The answer is No. Why then did the critics manifest such a cry for authority? If we assume that like their predecessors they were responsible men who inquired into the history and nature of lexicography (though perhaps we cannot assume this)[26] before they made their judgments, we must look to other sociological and psychological causes. Several penetrating analyses have explored these aspects of the outburst.

James Sledd saw the phenomenon of the fear of linguistic corruption recurring yet another time in history. "The scenario never changes," he remarked, "only the names of the actors; and the alarmists never learn, from the massive stability of the central structure of the language, that the causes of their alarm are insignificant. In retrospect their fears and forebodings are gorgeously absurd." Having established a historical (and perhaps somewhat mythic) perspective, Sledd put the present phenomenon even more specifically into place:

> An articulate minority of phony conservatives, already in flight from a disturbing present to an irrecoverable past, began to shout about the dictionary as they ran. The mob followed, and the American tradition was vindicated by the symbolic burning of a book and the lynching of its editors.
>
> To argue this hypothesis, a little history is needed. The folk beliefs that made the lynching possible, the ordinary American's ideas about English, were planted early and planted deeply. They were established in the eighteenth and nineteenth centuries by statesmen as well as teachers, and they were perpetuated no more by schoolmarms than by social pressure. The damnation of the *Third International*, one might argue, was foreordained in the lost childhood of the Republic. . . .[27]

Like Sledd, Albert Marckwardt saw the *Webster III* affair as having roots in the past. He stressed the point made earlier that "the concept of lexicographer as linguistic legislator or arbiter, if not absolute dictator, is still strong in the United States." Marckwardt attributed a good deal of the blame for the perpetuation of this conception to the Merriam Company which used the words "Supreme Authority" as their motto. He also blamed the educators whose failures he described as "a sad commentary on how inadequately the dictionary has been presented in the English classrooms of the nation, and how insufficiently English teachers are informed about one of the principal tools of their profession." Finally Marckwardt felt that there had been several unfortunate misunderstandings. One was "the mistaken notion that *Webster III* represents a change in lexicographical principle, an error fostered ironically by more complete coverage and greater accuracy of the editor"; another was that "the excision of certain kinds of non-essential material—Gazetteer, Biographical Titles of Works of Art, Names of Fictional Characters, Mottoes, Proverbs, Names of Battles, Organizations, Cities and States—caused alarm because it evidently represented a sudden departure from Time-Honored Practice." [28]

Even more than Marckwardt, Karl Dykema blamed educators in their academic ivory towers. He called their perpetuation of obsolete conceptions cultural lag. Even though the reviewers who caused the storm were not linguists, he said, they should have known better simply as college English or journalism majors, or even as college graduates, no matter what the major. The fact that they did not understand the descriptive nature of lexicography reflected extremely inadequate knowledge, if any at all, about the history and structure of the English language. "It is only too clearly the fault of the whole academic profession, with indictment falling most heavily on those in English. . . . The men who are responsible for the views in the popular press are, we may assume, the products of our universities, where none of them can have escaped contact with the English departments. Their attitudes towards language are fixed there. If they are Medieval, rigid, and Philistine, and occasionally hysterical, the colleges must blame themselves." [29]

Along other lines, Walter Ong, S.J., saw in the conflict over *Webster III* the forces of a new "oral-aural culture" at odds with an older "alphabetical culture." Preceding lexicographers, he said, even the descriptive ones

> took as their norm for usage the practice of persons in the community who were more or less professional or semi-professional *writers*. Oral influence was discounted. The new *Webster III* reverses this stand. As never before, what falls on the *ear* is recorded; pronunciation variants, words chiefly heard, seldom written. . . . *Webster III* represents the breakthrough to a more oral-aural culture which marks our day, characterized by electronic media of communication: telephone, radio, t.v. and the beep-beep of orbiting space-craft. . . . It is this breakthrough from quiescent to vibrant, temporarily fluid sound which, I believe, constitutes the most deep-seated source of anxiety in reactions to *Webster III*. Space is the great symbol of order and its primacy is now being compromised. The alphabet and print had made language as never before an instrument of constraint rather than openness, and therefore reorganized man's life world. . . . The alphabetically conditioned psyche, in other words, is terrorized by the fact that *Webster III* has abandoned the solid world of space for the uncertainties of time.[30]

Father Ong's theory was one that took account of a broad cultural movement. Raven I. McDavid, Jr., has called attention to a specific event in that movement that had a very significant bearing on the Webster affair, and he referred to other aspects that have already been touched on:

> One part of the climate of opinion in which *Webster III* appeared was the sputnik shock. Till 1957, despite the evidence of Russian tanks and artillery aircraft in World War II and Korea, Americans had been accustomed to laugh at the idea that a Communist country could outstrip us in scientific or technological achievement; even the Soviet achievements in nuclear weap-ons had been brushed off as due to German captives or defectors from the West. But the successful launching of a satellite (and the well-published failure of the first U.S. attempt) produced something like a panic from which we have not yet recovered. We sought an explanation for our discomfit in the inadequacies of our educational system; we have engaged in agonizing re-appraisals (admittedly long overdue) of the standards of elementary and high school education; we have become more conscious of standards than even before. In view of the lack of public awareness of the nature of lin-guistics or of language behavior, it was not unnatural that in English the maintenance of standards would be properly equated with an enforcement of the touchstone of "good English" as outlined in the usual school grammars—whether or not these touchstones (such as rules for *shall* and *will*, exposed by Fries as far back as 1925) have ever had any correlation with the actual usage of educated Englishmen and Americans. The Americans, notably the Amer-ican schoolteacher, had little opportunity to acquire a more sophisticated philosophy of language than that represented by these school grammars. He was nervously aware of certain linguistic practices as possible touchstones of his escape from an underprivileged environment, and was likely to resent any suggestions that these touchstones were of no value.[31]

McDavid's article is the most comprehensive analysis to date of the causes of the *Webster III* phenomenon. Because it was written as a report for the new publishers of *Webster III*, it is unfortunately unpublished as yet and unavailable. In it McDavid discussed in detail (1) certain technical aspects of *Webster III* that antagonized the critics, and (2) the problems in the relationships of the Merriam advertising men not only with the public but with the dictionary editors. McDavid contends that they have been responsible for many of the misunderstandings that resulted in the furor.

The analyses made by Professors Sledd, Marckwardt, Dykema, Ong, and McDavid substantiate many of the sociological, cultural, and even political factors that prepared the critics psychologically for their vehement reactions. These factors and the nature of the criticism itself seemed to suggest to me that there might be as well certain personality needs for authoritarian standards in the critics favoring prescriptive dictionaries. Work in the psychology of personality has described a general personality pattern or syndrome of *authoritarianism*, in which a person has a strong need for definite standards in all areas.[32] Thus the preference for a prescriptive dictionary expressed by critics may reflect a larger personality pattern. If this is true, there should be a relationship (a positive correlation) between a test developed to measure the psychological syndrome of authoritarianism and an expressed preference for prescriptivism. To test this hypothesis empirically, I combined a standard authoritarian measure (the California F-Scale) with a questionnaire developed by myself to determine preference (descriptive or prescriptive) towards dictionaries; the combined measures were then given to 105 subjects divided for purpose of analysis relevant to the *Webster III* situation into three groups—educators, non-educators, and students.

The description of the contents, methods, and statistical results of this "Authoritarian Personality–Dictionary Attitudes Study" are given *in toto* in the following appendix. But what can significantly be said here is that the hypothesis tested proved to be correct. *There was indeed a statistically strong relationship between the psychological personality variable of authoritarianism and a preference for a prescriptive dictionary.* What this means with relation to the rest of this essay is that the personality factor of authoritarianism—present in a person for any number of reasons related to his past—*can* significantly influence a critic's judgment of a particular dictionary. To what extent this factor operated in the *Webster III* critics cannot be exactly determined. It seems safe to infer, however, that if there is a familiarity on the part of the critic with the history and nature of lexicography and the English language, he will be more inclined to base his judgment on this knowledge rather than on his personality needs—or so tendencies displayed in American lexicographical criticism prior to 1961 seem to prove.

To conclude it remains only to summarize briefly what the purpose of this essay has been—an effort to understand at least part of the complexity of attitude, time, environment, and education that all played in the controversy over *Webster's Third New International Dictionary*. To do this I have presented in capsule form the attitudes of past American critics and analyzed their tendencies and developments. I have ended by relating this survey to other parts of the social and psychological milieu of one of history's greatest verbal battles about words.

Appendix
A DESCRIPTION OF THE METHODS AND RESULTS OF "THE AUTHORITARIAN PERSONALITY—PRESCRIPTIVE DICTIONARY PREFERENCE STUDY"

Hypothesis

In attempting to understand the psychological aspects of the outcry for authority made by the critics of *Webster III*, the hypothesis was made that the preference for a prescriptive dictionary expressed by some critics may reflect a larger personality pattern that social psychologists refer to as the syndrome of "authoritarianism." If this is true, there should be a positive correlation between personality scales developed to measure the psychological syndrome of authoritarianism and the preference for a prescriptive dictionary. To test this hypothesis, the California F-Scale of Authoritarianism was correlated with a scale of attitudes towards dictionaries developed by myself.

The California F-Scale

After World War II a group of psychologists at the University of California proposed a theory of the "Authoritarian Personality." According to the theory, authoritarianism is a basic personality trait, pattern, or dimension, like introversion or anxiousness. The trait was measured by an attitude scale (called the California F-Scale) consisting of twenty-seven items with which a person would agree or disagree on a six-point scale. These items covered a large number of areas, such as child-raising practices, obedience to authority, superstition, rejection of groups other than one's own, economic and political conservatism, etc. All of the items correlated positively with each other, so that a given person would tend to agree or disagree with the various items to a comparable degree. This pattern of agreement or disagreement was considered a measure of the general personality trait of high or low authoritarianism.[33] Later studies further validated the F-Scale by relating it to other personality variables and psychological processes.[34] Subjects taking the test were asked to indicate their agreement or disagreement with each statement by placing a number in front of the statement according to this key:

+3 strong support, agreement
+2 moderate support, agreement
+1 slight support, agreement
−1 slight opposition, disagreement
−2 moderate opposition, disagreement
−3 strong opposition, disagreement

The Dictionary Questionnaire

These questions were designed by myself to reveal the subject's preference for a prescriptive or descriptive dictionary by testing his atittudes towards (1) the basic purpose of a dictionary, (2) an Academy like the Académie Française to act as language arbiter, (3) certain words that had been particularly criticized for their presence or particular label in *Webster III*, (4) kinds of pronunciation description offered in the dictionary. The questions were stated in both positive and negative forms to balance what psychologists call the "acquiesence response set," that is, the tendency of people to agree with statements that are presented in a positive form; and the same plus-or-minus, one-to-three scale was used to register agreement or disagreement as in the F-Scale. This is the questionnaire:

1. This is not an acceptable dictionary description: "*Ain't*: though disapproved by many, and more common in uneducated speech, is used orally in most parts of the U.S. by many cultivated speakers."
2. A Dictionary is primarily responsible to provide a body of pure words for a consulting public that wishes a norm for correct speech.
3. A Dictionary should not try to tell people how to speak. It should not be based on the notions of correctness and superiority. It should not be prescriptive but descriptive.
4. There should be an American Academy (comparable to the French Academy) to arbitrate language usage, so that Americans will have a reliable authority for correct speech.
5. There should be both prescriptive dictionaries and an American Academy as language authorities.
6. The word *puff* as a verb meaning "to praise extravagantly" (e.g., as Willie Mays uses it: "Hit too many homers and people start puffing you up.") should not be labelled as "Standard English."
7. The word *goof* used as a verb (e.g., as President Eisenhower used it: "Somebody goofed.") should be labelled as "Standard English."
8. The word *fink* should be included in the dictionary.
9. The word *finalize* should not be included in the dictionary.
10. The word *goof* as a noun should be labelled as "Standard English" (e.g., "That fellow is a goof.").

11. The word *lousy* as an adjective should not be labelled as "Standard English."
12. General De Gaulle should not worry that too many American words are creeping into the French language (e.g., *le barman, le parking, le hot dog, le bar-bee-cue*).
13. A sophisticated reader is as good a judge of general dictionaries for public use as a trained linguist.
14. You are not competent to examine several dictionaries and make a judgment of which is best.
15. The use of French words lends a tone of refinement and breeding to a conversation (e.g., *tête-à-tête, de rigeur, carte blanche*).
16. A dictionary should state as many alternative pronunciations as possible of a given word.

It was decided that the first question concerning the labelling of *ain't* would be analyzed separately since it had been for so long the symbol of "bad grammar," and a person generally in agreement with descriptive principles might balk at a "liberal" label for *ain't*. The separate tabulation proved interesting, as will be seen in the paragraph on the results.

Subjects

There were 105 subjects in all, divided into three groups for meaningful analysis: (1) Educators, those who have apparently been perpetuating notions of prescriptivism, (2) Students, those whose academic training, hence the formation of their conceptions of language, is still in progress, and (3) Non-educators, the group into which the critics would fall. The Educators were evenly distributed on elementary, secondary, and college levels; with a few exceptions they were from Hardy Preparatory School for Boys, Chicago; Woodlands Academy for Girls, Lake Forest; Loyola University, Chicago; and the University of Nebraska. The Non-educators were for the most part employees of Cook Electric Company, Morton Grove, and their spouses; these were engineers, lawyers, contract administrators, book-keepers, secretaries, public relations men, and housewives. The Students were juniors and seniors at Loyola University.

Results

The first table gives the means of the average scores of the three groups on the two tests and on the *ain't* item which was scored separately. All three groups are negative, which signifies that the personalities involved are more "non-authoritarian" than "authoritarian." But there *is* a moderate difference between group means. The Educators are the most liberal or least authoritarian (−33.68), followed closely by the Students (−30.75), while the Non-educators trail considerable behind (−14.57). There are rather small differences (note the possible range) in reactions to the dictionary questions and fairly large differences in scores recording reaction to the *ain't* item. But the most important thing is the relationship of correlation of the dictionary and *ain't* scores with the authoritarian personality score.

TABLE OF MEANS

Group	Authoritarianism	Dictionary	Ain't
24 Students	−30.75	−3.12	−.46
37 Non-Educators	−14.57	−2.68	−.89
44 Educators	−33.68	−6.77	−.34
105 Total	−26.28	−4.50	−.54
Possible Range	−84 to +84	−45 to +45	−3 to +3

Let us look at the relationship of the *ain't* item with the authoritarianism test first. With the students it is not quite a statistically significant relationship (See table on following page), but tends toward it (.33 when .39 is needed); what this means is that the more authoritarian student tends to object to a liberal description of *ain't*, but not quite to the point that can be called statistically significant. Very strangely—and inexplicably, to me anyway—with the Educators the correlation is *negative* (and non-significant). *But the relationship (.42 when only .33 was needed) is very significant with the Non-educator group, the group into which the reviewers would fall who condemned Webster III's verbatim description of that word.*

Now let us look at the findings of the major relationship. With the Loyola Students there is not a significant correlation between degree of authoritarianism and preference for a prescriptive dictionary (.23 when .39 was needed for significance) although there is a trend. With the Non-educators the relationship is not quite significant, but very close (.29 when .33 was needed). With the Educators the relationship is indeed significant (.50 when .30 was needed)!

The major result is found in the composite subjects, and it is a statistically significant relationship (.47) that statisticians would term "fairly strong." We can understand better what this means if we look at several other established correlations. The correlation, for example, between I.Q. and college Quality Point Average is about .45 or .50, so the strength of the authoritarian personality–prescriptive dictionary preference is comparable to it. Typical correlations between various psychological variables and the F-Scale are about .20 to .30, so the relationship discovered by this study is considerably stronger.

There are two inferences I would like to make from the major results of the study just described. The first is that the very strong relationship in the Educators between the degree of authoritarianism and preference for a prescripive dictionary seems to bear out the point that there is a lack of understanding about the descriptive nature of a dictionary on the part of teachers

TABLE OF CORRELATIONS[1]

Group	Authoritarian-Dictionary	Authoritarian-*Ain't*	Statistical Critical Value[2]
24 Students	.23	.33	.39
37 Non-educators	.29	.42	.33
44 Educators	.50	−.20	.30
105 Total	.47	.28	.20

[1] *Correlation*: how two variables co-relate or vary together. The highest possible statistical relationship is + or −1.00. No relationship at all is .00. If one variable increases as the other increases, the correlation is *positive*, e.g., height and weight. The higher the correlation the stronger the relationship. If one variable increases as the other decreases, the correlation is *negative*, e.g., number of years of education and hours spent playing pinball. If no relationship at all exists, correlation is .00, e.g., grade on a test with the number of freckles on your nose.

[2] *Statistical Critical Value*: the value a correlation must exceed to indicate a significant relationship, the point between .00 (no relationship) and 1.00 (perfect relationship). Note that the size of the correlation necessary to show a significant relationship *decreases* as the number of persons increases. This is because we can be more certain that a larger sized group contains more representative people rather than unusual ones. For example, if you had only one person, he could be anything by chance.

(most of the educators who served as subjects for this study were language teachers); the strength of the relationship also seems to indicate that when they teach attitudes and conceptions of language they fall back on basic personality needs. The critics of *Webster III* may have done precisely the same thing; for the significant conclusion of this study is that *there is a statistically significant, fairly strong relationship between the psychological personality variable of authoritarianism and preference for a prescriptive dictionary.*

Notes

1. Morris Bishop, "So To Speak," *Horizon*, X (Summer, 1969), 44–47.

2. Dwight Macdonald, "The String Untuned," *New Yorker*, XXXVIII (March 10, 1962), 160.

3. See Philip Babcock Gove, "Linguistic Advances and Lexicography," *Word Study*, October, 1961, pp. 3–8. Here Dr. Gove has stated that the "five basic concepts of language behavior" the critics attacked *ad nauseam* are: (1) Language changes constantly, (2) Change is normal, (3) Spoken language is the language, (4) Correctness rests upon usage, (5) All usage is relative.

4. James Sledd and Wilma R. Ebbitt, *Dictionaries and THAT Dictionary* (Chicago, 1962).

5. *Ibid.*, p. v.

6. Albert C. Baugh, *A History of the English Language* (2d ed.; New York, 1957), pp. 306–55.

7. Upon being revealed as an English teacher to a member of the working class, I am no longer amazed when he invariably says, "Gosh, guess I'll have to watch my language," or "I wish you could learn me some good English." At the risk of

abusing a proverb I must add, "Scratch a janitor and you'll find a prescriptivist"—
at least in principle.

8. The best accounts of the Dictionary War are found in Eva Burkett, "A Study of American Dictionaries of the English Language before 1861" (unpublished Ph.D. dissertation, George Peabody College for Teachers, 1936), and Joseph H. Friend, *The Development of American Lexicography 1798–1864*, Janua Linguarum Series Practica, Vol. XXXVII (The Hague, 1967). The linguistic theories of Noah Webster, especially as they took specific forms in his *American Dictionary* in spellings, etymologies, and pronunciations, are brilliantly described and analyzed by Joseph Friend in *The Development of American Lexicography*. Detailed recounting of the lexicographical criticism of this period and following periods is found in Rosemary Laughlin, "The American with his Dictionary: A Historical Survey of Lexicographical Criticism in the United States" (unpublished Ph.D. dissertation, University of Chicago, 1968).

9. Harold Whitehall, "The English Language," *Webster's New World Dictionary of the American Language* (college edition; New York, 1960), xxxiii.

10. However, the voice of the purist had not yet disappeared from the land. Richard Grant White was still outspoken, especially devoting himself to condemnation of Bartlett's *Dictionary of Americanisms* in a series of essays in the *Atlantic Monthly* during 1877–78. Nor had the desire for an Academy died. One N.A. Campbell, "Protection for Our Language," *North American Review*, CXLIX (July, 1889), 127–28, submitted a plan which called for one member from "every first class college or university" to establish a standard of orthography and pronunciation. Such an organization would finally encourage England "to join hands" with it. Campbell did not say how an institution would be judged as "first class."

11. "*The Century Dictionary,*" *Atlantic Monthly*, LXIV (December, 1889), 846. It is interesting to compare this attitude with another expressed by Wilson Follett in the *Atlantic*, CCIX (June, 1962), p. 77, entitled "Sabotage in Springfield," with reference to *Webster III*: "The rock-bottom practical truth is that the lexicographer cannot abrogate his authority if he wants to. He may think of himself as a detached scientist reporting the facts of language, declining to recommend use of anything or abstention from anything; but the myriad consultants of his work are not going to see him so. . . . The fact that the compilers disclaim authority and piously refrain from judgments is meaningless; the work itself, by virtue of its inclusion and exclusions, its mere existence, is a whole universe of judgments, received by millions as the Word from on high."

12. The major collegiates comprise the various editions of Merriam's *Webster's Collegiate* (1898, 1910, 1916, 1931, 1936, and 1949 when it became the *New Collegiate*), Funk and Wagnalls' *College Standard* (1922, and 1947 when it revised title to the *New College Standard*), Random House's *American College Dictionary* (1947), World's *Webster's New World Collegiate* (1953), and Doubleday's *Thorndike-Barnhart Comprehensive Desk Dictionary* (1951). The Thorndike-Century school series appeared between 1935 and 1945.

13. "The Literary Zoo," *Life*, New York Edition (January 29, 1910), 180.

14. New York *Sun*, October 10, 1909.

15. For more lengthy coverage of the criticism of this period see Rosemary M. Laughlin, "The Predecessors of THAT Dictionary," *American Speech*, XLII (May, 1967), 105–14.

16. Kemp Malone, "Some Linguistic Studies of 1933 and 1934," *Modern Language Notes*, L (December, 1935), 515.

17. David M. Glixon, "One Hundred Thousand Words More," *Saturday Review*, XLIV (September 30, 1961), 19. One of the chief reasons given for the "new permissiveness" attributed to *Webster III* was the disappearance of status labels that

had been in *Webster* II. Actually, only *illiterate* and *colloquial* were removed; two more precise (but evidently more objectionable to the critics) labels replaced them—*substandard* and *nonstandard*. See *Webster III*, p. 18A for explanations.

18. Sidney J. Harris, "Good English Ain't What We Thought," *Chicago Daily News*, October 20, 1961, Section 1, p. 10.

19. Noah Webster himself followed prescriptive principles. In the Preface to the 1828 *American Dictionary* he stated: "It has been my aim in this work . . . to ascertain the true principles of the language in its orthography and structure; to purify it from some palpable errors, and reduce the number of its anomalies, thus giving it more regularity and consistency in its forms, both of words and sentences; and in this manner, to furnish a standard of our vernacular tongue, which we shall not be ashamed to bequeath to three hundred millions of people. . . ."

20. Clarence Barnhart, "General Introduction," *American College Dictionary* (New York, 1947), p. lx.

21. One of the best indicators of the upward mobility of classes is more widespread education, since there is a positive correlation between years of education and amount of income. According to the *U.S. Book of Fact, Statistics and Information for 1968* published by the Census Bureau, the 16.8% of high school graduates in 1920 has soared to 71.9% in 1965. The proportion of persons between the ages of 18 and 21 attending college in 1920 was 8.09%; in 1967 40% of the 18–21 year-olds were in college.

22. In countries where social classes are strictly defined and limited, such as England until very recent years, this is not so. A title is the mark of social class that guarantees acceptance and toleration. The eccentricities of ladies and baronets in the novels of Jane Austen and Charles Dickens were tolerated without question by the equally cultured but untitled characters. Even today Lord Harlech's daughters may be as "mod" or "hip" as they wish, but they are still deferred to as "The Honorables."

The difference in the situation found in the United States is exemplified in *The Rise of Silas Lapham*; though Lapham had a large fortune and a new home in the fashionable section of town, he and his family were not readily accepted by the society to which Silas aspired because of his countrified speech and behavior. In many American college fraternities it would not be uncommon for a bright young man to be refused membership because his speech betrays the accents of an ethnic working-class background.

One final example might be in order, from a country where class mobility has recently become possible after the "Economic Miracle" following World War II—West Germany. The *New York Times* published this account of attitudes towards speech:

> The discovery that many Bavarians, Rhinelanders, and Swabians are no longer proud of their rich, local dialects was made recently by a West German social research institute. The Allensbach Institute of Demography reported that more and more Germans consider it "socially degrading" to continue using their native brands of Goethe's language.
>
> Asked why they prefer words their elders would barely have understood, most Bavarians and Swabians told the pollsters that they merely wanted to speak "as most do." Many described their local idiom as uncouth and back-woodish.
>
> West German psychologists attribute the decline in use of dialect to a widespread wish to avoid easy recognition as Rhinelander, Bavarian, or inhabitant of Hamburg. Traditional cliches have it that Rhinelanders are untrustworthy, Bavarians pigheaded, and Hamburg's people anti-social and stiff. "Dialects Are

Losing Favor Among West Germans," *New York Times*, July 10, 1968, Sec. 1, p. 4.

23. Raven I. McDavid, Jr., "Herakles in Ellis," unpublished report prepared for the Britannica Company (the new owners of the Merriam Company), made available to me in a seminar on lexicography at the University of Chicago. More than a century earlier Dean Trench noted—after he had declared the dictionary to be "an objective inventory of language"—that "There is a constant confusion here in men's minds. They conceive of a Dictionary as though it has this function, to be a standard of the language; and the pretensions to be this which the Dictionary of the French Academy sets up, may have helped this confusion." *On Some Deficiencies in Our English Dictionaries* (London, 1857), p. 5.

24. James Hulbert, *Dictionaries British and American* (London, 1955), p. 101.

25. Laughlin, "The American with his Dictionary."

26. Some of them patently did not have their historical facts straight. The reviewer for *Business Week* ("Webster's Way-Out Dictionary," September 16, 1961, p. 89) wrote: "Since Dr. Johnson published his famed lexicon in 1755, dictionaries have been mostly prescriptive—establishing what is right in meaning and pronunciation."

27. James Sledd, "Lynching the Lexicographers," *Symposium on Language and Culture*, Publications of the American Ethnological Association, XI (September, 1961), 69–95.

28. Albert Marckwardt, "Dictionaries and the English," *English Journal*, LII (May, 1963), 336–45.

29. Karl Dykema, "Cultural Lag and the Reviewers of *Webster III*," *AAUP Bulletin*, XLIX (Winter, 1963), 364–69.

30. Walter Ong, S.J., "Hostility, Literacy and *Webster III*," *College English*, XXVI (November, 1964), 106–11.

31. Raven, I. McDavid, Jr., "Herakles in Ellis."

32. Roger Brown, *Social Psychology* (New York, 1965); T. Adorno, *et al.*, *The Authoritarian Personality* (New York, 1950); R. Christie and M. Jahoda, *Studies in the Scope and Method of "The Authoritarian Personality"* (Glencoe, 1954).

33. The F-Scale cannot be reprinted here, but can be found by anyone who wishes in T.W. Adorno, E. Frenkel-Brunswick, D.J. Levinson, and R.N. Sanford, *The Authoritarian Personality* (New York, 1950).

34. R. Christie and M. Jahoda, *Studies in the Method and Scope of the Authoritarian Personality* (Glencoe, 1954).

LACTANTIUS AND *BEOWULF*

DONALD W. LEE
University of Houston

The thesis of this introductory paper is that Lactantius' *Institutes* (*Divinae institutions*), particularly Book II of that work, was more or less constantly in the mind of the *Beowulf* poet during the composition of his ll. 86–183, that Lactantius' wording directly influenced many of these lines, and that some seeming difficulties and contradictions may be readily explained and clarified by considering the thought of Lactantius.[1]

In a paper with such a thesis it would be more or less standard procedure early to indicate that the *Beowulf* poet might have had access to the work of Lactantius. Alcuin's catalog of the York Library mentions him:

Quid Fortunatus, vel quid Lactantius edunt.

Ogilvy mentions that Aldhelm quotes from Lactantius and that Bede may have taken the idea of *Weltwoche* from the *Institutes*. Lactantius may or may not have written the Latin poem that served as source for the Anglo-Saxon *Phoenix*. This is probably enough to indicate that an eighth-century Anglo-Saxon poet might have had the opportunity to study Lactantius.[2]

Let us turn our attention first to ll. 90–98, given in Klaeber's edition as follows:

> Sægde sē þe cūþe
> frumsceaft fīra   feorran reccan,
> cwæð þæt se Ælmihtiga   eorðan worh(te),
> wlitebeorhtne wang,   swā wæter bebūgeð,
> gessette sigehrēþig   sunnan ond mōnan
> lēoman tō lēohte   landbūendum,
> ond gefrætwade   foldan scēatas
> leomum ond lēafum,   līf ēac gesceōp
> cynna gehwylcum   þāra ðe cwice hwyrfaþ.

These lines are so frequently explained as a recollection or quick epitome of the Caedmonian poems (and perhaps other similar works) that it seems rash to suggest another explanation. But the writer of this paper believes that it may be feasibly suggested that instead these lines recollect and echo Lactantius' rhapsodic passages about the creation of the world. In seeking to induce his readers to turn from idols—man-made creatures—and to recognize or "know" God as the creator of all of this wonderful world, Lactantius begins chapter 5 of his book II as follows:

> How much more correct it is, therefore, to disregard insensible and vain images and to turn the eyes to where is the seat, to where is the abode of the true God! He is the God who supports the earth, who has adorned the sky with gleaming stars, who has illuminated the sun—a most brilliant light for human affairs and a singular witness unto. His one majesty—who has spread the seas about the lands, who has charged the rivers to flow with everlasting roll, and who "did order the plains to stretch out and the valleys to subside, the woods to be covered with foliage and the rocky mountains to arise." [The quotation is from Ovid.] Surely not Jupiter, he who was born one thousand seven hundred years ago, did all these things, but rather "That maker of things, cause of a better world," who is called God, whose beginning since it cannot be comprehended ought not to be even sought. It is enough for man, until full and perfect wisdom, if he understand that that maker is God. Of this understanding the highest power is this, that it look up to and honor the common parent of the human race and the maker of wonderful things. Whence do certain people of blunt and dull heart adore the elements, things which have been made and which lack sensibility, as though they were gods? It is because, when they gazed in wonder at the works of God, namely: the sky with its various lights, the earth with its plains and mountains, the sea and rivers, lakes, and springs, struck dumb with admiration at these things, and forgetting their very Maker whom they were not able to see, they began to venerate and worship His works.[3]

This passage of course contains many of the details of the *Beowulf* lines quoted above. Some details not mentioned in the passage above—along with other matters relevant to *Beowulf*—occur in the first paragraph of chapter 9, about twenty-five pages later:

> Now, since we have refuted those who hold opinions contrary to the truth concerning the world and God, its Maker, we shall return to the divine workmanship of the world which is handed down in the hidden writings of holy religion. God made the heavens first of all and suspended them high above because His abode, the throne of God the Creator, was there. Then he established the earth and placed it under the sky, as the habitation of man with the other kinds of animals. He wished it to be surrounded and held in by moisture. He adorned his dwelling place and filled it with bright lights, the brilliant ornaments that are the sun, the gleaming disc of the moon, and the shining stars. Darkness, however, the opposite of these, He settled upon the earth; for it contains nothing of light of itself except what is received from the heavens where He put perennial light, the heavenly spirits, and perpetual life. Then again, in the earth He placed darkness and the infernal beings and death, and these are as far removed from those higher ones as evil is from good and vices from virtues.[4]

These two longer passages are, then, suggested as sources for most of the thoughts in ll. 90–98 of *Beowulf*. There are in addition a number of shorter passages in Book II of the *Institutes* that may be adduced as relevant and that may supply details missing from the long passages. L. 91A ("frumsceaft fíra") may perhaps be connected with Lactantius' chapter 2. In rebuking man for worship of idols, Lactantius says, "with an origin from heaven they adore lifeless things" and "You look directly upon the heavens to the sight of which that Artificer, your God, has aroused you. He gave you an erect bearing; you bend yourselves down to the earth." In discussing the stars in chapter 5 shortly after the first long paragraph quoted above, Lactantius says, "There is in the stars, therefore, a plan, arranged for the completing of their courses of motion, but it is the plan of God who made and directs all things. . . ." Chapter 5 likewise stresses that ". . . from the beginning the same God made man who made also the world," attacks the idea that either the world itself or man himself could be considered God or a god, and then continues as follows:

> And, contrariwise, if the world is a god, too, and its parts surely immortal, then man is a god, too, because he is part of the world, as you say. If man, then beasts of burden and cattle and the other kinds of beasts and birds and fishes, since these, too, feel or sense in the same way and are parts of the world. This is tolerable; for the Egyptians worship even these things. But the matter reaches such a point that frogs and mosquitoes and ants seem to be gods. . . .

It does not seem rash to suggest that this passage could underlie lines 97B and 98 of *Beowulf*.[5]

Does all this cast any light on 1. 90B—*sægde sē þe cūþe*? This half line is sometimes taken to refer to any competent poet or perhaps some one particular competent poet who sang of the creation. Could the author of *Beowulf* have had Lactantius in mind? Perhaps. If we read 90B-98 as a unit by itself this is possible enough. If, however, we read the *scopes* of 90A as referring to the same person as *sē þe cūþe* some of us may have momentary difficulties; reading the work of Lactantius today, some of us may find it a bit pedestrian, and we may wonder about the applicability of the wording *swutol sang*. But in the early medieval period Lactantius did have a reputation for lyricism.[6] But on the other hand if the *Beowulf* author had in mind Lactantius as the author of *De Ave Phoenice* in 90A and as the author of the *Institutes* in 90B— no great break in thought after all—then maybe both parts of line 90 may be read as referring to Lactantius. If, however, the author was not thinking of Lactantius he may well have been thinking in connection with line 90B of Virgil and his references to the creation in the *Aeneid*. It is even possible, although this writer thinks it implausible, that there may be behind 90B some thought of Ovid's accounts of the creation in the *Metamorphoses*, inasmuch as Lactantius refers occasionally to Ovid.

But let us turn from the creation song to considerations of Grendel. (The question of why heathen Danes in Heorot are regaled with a creation song will be dealt with later in this paper.) Ll. 102–114 of course stress the idea that Grendel is of Cain's kin. But Grendel is a composite figure, one whose attributes come from different sources. No one, I believe, would endeavor to explain Grendel *solely* as Cain, as a human descendant of Cain like Henoch, Irad, Mahujael, and so on, or even solely as a monster of the kin of Cain. Other considerations enter in. And the *Beowulf* poet seems to have passed rather freely in his own mind from stress on one characteristic to stress on another. Quite possibly he did so unconsciously, in the process of quick composition. Lactantius appears never to mention Cain, and we can therefore dismiss from consideration ll. 102–114 in this discussion. The Cain story will not obviously lead to an elucidation of ll. 164–183A, and I believe that another interpretation of Grendel may do so if interpreted against the background of Lactantius' thought.

What are the attributes of Grendel that are not necessarily closely connected with Cain in the lines that we have singled out for treatment? There is strong emphasis on the fact that Grendel is not entirely a purely physical monster but is also something of a demoniac spirit: *ellengǽst* (or *ellorgǽst?*), l. 86; *se grimma gǽst*, l. 102; *wergan gāstes*, l. 133. Although there are occasional suggestions that there exist others like Grendel (the plurals *untȳdras*, l. 11, *eotenas, ylfe, orcneas*, l. 112, *gīgantas*, l. 113, and *helrūnan*, l. 163), there are several indications that Grendel acts alone: *oð þæt an ōngan*, l. 100; *āna wið eallum*, l. 145; *atol āngengea*, l. 165 Grendel is the enemy, the adversary: *fēond*, l. 101 and l. 143. Grendel is closely connected with hell: *fēond on helle*, l. 101. Grendel is resentful and envious of the happiness of men in Heorot (l. 86–89). Grendel is thoroughly confirmed in and addicted to his crimes (ll. 134–137). He lies in ambush and plots (l. 161). There are other characteristics, too, but if we ask ourselves who or what is at least semi– or quasi–spiritual, who is alone, single, unique, who is the adversary, who is condemned to hell although with the privilege of excursions therefrom, who resents and envies a happy condition of man, and who is necessarily thoroughly confirmed in his procedures we must answer Satan or the devil, leader of demons, father of lies and heresies.

It is important to examine Lactantius' comments on the devil or devils in order to fully understand the thought of the *Beowulf* author, even though Lactantius was not much of a demonologist and contented himself with only a few observations on this subject in the *Institutes*.[7] None of his observations are in any way contradictory to the specifics listed in the preceding paragraph. Lactantius treats of the creation of the devil in chapter 8 of Book II; he says that after God "produced a spirit like to himself" and endowed with His virtues,

> Then He made another in whom the nature of the divine origin did not remain. And so this creation was infected as though by poison with envy of its own fashioning. The latter one passed from goodness to evil by its own will, and that which had been given it free by God, took up a name contrary to

itself [Gk. *diabolon*]. Whence it is clear that ill will or envy is the source of all evils. There was in that one envy of his predecessor, who by persevering was then approved of by God the Father and is still dear to him. The Greeks call this one, who became evil from good through himself, the devil.[8]

Later, in chapter 14, Lactantius tells that God sends messengers to the earth to protect men from the devil, to whom he had given power over the earth. The devil however seduced some of these messengers to his ways:

> Thus, the devil made them from angels into his satellites and ministers. Those who were sprung from these, because they were neither angels nor men, but having a certain middle nature, were not received into the lower world as their parents were not received into heaven. Thus, there are two classes of spirits, one heavenly, the other earthly. The latter are the unclean spirits, the authors of the evils which are done....

> These spirits, contaminated and lost, as I say, wander over all the earth, and they work toward a solace of their own perdition by destroying men.

> Thus, they fill all things with trickeries, frauds, deceits and errors. They cling to individual men and they seize all homes, indeed every last doorway....

There are many Grendels, actually. There is a Cain Grendel and a devil Grendel. Other infamous names could be listed here. Perhaps we could express the matter another way: there is a brute-force Grendel, the one who snatches away and eats thirty thegns. But there is a plotting scheming subtle Grendel, a devil-spirit given to trickeries, frauds, and deceits. The fusion between the two in *Beowulf* is imperfect. One may well ask why Grendel could be partly spiritual, could be interested in the destruction of men's souls, could resent men's joys at hearing creation songs, would need to lie in ambush or plot. The more subtle Grendel, the devil of Lactantius or one of the angel-messengers corrupted by him, may have been suggested in part by Lactantius' work.

There are a few interesting specific comments in the passages devoted to Grendel's raids in the section between line 86 and line 183, comments which, the writer thinks, may be taken to indicate that the *Beowulf* author did not at any time totally lose sight of the work of Lactantius while composing this section. In chapter 5, for instance, occurs the sentence, "It is possible for the world to be without man, just as it is for a city and a house to be without a man." [10] This of course recalls oð þæt idel stōd hūsa sēlest" (ll. 145B–146A). Certainly the most interesting of these details comes in connection with "nō hē þone giftstōl grētan mōste, maþðum for Metode" (ll. 168–169A), a little passage that many many critics and commentators have found most puzzling and difficult. It is often taken that here is a restriction on the power of Grendel as he inhabits Heorot at night. Superhuman as he is, Grendel cannot commit sacrilege with things pertaining to the Metod—God or a ruling or governing force. It is the feeling of the writer that a reference in Lactantius' chapter 4, about two pages before his first rhapsody on the creation, indicates at least the source for this line. Lactantius, as he often delighted in doing, held forth on the futility of man-made idols of the classical gods. He then turned to pay his respects to the gods themselves and asked why it was that men had to punish those guilty of sacrilege against these gods, suggesting that the latter were in themselves powerless to do so. He then recalled the story of Gaius Verres, quaestor of Sicily, accused by Cicero of lawless pillaging (to put the matter in very mild wording indeed):

> What about Gaius Verres, whom Cicero, his accuser, compares to this same Dionysius and to Phalaris and to all tyrants? Did not Verres pillage all of Sicily by taking away the images of the gods and the ornaments of the shrines? It is useles to go over the single incidents; it is enough to recall one in which the accuser, with all the powers of his eloquence, and with every effort of his voice and body, deplored the destruction done to a Ceres, either of Catina or Henna. The religious significance of the first of these was so great that it was a crime to approach the secret portions of its temple. . . . Ceres . . . was removed from its secret and ancient inner shrine by robber-slaves sent in with impunity by Gaius Verres. . . . Not without reason, Marcus Tullius, did the Sicilians run to you, that is, to a man, since for three years they had experienced that the gods were of no avail. They would have been utter fools if they had fled to gods for defense against the injuries of men, those very gods who could not be angry against Gaius Verres for themselves.[11]

Verres, fearing either the goddess Ceres herself or the popular reaction to any outrage done to her giftstōl with its maþūm or even his own approach to it ordered some of his gangster slaves to steal the statue. This incident of course figures prominently in the Verrine Orations; some twenty lines from the conclusion of the last of these Cicero speaks of Verres' causing "the image of Ceres in Catina, which none but women might touch or even see without sin, to be wrenched from its place in the shrine and carried away."

But what has Verres to do with Grendel? As we have seen, Grendel is a composite character made up from attributes and incidents from the lives of a quite considerable number of notorious figures. Verres (like Catiline and like Antony and Dolabella in the Philippics) shares some traits with Grendel. Both are merciless, nefarious, marauding ravagers. With the thought of Lactantius' second book in his mind, it is not unlikely that the *Beowulf* author would remember and utilize the comments on Verres, placed as they are so near the first of Lactantius' rhapsodies on the creation. But what would the audience of *Beowulf* make of the comment? This question will be answered later.

Mention of the Verres incident in the paragraph just above has, the writer is afraid, been a bit of a digression, although it is supporting evidence for the main thesis of this paper. Before going on ll. 171–183, which are extremely important, it is necessary again to digress, this time away from Lactantius, although the discussion will concern heresy. In our passage, filled as it is with extremely forceful epithets concerning Grendel, we find what appears to be an innocuous, even perhaps a sympathetic, epithet, *wonsǽlī wer* in l. 105. As this writer interprets the phrase, it is far from innocuous or sympathetic, and it is connected with the plotting devil Grendel who schemes at the destruction of the souls of men. In the last two decades of the eighth century there flourished, mostly in Spain, a heresy called adoptionism, which, put too simply and perhaps unfairly, regarded Christ as an adopted son of God the father. Bishop Elipandius of Toledo appears to have been the first prominent churchman of the period to espouse and support this belief. We can now quote from Richard Winston, *Charlemagne: from the Hammer to the Cross*:

> Looking around for allies, Elipand appealed to one of the finest theologians and most devout clerics in Spain, Bishop Felix of Urgel. Felix took up the cause, defying Pope Hadrian's condemnation of the doctrine of adoption as blasphemy and "serpent's venom," and made it his own—so much his own that it came to be known also as the Felician heresy; so much so that the ecclesiastics of the time were constantly punning on his name, which, since it meant "happy" in Latin, gave them the opportunity to refer to him constantly as "infelix"—"unhappy" or "unfortunate." But it took more than papal warnings and puns to silence a man who was not only eloquent and learned but whose reputation for purity and saintliness in behavior was so great that it reached Alcuin. . . .[12]

Wonsǣlī wer is of course a perfect translation for *vir infelix*. Preferring to date *Beowulf* relatively later than earlier, this writer feels that this epithet is a sarcastic reference to Felix and that it accords with much of the passage under consideration here in opposition to heresy.

We now come, however, to the story of how the Danes turned to the worship of heathen idols (ll. 171–183):

Monig oft gesæt
rīce to rūne;   rǣd eahtedon
hwæt swīðferhðum   sēlest wǣre
wið færgryrum   tō gefremmanne.
Hwīlum hīe gehēton   æt hærgtrafum
wīgweorþunga,   wordum bǣdon,
þæt him gāstbona   gēoce gefremede
wið þēodþreaum.   Swylc wæs þēaw hyra,
hǣþenra hyht;   helle gemundon
in mōdsefan,   Hethod hīe ne cūþon,
dǣda Dēmend,   ne wiston hīe Drihten God,
ne hīe hūru heofena Helm   herian ne cūþon,
wuldres waldend.

This writer feels that no contradiction whatever—or even any difficulty—arises in proceeding from the creation rhapsody of ll. 90–98 to these lines if—but only if—the thought of Lactantius is examined. Two things should be said before we try to examine that thought. One is that any summary of the thought of a theologian is likely to be too simple and a bit unfair in that the theologian's full development of his ideas is necessarily sacrificed. The second thought, which is somewhat similar to the first, is that, in the twelve lines above, the *Beowulf* poet has compressed into a very short time span (*twelf wintra tīd* in l. 147) Lactantius' account of many centuries of human existence.

As we have seen, Lactantius was impressed with the idea of the creation of the world. To him it was truly wonderful. He did not speculate much about the condition or thought of early men; he drew no picture of a pristine Golden Age. He did, however, postulate that the first generations of mankind appreciated the wonder and grandeur of the world around them. Doing so, they arrived, more or less intuitively, at the idea of a creator or, better, a Creator. They arrived at this conclusion by a half-intuitive, half-rational primitive ontology, if this wording is neither too awkward or too sophisticated. Lactantius would have said that in a sense they recognized, knew, and loved God the Creator. And that fact would have been quite adequate to Lactantius to find them good rather than bad, enlightened rather than ignorant. Acceptance of God the Creator was the most important merit or virtue that one could have; it was the corner stone of all virtue. But could persons in such condition, accepting and praising God but knowing nothing whatever of Christ, be called Christian? Lactantius never asked or answered that question. Actually Lactantius is among the least Christ-centered and the most God-centered of the patristic writers of the fourth century. Although he would doubtless have been deeply grieved if his essential Christianity had been questioned, he was not particularly interested in the *Institutes* in considerations of Christ; only two of the seven books of the *Institutes* even mention Christ.[13] Let us say, then, that Lactantius' notion of early men, accepting and loving God the Creator, was that although technically pre-Christian they were essentially good and capable of blessedness.

The notions explained in the paragraph just above keep reappearing in the *Institutes* frequently. Hence typical illustrative quotation is difficult. The following, from Book I rather than Book II, is useful:

> For there is no one . . . who, when he raises his eyes toward the sky, even though he does not know by the providence of what god all this which he beholds is governed, does not understand that there is something, however, from the very magnitude, motion, arrangement, constancy, utility, beauty, and proportion of nature, and that this could not be possible if it were not for the fact that it is established in a marvelous manner and has been fashioned by some greater plan.[14]

There is nothing at all necessarily *Christian* about ll. 90–98, the rhapsody on the creation; it has been a bit presumptuous on the part of the orthodox Christian critic so to presume. Thought and wording could have been adopted by believers in other religions, organized and codified or individual and intuitive. But it fits in very well indeed with Lactantius' ideas of pre-Christian blessedness in love and knowledge of God the Creator. Hence the men of Heorot enjoy bliss every day (l. 88). And hence the Adversary,

Grendel in his Satan phase, finds this hard to endure, his function being to bring about alienation between God the Creator and man. Our pre-Christian dwellers of Heorot, recognizing God, do not know sorrow, do not know the misery of men, until Grendel comes (ll. 119–120).

In Lactantius' reconstruction of the development of men's thoughts and practices and religions, what happens after this blessed pre-Christian knowledge of God? Is there advancement made by the contributions of the classical pre-Christian world? Emphatically not. Man takes a very decided turn for the worse; he suffers the dreadful catastrophe of loss of knowledge and love of God. He suffers this catastrophe through two causes. One is the machinations of the Adversary and his minions. Such machinations of the more subtle plotting and scheming Grendel to destroy men's souls have been dealt with previously. The quotations from Lactantius on page 401—especially the two concerning "a solace of their own perdition by destroying men" and "they fill all things with trickeries, frauds, deceits, and errors"—are illustrative. Although the following quotation, from chapters 18 and 19 of Book V, is not entirely satisfactory in that it is unclear whether Lactantius is thinking primarily of demons or of certain of their earthly followers (to be discussed shortly), it is worth inserting here:

> Of what punishments, then, is he deserving, who is a deserter of Him who is true Lord and Father except those which God Himself determined, who prepared eternal fire for the unjust spirits, because He Himself threatens the impious and rebellious through His prophets? Let these destroyers of souls, their own and those of others, learn, therefore, and admit how inexpiable is their crime; first, because they destroy themselves by serving the most depraved demons whom God has condemned to eternal punishment; then because they do not allow God to be worshipped by others, but strive to avert men to deadly rites, and strain with the utmost diligence lest there be any soul unharmed on the earth which may gaze toward heaven, its condition being unimpaired.[15]

To a degree the sheer presence of Satan-Grendel, of the Grendel demon (interpreting *demon* in the sense of "evil spirit" rather than "incarnate fiend"), would be expected to turn the men of Heorot from pre-Christian blessedness to idol worship. It was a natural development—so natural that anybody deeply grounded in Lactantius might rather expect it; certainly he would not feel it surprising or contradictory. As dogs and cats shed hair, as birds shed feathers, as certain snakes shed their skins, or as lack of plant life induces erosion or a long hot drought parches vegetation, so the sheer presence of Grendel the demon spirit would induce heathenism and heresy.

The *Beowulf* author, it may be said in passing, was probably quite aware of the irony of both situation and wording in which the aid of *gāstbona* (l. 177) might afford help to the men of Heorot against people's distresses brought by *se grimma gǣst* (l. 102) and a *werga gāst* (l. 133). He may well have had reason to believe that *some* of his original audience might follow his thoughts but that others would not. It is noticeable that the author does not seem to view Grendel's amazing raid which brings thirty thegns to their deaths (ll. 120–125) as seriously as he views whatever or whoever was instrumental in turning Heorot's men to worship in heathen temples. The thirty thegns died quickly if wretchedly. Furthermore, if the writer reads the thought of Lactantius correctly, they died in a state of pre-grace. Grendel's action, although monstrous, simply translated them from one kind of life to another—from the earthly to the heavenly. But turning Heorot from pre-Christianity to active worship at shrines of idols accomplished something infinitely worse—it destroyed the souls of those involved. This is one reason (but only one; there is another) for the bitter diatribe in ll. 183–186.

But there is in the thought of Lactantius another group of factors responsible for the falling away of early man from pre-Christian knowledge of God the Creator to the worship of heathen gods and idols. This group is composed partly of the bards, poets, myth-makers, originators of pagan religions, who receive some blame. But much more important—as much more guilty—than they were the philosophers. This paper cannot enter deeply into the cultural and philosophic problems faced by Lactantius in the first decade of the fourth century. Suffice to say, he was as baffled and as perturbed as any other Christian theologian of the period when he tried to deal with evaluation of pagan poet and philosopher. Perhaps his struggle with the problem posed by Cicero's work was even more acute than that of Jerome in the last part of the same century. He seems in general to have adopted a kind of eclecticism without, however, drawing up very firm or clear principles. As has been mentioned before, he can freely make use of tags from Vergil and Ovid. He has many references to and quotations from Cicero, many of them complimentary; in fact he makes more use of Cicero than he does of the Bible itself. In general, however, he condemns most of the work of the early poets and particularly of the philosophers as leading people away from knowledge and love of God the Creator—pre-Christian blessedness—into false beliefs. Whatever philosophy might contribute otherwise, it is, in the thought of Lactantius, futile unless it is based on and constantly operative toward knowledge of God the Creator. Know God. This may well be enough for you. Without knowing God nothing avails. There are many passages that might be quoted, but the following from the first part of chapter 9 of Book VI will serve:

> The first dogma of this law is to know God, to serve Him alone, to worship only Him. It is not possible to get at the reason of a man who does not know God as the parent of his life. This is the worst thing. This ignorance causes him to serve other gods, than which nothing more criminal can be committeed. Hence, his steps are inclined toward evil through his ignorance of the true and only good. . . . So, that the body may be alive and sensible, both the knowledge of God is necessary, which is, as it were, the head. . . . This is the reason that philosophers, although they have natural goodness, yet have no knowledge, have no wisdom. All their doctrine and virtues are without a head, since they

do not know God who is the Head of virtue and doctrine. . . . Wherefore, there is no doubt that whoever does not know God is impious, and all his virtues, which he thinks he holds or possesses, are found in that death-dealing way which is full of darkness.[16]

Many many other attacks on the Greek and Latin philosophers could be adduced. But we must return here and restate the thesis that the men of Heorot in the section under discussion are simply following the course taken by man from blessed pre-Christianity down into the evils of idolatry and paganism exactly as Lactantius had maintained. It needs to be said again that the poet has compressed all this most stringently and rigorously. Twelve winters (l. 147) or less elapse between the creation rhapsody that brings on Grendel's first raid and the praying at *hærgtrafum* in l. 175. Presumably this sort of praying could not have taken place during the period of pre-Christian blessedness, but it has hardened into a *þēaw* in the meantime (l. 178). With both more space for explanation and more time for composition at his disposal, the poet might have produced a more clear explanation. Evidently he had his reasons for not doing so.

Let us turn now to seeing whether some of the lines from 171 to 183 in *Beowulf* are strongly suggestive of wording in Lactantius' Book II. The following may have suggested ll. 171–174. Only the first of these quotations, adduced here in connection with *færgryrum* in l. 174, needs comment. Lactantius argues that sometimes in dire stress the true God is remembered, the false gods forgotten or ignored. But the *Beowulf* author seems at this point to present a complete reversal of Lactantius' thought. By this reversal—passage in the poet's mind from the God of Lactantius to the pagan gods that the poet has occasion to think of at the moment—the following passage may underlie the mention of *færgryrum*:

> 1. But whenever serious necessity should fall upon them, then they remember God. If the terror of war has raged, if the pestiferous blight of sickness has touched them, if a long period of drought has prevented their crops from nutritious yield, if harsh storms or hail has attacked them, they rush to God; they seek his help; they pray that he come to their aid. If anyone is tossed on the sea by a raging wind, he calls upon Him; if anyone is afflicted by any force whatever, he implores Him the more; if one is driven to the extreme necessity of begging, he appeals to the one God by prayers asking for his food . . . .

The following need no comments:

> 2. Cicero understood that those gods which men adore were false. When he had said many things which were strong enough for the overturning of the religions, he said, however, that those things ought not be discussed openly lest such a "discussion extinguish the religious beliefs that have been publicly accepted."
> 3. But, as I said, excuse can be found for the unlearned and those who do not profess to be wise, whereas for those who professing wisdom display rather foolishness, no excuse can be found.

4. And we prove, O philosophers, that you are not only uninstructed and impious, but even blind, foolish, and mad, for you have overcome the ignorance of the unlettered with emptiness.

5. The grammarians say that these were called spirits, like indwelling powers (*daemonas*), that is, skilled and knowing of things; for they think that these are gods. They do, indeed, know many future events, but not all, for it is not permitted for them to know the hidden plan of God, and, therefore, they are accustomed to arrange their responses into ambiguous terms. The poets also know them to be *daemonas* and speak of them as such. Thus Hesiod says: "These are the spirits of great Zeus, through counsels good, living on earth, and the guardians of living men." This was written because God had sent those guardians to the human race. But these very ones, since they are pervertors of men, want themselves to seem guardians so that they might be worshiped and that God might not be worshiped.

6. These are the mockeries or games of those who, lurking under the names of the dead, hold out wounds for the living. Thus, if that danger which threatens can be avoided, they want to seem to have averted it because they were placated; or, if it cannot be avoided, they do it so that it may seem to have happened because of some contempt shown to them. With this guile and these arts they tear away the knowledge of the one true God in all peoples. Destroyed by their own vices, they rage and go about that they may destroy. For this reason also they have contrived human victims, themselves enemies of the human race, so that they may devour as many souls as possible.[17]

In connection with ll. 175–178 some of the following may be relevant:

1. Why, then, do you not raise your eyes to the heavens and make sacrifices in the open after calling upon their [the heathen idols'] names? Why do you look to walls and wood and stones rather than toward where you believe them to be? What do the temples mean? The altars?

2. They take to themselves the name of genii; for thus they translate the word *daemones* into Latin. Men honor them in their inner chambers, and daily for them do they pour out wines. Knowing these demons, they venerate them as though they were terrestrial gods and dispellers of the evils which they themselves make and bring upon them.

3. Yet those same authors themselves work on their own presences, in order that they may be believed to be true; thus they delude the credulity of men through a feigned or lying divinity because it is not profitable to disclose the truth to them.

4. But the Magi and those whom the people actually call evil-doers, since they ply their execrable arts, summon those celestial ones which are read of in the holy books by their own names. These outright incestuous and horrid spirits, in order to confuse all things and overwhelm human hearts with errors, sow and mix the false with the true.

5. By means of oracles, however, they deceive especially, for the unitiated are unable to distinguish their deviations from and meddlings with the truth, and they think that empires and victories and wealth and prosperous outcomes are granted by them. In fact, they think that the state has been freed from imminent perils by their will, perils which they announced in their responses and averted because they were placated with sacrifices . . . . And whenever to some people or a particular city there is something good impending, according to the determination of God, they promise that they will do it either by prodigies or dreams or oracles, provided that temples or honors or sacrifices

be granted to them ... Hence, temples are vowed and new games consecrated and flocks of beasts are sacrificed.[18]

Other quotations could be taken from Book II, as well as from other books of the *Institutes*, but perhaps these are adequate. Turning now to ll. 178–184 of *Beowulf*, can we find in the *Institutes* quotations that are likewise suggestive? The following may be consequential:

1. Although I have shown in Book I that the religions of the gods are false, because these, whose varied and dissimilar cults men have adopted by custom, consent, and foolish conviction throughout the world ...

2. ... the causes by which men were deceived and believed in the beginning that such were gods, and then, later on with inveterate persuasion, continued in the mostly depravedly adopted religions.

3. I marvel that the majesty of the one God which holds and rules all things has fallen into such great oblivion, and that which alone ought to be worshiped is alone most neglected. I wonder that men themselves have been brought to such great blindness that they prefer dead gods to the true and living God, and earthly beings and those buried in the earth to Him who was the Founder of the earth itself. Pardon this impiety of men could be granted if it were absolutely from ignorance of the divine Name that this error came. But, since we often see that those very worshipers of the gods acknowledge and praise the highest God, what pardon for their impiety can they hope to win for themselves who do not acknowledge the worship of Him whom it is wrong for men not to know at all?

4. ... although we cannot see with our eyes the God whose abode the heavens are, we may contemplate Him with our minds ... the mind of man ought to look where his countenance is directed.

5. Rightly does Seneca in his moral books say that men venerate the likenesses of gods. "They supplicate them with bended knee; they adore them; through the whole day they sit or stand near them; they throw offerings and slay victims for them; and while they look up to these so much .... "

6. Why do you deprive yourself of celestial benefits and of your own will fall prone to the ground? ... When you submit yourself to the earth and make yourselves lowlier, you sink beyond to the infernal regions and condemn yourselves to death because there is nothing inferior to or more lowly than the earth except death and hell.

7. Nor is it to be wondered as if they do not see God since they themselves do not even see the man whom they think they see.

8. He is the God who supports the earth, who has adorned the sky with gleaming stars ...

9. These are the religions which, handed down to them from their ancestors, they persist in protecting and defending; they do not consider what sort they are, but they trust that they are true and approved from the fact that their ancestors handed them down.

10. From diverse and repugnant principles, therefore, man has been made as the world itself from light and darkness and from life and death. The Creator charged these two principles to struggle with each other in man, so that if the soul should win, which is of God, he may be immortal and live; but if the body wins and subjects the soul to its sway, he will live in everlasting shadows and in death. And that power of death is not to extinguish the unjust souls utterly, but to punish them for all eternity. We name that punishment a second death, which is itself, just as immortality is, also per-

petual. We define the first death this way: death is the dissolution of living things, or in this manner: death is a separation of body and soul. Of the second death, we say that it is the enduring of eternal pain, or we hold this: death is the condemnation to eternal punishments of souls according to their merits.

11. For God, just as I explained in the beginning, does not need a name, since He is the only One, nor do the angels, because they are immortal, either allow themselves to be called gods or wish to be. Their one and only duty is to serve the wishes of God and to do nothing but what He orders. Thus we say that the world is ruled by God as a province is by a governor. No one says that his assistants are his equals or colleagues in ruling the province, although the business is performed by their ministry. Still, these are able to do things besides the commands of the governor, because of his ignorance which is a condition of being human. That Ruler and Governor of the Universe, how-ever, who knows all things and from whose divine eyes nothing is shielded, alone has the power over all things, and there is not anything in the angels except the necessity of obeying. So they wish no honor to be attributed to themselves whose whole honor is in God.

12. With this guile and these arts they tear away the knowledge of the one true God in the peoples. Destroyed by their own voices, they rage and go about that they may destroy. For this reason also they have contrived human victims, themselves the enemies of the human race, so that they may devour as many souls as possible.[19]

The last quotation in this series needs especial treatment. It concerns ll: 180B–181 of *Beowulf*:

> Metod hīe no cūþon,
> dæda Dēmend,   ne wiston hīe Drihten God,

The translation of the *Institutes* here used, by Sister Mary Frances McDonald, has the following in chapter 16 of Book II:

> Thus, they spread darkness and cover the truth with a cloud of smoke, so that men may not know the Lord, may not know their Father.

Lactantius' original Latin is as follows:

> Offundunt itaque tenebras, et veritatem caligine obducunt, no dominum, ne patrem suum norint.

This paper is bold enough to suggest that the rhetorical repetition in *Beo-wulf* ll. 180B–181 is a reminiscence by the *Beowulf* author of Lactantius' sentence.[20]

One of the pecularities of poetic composition illustrated by the *Beowulf* author is that a more-or-less sustained passage may be followed in the next ten, twenty, or thirty lines, mainly concerned with something else, by an echo passage, a remembrance, a recollection, a kind of cadenza or final coda phrase or sentence. After l. 183—certainly after l. 188—the *Beowulf* author stops concentration on Lactantius and begins to go ahead with his narrative. But he does not—perhaps he can not—totally dismiss all thoughts of the *Institutes* from his mind. To the writer he seems to return to it in ll. 202–204:

Ðone sīðfæt him   snotere ceorlas
lȳthwon lōgon,   þēah hē him lēof wǣre;
hwetton hige (r) ōfne,   hǣl scēawedon.

A number of passages in Lactantius' Book II could be adduced as possible sources or influences on these lines, but the following will be adequate:

> Through demons have been discovered astrology, divination, the practice of augury, and those very practices which are called oracle-giving, necromancy, magic, and whatever other evils that men practice either openly or secretly....[21]

According to the interpretation here suggested, the *snotere* of l. 202 is to be interpreted as ironic and bitter.[22]

By way of summary, the argument here adduced depends on the following: 1) similarities in wording between Lactantius' praises of God the Creator and the creation rhapsody in *Beowulf*; 2) the picture of pre-Christian knowledge of God and ensuing happiness therefrom as explained in Lactantius and suggested by *Beowulf*; 3) the suggestions that Grendel shows traits of a demon likely to foster and abet paganism and heresy, traits over and above his immediate kin-of-Cain characteristics; 4) mention in Lactantius of Verres' unwillingness to approach the most sacred shrine of Ceres, which may suggest a source and an explanation for the puzzling ll. 168–169; 5) resemblances between the general story of mankind, as Lactantius recounted it, in which allegedly wise councilors turned men to paganism, and the story of the men of Heorot turning to heathen idols for aid; 6) a recollection passage dealing with examination of omens.

According to this series of ideas, the author of *Beowulf* is not necessarily describing or attempting to describe any conditions or events in Denmark or any other part of Scandinavia when he tells of the singing of the creation rhapsody and of the backsliding into worship at heathen idols nor yet any conditions or events in Geatland when he mentions the examination of omens. He is also not necessarily thinking of any backsliding into paganism after the first enthusiastic burst of Christianity in eastern England—in Kent, Sussex, East Anglia, or Northumbria, to be specific—although certainly in the composition of the lines about backsliding there would have been time and reason for the author to consider English events. In a creative mind, thought and association are rapid; we do not need to adopt an *either-or* argument in situations in which a *both-and* argument is satisfactory, safe, and enriching. But it may be important to note the probability that the author was thinking of the gods of the early Greek world and of other Mediterranean areas much more than of Woden, Thor, or Tiw—if indeed he thought of these latter figures at all at this point.

To what extent would an audience composed of persons from all ranks, classes, or groups of Anglo-Saxon England have understood the author's thoughts or message through ll. 86–183? The completely uneducated commoner would have understood it not at all. The thegn or dux or earl with no theological background or training would likewise have failed to make much of it. To persons of these groups *Beowulf* would have been only a story concerned primarily with fights against demons and dragons, secondarily with a variety of wars and feuds. This lack of understanding on the part of such persons made no difference in the eighth century and need make no difference to us now. Examination of the ultimate thought of the author should be the purpose of the critic or scholar. The notion that the author did not communicate much of his thought to many in his audience may not seem very complimentary to him. This difficulty, however, may be overcome by the suggestion that the first audience to hear *Beowulf* was composed at least partly of clerics and ecclesiastics who might be supposed by the author to have some familiarity with the thought of Lactantius.

Notes

1. This is an introductory paper and does not pretend to completeness. A variety of matters which the writer hopes to treat in the future have been omitted. This paper is furthermore intended as a *festschrift* contribution, and space is at a premium. Hence many provocative notes have been omitted. The works of Lactantius appear in volumes 6 & 7 of Migne's *Patrologiae Latinae*. This paper makes much use of Lactantius, *The Divine Institutes*, tr. by Sister Mary Francis McDonald, Washington, D.C., 1966, The Fathers of the Church Series. It also uses *The Works of Lactantius*, tr. by William Fletcher, Edinburgh, 1871, 2 v., The Ante-Nicene Christian Library.

2. Cf. Ogilvy, J. D. A., *Books Known to the English, 597–1066*, Cambridge, Massachusetts, 1957, p. 191. It should be indicated here that the reference in Alcuin's catalog *might* be to Lactantius' *Workmanship of God* or to his *Wrath of God* or to his *Deaths of the Persecutors* or to some combination of these three. It might also refer to *De Ave Phoenice*. One cannot be sure, but to the writer it seems likely that Alcuin refers to the *Institutes* alone or to the *Institutes* and some of the other works. Examination of *Workmanship of God*, *Wrath of God*, and *Deaths of the Persecutors*, along with Lactantius' *Epitome of the Institutes*, does not suggest any influence of these works on *Beowulf* or any connection between them and *Beowulf*.

3. *The Divine Institutes*, Washington, D.C., 1964, pp. 111–112.

4. *Ibid.*, p. 135.

5. *Ibid.* In order the quotations from Lactantius in this paragraph are to be found on pp. 100, 100, 114, 116, 117.

6. As has been indicated, Lactantius can arise to *swutol sang* in such passages as the creation rhapsody. He certainly attains to other heights of lyricism elsewhere in his works. The description of God's creation of the human body, for instance, in chapters 7–16 of the *Workmanship of God* could be described as *swutol sang*. If we could assume that the *Beowulf* author was for the time being thinking of Lactantius mainly as the author of these and similar passages, the paragraph to which this refers could be less guarded and tentative in its comments.

7. Cf. Schneweis, E., *Angels and Demons according to Lactantius*, Washington, D.C., 1942, Catholic University of American Studies in Christian Antiquity, no. 3.

8. *The Divine Institutes*, Washington, D.C., 1964, pp. 111–112.

9. *Ibid.* In order the quotations are to be found on pp. 152–153, 153–154, 154.

10. *Ibid.*, p. 116.

11. *Ibid.*, pp. 109–110.

12. Winston, Richard, *Charlemagne: from the Hammer to the Cross*, Indiana-polis, p. 214.

13. In Lactantius' *Epitome of the Institutes* somewhat greater attention is paid to the figure of Christ.

14. Lactantius, *op. cit.*, p. 21.

15. *Ibid.*, pp. 375–376.

16. *Ibid.*, pp. 413, 415.

17. *Ibid.* In order the quotations given in the series are to be found on the following pages: 1 pp. 95–96; 2. p. 101; 3. p. 104; 4. p. 113; 5. p. 153; 6. p. 159.

18. *Ibid.* In order the quotations given in the series are to be found on the following pages: 1. pp. 95–96; 2. p. 154; 3. p. 156; 5. pp. 157–158.

19. *Ibid.* In order the quotations given in the series are to be found on the following pages: 1. p. 94; 2. p. 94; 3. p. 95; 4. p. 97; 5. p. 99; 6. p. 100; 7. pp. 102–103; 8. p. 111; 9. p. 119; 10. p. 147; 11. p. 156; 12. p. 159.

20. *Ibid.*, p. 157. The direct quotation from Lactantius is from column 338 of volume 6 of Migne.

21. Lactantius, *op. cit.*, p. 155.

22. Fletcher's translation of *The Anger of God* has at the beginning of the last paragraph of chapter 4 the sentence, "The disputation of the wise man[3] extends thus far: he was silent as to other things which follow . . . ." Fletcher's note 3 to the page in question is as follows: "Epicurus: it seems to be spoken with some irony." See *The Works of Lactantius*, tr. by William Fletcher, Edinburgh, vol. 2, p. 6. To this writer it seems that Lactantius may have used words for *wise* and *wisdom* ironically elsewhere in his work. The *Beowulf* poet might likewise have taken such usages as ironic and used similarly ironic usages himself.

MAXIMILIAN Von SCHELE De VERE AND HIS *AMERICANISMS:* *THE ENGLISH OF THE NEW WORLD*

DAVID W. MAURER
University of Louisville

in collaboration with

ATCHESON L. HENCH
University of Virginia

I

For nearly a century Schele De Vere's *Americanisms* has been a neglected work in the study of the development of American English. This can be partially explained on the basis of the scarcity of copies of the first and only edition of 1871. In fact, up to the time that Mencken was preparing *Supplement One* of the Fourth Edition of *The American Language*, he thought that he had never been able to see one, though we now know that he had one but did not realize it at the time. This matter will be taken up later on. The point is that students of American English did not make wide use of his large and valuable collection because it was not generally available. Mencken was the first to recognize its importance, and he assembled most of the biographical data on Schele De Vere which is used in this study.

At about the same time, Professor Atcheson L. Hench of the University of Virginia was doing some work on Schele De Vere which resulted in a paper (1934) read before the Modern Language Association but never published. Mencken consulted Hench, and was in turn indebted to him for some information about Schele De Vere. Meanwhile, in 1968, the Gale Research Company had been interested in issuing a modern reprint of *Americanisms* and asked me to prepare some introductory material for that volume. This project led me naturally to Hench, whom I had known for many years as a productive researcher in the field of American English, and who had in the interim discovered Schele De Vere's personal copy of *Americanisms*, glossed with many manuscript notes for a projected Second Edition which never appeared.

Just as Gale was about to go to press (in fact they had already issued pre-publication announcements) Johnson Reprints released a reprint edition, and Gale deferred to their competitor. So now *Americanisms* is readily available and will undoubtedly be warmly welcomed. Both Professor Hench and I agreed that, since *Americanisms* may be widely consulted by all those working in American English, from the undergraduate level on up, some portion of our notes might well be useful, especially since this information is not available elsewhere. We suggest in passing that a critical edition of *Americanisms* would be in order, and might tempt some doctoral candidate interested in making a practical contribution to the field.

Maximilian von Schele (he dropped the De Vere after coming to the United States, but revived it on the title page of *Americanisms*) was born in Germany, the son of a Swedish army officer resident there, and a French mother. After taking the doctorate at the University of Bonn in 1841, he did further work at Griefswald in 1842, then migrated to the United States, where he pursued graduate work in Greek at Harvard. In 1844 he was appointed Professor of Modern Languages at the University of Virginia where, except for the four years he served in the Confederate Army, he taught until 1895. From 1893 until 1895 he served on the editorial staff of the *Standard Dictionary*. He lived until 1898, a distinguished scholar, teacher, writer, and pioneer in what was then a new and most unconventional field—the study of the American language.

He was admirably equipped for his work (as scholars went in his day) for he knew, in addition to English, the principal Romance languages, German, Latin, Greek, Anglo-Saxon, and Middle English. He had also made some very perceptive observations on current British usage and had a remarkable familiarity with various British and Scottish dialects, which stood him in good stead in America, where many obscure and semi-archaic dialect forms tended to reappear and thrive vigorously. Any modern linguist who peruses this volume can see immediately that he had a good ear for the spoken language, though without the precise tools of modern linguistics he often had to resort to "eye dialect," involving some rough and ready spelling tactics in order to render what he heard in printed form. In addition he had a wide reading acquaintance with the older English literature, from which he dredged up examples to confound the British purists who were damning the invasion of Americanisms; time and again he shows that many of these words and phrases (then hunted down like criminals in England) were simply old-fashioned, with a long history in the usage of respectable English authors.

For sources from which to draw basic historical data he was somewhat handicapped. Of course he knew the rather limited work of Witherspoon (1781), Pickering (1816), Bartlett (1848 and 1859) and Elwyn (1859) as the most prominent Americans, by birth or adoption, who ventured to write on Americanisms. He made good use of them, along with various minor commentators, and, naturally, Noah Webster's *Dictionary* which was available in several editions. Thornton's *American Glossary*, an imposing work, had not even been begun when Schele De Vere published his volume in 1871. On the British side he knew Harman, Grose, and Trench as compilers of slang, and quoted freely from obscure papers on British and Scottish dialects. Aside from his own sharp observations, Johnson's *Dictionary* (probably in one of the 19th Century editions revised and enlarged by Todd) seems to have been his guide to conventional British usage. The great renaissance in philology and linguistics had not yet taken place—though Schele De Vere was perhaps one of the men who sparked it—and he lacked the tools and technology which every modern researcher takes for granted. The magnificent *Oxford English Dictionary* was only a vague hope in the minds of several distinguished British scholars, most of whom did not live to see its tenative completion in 1928. The vast array of linguistic journals which we find so useful today simply did not exist. However, again Schele De Vere appears as a pioneer, for he was one of the founders of the American Philological Association, whose purpose was the production and publication of research bearing on language.

If he lacked modern research facilities, he compensated through his own wide background in languages, his intense interest in all phases of American life, his keen powers of linguistic observation, and his remarkable rapport with people. He believed that one must study language where ever one finds it, and he traveled everywhere. Also his familiarity with the major European languages enabled him to converse with and observe the endless waves of immigrants in all stages of assimilation.

In a sense, too, the age in which he lived afforded some advantage, for his work spanned the period between the frontier and the growth of an industrial civilization. During the years while he was collecting material, he could easily hear the speech of old people who recalled the days of the American Revolution, trappers and mountain men of the Northwest, Indian scouts, remnants of the Dutch in New York City and the Hudson Valley, steamboat men, railroad men, politicians and statesmen of a yeasty era, Frenchmen, Creoles, and Spaniards from the Gulf Coast through New Orleans to Texas and the Mexican border just freshly established, farmers from all over the settled lands East of the Mississippi as well as new emigrants in the West, intellectuals in the East-Coast cities North and South, Negroes both free and slave, hillbillies or "mean whites," backwoodsmen, hunters, stockmen, industrialists, seamen, mechanics, and practitioners of every trade and craft then practiced here. He was also quite familiar with what remained of the old Cavalier traditions in his adopted state of Virginia and throughout the Tidewater South. He constantly studied American modes of living and working, and usually made his linguistic observations in terms of the culture as he saw it, in which he to some degree anticipated the principle of modern sociolinguistics. At the same time he obviously began to form a crude picture of the geographic distribution of dialects in the United States.

Like other highly educated Europeans—Tixier, von Humboldt, de Tocqueville, Sir Richard Burton—who visited us while we were new, he often recorded and comprehended more of American life and language than did enlightened Americans themselves, for his viewpoint was fresh, his perspectives deep, and his own mind already shaped by sound scholarly discipline. But, unlike these other foreigners, he came to learn and he stayed to teach. Also, he developed an elegant rococo English style—as became an acknowledged scholar in the heart of the Gilded Age—which, except for very faint traces of Germanic idiom and syntax, probably ranks with the best of his day in his field on both sides of the Atlantic.

In his work with Indian languages and their contributions to American English, he had the advantage of knowing some of the men, ranging from scouts to scholars, who had spent their lives among the Indians. For notes on Indian languages no longer spoken in the East, or not available to him, he combed every diary and journal he could find, from Captain John Smith to the Reverend John Gottlieb Heckewelder. Here he tackled some rather controversial problems head-on, and although he was neither a Bloomfield nor a Hoijer, many of his etymological results compare favorably with those obtained by modern ethno-linguistic methods. Inevitably, he also made some king-size bloopers, which can be accomplished with astonishing ease in this area.

Although his book is a treasure-chest for anyone interested in the development of the American language, it is certainly not without its flaws, the results of inadequate data, bad judgment or even ignorance on the part of the author, or simply the stage at which linguistic science found itself at that time. For example, he suggests that the American *cuss* may derive from customer; for the phrase *to pass in one's checks* (to die) he could think only of a derivation involving *checks* as a name for a work-shirt worn in New England; either from ignorance or excessive delicacy—then an understandable weakness which plagued all scholars—he defines a *stud* as "an old horse who refuses to go on"; for all his knowledge of Anglo-Saxon, he had apparently never heard of flat adverbs, is much disturbed by the widespread confusion of *bad* for *badly*, *slow* for *slowly*, etc., and declares that "their use is, of course, unpardonable." While he was probably the first writer anywhere to chronicle the American institution of Groundhog Day and describe it with laudable exactness, he did not suspect the Algonkian origin of *woodchuck* and fell back lamely on English folk-etymology, which he roundly condemns when used by others.

Of the tall talk of the mountain men, the argot of criminals, the slang of gamblers, the speech of many vigorous, disreputable sub-cultures already imported from Europe and flourishing in America, he has nothing to say. And although he must aften have heard it, he is likewise silent on the vast store of profanity and obscenity known to every frontiersman, especially those who handled mules, and who, delivering it in great rock-shivering strophes and in cathedral tones, could hover delicately and indefinitely between prayer and blasphemy. But social pressures in those days were severe. We must recall that Mark Twain also knew this salty language, even unto the employment of it personally and with sulphurous proficiency, and also remained silent in print—

except for one lone surreptitious and unofficial publication now known to every graduate student. And although Schele De Vere is, to my knowledge, the first writer in English to gloss the name for the powerfully hallucinogenic drug *peyote* (unaware of its Aztec origin, he renders it *peioke*), at the same time he quotes the experiences of a group of desert travelers, introduced to the drug by an Indian scout, in terms sufficiently authentic to be readily recognized by any modern *acid-head* who has ever *taken a trip* on either peyote buttons or LSD.

Because of the relative scarcity of this book, which has only recently been reprinted, few students have had the pleasure of exploring it. Probably, when it appeared, it had a severely limited audience. Certainly in modern times it has not received the interest due it, though H. L. Mencken recognized its importance and gave it a brief note in *Supplement One* of *The American Language* (1945). To my knowledge, the only research done on it was performed by Professor Atcheson Hench of the University of Virginia some years ago, in which Professor Hench, who had discovered Schele De Vere's manuscript notes for a possible second edition, summarized the additions and revisions which the author recorded shortly after the first and only edition appeared. Since these notes give some insight into Schele De Vere's methods, as well as an indication of the state of linguistic scholarship in America in those days, I have persuaded Professor Hench to update some of this material, previously unpublished, for inclusion in this article.

There has been some doubt in the past about whether or not there were possibly two editions instead of the one dated 1872. I think these doubts are now resolved on the basis of book reviews, advertisements included at the end of the 1872 edition describing books already published and on the market in the fall of 1871, and other internal evidence. It now appears that the edition dated 1872 was actually released in 1871, and that there was no other edition. Professor Hench quotes George Watson, of Sir William Craigie's staff of the *Dictionary of American English* as confirming this date. My copy is inscribed as a Christmas gift to one David B. Scott, Jr. on December 25, 1871.

Following are Atcheson Hench's notes on the lines along which Schele De Vere optimistically planned his revisions for a second edition. Only a small number of specific revisions can be included here and it is hoped that the entire list may eventually be published elsewhere.

II

This is a report of a body of manuscript notes on English in America, comparatively small but worth being mentioned to people interested in the American language.[1]

In 1844 Baron Maximilian Schele De Vere, of Swedish birth, and of Prussian and French training, became—under the simpler name of Maximilian Schele—professor of Romance languages at the University of Virginia; and at times from then on he taught Anglo-Saxon as well. In 1871[2] Scribners published his volume *Americanisms, The English of the New World* under his earlier and longer name M. Schele De Vere. In 1895 he retired to Washington, and there in 1898 he died.

Somewhere in the stretch of years from 1844 to 1871 he re-took the name De Vere—for what reason, no one who knew him was able to recall. He had, however, been known so long by the people close to him as Professor Schele or Mr. Schele[3] that many of the older people whom I met here at the University of Virginia in the 1920's who had known him, still used the simple form "Schele." Many others had come to call him by his fuller last name "Schele De Vere." The result was that, until his name disappeared from conversation, he went by either name. I shall use Schele De Vere in this article.

Incidentally, not knowing correctly the parts of his name, the Oxford *New English Dictionary* and later the *Dictionary of American English*, understandably but mistakenly, called him "De Vere." I hope that this paper will help to bring him and his right name together again.

In 1931 or 32 I learned that one of the copies of his book in the University of Virginia library was his own annotated copy containing some 370 deletions, corrections, and additions to his text, about 260 of them being lexical in nature. The two quite different scripts that he used made me think at first that the notes were written from time to time, over the next 20-odd years. But George Watson of the staff of the *DAE*, in a study that he made, shows that the notes were probably all written by 1875 and that most of them were written probably by 1873.[4]

What I am giving in this paper is a resumé of the kinds of things that make up the lexical segment of the notes. Because we students of American English have had the advantage of more than ninety years of study since Schele De Vere's day, some of these are old matters to us now. It would also be misleading of me to say that these notes add greatly to Schele De Vere's contribution to the field. Many of them are corrections of spellings, as with some Indian words. Others improve the accuracy of his text. Now and then on the authority of "Sp," the *Spectator*,[5] he corrects his statement that this or that is an Americanism by noting that this is found also in Scotland, that in Ireland, and that in England.

Here and there he cancels passages. For instance, all that he wrote about the origin of the verb-phrase to *sugar off* (p. 106)—that it came from the "custom of eating the maple-sugar as it is poured off in its hot state on the snow"—goes out. In his text he advocated *I feel badly* (p. 438), but his instinct worked on him, for he has questioned the sentence and has written on the margin " 'I feel bad' seems correct."

On the subject of pronunciation, the notes are few, and the only method that he used to denote pronunciation was spelling. Most of his remarks are about varying pronunciation of words in different sections of America, such as that *fouty* meaning "despicable" (p. 603) was pronounced *fautty* in some parts of New England and *footy* in Pennsylvania; that *scranny* (p. 539) was *scrawny* in the West; that *pokeloken* (p. 20)—an Indian word meaning "marsh"—was "commonly pronounced *pope-logan* by the lumbermen of Maine."

The largest groups of manuscript notes contain either explanations or improvements of Schele De Vere's printed text, or new matter.

Here and there the writings of others, sometimes in the form of newspaper clippings, are the sources of small items. Certain explanations of Indian words he added on the authority of J. H. Trumbull: for instance, of *hominy* (p. 42) from an aspirated word *h'minne, maise* [maize]; of *buccaneer* (p. 71), a French word meaning originally a hunter and a curer of a Brazilian-Indian meat called *boucan*; and of *caucus* (p. 269) from *caucausu*, one who urges, encourages, or pushes on. Using unnamed sources Schele De Vere added the Indian originals of *pecan* (p. 416) and *kiskitomas nut* (p. 59): *pacan*, which to the Indians meant any hard-shell nut, and *s'kooskada'meme*, a name for the hickory nut, which came through American Dutch into American English.

The great bulk of his added matter came from his own experience or from miscellaneous gleanings. He has noted variant forms or spellings of words such as *sharavally* along side of *sherryvally* (p. 109) and *mooley-saw* beside *muley-saw* (p. 146).

In the case of a number of words he has enlarged upon his text by explaining meanings more thoroughly. For instance, he annotates *water-lot* (p. 183) as it was used in the Middle West; there in speculation towns on the Missouri and Mississippi Rivers, during the period of 1834–1840, a *water-lot* was "considered m[ost] valuable as being within reach of water-communication"; it was "in reality worth nothing at all." He describes in detail how the *dipsy* (p. 339), a special kind of whale-bone fish hook, known only in Pennsylvania, was made. He annotates his remarks on a religious *infare* (p. 236) or solemn installation, by saying that it was so called because of its resemblance to a wedding infare or festival. He enlarges the meaning of *snake*, to catch or draw swiftly from any place (p. 213), by adding: "To *snake* in the W. [west] [means] to drag or draw along slowly—especially a stick of timber which makes a snake track on the ground."

There are a good number of popular explanations of the origins of names or expressions in Schele De Vere's notes: of *galvanized Yankee* (p. 23), a *coon's age* (p. 52), a *Sucker*, a person from Illinois (p. 659), and others. I shall let one example stand for all. Kansans are called *Jayhawkers* (p. 282, a clipping) because back in the 1850's a Kansan riding a mule loaded with "plunder" when asked how he happened to be transporting such a load, said that he had been jayhawking and explained that a jayhawk was a bird that warned its prey before devouring it.

Schele De Vere makes no comment on the credibility of such stories; but in view of the fact that he cancelled stories of the same nature from his printed text, I should like to believe that he made these notes for their interest or humor rather than for their truthfulness.

One of these oddities seems to have the facts behind it. It is contained in an undated and unplaced clipping, pasted on p. 255, which reads in part: ". . . asked Professor Porter of Yale why the verb 'gerrymander' was not in the first edition of Webster. The reply was, the widow of Elbridge Gerry lived directly opposite Prof. Goodrich, and, as the families were on intimate terms, he did not have the heart to give 'gerrymander' a place in the *Unabridged*." Although the word seems to have been coined in 1812, the Merriam-Webster people inform me that the truth is that it missed the 1820, 1840, and 1847 editions; that Mrs. Gerry died in 1849, and that the word did appear in the next, the 1864 edition.

The most valuable notes that Schele De Vere has inserted in his volume are the new matter—Americanisms either through their being born here, or through their being diverted to new uses here.

In the realm of slang are such things as: *God-dam*, which he calls Indian English in the phrase (p. 607) "two how-haws and a god-dam," "a yoke of cattle with a driver"; and (p. 420) "*Gumsucking*=kiss'g in Ky & Tenn' coupl^d w[ith] *neck-sawing*."

In the realm of colloquial, regional, or standard American English are many notes. Unlocalized are *striffen* (p. 638), the membrane next to the hide of an animal; *kennel* (p. 506), meal of wheat midway in fineness between flour and bran; *bunty-tailed* (p. 380), descriptive of short frock coats; and *to deacon out* (p. 237), meaning *to line out* (hymn for a church congregation to sing).

Examples of words localized here and there are: *pison-truck* (p. 189), meaning medicine in West Virginia, North Carolina, and Tennessee; *buffalo* (p. 282), meaning, in North Carolina, a maurauder from either the Northern or the Southern army in the Civil War; *nan* (p. 434), meaning in Pennsylvania "What did you say?," a word that was dying out but had been "much used formerly"; *to hike up* (p. 488), to hitch up, descriptive of what in Philadelphia the back of a woman's dress did; and "*darkavised* (s sounded like c)" [=voiceless], dark-visaged, used in Western Pennsylvania of a person with "dark complexion, eyes, beard &c." (p. 594).

I am listing finally a group of samples labelled usually "In the W[est]." If a person belonged to the *Broad Gauge* Church (p. 242), he belonged to the Universalist Church or to no church at all. A *Broad Gauger* could be an infidel or an atheist. The bull-whacker crossed the plains with his terrible *flaggers* or bull whips (p. 225) with which he was "often seen to perform marvell[ou]s feats of cruelty." *Niggerhead* (p. 116) meant a round, hard, dark-colored stone or boulder. *Gopher-hole* (p. 101) meant a dug-out house "very common in Nebr (N Pacific RR & Swedes!) and warm in winter." A *stoop* (p. 89) was the roof of a house. If I interpret the next note right, there was in the West both *cold slaw* (p. 85) and *warm slaw* or *slaw*, which was "finely cut cabbage, slightly cooked & dressed with butter, vinegar, pepper and salt." As for the name for a ploughed field—a Western man "hardly ever calls a ploughed field anything else but a *breaking*. Breaking ploughs are quite distinct fr o [from other] ploughs" (p. 189). To what Schele De Vere said in his text about the use of *logy* (p. 86) meaning dull or boring as of "a *logy* preacher or *logy* talker," he added the note that in the West women used *logy* to describe their pregnant sisters.

I have given forty-odd examples of the 260 lexical notes that Schele De Vere wrote. They can afford only a hint of how much improved a second edition of his *Americanisms* would have been had he published it.

Notes

1. This is a revision of a paper read in December 1934, at a meeting of the Present Day English section of the Modern Language Association, and that I then laid aside. I laid it aside because, after I had sent copies of all Schele De Vere's manuscript notes that were of a lexical nature to Sir William Craigie for possible use in the *Dictionary of American English*, I could see no further value in it. The editing and publishing of the *DAE* was at the time diverting students of American English from an interest in lexicographers of an earlier time.

But, when Professor Maurer recently began studying Schele De Vere and his *Americanisms*, he found out about the existence of my paper and asked me to bring it up to date.

I have rewritten much of the paper, correcting mistakes and changing the text. I have also added information that in the later 1930's Mr. George Watson, of the staff of the *DAE*, sent me as he studied Schele De Vere's notes and prepared to use certain of them in the *DAE*.

A study that I wrote concerning what happened to the manuscript notes after they had gone into the *DAE* files was published recently under the title "The use by the *Dictionary of American English* and the *Dictionary of Americanisms* of Schele De Vere's manuscript notes on Americanisms," *Publications of the American Dialect Society*, No. 46, 1966 (published 1968).

2. On the title-page the date is 1872. But Watson writes: "In the Dictionary we are dating his *Americanisms* 1871, since we know from the reviews of the latter part of that year that it was then published." From a postal card dated 6/24/36.

3. Originally his name was pronounced "Shay-lay." Later it came to be pronounced as if it rhymed with "Bailey."

4. Letters of George Watson, June 5, 1935 and May 12, 1936.

5. George Watson identified *Sp* as meaning the London *Spectator*, Vol. LII, March 2, 1872, pp. 276–7: Letter of George Watson, June 5, 1935.

THE AUDITORY MASS MEDIA AND U

THOMAS PYLES
Northwestern University

In the era of auditory mass media in which we are privileged to live, an American may willy-nilly hear more talk in the course of a waking day than it would have been possible for him to hear in a similar space of time in any previous period of history. Even the day's news is read aloud to him, and frequently explained to him as well. Students of usage, most of whom are, fortunately for their sanity, able to attend mainly to the manner of speech while almost totally disregarding its matter, have thus an unprecedented opportunity of observing stylistic varieties occurring within the context of standard English, which from a democratic point of view can mean only "educated" English.

Our national ideal of equality, so highly esteemed that we are willing to surrender many individual liberties to ensure even its semblance, commits us to the proposition that standard speech is attainable by any man who makes an effort to acquire it. We must continue to assume that conscientiously following a set of reasonably easy precepts involving the avoidance of double negatives, split infinitives, dangling participles, and the like will enable any man to speak as well as any other man, and that such characteristics as those which in less enlightened times were embodied in what was referred to as a "good background" are or should be more or less negligible. Such an assumption implies among other things that a cultured tradition in the apparently outworn sense of the term is of linguistic significance only so far as the style of speech of those who used to be vaguely regarded as "privileged" might be easily imparted to those now fashionably regarded as "culturally deprived."

The subtleties and nuances of the style to which I refer—qualities which those who employ it are for the most part quite unaware of—are of course not teachable; not even, in fact, capable of any thoroughgoing analysis. It would be difficult indeed to say precisely what qualities differentiate the speech styles of, say, Ellsworth Bunker, Senator Hugh Scott, Henry Cabot

Lodge, the late Adlai Ewing Stevenson (but not his son Adlai III), William Frank Buckley, Jr., and William Averell Harriman from those of, say, Richard Milhous Nixon, the Kennedy brothers, Lyndon Baines Johnson, Melvin R. Laird, Nelson Aldrich Rockefeller, and Chester Robert ("Chet") Huntley. The two groups of speakers cited cover a fairly wide political, geographical, and cultural range, and all speak, or have spoken, what is definable as standard American English, despite widespread prejudice against the regional characteristics of Johnson's speech.

To designate these two varieties of standard American English, I shall henceforth, for want of any terms which might be less offensive to democratic sensibilities, use the abbreviations applied to British English by A.S.C. Ross in his well-known "Linguistic Class-Indicators in Present-Day English":[1] U (upper class) and Non-U. The terms were given wide currency by the Hon. Nancy Mitford's use of them in her article "The English Aristocracy," first published in *Encounter* and later in her anthology *Noblesse Oblige* (London, 1956). Miss Mitford gives full credit to Ross for having provided the terms and the specimens that she exhibits. *Noblesse Oblige* begins with Ross's "U and Non-U: An Essay in Sociological Linguistics," a condensed and simplified version of his earlier article.

Like Ross, I use the terms "factually and not in reprobation" and, as previously stated, I take them as designating varieties of standard American English. I do not regard U speech as particularly worthy of emulation by those who do not have it by tradition or as necessarily any more "beautiful" than any other type of speech. Like their British counterparts, American U speakers are, in Ross's words, "not necessarily better educated, cleaner, or richer" than Non-U speakers. They have by and large come from what are thought of, if only locally, as "old families"; and they are conscious of the fact without being particularly proud or ashamed of it. As a rule they give little thought to matters of linguistic usage, and it would probably not occur to most of them to consult a dictionary to find out the pronunciation of any word that they used themselves, since from their point of view the way to say it would obviously be the way they said it.

Although some will regard Ross's term U as snobbish, it is certainly as accurate as anything else that I have been able to come up with—*elite* has connotations of caste equally offensive to egalitarians as U—and it has the advantage of being widely known as a designation for a type or style of speech which almost inevitably must exist in all societies, including those that pride themselves upon their classlessness. It is, incidentally, unlikely that any adult takes this notion of classlessness very seriously, including the political spellbinders who pay lip service to it. Ross points out that even in present-day Russian the distinction between the two plurals of *ofitser* 'officer'—*ofitsery* and *ofitsera*—"is certainly one of class." As for Germany, although the "good Potsdam society of the late twenties," which frowned upon "küss' die Hand" (on being introduced to a lady), may be gone forever, Germans with all their talk about "democracy" are still very conscious of linguistic class-indicators. I was told by a tobacconist in Göttingen, upon my inquiring about the matter, that she had the impression that it was "eleganter" to ask for "ein Pakete (Zigaretten)" than for "ein Päckchen." Whether or not her impression has any validity I do not know, but the concept of German U was there. Germans of high status have informed me that *auf Wiederschauen* (for *auf Wiedersehen*) and *Mahlzeit!* (as a mealtime greeting or valedictory) were avoided by gentlefolk, though it seems likely that these may be merely regionalisms.

It has already been implied that, unlike the more or less standardized speech of those who speak professionally over mass media—the commentators ("news analysts"), the "anchor men," the interviewers, the announcers, and those who deliver the messages (sales talks)—and unlike its British equivalent, American U speech is by no means unmarked by regional characteristics. The speech of Franklin Delano Roosevelt bore the characteristics of his region as well as of his class, but the former were somewhat different from those of Albert Cabell Ritchie, Governor of Maryland throughout the 1920's until 1935. Yet both men were unquestionably U speakers; the usage of both was that of those whom they grew up with, without much regard for the schoolroom prescriptions—which does not mean that they made "grammatical errors"—and for the supposed necessity for euphemism of which Non-U is always keenly conscious.

Differences between U and Non-U word choice are fairly well known, despite the almost complete lack of any scholarly study of these differences as they are manifested in American English.[2] One salient characteristic of U has just been alluded to—the preference for plain and forthright terms instead of euphemistic ones, particularly when the latter are voguish terms smacking of advertising or social uplift, or appear to be employed by Non-U speakers as mealy-mouthed attempts to gloss over facts of life which they may regard as shocking, such as death, excretion, and sex. The male U speaker (for the female of the U species would probably not refer to the activity at all) would of course use some such learned term as *fornication* or *coitus* rather than the more "folksy" word for the same thing, but practically always with a vague sense that he was being foolishly and unnecesarily evasive and a bit pompous.

Where sex is not involved, however, the U term very often coincides with the term used by speakers of nonstandard(that is, sub-Non-U) English, who say *crazy*, *old man* (or *woman*), and, in formal circumstances at least, *toilet paper*, not so much as a matter of taste as because they are unfamiliar with such namby-pambyisms as *mentally ill*, *senior citizen*, and *bathroom tissue*.[3] But U speakers are generally quite tolerant of Non-U terms and may even find them faintly amusing; they respect the right of anyone to say *finalize*, *budgetwise*, *in depth*, and *breakthrough*, but they would not use these terms themselves, perfectly standard though they are. Perhaps it would be more accurate to say that they would not use them in talking to other U speakers, for it is an ironic fact that many such modish terms are the concoctions of men in popular journalism and advertising who are, as Fadiman points out in the article cited, U by birth and education, meaning that they come from "old" families and have gone to Ivy League schools.

U pronunciation, unhappily for those who may yearn for it but do not have it by tradition, is shot through with subtleties of one sort or another rather than being consistent or reasonable as the old textbook rules dictated. For instance, loss of the first /r/ in *February* might occur in U pronunciation, but never a similar loss in *secretary* and *library*. There is nothing Non-U about the loss of /n/ in the second syllable of *government*, but the assimilatory /m/ for /n/ at the beginning of the second syllable of *hypnotize* is decidedly Non-U. What is popularly called "dropping the *g*" in words ending in -*ing* is unquestionably U, though by now somewhat old-fashioned; this conservative practice is still widespread in nonstandard speech, but not in Non-U, where it has been "taught out." Such apparent inconsistencies, such infringements of regulations highly regarded by Non-U speakers, occurring as they do within a type of speech which is usually marked by a blithe self-assuredness, are both annoying and baffling to those who, like the aforesaid Non-U speakers, have learned by the book.

The pronunciations to be treated in the discussion which follows have been taken down from the mouths of persons who are much in the news, most of them professional commentators from the auditory mass media, but some from speakers who appear on the media as interviewees, panelists, and the like because of their importance in American life. If not invariably professional public speakers, all are by any conceivable definition prominent Americans, and most have political potency on a national or metropolitan scale. There are no citations from speakers who, deservedly or not, have been publicly pilloried for their malapropisms, fractured syntax, markedly regional speech, and the like. Thus Chicago's Mayor Richard Daley, who except for an occasional /d/ for /ð/ has spoken what I consider to be standard English on the few occasions when I have heard him, is not represented. My present concern is with a variety of speech which no one acquainted with the cultural and social vagaries of the "American way" could possibly impugn as nonstandard.

As for the pronunciations of network newscasters, commentators, "anchor men," and those of almost equal prestige who exhort us to buy their particular brand of deodorant, laxative, headache remedy, detergent, or shampoo cream, many may be regarded by a handful of U speakers as affected, naive, or simply in a vague sort of way Non-U. Nevertheless, all pronunciations cited represent what must be accepted by any truly democratic criterion as standard; all represent "educated" usage—the usage of expensively groomed, high-salaried, mellifluous speakers, whose voices exude a self-confidence which cannot but be tremendously impressive to their considerable following of admirers. If the usage of such high-powered speakers be not adjudged standard English, I know not what should be.

Usually, it is to be suspected, the auditory media do not originate but merely reflect Non-U usage and, because of the eminence in the popular mind of those who speak professionally over these media, lend it authority and prestige. Thus, when Eric Sevareid, a widely respected pundit, solemnly pronounces *particularly* and *regularly* with penultimate secondary stress, he is certainly not using idiolectal pronunciations but rather ones that have been fairly widespread in Non-U speech for some time, though as yet unrecorded in the dictionaries.[4] But the prestige of Mr. Sevareid is awesome; and it is likely that, even without supporting usage by other TV "personalities," his usage would suffice to give final sanction to the pronunciations cited. U speakers may consider them either affected or naive, or both, but U speakers are doubtless best regarded as a moribund species; it is certain that no U speaker is anywhere near as impressive as Eric Sevareid. Similarly, when an even more frequently audible and visible reporter-commentator-analyst—an LL.D. *honoris causa*, no less—charged by his network with "covering" Sir Winston Churchill's funeral some years ago inserted a svarabhakti vowel between the *n* and the *s* of *Westminster*, he was merely giving authority to a Non-U pronunciation of the word symbolized by the spelling *Westminister* which appeared on the TV screen in the same program. Although labeled "substandard" by *Webster's Third*, the pronunciation cited is used by many quite respectable and some quite prominent Americans in addition to the commentator cited, in view of which fact I should hesitate to call it even nonstandard. Non-U it certainly is.

Some of the pronunciations to be cited as Non-U seldom occur in non-standard or substandard speech for the obvious reason that the words themselves seldom occur in such speech; the pronunciations indicated are thus pretty much confined to standard Non-U. Others, like the common pronunciations of *premises* and *processes* as if these were third-declension Latin plurals in /ɪz/,[5] like *crises*, *analyses*, and *indices*, may have seeped down into nonstandard usage but certainly originated in rather rarefied intellectual circles, where they are heard from speakers of unquestionably high status. They are by no means unknown in the groves of Academe, which are not inhabited exclusively by U speakers nowadays, if indeed they ever were. U speakers, whether or not they are aware that *premises* and *processes* are not Latin loan-words, are in their stodgy traditional way likely to consider the Latinized pronunciation somewhat showy or, what is usually equally repugnant to the U linguistic psyche, newfangled.[6]

The increasing frequency in all positions of /ž/—earlier confined to medial position in loan-words taken into English from Old French, like *vision*, *pleasure*, and *azure*—is a phenomenon of recent times strikingly reflected in, and perhaps originating from, the auditory mass media. In all types of educated speech, U and Non-U alike, it occurs initially and finally only in a few quite recent loan-words from French, like *genre* and *beige*, in which it is taken directly from Modern French. Nonstandard speech lacks initial /ž/, since French words beginning with the sound are no part of the word stock of the unschooled; in final position, in a few words like *rouge* and *garage* having currency in such speech, /ǰ/ replaces standard /ž/. Non-U speakers, including those on the media, have extended this originally non-English consonant to a number of words in which there is no historical reason for it. It is, for instance, fairly usual in Italian *adagio* and may be heard in *Borgia, (Di) Maggio*, and *(Vesti la) Giubba*, although the Italian value symbolized by *gi* is of course /ǰ/; it is apparently also assumed to be the sound symbolized by *j* in *rajah* and *Taj (Mahal)* and by *sh* in *cashmere* and in other words recognized as non-English, no matter what their precise provenience. The pronunciations cited are almost certainly of American origin; some are recorded in American dictionaries, none in British dictionaries. The *g* of *menagerie*, genuinely French, has apparently been pronunced /ǰ/—the only pronunciation recorded in the *OED* and other British dictionaries—since its adoption into English in the early eighteenth century. Non-U has, however, Gallicized the consonant as /ž/. Less easily accounted for is the recent occurrence of /ž/ in the Latin loan-words *coercion, fission*, and *subterfuge*.

Although of genuine French provenience, *liege* has been a part of the English word stock since the thirteenth century, about as long as *marriage* has been. Its final consonant is nevertheless sometimes pronounced as if it had been recently adopted. Even Prince Charles, on the occasion of his investiture as Prince of Wales, swore to be his mother's /liž/ man, so that the pronunciation in question is obviously on its way to becoming the King's English—or so it is devoutly to be wished. The word is of course of rare occurrence in current English; it is thus not surprising, in view of its French "look," that it should have acquired a Modern French final consonant that has not as yet, it should be noted, occurred in the more familiar *siege*.

In U, particularly older-generation U, the Latin plural ending *i* is usually /aɪ/, as in *fungi, cacti, stimuli*, and *alumni*,[7] but otherwise final *i* in Latin loanwords is /ɪ/, as in the prefixes *anti* and *semi*. Non-U, however, pronounces the plural ending /i/ but usually has /aɪ/ in the prefixes when they are easily recognizable as such, as in *anti-intellectual, antisocial, antiaircraft, semiofficial*, and *semimonthly* (in contrast to *antiseptic* and *semicolon*, in which prefix and root are completely welded). Equally perverse from the point of view of the U speaker is Non-U's un-English /i/ for /aɪ/ in the first syllables of *biography* and *biotic*; in *antibiotic* Non-U reverses the traditional English vowels of the second and third syllables.

Overcareful speech, frequently based upon spelling, is characteristic of the professional mass-media speaker, whose standards of linguistic propriety demand something less devil-may-care than schwa in the first syllables of such words as *collaborate, occur(rence), opinion, obedient, official*, and *offensive*; typically, he uses /o/ in these and similar words, so that their traditionally unstressed initial syllables receive a very slight degree of stress lacking in less painstaking, if more traditional, U speech. Similarly, he prefers /i/ to traditional /ɪ/ (or schwa) is *essential, effect(ive), efficient, effeminate*, and the like.

The concern with giving every syllable what is regarded as its just dues is likewise evident in the mass-media treatment of the final syllables of the names of the days of the week and of *holiday*, which become /de/. Analysis of these previously amalgamated compounds is, it should be mentioned, now usual among younger-generation speakers, who pronounce the words in question with the same stressing as in *birthday*. John S. Kenyon's labeling of the use of the unreduced vowel in these words as "semiliterate formal" will not do for today's speech.[8]

Spelling is certainly responsible for the supposedly hifalutin (but decidedly Non-U) pronunciation of final *-or* with unreduced vowel, thus carefully distinguishing words with this ending from words in *-er*. There is not always complete consistency: I have recorded "senators and legislators' in the formal speech of a Non-U politician with /-ərz/ in the first word and /-ɔrz/ in the third. The unreduced vowel may nonetheless occur in *senator* or indeed in practically any word ending in *or*, whether or not an agentive suffix, for instance, *ambassador, competitor, juror, Bangor,* and *creator* (with reference to God, the full vowel giving the word a certain mouth-filling dignity felt to be appropriate to such elevated reference).

Unreduced final vowels also occur in the type of speech under consideration in *window, widow, narrow, thorough, borough*, and the like. The judgment of Kenyon and Knott in 1944 (unrevised in subsequent printings of the *Pronouncing Dictionary of American English*) that the ending *-ow* (or *-ough*) is "seldom pronounced" with a full vowel "except with artificial care" is no longer strictly accurate; the final /o/ is now usual not only in the auditory mass media but also on all levels of younger-generation speech. Older-generation U speakers continue to pronounce /-ə/.

Whether to their credit or not, network professionals have by and large given up certain pronunciations which have been the subject of puristic objurgation in the press, for example, that for *nuclear* as if written **nucular*[9] favored by Dwight David Eisenhower, Melvin R. Laird, Secretary of Defense in the Nixon cabinet, and Robert Miller, manager of the Nevada Test Site, among many others; that for *column* riming with *volume*, which used to be heard much more frequently than it is nowadays; and that for *escalate* as if written **esculate*, still preferred by many of high rank in our armed services. These and other pronunciations to be indicated which may by now be eschewed by the professionals nevertheless occur again and again from speakers or unquestioned status—government officials, physicists, social scientists, medical gurus, business leaders, and the like—who in our society are eminently newsworthy. (U speakers by and large have only a local prominence and thus are seldom in the national news.)

But subtler Non-U designators have hung on in network usage, such as *congratulate* as if written *congradulate; *dissect* riming with *bisect*; *minera-logy* and *genealogy* with antepenultimate /a/, by analogy with many words in -*ology*; *schedule* as if written *schedual; *potential* and *substantial* as if written *-*tual* (and *substantiate* as if *-*tuate*); *grievous* riming with *previous*; *insidious* and *invidious* as if written *-*duous*; *stupendous* and *tremendous* as if written *-*dious*; *portentous* as if written *-*tious*; *deteriorate* as if written *deteriate or *deterorate; *priority* as if written *priorority; and *beneficiary* as if written *beneficiarary.[10]

Non-U practically always has strongest stress on the initial syllables of *millionaire* (frequently with loss of /l/), *cigarette*, *magazine*, *dictator*, and *spectator*, though initial stress in the last two words is now so widespread that it can hardly be considered a Non-U designator in any American speaker under sixty. Perversely enough, from the point of view of the U speaker, Non-U reverses the traditional initial stress of *berserk*, *Barnett*, *Bernard*, *Purcell*, *Gerard*, and *Maurice*, perhaps to give these words what is felt to be a tony Gallic flavor. The first name of the actor Maurice Evans, now that he has become an American, is /mərís/ rather than /mɔ́rɪs/, though when the same name is spelled *Morris* the traditional pronunciation is always used.

Such pronunciations as have been here cited, taken from what I conceive to be standard speech as heard over the auditory mass media, will probably strike most older-generation speakers who are perceptive about such matters as Non-U designators. In any event, they are all innovations, which from the usually conservative U point of view amounts to much the same thing.

But, despite the conservatism of U, it is certain that much of the Non-U of one generation becomes the U of the next. When, in the latter part of the eighteenth century, conservative speakers like Dr. Johnson deplored the retraction of /æ/ to /a/ in what Kenyon calls the *ask*-words, they could not have been aware that such vulgar pronunciations (vulgar to their ears, at least) would ultimately prevail in Standard British English, though the older vowel survives in the speech of most Americans.

Likewise, in the early years of the present century pronunciation of the *t* in *often* was a Non-U designator; but pronouncing the *t* is now widespread in U speech, both American and British. Pronunciation as the spelling seems to indicate has occurred in formal broadcast speeches of two English kings, Edward VIII and George VI. Whether or not the present sovereign lady and her family pronounce the *t* I have not had the opportunity to observe, but I should be surprised if they did not.

It is thus likely that many of the pronunciations here cited (but not reprehended) as Non-U will occur in the U speech of the next generation. Such is the course of linguistic history. My own grandfather, born in 1857, thought my pronunciation of *a* before *lm* (the only one current today, except for *salmon*, in which U has /æ/) utterly reprehensible; an almshouse was to him an "amshouse," he read the "sams" in church, and, had he been an evangelical, would doubtless have been soothed by the "bam" of Gilead. His usage, it should be said, was somewhat retarded even for his generation.

There were no auditory mass media on which to blame newfangled pronunciations in Grandfather's day; they must then have been attributed to the natural perversity of what was regarded, always with disapproval, as the rising generation. In the more enlightened days in which we live, however, there can be little doubt that these mass media have hastened the dissemination of pronunciations which those of us who have the misfortune of being older-generation are quick to stigmatize as Non-U, albeit more in sorrow than in anger—untraditional pronunciations mostly stemming from a highly regarded if rather easily acquired literacy.

Without the media, on which we are all to some degree "hooked," it is doubtful that we should be particularly aware of such changes as have been discussed. With the media, we may witness the emergence, if not indeed the fruition, of a cultural and social level of speech that, though it may lack such outworn and undemocratic qualities as elegance and sophistication, must be regarded, as it has been here regarded, as a variety of standard English which is both widely admired and widely emulated. It is difficult to conceive of a more appropriate means of communication for the brave new world envisaged by our more advanced thinkers—a classless world in which tradition and elegance will, it is hoped, play no part.

Notes

1. *Neuphilologische Mitteilungen*, LV (1954), 20–56.
2. They are treated somewhat superficially by Vance Packard in *The Status Seekers* (New York, 1959), who cites (p. 41) contrasting examples of upper-class (U) and middle-class (Non-U) word choices from E. Digby Baltzell's *Philadelphia Gentelmen* (Glencoe, Ill., 1958), and by Clifton Fadiman in "On the Utility of U-Talk," which appeared in *Holiday* magazine and in his *Any Number Can Play* (Cleveland, Ohio, 1957) and is reprinted in *The World of Words*, ed. Barnet Kottler and Martin Light (Boston, 1967), pp. 179–87.
3. Ross points out that *toilet paper* is Non-U in British English, the U term being *lavatory paper* (in 1954). Both *toilet* and *lavatory* are of course euphemisms, but they supplanted plainer terms so long ago as to require other euphemisms for the squeamish: *rest room, comfort station, little boys'* (or *girls'*) *room*, and the like. The "plainer terms" referred to are not themselves very plain; one would have to go very far back to find really plain ones in general use. There is need for a sound historical study of cloacinal semantics.
4. The words in question may also in Non-U speech have an extra syllable, as if written *particularily* and *regularily*, perhaps by analogy with *ordinarily*, *primarily*, and other adverbs in *-arily*.
5. They are in fact not even taken from Latin. *Sequence*, which often has Non-U plural /-ìz/, is genuinely Latin, from *sequentia*; its Latin plural is of course *sequentiae*. For a few other spurious Latin third- declension plurals, see John Algeo, "More False Latin," *American Speech*, XLI (1966), 72–74.
6. The traditional English pronunciation of the Latin plural ending written

−es is of course /−iz/; but *mores*, a genuine third-declension Latin plural, usually has pseudo-classical /−es/ or /−ez/, pronunciations doubtless promulgated by the sociologists, for whom the word is a technical term. It is of fairly recent adoption into English.

7. Note that the Non-U pronunciation of *alumni* is thus identical with the older (and doubtless still U) pronunciation of *alumnae*, with traditional English-Latin /i/ for −*ae*; and that Non-U *alumnae* (with /aɪ/) likewise becomes identical with U *alumni*.

8. "Cultural Levels and Functional Varieties of English," *College English*, X (1948), 32.

9. Respellings and riming words, rather than phonetic transcriptions, will be used henceforth whenever possible; they have the virtue of suggesting analogies—in this instance with *circular*, *jocular*, *particular*, and the like.

10. The pronunciation cited for *beneficiary* was that used by our thirty-sixth President in a broadcast telephone conversation with the Gemini astronauts Cooper and Conrad on August 29, 1965. He did not originate it.

"OBSCENITIES" IN CONTEMPORARY AMERICAN ENGLISH

GEORGE L. TRAGER
Northern Illinois University

The social dialectology of American English has always been one of Raven McDavid's main interests. As a near-contemporary of mine, he has, I am sure, encountered in the spoken language of his own and others' children the use of what to him, and me, were tabu words when we were being taught how to behave "properly." I hope he will accept this note on some encounters of mine with two of these words as a contribution to the ethnology of speaking with which he and I have so long been concerned professionally as well as personally.

I shall consider what are probably the two most common items, /fək/ and /šít/, and their paradigmatic set-members. (I suppose I should apologize to the young users of these words for my "squareness" in writing them phonemically rather than in ordinary orthography. This probably emphasizes their being still, to me, "obscenities"; if I wrote them in ordinary spelling, they would be, perhaps, just lexical items. But this question of their status in this regard is precisely one of the things I want to discuss.)

1. It was noted long ago, in an article to which I no longer have the reference, that in England in the late nineteenth century the term /fəkiŋ/ as an adjective had become a sort of general "empty" modifier, without even emphasizing force, to any description, whether praising or derogatory; in the uses discussed there, it was a slightly more shocking (to the prissy) term than the more usual *bloody*. To Americans, the idea of *bloody* as an obscenity has always been laughable; to read that /fəkiŋg/ was a not necessarily stronger substitute was also amusing, but couldn't help being shocking too. With the passage of time, the American usage that I observe going on about me of /fəkiŋ/ as an adjective has grown somewhat along the lines of the British usage of another day; but the term doesn't seem to have become "empty" of meaning; it is, along with the other members of its paradigm, a strong word, a modifier with meaning, a word that is not complimentary, but—not an obscenity.

We might start with the World War II term written *snafu*. Despite the conventions of what was printable in those days, everybody knew that the term was made up of the initials of "situation normal—all /fɘkt/ up", but the explanatory euphemism "all fouled up" was invented immediately. The pronunciation /snæfúw/ seems to have arisen "naturally" from the spelling (the question of how that came about could certainly give rise to a separate long article!). The word *snafu* soon became a fairly usual item in colloquial speech, and has continued in use, with all the nominal and verbal paradigmatic forms. It is a printable and respectable term, and by now it is probably only we old-timers who know what the *f* "really" means, while everybody else has long forgotten that the word is an acronym (or remembers only the euphemistic explanation).

Let us now present a small corpus of usages, and after that we can try some generalizations.

1.1. A colleague and friend of many years, a "Southern gentleman" in speech and demeanor by upbringing and choice, began, a decade or so ago, to use, in the presence of "ladies", including students, such utterances as these:

"That's a lot of /fɘkiŋ/ nonsense." (gloss: 'unmitigated'.)

"/fɘk/ the administration." (Academicians need no gloss for this one.)

"That character is a /fɘk/." (Of a fellow academician with whom he disagreed strongly; gloss: 'fool', 'non-scientist', 'misleader of the young', etc.)

"Why /fɘk/ it all, dear, I'll show you if you don't believe me". (To the wife of a colleague, at a cocktail party. The gloss for the whole first clause here is something like 'Disregarding the usual proprieties, . . . '.)

The early instances of these utterances were, as far as I could judge, used sparingly, and were brought on by real emotional need. With the passage of time, they became more frequent, were used in more neutral situations, and with less reticence in the presence of women. Nonetheless, it is my impression that the term always had some kind of special paralanguage—a slight "thinning" perhaps, or, by overcompensation and contrast, greater resonance; or under-loudness, and a contrasting over-loudness on the immediately following occasion.

1.2. The uses alluded to are not, of course, new in themselves. Men have used these terms, in this way, in male company, for many years—and usually, I should judge, with the paralanguage variations mentioned. What is new is the use of the term in the presence of, and to, women.

All through the development of freedom of use of the term, there has continued the use of /fɘk/ in its literal meaning. When so used, in appropriate situations, it has no special paralanguage accompaniments. It is especially noticeable that as used by women, in intimate situations or as evidence of their "emancipation," it seems NEVER to have any special paralanguage.

This use of /fɔk/ as an ordinary word has come to be quite frequent among younger people especially. For instance, the supposedly "way-out" movies that get rated "X" (= 'No one under 18 admitted') are often referred to as /fɔk/-*films*; as one who has seen many of the old-fashioned stag-smoker type of film (without color or sound), I can only take this usage as a case of misunderstanding, since these technically excellent pictures seem utterly lacking in any but imaginary /fɔkiŋ/. For myself, I still exhibit a tendency to use at least some "thinning" when citing the term as a linguistic example (say as a cognate with Latin *pugnare!*).

When I first grew old enough (a long time ago!) to begin to understand the use of the term in its non-literal meaning, I was inclined to react with the thought that the usage as a derogatory or depreciative term was somewhat surprising, in view of the supposedly high value set on the "real thing." At that time I was, of course, considering the term as an obscenity, one to be relished and appreciated in its literal, "neutral"-paralanguage-accompanied, use, and to be used sparingly, but with the force of its obscene nature, in invective or as a derogatory term.

1.3. Interpreting the observed changes in frequency of use, I would now say that /fɔk/ has acquired polysemy, and in the process has lost its obscenity. It is, as it were, two words: one is a term of invective and degradation, but with little forcefulness, and no visible relation to the other term; the second is a term for copulation, used almost without hesitation on appropriate occasions, and by men and women, while words like *copulation* or *intercourse* are the ones now said with special paralanguage, having now become (perhaps?) obscenities.

A further observation is, I believe, justified: the very young (the high-school "pot" users?) seem not to employ the term as a manifestation of sophistication and worldliness. This is probably because they are victims, among other things, of the growing neo-monacisticism of our society—but that too is another paper, in another field.

Before turning to our second term, mention should be made of the originally Negro-dialect expression *mother-*/fɔkɨr/ and its paradigmatic associates. In the general white society, this term was once unknown—or known only to a few. Now, in the allusion "half a word," almost everybody in the "enlightened" middle classes knows the joke (the proud mother says of her baby, "He just learned half a word!"). This too is no longer an obscenity, I think.

2. The use of /šít/ as a general term of derogation, and with only peripheral, if any, reference to its literal meaning, has existed for a long time. I shall not adduce any historical data here, other than to say that the kids were using it well over half-a-century ago when I was in high school. And the usage was widespread enough, geographically and socially, to have given rise to euphemisms.

Early in my academic career, I was teaching in a church-related college in a part of the Bible-belt. A young lady of my acquaintance (a school-teacher in the town) was constantly using the expression "Oh, shoot!" to denote mild chagrin or disappointment or the like. She was (literally) a minister's daughter, and her general use of the language was very proper by the standards of the late '20s. Yet this expression was used by her in exactly the same ways that I, in masculine company, would have said "Oh, /šít/!" When our acquaintance had matured sufficiently to permit objective discussion of such scholarly matters, I mentioned this parallelism to her; she was greatly surprised, said she had learned the expression at home (in Iowa), that it was used freely by all kinds of people, and that it apparently had no connotations of impropriety about it. She accepted the argument that it must be a euphemism, but this in no way affected her free use of the term. The vocalic nucleus in her speech was /ɨw/, but there could have been no phonemic confusion even if she had used /i/ instead of /ɨ/, which she didn't.

2.1. A corpus of the uses of /šít/ is difficult to present, because it is used so frequently, and with little variation. A few common expressions will have to suffice:

"Oh. /šít/!" Well established, very frequent, devoid of even shock value.

"That's a lot of /šít/." This expression seems to have completely ousted "That's a lot of bull." The only relic of the latter that I seem still to hear is "Bull-/šìt/!", as an indication of disbelief in and lack of appreciation of something that has been said.

"That man is a real /šít/." Here the term is perhaps a little weaker than the older, and non-obscene in any way, term *jerk*.

"Why, /šít/, man!" The beginnings of a remonstrance or counter-argument. With *man* replaced by a proper name, or a kinship term, it gets used frequently and freely in innumerable situations, and quite without restraint, to old-fashioned parents who are "liberal" but yet "square" in many of their behavior patterns and reactions to the young.

"That was a /šítiy/ exam." This is the common adjectival form, and mans something like 'unfair, ill-conceived, designed to ensnare and mislead', or 'I was unprepared for it'.

2.2. Although /šít/ is used freely in the presence of females, I have noted little use of the term by them, but I am told by a reliable informant that it is freely used by women among themselves, as in women's dormitories.

Another limitation on the use of /šít/ is that, except by men in the least inhibited situations, the term seems not to be used in its literal meaning of 'feces' or 'defecate'. This may well be due to the long years of euphemisms imposed on us all by the middle-class preoccupation with toilet-training. Physicians use *B.M.*, *bowel-movement*, *stool*, and are literally shocked by the use by a layman of *feces* or *defecate* (I've never tried saying just plain /šít/ to one, but the experiment ought to be made, with sound film available to record the results). Mothers (and other relatives) invent all kinds of baby-words, among which the expression *do-do* is probably the most common nowadays. When the child gets older, he may learn /šít/ and try to use it, but will commonly get reproved for it. Many people end up using *crap* for the literal uses of /šít/ was well as for most of the uses of the kind cited above.

3. A learned paper must have a summary and/or a conclusion.

Both /fək/ and /šít/ have come to be more freely used in mixed company nowadays than 50 years ago. They are partially interchangeable, but /fək/ is more verbal, /šít/ more nominal. Both are no longer obscene, and on many occasions even have little if any shock value. The euphemisms and technical terms used for the literal meanings have come to acquire some of the obscene or improper connotations as the two terms themselves have lost the latter.

I think it safe to conclude, however, that, if /fək/ and /šít/ should some day go out of use, they will not be replaced by *copulate* or *feces* as "swear"-words. English is much too monosyllabic for that, though I must admit that I have been startled on hearing or reading a sentence beginning with "That's a lot of . . .", to find it ending with "data" instead of what I expected.

RESPONSES OF CO-WORKERS TO THE WORD *INFORMANT*

Gerald Udell

in collaboration with

John McKenna, Sara Chapman,
Francis Xavier, and Johnnie D. Ragsdale, Jr.
Ohio University

While interviewing for the Linguistic Atlas, the Dictionary of American Regional English, and for a study of speech in Akron, Ohio, I repeatedly became aware that I was carefully avoiding the use of the term *informant*: not only during the interviews themselves, but in the course of conversations preceding and following them: with the persons interviewed, with candidates for interviewing, and with intermediaries. Upon reflection I decided that I was censoring myself because of a feeling that *informant* and *informer* might very well have the same significance in the minds of the persons I was dealing with.

Anyone who has done dialect field work will not need to be told that securing properly qualified persons for interviewing can be difficult, frustrating, and occasionally even impossible. Manifestations of suspicion and hostility, which seem absurd to those who know that the motivations of linguistic geographers are, if not pure, at least harmless, provide any experienced gatherer of dialect with a stock of anecdotes. Field workers *are* commonly suspected of working for the Treasury, the FBI, or one of the locally present finance companies. Even sponsorship by the university of the state does not always resolve such problems. One dirt farmer in the Ozarks, sitting on the porch of his unpainted dwelling, looking over his clearing in the wooded hills, met my statement that I worked for the University of Missouri with blunt hostility, though I came recommended by his brother. He subsequently declared that the University was primarily engaged in wasting the taxpayer's money and had never discovered anything which would help farmers like himself. A few moments later he bluntly asserted that he would not participate in the project I was connected with, nor any other like it, whatever it was. It would seem clear that in situations of this type, in any negotiating to get someone to grant several hours to a stranger for the purpose of answering a set of unknown questions, unnecessary risks shouldn't be run.

But does the term *informant* actually involve a risk? Does the kind of speakers whose cooperation is sought in studies of dialect actually react unfavorably to the word in significant numbers? It does not seem that the question should be answered on the basis of intuition, as popular as that source of information has become in linguistics. This article will report an attempt to provide data, gathered objectively, on which a more informed judgment can be made. We may get some enlightenment, however, if we first glance at what the lexicographers have to offer.

Materials supplied by Merriam *Webster's New International Dictionary*, both second and third editions, and by the *Oxford English Dictionary* are pertinent. Merriam *Webster's Third* indicates that an *informant* is "one that informs: one who gives information: as a: INFORMER b: one who supplies cultural or linguistic data in response to interrogation by an investigator." A check at the entry *informer* turns up the following: "2: one that informs or imparts knowledge or news 3: one that informs against another: a: one that informs a magistrate of a violation of law: one that lays an information: esp. one that makes a practice of informing against others for violations of penal laws particularly when the informer may receive as reward a share of the money penalty imposed—called also *common informer* . . . b: one secretly in the service of the police or of a diplomatic agency (as an embassy) that supplies information."

If these materials are interpreted according to the instructions given among the prefatory sections to the dictionary and without introducing gratuitous suppositions, there is nothing in the entries to indicate that apart from the sense associated with linguistics the two forms are not interchangeable. The prefatory explanations make it clear that the context of an occurence and a feeling for that context will have to guide the user of the dictionary.

The second edition is bolder. It does not caution the reader that his selection of meanings is heuristic: the explanatory materials say nothing on the subject. The entries under *informant* and *informer* are substantially the same in the second and third editions, with the following important exceptions: the special sense of *informant* associated with linguistics is not yet noticed in 1934. Also, the statement is made in the second edition, in connection with the treatment of the synonymy of *informant* and *informer* that "*informer* is often, *informant* never, a term of opprobrium." The suggestion of the second edition entries seems then to be that the denotations of the two terms are nearly identical but that the connotative implications are often diverse. Evidence will subsequently be presented which will rather strongly suggest that the omission of the declaration concerning the possible opprobrium attached to *informer* and the impossibility of opprobrium being attached to *informant* represents one point at which the third edition advanced beyond the second. Nor can it be alleged with impunity that the second edition was reporting a state of the language existing in 1934 but no longer the same in 1961.

The O. E. D. says nothing about opprobrium being attached to either form but it gives as one of the senses of *informant* the legal one, "one who lays an information against a person; and 'informer'." The earliest citation of its occurrence with this sense is dated 1783. It reads as follows: "It was the last evidence of the kind; the informant was hanged." The citation makes it possible at least that *informant* had already begun the process which would attach to it some opprobrium.

The inevitable distance between dictionaries and the totality of phenomena they attempt to reliably report is not as widely known as it should be, but it can be presumed that it will be appreciated by readers of this report. At least it is hoped that the reader will agree that there is no guarantee that the generalizations of any dictionary or any set of them is sufficient for making practical judgments involving the data to which the generalizations presumably apply. So, here: it seemed desirable to investigate directly what the reactions of native speakers of English were to the term *informant* and specifically the reactions of persons qualified to serve as sources of data for the Linguistic Atlas.

The polling of *informants* regarding their reactions to the word *informant* was conducted in all its aspects in cooperation with graduate students in my class, *The Development of American English*, in the Fall of 1968, as a means of introducing them to the methodology underlying the Linguistic Atlas. These students participated fully in designing the questionnaire used, in finding qualified persons willing to grant interviews, in interviewing them, in analyzing the data collected, and in composing reports of the findings. The importance of their contributions is reflected in their being listed as co-authors of this report.

An objection to the methodology of this study may just as well be considered at the onset of the description of it. The number of persons interrogated is small: only twenty-eight. Furthermore the sample is not very well distributed either vertically or horizontally. Only natives of four states, Vermont, New York, Ohio, and West Virginia, are represented. There are seven Class III speakers, sixteen Class II speakers, but only five Class I.[1] Since Class I speakers, those most limited in education, are the most difficult to secure, at least in certain age groups and in urban areas, the desirability of having more such speakers is evident. To make matters worse, none of the speakers are residents of large urban communities. The solution to all this would have been to make the sample larger and more broadly representative. Why wasn't this done?

Well, in a day when data gathering has gone out of fashion (like the oil industry, linguists are now making use of accumulated fat), perhaps a sample made up of twenty-eight speakers needs no defense. Besides, there is no article of confederation that specifies that a study has to be overwhelmingly conclusive. Twenty-eight were what could be managed under the prevailing circumstances. It may turn out that twenty-eight speakers were enough to make some significant points.

At the heart of the investigation was the set of questions used. In addition to supplying information for vitae of the kind assembled for Atlas and D. A. R. E. studies, the persons interviewed were asked five questions. At the same time they were given a dittoed copy of the question sheet, one page at a time, so that the clues provided by the questions as to the specific intentions of the survey accumulated in programmed fashion. Those polled were told that the survey was simply an exercise in language study; its aim was to discover something about how a somewhat randomly selected sample of the population reacted to a particular set of words and phrases. The aim of the exercise was, then, to provide a glimpse into the vast universe of feelings and conceptualizations which surround the words and phrases people use. Each interviewer explained the purposes of the study in his own way, but the explanation was to be as nebulous as the preceding in every case.

The pages of the questionnaire read as follows: page one: "#1. As you hear each of the following words would you tell what your reaction to each of them is? Say whether the word strikes you as a favorable word to apply to a person, an unfavorable word, or a neutral word (neither favorable nor unfavorable when applied to a person): a discussant, a co-operator, a respondent, an interviewee, an informant, a collaborator, a donor, an assister, a researchant, a contributor, a helper, an answerer, a consultant, a correspondant (sic), an assistant, a conferee, a supplier, a source person, an answerant, a conferent. #2. What does each of the following words mean? Explain as best you can in your own words: an informant, a helper, a co-operator, a respondant (sic)." Page two: "#3. You will be given two lists of words that have to do with jobs people have or the kinds of activities people may carry on. For each of the words in list #1, see if there are any words in list #2 which have just about the same meaning. If there are, point them out. List #1: Attorney, Bricklayer, Spouse, Informant, Player. List #2: Mason, Lady, Warden, Lawyer, Astronomer, Police Spy, Coach, Pick-pocket. #4. If a friend asked you to serve in a study of how people in different parts of the country speak and told you that your job would be to answer some easy questions, which of the following ways of referring to this job would you like best (pick the three best in the order: best, next best, third best)? Which would you like least (name them in the order: worst, not as bad, least bad)? A respondent, a consultant, a source person, an informant, an answerer, a discussant, an assistant, a conferee, a co-operator, a co-worker, an interviewee." Page three: "#5. Select any terms from the list given you which *closely* fit the following definition: *A person who secretly reports to the police concerning the activities of some radical political group which is illegal or may be declared illegal and of which he is a member.* A reporter, a respondent, an undercover agent, an informant, a co-operator, a consultant, a hoofer."

Some comments on the rationale of the work sheet are in order. Questions one and two exploit certain sequential advantages. As has been suggested previously, cues as to the specific aims of the investigation are minimal at the point when the person being interviewed has seen only page one. Not only has he not seen the pages which follow it but in addition the questions he is confronted with supply the least specific cueing information. Furthermore questions one and two measure the most general kinds of emotional and intellectual reactions to the term *informant* and a number of alternate terms.

Questions three and four of page two more specifically relate to the aims of the investigation and thus supply more specific cues to these aims. It may also be noted that the third question involves some control mechanisms that may not be immediately apparent. This question, designed to test synonymy, includes some relatively close synonyms: *attorney-lawyer*, and *bricklayer-mason*. (I assume that most speakers of English would agree that these pairs constitute relatively close synonyms.) On the other hand the list includes some pairs that might be considered synonyms if the term were conceived very broadly and if rather peculiar contexts for the words were imagined. One such pair is *spouse-lady*, but other possible combinations could be designated synonymous. The interpretation of one such pair, *player-coach*, as being synonymous either involves stretching the concept of synonymity rather far (the same person may simultaneously function as a player and a coach) or possibly confusing synonymity with antonymity. Some indication of how strictly the person interviewed observed the injunction to point out pairs of words "which have just about the same meaning" is provided by considering all of his responses to this question.

Question five occurs at the point when cueing information supplied to the person being interrogated has been maximally provided. It is noteworthy in this connection that question five supplies the most specific cues. Question five, like question three, has controls built into it. Putting *informant* and the questions connected with it to one side, one item in the list, "an undercover agent", rather closely fits the definition upon which question five is centered. The other items on the list fit the definition in particular contexts, perhaps, especially if the matter of accident is ignored, but such contexts are not likely to suggest themselves to very many people (as an examination of all of the responses of the interviewees shows).

The responses to question one can best be analyzed when the statistics are considered in tabular form. Tables One and Two which appear in the Appendix of this report make such consideration possible. Table One reveals that of the twenty items involved in question one, *informant* received fewer *favorable* designations than twelve other items; only six items were in less favor. More important, *informant* received eleven *unfavorable* ratings. It received only three *neutral* ratings. One other term, *collaborator*, got more *unfavorable* responses. Its wide dissemination as a pejorative in the recent hot and cold wars going back to W. W. II is no doubt primarily responsible for its unsavoriness. In any case, if it is accepted that an ideal term for the person who supplies data to the field worker should invoke either a *favorable* or *neutral* response as frequently as possible the terms which come off best in

Table One are: *helper, contributor, respondent, assistant, assister, interviewee, donor, consultant, conferent,* and *co-operator.*

The breakdown of the data by socioeconomic classes in Table Two (see the Appendix) prompts one observation. It would seem that Class I speakers are reluctant to express unfavorable opinions, at least where there are no clear indications that unfavorable opinions are expected of them. The sample here is small, but I would venture the opinion that a very large sample would show the same patterns as the one available. Still, the inclusion of urban speakers, white and Negro, might provide evidence that a segment of Class I speakers are capable of forthrightness, even under the circumstances which prevail for an interview. It is probably this lack of assertiveness which makes for so much difficulty in securing the co-operation of Class I speakers for Atlas studies. And in any studies which aim at securing the opinions of Class I speakers concerning linguistic items, their chameleon tendencies will have to be reckoned with.

The responses to question two can best be appraised in lists. If the complaint is voiced that the lists involve too much repetition, too much slight variation, it can be replied that it is precisely in the repetition and slight variation that all the significance lies. Class III speakers offered the following definitions of *informant*: (1) "is one who informs," (2) "a person giving information," (3) "someone who gives information," (4) "a person who gives secret information," (5) " a person who is apt to give out secret information, to inform upon an acquaintance," (6) "one who gives information necessary to a case," (7) "one who gives information behind someone else's back."

Class II speakers gave the following definitions: (1) "one who tells you something," (2) "a person who offers free information," (3) "someone who informs," (4) "one who informs? um—, -ant, right? one who is informed/ one who informs," (5) "a person who can inform you or tell you how to do something," (6) "a person who informs, tells, explains or has information," (7) "someone who informs. The kind of informing depends on the job," (8) "a man of information who helps us with some decision—gives us infor. help the business better," (9) " a know-it-all," (10) "someone who tell *against* you," (11) "a person that informs on someone else," (12) "a) one who informs to police b) helps you gain knowledge," (13) "is a person who has information on unlawful practice," (14) "a person who has knowledge of activities and tells the police," (15) "one who informs on certain information a person who jumps to conclusions or would tell on people. This could be either good or bad," (16) "a person who would more or less tell on another person, give information about someone else. A bad connotation."

The definitions given by Class I speakers were: (1) "someone you go to for advice," (2) "a person who can tell you all about it," (3) "Somebody you'd go to get information from Somebody who tells you something about someone," (4) "Someone who talks about you," (5) "A person that tells on another."

The answers to question two constitute the strongest and most definitive evidence that *informant* has strongly pejorative connotations among a significantly large proportion of speakers at all social levels. The definitions were given without any prejudicial cues other than those provided by page one of the work sheet. It is worth repeating that the answers to questions one and two were given prior to seeing or hearing the last three questions.

The aim of question three was to investigate through synonymity whether *informant* was associated in the popular mind with secret, undercover activities for the police, when a general context was provided for the term. The results are shown by the following table:

TABLE 1
RESPONSES TO QUESTION THREE

Synonymous Pair	I	II	III	ALL
informant-police spy	4	13	6	23
informant-lawyer	1	1	1	3
informant-coach	0	1	1	2
informant-none	0	3	0	3

The responses to question three in some cases may have been influenced by the availability of question four to the person being interviewed. It can be presumed that such influence was not very great. The interviewer read the question aloud while the person interviewed read it silently. The business of understanding question three and making decisions immediately would contribute to the unlikelihood that the information supplied by question four would have much effect. In any case, twenty-three of twenty-eight speakers decided that *informant* and *police spy* were synonymous where the context given was highly generalized.

Question four provides each of the terms listed with a context. The services a speaker is asked to perform in the course of an Atlas interview constitutes the context. The description of these services is in the sort of terms used when negotiating with a candidate (though much abbreviated). The responses are tabulated in Tables Four, Five, and Six of the Appendix. Table Four is singly most useful. Significantly, of the twelve terms available *informant* was rated among the three most highly favored terms by only one person interviewed. Nor was any term in more disfavor. Only *discussant* was disfavored as many times (echoes of *disgust* and *cuss* subcutaneously at work?). The responses to this question provide the clearest positive evidence regarding alternatives to *informant*. The alternatives which come off well here are: *consultant, assistant, co-operator, respondent,* and *interviewee,* though a persuasive evaluation of the terms on the basis of this data alone does not seem possible.

Question five does not provide, as it turns out, any very useful data. It was designed as a kind of back up question in case the others failed to uncover any association between *informant* and the unsavoriness usually thought to be reserved for *informer*. No back up question was needed. Nevertheless the data is presented in Table Seven of the Appendix.

The conclusion seems adequately supported that *informant* carries with it pejorative connotations for a large number of speakers of American English, though it would be desirable to have a larger investigation of this problem conducted independently of this one. Before discussion begins as to what can or should be done if the conclusion is accepted, it might be well to consider a prior question: how *informant* got to be established as the favorite term among American linguistic geographers to designate the speaker interviewed.

The investigation of the history of *O. K.* has demonstrated how complicated this sort of research can be. I do not propose to offer here a definitive history of *informant*. Rather I will offer the results of a kind of preliminary research of the problem. It uncovered some interesting and clear cut facts which will provide, at least, a platform for further investigation. These facts should contribute something to a general understanding of the issues connected with *informant*.

A search through the articles which appeared most promising in all of the issues of *Dialect Notes* (1896–1934) did not turn up a single instance of *informant* earlier than 1932. The first occurrence of *informant* in *Dialect Notes* which I located was in Hans Kurath's "Progress of the Linguistic Atlas" in the issue of 1932. In previous reports and articles concerning the Atlas the term used is *subject*. So in a report of his visit to Dr. Scheuermeier in Europe, published in 1930, Kurath observes that "Dr. Scheuermeier's demonstration of his method of interviewing subjects was extremely enlightening." [2] In the 1931 report, "Progress of the Linguistic Atlas and Plans for the Future Work of the Dialect Society," Miles Hanley uses *subject* several times, even entitling one of the sections, "Choice of Communities and Subjects." [3] But after Kurath used *informant* he is followed in this by Miles Hanley in the next progress report, where the term occurs once.[4] In the progress report of the next issue, *informant* occurs so frequently that it is hard to escape concluding that it had by then become established as the technical term.[5]

A similar search through the early volumes of *American Speech* (volumes one through nine—1926–1934) uncovered parallels to the situation in *Dialect Notes*, though not much positive evidence was provided. *Informant* first occurs in that publication, seemingly, in 1934. Herbert Penzl uses it in the opening paragraph of "New England Terms for 'Poached Eggs.' " [6]

Important evidence is provided by Bulletin No. 4 of the Linguistic Society of America published in 1929. In a compilation of abstracts of the remarks of discussants participating in a conference held on August 2 and 3, 1929, *informant* never occurs.[7] G. Oscar Russell in a paper on "The Mechanical

Recording of Speech" used the term *subjects*. In discussion Kenyon refers to "the speaker", Hanley to "subjects", Kurath to "speakers and subjects." *Subject* is used repeatedly by Leonard Bloomfield and W. Cabell Greet.

It would seem that the term *informant* was imported into American dialectology from anthropological linguistics. A purview of volumes of *American Anthropologist*, which began publication in 1888, shows *informant* occurring as early as 1905.[8] The first volume of the *International Journal of American Linguistics* published in 1917 shows *informant* being used as does the first volume of *Language*, published in 1925. Leonard Bloomfield, for instance, uses it in his article, "A Set of Postulates for the Science of Language." [9]

The importance of historical evidence of this type is that it may indicate how *informant* came to be used in dialect study despite its clearly disadvantageous connotations. In anthropoligical field work the connotative potentialities of the term are not often of much practical importance, since the persons to be interviewed are not likely to have English as their first language. Early students of American dialect apparently made use of any of several terms available to them: apparently *informant* was not one of the set. It not only seems possible but even somewhat probable that *informant* would come up for consideration, independently of its currency among anthropological linguists. If so, it was apparently rejected by students of American English who considered it prior to 1932. In 1932 Kurath, brought into contact with Bloomfield and other anthropological linguists, in connection with the Linguistic Atlas project, adopted their terminology, or so it would seem. At this point field work for the Atlas was only being discussed. Sensitivity to practicalities would not have been so sharp as it would have been later.

Curiously enough, Kurath did evidence awareness of the effect of his choice of technical terminology on the persons the Atlas workers would be consulting with. The evidence is his well known distaste for the term *questionnaire*, and preference for *work sheet*.[10]

Perhaps one more point should be made before conclusions are drawn. Evidence is readily available to anyone that it is standard police practice today to issue all press releases concerning the receiving of information from underworld sources in terms of *informants*. So in a story released by the Associated Press appearing in the *Athens Messenger*, the opening paragraph read: "Newspaper reports said today investigators are checking the credibility of the informant whose story led police to arrest a Yemeni immigrant and his two sons in an alleged plot to Richard M. Nixon." [Sic.] On November 6, 1968 at 11:00 PM on a WBNS TV news program a Columbus police detective was recorded as saying concerning Robert Lingler, wanted for suspicion of murder, that "we had information today from an informant" that Lingler was a female impersonator. Even more significantly, on one of the Perry Mason shows being rerun on November 18, 1968 on TV (probably made five years or more earlier), the Police Chief said as he entered an apartment where a missing witness was hiding: "It's obvious my informant knew who she was talking about." Even those who report anti-revolutionaries to the Castro government of Cuba are referred to as *informants*, not *informers*. So Sandy Van Ocer, on January 7, 1969, on a TV documentary showing at 10:00 PM in Athens, Ohio, offered this explanation for the survival of Castro: "One reason is the block by block network of vigilantes and informants." (The program is called *The First Tuesday*.)

It can be generalized that *informant* has become a standard euphemism for *informer* in police jargon. It is well known that if euphemisms are used regularly over a period of time they cease to be euphemistic, acquiring all the unpleasant connotations of the word they substitute for. This process is clearly well under way if not already fully consummated in the police use of *informant*.

Should *informant* as a technical term in dialect geography be abandoned? Clearly it would be presumptuous and vain to attempt to prescribe to American dialect investigators on this point. *Informant* is fixed rather solidly, one suspects, in the habits of those who constitute this particular linguistic sub-culture. Not only may many be unimpressed by the evidence presented, they may remain unimpressed even if the evidence is amplified. It may be argued that the term *informant* may be retained for use in all situations except those involving persons being interviewed or arranging interviews. Some may feel this report smacks of using a hammer to swat a fly. I would be less than honest if I did not report my skepticism that *informant* will in fact be replaced.

Nevertheless I intend to replace it as much as shows itself to be practicable in my own work. My feeling is that where thousands of interviews are involved, and several times that many man-hours; where the whole frustrating and discouraging business of securing the cooperation of qualified speakers of dialect impinges, even in limited fashion, there can be no question of triviality. Having two sets of terms, one for the general population, another for the profession, may represent some kind of partial solution. I think, however, that it underestimates the sensitivity of the general population to any suggestion of a conspiracy against them. There is enough for them to be sensitive about in what is asked of them without exposing them to the added risks of slips of the field worker's tongue. More important is the consequences such a procedure would have on the attitudes a field worker has toward his *subjects* (we see why that term went by the board). In the final analysis each dialect investigator will have to decide for himself whether to use *informant* or some other term.

But what other term? For anyone who may be persuaded that alternate terms are advisable, it has been one of the intents of this report to suggest that dialect study itself has developed techniques which can contribute to a choice. It seems mildly ironic that a discipline, which has as its main object the gathering of linguistic data by moving out among the everyday speakers of the language, both the washed and the unwashed, should not consult those same speakers concerning the terminology to be made use of in such work.

I do not mean to suggest that it is my opinion that the choice should be made automatically—that the term selected should necessarily be the one that is most favorably received by a group representative of that section of the population which will be studied in the future. The terms offered for their evaluations are not as yet technical terms with special senses. They cannot be rated as such by anyone except on a kind of prognosticatory basis. Prognosticatory judgments would hardly seem to be the forte of the ordinary speaker. I cannot think of any group better qualified to select the term most likely to be a desirable and apt one for dialect work than dialect workers themselves, especially when they have consulted the visceral and cerebral reactions of ordinary native speakers and consciously deliberated on the wisdom of a choice.

My own predilection has wavered between *co-operator, co-worker,* and *respondent. Respondent* has some currency among dialect students at the present time, though I cannot document such a generalization. *Co-operator* has to recommend it, as well as to recommend against it, its use by agricultural extension offices, county agents, state foresters, federal conservation specialists, and the like, referring to farmers who voluntarily join any of various programs sponsored by these agents and their agencies. All three of the terms come off fairly well in the poll of sentiment reported in this article. Unfortunately, *co-worker* was not included in the terms evaluated by question one. It showed well in the responses to question four however. *Co-worker* is my present candidate to replace *informant.* The primary reason is that I believe *field worker* was an acceptable designation originally, now firmly established, and that *co-worker* meshes well with *field worker. Fellow worker* would get a friendlier reception from representative native speakers, I suspect, but it strikes me as somewhat ingratiating. Still, it was unfortunate that it was not included in the poll. Until I have reason to do otherwise, in future field work, then, I will try to secure co-workers. In reporting my findings I plan to make use of the same term and any other acceptable terms whose synonymousness seems self-evident.

Appendix
Statistical Tables

TABLE 2
RESPONSES TO QUESTION ONE: TOTAL SAMPLE

Term	*Favorable*	*Unfavorable*	*Neutral*
helper	27	0	0
donor	26	2	0
contributor	25	0	3
co-operator	23	3	2
assistant	21	1	6

TABLE 2 (Cont'd)

RESPONSES TO QUESTION ONE: TOTAL SAMPLE

Term	Favorable	Unfavorable	Neutral
consultant	21	2	5
respondent	20	0	7
assister	20	1	7
answerer	19	4	5
researchant	16	2	9
supplier	15	4	9
correspondent	15	4	8
interviewee	14	1	13
informant	14	11	3
source person	12	3	11
conferent	11	1	15
discussant	11	5	12
answerant	10	4	14
collaborator	10	15	2
conferee	9	3	16
TOTALS	339	66	147

TABLE 3*

RESPONSES TO QUESTION ONE: BREAKDOWN INTO CLASSES

	Class I			Class II			Class III		
TERM	F	U	N	F	U	N	F	U	N
helper	5	0	0	15	0	0	7	0	0
donor	5	0	0	14	2	0	7	0	0
contributor	4	0	1	15	0	1	6	0	1
co-operator	5	0	0	13	2	1	5	1	1
assistant	5	0	0	13	1	2	3	0	4
consultant	4	0	1	12	2	2	5	0	2
respondent	5	0	0	10	0	5	5	0	2
assister	5	0	0	9	1	6	6	0	1
answerer	5	0	0	9	4	3	5	0	2
researchant	5	0	0	8	2	5	3	0	4
supplier	4	0	1	9	3	4	2	1	4
correspondent	3	0	1	9	3	4	3	1	3
interviewee	4	1	0	9	0	7	1	0	6
informant	4	1	0	8	6	2	2	4	1
source person	2	0	2	4	3	8	6	0	1
conferent	5	0	0	4	0	11	2	1	4
discussant	3	1	1	6	3	7	2	1	4
answerant	4	0	1	4	3	9	2	1	4
collaborator	3	1	0	4	10	2	3	4	0
conferee	3	1	1	4	2	10	2	0	5
TOTALS	83	5	9	179	47	89	77	14	49

* In the table, "F" represents *favorable*, "U" represents *unfavorable*, and "N" represents *neutral*.

TABLE 4
RESPONSES TO QUESTION FOUR. TOTAL SAMPLE.
UNDIFFERENTIATED BEST AND WORST.

Terms	Best	Terms	Worst
consultant	13	informant	11
co-worker	11	discussant	11
source person	9	answerer	8
interviewee	8	source person	7
assistant	8	conferee	6
respondent	6	co-worker	6
answerer	6	respondent	5
co-operator	5	interviewee	5
discussant	4	co-operator	4
conferee	3	assistant	4
informant	1	consultant	3
NONE	7	NONE	10

TABLE 5
RESPONSES TO QUESTION FOUR. BREAKDOWN BY CLASSES.
BEST, NEXT BEST, AND THIRD BEST ELECTIONS
UNDIFFERENTIATED.

Term	Class I	Class II	Class III
consultant	3	7	3
co-worker	4	5	2
source person	0	3	6
interviewee	1	3	4
assistant	3	5	0
respondent	1	5	0
answerer	2	2	2
co-operator	0	3	2
discussant	1	3	0
conferee	0	1	2
informant	1	0	0

TABLE 6
RESPONSES TO QUESTION FOUR. BREAKDOWN BY CLASSES.
WORST, SECOND WORST, THIRD WORST ELECTIONS
UNDIFFERENTIATED.

Term	Class I	Class II	Class III
informant	2	4	5
discussant	2	5	4
answerer	1	5	2
source person	2	5	0
conferee	3	2	1
co-worker	0	5	1
respondent	1	2	2
interviewee	2	2	1
co-operator	0	1	3
assistant	2	2	0
consultant	1	2	0

TABLE 7
RESPONSES TO QUESTION FIVE.

Term	All Classes	I	II	III
informant	24	4	14	6
undercover agent	20	4	10	6
reporter	7	4	10	6
co-operator	4	0	2	2
consultant	1	0	1	0
respondent	0	0	0	0
hoofer	0	0	0	0

Notes

1. These are the classes set up by Hans Kurath for the Linguistic Atlas, dispensing with his age qualifications. For definitions see: Hans Kurath, *Handbook of the Linguistic Geography of New England*, (Linguistic Atlas of New England, Vol. 1.) Providence: Brown University Press, 1939, pp. 41–44.

2. P. 93 of "Report of Interviews with European Scholars Concerning Our Plans for a Linguistic Atlas of American English," Vol. VI, Part 2 (1930), pp. 65–78.

3. P. 94. *Dialect Notes*, Vol. VI, Part 3 (1931), pp. 91–98.

4. "Progress of the Linguistic Atlas," *Dialect Notes*, Vol. VI, Part 6 (1933), p. 335.

5. "Progress of the Linguistic Atlas," *Dialect Notes*, Vol. VI, Part 7 (1933), pp. 365–367.

6. Vol. IX (1934), pp. 90–95.

7. "The Conference on a Linguistic Atlas of the United States and Canada; Held at New Haven, August 2–3, 1929 . . . ," Compiled by Hans Kurath. September, 1929, pp. 20–47.

8. See Roland B. Dixon's "The Shasta-Achomavi: A New Lingiustic Stock, With Four New Dialects," Vol. VII, New Series, pp. 213–217. *Informant* occurs on p. 214.

9. pp. 153–164.

10. See Miles Hanley's statement in "Progress of the Linguistic Atlas and Plans for the Future Work of the Dialect Society," *Dialect Notes*, Vol. VI, Part 3, 1931, pp. 91–98: "The questionnaire (commony called 'work sheets' to avoid the *odium pedagogicum*) is the work of Professor Kurath." p. 93.

SPONSORS

John Algeo
University of Georgia

Albert C. Baugh
University of Pennsylvania

Clarence L. Barnhart
Bronxville, N.Y.

Ruth M. Blackburn
State University of New York at Albany

Jean Bressler
University of Nebraska at Omaha

Arthur J. Bronstein
City University of New York, Herbert H. Lehman College

Margaret M. Bryant
Brooklyn College, The City University of New York

Daniel N. Cárdenas
California State College at Long Beach

Thomas L. Clark
University of Nevada, Las Vegas

Walburga Von Raffler Engel
The University of Ottawa

William W. Evans
Louisiana State University

Louis J. Feldstein
New York, N.Y.

Victoria A. Fromkin
University of California at Los Angeles

Furman University Library

Ruth I. Golden
Wayne State University

Eva and Einar Haugen
Harvard University

Allan F. Hubbell
New York University

Kellog W. Hunt
Florida State University

Marian Hutchison
New York, N.Y.

Hilda Jaffe
University of Houston

E. Gustave Johnson
Miami, Florida

Harold Kirshner
New York City Community College City University of New York

Vernon S. Larsen
Chicago, Ill.

James B. McMillan
The University of Alabama

Anne Malone
University of Montevallo

Albert H. Marckwardt
Princeton University

Dr. Marie Marcus
Louisiana State University

Elizabeth J. Moffet
Moody Bible Institute

Claude Henry Neuffer
The University of South Carolina

Don L.F. Nilsen
University of Northern Iowa

Mr. & Mrs. Raymond K. O'Cain
University of South Carolina

Roy C. O'Donnell
The Florida State University

George B. Pace
University of Missouri

Robert C. Pooley
University of Wisconsin

Princeton University Library

Allen Walker Read
Columbia University

Melvyn C. Resnick
Florida Atlantic University

A. Hood Roberts
Washington, D.C.

I. Willis Russell
University of Alabama

John W. Schmaus
Iola, Kansas

Garrett H. Scott
Bloomington, Ill.

Walter A. Sedelow, Jr.,
The University of Kansas

Claude L. Shaver
Louisiana State University

Jess Stein
New York, N.Y.

Edward A. Stephenson
University of Georgia

Peter Tamony
San Francisco, Calif.

Zacharias Thundyil, C.M.I.
Northern Michigan University

Gary N. Underwood
University of Arkansas

Dennis Wepman
Miami, Florida

Oliver M. Willard
University of Oregon

INDEX OF NAMES